Napo

1814

The Battle of Montmirail: Napoleon's Old Guard assaulting Russian infantrymen.

Napoleon 1814
The Defence of France

ANDREW UFFINDELL

Pen & Sword
MILITARY

First published in Great Britain in 2009
and reprinted in this paperback format in 2015 by
Pen & Sword Military
an imprint of
Pen & Sword Books Ltd
47 Church Street
Barnsley
South Yorkshire
S70 2AS

Copyright © Andrew Uffindell, 2009, 2015

ISBN: 978 1 47384 256 4

The right of Andrew Uffindell to be identified as author of the work has been asserted by him in accordance with the Copyright, Designs and Patents Act 1988.

A CIP catalogue record for this book is available from the British Library

All rights reserved. No part of this book may be reproduced or transmitted in any form or by any means, electronic or mechanical including photocopying, recording or by any information storage and retrieval system, without permission from the Publisher in writing.

Typeset in Ehrhardt by S L Menzies-Earl

Printed and bound in England by
CPI Group (UK) Ltd, Croydon, CR0 4YY

Pen & Sword Books Ltd incorporates the imprints of:
Pen & Sword Archaeology, Atlas, Aviation, Battleground, Discovery, Family History, History, Maritime, Military, Naval, Politics, Railways, Select, Social History, Transport, True Crime, Claymore Press, Frontline Books, Leo Cooper, Praetorian Press, Remember When, Seaforth Publishing and Wharncliffe.

For a complete list of Pen & Sword titles please contact:
Pen & Sword Books Limited
47 Church Street, Barnsley, South Yorkshire, S70 2AS, England
E-mail: enquiries@pen-and-sword.co.uk
Website: www.pen-and-sword.co.uk

Contents

Key to Maps vii
List of Maps viii
Author's Note ix
Introduction x

Part One: The Gathering Threat
 1. 'No language can describe the horrible devastation' 1
 2. France in 1814 9
 3. The Allied armies 18

Part Two: The Campaign of France
 4. Invasion! 25
 5. The campaign theatre 32
 6. Napoleon takes command 42
 7. 'Where will we stop?' 50
 8. A salvo of victories 56
 9. 'They were swept away in the whirlpool' 69
 10. Stalemate 82
 11. 'We are afraid of fighting' 100
 12. Paris 113
 13. The end of the war 122

Part Three: Analysis
 14. Napoleon's finest campaign? 128
 15. A protracted, attritional struggle? 142

Part Four: The Civilian Experience
 16. Occupation 150
 17. The struggle to survive 164
 18. Resistance 177
 19. The propaganda war 188
 20. Population displacements and prisoners-of-war 202
 21. The sick and wounded 215
 22. Reconstruction 221

Appendices
   I. The weather during the campaign 238
   II. Sunrise and sunset at Paris on selected dates 245
   III. Allied order of battle 246
   IV. Napoleon's order of battle 250

Glossary 260

References 267

Bibliography 300

Index 317

Key to Maps

☐	Infantry	☐	Company
◨	Cavalry	◨	Squadron
⊢⊣	Artillery	☐	Battalion
○	Skirmishers	☐	Regiment
■	Napoleon's units	☐ˣ	Brigade
☐	Allied units	☐ˣˣ	Division
		☐ˣˣˣ	Corps
		☐ˣˣˣˣ	Army
		(+)	Strengthened
		(−)	Reduced

List of Maps

	Page
1. Europe at the end of 1813	5
2. The Allies cross the Rhine: December 1813–January 1814	26–7
3. 1814: the campaign area	35
4. Napoleon's counter-offensive: 26–29 January 1814	43
5. Battle of Brienne: 29 January 1814	45
6. Battle of La Rothière: 1 February 1814	48
7. Blücher's first advance on Paris: 2–10 February 1814	54
8. Battle of Champaubert: 10 February 1814	57
9. Battle of Montmirail: 11 February 1814	60
10. Battle of Château-Thierry: 12 February 1814	62
11. Battle of Vauchamps: 14 February 1814	65
12. Napoleon's concentration against Schwarzenberg: 15–17 February 1814	71
13. Battle of Montereau: 18 February 1814	75
14. Schwarzenberg retreats on Troyes: 17–22 February 1814	78
15. Blücher's second advance on Paris: 24 February–6 March 1814	83
16. Battle of Craonne: 7 March 1814	87
17. Battle of Laon: 9 March 1814	92
18. Napoleon's descent on Schwarzenberg: 17–19 March 1814	102
19. Battle of Arcis-sur-Aube: 20 March 1814	104
20. The final Allied advance on Paris: 22–30 March 1814	110
21. Battle of Paris: 30 March 1814	115
22. The Allied occupation of France: the general-governments	152
23. Schwarzenberg's main lines of communication: early February 1814	171

Author's Note

I am most grateful to my family and friends for their help and encouragement during the writing of this book. I am much indebted to the team at my publishers, Pen & Sword, and particularly to Rupert Harding, who not only suggested the subject in the first place, but read the draft and advised me throughout the publishing process. I also wish to thank Sarah Cook for all her hard work in editing the book. In addition, I am much obliged to the extremely helpful staff of the *Archives nationales*, the *Bibliothèque nationale de France*, and the *Bibliothèque Sainte-Geneviève* at Paris; the *Archives départementales de l'Aube* at Troyes; and the British Library, including the Newspaper Collection at Colindale. I am greatly indebted to the staff of the Hertfordshire Library Services for their efficiency in obtaining books, and to John Richards, who drew the twenty-three superb maps that you will find throughout these pages.

Names of towns are the modern French versions. To avoid confusion, I have made an exception for Châlons-sur-Marne, which was the name in use in 1814. It was originally known as Châlons-en-Champagne, and officially reverted to that title in 1998. Note that Bar-le-Duc is sometimes known as Bar-sur-Ornain, which was the politically correct form during the Revolution.

I have given French and German ranks in the relevant language, but Russian ones in their nearest English equivalent, for the sake of simplicity. The Russians used the Julian calendar, which was twelve days behind the Gregorian calendar used by the other powers. All dates in this book conform with the Gregorian calendar.

All temperatures are in degrees centigrade. Sources at the time often used the Réaumur scale, on which water froze at 0 degrees and boiled at 80. To convert Réaumur temperatures into centigrade, multiply by 1.25.

Introduction

Napoleon's conduct of the intense and fast-moving campaign of 1814 has been widely hailed as one of his finest feats as a commander: a struggle in which, after two successive years of disaster, he seemed to rediscover all the flair and brilliance he had shown eighteen years earlier as the brash, young commander of the *Armée d'Italie*.

Yet despite this acclaim, his defence of France has never been properly understood, nor examined as closely as the epic invasion of Russia two years earlier, or the subsequent, dramatic defeat at Waterloo. It is, in fact, an artist, not a writer, who has come closest to capturing the essence of the campaign. Jean-Louis-Ernest Meissonier's masterpiece, *La Campagne de France (1814)*, is one of the world's great, iconic images. First exhibited in 1864, it shows Napoleon riding at the head of his staff along a frozen track, and is often mistaken for a depiction of the retreat from Moscow.

Meissonier actually intended to produce a cycle of five historical pictures showing Napoleon's rise and fall, but completed only two. The first, based on the Battle of Friedland in 1807, shows Napoleon in his years of victory, surrounded by masses of enthusiastic troops, and is entirely filled with light, colour, noise, and energy. In contrast, *La Campagne de France* depicts him as a more isolated figure, at the head of a clearly drained and demoralised army trudging through the emptiness of a barren landscape, under a leaden and overcast sky. The predominant colours are grey, brown, and black, relieved only by the brilliant whiteness of Napoleon's horse, and a few areas lightly dusted by snow. Reds and golds are deliberately dulled, and the only brightness in the sky is a sliver behind Napoleon's entourage, hinting at the final setting of the sun on his Empire.

Meissonier was a perfectionist. He even had a copy made of Napoleon's grey overcoat and, since he had the right physique, sketched himself wearing it in a mirror. From a former valet he learned that when Napoleon put on his overcoat, he never bothered to undo his epaulettes, as was customary at the time. Instead, he had his coat specially made to fit over the epaulettes, which accounts for the odd shape of his shoulders in the painting. Similarly, a medical officer who served with Napoleon's army told Meissonier that *Maréchal* Michel Ney never put his arms into the sleeves of his overcoat and that the feathers of his hat were always dirty, and so that is how the 'bravest of the brave' is shown.[1]

Despite Meissonier's admiration for the Emperor, he did not paint an overt piece of propaganda, showing him as a semi-deified hero. His Napoleon is a very human figure, with a grim face and mud-spattered boots. In fact, the painting is so crisp and realistic that it captures the very veins on the horses' legs, and the frozen breath from their nostrils. Yet it is more than just a painstakingly accurate historical image: it is a timeless psychological study. Meissonier stated that he had the general idea of Napoleon retreating after being checked at the Battle of Laon in the middle of March, but really intended to represent the campaign as a whole, so as not to feel constrained by a specific moment:

In my *1814*, I have shown the overall conditions and impending results of the campaign of France in the form of an episode. Napoleon is reduced to the defensive and those who follow him, under an overcast sky and on a devastated land, feel more or less overcome with doubt. They are very close to losing their faith in him.[2]

Everyone is silent, isolated, and wrapped up in his private thoughts. Only some elements of unity remain between Napoleon and his entourage. *Maréchal* Louis Berthier, for example, has a similar overcoat and expression, but is visibly older and has his head lowered. The other officers display different degrees of demoralisation. Ney alone holds his head up and looks straight ahead, like Napoleon himself. Further to the rear, the doubts are more obvious. Some men have their heads down, in either exhaustion or despair, while others look to the left or right, or directly at the viewer, as if seeking answers to the questions assailing them. The motley collection of hats, shakos, and helmets adds to the lack of cohesion. Only Napoleon wears his hat parallel to his shoulders. Ney has his set at a cocky, individualistic angle, while the rest wear their hats fore and aft, some with the shorter side on the left, others on the right.

Napoleon's dominance is unmistakable. His central position in the foreground, the brightness of his white horse, and the clever manipulation of the perspective so that the column of riders rapidly recedes into the distance all reflect his paramount role in the struggle. Meissonier emphasised Napoleon's solitude as leader, and his overriding determination to continue the war and carry his army and people with him. It is the emotional rawness of the painting, and the way it captures the unstable mix of hope and despair, that form the secret of its enduring hold.

In this way Meissonier grasped the crux of the campaign: it was a psychological struggle, waged for the minds of the population, soldiers, and senior commanders, and driven by Napoleon's relentless, almost obsessive resolve. *La Campagne de France* is not a battle painting. Only a discarded shako suggests death or injury, and this reflects the small proportion of the total losses accounted for by battle casualties. Even at Montmirail, its heaviest action in 1814, the Prussian I Corps lost fewer than 900 men, and yet it was so worn away by the demoralising winter conditions that it was left with barely more than half its initial strength by the end of the three-month campaign.[3]

What the painting does not show is equally significant. There are no civilians in Meissonier's image, and yet the number of inhabitants caught up in the campaign was at least twenty-five times that of the soldiers who fought in it, and they often suffered proportionately heavier losses.[4] Napoleon's decisions, and the course of the military operations, can not be fully appreciated without examining the parallel events that occurred off the battlefield, in both the occupied and unoccupied areas. The French authorities were overwhelmed by a combination of different challenges, not just the task of supplying thousands of troops in mid-winter, but also the mass evacuations of prisoners-of-war, the population displacements, the threat of social disintegration, and a deadly typhus epidemic that had already devastated Germany. As the campaign progressed, its associated burdens were thrown more and more on to the civilian population because of the progressive paralysation of the central government.

By focusing so narrowly on Napoleon's battles and manoeuvres, historians have underrated the sheer scale and complexity of the problems he faced. He had to fight a multi-dimensional contest, not only co-ordinating the military operations in several theatres, but integrating them with economic measures, diplomatic negotiations, and a pervasive propaganda war, while at the same time trying to negate the Allied advantage of numbers by rousing popular resistance and transforming the campaign into an asymmetrical struggle.

Using previously unpublished material from the archives in Paris and in one of the most heavily contested *départements*, the Aube, I have set out to fill these gaps and provide a more balanced picture of Napoleon's defence of France. I have walked the campaign area to gain an insight into the decisions of the commanders, and to understand the full achievement of the soldiers who fought there.

I have also looked again at some of the most cherished incidents of the Napoleonic Legend, for on closer examination the best-known stories about the campaign often turn out to be no more than popular myth. Foremost among them is the celebrated occasion when Napoleon supposedly reassured men concerned about his safety by exclaiming: 'Come now, my friends, have no fear. The cannonball that is to kill me has not yet been made.' These words have been repeated in hundreds of books, and even inscribed for posterity on a stone slab on the heights overlooking the town of Montereau, and yet, ironically, Napoleon almost certainly never said them.

Above all, I have sought to bring these extraordinary events to life by describing what they were really like for those soldiers and civilians who lived through them, for it is their rich variety of individual human experiences that no one painting can ever hope to capture.

Part One
The Gathering Threat

Chapter 1
'No language can describe the horrible devastation'

At Leipzig in October 1813 Napoleon suffered his greatest ever battlefield defeat. It was the biggest and bloodiest battle of the entire Revolutionary and Napoleonic era, with the Allies alone suffering 54,000 casualties, almost as many as the British would on the first day of the Somme in 1916.[1] In terms of the number of troops present, Leipzig was twice as big as Borodino (1812), and three times the size of either Waterloo (1815) or Gettysburg (1863). Not until 1914, with the opening engagements of the First World War, did the western world see a bigger battle.

Cossacks attacking French infantry.

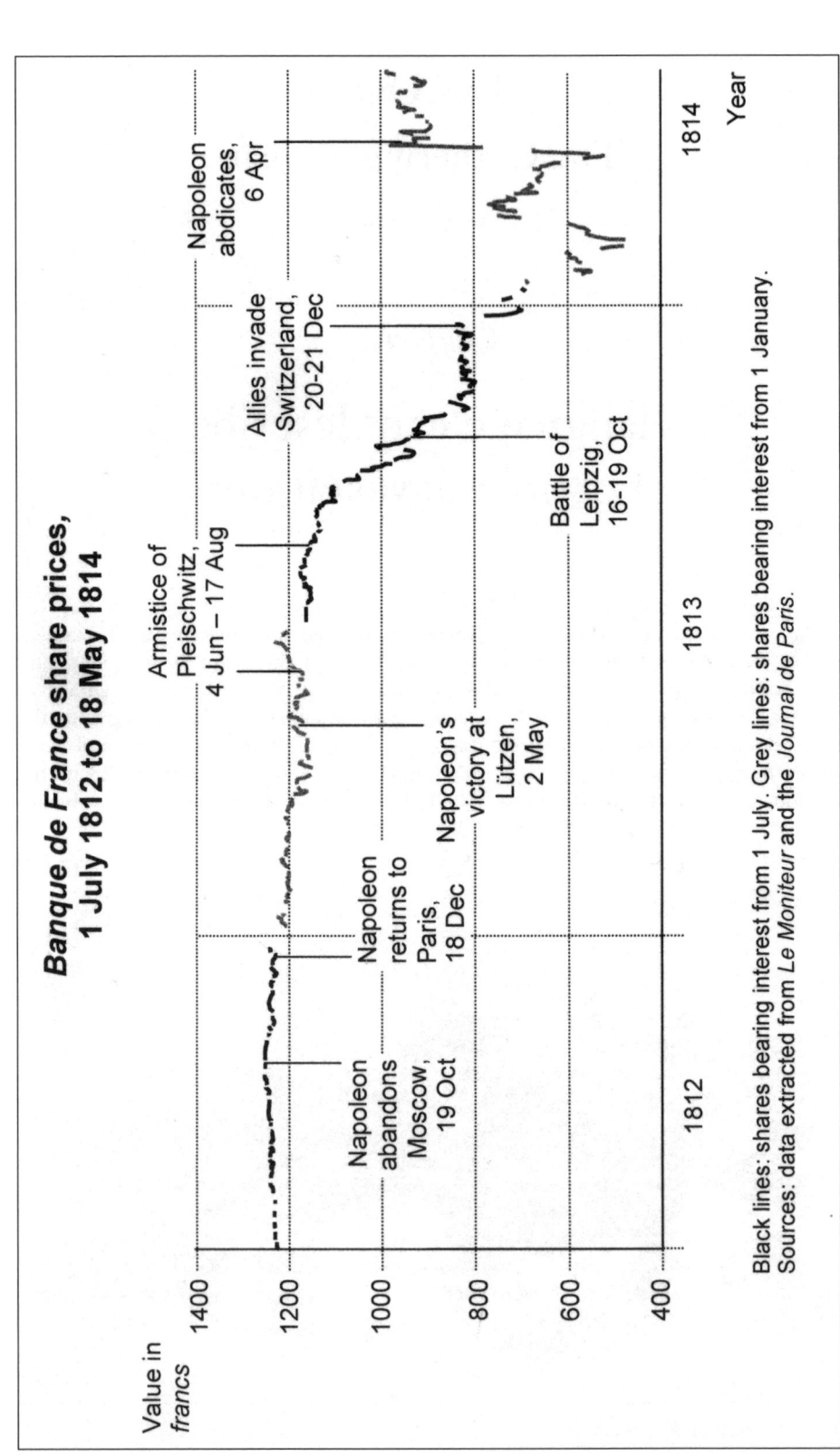

For Napoleon, the impact of Leipzig was even more catastrophic and immediate than the destruction of his *Grande armée* in Russia in 1812. On that occasion, he had been able to raise a fresh army, and take the field again in Germany in the spring of 1813 to try to reverse the setback. But his hopes of continuing to dominate central Europe were destroyed by the disaster of Leipzig, and by the loss of nearly all his allied and satellite states. Public confidence in France itself was shattered: share prices of the *Banque de France*, which had previously remained steady even in the wake of the retreat from Moscow, suddenly slumped in the autumn of 1813, as hopes collapsed that Napoleon could secure a favourable peace and avert an invasion.

When the remnants of Napoleon's army reached the Rhine, the eastern frontier of France, they found few supplies and little organisation, and fell victim to a deadly typhus epidemic. At Mainz alone, as many as 30,000 troops are thought to have died over the next six months, along with 10 per cent of the city's inhabitants.[2] Wellington's niece, Priscilla Fane, Lady Burghersh, was appalled at the desolation she found when she travelled through Germany to rejoin her husband, the British military commissioner with the Austrian forces:

> We have come all along the line of the French retreat, and as it is not a month since they passed, the roads are covered with dead horses and remains of dead men. . . . No language can describe the horrible devastation the French have left behind them, and without seeing it no one can form an idea of the country through which such a retreat as theirs has been made. Every bridge blown up, every village burnt or pulled down, fields completely devastated, orchards all turned up, and we traced their bivouaques all along by every horror you can conceive. None of the country people will bury them or their horses, so there they remain lying all over the fields and roads, with millions of crows feasting . . .[3]

In the wake of Leipzig, attention shifted to the city of Frankfurt-am-Main, where the Allied monarchs, generals, and statesmen assembled in the first fortnight of November to discuss the political settlement of central Europe, and future strategy against Napoleon.

The Allied coalition

The Allied coalition of 1813–1814 emerged fitfully in the wake of Napoleon's retreat from Moscow, and had to be created during the course of active operations. Apart from the four major powers, Russia, Prussia, Austria, and Britain, the coalition included Sweden, Spain, Portugal, Sicily, and also a host of German states that had hitherto been aligned with Napoleon but now joined the Allies. The cycle of imperial expansion had gone into reverse, for whereas Napoleon had used his conquests to sustain further wars, the manpower and resources of central Europe were now transferred to Allied hands. For the Allies, the costs of the war were also defrayed by British funds, weapons, and equipment: in 1814 Britain supplied £10 million of subsidies, an amount unprecedented during the entire Revolutionary and Napoleonic Wars.[4]

What the coalition did not have was a comprehensive alliance treaty, and it was therefore limited in its effectiveness by the looseness of its bonds. Agreement on war aims was all but impossible, since the addition of more states complicated the coalition, and the evolving situation forced the partners continually to adjust their ambitions. At the same time as they fought Napoleon, they were faced with crucial decisions about the future settlement of Europe. It did not help that the key members of the coalition were long-standing rivals and had recently been enemies: Napoleon had forced Prussia and Austria to provide contingents for his invasion of Russia in 1812.

Vagueness actually helped to keep the coalition together given the incompatible interests of its partners, especially over the two most controversial issues, the future of Poland and the question of regime change in France. Whereas Tsar Alexander I saw the removal of Napoleon as an essential precondition for an era of international peace and stability, the Austrian Foreign Minister, Klemens, *Fürst* von Metternich, sought a more limited outcome. Not until August 1813 had Austria declared war, for she had hoped to broker a peace in which she could prevent either France or Russia from being a dominant superpower. A compromise settlement remained her preferred outcome, lest a complete Allied victory endangered her position in central Europe by allowing Russia to absorb Poland, or Prussia to annex the Kingdom of Saxony.

As Metternich was also aware, heavy Austrian casualties would undermine the ability of the Habsburg Empire to survive internal unrest or protect its interests in post-war Europe. By the end of 1813 Austria's main objective in terms of territory and influence was to recover her position in northern Italy, and she had little interest in invading France except to force Napoleon to make a compromise peace. Since he had married the daughter of the Austrian Emperor, Franz I, three years earlier, his throne, if he remained in power, would eventually be inherited by his half-Habsburg son. But an invasion that ended with the occupation of Paris and a change of regime could turn France into either a Russian satellite or a failed state vulnerable to revolutionary extremists. Openly seeking Napoleon's removal was likely to harden his intransigence, and Austrian leaders had no confidence that Alexander would persist in his desire to capture Paris should the Allies suffer a setback.

Prussia, weakened by six years of French domination, was more dependent on Russia, and could regain her great power status only by annexing territory, including French lands on the left bank of the Rhine, so senior Prussian soldiers were intent on inflicting a total defeat followed by a punitive peace. Yet Prussia's leaders were not united: King Friedrich Wilhelm III was alarmed by the aggressive and independent attitude of some of his generals, and the Chancellor, Karl August von Hardenberg, was concerned that Russia could become too powerful.

Authority within the Allied coalition was diffused, with important decisions being made either in councils of war, which often involved delay, deceit and unsatisfactory compromise, or through unilateral action by an army, or even corps, commander. No one Allied leader was able to dominate the others, except momentarily. The indispensability of bringing Austria into the coalition had ensured the appointment of one of her generals, *Feldmarschall* Karl Philipp, *Fürst* zu Schwarzenberg, as the supreme commander. On the other hand, it was Russia that fielded the largest contingent in the main campaign theatre in 1814, and this increased Alexander's influence, even though he encountered resistance to his wilder ambitions from some of his own advisers. 'I don't know how far we are going to advance', complained the Russian diplomat Karl, Count von Nesselrode on 16 January:

> Some people want to push as far as Paris, but I want to push only the negotiations. I regard peace as more necessary than ever, and the moment as come when we can obtain a good, solid, and glorious one. In addition, I consider any further operation or enterprise as extremely dangerous.[5]

Many Russian generals had been reluctant after the 1812 campaign to continue the pursuit into central Europe, let alone invade France, and wanted simply to occupy Poland and avoid further casualties.

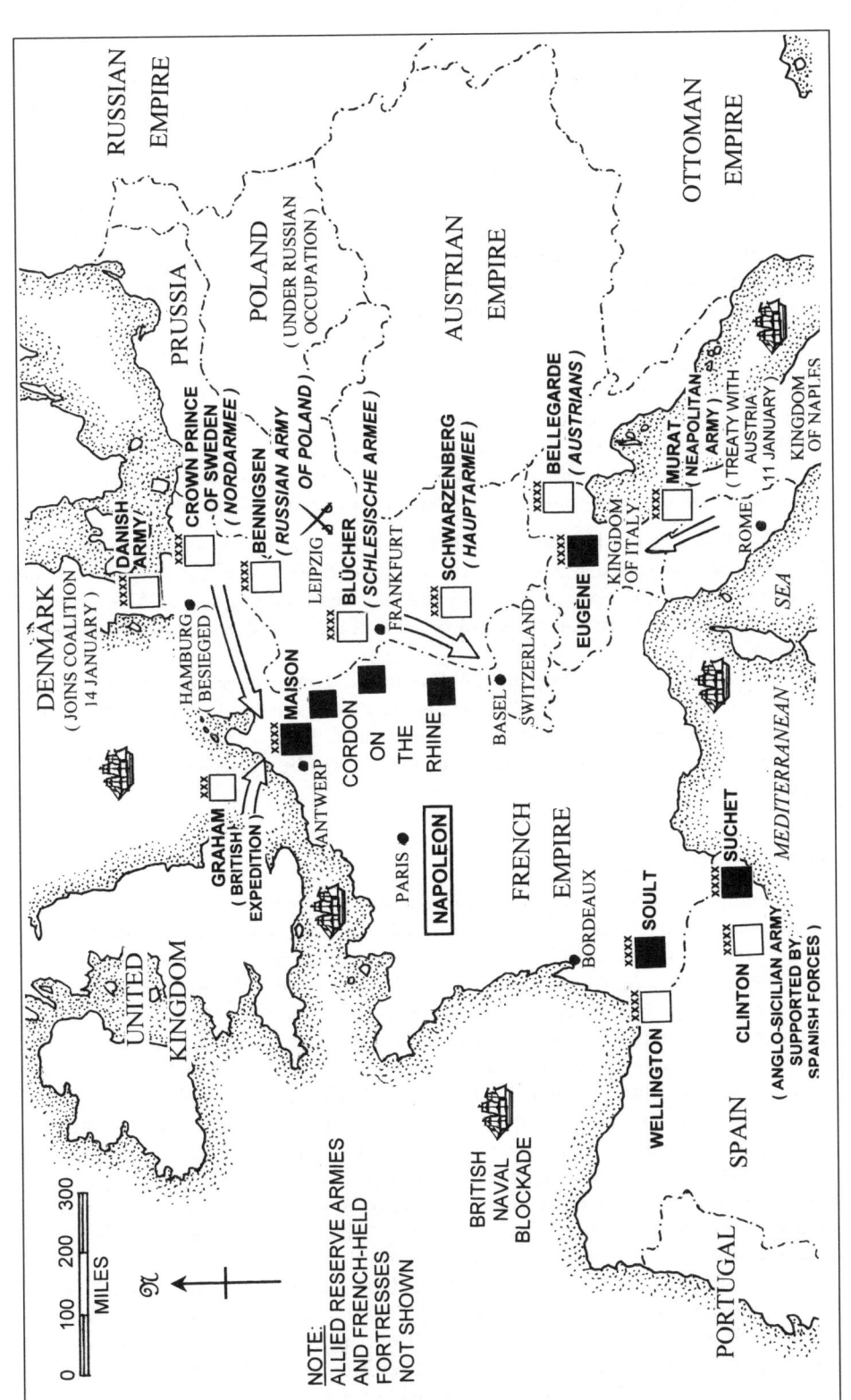

Europe at the end of 1813.

Decision-making was therefore inhibited by a complex web of distrust, as the British Foreign Secretary, Robert Stewart, Viscount Castlereagh, reported on 30 January:

> I think our greatest danger at present is from the *chevalresque* tone in which the Emperor Alexander is disposed to push the war. He has a *personal* feeling about Paris, distinct from all political or military combinations. He seems to seek for the occasion of entering with his magnificent guards the enemy's capital, probably to display, in his clemency and forbearance, a contrast to that desolation to which his own was devoted....
>
> You may estimate some of the hazards to which affairs are exposed here, when one of the leading monarchs, in his first interview, told me that he had no confidence in his own Minister, and still less in that of his ally. There is much intrigue, and more fear of it. Russia distrusts Austria about Saxony; and Austria dreads Russia about Poland, especially if she is mistress of the question after a peace.... Suspicion is the prevailing temper of the Emperor, and Metternich's character furnishes constant food for the *intriguants* to work upon.[6]

War aims had still not been settled when the Allies invaded France, so confusion, disputes, and contradictory moves were inevitable. In fact, it was mainly the fear of Napoleon that kept the powers together and subdued their suspicions. The coalition was more likely to break up if Napoleon was defeated and Alexander felt able to achieve his aims single-handed.

The frustrations of operating as a coalition commander took their toll on Schwarzenberg. 'We are not wholly idle', he wrote to his wife on 25 December 1813, 'but the coalition is an awful obstacle in all measures.' Even so, he recognised that 'we would not have come here without it, so we can not be aggrieved at it and all its imperfections'.[7]

Military strategy

At the end of 1813 Napoleon still occupied much of northern and central Italy, part of Catalonia in north-eastern Spain, and isolated fortresses across central Europe. Even so, the invasion of the French Empire, those lands ruled directly from Paris, had already begun, first in March when a Cossack raid temporarily occupied the city of Hamburg (which Napoleon had annexed in 1810), and then in October when Wellington crossed the Bidasoa river and carried his offensive from Spain into south-western France, before it petered out by the end of the year south of Bayonne.

Yet it was the Rhine frontier that most directly threatened Napoleon. When they gathered at Frankfurt in November, the Allies had to decide whether to launch an invasion across the Rhine, and when and how to do so, and these debates dragged on into December. Disagreements arose not simply between different coalition partners, but between a country's representatives. Generals who had commanded an army against Napoleon clashed with royal military advisers still wedded to the more cautious and methodical strategies of the eighteenth century.

Some feared that an invasion could reunite France around Napoleon and revive the popular resistance encountered during the Revolution. They were also intimidated by the belts of fortresses protecting the French frontiers, but others pointed out that the strongpoints were in need of repair and that threatening them would actually reduce Napoleon's field army by forcing him to provide garrisons.

Schwarzenberg and *Feldmarschall* Gebhard Leberecht von Blücher, the other leading army commander, both favoured an immediate invasion, to exploit the French demoralisation and confusion and pre-empt Napoleon's attempts to mobilise fresh resources. Yet, however desirable in military terms, a prompt invasion was logistically doubtful and politically impossible. After advancing more than 190 miles from Leipzig, the Allies needed to incorporate replacements, issue new equipment, and overhaul their supply system. The Prussian *1. Garde-Regiment zu Fuß*, for example, had lost 870 officers and men, or one-third of its strength, between 12 August and 14 November, despite barely seeing action except at Leipzig, where it had just 67 casualties.[8] How much worse would the haemorrhaging of men be if the Allies invaded a hostile land in the middle of winter, and extended their lines of communication another 300 miles to Paris?

Delay would also give time for the incorporation into the coalition of the princes who had hitherto belonged to the *Rheinbund*, Napoleon's confederation of German satellite states, which had collapsed at the time of Leipzig. The Allies needed the support and resources of the princes in order to secure their lines of communication, but admitting them to the alliance raised intricate questions about the future settlement of central Europe, since the great powers sought to secure influence over individual German states.

Yet postponing an invasion would cause problems of its own, for it was difficult to feed large numbers of men and horses concentrated in one region for long. The Allies were soon short of supplies at Frankfurt, and by invading France could relieve the burden on the recently liberated German lands.[9]

Where should they invade? The three alternatives were the Lower, Middle, and Upper Rhine. A thrust across the Lower Rhine would exploit unrest in Napoleon's annexed Dutch and Belgian *départements*, and would then have to cross just 125 miles of the old French heartland to reach Paris. A central advance across the Middle Rhine would use the most direct road to Paris, but would have to force several major river crossings, and pass through the fortress belts. Finally, a detour 190 miles to the south to cross the Upper Rhine would outflank the fortresses and rivers, but take longer to put pressure on Napoleon.

In making these strategic choices, the Allies had to subordinate purely military considerations to political ones, in order to hold the coalition together. The victory at Leipzig offered the prospect of a prompt peace, and hence brought underlying strains and divergent objectives to the fore. The result was a compromise, with the Allies dissipating their strength along a broad front, for whereas Britain for her own security needed the French expelled from the Low Countries, Austria had vital interests in Switzerland and Italy, and this emphasis on both flanks militated against a powerful central punch.

The general concept that emerged was for the main Allied force, the *Hauptarmee* under Schwarzenberg in person, to swing southwards across the Upper Rhine, pass through the gap between the Jura and Vosges heights, and reach the strategically important high ground of the Langres plateau, 110 miles inside France. Blücher's *Schlesische Armee* would have a secondary role on the Middle Rhine, where it could cover the *Hauptarmee*'s communications, while elements of a third force, the *Nordarmee*, would cross the Lower Rhine. By occupying the Langres plateau, Schwarzenberg hoped to induce Napoleon to seek peace without having to fight a major battle. While negotiations progressed, he could sustain the *Hauptarmee* logistically by having the fertile and densely populated Saône valley in his rear.

The Allies did not, therefore, agree a masterplan for the entire invasion. They decided simply to invade France, and would not necessarily advance all the way to

Paris. Decisions on military operations after the occupation of Langres would have to await political developments. Metternich was determined to control the pace of the campaign, and integrate military pressure with negotiations. Recovering their territory and influence in the Italian peninsula was more important to the Austrians than capturing Paris, a longer venture, and one laden with military and political risks.

Austria's focus on her own vision of a stable European settlement would cause bitter resentment, but was no different in principle from many Russian and Prussian attitudes. The key distinction was that Austrian priorities made her military moves more cautious than those of her Allies, and that invited contemptuous comparisons. Yet there was no reason why the more extreme war aims of Alexander or the Prussian generals should take precedence over Austrian concerns. The war did not have to end with an occupation of Paris. Without Austrian co-operation, the coalition would not have been able to defeat Napoleon in central Europe, let alone invade France.

The Frankfurt Proposals

Already, in the aftermath of Leipzig, Metternich had made peace proposals in a bid to pre-empt Alexander's desire for a military solution. On 10 November he informally offered moderate terms, the so-called Frankfurt Proposals, under which France would retain her natural frontiers, the Rhine, Alps, Pyrenees, and the sea, instead of returning to the former frontiers of the *Ancien Régime*, which would have entailed the loss of Belgium and the left bank of the Rhine.

Rather than give a direct response, Napoleon advocated a peace conference, but Metternich insisted that the Frankfurt Proposals had to be accepted first as the basis for negotiations. Then, on 1 December, he put pressure on Napoleon to negotiate in earnest by issuing the Frankfurt Declaration, which publicly portrayed him as an obstacle to peace by stating that the Allies were waging war not against the French people, but against his disproportionate power.

These proposals and counter-proposals were not merely cynical bids to win time or undermine an opponent. They sought, step by step, to clarify each side's position, and develop the initial proposals into more formal and precise undertakings, a process that was all the more necessary since the Allies themselves had yet to agree their war aims.[10]

In reality, the Frankfurt Proposals could never have formed the basis for a durable peace because of the fundamentally incompatible interests both within the coalition, and between it and Napoleon. The natural frontiers that Metternich had offered were, in fact, unacceptable to Britain, since they would have left the great naval base of Antwerp in French hands.

On 5 December the Allies were informed that Napoleon had accepted the Frankfurt Proposals, but British and Russian opposition to the terms had now hardened, and further negotiations were postponed until Lord Castlereagh could arrive from London to give Britain an effective voice within the coalition. Thus, the proposed peace conference would not open until February 1814, and by then the transformed military situation would enable the Allies to insist on the former frontiers as the basis of negotiation.

Chapter 2

France in 1814

Had Napoleon been two years older, he would have been Genoese by birth, as it was only in 1768 that France annexed Corsica, his homeland. For the first 23 years of his life, until his family had to flee the island in 1793, he saw himself as a Corsican patriot, and regarded France as an oppressor.

Napoleon's own background showed how disparate and disunited much of France was as a nation. Vast swathes in the north and east had been added to the central core around Paris only in the previous 160 years: Lorraine, for example, had been acquired as recently as 1766. More outlying areas had been annexed since the start of the Revolutionary Wars, including Belgium, Holland, the left bank of the Rhine, and parts of Switzerland and the Italian peninsula. Even the old heartland had strong regional identities, and was still riven by the bitter political, social, and religious schisms of the Revolution.

War-weariness

France was exhausted. For a quarter of a century she had been beset by Revolution or war, and ever since 1808, following Napoleon's disastrous intervention in the Iberian peninsula, she had been fighting continuously on the continent of Europe. Besides military setbacks, Napoleon had suffered a series of blows to his prestige, including excommunication by Pope Pius VII in 1809, an economic crisis in 1810–1812, and an abortive *coup d'état* in 1812. With the collapse of her wider Empire, France now had to bear the full burden of the war herself. Napoleon needed men, money, weapons, and time, and it was money that was the most pervasive problem. Having exhausted his credit, he had to resort to increasing taxes, cutting state salaries, and relying more heavily on requisitioning, all of which cost him political support.

France had regressed to the disarray that had dogged the dying days of the Directory, shortly before Napoleon had seized power in 1799. Yet the disillusionment was not translated into effective political opposition, for this required leaders, organisation, and large numbers of people with the motivation to take action. Passive resistance was more common than open revolts, and when disturbances did occur, as in the *département* of the Nord, which saw anti-conscription riots in November 1813, they were generally directed against specific grievances, or simply the principle of control from Paris, rather than against Napoleon personally.[1] Equally, those Frenchmen who were keen to fight the invasion might have patriotic rather than Bonapartist motives. Republicans such as Lazare Carnot, the 'organiser of victory' of the Revolutionary Wars, had hitherto remained aloof from the Empire, but now rallied to defend France.

The final months of Napoleon's regime revealed its moral hollowness. By demanding blind obedience, he had deadened the spirit of initiative, and even before the invasion began, his administrative control over France had begun to disintegrate, as cynicism, self-interest, and preoccupation with local matters frustrated his attempts to generate a sense of national unity. Officials might carry out their duties, but they did so simply out of a habit of compliance, while *maires* tended to empathise more with their communities than with the Empire.

In response, Napoleon superimposed high-ranking *commissaires extraordinaires* on the existing administrative machinery in the provinces, as direct agents of the central government. They were meant to overcome inertia, and hasten the mobilisation of resources, but were mostly aged between 57 and 64, were despatched only after the start of the Allied invasion, and all too often found themselves overwhelmed by the situation.[2]

The *commissaires extraordinaires* were an echo of the famous *représentants-en-mission* of the Revolution, and this was no accident. Napoleon consciously sought to evoke the spirit of 1792–1793 when France had last faced danger from invasion on this scale. The *Marseillaise*, which had fallen out of favour during the Empire, was once again performed on barrel organs in the streets of Paris, although the actual words might be replaced by verses praising Napoleon.[3] On three occasions during the winter of 1813–1814, he appeared in the streets of the capital to strengthen his links with the common people.

Evoking Revolutionary precedents ran the risk of alarming the respectable classes. Napoleon hoped to rally them around him by having a commission of the *Corps législatif* examine the record of his foreign policy and endorse his claim that he had never rejected a reasonable peace. But instead of providing unreserved support, the deputies sought to extract guarantees of liberties, and make him renounce wars of conquest. When Napoleon responded on 31 December by adjourning the *Corps législatif*, he widened the gulf between himself and the social élites. This was all the more dangerous in that they had been the bedrock of support on which he had established his Empire, and many liberals held posts within the government.

By suppressing open opposition, Napoleon had driven it underground, and had forced those who disagreed with him either to serve him regardless, or to resign from office and enter the political wilderness. The result had been to accumulate a critical mass of discontented political figures in Paris, who could be contained only so long as the Allied armies were kept at a distance.

Napoleon was distracted from the danger within his regime by more pressing military concerns. He was instinctively reluctant to change servants with whom he was familiar, and found it hard to believe that men who had come to the fore during the Revolution could secure a political future under the most obvious alternative regime, a restored Bourbon monarchy. Imprisoning disillusioned senior figures, such as Charles-Maurice de Talleyrand-Périgord, the *Vice grand électeur*, would have shaken public confidence, and could actually have increased the danger by removing moderate opponents whose influence contained more headstrong men.[4]

Napoleon's methods ranged in degree from the subtle to the overt. The overt tended to be a sign of failure, as the adjournment of the *Corps législatif* demonstrated. He preferred to use soft tactics of influence and surveillance. In any case, as the *Ministre de la police générale* later explained, the sheer number of suspects made it impossible to arrest them all.[5] So long as the regime maintained a show of confidence, and the possibility remained of the war ending in a negotiated peace with Napoleon still in power, most opponents would be content to grumble.

Peace was what the French people wanted, but peace without the dishonour of defeat or the social disintegration that could accompany a complete collapse of the regime. The bulk of the population constituted an inert mass that, although resigned to events, could eventually stir and become an overwhelming groundswell of opinion.

Everything depended on whether Napoleon could secure peace by repelling the invading armies. If he succeeded, he could rally France behind him, and make irrelevant any political intrigues in the capital. If, on the other hand, he failed, he might see support swinging behind his opponents once they moved openly against him.

Military resources

It was the second time within a year that Napoleon had to rebuild his army, and France had already been drained by the unprecedented demands on her manpower since 1812. Nevertheless, between 9 October 1813 and 6 January 1814 Napoleon ordered the raising of another 936,000 soldiers or *gardes nationaux*. But this impressive figure hid a more disappointing reality, for Napoleon lacked the time to organise, train, and equip all the men, and had no weapons with which to arm them, and he encountered high levels of desertion and evasion. In fact, of the theoretical total of 936,000, only one man in eight actually fought in the campaign.[6]

After his disaster in Russia, Napoleon had been given four months in which to raise a new army for the 1813 campaign. He calculated on having a similar lull before the Allies invaded France in the spring, but they actually crossed the Rhine on 21 December 1813, just six weeks after he had returned to Paris. This disrupted his plans, forced him to react to successive crises, and deprived him of the resources of the frontier regions.

Napoleon did have a pool of 100,000 mostly experienced troops in south-western France and Catalonia. Commanded by *Maréchaux* Jean-de-Dieu Soult and Louis Suchet, they had become toughened in the Peninsular War, but were tied down garrisoning fortresses and containing the Spanish and Anglo-Portuguese armies. Desperate to release them, Napoleon offered to return the detained Spanish King, Ferdinand VII, provided Spain took no further part in the war. On 10 December Ferdinand duly signed the Treaty of Valençay, but had no intention of honouring it, and in any case the Spanish Regency and *Cortes* would reject it in February. As a result, Napoleon was able to withdraw only 24,000 troops from Soult and Suchet in January, followed by another 10,000 from Suchet at the beginning of March.

Thousands more troops had been left trapped in fortresses in central Europe, along with capable commanders, like *Maréchal* Louis Davout. Frontier fortresses in France itself also required garrisons, but could be held mainly by second-rate troops: only the two most important, Antwerp and Mainz, had large contingents of regulars.

A successful defence of France depended on horses and muskets as much as manpower. But Napoleon had lost the prolific horse-breeding regions of Germany, and while he could find plenty of smaller horses in France, he no longer had an abundance of the larger animals that were suitable as cavalry mounts. He had also squandered immense quantities of weapons, left behind in fortresses in central Europe, where they had been sent for the *Grande armée* in 1812 and 1813. Napoleon ordered the manufacture of new muskets, the arming of the *gardes nationaux* with foreign ones, the repair of firearms in arsenals, and the fitting together of muskets from existing parts. During the campaign, muskets were collected from the battlefields, and taken from prisoners, deserters, and the wounded.[7]

Inadequate clothing also plagued the army, which helps explain the high desertion rates. Despite the extreme coldness, many of the men in newly formed regiments wore cotton trousers and lacked overcoats. Napoleon was reduced to ordering shakos and greatcoats to be taken from Allied prisoners-of-war, but had to abandon even that idea when they were found to be infested with lice.[8]

Napoleon's subordinates

Nine years earlier, in the 1805 campaign, Napoleon had eleven *maréchaux* in the *Grande armée*, and all but three of them were aged between 35 and 38.[9] But by 1814 his senior command team bore the scars of a decade of almost constant war. Of the twenty-five *maréchaux* that he had appointed up to then, three (Lannes, Bessières and Poniatowski) were dead; four (Kellermann, Moncey, Pérignon and Sérurier) were honorary *maréchaux* and unfit for active commands with the field army; three (Massena, Brune and Jourdan) were worn out, disgraced or relegated to sedentary commands in the interior of France; and two (Soult and Suchet) were containing Wellington and the Spaniards in south-western France and Catalonia. Of the others, Augereau was entrusted with the defence of Lyon; Davout was besieged in Hamburg; Gouvion Saint-Cyr was a prisoner-of-war; and two (Bernadotte, now the Crown Prince of Sweden; and Murat, the King of Naples) were either in the Allied coalition or about to join it. Apart from Berthier, the *major-général*, that left only seven *maréchaux* directly under Napoleon in the *Grande armée*: Lefebvre, Macdonald, Marmont, Mortier, Ney, Oudinot and Victor. They ranged in age from 39 to 58, with the average being 47.[10]

Marmont was the youngest and most able, but he was also vain and impulsive, which meant that his performance could be erratic. Of the others, Oudinot repeatedly demonstrated his incompetence when entrusted with a detached force, while Victor proved so lethargic that he was eventually transferred to a less demanding post. Macdonald fell ill towards the end of February and had to be replaced temporarily. Lefebvre was past his prime, and had no permanent combat command, being instead attached to Napoleon's headquarters and entrusted with specific tasks on a battlefield as they arose. Ney was an inspiring, fighting general, but too headstrong, and in need of close supervision. Mortier was bold, energetic, and experienced, but not particularly intelligent.

Napoleon could not expect his *maréchaux* to serve willingly under each other when he had to detach more than one of them to cover a sector. Even Marmont and Mortier, who co-operated well, required time to concert their plans, partly as the more capable Marmont, who was effectively in command, had to show deference to Mortier, his senior in age and order of appointment.[11]

Outside the marshalate, some of Napoleon's generals had become sick or worn out, including *Général de division* Etienne Champion, *comte* de Nansouty, who had to give up command of the Imperial Guard cavalry in mid-campaign and would die within a year. But many of the generals belonged to a younger generation of capable and ambitious men. More than three-quarters of the divisional commanders who fought directly under Napoleon in 1814 were under the age of 45. They had already served on average for twenty-four years, eight of them as a general. A staggering 89 per cent had previously been wounded, and one in every three of them became a casualty or a prisoner in 1814 itself.[12]

By 1814 Napoleon's army had been degraded by years of massive casualties, overwhelmed by the influx of poorly trained conscript replacements, and was composed partly of hurriedly assembled provisional units. Yet he still had scores of capable and formidably experienced generals, who could act aggressively under his direct supervision, and this is often forgotten. Nowhere was the quality of his generals more obvious than in the cavalry. Despite often being outnumbered and handicapped by mediocre men and horses, his cavalry commanders repeatedly demonstrated their superiority over their Allied counterparts. They supplied Napoleon with accurate and timely intelligence, successfully screened his army's movements, and achieved some outstanding battlefield successes.

'Forwards, the *Marie-Louises*'

Following Leipzig, Napoleon had dispersed the survivors of the *Grande armée* in a cordon along 400 miles of the Rhine to cover his eastern frontier between Switzerland and the North Sea. These forces were further reduced through sickness and desertion in November and December, but their quality increased, since the weaker soldiers were eliminated.[13]

Napoleon had to raise thousands more men to reinforce these units. Since the line formations were too weak to provide enough cadres around which to organise so many new conscripts, Napoleon massively expanded the Imperial Guard, which had a more efficient administration, the necessary numbers of experienced personnel, and the prestige to make military service in its ranks more attractive. As a result of this enlargement, Napoleon effectively turned the Guard into his army, and reduced his other troops to the role of auxiliaries. For this reason, 1814 has been called 'the campaign of the Guard'.[14] Overall, the Imperial Guard amounted to one-third of the field army under Napoleon's direct command, but because of his reliance on its superior combat power, it constituted well over half the troops he had on some battlefields, and even, at Château-Thierry, his entire force.

Unfortunately, expansion on such a scale diluted the Imperial Guard's quality. The Old Guard was still reliable, but some of the most junior units were little better than the line. 'I hardly count on the conscripts of the Young Guard', complained *Maréchal* Etienne Macdonald. 'Their officers say that they do not know how to turn to the right, and I fear they know the about-turn only too well.'[15]

The conscripts who filled the army were dubbed *Marie-Louises*, since it had been Napoleon's wife, the Empress Marie-Louise, who had decreed the levies during his absence on campaign in 1813. The nickname contained an undercurrent of pity, yet one of their officers, *Colonel* Charles, *baron* Fabvier, proudly remembered how:

> Hastily raised and absorbed into the ranks, they amused the old soldiers with their innocence and simplicity. Their uniform consisted of a grey greatcoat and an effeminate-looking cap. . . . These children lacked training and physical strength, but their sense of honour made up for everything and their courage was indomitable. At the shout, always repeated by a thousand voices, 'Forwards, the *Marie-Louises*', you could see their pale faces flush most nobly, and their knees, weakened by hunger and exhaustion, became firmer as they prepared to dash at the enemy.[16]

At Champaubert in February, one conscript said that he would willingly fire his musket, if only he had someone to load it for him. Another told his *lieutenant*: 'Sir, you have been in this profession for a long time. Take my musket and fire and I will pass you cartridges.'[17]

Teaching men how to load and fire did not, in fact, require much time, and could be done even during the campaign.[18] But training them to manoeuvre, and to deploy out of column, was more difficult, and this limited a commander's tactical options and increased the likelihood of heavy casualties.

However brave and enthusiastic they were in combat, young conscripts were unsteady in adversity, and lacked the experience and forcefulness to be able to fend for themselves. They suffered an appalling wastage rate from desertion and straggling. 'I need men and not children,' Napoleon complained in October 1813:

> No one is braver than our youths, but, since they have no physical strength, they fill the hospitals, and they behave as is natural at their age whenever things are at all uncertain. Men are needed to defend France.[19]

Thus, only some of the *Marie-Louises* were teenagers. The class of 1815, which had an average age of 19, was meant to contribute 150,000 men, but the call-up was not pressed, precisely because of their youth. Conscription fell more heavily on the earlier classes, and so it was more common for the *Marie-Louises* to be in their early 20s.[20]

In any case, Napoleon's troops varied widely in quality, and included not just conscripts, but Old Guardsmen, veterans withdrawn from the Peninsular armies, and naval personnel, *gendarmes*, and *douaniers*, many of whom were former soldiers. Even some retired or mutilated veterans were recalled to active service as NCOs. The state of discipline also varied. The experienced Peninsular troops were a welcome reinforcement, but had acquired bad habits while serving in Spain, and caused much discontent during their disorderly passage through France.[21]

Cavalry and artillerymen took longer than infantry to train. Napoleon had been crippled during the 1813 campaign by a shortage of cavalry, a legacy of his massive loss of horses in Russia the previous year. But by 1814 the shortfall had been overcome, even if the quality and stamina often remained low, and on some battlefields Napoleon actually had more cavalry than his opponents. In general, he also had plenty of guns, which helped offset the deficiencies in his other arms. 'We did not have an army,' he later recalled, 'we had only cannon', and he claimed that the Allies overestimated his strength because they judged it by the number of his guns.[22] But the artillery itself varied in quality, and was short of horses and trained gunners.[23]

A 39-year-old carpenter called Jean Caupeil believed he had the answer to the superior Allied manpower. He actually invented an armoured personnel carrier, and on 22 January handed a petition to a valet at the Tuileries palace, asking to see Napoleon. But instead of being given the opportunity to explain his invention personally, he was questioned by the police, who seemed more interested in why he had never done any military service. During the interrogation, he described how:

> As soon as I knew that the enemy had invaded part of our territory, I thought that it would be impossible to have too many means of destroying and chasing them away. Since I am very interested in mechanics, I dreamed up a specially-constructed vehicle, in which you can place two or three men, and as many horses, with all the necessary ammunition and equipment for going on campaign.
>
> These vehicles are covered and lined with metal sheets, so that they hide their contents and are protected from musket shots. Even the horses that are harnessed to it will be sheltered from shots, since they are also to be coated in a covering, likewise of sheet metal, which will protect them from head to foot, and in a way as not to hinder their movement. The soldiers who are placed inside the vehicles, with their horses, will be able to take action and fire very easily, without being seen, and without danger.

Caupeil had even constructed a model of his carriers. But they would not, in fact, have proved practicable, since there was no time or money to build them, or suitable horses to pull them. Small horses weighed down by armour, or heavy animals more used to ploughing fields, could hardly have made a sweeping charge, and Caupeil's carriers were more likely to have plodded slowly around the battlefield, or broken down as their horses collapsed in exhaustion. Yet his concept was a truly visionary one:

> If you sent a great number of these vehicles off against the enemy, equipped in this way with men, horses, weapons, and ammunition, you would certainly do him much harm. What is more, if it becomes necessary, the soldiers can easily get out, with their horses and ammunition, draw up in ranks, and fight as cavalry or infantry.[24]

'My confidence was unshaken'

Napoleon had a largely French army, in contrast to the multi-national composite armies of 1809–1813. By 1814 he was left with only one satellite state, the Kingdom of Italy, and had disarmed many of his remaining foreign corps, for he had little confidence that men like the Dutch and Germans would remain loyal, and he needed their muskets. But his field army did still include some men from the annexed regions of Belgium and Italy, as well as Poles and Swiss. Their presence could result in misunderstandings. At Reims in March six Polish soldiers tried to re-enter the city, but were unable to reply in French when challenged by the sentry. Mistaken for Russians, they were fired on, and two of them were seriously wounded.[25]

In order to supply a stream of reinforcements, Napoleon wanted an *Armée de réserve* based at Paris and composed of provisional divisions formed successively from the resources of the city's depots and the influx of conscripts from elsewhere in France. The divisions would be composed of assorted battalions, and could be pushed forward to outlying towns or camps before joining the field army. Napoleon explained to the *Ministre de la guerre* on 2 January:

> You will notice that these battalions all belong to regiments in the *Grande armée*. Each battalion will rejoin its regiment in the *Grande armée*, when the reserve is disbanded and the enemy has been driven from our territory. The organisation of the *Armée de réserve* is therefore only a way of getting these battalions to their destination . . .[26]

The existence of this *Armée de réserve* also ensured that troops were always present at Paris to maintain order and guard against an attack by an Allied raiding force. In theory, Napoleon could expect the capital to have a reserve of 30,000 to 40,000 men by early February, but the want of muskets made these strengths unrealisable.[27] Nor, despite all the reinforcements that reached his field army, did he ever have more than 45,000 troops on a battlefield: the reinforcements did no more than replace his losses.

Napoleon repeatedly reorganised his army during the campaign according to the turnover of men and the availability of subordinate commanders. This constant improvisation made it difficult for the Allies to realise the full extent of his army's weakness, but also undermined its cohesion.[28] Since so many units were cobbled together from assorted detachments, strong leadership was essential. Battalions were deliberately kept smaller than usual, so that the cadres of officers and NCOs could supervise their conscripts more closely. The fact that battalions were understrength meant that higher formations, such as divisions and corps, were correspondingly weak, which enabled the French generals to exercise more direct and personal leadership. *Maréchal* Auguste Marmont noted that he often had to do the job of every rank down to second-in-command of a regiment.[29]

What of the morale of the troops? It varied between units, between officers and men, conscripts and veterans, and with the fluctuations in military fortune. Napoleon had seized power 15 years ago and few of his young conscripts could remember any other ruler. Nor was it was obvious at the time that he would lose the campaign, for a string of victories can give even a largely conscript army a heady sense of invincibility, and he was both prompt and generous in rewarding men who distinguished themselves. As many as 300 decorations were granted to the 1st Old Guard Division in the middle of February, and 500 to the Guard cavalry.[30] *Capitaine de vaisseau* Jean Grivel of the *Marins* of the Guard explained that as late as the middle of March:

> My morale was still high, despite our daily misfortunes, and my confidence in a good outcome was unshaken. Yet you did not need much insight at this time to foresee a catastrophe. Had I realised a little how our matters stood, it is clear that I would have sensed the terrible situation. But I was far from these thoughts and lived wholly in the present, absorbed as I was by my day-to-day tasks.[31]

Second-line units

In support of the regular army were various forces of the interior, including the *compagnies de réserve* (a company of reservists at the disposal of each *préfet*), and the *Gendarmerie* (a paramilitary police force distributed throughout the country). Above all, there was the *Garde nationale*, initially a politically active Revolutionary militia, which Napoleon had neutralised and placed in suspended animation before reviving it as a territorial reserve that could be mobilised for home defence in the event of a crisis while his army was absent on campaign.

The *Garde nationale* existed largely on paper, and would require time and resources to become fully organised, trained, and equipped. In rebuilding his regular army after the disaster in Russia, Napoleon had been obliged to incorporate eighty-eight *cohortes* of the *Garde nationale* into the line infantry, instead of using them to train large numbers of civilians on a rotational basis. At the end of 1813, therefore, he had available neither a great pool of trained reservists, nor sufficient firearms.

Activating too much of the *Garde nationale* under these circumstances would have been counter-productive. Napoleon could not mobilise men by every available means at the same time without overwhelming the administration, and he realised that mass levies of *gardes nationaux* would encroach on resources that could be raised more quickly and effectively through conscription. Apart from causing concern about the potential political risk of arming citizens, ordering levies of the *Garde nationale* increased discontent, especially among married men who had escaped conscription, as it was seen as a way of imposing military service by stealth.

The *Garde nationale* was therefore activated only partially, in specific locations when required, starting in particular with the coastal areas and, in October 1813, the eastern *départements*. Since Napoleon expected a lull before the Allies invaded, he gave priority to conscription, but after the invasion began on the Rhine, he issued decrees on 30 December and 6 January for over 100,000 *gardes nationaux* to form two reserve armies for Paris and Lyon. The results were disappointing, for the orders had come too late to be effective, and were undermined by the dislocation caused by the invasion.

Some *gardes nationaux* helped garrison fortresses, and Napoleon wanted to use other units actually on the battlefield:

These troops are no longer *gardes nationales*, but real troops of the line, since they are composed of men who have already covered 200 leagues to come and cover the capital. They must be armed and made ready to serve.[32]

Garde nationale units did occasionally see action in the field, but were restricted in numbers, and varied considerably in quality, partly because they had been activated at different times. Regiments from the western coasts had been mobilised as early as April 1813, and had been able to complete their organisation and equipment, unlike units raised hurriedly at the end of the year. Napoleon himself admitted:

The *gardes nationales* are good only when the cadres are of line troops and are full. Otherwise, the *gardes nationales* are pitiful, for without officers and cadres, they really have nothing good.[33]

Besides the active *gardes nationaux*, who could be moved from their *départements* of origin to the campaign area, there were sedentary *cohortes urbaines*, which were tied to their local towns as a security force. They were activated in December 1813 to help the *Gendarmerie* contain the perceived threat from the tens of thousands of prisoners-of-war disseminated throughout France, but had limited combat value. At the town of Provins they were armed with pikes, and could offer no serious resistance. When an Allied force approached in February, their commander simply hid his uniform until the French army returned five days later.[34] Even so, the sedentary *gardes nationaux* were useful in other ways, for by undertaking routine, rear-area duties, they left the field army free to fight. They rounded up stragglers, deserters and Allied fugitives, escorted supply convoys or prisoners-of-war, and guarded roads, bridges, prisons, and magazines.

In addition to raising conscripts and *gardes nationaux*, Napoleon sought to mobilise the remaining population in the threatened frontier districts by decreeing the *levée en masse*. The existence of the sedentary *gardes nationaux*, and the *gardes champêtres* and *gardes forestiers* (rural and forestry wardens), provided a nucleus around which to organise popular resistance.

The distinction between the regulars, *gardes nationaux*, and armed civilians was often blurred in terms of morale, experience, and the state of their equipment. Some conscripts received only rudimentary uniforms, or none at all, as an ADC, *Sous-lieutenant* Lefol, noted at Vitry-le-François on 26 January:

Waggons, filled with items of equipment and weaponry, were drawn up in front of each regiment in order to provide the arriving masses of conscripts with the uniforms of the units that they were going to join. Hardly had they reached their companies than these poor youths undressed in the open air and exchanged their peasant clothes for a soldier's greatcoat. They were issued with muskets, which the NCOs taught them right away how to load, for there was no time to teach them the drill. Many of these improvised soldiers, unable to find uniforms that fitted them, set out that same evening in the state in which they had come; several of the unfortunate men were killed the very next day at Saint-Dizier, without having the satisfaction of wearing a French uniform before they died.[35]

Chapter 3

The Allied armies

By the start of 1814 the Allies had mobilised over a million troops against Napoleon, more than one-and-a-half times as many as he had assembled for his mighty invasion of Russia two years earlier.[1] Yet on no occasion during the campaign did they manage to confront him on a battlefield with more than 10 per cent of their total manpower, for they also had to field an array of armies in secondary theatres around the periphery of France, besides reserve, siege, and blockade corps. Britain, moreover, had to maintain her global commitments, and fight a parallel war against the United States.

The two most important Allied formations were the *Hauptarmee* under Schwarzenberg, and the *Schlesische Armee* under Blücher, which together constituted the main invasion. These two armies, including the corps that reinforced them during the campaign, amounted to 350,000 troops, or about one-third of the total Allied strength.[2]

The nearest of the supporting armies was the *Nordarmee*, under the Crown Prince of Sweden, which detached two corps into the Low Countries. The other Allied armies could offer only indirect support, by distracting and tying down French troops. Wellington, for example, had fought his way over the Pyrenees, while an Austrian army had begun an invasion of north-eastern Italy.

The *Hauptarmee*

The *Hauptarmee*, or Grand Army, had three Austrian corps (the I, II and III), and the IV (Württemberg), V (Bavarian), and VI (Russian) *Armee-Abtheilungen*. It also contained an Austrian reserve corps, and a Russian reserve army of Guards, grenadiers, *cuirassiers*, Cossacks, and reserve artillery.

At its head was Schwarzenberg, the Allied supreme commander. His appointment in 1813 reflected the lack of an acceptable alternative, and the need to block Alexander's desire to fill the role himself, an ambition that threatened both military defeat and undue Russian political influence. Yet Schwarzenberg was only 42, and had previously led nothing larger than a cavalry division at Wagram in 1809, and a corps of 30,000 men in 1812. By January 1814 he had just four-and-a-half months' experience of actively commanding an army, too short a time in which to become confident. But he had also served as a diplomat in Paris and St Petersburg, and was appointed because of his negotiating skills, and the fact that he could be trusted to work closely with Metternich and Emperor Franz in protecting Austrian interests.

Thus, Schwarzenberg's role has been misunderstood: he had a broad, managerial responsibility, rather than being purely a military leader. He had to subordinate military considerations to Austria's political strategy, and his apparent hesitations and delays were sometimes the result of him being ordered to halt for political reasons, torn between conflicting pressures, or constrained by the logistical challenge of supplying his large army. He was further inhibited by an awareness that the Austrian

Empire was already drained of money and manpower and that further heavy casualties would endanger its ability to defend its interests in post-war Europe and hold together its numerous subject peoples.

As supreme commander, Schwarzenberg had nominal co-ordinating authority over the *Schlesische Armee* and *Nordarmee*, but the reality of his power was limited by distance, disobedience, and intermittent communications. Even within his own *Hauptarmee*, he had restricted control, particularly over the Russian reserves, which tended to be shielded from action even though they accounted for over 20 per cent of the army's strength. His corps commanders tended either to lack drive, like *Feldzeugmeister* Ignaz, *Graf* Gyulai, or to have too much, like *General der Kavallerie* Karl, *Graf* von Wrede, the abrasive and insubordinate commander of the Bavarian V *Armee-Abtheilung*.

Schwarzenberg also had to contend with the presence in his rear of the Russian, Prussian, and Austrian monarchs. Alexander seemed particularly prone to intervening in the conduct of operations, yet the *Hauptarmee*'s operations were actually shaped more by Metternich's subtle control. Alexander's interference was especially noticeable because he was more charismatic and forceful than his two fellow monarchs, because he could be infuriatingly inconsistent and carried away by the enthusiasm of the moment or persuasive advisers, and because he was obliged to exercise his influence more overtly since the *Hauptarmee* was under Austrian, and not Russian, command.

The presence of the monarchs and their advisers complicated Schwarzenberg's task as a commander, created concerns for their safety, and reduced him to despair:

> It is really inhuman what I suffer and endure, surrounded as I am with weaklings, fops of all sorts, eccentric planners, intriguers, idiots, gossips, and petty critics – in short, immense numbers of vermin gnaw at me and torment me right into the marrow of my bones.[3]

Even so, the disadvantages have been exaggerated. The three monarchs had all ruled for between 13 and 22 years, knew Napoleon personally, and had first-hand experience of several campaigns since 1792. Their authority could smooth difficulties and compel obedience from those of their generals who resented being placed under an Austrian supreme commander.[4] Their presence made it easier to combine military and political measures into a cohesive strategy than if the commanders had been obliged to refer decisions to their capital cities, between 500 and 1,300 miles to the east.

In fact, the campaigns of 1813–1814 constituted an intermittent, one-year conference of the foremost monarchs and statesmen in Europe. Decision-making remained slow and difficult and required frequent councils-of-war, but this was a problem inherent in coalition warfare, rather than one caused by the presence of the monarchs. Swift military operations would have been possible only if the contentious political issues dividing the Allies could have been settled before the invasion, and that was practically impossible, since the very basis of those political problems would be changed by the course of the military campaign.

The *Schlesische Armee*

Even though it was initially just two-fifths the size of the *Hauptarmee*, the *Schlesische Armee* (Army of Silesia) did more to shape the course of the campaign because of the energetic leadership of its commander, *Feldmarschall* von Blücher.

An hussar in temperament and training, Blücher was one of the few Allied generals undaunted by the prospect of a battle with Napoleon in person. His appointment in 1813 had not been universally welcomed. At 71 years of age, he was thought by some to be too old and unstable. Shrewd rather than well-educated, he had risen slowly, reaching general officer rank only at the age of 51, and had suffered from bouts of depression and alcoholic delusions during the troughs in his career.

Blücher's limitations, and the fact that he had actually commanded an army for no longer than Schwarzenberg, were offset by the existence of the Prussian *Generalstab* (General Staff).[5] Systematically trained staff officers were attached to generals at all levels, as full partners in managing and directing the army, rather than mere assistants. In a doctrine now known as mission command, subordinates were kept informed of the overall situation, and encouraged to react immediately to developments using their own initiative, instead of referring everything to higher authority. The common training of the staff officers provided the necessary framework to ensure that this decentralisation of authority did not cause the army's actions to lose their cohesion.

It was therefore a team that directed the *Schlesische Armee*. The *Chef des Generalstabes, General-Leutnant* August Neidhardt von Gneisenau, and the *General-Quartiermeister, General-Major* Karl von Müffling, would jointly present plans for Blücher's approval, and the headquarters would often debate key issues. They were talented, but flawed men: Gneisenau was headstrong and often wildly optimistic, while Müffling, although more affable, was vain and veered between over- and under-confidence.

The *Schlesische Armee* contained a combination of Prussian and Russian corps. With an average age of 53, the corps commanders were notably older than their counterparts in the *Hauptarmee*, who were, on average, just 41.[6] But their age did not make them less active, and most of them were capable and independent-minded, which also meant that they were difficult to handle. The more traditional Prussian generals, like *General der Infanterie* Hans von Yorck and *General-Leutnant* Friedrich Wilhelm von Bülow, disapproved of the way the army command strained the troops with forced marches in order to take the war to the enemy, and they distrusted Gneisenau because of his desire to regenerate Prussia with sweeping social reforms.

This friction undermined Gneisenau's delegation of authority through the *Generalstab* system, for distrust between army and corps headquarters was hardly conducive to effective mission command. Instead of reacting promptly to developments, the *Schlesische Armee*'s moves could be cautious, disjointed, and inflexible.

As the commander of a composite army, with so many fractious subordinates, Blücher had to lead more by encouragement than coercion. He made a point of asking Russian soldiers for some brandy, or a light for his pipe, in order to encourage the Prussians to see them as comrades, and the Russian officers to respect their men.

It took Wellington five years to establish an unquestioned dominance over his Peninsular army and bring it to a peak of efficiency and cohesion. Yet by the start of 1814 the *Schlesische Armee* had existed for just five months, and had initially been riven with discontent.[7] Blücher had not fully established his authority until the end of August 1813, when he led the *Schlesische Armee* to its first major victory on the Katzbach river, and he would face renewed problems in March 1814.

The German *Bundes-Corps*

To support the invasion of France, the Allies created eight corps from contingents extracted from German states. Bavaria, Württemberg, Hesse-Cassel, and Baden each provided one corps. Another four corps were formed by combining several contingents from lesser states.

The *1.* and *7. Bundes-Corps* were incorporated into the *Hauptarmee*, and became the IV (Württemberg) and V (Bavarian) *Armee-Abtheilungen*. The other six corps were divided equally in support of the *Hauptarmee, Schlesische Armee*, and *Nordarmee*.[8] They were intended mainly for rear-area duties, protecting communications, and blockading fortresses, but in the event, the *3.* and *6. Bundes-Corps* saw serious fighting against French field forces in the secondary theatres of Belgium and Lyon.

It proved difficult to form and equip the *Bundes-Corps* in time for the campaign, partly because of a shortage of weapons and equipment, but also because of obstructiveness. Many German princes were reluctant to raise a *Landsturm*, or home defence force, to enable their regular and *Landwehr* (militia) troops to take the field, partly as they were concerned about the potential risk of revolt if they armed their people. The delays obliged the invading Allied armies to detach units to protect their rear until they could be relieved by the *Bundes-Corps*.

Quality of troops

It was not just Napoleon who had to fight the 1814 campaign with an army of dubious and uneven quality. All the major European states had suffered massive losses since 1792, and had been forced to adapt and expand their armies to meet the threat from France and address the deficiencies revealed by their defeats, with mixed results.

Military doctrine, army organisation, staffwork, and command and control were all improved. Permanent higher formations were created for greater resilience and responsiveness. Tactics became more flexible and integrated, with more emphasis on attack columns and skirmishers, and attempts were made to ameliorate conditions for the rank and file. But reforms took time to be effective, and rulers would tolerate no more than the minimum required to meet the challenge posed by Napoleon. The emphasis was on improving the army and the administrative machinery of the state, rather than on transforming society as a whole to produce a true nation-in-arms, lest it endangered the established order. Even in Prussia, the most comprehensively defeated state, which undertook the most far-reaching reforms, the impact was limited. The benefits were also undermined by the simultaneous expansion of the armies, which saw officers promoted above their capabilities and the quality of units diluted by large numbers of recruits. When the Austrians took the field in August 1813, only one-third of their men were fully trained, the rest being no more than uniformed peasants.[9]

The Allied armies gained valuable experience during the 1812–1813 campaigns, but also took heavy casualties: many Russian regiments were no stronger than a single battalion. Recruiting standards had been progressively lowered to meet the demands for manpower. In the Russian army the upper age limit had been increased to 40 by 1812, while the height requirement was lowered, and the assessment of physical fitness was often hurried and superficial.[10]

Yet recruits could soon become effective soldiers, provided they were well-led. Lieutenant-General Prince Eugen von Württemberg boasted of the combat effectiveness of his Russian 2nd Infantry Corps by the end of the 1814 campaign:

> The example of the veterans influenced the mass of recruits. At that time, two-thirds of the corps were recruits, and yet I would dare to say that the corps never did its duty better than on this occasion, which proves the ease of

forming good infantry by means of war-hardened officers and cadres. But the main reason for the worth of the troops by that stage was the quality of the brigade and regimental commanders.[11]

Prince Eugen added that his newly joined recruits had to resort to taking uniforms from the dead, with the result that his corps looked more like a French formation, but his was not the only Allied unit with an odd appearance. A Prussian officer, *Leutnant* Wilhelm von Rahden, described the state of his *2. Schlesische Infanterie-Regiment* in January:

> As a result of the enemy fire, the relentless strains of the long campaigns, and the illnesses that had occurred before Erfurt, the fine regiment was almost unrecognisable. Replacements had generally filled up the gaps again, but their young faces still showed that they were no longer the war-hardened soldiers who had formed the magnificent army corps of *General* von Kleist after the [summer 1813] armistice. Nor had any great improvement been made in the clothing, even though we had enjoyed a six to eight-week break in the fighting since Leipzig. I remember very clearly being struck in this regimental inspection by the greatest variety, particularly in the headdresses.[12]

Combat performance depended as much on circumstances as on the quality of the troops. Rain, cold, and hunger all affected morale, and the loss of a unit's officers could be decisive. Much nonsense has been written about how Russian soldiers were so formidable that they had to be killed where they stood. In fact, they did not always fight doggedly in defence, and at Reims in March collapsed in panic after the fall of their commander, Lieutenant-General Emanuel, Count Saint-Priest.

Few Allied soldiers were genuine volunteers. Patriotism was a limited force, for none of the armies was nationally homogenous. The Austrian Empire was a sprawling, supra-national entity, held together by the Habsburg monarchy, while the Russian Empire had expanded to absorb such diverse peoples as Finns, Poles, Lithuanians, Georgians, Armenians, Belorussians, and Cossacks. Poles were also found in the Prussian army, along with men from a variety of German states.

Muskets were of several different calibres, and often unreliable, which helps explain the emphasis, in the Russian army in particular, on bayonet charges. The Austrians and Russians had a poor reputation as skirmishers, but this has to be qualified by the knowledge that many French conscripts barely knew how to load their firearms.[13]

All three powers had to supplement their regular forces with militia. Prussia had actually incorporated *Landwehr* regiments into her field army, for she had needed all the manpower she could muster in order to break free from French occupation.[14] In contrast, the Austrians had been reluctant to arm and train their subject peoples, in case of a future revolt: although one or two *Landwehr* battalions were included in their regular infantry regiments, they were detached for rear-area duties while on campaign. Similarly, hardly any use was made of the Russian militia, or *opolchenie*, except in supporting armies outside France.

The Austrians and Russians tended to be slow-moving, partly because they were encumbered with too much baggage. The Russian artillery was impressive, and commanded by officers who were generally better-educated and trained than their counterparts in the other arms, but the infantry were sometimes over-reliant on the artillery, and unwilling to fight without its support.[15] Allied commanders tended to deploy their artillery to stiffen their infantry and cavalry, rather than using it in the

French manner as a powerful, offensive arm in its own right. The Russians did sometimes mass their guns, but more to defend a position than to spearhead an attack.

Command and control

Only a few Allied commanders were outstanding generals, but the majority were at least brave and experienced. More than 70 per cent of the Russian corps commanders who took part in the invasion of France had already been wounded at least once in their career, and they had held general officer rank for an average of eleven years.[16] It is true that some Allied generals owed their position partly to birth and patronage, but that did not necessarily make them incompetent.

In 1813 Prussia's three front-line corps had been assigned to three different armies, but during the invasion of France they were gradually concentrated under Blücher, because of the need to strengthen the *Schlesische Armee*.[17] The Austrians had always been concentrated in the *Hauptarmee*, but the Russians were more dispersed. This, and the size of the Russian contingent, meant that their troops fought at every major battle in the main theatre of the campaign with the exception of Montereau, whereas the Prussians and Austrians were each engaged in only about half of them.

It could be challenging for contingents to operate effectively alongside one another, because of their different traditions, tactics, organisation, and sometimes languages. The relationship between the Prussians and Russians was one, at best, of good-humoured contempt, intensified by their frequent arrogance and boastfulness. Initial ideas in 1813 of standardising Russian and Prussian tactical doctrine had soon been abandoned in the face of opposition on both sides, and there was no attempt to form mixed Russo-Prussian corps in the *Schlesische Armee*.[18] In the *Hauptarmee*, in contrast, a shared language made it feasible to add Austrian units to the IV (Württemberg) and V (Bavarian) *Armee-Abtheilungen*, and some units from different states formed close ties. When Austrian *Kürassiere* had a dispute with the Württemberg *Jäger-Regiment Nr. 2*, they appealed to the Austrian *Ferdinand-Husaren* for support, but to no avail because the hussars had become used to serving alongside the Württembergers and saw them as their comrades.[19]

Cavalry

Throughout the 1814 campaign the Allies failed to use their cavalry boldly and ambitiously, either on the battlefield or in reconnaissance. The problem lay not simply in co-ordinating units from five different countries, but in deficiencies of morale, leadership, and organisation. It was difficult to assemble a mass of cavalry because of poor co-operation between corps, the rarity with which the *Hauptarmee*'s reserves saw action, and the fact that the *Schlesische Armee* remained weak in cavalry until it was reinforced in the second half of the campaign. Blücher did try to mass his cavalry in March, but lacked a commander who was senior and capable enough to handle a large force. 'It would certainly be good to push forward a large cavalry corps,' lamented Gneisenau:

> But where can we find someone to command it? Even in the Russian corps it is difficult, if a cavalry commander is to be placed under that of another corps. The best of them, Vasilchikov, is younger than the worst, Korf. Recently, we tried it with Winzingerode, but he did not do us any good. Our [Prussian]

commanders are too young compared with the Russians. In any case, it is no small task to lead a cavalry corps of 10,000 men with both boldness and caution at the same time.[20]

The Russian army included various types of irregular cavalry. Some were of dubious value, such as the Bashkirs, who wore chainmail armour, were armed with bows and arrows, and were used almost entirely in rear-area duties. The Cossacks, tribesmen from the frontiers of the Empire, were more ubiquitous. They were very light cavalry adept at raiding and reconnoitring. Their reputation as murderous barbarians was only partly deserved, for the term 'Cossack' was often applied indiscriminately to any Allied looters, thus inflating the terror they caused.[21]

Both Blücher and Schwarzenberg used flying corps to ease their advance. Formed from regular units, volunteers, or Cossacks, these mobile detachments were used to gather intelligence, protect an army's flanks, interdict French communications, and disrupt the mobilisation of conscripts and popular resistance. The flying corps had made great, sweeping raids in 1813, but became more cautious in France, where they had to operate in a more restricted and hostile region. They were also hindered by some of their more lacklustre leaders, including General Matvei Ivanovich, Count Platov, the *Ataman* of the Don Cossacks, who failed to live up to the fame he had won while harassing Napoleon's retreat from Moscow. He was now 60 years old, had just four years left to live, and, according to one of his Colonels, was 'good for nothing except drinking and sleeping':

> His feebleness and torpor increase every day, and obviously do serious harm to His Majesty the Emperor's service, and even more now than in the past. If General Kaisarov was not always there to drive him, if I myself did not act on the same lines, and if we did not force him to make at least some small marches, he would fall completely asleep. If we had an active leader at our head, we could do wonders and undertake diversions that would strike terror into the enemy.[22]

Just what could have been accomplished was demonstrated by Colonel Fedor Klementievich, Baron von Geismar. Operating from Belgium, ahead of the *Nordarmee*, he led a flying corps of 800 Cossacks and Saxon cavalry deep into northern France. In under two months, between 14 February and 11 April, he covered 500 miles, fought nine combats, and seized 118 guns, besides despatches, equipment, weapons, and a military pay chest. He destroyed semaphore telegraph posts, and took the towns of Messines, Bailleul, Cassel, Hazebrouck, Saint-Pol, Doullens, Arras, Roye, Noyon, Chauny, Saint-Quentin, Clermont, and Montdidier. French commanders became so alarmed by the depth of his raid that they feared it heralded imminent British or royalist landings on the Channel coast. It was an outstanding example of how a small corps, boldly and intelligently handled, could have an impact out of all proportion to its size.[23]

Part Two
The Campaign of France

Chapter 4

Invasion!

The Allied invasion plan, involving crossings all along the Rhine, emerged mainly for political reasons, and has rightly been criticised on military grounds. But it did have an important and often overlooked benefit: its very irrationality misled Napoleon and forced him to react to a whole series of unexpected threats.

The first crisis exploded in the middle of November, when the Dutch *départements* revolted against French rule and welcomed units detached from the *Nordarmee* as liberators. Belgium and northern France were now open to invasion, but Napoleon managed to contain the threat with reinforcements. At this stage the single Prussian corps in the Netherlands was too weak to continue the offensive southwards, and was not properly supported. The Crown Prince of Sweden, who commanded the *Nordarmee*, was more intent on wresting Norway from the King of Denmark, while the British, despite their keenness to seize Antwerp, could spare only a second-rate expeditionary force of 8,000 men. The Dutch revolt was therefore a missed opportunity for the Allies, but did at least distract Napoleon from Switzerland, where Schwarzenberg was preparing to launch the main offensive.

Switzerland

Since the Austrians sought a compromise peace, they needed to secure their key areas of interest at the outset, so they could negotiate from a position of strength. Switzerland was central to Metternich's strategy, for its occupation would not only secure the *Hauptarmee*'s southern flank and rear, but also isolate Italy. Unfortunately for him, the Swiss *Diet* at Zürich declared its neutrality, and Alexander now agreed only to the *Hauptarmee* passing through the northern tip of the country, so as to cross the Rhine by the bridge at Basel.

Yet despite her claim of neutrality, Switzerland had effectively been a French satellite since 1803, when Napoleon had mediated a settlement to her internal strife. Metternich could not risk leaving the country unoccupied in the Allied rear in case of a military setback. He therefore convinced Emperor Franz of the necessity of proceeding as originally planned, even though this would poison relations with Alexander for the rest of the campaign. To justify the intervention, Metternich

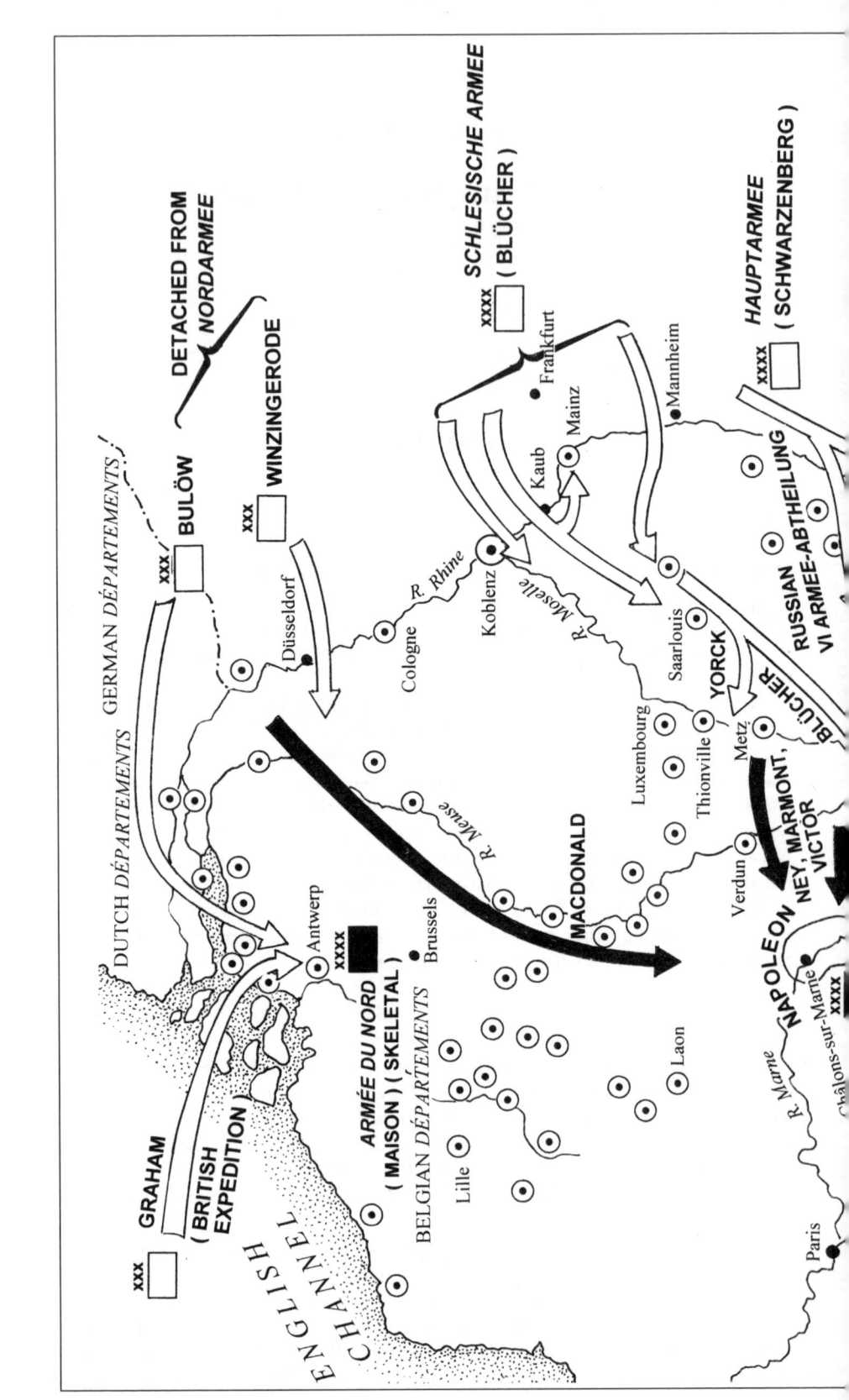

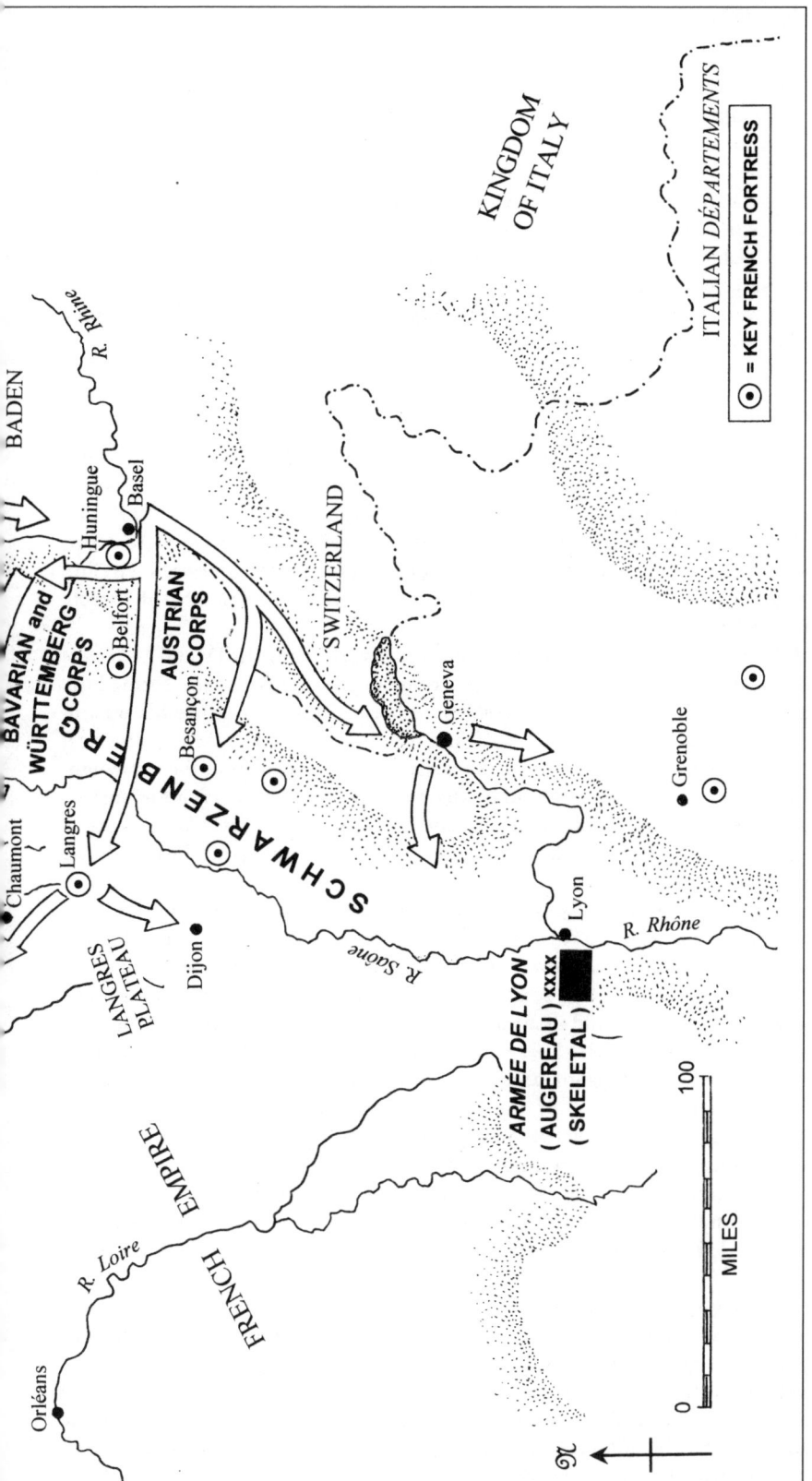

The Allies cross the Rhine: December 1813–January 1814.

exploited the divisions between Switzerland's cantons and political factions, and encouraged a counter-revolution at Berne by the conservative patricians, who wanted to restore the old confederation that had existed before the French Revolution.

Although the Allied invasion provoked the overthrow of the French-sponsored Mediation regime, Metternich would then be forced to step back from further political interference, partly because of Alexander's suspicions about his aims, and partly because of the risk of igniting a civil war. A final settlement of Switzerland's internal disputes would have to await the Congress of Vienna, and in November 1815 the great powers would guarantee the country's neutrality, one of the most significant side-effects of the campaign.[1]

The *Hauptarmee*

On 21 December the *Hauptarmee* began crossing the Upper Rhine, so it could swing clockwise through Switzerland and into France. Negotiations ensured that the small Swiss army offered no resistance. The Austrian corps were the first to cross the Rhine, and they alone moved through the interior of Switzerland. The other, non-Austrian, corps crossed later, since they were on the inside of the *Hauptarmee*'s circling movement, and had less distance to cover. Those that entered Switzerland at all merely passed through Basel.

Thus the Austrians constituted the left wing and centre, while the IV and V *Armee-Abtheilungen*, composed predominantly of Württembergers and Bavarians, formed the right wing, and the Russian VI *Armee-Abtheilung* was on the far right. This was, in fact, a logical arrangement, with the IV, V, and VI *Armee-Abtheilungen* in numerical order from left to right, and one that was generally retained throughout the campaign. The IV and V *Armee-Abtheilungen* would be able to draw resources and reinforcements more directly from their home countries, and the VI *Armee-Abtheilung*, being a Russian corps, was the most suitable formation to act as a connecting link with the Russo-Prussian *Schlesische Armee*.

This arrangement meant it was the Bavarians and Württembergers, and the advanced guard of the Russian VI *Armee-Abtheilung*, that bore the brunt of what fighting actually fell to the *Hauptarmee* in the main theatre of operations. This, too, suited the Austrians, for they had scraped the barrel of their resources to assemble Schwarzenberg's army, and could ill afford heavy casualties among their own men. Of the Austrian corps, only the III *Armee-Abtheilung* remained in the main theatre of operations for the whole campaign, and it was heavily engaged at just one battle, La Rothière.[2] In the bloodiest action of the entire campaign, the battle fought outside Paris on 30 March, Austrian casualties were fewer than 100.

Instead of concentrating for an immediate thrust to occupy the Langres plateau, the *Hauptarmee* fanned out in nine main columns, with some moving south-westwards through Switzerland, and others northwards into Alsace. By the first week of January, it was over-extended along an arc of 150 miles, and had penetrated less than 70 miles into France.

There were logistical advantages to the dispersal of Schwarzenberg's army, and sound political reasons for the slowness of his advance. Furthermore, he was hindered by inadequate intelligence, for his outposts and flying corps repeatedly allowed the French to break contact, and by Alexander's insistence of waiting until 13 January to lead his Guards and reserves across the Rhine, because that was the New Year by the Russian calendar and the anniversary of the occasion when he had crossed his own frontier, the Niemen river, a year before.

Yet Schwarzenberg's pace was dictated as much by caution as by any other reason. He was opposed by just 10,000 troops under *Maréchal* Victor, or 5 per cent of his own strength, yet whenever he felt seriously threatened, or alarmed by rumours of Napoleon's arrival with a powerful army, he tended to temporise, manoeuvre, call forward reinforcements, and instruct Blücher to make a diversion.

Schwarzenberg was also concerned at the threat from the fortresses on his lines of communication, and besieged or blockaded them rather than simply leave a small observing force. Some of the lesser strongpoints were able to resist for only a few days, but the three most important, Huningue, Belfort, and Besançon, held out until after Napoleon's abdication, and immobilised large detachments of the *Hauptarmee*, including the whole of the Austrian II *Armee-Abtheilung*. Yet the cost of resistance was high: over 11 per cent of the population of Huningue died between 21 December and 15 April, along with 16 per cent of the garrison, and few homes were left with an intact roof.[3]

Apart from minor clashes, for instance at Epinal on 11 January, the *Hauptarmee* saw little actual fighting during the first month of the invasion. Staff Captain Karl von François, who was serving with the Russian VI *Armee-Abtheilung*, later confessed:

> The campaign in France was not very interesting for us at first. It consisted of marches and more marches, with not too bad quarters in between. The inhabitants greeted us not with fiercely expressed hatred, but in a sort of numbed despair. They had lost faith in the fortune of their army, and Napoleon's haughty harangues made no more impression, for everyone longed for peace.[4]

At the end of the first week of January, Schwarzenberg heard that Langres was held by 80,000 French troops. In fact, *Maréchal* Edouard Mortier occupied the town with barely 12,000 Old Guardsmen, but he was able to hold it for a week by making his force seem larger than it was through constant activity. Only after causing Schwarzenberg to concentrate three corps ready to attack him did Mortier withdraw.

Schwarzenberg did not attempt a serious pursuit, having been instructed by Metternich to halt his advance for political reasons. The Langres plateau offered a security that was difficult to abandon lightly for the more exposed country to the north-west, and the Austrians hoped that its occupation would be sufficient to secure a negotiated peace. Hence Schwarzenberg dispersed his army again, and created a new, central reserve based on Dijon, from where it could cover his lines of communication against a potential advance from the south by those French forces that were assembling at Lyon.[5]

It was only after Alexander personally reached Langres on 22 January that the *Hauptarmee* made a further, limited advance. On the 24th Mortier was attacked by elements of the III and IV *Armee-Abtheilungen* outside Bar-sur-Aube, but again broke contact, and withdrew on Troyes, 29 miles to the west.

Schlesische Armee

Blücher's *Schlesische Armee* was supposed simply to support the *Hauptarmee* and cover its northern flank, but assumed a more prominent role because of the aggressiveness of its command team.[6] On 1 January it began crossing the Middle Rhine at Koblenz, Kaub, and Mannheim, encountering minimal opposition, partly as it achieved surprise and partly as Napoleon had shifted his forces southwards in response to Schwarzenberg's invasion just over a week earlier.

Blücher could advance into France with little more than two corps under Yorck and General Fabian, Baron von der Osten-Sacken, or just 50,000 men in all, for he had to leave the rest of his forces behind to contain Mainz and other fortresses.[7] Only after being relieved by the *4.* and *5. Bundes Corps* would they be able to follow, and this left the *Schlesische Armee* dangerously weak for the first two months of the invasion.

Despite this, Blücher pushed rapidly into France, inclining southwards as he did so, in order to draw nearer to the *Hauptarmee* and avoid a cluster of fortresses in the area of Metz and Luxembourg. He temporarily detached Yorck's corps to observe these strongholds, and hoped to secure at least one of them to anchor his lines of communication, but when none of them capitulated he was forced to use Nancy, an open town, as his main rearward base.

By 21 January Blücher realised that the French army was concentrating around Châlons-sur-Marne. Rather than attack it directly, he shifted further south, so as to outflank it, and be in a position for a joint advance with Schwarzenberg along the Seine, for he was intent on dictating peace in Paris. 'We are still waging the war much too systematically,' complained Gneisenau on 15 January.[8] Yet Schwarzenberg was also right to complain about the recklessness of the *Schlesische Armee*'s advance:

> Blücher, and even more so Gneisenau, to whom the good old man must lend his name, thrust on Paris with such a great and quite childish rage, and they trample on all the rules of war. They run madly to Brienne without covering the highroad from Châlons to Nancy with a considerable corps. Without worrying about their rear and flanks, they make plans only for fine parties in the Palais Royal, which is ridiculous at such an important moment.[9]

Besides allowing a gap of 60 miles to open up between himself and Yorck, Blücher exposed both the Allied armies' lines of communication to a counter-offensive from the north. Furthermore, the strain of his swift advance took an alarming toll, even in the absence of serious resistance. Yorck, for example, lost one-quarter of his men in the first twenty-five days of January, although this was partly offset by the arrival of reinforcements.[10]

The Langres Protocols

The mounting political tensions within the coalition came to a head in the second half of January. The Allied leaders had yet to agree their aims, and indeed could not have done so until a number of defeats at Napoleon's hands forced them to become more realistic and readier to compromise between themselves. Inevitably, therefore, they lacked a coherent military plan, but having attained their initial objective of occupying the Langres plateau, they could no longer defer serious discussion of the interrelated questions of their war aims, military strategy and approach to peace negotiations. They did so at Langres, in a series of private meetings and general conferences between 26 and 31 January. These deliberations were possible as Castlereagh had now joined the main Allied headquarters to represent Britain. His arrival strengthened Metternich, since the two men quickly reached a mutual understanding over key issues, although they differed on some proposals.

Alexander wanted to advance directly on Paris, and postpone both negotiations with the French and the settlement of war aims until after the end of hostilities. Metternich, on the other hand, insisted on the immediate opening of a peace conference to secure a negotiated outcome. He was equally alarmed by Alexander's plans to remove Napoleon from power and allow the French nation to decide its ruler under the supervision of a Russian governor. Apart from setting a dangerous precedent by recognising the will of the people, this revolutionary proposal was likely to turn France into a Russian satellite.[11] The result was deadlock. Metternich threatened that Austrian forces would take no further part in the campaign if Alexander insisted on deposing Napoleon. For his part, Alexander indicated that he would march on Paris without them, by taking the Russian reserves from the *Hauptarmee* to reinforce the *Schlesische Armee*. In fact, Alexander was not strong or willing enough at this stage to act independently, and Metternich knew that Austria's interests could subsequently be ignored if she withdrew from the war. Thus, the Allies reached a compromise agreement, known as the Langres Protocols.

Alexander agreed not to interfere in the question of the French regime, and accepted that a peace conference should open at Châtillon. But at the same time, military operations would continue, with the *Hauptarmee* resuming a cautious advance. Napoleon would be offered peace provided he accepted a return to the former frontiers of France: the more generous natural frontiers, which Metternich had offered two-and-a-half months earlier in the Frankfurt Proposals, had been invalidated by events.

The Langres agreement restrained Alexander, and kept the coalition intact. Yet it did not address all the issues, and was based on the coalition partners' mutual dependence, something that would vanish if they either won or lost a decisive battle.

Napoleon

So far, the invasion had not unfolded as Napoleon expected, for he had wanted his cordon of troops to hold the Allies near the Rhine and win time for him to organise a new army and prepare a counter-offensive. A deep Allied penetration would cause panic, induce large numbers of soldiers to desert so they could protect their families, and reduce the territory from which Napoleon could extract resources.

Yet he failed to explain his intentions adequately to the *maréchaux*. Rather than wage an aggressive defence to delay the Allies as long as possible, they retreated too hurriedly, lest they were destroyed or trapped inside fortresses. To encourage them, Napoleon had given the misleading impression that he was assembling a massive army, but this actually undermined their motivation, since they expected him to be able to retrieve the situation if they simply retreated to join him. Their prolonged withdrawal undermined morale, which resulted in defeatism, negligence, and widespread indiscipline.[12]

Only by acting jointly could the *maréchaux* have imposed on the superior Allied numbers, and that required a mutual confidence that did not exist. Napoleon was unable to provide close supervision from Paris, and yet he had failed to appoint an overall theatre commander, with the result that the *maréchaux* repeatedly uncovered each other's flanks as they fell back. His instructions were often out-of-date even when they were issued, and his goadings simply made his subordinates blame each other. It was clear that his personal presence alone could now retrieve the situation.

Chapter 5

The campaign theatre

By the time Napoleon joined his field army on 26 January, the Allies were more than halfway to Paris. He would have to launch an immediate counter-offensive to regain the lost territory, divert the threat to the capital, and restore his prestige with a victory. During the two months that followed, his operations were shaped to an unusual degree by a combination of extreme weather conditions and the region's remarkably varied geography.

Weather

'I would never have believed it could be so cold in France,' grumbled *Leutnant* Heinrich von Jordan of the Prussian *1. Garde-Regiment zu Fuß*. He described how bread froze in the bags in which it was carried, and how it had to be warmed over a fire before it could be eaten. His complaints were echoed by the Russian diplomat Karl, Count von Nesselrode, who wrote to his wife on 26 January: 'Here we are in the heart of France, my love, and more frozen than we could be at St Petersburg.'[1] In fact, a study carried out in England during the Second World War found that 1814 had been the harshest winter in 160 years of records since 1783.[2]

The period before 1850 is known as the Little Ice Age, as it was generally colder than subsequent decades, and a major volcanic eruption in 1809 lowered the average temperatures even further during the 1810s.[3] Yet the exceptional bitterness of the winter of 1814 may also have been linked to the El Niño Southern Oscillation (ENSO), a recurrent phenomenon in the Pacific Ocean that can dramatically influence the climate elsewhere in the world. A strong ENSO event is known to have occurred in 1814, and a previous event in 1789–1793 had been preceded in western Europe by an unusually cold winter and by crop failures that helped trigger the French Revolution. However, it is difficult to establish a definite link between an ENSO event and specific anomalies in the weather, because of the complexity of the world's atmospheric systems.[4]

The cold made it more difficult for soldiers to sleep, and reduced their ability to fight by numbing their fingers and forcing them to swaddle themselves in layers of clothing. They huddled indoors when they could, but found some houses almost as cold and uncomfortable as a bivouac, with rooms often bare and fuel non-existent. Frozen ground could make it impossible to erect earthworks, and could cripple a cavalry regiment more effectively than a battle, as horses that were not specially shod for ice tended to slip and break their legs.[5] Yet the periods of frost alternated with thaws, since the temperatures fluctuated wildly. The coldest spells, when even the maximum daytime temperature at Paris fell below 0°C, were 10–14 January, 21–25 January, 4–5 February, 20–25 February, and 6–9 March. On one occasion, the thermometer dropped as low as –12.5°C even during the day.

During the intervening thaws the maximum daytime temperature could reach as high as 12°C, and it climbed still further in the second half of March with the onset

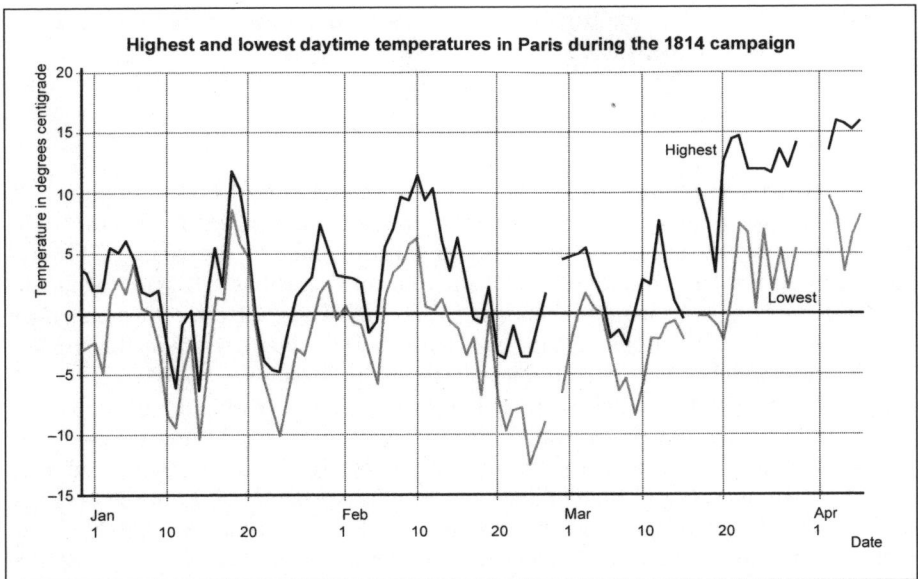

of spring. Rivers became swollen, valleys flooded, and armies restricted to the main roads, since unpaved tracks dissolved into viscous trails of mud blocked by broken-down guns and vehicles. Shoes disintegrated, and it became more difficult to keep an army supplied. At the same time rain and fog reduced visibility, undermined morale, and prevented muskets from firing by dampening the powder.

Such swift oscillations in the temperature helped determine the course of the operations, and yet their full implications have never been grasped. One reason, for example, why Napoleon was able to win a spectacular series of victories over the *Schlesische Armee* in the middle of February was because it was bogged down in mud and congested roads. In contrast, when he then switched his attention to the *Hauptarmee*, it was able to escape, partly as a plunge in the temperature enabled it to leave the roads and move over fields that were now rock-hard.

Several veterans later claimed that 1814 was their most gruelling campaign.[6] They exaggerated in that it could hardly be compared to the rigours of the retreat from Moscow, when the temperature once fell to −37°C. But few campaigns called for such a relentless succession of marches and battles, nor such swift alternations between snow, rain, frost, and mud. 'Since yesterday, the welcome sun has begun to cast milder rays on us', wrote 19-year-old *Leutnant* Wilhelm Alberti of the Prussian *6. Reserve-Infanterie-Regiment* to his parents on 17 March. Yet the nights, he added, were still very raw:

> All of us have a severe tingling in our fingers and feet, which is not gout, but rather frostbite. I have not noticed my gout and my chest is not so bad. Nearly all our soldiers are in the grip of just a great tiredness and weakness, but this is really no wonder since we have had so strenuous a campaign. Even so, I endure to the bitter end, despite my not exactly over-robust constitution. . . .
>
> I swear to God, it has to be admitted that we become deadened by seeing every day the deepest misery on earth, but it goes on for too long, and in the end everyone finds it loathsome and repulsive once more. By God, this dreadful war, which we have waged and are continuing to wage, is almost

indescribable, and no description or analysis of the most terrible events on earth can include the whole scale of the misery it has caused.[7]

Terrain

The campaign area lay in a surprisingly small swathe of land that extended just 120 miles from Paris in the west to Saint-Dizier in the east and was contained between the Marne river in the north and the Seine about 40 miles to the south. This was equivalent to the land area of Connecticut, the third smallest US state, or, in the United Kingdom, to little more than half the size of Wales. Of the campaign's main battles, only three (Craonne, Laon, and Reims) were fought outside this narrow region, when Blücher retreated 30 miles north of the Marne early in March. In fact, during his entire career Napoleon never fought a campaign in a smaller zone.

But unlike Wales or Connecticut, or most other similarly sized lands, the contested area contained a remarkable variety of geographically distinct regions, and it is impossible to understand the military operations without being aware of these differences. The campaign was fought within the Paris basin, a vast oval 300 miles long, with the low-lying capital at the centre. The underlying layers of rock of this basin were tilted by the upthrusts that formed the heights at its fringes. Since the harder layers were more resistant to erosion than softer ones, their edges left steep escarpments, or *côtes*. Travellers moving eastwards from Paris crossed a series of plateaux and plains, separated by these *côtes*.[8]

Each successive band of the campaign theatre had its own set of characteristics, with its wetness being determined by the permeability of the substrata, and its fertility by the presence of a top layer of silt deposits. These two qualities determined not simply what crops the land could grow, but its population density, the pattern of its settlements, and its ability to support an army. Close to Paris, for example, the Brie plateau was largely damp and fertile, and it ended dramatically in the *Côte de l'Ile-de-France*, an abrupt escarpment that swept in an arc past Epernay and Sézanne. Further east, in contrast, lay an open plain known as *pouilleuse*, or barren, *Champagne*. Some 35 miles wide, it was dry because of its permeable, chalky substratum, and infertile because of the thin topsoil almost devoid of silt. It was good country for a cavalry charge, but a difficult one in which to keep an army supplied, as it was so impoverished and sparsely populated. Many homes were simply thatched wooden huts, with a single room, an earth floor, and barely any light.[9] Even today, with the crop yield transformed by the use of fertilisers, a glance at a map shows that the villages are more widely scattered here than elsewhere, a striking testimony to its past poverty.[10] A Bavarian ADC, August, *Fürst* von Thurn und Taxis, vividly remembered the wretchedness of the region, for he had to retreat through it in February:

> The land was as desolate as can be, since it was the most miserable part of *Champagne pouilleuse*. Only extremely rarely did we see a village and the inhabitants were so poor that I believe they went hungry even in peacetime, never mind at such a moment, when our advance had already exhausted all the resources. The soldiers therefore suffered from a shortage of the essentials of life and also from the complete lack of wood in this land.[11]

The barren plain ended with another escarpment, which introduced a wetter region known as *Champagne humide*, covered with ponds, lakes and woods. This, in turn, gave way to the *Côte des Bars* and the Barrois plateau.

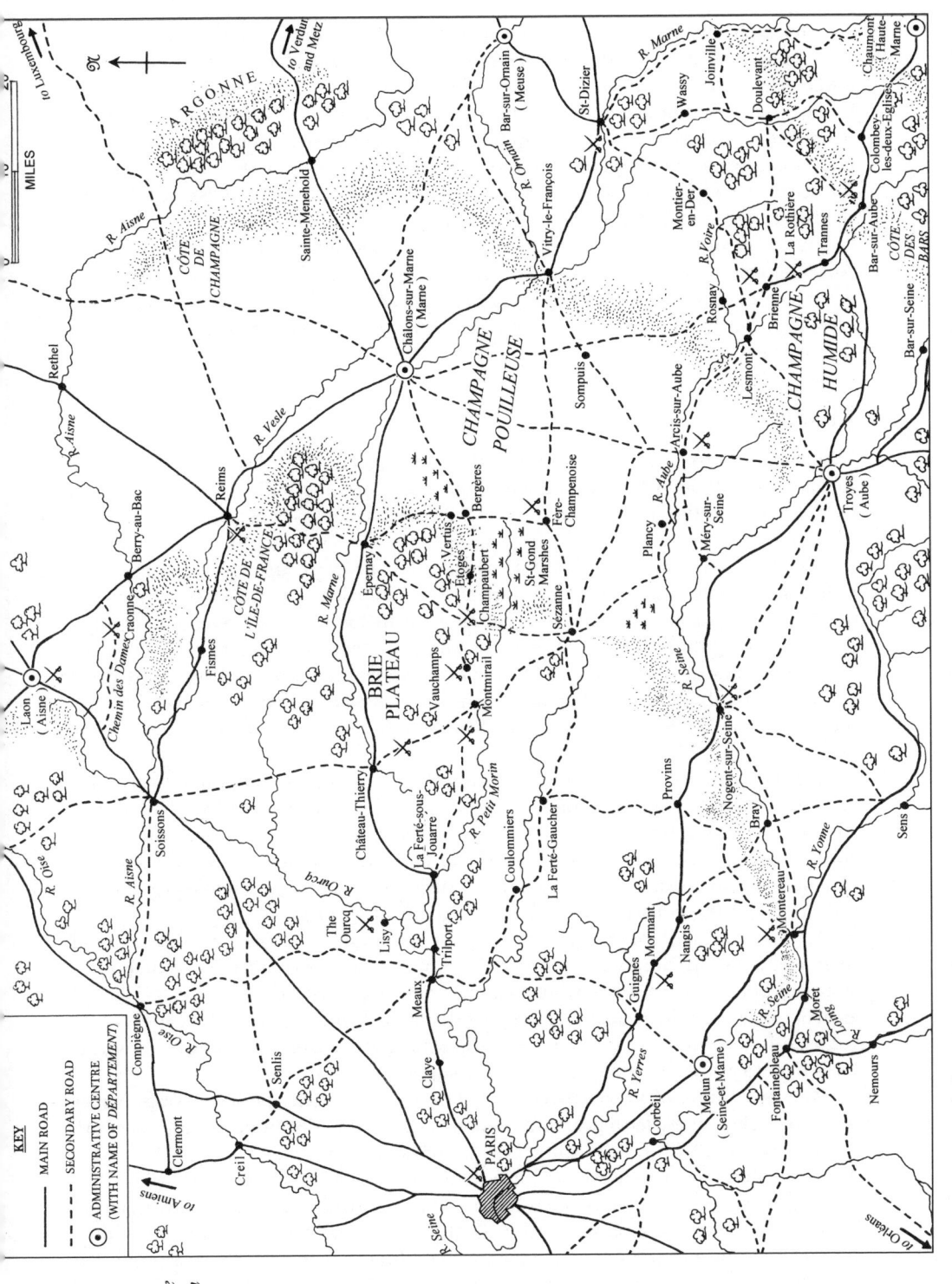

1814: the campaign area.

To reach Paris or attack Napoleon, the Allied armies would have to cross *Champagne pouilleuse*. Yet the *départements* of the Aube and Marne, which were partly covered by it, had a population density of no more than 3.9 inhabitants for every 10 hectares, less than the average of 5.4 for old France as a whole. Napoleon, on the other hand, had all the resources of the capital at his back, and could draw supplies from its often rich, fertile, and populous hinterland. The *département* of the Seine-et-Marne, for instance, had 5.1 inhabitants for every 10 hectares, the Seine-et-Oise had 7.5, and the Seine, which included Paris itself, had 137.

As the campaign progressed, the swathe of impoverished land confronting the Allies became an even wider barrier, since the armies gradually exhausted even the more fertile regions to the west of *Champagne pouilleuse*. This also posed problems for Napoleon when he attempted to pursue them, thus confounding his quest for a decisive victory.

Roads

Napoleon inherited a road network that had fallen into disrepair during the Revolution. Although he restored and improved routes, he built few new ones, and concentrated on the nation's strategic and commercial arteries at the expense of the local networks.

The best roads were the first two classes of *routes impériales*.[12] From Paris, they radiated outwards to the coast and frontiers. The campaign area was crossed by several of these great *chaussées*, with one running north-eastwards to Soissons, another eastwards along the Marne to Strasbourg, and two others south-eastwards, along the Seine valley, one of which was used by the *Hauptarmee* in its advance from Basel. Such was the width, directness, and quality of the *routes impériales* that it took just five days for a *diligence* to travel from Paris to Strasbourg, a distance of 300 miles on the ground.[13]

Just as the main roads radiated out from Paris, the local ones in each *département* centred on the *chef-lieu*, or administrative centre. This was partly why Châlons-sur-Marne and Troyes, the *chefs-lieux* of the two most contested *départements*, the Marne and the Aube, were so useful strategically to both sides, quite apart from their size. Napoleon returned three times to Troyes during the campaign, and slept a total of eight nights there, twice as long as he spent at any other location.

Yet the secondary roads were often in poor condition. Even the most important of them could consist simply of compacted earth, perhaps covered by layers of broken stones or gravel for either the whole length, or just wet sections. Bad roads exhausted an army, increased the problem of keeping it supplied, and damaged the wheels of its vehicles. It was therefore easier for the Allies to advance along the *chaussées* towards Paris than to move either north or south to support each other.

The most minor of the roads tended to be mere mud tracks, perhaps overgrown or partly ploughed up by local peasants, and often difficult to distinguish amid a network of other paths, which readily shifted or disappeared with time. Many of them were wide enough for just two horsemen, and almost impassable in winter except when they froze. In any case, the troops often had to leave the road clear for the artillery, and march over the fields on either side, with the men at the front of a column wading through mud up to their knees. Under such conditions, it was hardly surprising that they shed so many stragglers on the march.[14] A French ADC, *Capitaine* Nicolas Planat de la Faye, vividly remembered the road leading north-eastwards from Nogent-sur-Seine to Sézanne:

This road was an unimaginable quagmire and my horse had much trouble in moving through the heavy, clay soil. At this period, no one attended to the transverse roads, so they were in a deplorable state throughout France and even at the gates of Paris. The more I advanced, the more difficulty I had in seeing how artillery could pass along such tracks.[15]

Indeed, the greatest difficulty lay in moving large numbers of heavy guns and caissons. Napoleon did use the transverse roads, and surprised the Allies by managing to do so, but he took with him just a small, mobile core of his army. He also sought to upgrade key routes in his rear, although the situation elsewhere was not improved when the opposing sides deliberately broke up or barricaded roads to impede each other's progress.[16]

Rivers and bridges

As with the roads, the major rivers generally flowed westwards and converged on Paris. The two most important were the Marne and, further south, the Seine, the great trunk stream of the Paris basin. During the winter, they were unfordable except in the upper reaches, and often flooded.[17] They offered multiple locations in which to block an advance on the capital: they were repeatedly crossed and recrossed by the main roads, and were joined by numerous tributaries, which offered additional defensive lines. Two of the Seine's tributaries, the Aube and the Yonne, were major rivers in their own right, as was the Aisne, 25 miles north of the Marne. But rivers were communication arteries as well as obstacles, and enabled Napoleon to ease the pressure on the roads by moving supplies and casualties by boat.

The importance of the rivers meant that the timely capture of a single bridge could be pivotal. One reason why Schwarzenberg was so cautious about pushing along the south bank of the Seine was that Napoleon might manage to seize a bridge in his rear and sever the head of his army. His advanced guard would have difficulty in escaping, since it would have further to retreat round the outside of the bend formed by the river than Napoleon had to cover in attacking directly southwards.

Equally, a bridge that was destroyed in time could check an offensive. A stone bridge could be repaired temporarily with a wooden roadway placed over the ruptured arch, but even when the necessary materials were at hand, the work usually took about a day, long enough for a retreating enemy to reach safety. The Allies did not even try to rebuild the wooden bridge at Lesmont after it was burned down at the start of February, because it would have taken too long, and they instead replaced it, first with a ferry and then with a trestle bridge erected nearby.[18]

The Allies regularly forced the local authorities to restore broken bridges. The provisional *préfet* of the Aube was obliged on 15 February to order the repair of the bridges on the Seine and Aube rivers within his *département* after the Allies threatened to resort to armed force if the work was not done within a week.[19] Sometimes French troops then forced the inhabitants to destroy the bridges again: *Sous-lieutenant* Pierre Auvray of the *23e Dragons* reconnoitred the Aisne in the middle of March and requisitioned peasants to break a wooden bridge that had just been rebuilt.[20]

An alternative to capturing or repairing a bridge was to use pontoons, and here the Allies enjoyed a significant advantage, for both their armies had mobile bridging trains. Blücher, for example, had Russian pontoons made of tarred canvas stretched over a wooden framework. They were vulnerable to chunks of ice floating down a river, but were more easily transported than heavy, copper pontoons, and could be assembled, secured with small anchors, and covered with a roadway.²¹

Napoleon, on the other hand, lacked a pontoon train as a result of his disaster at Leipzig, and was forced to spend time gathering boats from along the main rivers, and felling trees to make girders of sufficient length. He therefore demanded a mobile bridging unit, using boats assembled at Paris. But only twenty suitable craft were found, and others had to be specially constructed, along with rope and pulley mechanisms of sufficient strength.²² 'If I had possessed a bridging train of ten pontoons, the war would be over and Prince Schwarzenberg's army would no longer exist,' Napoleon berated the *Ministre de la guerre* on 26 February:

> In the absence of boats, I was unable to cross the Seine where I needed to cross it and whenever I wanted. It is ridiculous to tell me that Paris lacks the necessary boats to form a bridge on the upper Seine. . . . The steps you have taken mean that the war will be over by the time the boats arrive . . . This is just ineptitude.²³

It was 2 March before Napoleon was informed that a bridging train had left Paris. 'It is my greatest need,' he noted. But when it arrived, he found that it was too heavy to be readily transported, and he demanded one that was as light as possible, with canvas pontoons. Ironically, he captured at least two bridging trains like this from the *Hauptarmee* in the second half of March, but by then the campaign was almost over.²⁴

Yet pontoons were not always the best or quickest solution, for they could not be kept near the head of an army without being at risk of capture or destruction.²⁵ Swollen rivers could flood their valleys, or have too swift a current. Pontoon bridges were not always safe enough for heavy vehicles, and cavalrymen might have to dismount and lead their horses over on foot. Sometimes, pontoons could not be used where they were most needed, for the rivers in the campaign area often had high banks, and in 1815 Gneisenau wanted the Prussian army to be equipped with rope bridges, of the sort that Wellington had used in the Peninsula, specifically to overcome this predicament.²⁶ Access could also be a problem: after the permanent bridge was broken at Nogent-sur-Seine, vehicles had to negotiate narrow side-streets in order to reach the pontoon crossing. In any case, there were practical limits to the number of temporary bridges that could be established, imposed by the availability of materials, the financial cost, and Napoleon's concern that building them immediately outside Paris could alarm the inhabitants.²⁷

It was therefore vital to control the permanent crossings. These were often entrusted to *gardes nationaux*, who were usually sufficient to deter roving detachments of Cossacks or cavalry, and the French government issued detailed instructions for their defence and destruction.²⁸ To break a stone bridge, it had to be blown up by digging a trench on the crown of an arch, filling it with powder, and covering it with weighted planks of wood. Wooden bridges, on the other hand, could be burned, blown up, or pulled apart.

A defender was normally reluctant to destroy a bridge until it became unavoidable, partly because his own army might need to use it, and because of the social and economic impact on the local community. Yet it was difficult to demolish a bridge under fire, in a hurry, or without proper tools and experienced engineers.²⁹ Wooden bridges were difficult to burn if they were wet, and the *Schlesische Armee* found it impossible to burn or pull down the one at Méry-sur-Seine on the morning of 22 February.³⁰

Thus, a surprise attack, with artillery support, had a good chance of seizing a bridge.

'River crossings', noted Napoleon, 'are a matter of cannon.'[31] This made fortifications essential to win time. Buildings could be loopholed, ditches dug across the approach road, and barricades formed from felled trees. More formidable defences could be constructed to form a bridgehead, with either end resting securely on the river, using either earthworks or, if time was short, stockades made from tree trunks or planks of wood.[32] Civilian workers were requisitioned by the local authorities to erect fortifications; those who refused to obey were threatened with fines, with having to billet troops at their own expense, and even, if it proved necessary, with corporal punishment.[33]

Towns

The campaign area had few large towns, since Paris sucked migrants from its hinterland and prevented places within a radius of 60 miles from developing into major regional centres in their own right. Even Reims, the largest town occupied by Napoleon during the campaign, had barely 30,000 inhabitants, or less than 6 per cent of the population of Paris, and it stood more than 80 miles north-east of the capital, beyond the reach of its most potent influence. The only other large town, Troyes, with little more than 20,000 people, lay 90 miles south-east of Paris. Châlons-sur-Marne had 11,000 inhabitants, and Soissons and Laon about 7,000 each, but most of the other towns in the campaign area, like Montereau, Nogent-sur-Seine and Château-Thierry, had fewer than 5,000. Versailles, which had been the residence of the royal court, was exceptional, in that it had a population of 23,000 and lay just 10 miles south-west of the capital.[34]

Some provincial towns were beautiful, such as Orléans, Nancy, and the smaller, picturesque Provins, with its walls, medieval buildings, and hill-top location overlooking the surrounding countryside. Yet many others were dull, dirty, and dismal places in winter, with narrow streets devoid of pavements, and wretched inns where it could be difficult to obtain food or accommodation if the area was overcrowded with troops and displaced persons.[35] 'Nothing was as sad as the sight of the town of Laon,' noted a royalist emissary, Jean de Gain de Montaignac, at a time when it was occupied by the *Schlesische Armee*:

> A foot of mire, produced by the bivouacs of the baggage train, made walking unbearable. All the houses were closed. You met no inhabitants. Every street was cluttered by the passage of soldiers and horses, and by the numerous caissons and every type of vehicle that were all over the place.[36]

Towns offered armies shelter from the cold and rain, and resources that could be requisitioned in large quantities. Key road hubs of sufficient size could accommodate hospitals or supply dumps. Other places, like Soissons and Meaux, were strategically important primarily because of their bridges. But few of the towns had proper fortifications, for the campaign area had ceased to be a frontier district as France expanded eastwards to the Rhine during the seventeenth and eighteenth centuries. Their defences had become ruined or obsolete, and it was difficult to spare enough troops to garrison large towns properly: the walls encircling Reims, for example, were over 4 miles long.[37]

Open towns, which lacked any permanent fortifications, were even more vulnerable. The government issued instructions for their defence, so they could at least be protected from minor cavalry raids.[38] A continuous perimeter had to be formed by incorporating existing buildings, walls, hedges, and fences, filling the gaps with stockades and abattis, and digging a ditch all the way around. Rivers could be dammed to create inundations, streets blocked, and the approaches to the town cleared of any cover. If time was short, makeshift barricades could be established simply by removing the wheels from a cart and filling it with earth or dung. A large building inside the town, such as a church or *château*, could be converted into a keep.

But many towns were built largely of wood, for timber was often more readily available than stone, and this made them vulnerable to fire. Brienne, Méry-sur-Seine, and Nogent-sur-Seine were all burned down to a greater or lesser degree. Much of Arcis-sur-Aube was destroyed by flames during the battle of 20–21 March, leaving the surreal sight of brick chimneys standing isolated amidst the charred remains of houses. Early in February the Allies warned that they would set fire to Châlons-sur-Marne with their artillery unless *Maréchal* Macdonald abandoned it, and later that month they secured an unharassed retreat from Troyes by threatening to burn it.[39]

Exploiting the terrain

Roads, rivers, bridges, towns, hills, marshes, and forests combined to form barriers that restricted the Allied armies to just a few avenues of advance. This made it easier for Napoleon to check them at key choke-points, or outmanoeuvre them from a central position by exploiting the road network, seizing vital bridges, and striking at their communications.

The most effective barrier lay on the western edge of *Champagne pouilleuse*, where the escarpment of the *Côte de l'Ile-de-France* suddenly rose 120 metres above the plain. It was completed by a chain of forests and marshes that shadowed the line of the escarpment. The only points between the Marne and Seine valleys at which roads of any significance allowed an army to ascend this escarpment were Etoges and Sézanne.

To the north of the Marne, the defence line was extended up to the Vesle river by the forested hills south of Reims. South of the campaign area, the Loing and then the Briare canals connected the Seine with the Loire, 50 miles to the south. They had fallen into disrepair, and could be crossed at numerous locks, but were backed up by the Loing river, which provided a double line of defence for nearly the whole stretch.[40] The line was supplemented by the advanced position of the Yonne river 25 miles to the east.

To be militarily useful, bridges had to have good access roads. The Yonne river, for example, could be crossed between Montereau and Auxerre, 50 miles to the south-east, by four bridges, at Joigny, Villeneuve, Sens and Pont. But only Sens, along with Auxerre and Montereau, had roads practicable for an army. The Yonne could therefore be held simply by occupying these three points strongly, destroying the other bridges, and observing the line with cavalry posts.[41] Thus, Napoleon was able to cover the approach to Paris along the south bank of the Seine with just a cordon of assorted troops under *Général de division* Claude, *comte* Pajol and *Général de brigade* Jacques Allix de Vaux.

In short, a string of natural obstacles drew a diagonal line of defence from Reims and the Vesle river 150 miles south-westwards to the Loire, which itself served as a moat protecting the central rump of France. The most likely Allied lines of advance were the valleys of the Marne and Seine, which had superior-quality roads. Napoleon appointed *Maréchal* François Kellermann to organise the defence of the Marne, and *Général de division* Pajol to take charge of the Seine. As well as raising the *Garde nationale*, they were ordered to assemble supplies, fortify towns, and secure the bridges.[42]

A camp was established towards the western end of each valley: at Meaux on the

Marne and Melun on the Seine. The camps lay exactly the same distance, 25 miles, east and south-east of Paris, and were large enough for 15,000 men. They blocked the Marne and Seine valleys, and were points where supplies could be stockpiled, and conscripts, volunteers, and *gardes nationaux* assembled and trained.[43]

More distant camps were established at key towns such as Châlons-sur-Marne, Soissons, and Troyes, to form an outer ring of advanced bases 60 to 90 miles from Paris. The existence of this network of locations would allow Napoleon constantly to improvise, switch his lines of communication, and manoeuvre throughout the area. At one time or another, each of these camps would temporarily become his centre of operations, as would other important road hubs, such as Reims and Doulevant.

The establishment of these camps was a lesson learned from the Revolutionary Wars. In 1792 the *Garde nationale* had been assembled and trained at Paris and four other points: Meaux, Soissons, Reims, and Châlons-sur-Marne.[44] A string of such camps could make it possible to wage a flexible defence in depth, with the field army delaying the Allied advance, and second-line units in the camps attacking the Allied rear from either side, whenever they could do so advantageously. Yet the effectiveness of the system was limited by the fact that the camps were often bereft of tents, weapons, and equipment, and that many of the *gardes nationaux* reached them in a state of destitution.[45]

Paris itself constituted a massive, central base. Politically dangerous it may have been for Napoleon to have the city right at his back, but it had major military and logistical advantages. Since the best roads radiated out from the capital, he could draw resources from it, and manoeuvre more easily than his opponents. Blücher and Schwarzenberg, in contrast, would find it difficult to obtain supplies while they were in *Champagne pouilleuse*, and hard to support each other once they left it and entered the barrier zone along the *Côte de l'Ile-de-France*. Everything now depended on the skill and ruthlessness with which Napoleon exploited these advantages.

Chapter 6

Napoleon takes command

On 26 January Napoleon reached Vitry-le-François, the concentration point of his army and the pivot of his forthcoming operations. His arrival boosted morale, and marked a new phase in the campaign, with the disjointed retreat of his subordinates giving way to a bold and co-ordinated offensive.

During the opening weeks of the invasion, it had taken two or three days for Napoleon's orders from Paris to reach his *maréchaux*, but now that they had fallen back they were more concentrated, and easier to control. The Allied armies, in contrast, had become dispersed over a distance of more than 150 miles, giving Napoleon a chance to defeat them piecemeal.[1]

The first clashes

Napoleon hoped to concentrate as many as 70,000 or 80,000 troops for his counter-offensive, but fewer than 50,000 were immediately available near Vitry.[2] Another 9,000 under *Maréchal* Macdonald were falling back from Belgium, and were still 70 miles to the north, while Mortier had 20,000 men, including the Old Guard, around Troyes, 38 miles to the south-west.

Napoleon had joined his army a day later than planned, and it turned out to be a crucial delay. He found that Victor had abandoned the important road hub of Saint-Dizier, 18 miles to the south-east, giving Blücher an unimpeded route to join Schwarzenberg. Napoleon was therefore intent on immediately recapturing Saint-Dizier on the 27th, and in doing so expected to fight a considerable battle with Blücher's army. 'If there are only 25,000 to 30,000 men, we will be able to beat them', he informed *Maréchal* Berthier, 'and if we succeed in this operation, it will change the entire situation.'[3] After defeating the *Schlesische Armee*, Napoleon could press southwards, up the Marne valley, and plunge into Schwarzenberg's flank or rear towards Chaumont and Langres.[4] But, he emphasised, it was essential to prevent the junction of the two Allied armies: 'If we let them concentrate, we would have no more chances in our favour.'[5]

As it happened, when Napoleon occupied Saint-Dizier on the 27th, he encountered only some cavalry units, for the main body of the *Schlesische Armee* had already passed by on its way to Brienne, 26 miles to the south-west. He decided to pursue and crush it against the Aube before it could unite with Schwarzenberg or take the city of Troyes. The most direct route towards Brienne was a bad transverse road, but its very impracticability could help Napoleon achieve surprise, and the mud seemed likely to freeze.[6]

Instead, it poured with rain. *Lieutenant* Octave Levavasseur, ADC to *Maréchal* Ney, recalled the state of the troops when they reached the town of Montier-en-Der on the 28th:

> The army arrived there in the night, but no preparations had been made to feed it. The staff officers took possession of the houses. As for the rest of the army,

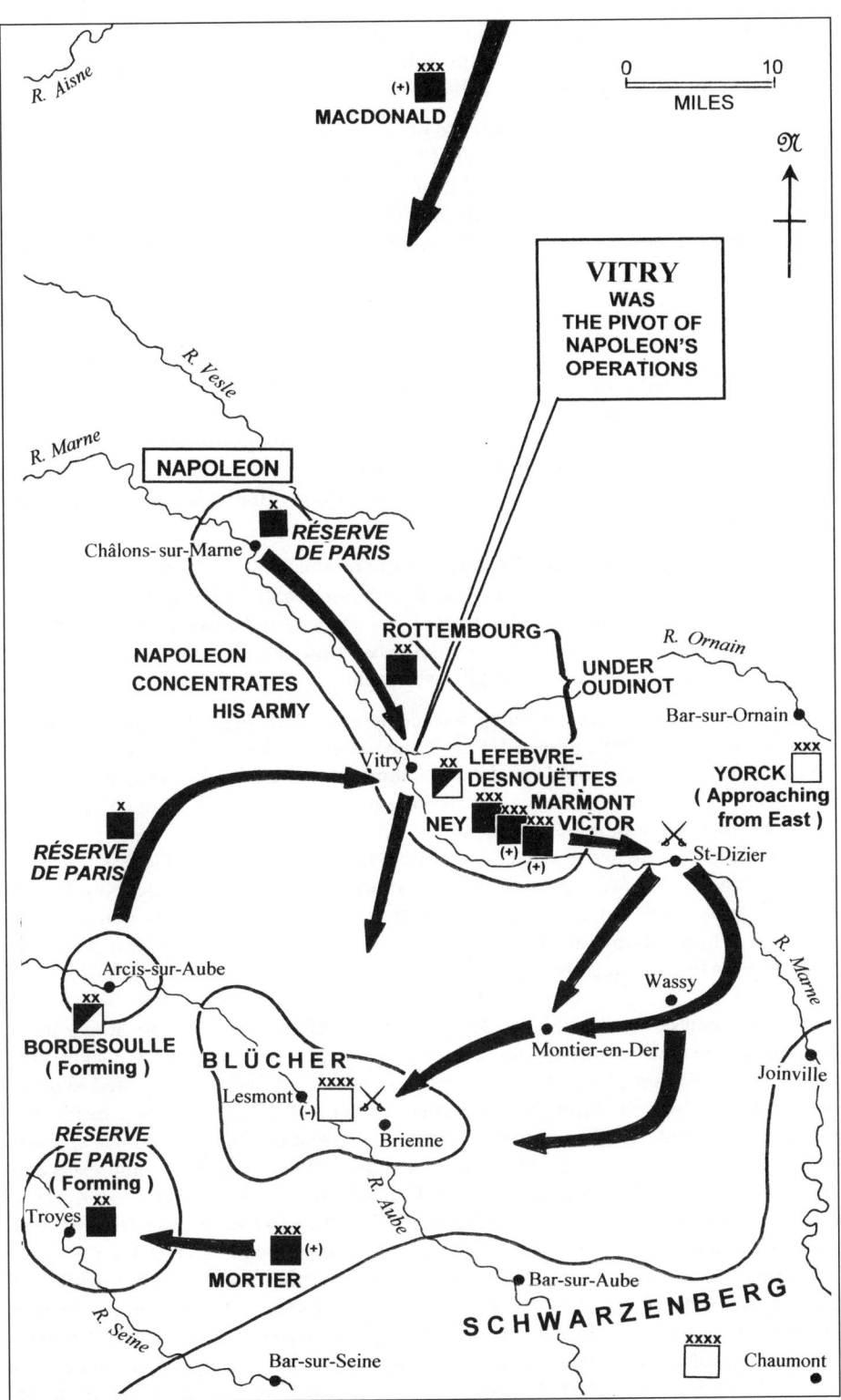

Napoleon's counter-offensive: 26–29 January 1814.

imagine masses of young conscripts, soaked to the skin, wandering the streets, knocking on the doors, which the inhabitants did not want to open, and begging for a potato, which they could not give.[7]

Next morning, the 29th, Blücher learned of the danger descending on him at Brienne from the north-east, and even discovered Napoleon's plan from captured despatches. Yet he could not simply avoid battle, fall back, and unite with Schwarzenberg until he had reassembled his scattered formations. Hence, he had to hold the town of Brienne until Sacken's exposed corps could rejoin him from Lesmont, 6 miles to the north-west.

Battle of Brienne

At midday the leading French cavalry units started to deploy in the plain north-east of Brienne. Opposite them was the Russian cavalry of Lieutenant-General Peter Petrovich, Count Pahlen III, drawn up to cover Sacken's withdrawal.[8] It was another two hours before the French were strong enough to advance in earnest, but they then pushed Pahlen back on Brienne. One of his officers, Staff Captain Eduard von Löwenstern, recalled how:

> I found Count Pahlen under the heaviest fire on the heights of Perthes, not far from the town. Cavalry attacks were almost impossible in the quagmire, but even so, our Tchougouiev Uhlans made some splendid attacks, overthrew the enemy and took 4 guns. The cannonballs could not ricochet and instead smacked into the ground. Doggedly, we fought the enemy's advance.[9]

Pahlen won valuable time, enabling Sacken to retreat through Brienne. Napoleon himself was now on the battlefield, but the poor state of the roads delayed the build-up of his forces, and he could see the opportunity to defeat Blücher slipping through his fingers. Already, it was 1500 hours, leaving little more than two hours of daylight, and this explains the hurried and disjointed nature of his attacks on Brienne.

The failure of the first French onslaught on the town, by part of Victor's II Corps, obliged Napoleon to await the arrival of the Young Guard infantry under Ney. By the time a second, more general, attack was made, it was more than twenty minutes after sundown. Three columns advanced on Brienne, with the main, central, thrust coming from the north-east, and the right-hand column circling round to attack from the north.

Blücher had established his headquarters at the *Château* de Brienne, atop a steep hill that dominated not just the town but the whole plain to the north and south. He had watched the first phase of the action from the terrace, and was delighted to make out Napoleon himself through a telescope.[10] Eventually, he went back inside the *Château* to eat, but the dining room, at the northern end of the building, was exposed to French artillery fire, and the meal was accompanied by the crash of cannonballs and crack of falling panels in the walls above. Blücher offered his apologies to a guest, a captured French officer, and instructed him to be taken to a safer place, but the man politely declined, saying that he was enjoying the company too much to leave.

When Blücher returned to the terrace, he noticed that the French left flank had become exposed. His cavalry was ordered to attack, and fell on the easternmost French column, throwing it into disorder before becoming scattered in the gathering darkness.

The central French thrust gained a foothold in Brienne, but was then fought to a standstill. *Lieutenant* Octave Levavasseur was shocked by the cowardice of many conscripts:

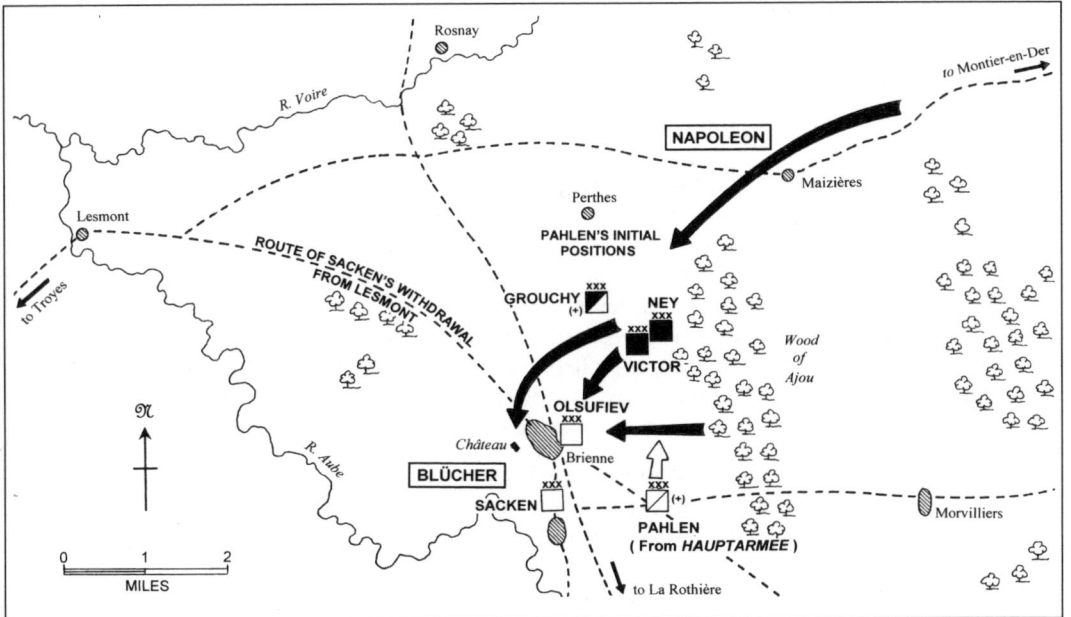

Battle of Brienne: 29 January 1814.

> Whole packets of cartridges were soon being thrown on the ground. Despite the ardour of the officers, our soldiers did not respond to the command of 'Forwards!' Many hid behind the trees, while others retired either wounded or claiming that they had run out of cartridges.[11]

Blücher had personally mounted his horse to see the situation for himself, but rode back to his headquarters since the battle seemed to be at an end. He was inside the *Château* when the action suddenly flared up again, for the remaining French column had penetrated into Brienne along the road from the north-west, which had been left unguarded after Sacken's retreat along it. French skirmishers climbed up to the *Château*, sent musketballs whistling across the terrace, and forced Blücher to leave and hurriedly descend the main avenue towards the town.

Then a Cossack dashed back with a warning that French troops were blocking the way ahead, so Blücher turned off to the right, left the grounds by an alternative exit, and passed through a narrow street to reach the open countryside. The danger was later inflated, not least by Blücher's adjutant, *Major* August, *Graf* von Nostitz, who claimed to have saved his life several times during his campaigns while playing down the role of other rescuers. It actually seems to have been an inhabitant of Brienne, a German-born man, who used his local knowledge to guide Blücher to safety.[12]

Towards 2200 hours, Blücher ordered a counter-attack to regain his headquarters and deny Napoleon a claim to victory. His troops retook nearly all of Brienne, but not the *Château* on the hill above, for the town had been set alight by artillery fire and the flames illuminated anyone who tried to approach. 'Brienne burned like a torch, and many wounded suffocated in the houses and streets,' recalled Staff Captain Eduard von Löwenstern. He bivouacked south of the town, and described how:

> Everyone slipped about in the terrible clay, the horses sank far above their knees and we had the greatest difficulty extracting ourselves from the morass into which our horses had half sunk. . . . We were all so exhausted that no one thought of eating, although we had gone without food the whole day.[13]

That night Blücher retreated to a strong position at Trannes, 7 miles to the south-east, where he could cover the *Hauptarmee* as it emerged from the hills around Bar-sur-Aube.

The fighting had lasted nine hours, and even Napoleon, who habitually minimised his losses, admitted to having suffered as many as 3,000 casualties. 'It was less a battle than a butchery,' wrote a young French officer, *Sous-lieutenant* Lefol, who had just witnessed his first action.[14] Napoleon had needed a stunning success in order to shock the Allies, establish his moral supremacy, and destroy any notion that the French army was unfit to offer further serious resistance. Yet he had won no more than a bloody and indecisive victory, partly because he had enjoyed only a slight advantage of numbers, and partly because the Old Guard had been unable to join him from Troyes. His disappointment was obvious when he wrote to the *Ministre de la guerre*:

> If I had had old troops, it would have been possible to do better and to take all the parks and baggage that I saw filing past in front of us . . . If Brienne could have been occupied earlier, all would have fallen into our hands, but in the present circumstances, and with the sort of troops that we have to handle, we must be content with what has happened.[15]

Like Blücher, Napoleon had a brush with danger that evening. While returning to his headquarters at Maizières, 4 miles north-east of Brienne, he and his staff were surprised by Cossacks, and amidst the confusion one of the attackers is said to have come dangerously close before being shot down by *Colonel* Gaspard, *baron* Gourgaud, the *premier officier d'ordonnance*. But the incident was later embellished, especially by the notoriously vain and touchy Gourgaud, and some accounts even claimed, ludicrously, that Napoleon had to push a Cossack back with his hand, and draw his sword in his own defence.[16]

Next morning, Napoleon returned to Brienne, expecting to resume the battle, but found that Blücher had abandoned the town.[17] 'It had been cold during the night,' noted *Lieutenant* Octave Levavasseur:

> The wounded were still on the battlefield, stuck to the ground by the ice, and so the plain offered the most horrible sight, with the wounded giving dreadful groans. The Emperor ordered a review on this very ground. In order to remain aligned, the soldiers stood with comrades lying on the ground between their ranks, either dead or drawing their last, agonised breaths. On young soldiers, this made an unforgettable impression, and the review was held in gloomy silence.[18]

Battle of La Rothière

From Brienne an almost flat plain extends 6 miles southwards, past the village of La Rothière and up to the rising ground near Trannes. To the west is the Aube river, while 4 miles to the east the plain ends in woods and gentle hills near the village of Morvilliers.

Napoleon had merely driven Blücher back on to the *Hauptarmee*, and could not hope to defeat him in a second battle. Yet neither could he withdraw until his rearguard under Marmont had rejoined him from Saint-Dizier, and until the broken bridge at Lesmont had been repaired to open a line of retreat to Troyes.

Napoleon's inactivity puzzled the Allies, who had expected him either to retreat or renew the attack. Since Schwarzenberg could not keep both the Allied armies concentrated for long without exhausting their supplies, he agreed that Blücher should take the offensive on 1 February. In order to do so, Blücher needed reinforcements, for he still had only part of his own army with him. Schwarzenberg therefore placed the III and IV *Armee-Abtheilungen* at his disposal, but stipulated that they were to revert to the *Hauptarmee*'s control once Brienne had been recaptured.

Schwarzenberg has been criticised for not using a greater proportion of his strength. The fact that another corps, Wrede's V *Armee-Abtheilung*, marched against Napoleon's eastern flank was due to the initiative of its commander, and was a move that Schwarzenberg simply approved. Nor was Blücher given control over the *Hauptarmee*'s reserves, although some were placed behind him in support.[19] Crushing Napoleon was simply not in Austrian interests: a limited defeat could oblige him to negotiate in earnest, without causing his regime to collapse. Schwarzenberg therefore left the tactical direction of the battle to Blücher, who knew the ground and had more experience of fighting Napoleon, but sensibly retained control of the wider, strategic options.[20]

Despite these self-imposed restrictions, 85,000 Allied troops and 150 of their guns would see action, making La Rothière one of the bigger battles of the campaign. Napoleon was heavily outnumbered. Despite being joined by Marmont on the morning of 1 February, he had just 45,000 men, and, since the plain was so extensive, he was over-stretched along a front of 7.5 miles. To cover his line of retreat, his left wing was bent back at right angles, and ran north along the low hills that marked the eastern edge of the plain.[21]

Napoleon used his infantry to hold a chain of villages that anchored his position, but had to fill the wide gaps in between with cavalry. He did have plenty of artillery, 128 guns in all, but that was actually an encumbrance, since his batteries were vulnerable to capture on such a long and weakly held front. In the face of such odds, Napoleon had no desire to fight, and knew that the Allies might simply pin him down, while they moved the bulk of their strength westwards to seize the city of Troyes and gain a head start on the road to Paris. He had actually begun to withdraw units north-westwards when, towards noon, he was informed that an Allied attack seemed imminent. Realising that it was too late to break contact, he found himself forced to fight an action that he could not win. The most he would be able to do was contain the Allies until dusk and then extricate his army under cover of darkness.

As happened so often during the campaign, he was fortunate in both the weather and the geology of the battlefield. Falling snow reduced visibility at times to a few paces, masking the full extent of his weakness and making it difficult to co-ordinate an offensive. The ground delayed the Allies as they took up positions ready to attack, for the battlefield lay in *Champagne humide*, a wet region made worse by the recent rain, and a frost during the night had covered the mud with a thin but slippery crust of ice. In fact, Sacken's Russian corps had to deploy its artillery in two stages, doubling the teams of half the guns and then sending the horses back for the remainder.[22]

Not until the middle of the afternoon were the Allies ready to launch their main attack. It was difficult for them to move anywhere except along the main road to Brienne, and this led directly through La Rothière, the centre and strongest part of Napoleon's line. Blücher intended to fix the French frontally here with the *Schlesische Armee*, supported on either side by the III and IV *Armee-Abtheilungen*, until Wrede could arrive from the east to threaten Napoleon's line of retreat.

Despite repeated attacks, Blücher was brought to a standstill. So bad were the tracks used by the IV *Armee-Abtheilung* that the skirmishers leading its advance came across an abandoned donkey stuck in a hole up to its ears.[23] When the corps

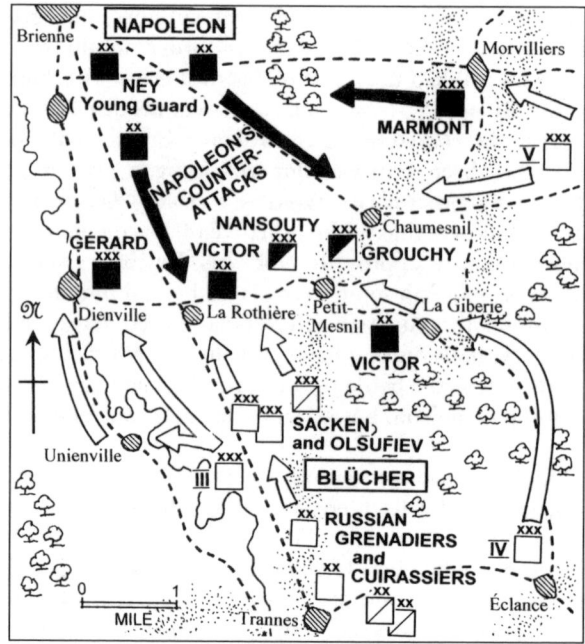

Battle of La Rothière: 1 February 1814.

commander, *Kronprinz* Wilhelm von Württemberg, requested support, he sparked a dispute about how the battle was being fought, and where the *Hauptarmee*'s reserves should intervene. Alexander's Adjutant-General at Schwarzenberg's headquarters, Lieutenant-General Karl Fedorovich Toll, tried to convince Blücher to reinforce the *Kronprinz*, instead of battering away at La Rothière. But Blücher rebuffed him. Weakening his centre could have exposed it to a counter-attack, and in any case he could not readily transfer units away from the main road because of the state of the ground, the limited visibility, and the shortness of daylight.

Toll then rode to the rear and appealed to Alexander, who compromised by sending Blücher a division of Russian grenadiers from reserve, with the request that he send one of its brigades to the *Kronprinz*. When Blücher persisted in objecting that La Rothière was the key point, Alexander directed the rest of the Russian reserves to move forward in support, but they were too far in the rear to have a timely effect.[24]

It was therefore Wrede's arrival that did more than anything to break the stalemate. By driving in Napoleon's eastern wing, he eased the *Kronprinz*'s advance, endangered the French line of retreat on Brienne, and made their entire position untenable.

Fortunately for Napoleon, the sun had already set by 1640 hours. Before he could disengage, he had to counter-attack and shore up his front line. On his eastern wing, he committed a Young Guard brigade, supported by cavalry and 16 guns. When La Rothière finally fell to the Allies, he retook it with a Young Guard division. Then Allied reinforcements joined the fray, the tide swung decisively against the French, and La Rothière was lost for good, obliging Napoleon to form a massed battery north of the village to cover his retreat.

More by luck than design, the Allies assembled a mass of cavalry, which drove the French back towards Brienne, but its advance then petered out, partly through exhaustion, and partly because of the darkness and confusion. Bavarian and Württemberg light cavalry had already clashed after mistaking each other for an enemy unit. When Blücher sought guidance from Alexander and Friedrich Wilhelm III on whether he should continue the battle through the night, he was instructed to allow the troops to rest rather than risk a setback.[25]

Casualties are thought to have been roughly equal, about 6,000 men on each side, but the French had also lost between 54 and 83 guns, and thousands more of their men would desert in the days that followed.[26] The lost cannon could be replaced, but in such large numbers were proof of a major French defeat. Indeed, La Rothière boosted the confidence of the Allies. It was their first victory over Napoleon on French soil, and promised a quick end to the war. For Blücher it was a personal triumph, being the first battle he had won in his own right over Napoleon. (At Leipzig, he had been just one of several Allied army commanders.)

Even so, the outcome fell short of the decisive victory that the Allies could have won. They failed to crush Napoleon, despite having almost twice his numbers on the battlefield. They found it difficult to co-ordinate their attacks, and made the mistake of concentrating against the villages, instead of penetrating through the weakly held gaps in between.[27]

Napoleon had claimed Brienne three days earlier as a tactical victory, but it and La Rothière make more sense when seen as parts of the same battle, separated by a brief interval, and jointly constituting a costly and demoralising French defeat. During the campaign as a whole, Napoleon lost seven generals killed or mortally wounded. Four of them fell at Brienne or La Rothière. This reflected the widespread confusion, the prevalence of street fighting, and the need for commanders to set their conscripts a personal example of bravery in the absence of the Old Guard infantry, but it was a high price to pay for failure.[28]

Chapter 7

'Where will we stop?'

'The great battle has taken place', bragged Blücher in a letter to a friend after La Rothière:

> Yesterday, I gave the Emperor Napoleon a blow on the head and he is in full retreat on Paris. . . . If Napoleon keeps his crown, he will have to regard it as a present from the hands of our monarchs, but I doubt that he will keep it – we will be before Paris within a week.[1]

Whereas Blücher brimmed with confidence, more moderate Allied leaders were filled with alarm at the prospect of a complete French collapse, the overthrow of Napoleon, and peace dictated in Paris on Alexander's terms. It was this schism in the attitudes of the Allies, and the consequent disjunction of their military manoeuvres, that would give Napoleon a chance to reverse his defeat.

The Allied pursuit

On the morning of 2 February the Allied leaders assembled in a council-of-war at the *Château* de Brienne. Napoleon had withdrawn during the night, and the Allies now needed to decide their future operations following the transformation of the situation. Their key decision was that the *Hauptarmee* and *Schlesische Armee* should separate once more, and advance on Paris along routes 30 miles apart, meaning that it would take at least two days for one army to rejoin the other should it need support.[2] Commentators have condemned it as one of the worst mistakes of the campaign, as it enabled Napoleon to seize a central position between the Allies and attack them piecemeal. Yet such criticisms are made with the benefit of hindsight, and are themselves flawed: a single-pronged advance would simply have provoked a different response from Napoleon, and indeed would have made it easier for him to undertake his alternative strategy, the *manoeuvre sur les derrières*, a sweep round to the Allied rear to cut both their armies' supply routes in one swoop. Nor could the Allies have reacted quickly to such a manoeuvre, for a single axis of advance would have caused their forces to become strung out in immense, ponderous columns, and turned the road hub of Troyes into a congested bottleneck. Logistically, it would have impossible to sustain their combined strength of 180,000 men along a single route in mid-winter and across the barren countryside of *Champagne pouilleuse*.

In any case, different imperatives pulled the armies apart. Schwarzenberg was retained in the south so he could cover his supply lines to Basel, whereas Blücher had to move back northwards, nearer the Marne valley, so he could collect both Yorck's detached corps and reinforcements on their way from the Rhine. Thus, while the *Hauptarmee* took the most direct route to Paris, through Troyes and then along the Seine, the *Schlesische Armee* would circle round to the north.

For the Allies the 2nd was a day of lost opportunities. Napoleon had broken contact, partly because of the usual inattentiveness of the Allied outposts, and it was not even clear at first if he was retreating westwards on Troyes or northwards on Vitry. Direct pursuit of him fell to Schwarzenberg, the less dynamic of the two Allied commanders, and it did not help that the region was already exhausted of supplies and obscured by snow. Two rearguard actions effectively checked Schwarzenberg: one north-west of Brienne at Lesmont on the Aube river, and the other on its tributary, the Voire, 4 miles north of Brienne, where Marmont inflicted heavy casualties on the V *Armee-Abtheilung* before withdrawing.[3]

'The disorganisation was dreadful'

Napoleon reached Troyes on 3 February. By falling back on the city, the second most populous in the campaign area, he could replenish supplies and unite with Mortier's detached group of 20,000 men, which had been absent from the first battles. But he had a cold reception from the inhabitants, who could not be expected to cheer the arrival of defeated and undisciplined troops, or willingly provide food for an army that would clearly be unable to protect them from Allied occupation. A week later, *Prinz* Wilhelm, the second son of the Prussian King, wrote to his sister from Troyes:

> A very great, but unprepossessing town. N[apoleon] withdrew with his army through here . . . . Really immense numbers have deserted from him for the past two days, mostly from the Guards. He has allowed his Guards to plunder everything here, while the line regiments went from door to door asking for a piece of bread. This has made the inhabitants very angry, and very favourable to us.[4]

The lack of enthusiasm at Troyes reflected a more general crisis of confidence that pervaded Napoleon's army. In a single night the *37e Légère* lost over 250 deserters. The regiment had behaved well in action just a day or two earlier, but was composed of men conscripted from the local *département*, the Aube, men who naturally wanted to return home and protect their families.[5]

Apart from a cold snap on 4 and 5 February, the daytime temperatures remained above freezing. Heavy rain, disintegrating roads, and the temporary collapse of Napoleon's logistics help explain why he lost so many men. Muskets, shakos, and cartridge pouches lay abandoned all along the roads, and, as *Colonel* Fabvier of the VI Corps noted:

> The Paris road was covered with soldiers of all arms, especially of the Young Guard. They said that they were ill or wounded, as an excuse to leave the army. Others, who were shrewder and more reprehensible, moved away from the roads and went, armed, to establish themselves in remote villages, where they forced the inhabitants to feed them. The disorganisation was dreadful.[6]

Napoleon's response was drastic. Mobile columns of *gendarmes*, each 20 men strong, were ordered to sweep the army's rear and arrest any stragglers, looters, or deserters: any man, in short, who lacked a legitimate reason for being absent from his unit. These men would then be literally decimated, with one in ten being brought before a board of commissioners under the army's provost-in-chief and shot.[7] Napoleon added that this order was to be read at the head of all the corps, but Fabvier thought little of such steps:

> The Emperor ordered rigorous measures, which had no effect. More men were brought back by some days of rest than by the threats. We were told that peace

had been made. The joy was universal, and the most frightened rejoined their corps.[8]

On 4 February a peace conference had finally opened at the town of Châtillon, 38 miles south-east of Troyes, as a consequence of the diplomatic exchanges arising from the Frankfurt Proposals, but agreement proved elusive. Napoleon's representative, *Général de division* Armand, *marquis* de Caulaincourt, received contradictory instructions to accept either any terms, or only reasonable ones.[9] This reflected Napoleon's changing mood. Despite his initial setback, he still hoped to win the campaign, and had immediately anticipated that the Allied armies might separate. Since Troyes was a road hub, he could use it to cover Paris indirectly, by threatening to strike into the flank of any Allied advance as it moved past him to either the north or the south.

Napoleon's first move was a probe south-eastwards by *Maréchal* Mortier on the 5th to ascertain what the *Hauptarmee* was doing. Schwarzenberg had already run into difficulties east of Troyes, where the ground was cut by branches of the Barse river and further obstructed by flooded meadows and disintegrating roads.[10] He was therefore seeking to move the *Hauptarmee* round Troyes to the south, but this shift in its centre of gravity, and the transfer of its northernmost units to the south bank of the Aube, would widen the gap between the Allied armies and leave Blücher exposed.

By holding Troyes, Napoleon sought to delay Schwarzenberg, but he knew that the city was indefensible, for despite the broken ground covering it to the east, its ramparts were ruined and its largely wooden houses vulnerable to fire. In any case, he did not have the strength to fight a defensive war by holding fixed points for long against a concentrated opponent. Instead, he had to retain the initiative and impose on the superior Allied numbers by bluff and constant manoeuvre. On 6 February he therefore fell back on Nogent-sur-Seine, 29 miles to the north-west, where he could collect reinforcements and occupy a more central position. This new withdrawal increased the demoralisation of the army, as the chief secretary of the cabinet, Agathon, *baron* Fain, noted: 'The abandonment of Troyes and the continuation of our retreat caused our last hopes to vanish. The soldiers marched in a gloom that can not be described. "Where will we stop?" was the question on everyone's lips.'[11]

Reorganisation

Napoleon's retreat from La Rothière hid the fact that, in the first half of February, he was able almost to double the size of the forces under his immediate command by falling back and gathering detachments. More than half of his reinforcements were veterans: the Old Guard infantry, which he collected at Troyes, and two divisions of Peninsular infantry arriving in the Seine valley from the Pyrenees. For the next phase of the campaign, therefore, Napoleon's army had a backbone of hardened troops, and was no longer the spineless instrument of Brienne and La Rothière.[12]

According to a heavily dramatised account by *baron* Fain, Napoleon was thrown into despair when he received news on the night of 7/8 February that the Allies were insisting on the harsher formula of the former frontiers as the basis for the peace talks at Châtillon. Eventually, he agreed that the discussions should be allowed to continue, but when the necessary despatches were taken to his room the next morning for signature, he was found stretched out on his maps, having supposedly recovered his spirits after suddenly deciding to attack Blücher.[13]

The truth was that Napoleon had already begun to push units northwards on the

7th, even before the arrival of the news from Châtillon. Leaving behind *Maréchaux* Victor and Oudinot to contain Schwarzenberg on the Seine, he intended to attack the *Schlesische Armee* with 30,000 troops. As much as one-third of this mobile strike force consisted of cavalry, and, equally significantly, three-quarters were from the Imperial Guard.[14]

Directly opposed to Blücher's advance was an outnumbered detachment under *Maréchal* Macdonald, which was being progressively pushed down the Marne valley. Rather than simply move north-westwards to join Macdonald and check the *Schlesische Armee* frontally, Napoleon took the bolder, and potentially decisive, option of thrusting northwards into its flank.

The route lay along transverse roads, and, since the milder temperatures persisted, some sections were all but impassable, so much so that local horses had to be used to double the teams hauling the cannon. *Général de brigade* Philippe, *comte* de Ségur, who was at the tail of the march with a brigade of *Gardes d'honneur*, vividly recalled how:

> The road was so dreadful, . . . that our night march became intermingled with the stragglers of the divisions that had gone before us. Their trail was all strewn with horses, soldiers, and even guns, lost or drowned in these ruts. Many of the infantrymen had left their shoes there, and several hundreds had become scattered through the marshes.[15]

The very difficulty of the road increased the chances of achieving surprise. Yet even on the 9th, just a day before colliding with Blücher's army, Napoleon misjudged the situation, for he thought that the *Schlesische Armee* had little more than 40,000 men, which was an underestimate of at least 15,000. Even so, he rightly anticipated that he would be able to fall on Blücher's leading corps and defeat them piecemeal.[16]

Blücher

The head of the *Schlesische Armee* had been pushing westwards along two axes from the area of Châlons-sur-Marne. Yorck's Prussian corps followed the *chaussée* down the Marne valley, while Sacken's Russians took an inferior but more direct road, 10 or 12 miles further south, which passed through Champaubert and Montmirail.

Blücher himself remained in the rear, for he expected to be joined imminently by two corps of reinforcements, which were on their way from the Rhine under *General-Leutnant* Friedrich von Kleist and Lieutenant-General Peter Mikhailovich Kaptsevich.[17] Once they arrived, he reckoned he would be strong enough to advance all the way to Paris, which he was anxious to reach before a negotiated peace could end hostilities.

By the morning of the 9th the *Schlesische Armee* had become stretched out over a distance of more than 37 miles, from Montmirail to Châlons-sur-Marne. Each of its corps was at least a day's march from its nearest neighbour, beyond the reach of prompt support. Blücher was also handicapped by a shortage of cavalry. Too much of it was still observing fortresses in his rear, and those units that were present were needed to spearhead the advance, making it impossible to link the rearward corps with a string of cavalry posts.

The danger of Blücher's over-extension was not obvious at the time. He believed that Napoleon was being contained by the *Hauptarmee* in the south, and underestimated his ability to recover from his defeat at La Rothière. Nor could he have anticipated that Napoleon would be able to move an army through the difficult region

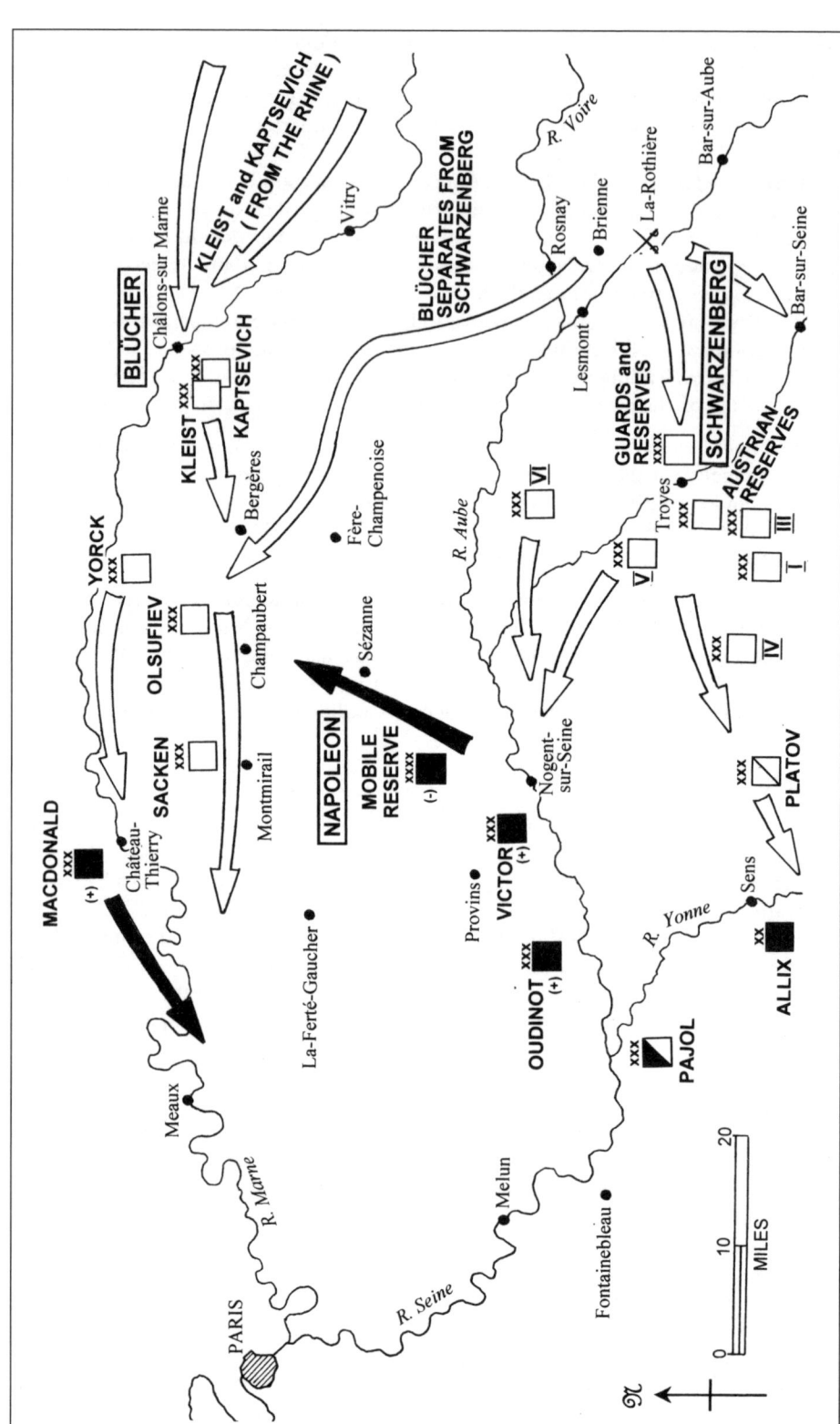

Blücher's first advance on Paris: 2–10 February 1814.

between the Seine and the Marne in the middle of winter, let alone that he would do so at such speed.

As a result of the *Hauptarmee* shifting southwards to outflank Troyes, Blücher received instructions to send Kleist's corps to reinforce Schwarzenberg's northernmost unit against Napoleon in the Seine valley. To compensate, a Russian corps under General Ferdinand Fedorovich, Baron Winzingerode would be detached from the *Nordarmee* and placed under Blücher, but it would take well over a week to arrive from Belgium.[18] Blücher's command team decided to march both Kleist and Kaptsevich towards the Seine, but this would extend the *Schlesische Armee* even further, by pulling it southwards as the same time as it thrust to the west. Thus, it was actually the caution at the *Hauptarmee*'s headquarters, and not just Blücher's boldness, that exposed the Allies to their forthcoming string of defeats.

At this stage Blücher's headquarters knew that some French troops had reached Sézanne, 11 miles to the south, and had even probed northwards towards the crossroads of Champaubert before falling back. But the overriding impression was that the move was merely a reconnaissance, and so the *Schlesische Armee* was allowed to continue its advance instead of being ordered to concentrate.[19]

By the morning of the 10th Blücher knew that Napoleon himself was moving north from the Seine, but was unsure whether he intended to strike northwards into the *Schlesische Armee*'s flank, or simply to join Macdonald. Later that day confirmation arrived of Napoleon's presence at Sézanne with as many as 30,000 troops, mainly Imperial Guardsmen, and there came the ominous sound of firing from near Champaubert.[20]

Chapter 8

A salvo of victories

The Battle of Champaubert was the first in a dramatic series of French victories that nullified the defeat of La Rothière and temporarily reversed the course of the campaign. In itself, Champaubert was only a minor village, but it stood at a strategically important crossroads, and was covered by the Russian 9th Infantry Corps under Lieutenant-General Zakhar Dmitrevich Olsufiev I.

When Napoleon thrust northwards from Sézanne on 10 February, he enjoyed an overwhelming superiority of numbers. Olsufiev had only 4,000 infantry and 24 guns, and had been left isolated in the middle of the *Schlesische Armee* by its over-extension. The other corps were between 10 and 30 miles away to the west, north-west, and south-east. Yet, despite his inferior numbers, Olsufiev could have checked the French long enough to escape by destroying the bridge over the Petit Morin river at Pont-Saint-Prix, 4 miles south of Champaubert. This would have blocked the only axis of advance open to Napoleon, for the Petit Morin valley was a major military obstacle, especially to the east where it was filled with the boggy expanse of the Saint-Gond marshes. But Olsufiev failed to do so, partly because he had barely any cavalry with which to reconnoitre and ascertain the full danger of his position.

Battle of Champaubert

It took time for a succession of French units to cross the narrow bridge at Pont-Saint-Prix and deploy ready to attack up the slopes on the far side. The assault began in the morning, and was spearheaded by Marmont's VI Corps.

Despite being urged by his subordinates to retreat, Olsufiev decided to hold a strong position above the Petit Morin valley, anchored on the villages of Baye and Bannay. He still underestimated the threat, for the initial French attacks were purely frontal and in limited strength. Just a fortnight earlier he had been rebuked for his failure to guard a road into the town of Brienne, which had enabled the French to surprise Blücher at his headquarters. He therefore stuck to the letter of the orders he had previously received to hold Champaubert, lest he incur further displeasure.[1]

Not until the afternoon, after more than three hours of fighting, did the French take Baye and Bannay. It was the turning point of the battle. Hitherto, they had been obliged to fight their way uphill, using just two roads, and had difficulty bringing forward their artillery. But they could now deploy superior numbers on top of the plateau, dominate the battlefield with their cavalry, and press home their advance on Champaubert, less than 2 miles to the north.[2]

On the flanks French cavalry pushed forward to sever the Châlons-sur-Marne road on either side of Champaubert, thus threatening to trap Olsufiev's reserve. He began a retreat northwards, which he covered by sacrificing a rearguard of 1,000 infantry under Major-General Constantine Markovich Poltoratsky. Driven into Champaubert and pounded by French artillery, Poltoratsky refused a surrender summons and instead tried to reach the safety of some woods. His infantry were charged by cavalry,

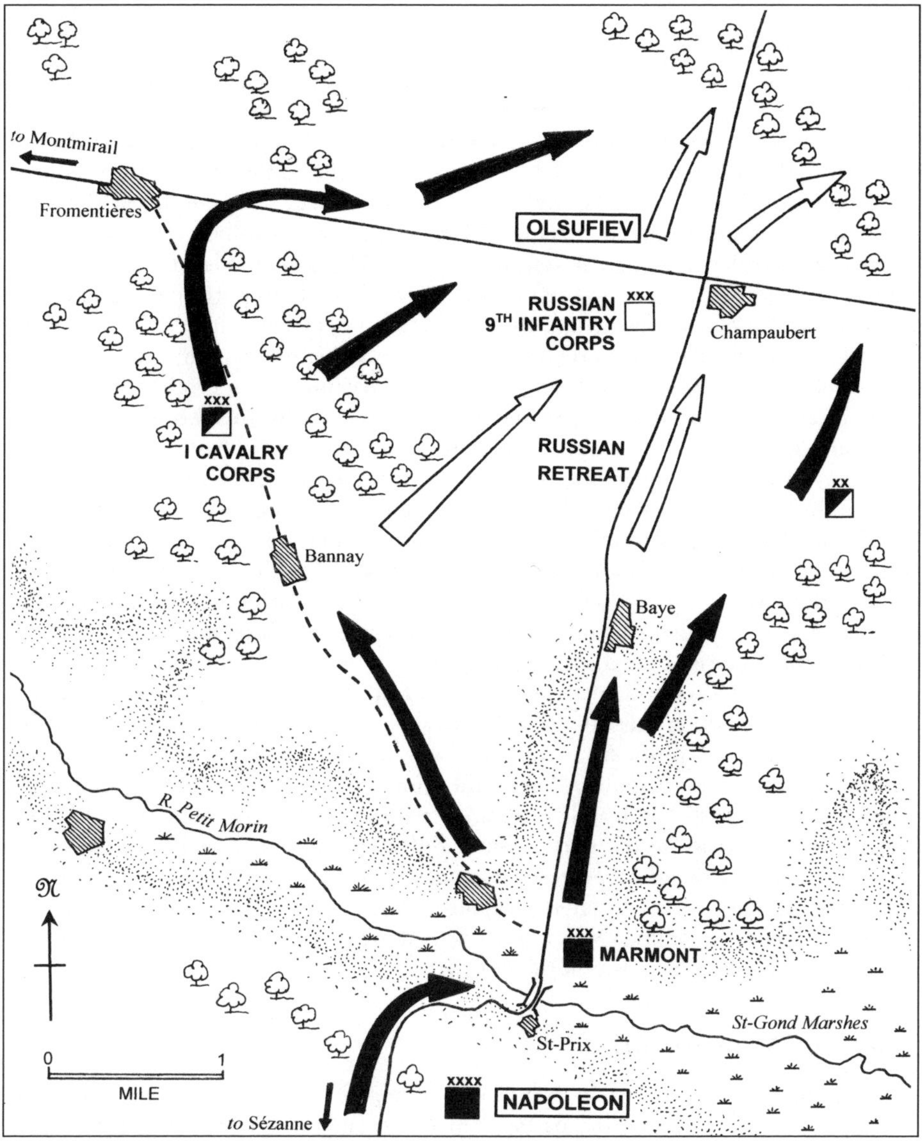

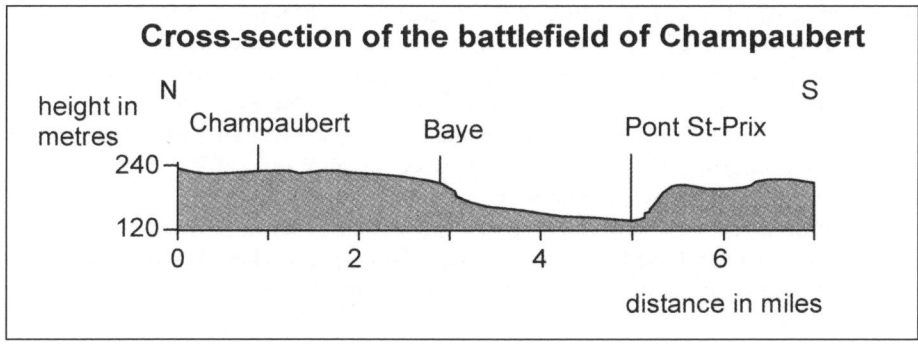

Battle of Champaubert: 10 February 1814.

but fought on until they exhausted their ammunition, and only then laid down their arms. The rest of Olsufiev's troops, finding their retreat blocked by French cavalry, headed eastwards for the woods, but were dispersed by French *cuirassiers*.

In all, 60 per cent of Olsufiev's men were killed or taken prisoner, and he himself was captured along with 9 guns.[3] Yet by no means did the battle disgrace the Russians, for despite the numerical odds, the French had taken half a day to defeat them. In terms of the numbers of combatants, Champaubert was a minor clash, twenty or thirty times smaller than the colossal battles of 1813, and too modest to have a lasting impact on its own. But its moral significance was out of all proportion to its size, as it marked the end of the misfortune that had dogged Napoleon since the start of the campaign, and enabled him to revive enthusiasm both within his army and in France as a whole by brazenly exaggerating the results. Writing to his brother Joseph that night, he claimed to have taken at least 6,000 prisoners and 40 guns, which was actually one-and-a-half times Olsufiev's total strength at the start of the battle.

In any case, Champaubert was just the beginning, for it opened a whole plethora of opportunities. Having broken right into the middle of the *Schlesische Armee*, Napoleon could now defeat it piecemeal, and he decided to swing westwards and trap its two leading corps, under Yorck and Sacken, against the Marne. To cover this move, and observe the severed tail of Blücher's army, he detached Marmont with 4,300 men to occupy Etoges, 3.5 miles east of Champaubert, where the escarpment of the *Côte de l'Ile-de-France* offered a good, defensive position.

Napoleon had lost the element of surprise on an operational level, for his onslaught had alerted the Allies to his offensive, but so long as he maintained the tempo of his operations, he could profit from the initial advantage he had won. His seizure of a central position at Champaubert did not completely interdict Blücher's communications with Yorck and Sacken, since messengers were able to take a detour along transverse roads to the north.[4] But it did delay the arrival of Blücher's orders, and contributed to the disagreements that ensued between the aggressive Sacken and the more cautious Yorck. In short, Napoleon had already dislocated the *Schlesische Armee*'s system of command and control, and could undermine its cohesion still further by exploiting his position the next day.[5]

Battle of Montmirail

Montmirail was the second in Napoleon's string of victories over the *Schlesische Armee*, and a more substantial battle than Champaubert. In fact, in terms of the numbers of troops he defeated, it was his greatest success of the entire campaign.[6]

Leaving Champaubert on the morning of 11 February, Napoleon rode 11 miles westwards to the town of Montmirail. He hoped to crush Yorck and Sacken between himself and Macdonald's detached corps, which was holding the Marne near Meaux. To complete the trap, and block any escape to the south, he instructed Oudinot to send an infantry division or two northwards from the covering forces on the Seine.[7]

Alerted to their danger by messages from Blücher, Sacken and Yorck were already moving back towards each other. Sacken retraced his steps eastwards during the night of the 10th/11th, and by the middle of the morning was less than 7 miles west of Montmirail. Yorck was moving south-eastwards from Château-Thierry to join him, but his corps was barely fit for action following its recent marches. The commander of one of its cavalry brigades, *Oberst* Wilhelm, *Graf* Henckel von Donnersmarck, later explained:

The whole corps was extremely run down. Many of the horses were dejected, had lost their shoes, were lame or emaciated, while the infantrymen often went barefoot on the abominable tracks. In short, our corps was very much exhausted.[8]

Yorck had to leave one of his infantry brigades behind to cover his line of retreat over the Marne at Château-Thierry, and would be prevented by the state of the road from intervening in the battle until the middle of the afternoon. In fact, no more than 4,000 of his men, or barely a quarter of his total strength, would be seriously engaged that day, and they would have little artillery support.[9]

Yorck sent an officer to try to persuade Sacken to retreat immediately on Château-Thierry. But Sacken was Russian, and not under Yorck's authority. He underestimated the size of the French forces opposed to him, and did not realise that Napoleon was present. He intended, if not to crush the French, then at least to drive them back and ease his junction with Yorck.

The fighting did not begin in earnest until the early afternoon, and until then both sides raced to build up their forces on the battlefield. All sides converged on the plateau 2 miles north-west of Montmirail, where the road from Château-Thierry joined the main lateral road from the east. By occupying this key junction, Napoleon would make it difficult for Sacken to unite with Yorck and escape to Château-Thierry, as vehicles could not move easily across the sodden countryside.

Sacken had about 16,000 troops, and occupied a ridge 2 miles west of the junction with the Château-Thierry road. Towards 1100 hours he pushed along the main road to occupy the *Ferme* des Grenaux, and drove the French from the village of Marchais 900 yards to the south. Both these positions stood on high ground and were the salient points on the battlefield. To the north of the main road the ground was relatively flat and open, and thus suitable for cavalry charges, whereas to the south it was intersected by tributaries, which made it more difficult to advance either east or west.

Napoleon could not attack until he was joined by enough units to have a sufficient reserve. During the first phase of the battle, he merely contained Sacken until the arrival of the 2nd Old Guard Division towards 1400 hours brought his total strength to 19,000 men, giving him a considerable numerical superiority over the Russians. He now unleashed a series of carefully co-ordinated attacks, which systematically dismantled the opposing forces. After a preliminary artillery bombardment, the onslaught opened with *Maréchal* Ney punching through the Russian centre with four Old Guard battalions. Casualties were high, with the *2e Chasseurs à pied* losing seven officers killed or wounded that day, but Ney's assault took the *Ferme* des Grenaux, silenced much of the Russian artillery, and dislocated Sacken's corps.

Napoleon immediately exploited the success with a sequence of charges by the Guard cavalry, designed to destroy Allied cohesion by severing communications between Sacken's unit commanders and isolating them from Yorck. Part of the Russian southern wing managed to escape, but the rest was cut off when the Old Guard *Dragons* swept down from the main road and into its rear. French infantry followed up the breakthrough by eliminating a pocket of resistance at the village of Marchais, and by countering Yorck's belated intervention from the north.

By the end of the battle the French were masters of the battlefield, and their leading units had penetrated 2.5 miles behind Sacken's original position. The Allies lost a minimum of 3,600 men killed, wounded, or captured, compared to French

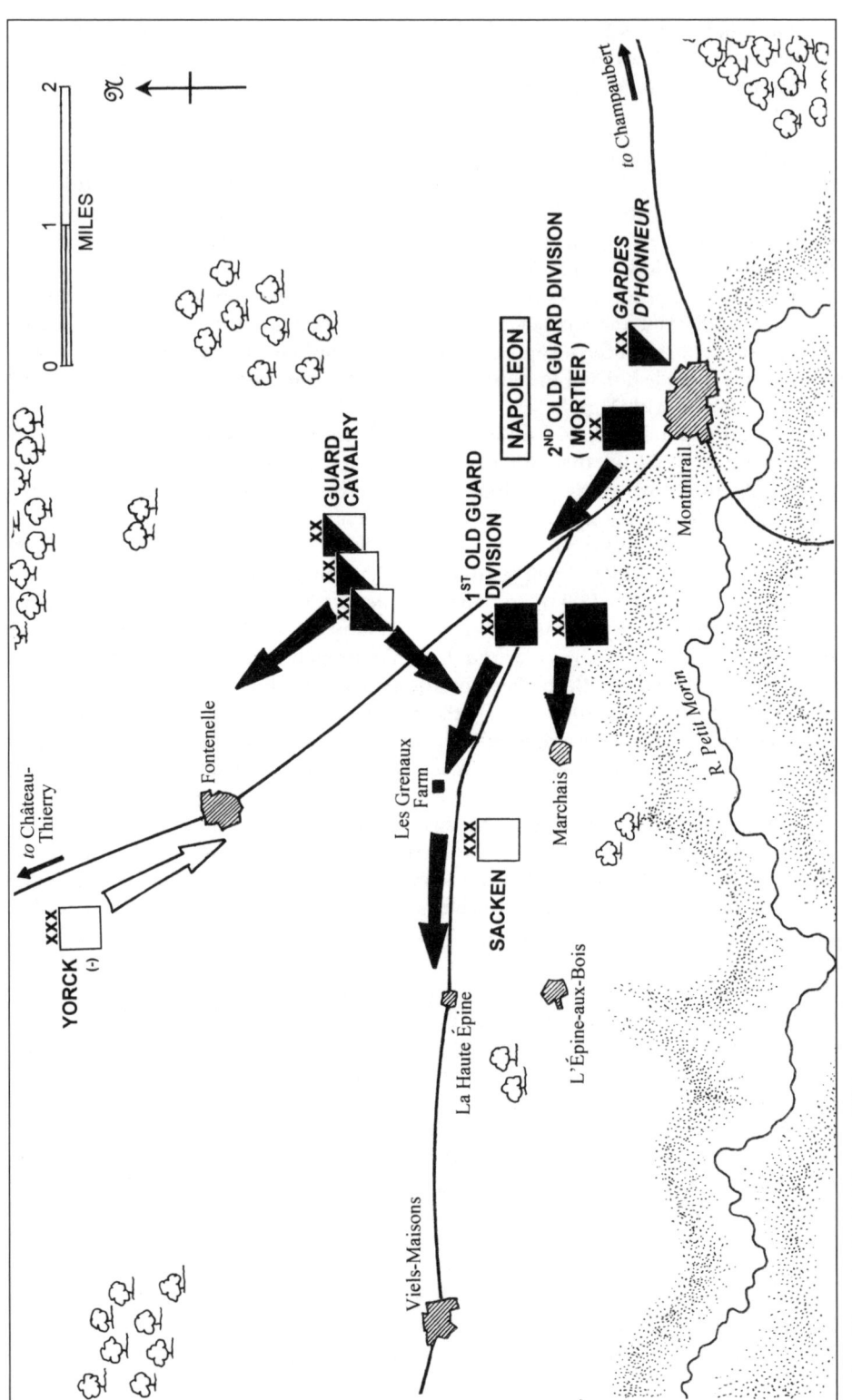

Battle of Montmirail: 11 February 1814.

casualties of about 2,000. That evening, Napoleon boasted to his brother Joseph:

> It is eight o'clock and, before going to bed, I send you this brief note to inform you that today has been decisive. The enemy's Army of Silesia no longer exists. I have completely routed it. We have taken all its cannon, its baggage and have taken thousands of prisoners, perhaps more than 7,000. They are coming in all the time. There are 5,000 to 6,000 enemy lying on the battlefield. All this has been obtained by engaging only half of my Old Guard, which has done more than can be expected of men. . . . My Guard infantry, my *Dragons* and my *Grenadiers à cheval* have done miracles. . . . I think that these two days will therefore dispel every threat to Paris, since this Army of Silesia was the best Allied army.[10]

Battle of Château-Thierry

It poured with rain during the night, adding to the demoralisation of the defeated Allied troops. As Sacken's units struggled northwards across the soaked countryside in the darkness, they were forced to abandon several guns and many other vehicles.

By the morning of the 12th Yorck and Sacken had united on the Château-Thierry road, and were able to retreat along it to the north-west, in order to cross the Marne to safety. But at 0900 hours Napoleon launched a full-scale pursuit with two converging prongs. Mortier advanced directly along the Château-Thierry road, while Napoleon himself moved along transverse roads 2.5 miles to the west, so he could outflank any rearguards that tried to check Mortier, and mop up the stragglers along Sacken's line of retreat.

Napoleon left some units in reserve near Montmirail, for there was no point in using more troops than necessary, or in forcing tired and depleted formations to make needless marches. What is notable is that the pursuit was made entirely by Imperial Guard troops, and that it included all the Guard cavalry.[11]

The countryside undulated deeply, providing the Allies with a series of defensive positions. It was Yorck's relatively intact corps that covered the retreat, with the support of some of Sacken's Russians, and his rearguard made a stand behind the Dolloir stream halfway to Château-Thierry. But it could not resist Napoleon for long, since the *Grenadiers à pied* of the Old Guard stormed up the slopes and seized the village of Les Caquerets, while French cavalry began to turn the Allied flanks. Yorck fell back to a new position on the southern edge of a plateau that covered the final 1.5 miles up to the Marne valley.

Colonel Charles, *baron* Griois was supporting the French advance with part of the Guard artillery, and recalled how impatiently Napoleon waited for his troops to come up:

> I was right in front with the skirmishers and with one of my batteries that was ahead of the others. Having left his escort in the rear, the Emperor came on his own to my post, and examined the position with his telescope. He particularly looked towards the point where the Guard cavalry would emerge, and asked if I could see it. He was not distracted for an instant by the musketballs and canister that whistled past us. . . . At last, the longed-for cavalry appeared – I was the first to spot it and point it out to the Emperor.

The action that followed was brutally unequal. A series of clashes on the eastern wing

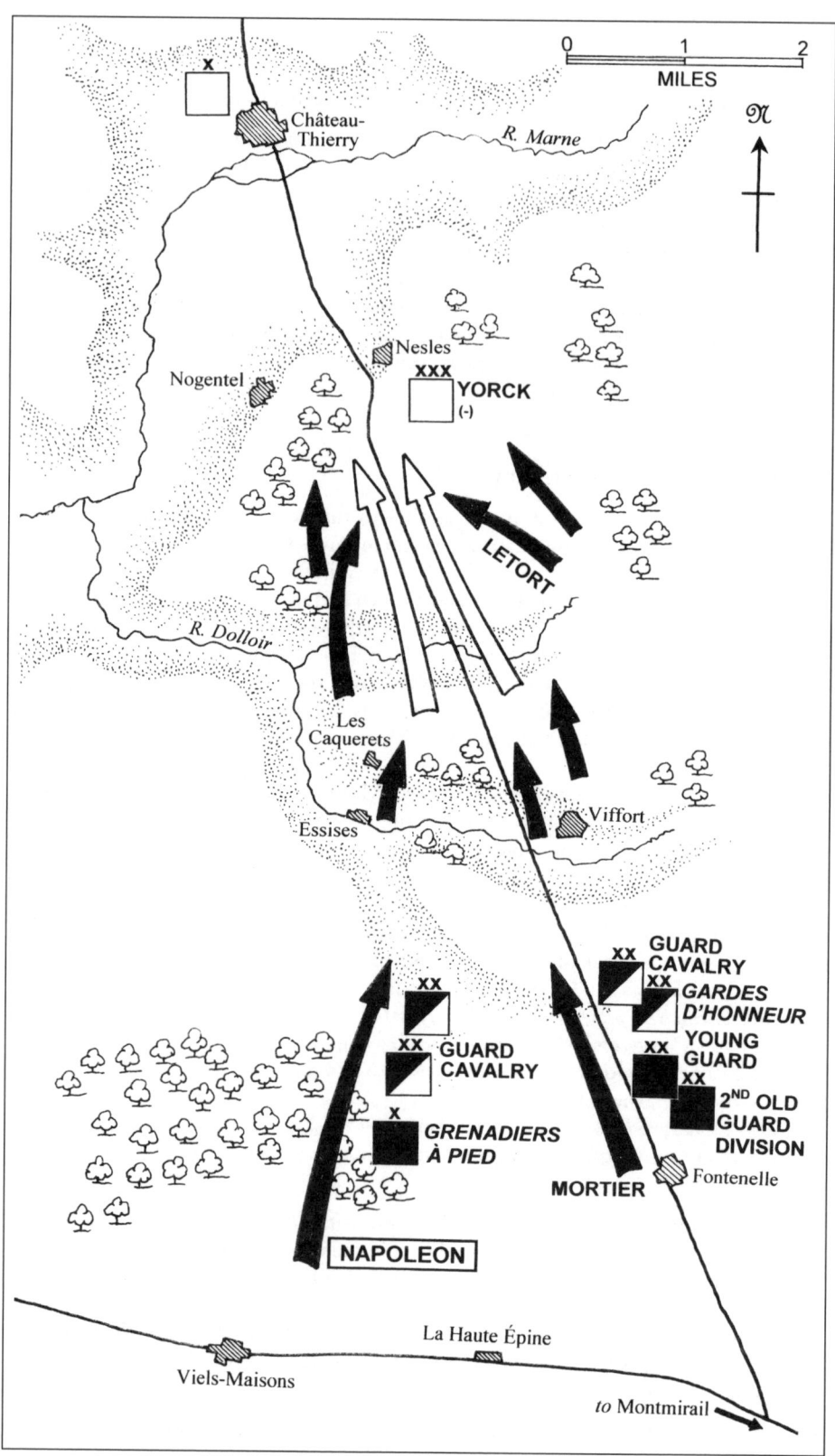

Battle of Château-Thierry: 12 February 1814.

ended with the Prussian cavalry being driven from the field and Yorck's infantry exposed to the French horsemen, who now dominated the plateau. On the western wing two Russian regiments were caught in a devastating pincer move when Napoleon committed his own escort squadrons, seconded by *Général de brigade* Louis, *baron* Letort charging from the opposite flank with the *Dragons* of the Young Guard. *Colonel* Griois described how:

> The *Dragons*, who were in front, headed in column for the Russian line, which immediately formed squares. The *Dragons* attacked the nearest one and, despite the heavy fire and its rampart of bayonets, rushed at it with their heads down. In a moment, the square ceased to exist and only the fallen men and broken weapons marked the spot where it had been.
>
> After destroying this square, the *Dragons* fell on the other two, one after the other, with the same outcome. The rest of our cavalry routed that of the enemy, while the Russian infantry, seeing three of its squares broken, retired in disorder. This charge by the *Dragons* of the Guard is one of the finest cavalry feats I have seen.[12]

Fortunately for Yorck, the French cavalrymen were slowed by the mud as they pursued his surviving units. Horses sank up to their hocks in the mud, and squadrons had to halt and reform. Once they reached the edge of the plateau, the French could see the Allied troops pouring in disorder into the Marne valley. Cheers of *Vive l'empereur!* echoed along the heights, and were immediately followed by chilling calls of 'Forwards! Kill! Kill!'[13]

But the steep and uneven slopes were covered with vineyards, making it difficult for cohesive units of French cavalry to swoop down on the river. The road itself was wide enough for just four horses, and laboriously zig-zagged its way down the hillside.[14] Even after reaching the valley floor, and throwing back two fresh battalions that tried to cover the retreat, the French were checked by Yorck's destruction of the bridges, and by artillery fire sweeping the open meadows from the far side of the Marne.[15]

Yorck and Sacken lost 2,750 men that day. Yet the victory, like Montmirail, fell short of Napoleon's hopes, for he had again failed to annihilate the Allied forces.[16] He owed the outcome, such as it was, primarily to his superior numbers of cavalry, and the tactical skill of its leaders: men like Letort, whom he promoted to *Général de division*, and *Colonel* Jean Curély, the commander of the *10e Hussards*, who became *Général de brigade*.

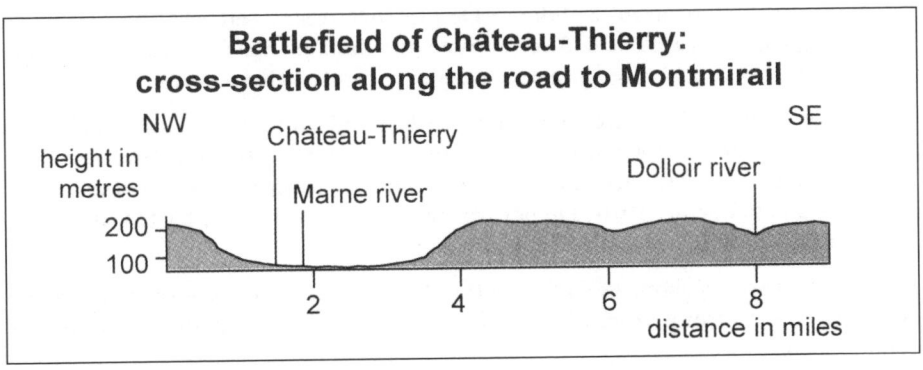

'Announce that sixty regiments have been destroyed'

Next day, the 13th, Napoleon had the broken bridge at Château-Thierry repaired, and then pushed Mortier across with the 2nd Old Guard Division and two divisions of cavalry to resume the interrupted pursuit. But Yorck and Sacken were now more than 10 miles to the north-east, and would safely rejoin Blücher at Châlons-sur-Marne on the 16th by way of Reims.

To complete the *Schlesische Armee*'s disorientation, Napoleon sought to rouse the population along the entire Marne valley. Officers were detached to establish observation posts and organise the *gardes nationaux* using abandoned muskets collected from the battlefields. Marmont was instructed to issue proclamations deliberately exaggerating the results of Montmirail:

> Announce that sixty Russian regiments have been destroyed, that we have captured 120 guns, that the commanding general has been killed or mortally wounded, that it is time for the French people to rise in order to fall on them, that the Emperor is pursuing them, that all Cossacks and detachments must be stopped, the bridges cut before them, the baggage halted and no food given to them.[17]

Major Friedrich von Colomb, the commander of a Prussian *Streifkorps*, was observing the Marne valley, and testified to the effectiveness of Napoleon's measures. 'The proclamations had further increased the over-excitement of the population, and it was interesting to note how far public opinion had changed,' he noted. His patrols were greeted everywhere with musketshots, and he had to operate with great caution, without straying far from supporting formations. In sending a report to Reims, he had to detach an escort of as many as twenty men.[18]

Battle of Vauchamps

To his mounting frustration, Blücher had been forced to remain inactive at Bergères during the 11th and 12th, despite hearing the cannonade from Montmirail, 23 miles to the west. With him was the tail of his army: Kleist and Kaptsevich's men, and the smashed remnants of Olsufiev's corps from Champaubert, a total of 15,000 troops. But he was actually weaker than Yorck and Sacken, who together had well over half his troops at that time and, crucially, almost all his available cavalry, and he could not risk advancing to their support until the 13th, when he was reinforced from the rear by two Prussian *Kürassier* regiments.

All that stood in Blücher's way was Marmont's weak covering force at Etoges, which he easily forced to withdraw. Despite his recent setbacks, he remained undaunted, partly because he had been misled into thinking that Napoleon had begun to withdraw. 'I have had three unpleasant days,' he wrote to his wife on the 13th:

> Napoleon attacked me three times in three days with all his strength and all his Guards, but he did not achieve his aim and is today retreating on Paris. I will follow him tomorrow, then our armies will unite and everything will be decided by a big battle before Paris. Do not fear that we will be beaten, for that is not possible, unless an unheard-of mistake happens.[19]

In fact, Blücher was about to suffer another heavy defeat, for his advance provoked Napoleon into returning from Château-Thierry and joining Marmont for a ferocious counter-attack.[20]

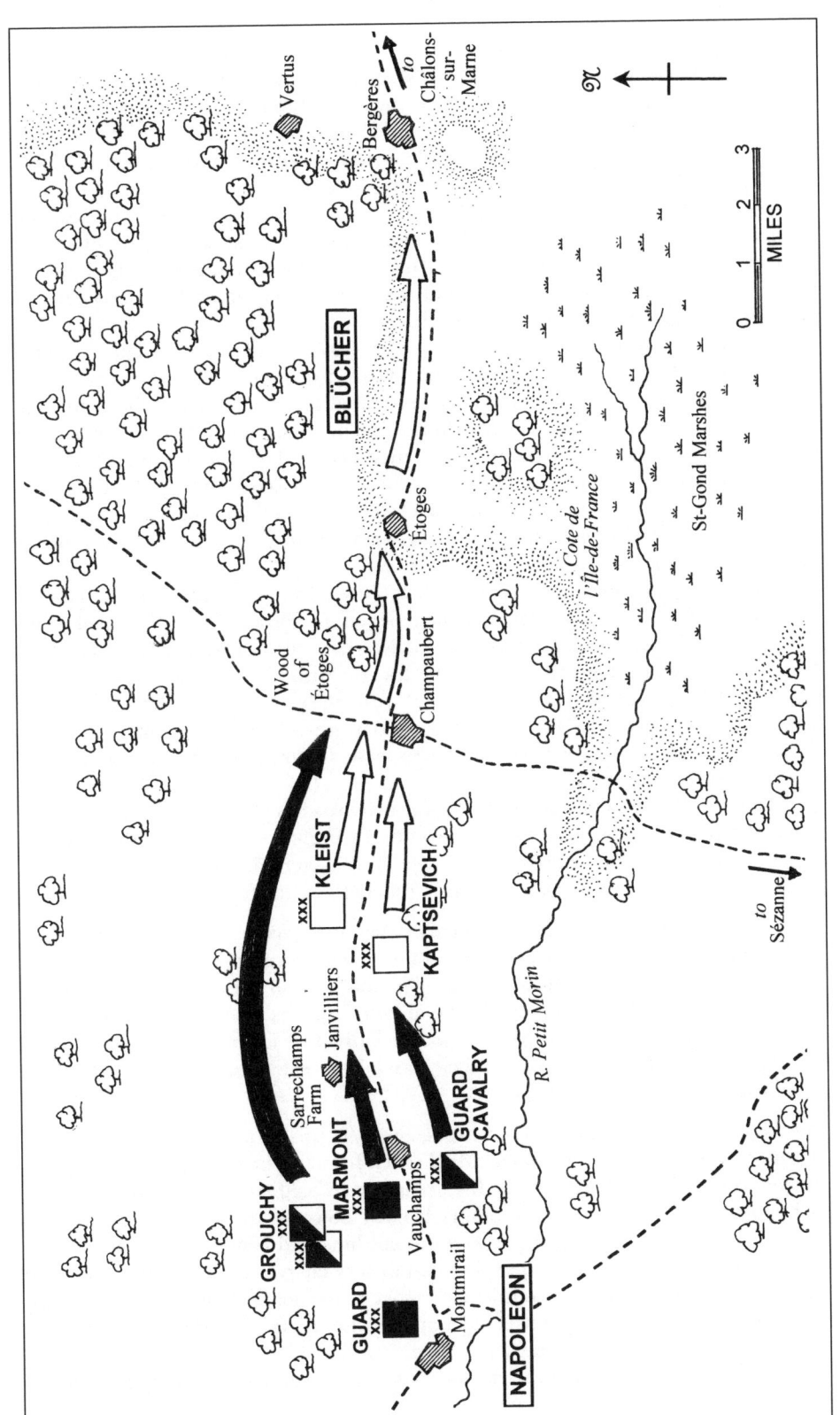

Battle of Vauchamps: 14 February 1814.

On the morning of the 14th Blücher's advanced guard under *General-Leutnant* Hans von Zieten took the village of Vauchamps, just 4 miles east of Montmirail. But that was the limit of its progress, for strong French masses were now drawn up in support of Marmont. Zieten had become dangerously isolated, since the bulk of Kleist and Kaptsevich's troops were a three-hour march to the rear.

Napoleon unleashed his offensive. As at Champaubert four days earlier, Marmont's infantry would spearhead the move with a frontal attack along the main road, while cavalry advanced on either flank to cut the escape routes: the Imperial Guard cavalry to the south, and the I and II Cavalry Corps under *Général de division* Emmanuel, *comte* de Grouchy to the north.

Evicted from Vauchamps, Zieten was mercilessly crushed in the open country further east. With his cavalry overpowered, his five infantry battalions were left exposed to charges from all sides as they retreated to rejoin Blücher. One unit, the *1. Schlesische Infanterie-Regiment*, lost four-fifths of its strength. The flag of its 2nd Battalion was carried off in triumph by French cavalry, but that of the 1st Battalion was broken and buried by the soldiers. Napoleon later asked a captured ensign where it was. 'Sire, we know, but we will not say,' came the resolute reply. For a moment, Napoleon's eyes flashed with anger, but then a smile softened his face, and he ordered the prisoners to be treated well.[21]

Blücher's main body had now reached Janvilliers, less than 2 miles east of Vauchamps. By 1400 hours he, too, had begun to retreat, having learned from prisoners that Yorck and Sacken had been driven over the Marne, and that Napoleon himself was present. His retreat would be fraught with risk because of the superior numbers of French cavalry, and the open nature of the ground for the first 6 miles. To cover the withdrawal, the Prussians had to sacrifice a battalion of the *7. Reserve-Infanterie-Regiment* by throwing it into Sarrechamps farm, where it was overwhelmed after an obdurate resistance.

Blücher withdrew along either side of the main road, with Kleist's Prussians to the north and Kaptsevich's Russians to the south. To French eyewitnesses, their cavalry seemed like a swarm of bees hovering around Blücher's battalions, harassing and goading them with lance thrusts.[22] Nostitz, Blücher's adjutant, noted how:

> It was impossible to prevent the enemy cavalrymen, some individually, others in smaller or larger units, from flooding the whole terrain and roaming through the intervals between the battalions. This obliged all the leaders and their retinues to shut themselves inside the infantry squares for their safety. There was no longer any overall control, so the individual formation commanders were left to their own devices and their own initiative. Each of them had to help himself as best he could.[23]

But the horsemen made piecemeal charges, and were unable to halt the retreat, which continued in good order, even though the French formed a massed battery of 36 guns. Blücher could offer little reply to its fire, as he had to keep most of his artillery on the main road to prevent it from becoming bogged down in the mud and exposed to capture. Yet on this occasion the soaked ground hindered Napoleon even more than his opponents. It limited the Imperial Guard cavalry charges on the southern wing to a trot, and impeded Grouchy's outflanking move to the north. Two batteries had been ordered to follow Grouchy, but could not keep up along the difficult tracks, thus depriving him of supporting fire.

Blücher's men could see the dark, ominous mass of cavalry shadowing them to the north, and moving inwards to threaten their line of retreat. As the sun set towards 1700 hours, they passed through the village of Champaubert and emerged to find French squadrons blocking the main road further to the east.[24] In response, Blücher adopted a new and tighter formation that enabled him to brush aside the cavalry. Kleist and Kaptsevich's corps closed in towards the road, so their battalion columns formed a long, hollow rectangle, in which they could cover each other and prevent the cavalry from penetrating between them.

Leutnant Wilhelm von Rahden of the *2. Schlesische Infanterie-Regiment* recalled how his commander, *Major Graf* Reichenbach, instructed him to sally forth with his skirmishers as soon as a French charge was repulsed. Rahden thought that he was charged up to fifteen times that day:

> *Graf* Reichenbach always let them come up to fifty or sixty paces and only then halted, formed square, and gave a heavy and controlled battalion volley, which dispersed the enemy each time. I immediately bounded thirty or forty paces after them with my men and fired well-aimed shots until a new squadron rode up. I then withdrew just as quickly with my skirmishers to the battalion's rearmost platoon . . .
>
> *Graf* Reichenbach always remained outside the square and never took his place inside it. Instead, he rode on the battalion's left flank, which could not fire as it faced the road where our artillery stood. Our excellent *Major* gave the necessary commands with the utmost precision, composure and cool-headedness, as if on the drill and parade ground (and even far surpassing that). All you could hear was his voice and our volleys, and certainly for the brave *Graf* Reichenbach, as a soldier and superior, it was the finest afternoon of his life.[25]

The rest of the retreat was soon covered by Etoges wood, which stood near the northern side of the main road. The artillery was now sent on ahead to safety, and the rectangle of infantry battalions compressed to form a single column marching along the road. In the dusk, it took time to redeploy in this way, and French cavalrymen managed to penetrate between the wood and the road, and even cut down some staff officers after becoming mixed with Blücher's entourage. Others dismounted, and fired their carbines from the cover of the trees, until the darkness finally brought the action to an end, at least for the time being.[26]

Napoleon returned with his Imperial Guard to Montmirail, as he intended to leave the area and move against Schwarzenberg in the Seine valley. But to screen his departure, he ordered Marmont's VI Corps to take up the pursuit of Blücher again in the evening.

Blücher continued his retreat towards Bergères, 7 miles further east, but left Major-General Alexander Petrovich, Prince Urusov with a Russian rearguard at Etoges, where the main road narrowed and wound its way down the escarpment. It was here that Urusov's men were suddenly attacked by Marmont, and quickly routed. *Leutnant* Rahden, whose Prussian brigade was caught up in the panic, frankly admitted:

> Very many men of my regiment, too, were killed or taken prisoner, as all order and discipline completely disintegrated in the darkness and as a result of the terror, among the same troops who had defended themselves heroically the whole day.[27]

During the battle as a whole, Kleist and Kaptsevich lost one in every four of their men.²⁸ Blücher resumed the retreat before dawn on the 15th, in order to leave the exposed plain of *Champagne pouilleuse*. By the afternoon he had reached Châlons-sur-Marne, where he could draw supplies from magazines and concentrate his scattered corps behind the protection of the Marne.

Taking stock

In just five days Napoleon had inflicted four defeats on the *Schlesische Armee*. Not since April 1809 had he won such a swift succession of personal victories, and never before had any of his battles been fought so close to Paris, or had a more immediate or intense an impact on French public opinion.

Napoleon had thrown the *Schlesische Armee* back 55 miles and inflicted losses of at least 13,000 men, or about a quarter of its strength.²⁹ He had done so through surprise, manoeuvre, and the skilful and ruthless concentration of forces to defeat his opponents piecemeal. He exploited the *Schlesische Armee*'s paucity of cavalry and its limited ability to support itself with artillery as a result of the soaked ground. He explained to Joseph how he won at Vauchamps:

> The enemy had no cavalry, whereas I had 6–8,000 very good cavalrymen, with whom I constantly had him surrounded and outflanked. He had to send most of his artillery to safety in case he lost it and for the whole day I crushed him with canister fire from 100 guns.³⁰

Napoleon himself is thought to have lost just 4,000 men in these four recent battles, but, because of his increased reliance on the Imperial Guard, an unaffordable proportion of his losses were from his most experienced units. Brilliant though they were, his victories over the *Schlesische Armee* were won at an unsustainable cost in both casualties and stragglers as a result of the relentless marching over poor-quality roads.

Nor was Blücher's army cowed. Colonel Hudson Lowe, who was attached to its headquarters, wrote enthusiastically of Vauchamps:

> I want words to express my admiration of the intrepidity and discipline of the troops. The example of Field-Marshal Blücher himself, who was everywhere, and in the most exposed situations; of Generals Kleist and Kapsiewitz; of General Gneisenau, who directed the movement on the chaussee; of General Zieten, and Prince Augustus of Prussia, always at the head of his brigade, animating it to the most heroic efforts, could not fail to inspire the soldiers with a resolution that must have even struck the enemy with admiration and surprise.³¹

Over the days that followed, the various beaten detachments of the *Schlesische Armee* reassembled at Châlons-sur-Marne, and were reorganised and re-equipped. The most badly hit units had to be amalgamated. Kleist's corps, for example, was reduced from thirty-one battalions to thirteen, and three of its infantry brigades had to be fused into just one.³² But a stream of reinforcements arrived, including replacements and also part of General Louis, Count Langeron's corps, which had now been relieved before the fortress of Mainz. Thus the *Schlesische Armee* soon made good most of its losses, 'and so', wrote Blücher on the 16th, 'the business will now assume another character'.³³

Chapter 9

'They were swept away in the whirlpool'

Blücher's defeats owed much to the cautious and ponderous nature of the *Hauptarmee*'s advance from La Rothière. After occupying the city of Troyes on 7 February, a day after Napoleon had evacuated it, Schwarzenberg gradually pushed two prongs along the main roads that led to Paris along either side of the Seine: one north-westwards through Nogent and the other westwards through Sens.

To contain the *Hauptarmee*, Napoleon had left behind Victor and Oudinot, but they were outnumbered and lacked an overall sector commander to co-ordinate their moves. Schwarzenberg's southern prong breached the line of the Yonne by taking Sens on 11 February, and by the 16th the light troops at the tip of its advance had penetrated as far as Fontainebleau, just 35 miles south-east of Paris.

The northern prong, consisting of the V and VI *Armee-Abtheilungen*, was blunted by a fierce action at Nogent on 11–12 February, when a detachment of 1,000 French troops, supported by the civilian population, bloodily checked a series of disjointed assaults. Only after the Allies secured bridgeheads across the Seine several miles on either side of Nogent did the French finally evacuate the town and blow up its bridge. It was one of the most heroic actions of the campaign, and, as was later admitted by a Bavarian officer, August, *Fürst* von Thurn und Taxis:

> We must, in general, do the French the justice of allowing that they are masters of the defence of a town. It was very noticeable here how obstinately they defended each individual house against our troops and against the Russian *jägers* on our right.[1]

The coalition in crisis

The slowness of Schwarzenberg's advance was due partly to Austrian concerns about the potential consequences of the fall of Paris. Victory at La Rothière upset the very basis of the Langres Protocols, for it made Alexander believe he could now reach Paris without active Austrian assistance. The battle was therefore a defeat not just for Napoleon, but for Metternich, as it nullified his strongest bargaining tool: the threat that Austria would make a separate peace.

The peace talks at Châtillon were suspended on 10 February because of Napoleon's reluctance to make concessions and Alexander's expectation that he could soon impose his own settlement in Paris. The Austrians have been condemned for subordinating the progress of military operations to their own political timetable, yet the sluggishness of Schwarzenberg's army was simply the counterpart of the delays that Alexander imposed on the Châtillon conference.

The prospect of a prompt peace brought the coalition's underlying tensions to the fore, and caused a crisis to erupt at the main headquarters at Troyes. Metternich was not prepared to continue military operations until he had a guarantee of diplomatic support from Britain and Prussia, and so Schwarzenberg was instructed on 13 February not to cross the Seine. The next day Metternich, Castlereagh, and the Prussian Chancellor, Hardenberg, secretly agreed not to allow France to be reduced beyond her former frontiers. This would preserve her as a counterbalance to Russian power and influence. It would also hinder Alexander's hopes of restoring a powerful Kingdom of Poland as a Russian satellite, for he would now be unable to use French frontier provinces to compensate other powers for lands that had been absorbed by them during the partitions of Poland at the end of the eighteenth century.

Nonetheless, the accord failed to restrain Alexander, who refused to accept the idea of an armistice with Napoleon. Nor, whatever Hardenberg's views, was King Friedrich Wilhelm III prepared to split from Russia. It was actually the reports of Napoleon's victories over the *Schlesische Armee* that saved the coalition from disintegrating, for they dispelled the illusion that Alexander could end the war through unilateral action. The result was a compromise agreement on the 15th that military operations and peace negotiations should once again proceed simultaneously. Napoleon would be allowed to retain power provided he accepted the former frontiers, but if he was rejected by the French people, he could be replaced only by the Bourbon monarchy, which ruled out the alarming alternatives proposed by Alexander.[2]

The *Hauptarmee* in danger

Despite the paralysis caused by the crisis at Troyes, Schwarzenberg had breached the line of the Seine and was now threatening Paris enough to divert Napoleon from the *Schlesische Armee* at a critical moment. Napoleon had planned to complete Blücher's defeat at Vauchamps on the 14th by pursuing him to Châlons-sur-Marne, and then boldly sweeping south-eastwards through Vitry to fall on Schwarzenberg's rear. It was, in fact, the best chance he had during the campaign to secure a victorious peace, but the alarm in Paris was too great and made it imperative to defend the city more directly.

Like Blücher a week earlier, Schwarzenberg had allowed his forces to become over-extended, for he was unable to feed his large army if it was concentrated for long, and had to cover his rear at the same time as he threatened Paris. By the evening of the 14th the *Hauptarmee*'s corps were dispersed over a distance of 50 miles from east to west, and unable to lend each other prompt support. The next day, after learning that Blücher would probably have to retreat to Châlons-sur-Marne, Schwarzenberg issued new orders for the *Hauptarmee* gradually to pull back so it was more concentrated in the area of Troyes, and covered on three sides by rivers: the Aube to the north-east, the Seine to the north, and the Yonne to the west. Only two corps, the V (Bavarian) and VI (Russian) *Armee-Abtheilungen*, would be exposed north of the Seine and Aube, since they were directed to advance towards the *Schlesische Armee*, thus diverting pressure from it and covering the concentration of the rest of the *Hauptarmee*. When reports subsequently arrived that Napoleon was pulling back away from Blücher, apparently in order to strike at the *Hauptarmee*, Schwarzenberg switched completely to the defensive and sought to pull all his corps back behind the rivers.

But Napoleon would not give the *Hauptarmee* time to complete its concentration, and so it was still over-extended along the Seine. Not only was the northern prong, comprising the V and VI *Armee-Abtheilungen*, exposed on the far side of the river, but the head of the southern prong ran the risk of being severed if Napoleon managed to seize a bridge in its rear.

Napoleon concentrates against Schwarzenberg

After abandoning the Seine in the face of Schwarzenberg's advance, Victor and Oudinot had used a tributary, the Yerres, as a defence line to cover Paris. Napoleon's initial response to their appeals for support had been to send reinforcements under Macdonald, who joined them on the evening of the 14th at Guignes, 25 miles south-east of the capital. Then, on the 15th, Napoleon personally left the northern sector, and carried out one of the most brilliant manoeuvres of his entire career. Within just two days he concentrated over 50,000 troops at the road hub of Guignes, thus blocking the most direct route from Nogent-sur-Seine to Paris.[3] He assembled these forces from all directions – some had initially come from as far away as the Pyrenees, 400 miles to the south – and yet they arrived at precisely the right time and place. The *Hauptarmee* was twice as numerous as the forces Napoleon had to oppose it, but so widely scattered that his immediate target, the advanced guard of the VI *Armee-Abtheilung* under Lieutenant-General Pahlen, consisted of just 4,300 Russians and 14 guns, giving the French a massive local superiority of ten soldiers to one. The manoeuvre was all the more impressive in being improvised, and accomplished without alerting the Allies to the danger in time for them to escape.[4]

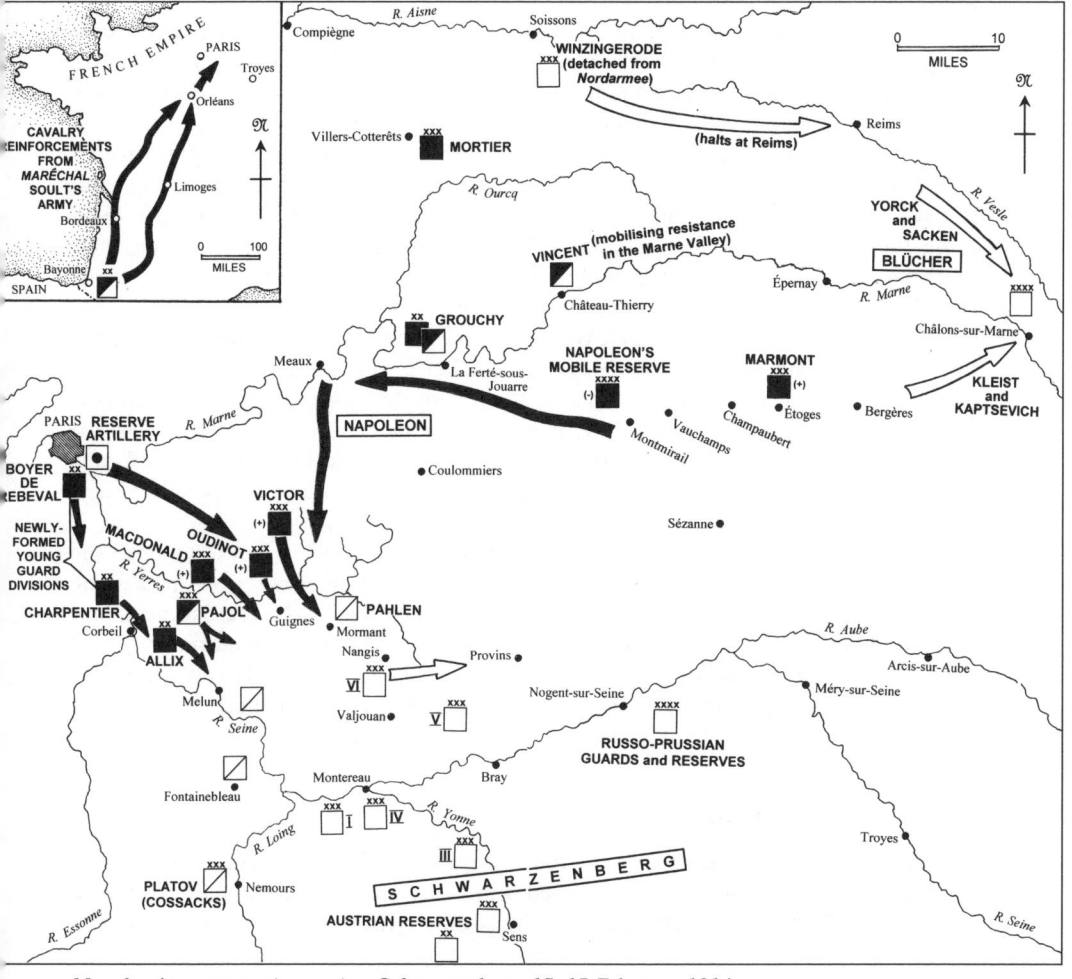

Napoleon's concentration against Schwarzenberg: 15–17 February 1814.

To contain Blücher, Napoleon left Marmont's covering force on the escarpment at Etoges. Another corps, under Mortier, was based around Villers-Cotterêts, 20 miles north of the Marne, to cover the north-eastern approaches to Paris.

In moving from Montmirail to Guignes, Napoleon brought with him the mobile core of his army. He could have taken the direct route to the south-west, but although Guignes was just 38 miles away, he would have had to use bad transverse roads, and would have been delayed too long. Instead, he took a detour, using a longer but better-quality route, heading first west to Meaux and then south. On the first day of the move, the 15th, the 1st Old Guard Division under *Général de division* Louis, *comte* Friant marched as much as 30 miles, leaving Montmirail at 0600 hours, and reaching Meaux that night.

Ordered to set out again at 0800 hours the next morning, Friant covered the remaining 23 miles southwards to Guignes, this time using carts requisitioned from nearby villages to lift his troops forward.[5] The use of such vehicles was known as *transport en poste*, and it enabled Friant to cover the total of 53 miles from Montmirail in just thirty-six hours. The same route was also used by the Imperial Guard cavalry, and by Ney's two Young Guard infantry divisions bringing up the rear. Unlike the Old Guard, they marched the entire distance, and by the end of the 16th the head of their column was still 2.5 miles north-east of Guignes.

From the opposite direction a division of *dragons* under *Général de division* François, *baron* Trelliard arrived near Guignes on the 16th, exactly a month after setting out from south-western France, where it had been detached from Soult's army in response to Napoleon's demands. Napoleon also drew reinforcements from the capital's depots, and could now do so more easily because of his proximity to Paris.

To cover the concentration, the three *maréchaux*, Victor, Oudinot, and Macdonald, had advanced a couple of miles, so they could screen the arrival of the mobile force along the road from Meaux. Similarly, Pajol pushed his cavalry forward on their southern flank, while other units, including two newly formed Young Guard divisions from Paris, covered the capital's approaches on the western bank of the Seine.

Napoleon had been obliged to leave his reserve artillery behind when he had used the transverse roads to move north against Blücher a week earlier. For safety, it had withdrawn as far as the outskirts of Paris, along with the other cumbersome elements of the army, such as the treasury. This mass of vehicles was now ordered forward again, and during the night of the 16th/17th the reserve artillery arrived at a village 2 miles north-west of Guignes. Its arrival was particularly timely as the 1st Old Guard Division had outpaced its own attached batteries.

Napoleon wanted every gun of the reserve artillery and at least some of the caissons to have a full team of six horses, so *Colonel* Griois was sent to pick some suitable horses from those that had been requisitioned locally. In the darkness, and with time so short, he found it difficult to judge their height and condition. He had been given 100,000 *francs* in gold to pay for the horses, but found only sixty that were suitable, and spent just 18,000 *francs*.[6] Nonetheless, the reserve artillery would play a prominent role in the impending action.

Battle of Mormant

Napoleon dictated his final orders at 0100 hours on the 17th. He expected to run into a battle later that morning, as he advanced south-eastwards along the main road from Paris. By 0700 hours, soon after sunrise, the advance was under way, spearheaded by

Victor's II Corps, which marched along the main road in three columns. On either flank were *Généraux de division* Edouard, *comte* Milhaud and François Kellermann, *comte* de Valmy, each with two cavalry divisions, making a total of about 7,000 horsemen. The ground was a vast, open plain, more than 4 miles wide, and ideal for sweeping charges.

The nearest Allied force, Pahlen's Russian detachment, had already begun to retreat, but was swiftly overtaken by disaster near the village of Mormant, where its rearguard made a stand. As Victor's infantry stormed the village, cavalry outflanked the defenders on either side and then swung inwards to trap them on the far side. Other squadrons charged home against Pahlen's cavalry units, forcing them to abandon the rest of the Russian infantry, most of which was brought to a halt 4 miles beyond Mormant, crushed by a massed battery of 32 guns, and ridden down.

The attack on the southern wing was led by the *4e Dragons*, one of the veteran regiments that had just joined Napoleon from the Pyrenees. One of its officers, *Capitaine* d'Agout, recalled how:

> Four years in Spain had made neither the men nor the uniforms younger, and their appearance had something of that of Robinson [Crusoe] on his island. Many were dressed not in green, but in brown cloth, which they called curate's cloth, because the coat of more than one priest had become a soldier's garment. But what most bore the marks of time and decay were the helmets and bearskins: the horsehair manes were no more, and the bearskins had only their leather left. All this gave us an extraordinary look.[7]

But the regiment was mounted on superb Andalusian horses, and was so used to fatigue that it had left few men behind while marching across France.

Napoleon controlled the battle closely, sometimes bypassing senior commanders to send an order directly to the *Colonel* of a regiment. In the morning he had gathered the officers of the *4e Dragons* around him and questioned their commander, but had to cut the interview short as the cannonade increased in intensity. 'Mount up, gentlemen!' he instructed.

When the *4e Dragons* charged, the Russian infantry quickly formed defensive squares. The skirmishers, left out in the open, stood their ground, fired at a range of four paces, thrust at the horsemen with their bayonets, and were cut down. The *dragons* were still a compact formation when they galloped up to the squares. *Capitaine* d'Agout rode at a Russian officer, but found his way blocked by a bayonet as an infantryman took the officer's place, and then felt a violent blow to his right leg as it was broken by a shot. As he was carried from the field, he saw Napoleon clasping his hands together in a gesture of sympathy, and a staff officer came and asked his name.[8]

On the Russian side of the battlefield Pahlen's adjutant, Staff Captain Eduard von Löwenstern, vividly recalled the awesome power of the French onslaught, and the sheer suddenness with which it overwhelmed a hitherto orderly retreat:

> We withdrew for about one-and-a-half hours like this, and had our hands full containing the enemy's advance. Then, all at once, the ground seemed to open up and spew death and destruction at us. On all sides, the enemy trumpeters sounded the attack, and an immense cavalry force deployed in the plain and fell on us at full speed. Anyone who tried to resist was cut down: our weak forces were immediately overthrown, and the French went round both our flanks at full tilt.
>
> Panic spread, and now everyone thought only of striving to save his own

life. Many pushed their way along the *chaussée*, which was soon blocked with dismounted guns. . . . It continued relentlessly. . . . Anyone who could not ride, who was useless or who fell, was lost. . . . Everyone shouted 'Halt! Halt!' – and everyone ran.

Other Allied units now became caught up in the French pursuit. At Nangis, 5 miles south-east of Mormant, the advanced guard of Wrede's V *Armee-Abtheilung* was immediately carried away in the avalanche of men and horses. 'Here and there some brave men rallied, but what was the point?' asked Löwenstern: 'They were swept away in the whirlpool, for it was like a child trying to stop the sails of a windmill with its hands. Only if you have been in such a stampede can you really imagine what it was like.'[9]

Pahlen lost half his men that day, and at least 9 of his 14 guns.[10] It was sheer exhaustion, rather than resistance, that finally brought the French cavalry to a halt. The *16e Dragons*, for instance, slept that night at Savins, more than 18 miles from Mormant, after being on the move or in action for thirteen hours.[11]

Nangis was a road junction, and Napoleon split his forces to pursue the defeated Allied units along different routes as they sought the safety of the south bank of the Seine. In order to burst over the river and into Schwarzenberg's rear, Napoleon would have to capture crossings before they could be destroyed, and this would require luck as well as speed. He himself remained with a central reserve around Nangis, and sent two prongs eastwards and south-eastwards to the bridges at Nogent and Bray, while a third, under Victor, headed southwards for the nearest and most important passage, 12 miles away at Montereau.

Victor attacked one of Wrede's Bavarian divisions at Villeneuve, 5 miles south of Nangis, but, to Napoleon's fury, broke off the action and failed to continue his advance to take Montereau that evening. In fact, Victor's men had already fought and marched over 17 miles that day, and would have been unable to seize the town in a night action. But Napoleon had noted his lack of drive and determination since the start of the invasion, and the next day replaced him with the younger and more energetic *Général de division* Etienne, *baron* Gérard. (A few days later, the chastened Victor was given command of a newly created Young Guard corps, which enabled Napoleon to supervise him more directly as it was added to the army's mobile reserve.)[12]

Battle of Montereau

Faced with Napoleon's sudden onslaught, Schwarzenberg needed to win time for his army to pull back out of the danger zone. On the evening of the 17th he therefore wrote to *Maréchal* Berthier, claimed that the preliminaries of peace were being signed at Châtillon, and requested that the French halt their offensive so as to avoid unnecessary bloodshed. Napoleon realised that it was a ruse, and delayed replying for three days.

Schwarzenberg also ordered the *Kronprinz* von Württemberg to cover the retreat of the *Hauptarmee*'s most advanced units by holding Montereau and its twin bridges over the Seine and Yonne until the end of 18 February. Apart from one suburb the town lay on the south bank, but was dominated by the Surville heights, which abutted on to the far side of the Seine. This meant that the *Kronprinz* had to defend Montereau by placing the bulk of his troops on top of the plateau north of the rivers, even though he would find it difficult to extricate them if he was defeated. He deployed them in a semi-circle so they covered the town, with the flanks resting on the edges of the plateau and the centre anchored by the village of Villaron. The wet ground was likely to swallow up cannonballs and prevent ricochets.[13]

'They were swept away in the whirlpool' 75

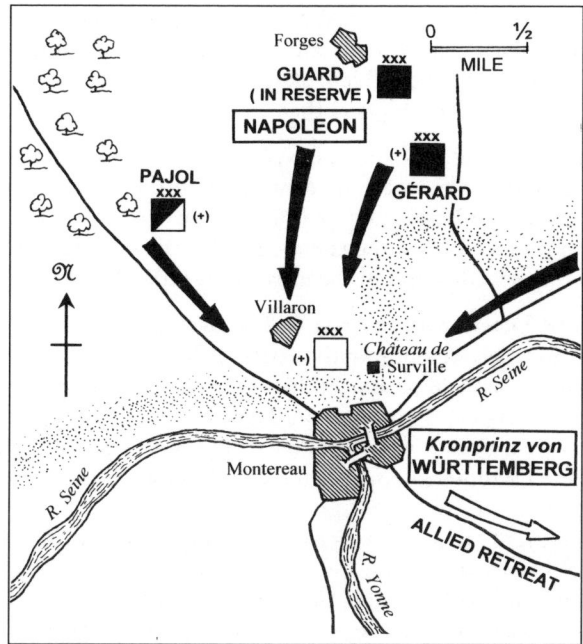

Battle of Montereau: 18 February 1814.

The 18th was cold, but sunny. French units descended on Montereau from the north-east and north-west, and began to arrive before the *Kronprinz*'s position from 0800 hours. Their initial assaults were repulsed, partly because the exposed ground on top of the plateau offered a superb field of fire. But the French steadily built up their strength and began to silence the *Kronprinz*'s artillery with superior numbers of guns.

By 1500 hours Napoleon himself had arrived with the Imperial Guard, and now had 30,000 men available, more than three times as many as the *Kronprinz*. The Allied troops had been in action for over six hours: they were tired, had suffered considerable casualties, and were left with more than half their guns dismounted and with muskets fouled from repeated firing. Now they had to face a general offensive launched from four different directions at once.

As the *Kronprinz*'s men began to retreat, they fell into disorder under the pressure of the attacks. Amidst the confusion, a torrent of French cavalry suddenly burst into Montereau from the north-west and over the twin bridges. It was Pajol who ordered one of his brigadiers, *Général de brigade* Jacques, *baron* Delort, to undertake the charge. Delort thought the order was madness, for many of his men had been on campaign for less than a fortnight, and could barely ride, let alone wield a sabre at the same time.

Despite his doubts, Delort formed his brigade into a column and moved off, progressively picking up pace to a trot, a gallop, and then an all-out charge down the slope. Ignoring the gauntlet of fire from the Allied troops in the first houses, he hurtled into the suburb that lay on the north bank. The very inexperience of the men worked in their favour, as they would have found it difficult to stop their horses even if they had wanted. They instinctively dug their heels into their horses' bellies to feel more secure in the saddle and found that it simply increased their speed. Since the road inside the suburb was hemmed in by houses, and barely wide enough for two vehicles, the men could not have turned aside, or even had much time to think, and were instead propelled over the bridges and into the streets of Montereau.

'I admit that I was far from confident about the outcome of our frantic stampede,' recalled Pajol's ADC, *Capitaine* Hubert Biot:

> As we were going through the town, I even glanced quickly to try to spot some escape route on our flanks where we could dash in the event of a setback. . . . Luckily, our exhausted horses stopped of their own accord at the town's exit. We quickly reformed and saw the enemy, terrified by our bold and impetuous charge, retreating speedily and in the greatest disorder.[14]

Pajol, who followed Delort with the rest of his cavalry, had still not fully recovered from wounds he had received four months earlier at Leipzig. As he crossed the bridges his horse was shot beneath him, and he had to give up his command since the fall caused his injuries to reopen. Two days later Napoleon told him that if all his generals had served him as well, France would not have been invaded, and that if he had been offered the bridges of Montereau in exchange for 4 million *francs*, he would have paid without hesitation.[15]

That did not prevent other generals from claiming the credit. Berthier reported to Napoleon on 21 February that Gérard was asking for one of his infantry commanders, *Général de division* Philibert Duhesme, to be given the title of *comte*. 'He explains that it is to this general that we owe the preservation of the bridges of Montereau, on which he arrived at the same time as the enemy.'[16]

Duhesme was granted his title, and it was, of course, true that Pajol's spectacular charge could not have occurred at all if the French infantry had not already driven the *Kronprinz* von Württemberg from his positions on the plateau after several hours of fighting. By the time Pajol charged, the Allies had already begun their retreat, and were distracted by attacks from all sides. He also benefited from the difficulty they faced in trying to destroy the bridges in a hurry, with his cavalry pressing the fugitives so closely. They did, in fact, explode a mine on the Seine bridge, but failed to bring down the arch, and the sappers who clumsily tried to cut a wooden span of the Yonne bridge fell into the river.[17]

By this stage Napoleon had reached the edge of the heights overlooking Montereau, and had a heavy calibre gun of the Imperial Guard artillery brought forward to a point 200 yards from the *Château* de Surville, from where it could fire at the Allied retreat in the plain beyond the town. According to popular legend, Allied artillery replied without much effect, but sent cannonballs whistling through the air. Soldiers murmured that Napoleon was exposed to the fire, which supposedly provoked the reply: 'Come now, my friends, have no fear. The cannonball that is to kill me has not yet been made.'[18]

The story became one of the most celebrated incidents of the campaign, and its repetition resulted in different versions, with some accounts and engravings locating it at Arcis-sur-Aube a month later, when Napoleon's horse was brought down beneath him. In fact, he probably never made the remark at all. Commanders directing operations in the heat of a battle have more important tasks to occupy their minds than devising memorable phrases, and the words attributed to Napoleon were in all likelihood invented, possibly by Michel Balisson de Rougemont, the same journalist who invented the defiant retort ascribed to *Général de brigade* Pierre, *baron* Cambronne at Waterloo: 'The Guard dies, and does not surrender.'[19]

Being so memorable, the phrase of Montereau was repeated by a succession of authors and thus found a niche in history. Even men who took part in the campaign, like Napoleon's chief secretary, Agathon, *baron* Fain, included the remark in their accounts as if they had personally heard it, for they wanted to be associated with such a famous incident. Yet the French cannon gun was firing at extreme range from a height, so it is unlikely that Napoleon was in any significant danger from return fire from below. It is not even certain whether he aimed the gun himself, despite being depicted doing so in engravings.[20]

The outcome

The *Kronprinz* von Württemberg fell back eastwards, covered by a rearguard. Of the troops he had at Montereau, over half had been killed, wounded, or captured.[21]

In French accounts Montereau is often portrayed as an easy victory, won triumphantly by the headlong charge of Pajol's inexperienced young cavalrymen. But Pajol's irruption into the town was just the climax of a eight-hour battle, which cost Napoleon about 2,500 casualties, and many of the *Kronprinz*'s men fought heroically even as the defence collapsed. *Feldwebel* Josef Mattauschek of the Austrian *Infanterie-Regiment Josef Colloredo* defended himself and his Colonel on the bridge at Montereau against six Frenchmen. One man levelled a musket ready to fire, but Mattauschek hurled it aside, took several sabre cuts, and saved his Colonel's life, even if they both ended up as prisoners. During the retreat towards the bridges, another two men of the regiment, *Feldwebel* Anton Melzer and *Korporal* Josef Seiferth, actually advanced back towards the *Château* de Surville to win time for their comrades to withdraw: one was captured and the other shot through the leg.[22]

Napoleon had seized the Montereau bridges. But otherwise, the results of the battle, and the fact that it had to be fought at all, were disappointing. The *Kronprinz*'s stand had averted a disaster for the *Hauptarmee*, whose leading units had penetrated 12 miles further west along the south bank of the Seine and had therefore been in danger of being trapped by Napoleon's descent from the north. By fighting at Montereau, the *Kronprinz* delayed Napoleon for a vital day, and enabled the most advanced formations to reach safety.

It snowed on the evening of the 18th, and next day the corpses strewn over the battlefield lay frozen under a blanket of white. The plunging temperatures contributed to a parallel collapse in Napoleon's fortunes, for, as he complained to Joseph on the 20th, the hardened ground eased Schwarzenberg's escape to the east:

> He has had an exceptional stroke of luck, in that the severe frost enabled him to go across country. Had it not been for this, half of his baggage and artillery would have been taken. It is so freezing that it inconveniences us.[23]

Napoleon was inconvenienced, too, by the geography of the area. Montereau was a chokepoint, and the battle had caused units to pour into it from all sides. Many soldiers then found shelter for the night in the houses, making it difficult the next day to find them, sort out the chaos, and move the army off to the east. 'We needed the whole day to pass this dreadful defile of Montereau,' Napoleon lamented on the evening of the 19th.[24]

Even after crossing to the south bank of the Seine it was hard to mount a close pursuit. Napoleon had won his recent victories in the relatively fertile Brie plateau, close to his main supply base of Paris, but now had to move further afield and cross the ravaged and barren region of *Champagne pouilleuse*. By 20 February *Maréchal* Macdonald was complaining that some of his divisions had left more than two-thirds of their men in the rear, and that the Imperial Guard had pillaged a convoy of supplies

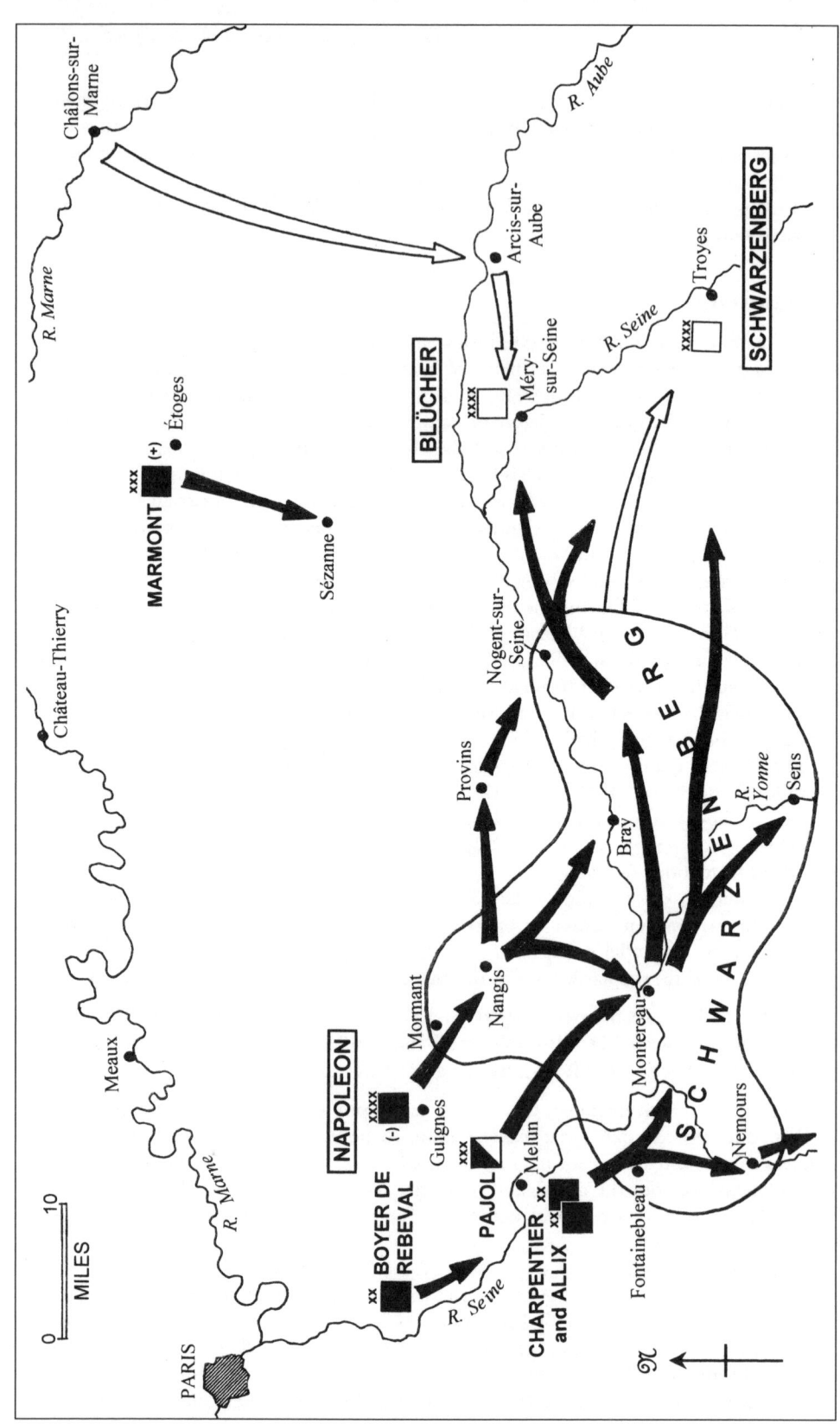

Schwarzenberg retreats on Troyes: 17–22 February 1814.

for his corps. 'We are in the middle of immense plains,' he added. 'The villages are no more than hamlets, and all of them are devastated.'[25]

Montereau was therefore the last in the spectacular series of six victories that Napoleon won in nine days, and it marked the end of this phase of the campaign. Whereas he had defeated all of Blücher's available forces a week earlier, he had managed to maul only two of Schwarzenberg's seven corps at Mormant and Montereau.

The unfought battle of Troyes

At first Schwarzenberg decided to halt his retreat and fight a major battle immediately west of Troyes, which had become his army's forward command and logistic base, and he requested Blücher to come to his support from Châlons-sur-Marne, 45 miles to the north. Once Blücher arrived, he explained in a letter to his wife on the 20th, 'I will accept battle, hoping for the Almighty's help.'[26]

The next day Blücher reached Méry-sur-Seine, 17 miles north-west of Troyes. Limited clashes occurred on the 22nd as the French arrived from the west and attacked the bridge at Méry. The town was burned down, and Blücher himself received a painful blow on the leg from a spent ball, but one of his officers, *Leutnant* von Rahden, waited in vain for a pitched battle:

> We stood on a large plain unbroken by either woods or villages. . . . A real February weather blew down on us. Immense flakes of snow fell from the sky and immediately wasted away on the miry ground. We froze above from the snow and ice, and were soaked below in mud and mire. Our only hope, to warm ourselves up in a sharp firefight, likewise remained unfulfilled, as neither the enemy commander-in-chief nor our own showed any interest in shortening the very unpleasant existence of us poor soldiers one way or another.[27]

Napoleon realised that he faced both the Allied armies. He had only 70,000 men immediately available, about two-fifths of the combined strength of the opposing forces, but noted that Schwarzenberg had deployed his army on the west bank of the Seine in order to cover Troyes, whereas Blücher was still on the opposite side and would need a day to force a crossing at Méry. Napoleon therefore planned to attack Schwarzenberg in the south, while containing Blücher with a small covering force.

During the night Schwarzenberg abandoned the idea of a battle and ordered a resumption of the retreat. His decision was ratified at a council-of-war in the morning of the 23rd, and so Troyes remained the great unfought battle of the campaign. Events outside the campaign theatre had intervened at a pivotal moment. Always nervous about his left flank and line of retreat, Schwarzenberg had been alarmed by news that *Maréchal* Pierre Augereau's forces based at Lyon, 175 miles to the south, had launched an offensive against Dijon and Geneva, thus threatening his lines of communication to Switzerland.

Schwarzenberg was also conscious that he could not keep his army concentrated for long in the barren and exhausted region near Troyes in mid-winter. 'Just as I foresaw, my situation is extremely wretched,' he wrote on the 21st. 'If I divide my army, I can be beaten in detail, but if I concentrate it, I starve to death.'[28]

A Prussian *Garde* officer, *Major* Wilhelm von Ditfurth, revealed the full extent of the *Hauptarmee*'s sufferings at this time:

> I cannot describe to you what appalling fatigues we have endured: the night marches are particularly frightful. The cold was very great and we spent day

and night under the open sky. We were often without a fire for a long time and rarely managed to eat a little soup. However, we had all the wine in the villages through which we passed or near where we bivouacked, in the greatest quantity, although we had to thaw it first, as it was frozen. The cold was so great that I put on all my clothes, even my sleeping pelt, with my coat on top, but I could not ride because of the cold and so I walked instead. My boots, which I had burnt on the fire, now came apart and, like many of the officers, I had wholly worn-out footwear.[29]

Faced with such logistical problems, Schwarzenberg needed not simply to win a battle, but to win it decisively, and since he had no confidence of being able to do so, he had to retreat out of the *Champagne pouilleuse*. It did not help that he had gained an inflated impression of Napoleon's strength from reports.

The *Hauptarmee*'s retreat was covered by the V *Armee-Abtheilung*, whose commander, Wrede, secured an unhindered evacuation of Troyes by threatening to set fire to it.[30] Napoleon finally occupied the city on the morning of the 24th. He pushed pursuits eastwards along the road to Bar-sur-Aube, Schwarzenberg's main line of retreat, and south-eastwards up the Seine valley, while keeping the rest of his army in reserve around Troyes.

Schwarzenberg was falling back to a strong central position based on the Langres plateau, from where he could readily move reserves to contain either Napoleon in the north-west or Augereau in the south. To meet the latter threat, he had decided on the 21st to create a *Südarmee* under *General der Kavallerie* Friedrich, *Erbprinz* zu Hessen-Homburg, by detaching 30,000 Austrian troops from the *Hauptarmee*, including the whole of the I *Armee-Abtheilung*, to reinforce the units that were already in the Lyon theatre. This Austrian *Südarmee* would be strengthened by the German 6. *Bundes-Corps*, which was on its way westwards from the Rhine.

Schwarzenberg has been criticised for weakening the *Hauptarmee* at such a critical moment, but he was still left with 130,000 men, and had found it difficult to feed a larger army. By detaching such a sizeable force against Augereau, he could decisively reverse the tide in the southern theatre, and gain the secure flank he needed. The creation of the *Südarmee* had another important consequence, which is often overlooked. Apart from a handful of units, including some *Grenadier* and *Kürassier* divisions of the reserves, it left just one Austrian corps, the III *Armee-Abtheilung*, with the *Hauptarmee*, and so reduced still further the risk of Napoleon inflicting heavy Austrian casualties.

Peace negotiations

The reversal of the military situation had transformed both sides' attitudes to the idea of a negotiated settlement. Defeats shook Alexander's opposition to talks, and led to the resumption of the Châtillon conference on 17 February, a week after its suspension. But at the same time Napoleon was emboldened by his victories, and had renewed hopes of driving the Allies from France. He therefore returned to his original demand for the natural frontiers, and wrote to Emperor Franz on the 21st in an attempt to detach Austria from the coalition with a separate peace.

Schwarzenberg had already sought an armistice to secure a safe retreat for his army. When the Allies renewed the request on the 23rd, Napoleon agreed that commissioners from the two sides should meet for ceasefire talks at Lusigny, 9 miles east of Troyes, but insisted that the Allies accept the natural frontiers as the basis for peace before he would halt his advance. The Lusigny talks ran parallel with the wider peace conference at Châtillon, but collapsed within a week, for the danger to the *Hauptarmee* receded, thus undermining the Allied rationale for requesting an armistice in the first place.

Napoleon has been accused of over-confidence in the wake of his victories, and of arrogance in demanding the natural frontiers, yet it was not obvious at the time that his military advantages would dissipate so soon. Nor is it certain that he could have secured peace even by accepting the former frontiers.

Treaty of Chaumont

Napoleon's dramatic recovery following his defeat at La Rothière injected a greater sense of realism into the Allied headquarters and helped transform the coalition into a more substantial and permanent alliance. Under the Treaty of Chaumont, dated 1 March, the four great powers, Austria, Prussia, Russia, and Britain, specified their war aims, ruled out a separate peace, and undertook to maintain their Quadruple Alliance against France for twenty years after the end of hostilities, in case of a renewed attempt to disturb the peace.[31]

The Treaty of Chaumont had at last bound the Allies into a general partnership, and replaced the series of separate, and sometimes contradictory, accords that had been made in the course of the previous year. The war aims agreed under the treaty would surround France with a ring of strong buffer territories: a German confederation, an independent Switzerland, an enlarged Netherlands, a Bourbon Spain, and an Italy freed from French control and restored to the old order.

The Treaty of Chaumont was an anti-French alliance, and not a general resolution of outstanding issues between the Allies. It did not attempt to settle the fate of Poland or offer collective security against Russian ambitions. Nor did the Allies exclude the possibility of jointly making peace with Napoleon, for the Treaty developed out of their previous resolutions at Langres and Troyes, under which they agreed that Napoleon could keep his throne provided he accepted the former frontiers. He would no longer be able to detach Austria from the coalition, but might still remain the French ruler, and hence peace negotiations continued at Châtillon.

Despite its limitations, and the persistence of tensions within the coalition, the Treaty marked a pivotal moment in the campaign, and it is no mere coincidence that it was followed by the Allied occupation of Paris before the end of the month. Cemented by promises of another £5 million of British subsidies, it marked the culmination of Britain's lengthy attempts to form a powerful coalition of all the European great powers.

Chapter 10

Stalemate

At a council-of-war on 25 February Schwarzenberg had agreed under pressure from Alexander to allow Blücher to operate independently, without having to conform to the *Hauptarmee*'s retreat. The Allies have been condemned for repeatedly allowing their armies to separate, yet releasing Blücher was actually one of their most effective decisions of the campaign. It reclaimed the initiative, and, by diverting Napoleon, averted a general unstoppable retreat that might have caused the *Hauptarmee* to disintegrate completely. By using different avenues of advance, the Allied armies forced Napoleon to march back and forth, and it was primarily this constant marching that wore down his army, even when he was winning the actual battles.

Blücher's renewed advance

Blücher therefore advanced on Paris, just a fortnight after being mauled during his previous attempt. Even after detecting his departure, Napoleon remained unsure of his objective, and initially thought that he might simply be withdrawing northwards to Châlons-sur-Marne. Not until the morning of the 27th were all Napoleon's doubts dispelled: Blücher was heading directly for Paris. Two detached corps under *Maréchaux* Marmont and Mortier were covering the approaches to the capital, but would be too weak to hold Blücher for long, and so Napoleon launched a full-scale pursuit with 35,000 troops. To contain Schwarzenberg, he left behind a covering force of 42,000 men under Macdonald's overall command.

Since Blücher had three days' head start over Napoleon, Marmont and Mortier would have to contain him on the line of the Marne at Meaux, despite having just 10,000 troops, little more than one-fifth of the *Schlesische Armee*'s available strength. On 27 February Blücher used pontoon bridges to begin crossing to the north bank of the Marne 9 miles east of Meaux, but the *maréchaux* countered this outflanking move by thrusting north-eastwards on the 28th. They collided with Blücher's leading corps under Kleist, which had crossed to the west bank of the Marne's tributary, the Ourcq, and drove it back more than 5 miles.

That night Marmont and Mortier received 6,000 reinforcements from Paris. They held a strong position, for most of the bridges over the Ourcq had now been destroyed, enabling them to contain Kleist's corps on the west bank, while the rest of the *Schlesische Armee* was still on the far side of the river. On the next day, 1 March, Blücher renewed the action with as many as four corps, but was hindered by the state of the roads as the rawness of late February gave way to a temporary thaw. His attacks were disjointed and easily checked, especially as Kleist received his orders too late to mount a serious offensive.

The *Schlesische Armee* was not given another chance, for Napoleon himself had now reached the Marne in its rear, forcing it to break off the battle and retreat north-eastwards on the 2nd. Blücher had nullified his advantage of numbers by making his

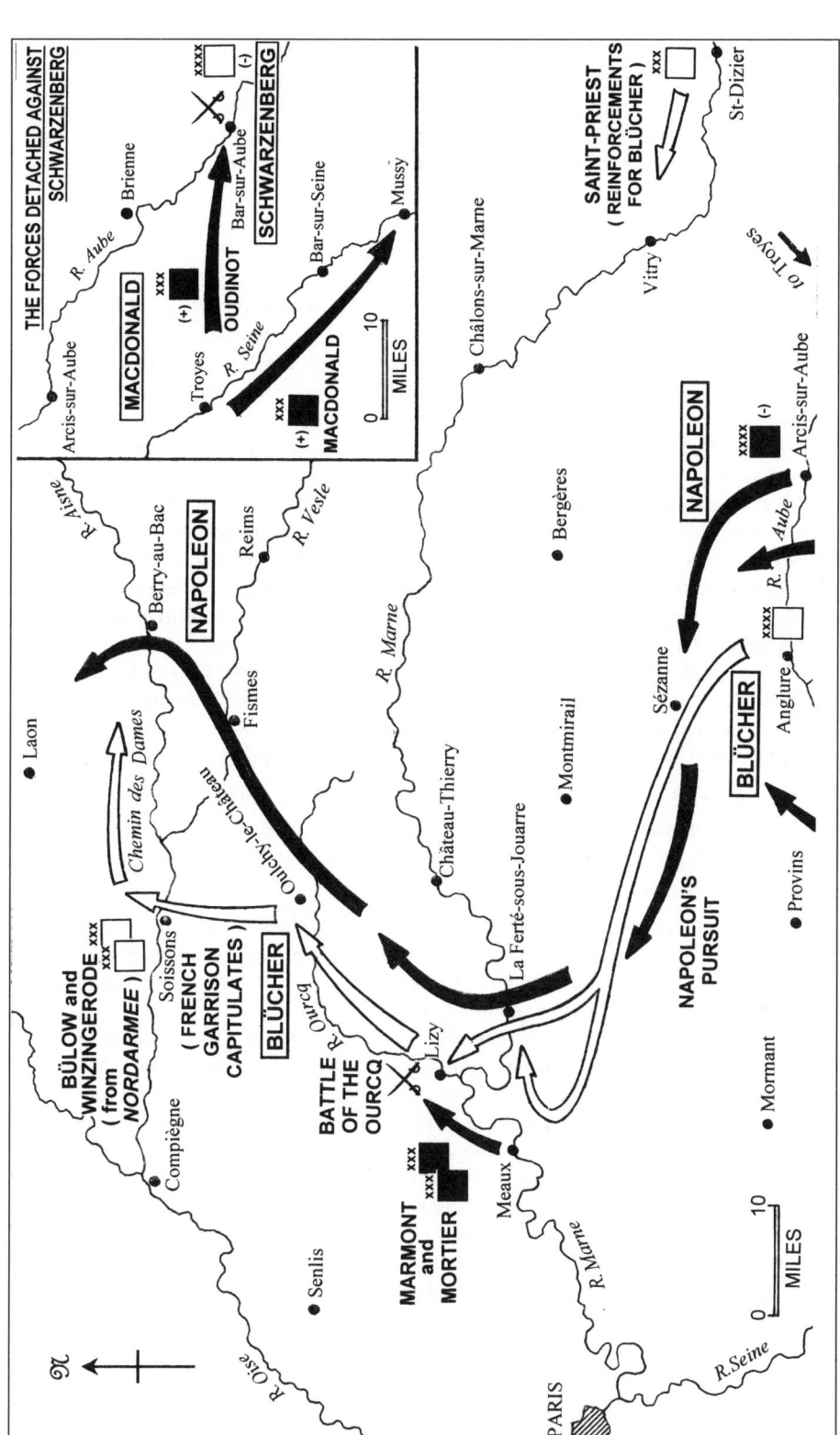

Blücher's second advance on Paris: 24 February–6 March 1814.

usual mistake, repeated throughout the campaign, of failing to co-ordinate his units and exposing individual corps by pushing them too far ahead of the rest of the army. The battle on the Ourcq was one of the most notable French successes of the campaign. It owed much to the skill and boldness of the *maréchaux*, and was actually larger and more impressive than Napoleon's better-known victory at Champaubert eighteen days earlier.

'I command a band of robbers'

Napoleon found himself brought up short by the Marne and its destroyed bridges, for he lacked a pontoon train. It was only on the morning of the 3rd, after repairing the bridge at La Ferté-sous-Jouarre, that he could cross the river and resume a full-blooded pursuit. Having failed to destroy the *Schlesische Armee* against the Marne, he resolved to harry its retreat and drive it well to the north, out of range of Paris.

Blücher was falling back on reinforcements, having learned that three corps were being transferred to his command from the *Nordarmee*. Two of them, under Bülow and Winzingerode, had already moved into northern France, while the other, the *3. Bundes-Corps*, was covering their communications through Belgium. By uniting with Bülow and Winzingerode, Blücher would almost double the size of the *Schlesische Armee* to more than 100,000 troops, and make it strong enough to operate on its own.[1]

But as he retreated towards them Blücher shed alarming quantities of wounded and baggage. His troops were demoralised by their defeat on the Ourcq, and had to contend with disintegrating roads. Supplies were short, for the *Schlesische Armee* had temporarily lost its communications with the Rhine and was crossing a less fertile region than the Brie plateau south of the Marne. As discipline began to break down, men plundered everywhere, causing Yorck to berate his unit commanders on 2 March:

> Gentlemen, I thought I had the honour of commanding a Prussian army corps, but I command a band of robbers. Gentlemen, I will not act Aballino the Great [a fictional outlaw], and I will court-martial anyone who does not rigorously restore order among the troops![2]

Just then, his point was underlined when two female sutlers galloped past, improbably wearing elegant silk dresses and hats decorated with feathers, which they had clearly stolen. 'There you see, gentlemen!' Yorck shouted indignantly. 'Get rid of these damned people!' The women had already vanished.

Once he joined Bülow and Winzingerode, Blücher would also be able to use their shorter supply lines to the north-east, in place of his old, intercepted ones. Yet he did not know the exact location of their corps, and needed their support if he was to give battle and check Napoleon's pursuit. He wanted to concentrate near Oulchy-le-Château, 11 miles north of the Marne, but when he arrived there in the night of 2/3 March he still had no news from them because a despatch rider had been intercepted.

On the morning of the 3rd Blücher finally discovered that Bülow and Winzingerode were 12 miles further north, for they had decided on their own initiative to try to capture the city of Soissons in order to open his line of retreat across the Aisne river. They had previously served in the *Nordarmee*, under the undynamic Crown Prince of Sweden, and by necessity had grown accustomed to acting independently. It was unrealistic to expect them suddenly to switch their mindset to one of strict obedience as soon as they were transferred to Blücher's command.

Soissons capitulated on the 3rd. Its surrender sparked bitter controversy, for the commandant, *Général de brigade* Jean, *baron* Moreau, could actually have held out for another day, and knew from the sound of gunfire that French field forces were approaching from the south. It has often been claimed that Moreau's timidity saved the *Schlesische Armee* from imminent disaster by unblocking its retreat, and it certainly seemed that way to Napoleon, who wanted him shot for cowardice. 'This business does us incalculable harm,' he wrote to Joseph on the 5th: 'I would have been at Laon today and there is no doubt that the enemy army was done for and disintegrating. Now I have to manoeuvre and lose much time building bridges. See to it that an example is made at last.'³

In fact, Blücher would probably have escaped with most of his army, even if he had been deprived of the bridge at Soissons.⁴ Yet the city's fall did ease his retreat, and enabled him to transfer all his troops over the Aisne by the morning of the 5th.

'Some rest will do the men good'

Having united with Bülow and Winzingerode, the *Schlesische Armee* was now strong enough to operate on its own without undue danger, but it was neither a cohesive nor an efficient fighting machine. Relations between its Russian and Prussian contingents were strained, and the two fresh corps would need time to become integrated. Müffling, Blücher's *General-Quartiermeister*, vividly described the appearance of the *Schlesische Armee* at Soissons after nine weeks of campaigning:

> Our men looked peculiar. Their gaunt faces were blackened from the smoke of bivouac fires and had long been strangers to the luxury of a razor, but had an expression of energy and physical strength. They wore tattered coats, badly patched trousers, unwhitened or unblackened leather straps, and had unpolished weapons. The cavalry rode thin, ungroomed, but spirited horses, and everything looked really geared for war.

They were a striking contrast to Bülow's men, who had not been driven so relentlessly. 'Some rest will do the men good,' said Bülow of the ragged troops parading past him, and Müffling thought that what he really meant was: 'My men, too, may soon look like this!'⁵

Deeper and more destructive problems blighted the *Schlesische Armee*'s leadership. Many Prussian generals resented the power wielded by Gneisenau and other headquarters officers, who were junior to them in rank and had not won distinction, as they themselves had done, in combat commands the previous year. Bülow's arrival revived these antagonisms by reuniting him with Yorck and Kleist, his fellow Prussian corps commanders.

Gneisenau himself lost his usual boldness under the influence of a close colleague, *General-Major* Hermann von Boyen, Bülow's *Chef des Generalstabes*. Boyen was anxious that if the *Schlesische Armee* was defeated, Schwarzenberg would retreat in alarm all the way back to the Rhine. He was also concerned that Prussia would need an intact army to protect her interests during peace negotiations, and yet she had already suffered alarming losses during the campaign: Yorck, for example, was left with just two-thirds of his original strength. The contrast with Bülow's corps sharpened such anxieties, and encouraged the idea of a more passive role to oblige the *Hauptarmee* to share the burden.⁶

Napoleon crosses the Aisne

After crossing the Aisne, Blücher deployed along a 15-mile stretch of the north bank, on either side of Soissons, with cavalry posts in observation further afield. Napoleon decided to outflank him by seizing the bridge at Berry-au-Bac, 26 miles east of Soissons. Sweeping round the *Schlesische Armee*'s eastern wing, he would then thrust to the north-west and seize the hilltop city of Laon, 10 miles in its rear. This ambitious manoeuvre could have decisive results, and after disabling Blücher Napoleon intended to return south-eastwards to Châlons-sur-Marne, from where he could descend on Schwarzenberg.[7]

Napoleon's cavalry captured the crossing at Berry-au-Bac on 5 March, and his army began to pour across the river. The next day Blücher countered the manoeuvre by shifting his army eastwards so he could fall on the French flank while their units were still strung out as they advanced along the road to Laon.

The ground north of the Aisne was particularly hilly, for the rivers had eroded the top layer of limestone and then cut deep valleys into the soft, sandy substrata. Some 4 miles north of the Aisne, and parallel to it, rose a narrow 15 mile-long plateau, along the crest of which ran a road built in the 1780s for the daughters of Louis XV, and hence named the *Chemin des Dames*. It was along this road that Blücher pushed his army on the 6th in response to Napoleon's manoeuvre, but he was delayed by congestion caused by the narrowness of the plateau. By the time he arrived he found that Napoleon had already seized the eastern end of the *Chemin des Dames* and the village of Craonne with a detachment in order to cover his advance on Laon.

Instead of being able to strike into the middle of Napoleon's advance, the *Schlesische Armee* would now be stuck on top of the plateau like wine inside a corked bottle. Forced to revise his plan, Blücher ordered Winzingerode to assemble 10,000 cavalry and use them as a mobile force with which to circle round to the north of the *Chemin des Dames* and fall on Napoleon from the north-west. It was a modified and limited version of Blücher's original scheme, but underlined the fact that the *Schlesische Armee* had become a more robust instrument than it had been the previous month. It now had a powerful cavalry force, which its high command was prepared to use offensively and *en masse*, rather than dispersing it in small detachments as a mere supporting arm. Yet success was not guaranteed: the move would have to be made at night, along transverse roads and through difficult, hilly terrain. In order to be in position to attack in the morning, Winzingerode would have to cover up to 20 miles in twelve hours.

Far from expecting such an attack, Napoleon suspected that the *Schlesische Armee* was withdrawing. At 0400 hours on the 7th he issued orders for Ney to pursue its rearguard westwards along the *Chemin des Dames*. He himself planned to march north-westwards and occupy Laon that same day, but was prepared instead to support Ney with a full-scale onslaught should that prove necessary to dislodge Blücher.[8]

Battle of Craonne

Both sides planned bold and sweeping manoeuvres, but would actually end up fighting a brutal attritional battle near Craonne to control the high ground of the *Chemin des Dames*. What Napoleon thought would be a limited action to evict a rearguard soon developed into something altogether more serious.

The plateau favoured a stubborn defence, for the steep slopes made it difficult to reach the crest from either the Aisne to the south or the Ailette valley to the north. Protected on both flanks, a defender would face mainly frontal attacks, and could defy them by deploying his forces in depth across the *Chemin des Dames*.

Spurs on either side meant that the plateau varied in width, and sometimes

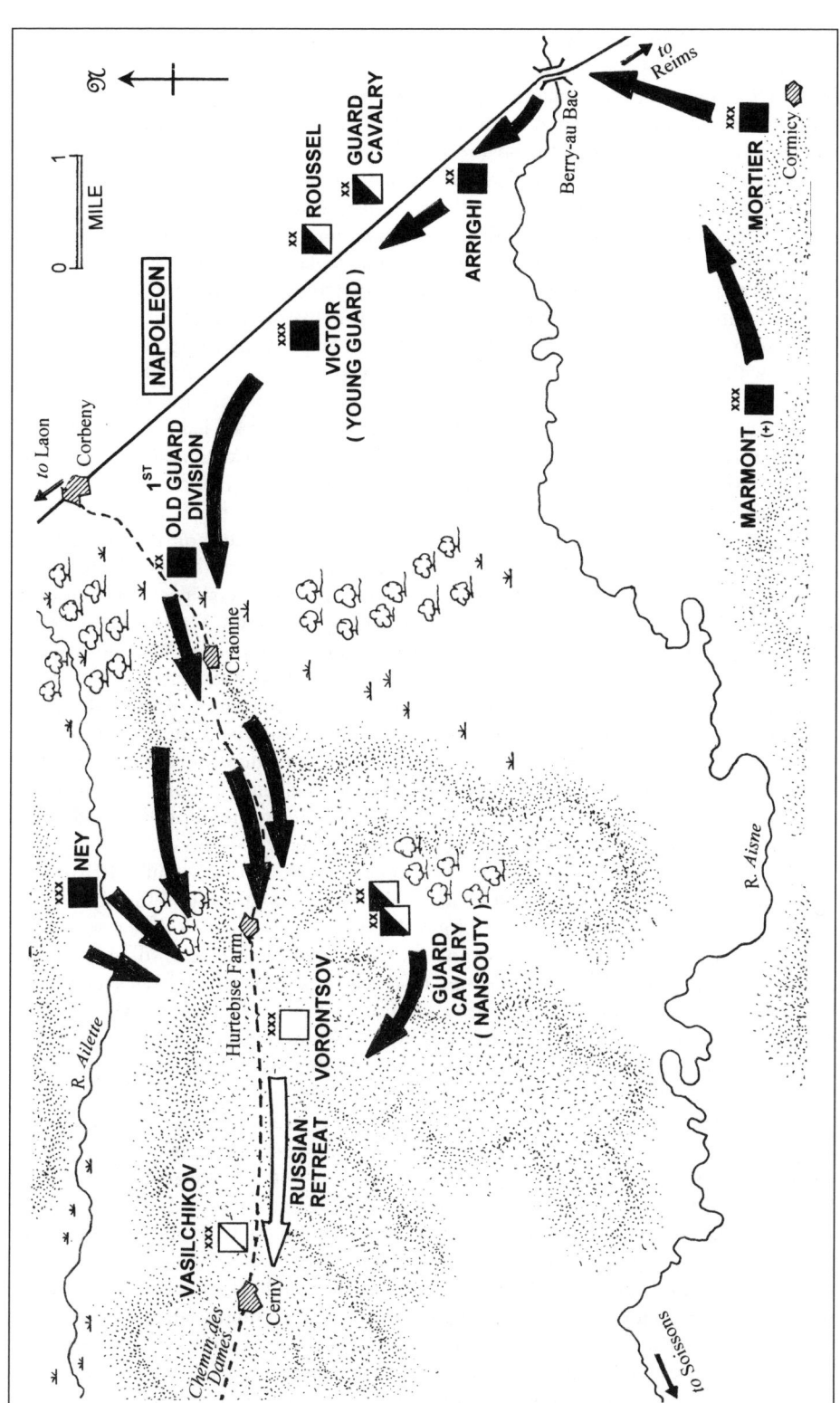

Battle of Craonne: 7 March 1814.

narrowed into a bottleneck before suddenly opening out again into an expanse as much as 2 miles wide. The most significant of these constrictions occurred at the Hurtebise farm, 2.75 miles from the eastern end of the plateau, where the crest was only 140 yards wide and was dominated by wider and higher ground to the west. This was where Blücher would defend the position, and such was the nature of the ground that he could do so with just 18,000 Russian troops under Lieutenant-General Mikhail Semenovich, Count Vorontsov, or less than one-fifth of his army. Some 6 miles to the rear was Sacken's corps, whose cavalry was pushed forward in support.

Vorontsov occupied Hurtebise farm as an advanced post with 800 *jägers*, and deployed the rest of his infantry in three successive lines, each of which consisted of a row of battalion columns. The first line stood 1,300 yards west of the farm, where the plateau widened again after the bottleneck, and had a cavalry brigade covering its southern flank in case the French attempted the ascent up the side of the plateau. Vorontsov's second and third lines were each 550 yards behind the one in front.[9] Vorontsov also had a mass of artillery, 96 guns in all, and posted half of it to create a deadly crossfire over the narrow neck of ground that any attack along the crest would have to pass. Another 18 guns covered the Ailette valley on the northern side of the plateau, while the remaining 30 formed a reserve.

Napoleon had no intention of making a purely frontal assault on this formidable position. Instead, after pinning the Russians down with artillery fire, he would try to assail both their flanks, despite the difficulties of climbing the slopes. The Imperial Guard cavalry would threaten the southern side, while Ney's Young Guard corps attacked from the north. But the French deployment was delayed by the ground, which was slippery with ice, and this, combined with Ney's characteristic impatience to see action, contributed to the disjointed nature of the first phase of the fighting.

It was after 0900 hours before the first French batteries arrived on the plateau near Craonne and opened fire. Napoleon still lacked sufficient troops in hand to begin the battle in earnest, and would actually need the whole morning to build up a force as strong as Vorontsov's. Yet when Ney heard the sound of the gunfire, he attacked prematurely from the north, and was repeatedly repulsed.

Eventually, Napoleon was able to reinforce Ney with the leading division of *Maréchal* Victor's corps. The Russian *jägers* were forced to abandon Hurtebise farm and withdraw to Vorontsov's main position. Having thereby opened the narrow neck of ground near the farm, Napoleon pushed some artillery across it to support the onslaughts. But when a brigade of *dragons* followed some time later, it was overthrown by a counter-attack and fled, spreading panic among Ney's infantrymen, who recoiled back down the northern slopes. On the opposite flank two divisions of Imperial Guard cavalry were checked by artillery fire after reaching the crest of the plateau from the south.

The intensity of the battle reminded Russian veterans of Borodino two years earlier. Vorontsov was everywhere, encouraging his troops, setting an example of coolness, and showing delight rather than fear at directing a battle against Napoleon for the first time. 'With regard to the artillery,' he later reported, 'I had only to look on with admiration, and rejoice in the destruction which it wrought among the enemy.'[10] His guns practically destroyed a Young Guard division under *Général de division* Joseph Boyer, *baron* de Rebeval on the northern side of the plateau. Its barely trained conscripts had to be kept exposed in tightly packed columns because they were incapable of manoeuvring, and were liable to break and flee if they attempted to deploy or fall back under cover. One regiment, the *14e Voltigeurs*, lost a staggering 85 per cent of its officers and 70 per cent of its men.[11]

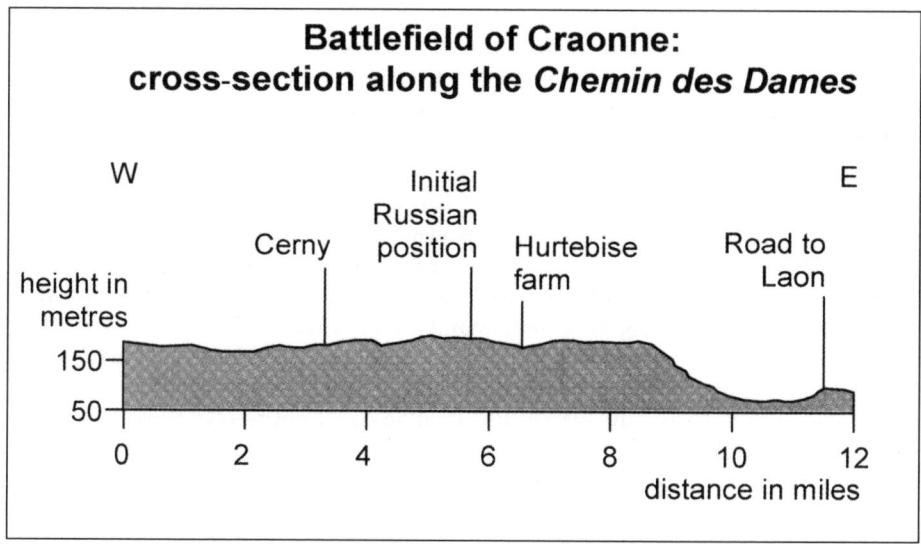

Only at 1300 hours was Napoleon in a position to launch a properly co-ordinated general offensive, in place of the hasty and piecemeal assaults that had been made throughout the morning. More of his units had come up from the rear, and these fresh formations now crossed the neck at Hurtebise, while the troops on either flank renewed their assaults. Then the reserve artillery of the Imperial Guard rumbled forward along the crest, and helped form a massed battery of 72 guns.[12] Outflanked, shaken by repeated attacks and relentlessly pounded by artillery, the Russians were at last being prised from their positions.

Vorontsov's superior, Sacken, twice sent him the order to retire if the French pressed him with overwhelming numbers. But Vorontsov thought that it was safer to hold his ground than attempt a retreat, and expected Winzingerode's cavalry to assail Napoleon's rear. Sacken sent a third order, this time informing him that Winzingerode's turning move had miscarried, and commanding an immediate withdrawal.[13]

Vorontsov finally began to fall back, with his infantry squares taking it in turns to retire at the usual unhurried pace. Even now, some of his subordinates were loath to abandon their positions. One brigade commander, Major-General Mikhail Ivanovich Poncet, received two orders to withdraw, but answered hotly that he was determined to die where he stood. His superior, Major-General Nikolay Vasilievich Vuich, went up to him and calmly explained that if he wanted to die there, it was up to him, but his brigade had to retire.[14]

The French redoubled their efforts when they noticed the retreat. Sacken sent forward the cavalry of his corps to help cover the retreat, and deployed a massed battery across the plateau. Its guns were arrayed in two lines, sixty paces apart, with those in the second line able to fire through the intervals between those in front. Once the Russian infantry had passed by, the battery opened up, but was later countered by the powerful French artillery and forced to withdraw. That night the French bivouacked towards the western end of the *Chemin des Dames*, having pursued the Russians more than 9 miles from their initial positions.

What had become of Winzingerode's ambitious manoeuvre to turn Napoleon's flank? He was supposed to have been ready to attack down the road towards Berry-au-Bac that morning, but was encumbered with 60 guns and hindered by the darkness of the night and by the Ailette valley north of the *Chemin des Dames*, where some of the congested tracks allowed only a single file of horsemen. 'I have never made a more tedious march in my whole life,' claimed *Oberst* Wilhelm, *Graf* Henckel von Donnersmarck. 'We marched the whole night, stopping infinitely often and for a long time, before proceeding again without any plan or a definite direction of march.'[15]

It did not help that Winzingerode crossed the Ailette at Chevregny, 5 miles further west than necessary, thereby reducing the chances of his move being discovered but also delaying it by several hours.[16] 'As an eyewitness', complained a Russian staff officer, Lieutenant-Colonel Vladimir Ivanovich, Baron von Löwenstern, 'I could see for myself an uncertainty and blundering around that were unimaginable and that should have resulted in a rigorous inquiry and a court-martial'.[17]

When Blücher learned on the morning of the 7th that Winzingerode's cavalry was still stuck in the Ailette valley, he left Sacken in overall command on the *Chemin des Dames* and went to hasten the march. But even he could not resolve the confusion in time to mount an attack that day, and so he ordered a retreat on Laon. Winzingerode's mass of cavalry was broken up, with its units returning to their parent corps.

The impact of the battle

Craonne is seen by the French as a victory for Napoleon, albeit a bloody and indecisive one, and by the Russians as an heroic rearguard action and one of their finest feats of arms. Both sides exaggerated their achievement. Napoleon claimed, preposterously, that he had lost fewer than 800 men killed or wounded, but in reality had suffered about 5,400 casualties, perhaps slightly more than his opponents. For their part, the Russians boasted of having left not a single gun as a trophy, and ignored the fact that Napoleon had managed to take their strong position by engaging only 20,000 of his troops, about the same number as they had defending it.[18]

Artillery played a particularly prominent role in the action, since both sides deployed as many as 5 guns for every 1,000 men, an unusually high ratio, and the effect of the fire was intensified by the cannonballs ricocheting on the frozen ground.[19] The consequences were clear from the casualty figures. On each side a staggering one in every four soldiers engaged was killed or wounded, a proportion unequalled in any other battle of the campaign.[20] Napoleon also lost a disproportionate number of senior subordinates – as many as eleven generals, including *Maréchal* Victor, were hit – and he knew that such experienced leaders were even harder to replace than troops.[21] The Russian high command also suffered severely, with seven generals being injured, two of them mortally.[22]

In fact, it makes more sense to see Craonne as a defeat for both armies, since the heavy losses and ensuing recriminations did lasting damage to their morale and cohesion. Napoleon simply could not afford to win battles like Craonne, and the impact of the action was one of the main reasons why, just three days later, the *Schlesische Armee* would become paralysed for well over a week.

Blücher's army rallied at Laon on the morning after the battle, but had now been retreating for a week and was riven by discord. The Russians resented the fact that their troops alone had fought at Craonne, seemingly to no purpose, and suspected that the Prussians were using them to bear the brunt of the campaign. In fact, the reason why the Russians had defended Craonne was simply the result of Blücher's previous dispositions behind the Aisne. Winzingerode had been on the eastern wing to avoid entangling his supply lines with those of the other corps, and the natural consequence was that his infantry, commanded by Vorontsov, ended up holding the eastern end of the *Chemin des Dames*. In any case, Winzingerode's corps was fresher than any other in Blücher's army except for Bülow's Prussians, who were too far away, on the extreme western wing. As for the failure of the encircling cavalry move, which included both Prussian and Russian cavalry, that was largely the fault of Winzingerode, a Russian general. Yet the mistrust persisted, and only a decisive victory would be able to heal the divisions.[23]

Battle of Laon

Despite such deep dissent, Blücher had now massed over 100,000 troops at Laon, ready for another action.[24] Never before in this campaign had the *Schlesische Armee* been so strong on a battlefield, nor so concentrated, for in all its previous actions it had been engaged piecemeal. It no longer had to rely on support from the *Hauptarmee*, as at La Rothière, or fight at a disadvantage because of inadequate numbers of cavalry, as had happened at Vauchamps. Laon was, in fact, the second largest battle of the entire campaign.

As the *chef-lieu* of the *département* of the Aisne, Laon was a key road hub and also happened to be a superb defensive position as it stood on a solitary hill rising 100 metres above the Ardon river. The broken terrain on the southern and western horizons ended at least 2.5 miles from Laon, leaving it isolated in the middle of an open, snow-covered plain that stretched far to the north.

Laon was the obvious site for Blücher to rally his army. The hill itself formed the centre of his position and was held by Bülow's Prussians, with batteries carefully sited to cover the approaches. To the west was Winzingerode's Russian corps, while the eastern wing was formed by the Prussians of Yorck and Kleist, who had now been amalgamated into a single corps. The rest of the army, Langeron and Sacken's Russian troops, constituted the reserve and remained hidden behind the hill.

Merely having to fight the Battle of Craonne had upset Napoleon's plan of sweeping round Blücher's eastern flank to seize Laon in his rear. The fighting had pulled his army westwards along the *Chemin des Dames*, so that by the end of the day his units were scattered over a distance of more than 20 miles from the western end of the road all the way to Berry-au-Bac in the rear.

Instead of retracing his steps along the *Chemin des Dames*, Napoleon continued westwards and joined the Soissons road, which he used to march on Laon from the south-west with 30,000 troops. Only the tail of his army, Marmont's 10,000 men, advanced on Laon along the Reims road from the south-east as originally planned.[25] By dividing his forces in this way Napoleon could magnify his apparent strength and confuse his opponents as to which prong constituted his main attack. It was potentially dangerous, since rough, wooded, and marshy terrain separated his two wings and would make it difficult for them to support each other. The danger would lessen as the roads converged on the city, but would still limit Napoleon's freedom of manoeuvre and force him to attack Laon frontally, for outflanking it to the west would leave Marmont's small detachment isolated. Even so, he was confident of being able to take the city, since the outcome of Craonne had deluded him into thinking that Blücher would now continue his retreat far to the north and that another attack would hurry him on his way.

Never before had Napoleon strayed so far from the main campaign area. He was now 30 miles north of it, for his failure to trap Blücher against either the Marne or the Aisne had forced him to prolong the pursuit further than he had anticipated. But the extension of his advance had its advantages. He apparently thought that Laon was held

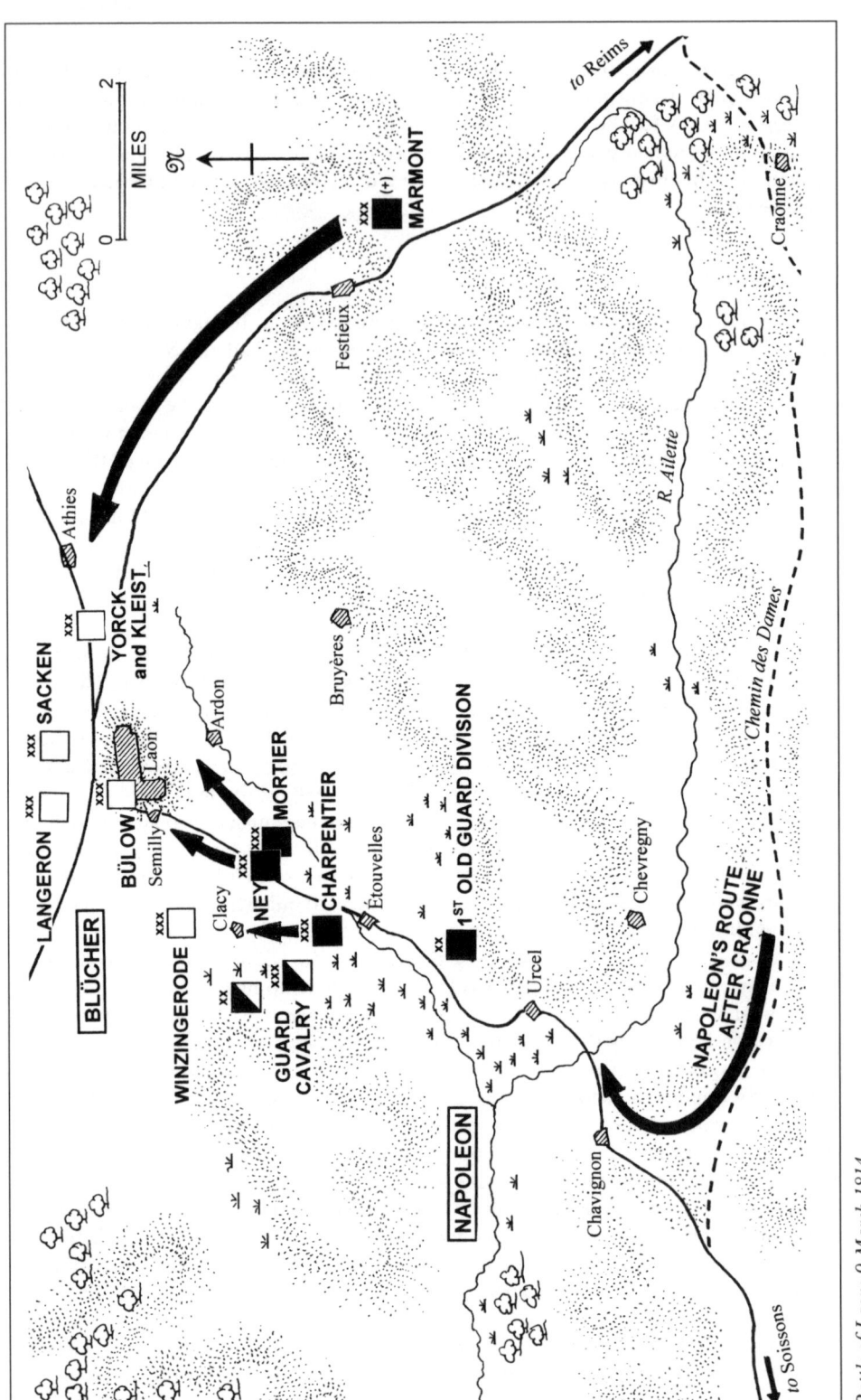

Battle of Laon: 9 March 1814.

merely by a rearguard, that he could easily seize it, and that it would then form a bulwark where a covering force could contain the shaken *Schlesische Armee* far from Paris, while he returned southwards to fall on Schwarzenberg. Laon was also far enough north for Napoleon to summon reinforcements from his nearest fortresses in the Ardennes, just 55 miles to the north-east. The regular garrisons were to leave the *gardes nationaux* in the strongholds, and march to join the field army, brushing aside the weak forces that had previously been detached by the *Schlesische Armee* to observe them.

Napoleon hoped to take Laon by surprise in the early hours of the 9th by detaching a mass of cavalry to burst into it from the flank or rear. But all chance of surprise was lost when the advanced guard was fatally delayed by a Russian detachment at the village of Chivy, 2.75 miles south-west of the city. As the French forces belatedly arrived, heavy fighting developed in the villages at the foot of Laon. Towards 1100 hours *Leutnant* Wilhelm Alberti of the Prussian *6. Reserve-Infanterie-Regiment* was writing a letter to his parents when he was interrupted by orders for his corps to move to a new position:

> At last, my dears, I can give you another sign that I am alive and more or less in good health. I have endured much this last week: contending day and night with the weather, marching without a break, often without the precious bread and water, and always in action! On the 4th, during a very heavy cannonade, I received your dear letter no. 3, of 9 February, which had gone by way of Berlin. Oh, how blissfully happy these few lines of comfort made me! I am still well. In a moment, I must be away, as the summons will be blown. Everything is still fine, God is with us all. The cannonfire begins once again! If only this letter reaches you. Farewell, God bless.[26]

Blücher wanted to launch a counter-offensive, but was thwarted by a thick blanket of fog that covered the battlefield for most of the morning. Even including Marmont's detachment, Napoleon had only 40,000 men, or just two-fifths of the *Schlesische Armee*'s strength. But with the fog helping to hide the actual odds, Blücher's command team readily accepted a report from a captured French headquarters official indicating that Napoleon had 70,000 troops. Nor was Blücher able to enthuse his army with his usual personal leadership. Stricken with fever and inflamed eyes, he had to direct the battle from a chair on the south-western side of Laon, from where he could watch the fighting below him once the fog lifted.[27]

Towards 1200 hours Blücher was informed that a separate French column was advancing on Laon from the south-east. This was actually Marmont's detachment, but its strength was uncertain and it was unclear whether it constituted the main attack or just a feint. Blücher therefore made a limited assault on the French western prong, in order to gauge its reaction. Its fierce resistance indicated that it was, in fact, Napoleon's main force, and that the eastern column was merely a diversion. Nonetheless, the *Schlesische Armee* would wait for the battle to develop further before committing its reserves to a general offensive.

Napoleon, too, misjudged the situation, for he initially failed to realise that his subordinates had run into a full-scale battle. Throughout the morning he remained at his headquarters 7 miles south-west of Laon, and did not move forward to take personal command until after midday. Even then, his presence had little effect in the face of such numerical odds and the natural strength of Blücher's position. When the sun set towards 1740 hours, the hill of Laon remained stubbornly in Allied hands.

But the fighting was not yet over. Towards 1700 hours Marmont had belatedly arrived east of Laon with his column, having been delayed in the morning by the fog. Finding himself confronted by superior forces, he could do no more than take the village of Athies before settling down for the night. Blücher and his staff were now confident enough to launch their long-delayed offensive, and they did so in the east, for whereas Napoleon's western wing had hills close behind it, Marmont was more exposed in the middle of the open plain.

The night attack began with Yorck's Prussian infantry storming Athies, while cavalry turned Marmont's flank. Surprise was complete, for Marmont's men were in bivouac, and had failed to take proper precautions.[28] Panic set in and most troops quickly broke and fled, as *Oberst* Wilhelm, *Graf* Henckel von Donnersmarck of the Prussian cavalry vividly recalled:

> We now heard firing, shouts of 'hurrah!', drums beating (it was always our Prussian quick march), the clatter of cannon and ammunition waggons as they tried to flee along the *chaussée*, and so on. Always, inexorably, the noise went forward. You can imagine the enemy's confusion, for several hussars in light blue uniforms approached, thinking that we were their people, and in this way some of them were cut down.[29]

Marmont had to fall back 4.5 miles to Festieux, where the Reims road left the exposed plain and entered hilly country that continued southwards to the Aisne. Fortunately for him, many of his men recovered their nerve and repelled repeated cavalry attacks as they withdrew. Their retreat was eased by Marmont's ADC, *Colonel* Fabvier, who had earlier been detached with 1,000 men to re-open communications with Napoleon. When Fabvier heard the fighting, he marched back eastwards, and managed to clear the road through the plain, while the escort of a convoy secured the entrance to the hills at Festieux. Marmont was able to rally his corps, but had lost 3,500 men and all but 10 of his 55 guns.

Laon: the second day

Napoleon was furious when he heard of the reverse but resolved to continue the battle south-west of Laon in order to cover Marmont's withdrawal, and also, it seems, as he still hoped that the *Schlesische Armee* would evacuate the city and resume its retreat. He should have paid a heavy price for remaining in his exposed positions. Blücher's headquarters issued orders for a bold outflanking move for the morning of the 10th, with Winzingerode and Bülow pinning Napoleon down frontally while the remaining corps thrust southwards and threatened his line of retreat.

Yet by daybreak Blücher had become too sick to leave his room, and suddenly lost interest in life. Several other senior officers fell ill at this time. Blücher's *General-Quartiermeister*, Müffling, had been suffering intermittently from fever for the past two days, while Schwarzenberg was ordered by doctors to stay in bed on 18 March and was still fairly weak on the 22nd. The strain of the campaign, and the recent freezing temperatures, were taking their toll. Even Napoleon had a heavy cold on the 14th.[30]

Blücher's collapse unnerved his subordinates. Gneisenau, the *Chef des Generalstabes*, effectively commanded the army, although, since he was too junior to do so openly, nominal authority remained with Blücher. Suddenly saddled with responsibility, Gneisenau cancelled the plans to outflank Napoleon, and settled instead for the safe and unambitious policy of holding Laon. The hilltop city was simply too good a defensive position: it offered a security that Gneisenau was loath to leave for the hazards of the country further south, in the same way that Schwarzenberg had been reluctant to advance beyond the fortified cities of Langres and Chaumont in January.

Napoleon's bold decision to stand his ground therefore intimidated the *Schlesische Armee*, and, by reinforcing Gneisenau's caution, negated the numerical odds. Fighting continued indecisively throughout the day. Professor Steffens, who was attached to Blücher's headquarters, watched from the top of the hill. Since he was billeted in Laon, he could enjoy a good night's sleep and then simply ride to the edge of the city, watch the battle, and return to his quarters in the evening for supper. It was a convenient, if unusual, way of witnessing an action, and he vividly recalled what he saw:

> It was not one continued battle, but different corps of the enemy as they came in sight were attacked, and engagements were taking place at several points distinct from each other at the same time. We saw all with perfect ease.... In one place a Russian square was furiously attacked; they were shot at with musket-ball[s], while a mass of cavalry tried to hew a road into the midst of them; but they were not to be broken; they waved every way, and curved and bent, but always drew closer again into a dense mass as if they had been one single living body. It was a grand, a wonderful sight![31]

Towards the end of the day, Napoleon finally slipped away under the cover of darkness, and fell back on Soissons, 18 miles to the south-west. The two-day battle cost him 6,500 casualties, as high a price as he had paid for his earlier defeat at La Rothière. He had also lost large numbers of men through desertion and straggling, for in pursuing Blücher to Laon he had marched his army more than 165 miles in eleven days.[32] Although he blatantly played down the outcome of the battle when he wrote to Joseph on the 11th, he could not ignore the way the campaign was relentlessly grinding down his army:

> I have reconnoitred the enemy's position at Laon. It was too strong to be attacked without heavy losses, so I decided to return to Soissons. The enemy would probably have evacuated Laon out of fear of being attacked there, if the *duc* de Raguse [Marmont] had not had a little action and behaved like a *sous-lieutenant*. The enemy has suffered enormous losses: yesterday he made five attacks on the village of Clacy and was repulsed each time. The Young Guard is melting away like snow. The Old Guard bears up. Much of my Guard cavalry also melts away.[33]

Napoleon reorganised his army at Soissons. The five Young Guard infantry divisions had lost so heavily, in both men and commanders, that they had to be amalgamated into just two.[34] Nonetheless, despite his losses, and despite failing to seize Laon, Napoleon had skilfully extracted himself from a potential disaster by imposing morally on his opponents. However battered, his army remained intact, and he could still hope to salvage some benefit from having driven Blücher so far north of the Marne.

'We will die of hunger'

Despite Napoleon's repulse, the *Schlesische Armee* remained paralysed for a week after Laon. Ironically, it was now finally at full strength and had a powerful cavalry force, which meant that, in theory, it could pursue and exploit victories, and was unlikely to suffer a decisive defeat itself.

Gneisenau's caution was one problem, but so, too, was his shortage of supplies, his limited information about Napoleon's movements, and his deep mistrust of the *Hauptarmee*. He was even concerned that the Crown Prince of Sweden might switch sides in the event of a serious Allied defeat, and use the *Nordarmee* to endanger the *Schlesische Armee*'s rear.[35] 'Still no news has arrived', he complained on 16 March:

> However, we must expect that Napoleon will continue to concern himself with us for a considerable time. We can not count on the *große Armee* [*Hauptarmee*]. Even if its leaders wanted, it could not achieve much, simply because of the nature of its composition, with its three courts. In the meantime, our situation here becomes ever more critical. If we remain concentrated, we will die of hunger. If we spread out, the enemy's skilfully led cavalry will fall on one of our corps.[36]

Two-and-a-half months of campaigning had crippled the *Schlesische Armee*, and exhausted its troops, as Colonel Hudson Lowe, a British observer attached to its headquarters, explained on 11 March:

> For forty-two days past this army, which appears to have been peculiarly the object of the enemy's disquietude and attacks, has been constantly marching or fighting; for, exclusive of the general actions, only two days have elapsed, in which the advance or rear of it has not been seriously engaged.[37]

The very fact that the *Schlesische Armee* had been reinforced also worked against it, for it now suffered from the same problem that had long afflicted the *Hauptarmee*: it had become too large. The addition of Bülow and Winzingerode's corps had enabled the *Schlesische Armee* to fight Napoleon single-handed, but also reduced its mobility and increased its supply difficulties. By the evening of the 12th Gneisenau had been obliged to disperse his troops over a distance of more than 35 miles, from Berry-au-Bac in the south-east to beyond La Fère in the north-west, but by thus extending the army towards the less-exhausted region west of the Oise river, he shifted its centre of gravity away from the *Hauptarmee*.

The *Schlesische Armee* never fully recovered its cohesion for the rest of the campaign. The removal of Blücher's iron will threatened to allow the fabric of his army to unravel, for he alone had held all the disparate threads together. During the rest of the campaign he recovered enough to listen to reports and sign decisions, but he had to shade his eyes and could not remain on horseback for long, let alone lead his men in battle.[38]

The corps commanders, independent-minded men at the best of times, were reluctant to obey Gneisenau. Nor had tensions eased between the Russian and Prussian contingents, for the Russian generals suspected that Gneisenau had cancelled the planned offensive on the 10th in order to limit Prussian casualties. The issue of who would assume command if Blücher became completely incapacitated further undermined relations. General Langeron was the most senior corps commander, but he was Russian and believed that the Prussians were intriguing for the appointment of one of their own men.[39]

Part of the problem lay with Blücher himself, for some of his subordinates had become disenchanted and blamed him for their setbacks on the Ourcq river and the excessive exertions of their troops.[40] Yorck had already clashed with Blücher and Gneisenau the year before over the way they pressed their men beyond reasonable limits. Now, inflamed by Gneisenau's actions, including the assignment of his corps to an area already deprived of resources, Yorck abruptly left in his coach, obliging Blücher to write, with an ADC guiding his hand, to beg him to return.

Yet for all the *Schlesische Armee*'s problems, its victory at Laon reinvigorated the Allies. Before learning of the outcome of the battle, Schwarzenberg had written anxiously to his wife on the 12th:

> Once again, I fear the worst. . . . If Blücher is beaten, although admittedly he has very good and more numerous troops than Napoleon, the question arises whether it is wise to risk a battle with this army. If this army is also beaten, what a triumph it will be for Napoleon. . . . I am so anxious for Blücher that I will be tormented the whole night.[41]

But the next day confirmation of the victory at Laon reached Chaumont, the headquarters of the Allied monarchs. 'The news came to the Russian mess, where we all happened to be,' recorded *Prinz* Wilhelm, the Prussian King's son: 'Immediately, the simply wonderful *Te Deum* was sung. Then Tsar Alexander went to Papa, and everyone congratulated each other. Alexander read out the report. Then to Emperor Franz. Same scene. Everyone happy.'[42]

Napoleon recaptures Reims

It was not immediately obvious what Napoleon would do after Laon. But then, on the 12th, he learned that the city of Reims, 32 miles east of Soissons, had just been taken by Lieutenant-General Count Saint-Priest, who was on his way from the Rhine with part of the Russian 8th Infantry Corps to join Blücher. This was actually the third time that Reims had changed hands, for it offered all the resources of a large city and the advantages of a road hub. Napoleon was determined to recapture it, and could thereby cut direct communications between Blücher and Schwarzenberg, and draw closer to his fortresses, making it easier for them to send him reinforcements.

Leaving part of his army at Soissons, Napoleon marched more than 20,000 troops to Reims. The advance began that night, the 12th/13th, and demonstrated the remarkable mobility of his army. The 1st Old Guard Division took just fourteen hours to cover a distance of between 35 and 40 miles, taking into account the twisting roads.

The speed of the French descent, and the fact that their army was able to take the offensive at all so soon after Laon, caught Saint-Priest by surprise. When their leading troops arrived west of Reims, he took up a position on the hills immediately outside the city, for at this stage he found it difficult to believe that he faced a major offensive. Only after Napoleon himself arrived with the bulk of his forces in the late afternoon did Saint-Priest belatedly order a retreat. Then an artillery shot smashed into his shoulder and he fell mortally wounded. As his men withdrew in disorder, his subordinate on the scene, Major-General George Arsenyevich Emmanuel, lost his head and, instead of taking command, went personally to find the most senior Russian officer, Lieutenant-General Ivan Davydovich Panchulidzev I, who was inside the city and unable to mount a horse following an accident that morning. For an hour, therefore, the Russians were left without a leader, at a time when they desperately needed one.

From his initial command post on a low mound, Napoleon could see the towers of Reims cathedral dominating the city 3 miles to the east. He unleashed a general offensive, with the main attack rolling directly down the road from the west, while the cavalry division of *Gardes d'honneur* circled round to the south to outflank the Russians and threaten their line of retreat into the city.

Led by *Général de brigade* Philippe, *comte* de Ségur, elements of the *Gardes d'honneur* made a spectacular charge, first overthrowing some Russian dragoons and then pursuing a tide of fugitives that poured back towards the Vesle river and the entrance to Reims. A Russian officer, Prince Golitsyn, frankly admitted:

> The confusion and disorganisation at the bridge over the Vesle were beyond all imagination. Men were already hurling the cannon into the water in order to clear a passage for themselves, and the congestion was such that those who could not keep their footing on the bridge fell into the river. This chaos reached a climax with the approach of the enemy cavalry, which fell *en masse* on this dreadful disorder and was able to pick off its victims at will. Only the [Russian] dragoons put up a desperate resistance, and so it was a hand-to-hand fight of one man against ten.[43]

But the sheer mass of fugitives brought Ségur to a halt, and he then found himself caught in a crossfire, for he had managed to penetrate behind some of the retreating Russian troops. A battalion of the Ryazanskii Infantry Regiment emerged in his rear, opened fire, and left the ground strewn with fallen Frenchmen. The *1er Gardes d'honneur* lost one in three of its men killed or wounded, Ségur himself was seriously injured, and the division as a whole was disabled for the rest of the campaign.[44]

Three days later Napoleon awarded seven crosses of the *Légion d'honneur* to the *gardes*. It was politically expedient for him to celebrate their deeds, as he had sought to recruit them from privileged young men in order to bind the nobility and upper bourgeoisie to his regime. Ségur himself came from a great aristocratic family, and his regiment, the *3e Gardes d'honneur*, had already been mentioned in the official accounts of the Battles of Hanau and Château-Thierry.[45]

Yet Ségur's charge was just one element of the French onslaught. In reality, as *Général de brigade* Pierre, *baron* Pelleport of Marmont's VI Corps pointed out, the *gardes* lost control and had to be rescued by the infantry.[46] Besides, it was the artillery that had mortally wounded Saint-Priest in the first place, thus causing the disorder that was exploited by Ségur. As so often in the campaign, the role of ordinary line units was overshadowed by dramatic, but not necessarily cost-effective, actions by prestigious regiments.

A Russian rearguard checked the French by holding the entrance to Reims, and the Vesle river prevented Napoleon from bypassing the city and cutting the escape route to the north.[47] It was the early hours of the morning before he could finally enter the city, but the inhabitants placed candles in their windows to illuminate the streets as a welcome.

Napoleon had inflicted a loss of 3,000 men and 11 guns, but the significance of the recapture of Reims went beyond mere statistics.[48] He had offset the impact of his defeat at Laon and once again secured a central position between the two Allied armies, from where he could threaten both simultaneously and reduce them to a state of nervous indecision. The *Schlesische Armee*, for example, had begun a southward advance to the Aisne on the 13th but came to a sudden halt the next day after learning of the action at Reims. Only on the 18th, after Napoleon left the area, would it end its week of hesitations and counter-orders and advance in earnest.

Despite its local impact, the victory at Reims had a negligible effect on morale in Paris, because it was unable to resuscitate the peace negotiations at Châtillon, which ended six days later.[49] Diplomatic efforts did not cease altogether, and Napoleon would make subsequent overtures when his prospects became desperate, but it was becoming clear that he was in danger of losing his throne unless he could quickly find a military solution to his predicament.

Napoleon remained at Reims for three days after recapturing the city, so he could gather information before deciding his next move. He also wanted to give time for reinforcements to arrive from the fortresses, but in the event only 6,000 men came from Mézières and were used to form an infantry division. Some of Napoleon's troops made preparatory moves during this brief lull, but others were able to enjoy the respite, as *Capitaine adjudant-major* Charles Faré of the *2e Grenadiers à pied* explained to his parents on the 16th:

> I take advantage of a moment's rest, which we have at last been granted, to tell you my news. With our forced marches and continual bivouacs, it has been impossible to find a single chance of writing to you. I now receive hardly anything from you. Admittedly, I believe that the running of the mail services is often interrupted, and I hold this responsible for my total deprivation of money and possessions. I believe I have never been in such a situation. I no longer have either boots or trousers. I had a new greatcoat, but it was stolen. . . . To crown it all, the barbarians of the north [the Russians] seem to have brought with them their country's frosts. We have never marched so much and with so little rest. We are doing a tough campaign, and if we finally manage to drive the enemy from our country, I think we will have deserved well of her.[50]

Chapter 11

'We are afraid of fighting'

In the southern sector, meanwhile, the situation had deteriorated dramatically for the French. On moving north against Blücher, Napoleon had left behind 42,000 men to continue pursuing the *Hauptarmee* beyond Troyes, but his departure soon resulted in setbacks. Schwarzenberg halted his retreat, and on 27 February crushed *Maréchal* Oudinot on the hills above Bar-sur-Aube. In the wake of this defeat, the French forces rallied at Troyes under the overall command of *Maréchal* Macdonald, and then fell back to the north-west.

Fortunately for Napoleon, Schwarzenberg lapsed into a week of inactivity around Troyes. As in the previous month, he did not hurry to assist Blücher with a powerful diversion, and instead awaited confirmation that the *Schlesische Armee* was still intact before risking an advance of his own. 'Our operations are, in my mind, very singular,' wrote Colonel John Fane, Lord Burghersh, the British military commissioner with the Austrian forces:

> The fact is, we are afraid of fighting. I am convinced this army will not be risked in a general action; without one, I don't see how we are to break down Buonaparte. Schwarzenberg would almost wish to be back upon the Rhine; he has so many difficulties to face in his present advanced position, that nothing but a victory could extricate him; but this he thinks a dangerous remedy: to go back without being forced, would require great nerve to bear the responsibility, so he continues where he is, without, I fear, any great prospect of doing much, unless the way was made easy for him by victories gained by others of the Allied armies....
>
> Peace is the constant cry of every officer in this army. It is very disgraceful, but it is my duty to tell you of it – the army is in a state of great disorganisation, pillage and plundering at its utmost.[1]

The *Hauptarmee* was simply too large to supply itself efficiently, and needed to recover from the strain of its recent retreat. Only on 13 March did Schwarzenberg resume the offensive in earnest. Breaching the line of the Seine, he drove Macdonald back a further 10 miles, but then halted his advance by the end of the 16th. His army was now extended along a depth of over 40 miles from the area of Nogent-sur-Seine eastwards to Lesmont.

Schwarzenberg had been alarmed by news that French forces had occupied Châlons-sur-Marne, 30 miles north of his army, following Napoleon's recapture of Reims. Over the next three days he issued a series of counter-orders, as he veered between retreating eastwards on Bar-sur-Aube and advancing northwards to support Blücher. His indecision has been severely criticised, but is understandable in view of the dilemma he faced. If he concentrated the *Hauptarmee*, he could be outflanked, whereas if he dispersed it to cover his communications, he could be defeated in detail. He had to deploy his army to face two potential threats at the same time – Napoleon to the north and Macdonald's detached force to the west – and received conflicting reports about their moves.

Napoleon descends on Schwarzenberg

On 17 March Napoleon dictated a memorandum in which he considered the merits of three alternative strategies against Schwarzenberg. The first was to fall on the *Hauptarmee*'s northern flank and rear by advancing southwards from Reims towards Arcis-sur-Aube and Troyes. The second was to move south-westwards to Sézanne and Provins, which would give him a central position between Blücher and Schwarzenberg so he could act against either of them. The third option was to withdraw by the main road to Meaux, 25 miles east of Paris, and cover his capital directly. Napoleon summed up the dilemma:

> All these three plans have their good and bad points.
>
> The first is the boldest, will greatly terrify the enemy and produce unforeseen results.
>
> The second has the disadvantage of always using the transverse roads, but in the end it cuts off the enemy on the right [north] bank of the Seine.
>
> The third is the most certain, because it leads swiftly to Paris. But it is also the one which has no moral impact and therefore leaves everything staked on a big battle. Now, if the enemy has 70,000 to 80,000 men, this battle will be a tremendous gamble, whereas by marching on Troyes and arriving in his rear whilst [Macdonald] retreats and disputes every position with him, there can be very great opportunities.[2]

Napoleon opted for the first, and most ambitious, option. Leaving 17,000 men under Marmont and Mortier to contain the *Schlesische Armee* on the Aisne, he set out from Reims on the 17th. He took with him the 1st Old Guard Division, the attached artillery, and two divisions of Imperial Guard cavalry, and by collecting other units as he moved south would swell his numbers to 23,000 men.[3] He now finally had a pontoon train, which removed the need to capture an intact bridge and gave him the freedom to cross rivers wherever he wanted. After reaching the Aube, he could either continue southwards on Troyes, or turn aside and try to trap part of the *Hauptarmee* between himself and Macdonald's detachment of 30,000 men, which was near Provins, 35 miles to the west.

On the 19th Napoleon duly crossed the Aube at Plancy, 8 miles west of Arcis, and had his cavalry cut up an Allied rearguard near Méry-sur-Seine to the south-west. Yet the *Hauptarmee* was retreating too quickly for him to fall on its centre as he had hoped. He therefore changed his plan, and instead of continuing southwards decided simply to advance eastwards along the Aube and seize Arcis in order to increase the Allies' alarm and confusion. Having thereby prodded the *Hauptarmee* into a faster retreat, he could leave Paris uncovered and strike boldly eastwards with his whole army, including his detached forces, and thus shift the campaign into a new and more fruitful phase as he penetrated deep into the Allied rear, collected reinforcements from his fortresses, and fanned resistance to the occupation.

Battle of Arcis-sur-Aube

Napoleon did not expect to fight the pitched battle that ensued at Arcis-sur-Aube on 20–21 March, and it was in fact the first and only time in the entire campaign that Schwarzenberg personally fought an action against him.[4] That the battle occurred at all was due to an uncharacteristically bold decision by Schwarzenberg on the evening of the 19th to switch to the offensive the next day. Once he knew that the French were

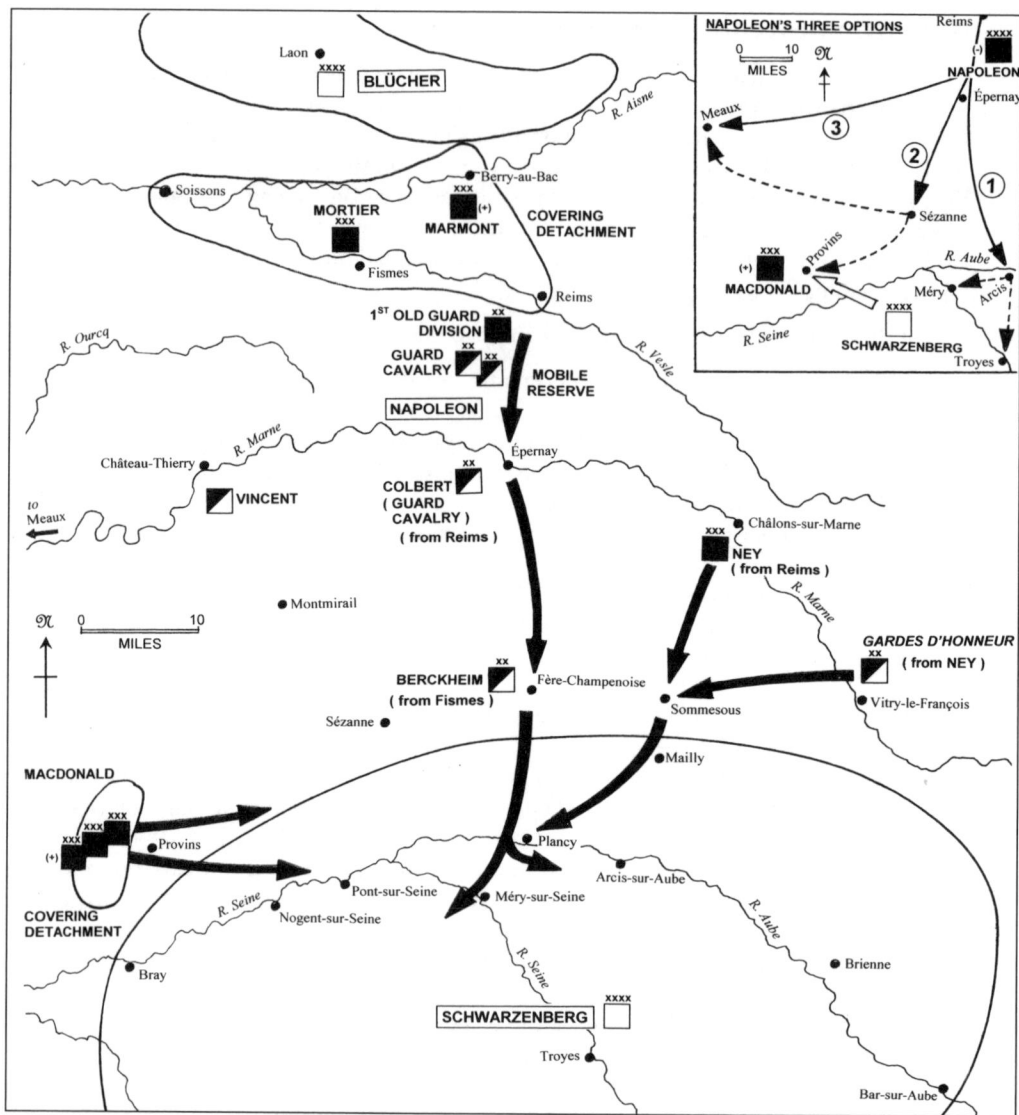

Napoleon's descent on Schwarzenberg: 17–19 March 1814.

crossing the Aube at Plancy, he concluded that they were moving southwards on Troyes, instead of trying to outflank him to the east by descending on Bar-sur-Aube.

No longer, therefore, was Schwarzenberg alarmed for his communications, but at the same time he knew that he had to contain Napoleon in the constricted triangle of land between the Aube and the Seine before he had a chance to manoeuvre and threaten Troyes, the *Hauptarmee*'s advanced base. He hence decided to check him by having his corps converge on Plancy from the east and south-east. By attacking Napoleon close to his bridgehead, Schwarzenberg could minimise the *Hauptarmee*'s main handicap, its limited ability to manoeuvre, and instead use brute force by concentrating superior numbers of troops and relying heavily on massed batteries.

But events on the morning of the 20th failed to unroll as either side expected. By 1100 hours French cavalry had occupied Arcis from the west. Napoleon himself arrived two hours later, and believed that he faced only a rearguard, since the bulk of the *Hauptarmee* was hidden from him in the folds of the ground further south. Most of Napoleon's units were still moving on Arcis, and would gradually reinforce him over the next forty-eight hours.

Schwarzenberg's own offensive had been delayed, since three of his corps were still on their way from Troyes under the overall command of the *Kronprinz* von Württemberg. In any case, Napoleon's unexpected move on Arcis changed the entire situation. It meant that Schwarzenberg's objective had now shifted to the east, yet the *Kronprinz* was heading north-westwards in accordance with the original plan and was on the far side of the Barbuisse stream.[5] As a result, Schwarzenberg had little more than Wrede's V *Armee-Abtheilung* immediately available for an attack on Arcis, giving him a comfortable advantage of numbers, but not the overwhelming force on which he had calculated.

At 1400 hours Schwarzenberg could wait no longer and gave the signal to launch the attack. Neither army, therefore, had more than a fraction of its strength present when the battle began. Napoleon had just two Imperial Guard cavalry divisions covering Arcis, and an infantry corps under Ney at the village of Torcy-le-Grand, a mile to the east. Ney was soon fiercely engaged trying to prevent Wrede from rolling up Napoleon's flank, while a superior mass of Allied horsemen overwhelmed the Imperial Guard cavalry and sent it pouring back towards Arcis.

Napoleon was reconnoitring when the action began and had to gallop back to check the rout. A torrent of fugitives swept into Arcis and exposed its vital bridge to capture. Historians have described how Napoleon heroically stemmed the tide by asking if anyone dared to pass him, and how he then organised a counter-attack, with his staff officers joining the charge and shouting encouragements of *Vive l'empereur!* In fact, the incident seems to have been comical as much as courageous. When Napoleon tried to draw his sword, he apparently found it had become rusted in the scabbard, so two equerries had to extract it for him, and they had such difficulty that one of them injured himself when it finally came free.[6]

Napoleon sent ADCs to hasten the rest of his army, and was fortunate that the Old Guard infantry soon arrived over the bridge. It was the deployment of these bearskinned veterans, as much as Napoleon's own presence, that restored the situation. Their effect on the battle was dramatic, as Wrede's ADC, August, *Fürst* von Thurn und Taxis, recalled:

> All seemed set for a brilliant success, when all at once . . . the enemy columns, which had practically withdrawn into the town, turned round before our eyes, and advanced towards us again, with reinforcements and supported by the fire of many guns.[7]

Arcis-sur-Aube was one of the most critical battles of Napoleon's career, and parallels have been drawn with Marengo and Lützen because of the degree of danger to which he exposed himself as he tried to steady his men. When a howitzer shell fell nearby, he reputedly rode over it in order to set an example of bravery. The explosion brought down his horse, but left Napoleon himself unharmed.[8] To some, it seemed that he consciously sought to get himself killed, for as his chief secretary, *baron* Fain, wrote:

> Far from avoiding dangers, he actually appeared to defy them. A shell fell at his feet. He awaited the explosion and soon disappeared in a cloud of dust and smoke. We thought we had lost him, but he got to his feet, mounted another horse and again placed himself under the fire of the batteries. . . . Death did not want him.[9]

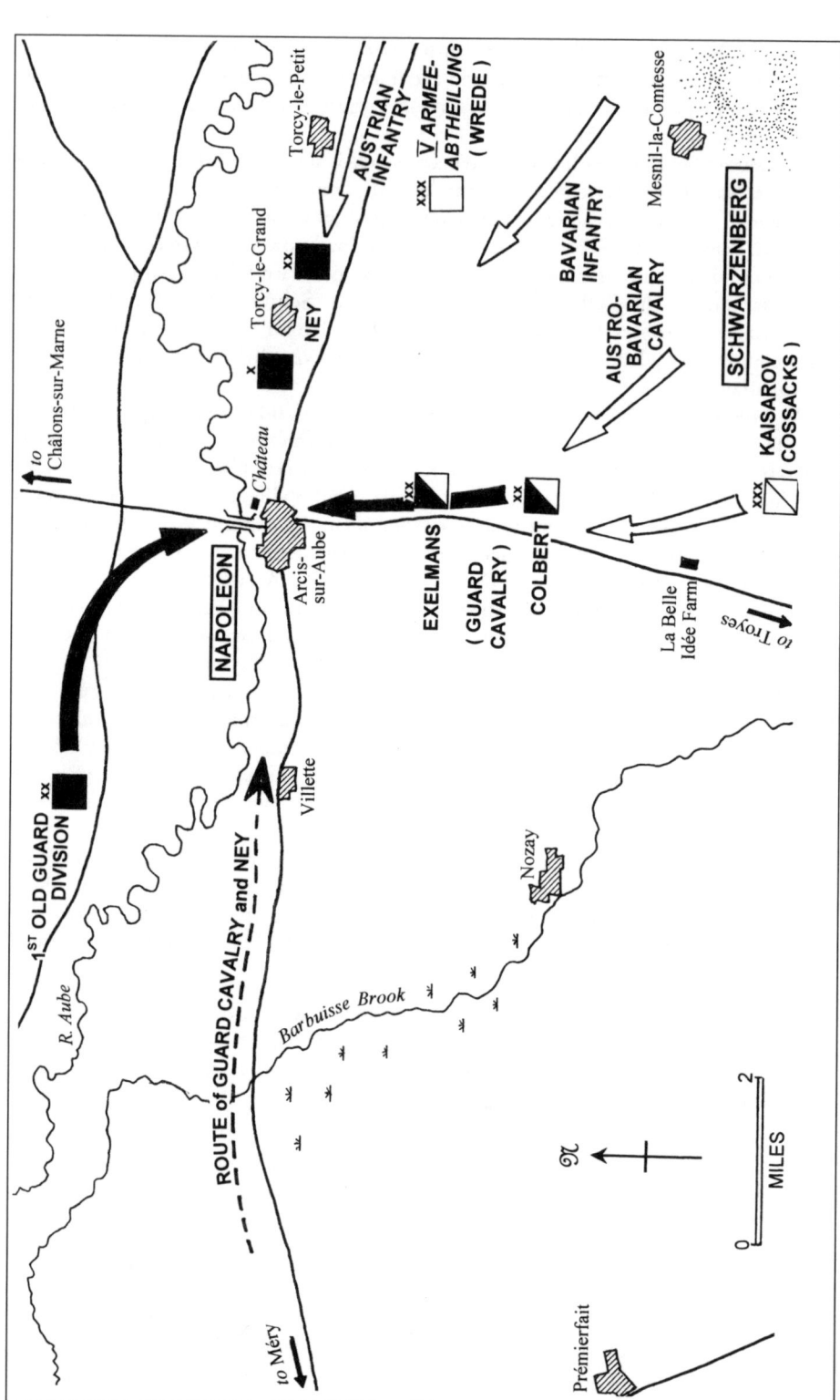

Battle of Arcis-sur-Aube: 20 March 1814.

The incident was later immortalised in prints and became part of popular myth. It did have some basis in fact, for word of it even reached the Allies. 'Napoleon himself is said to have lost a horse,' Schwarzenberg informed his wife two days later.[10] But the incident was actually less dangerous than it seemed, as the powder in a shell lacked the blast effect of more modern, high explosive projectiles, and tended to split the metal casing into just a few large fragments, which could leave a man unscathed even at close quarters. It was actually safer for Napoleon to place his horse over the shell as a living shield than to remain a few feet away. There is no hard evidence that he was attempting suicide, nor indeed that he despaired of the situation, or thought that he was confronting anything more at Arcis than an obstinate rearguard, since only part of the *Hauptarmee* had yet been engaged. He had every reason to hope that by manoeuvring against Schwarzenberg's communications in the coming days he could induce him to retreat.

The French occupied an unfavourable position, since they were concentrated near the low-lying town of Arcis, whereas the Allies were deployed in more dispersed and less exposed positions around it, and could direct their fire inwards for added destructiveness. By the evening *Colonel* Griois of the Guard artillery saw that a nearby infantry battalion had been reduced to a mass of mutilated bodies and weapons, and Arcis itself caught fire several times from the exploding howitzer shells. Yet the Allies also suffered heavily, for the French gunners kept up an incredibly intense fire, inflicting heavy damage, knocking out several guns, and having an effect at a range that surprised even experienced Bavarian artillerymen.[11]

Wrede was belatedly reinforced in the evening with 5,000 men from the Russian reserves, but still could not wrest Torcy-le-Grand from Ney's obstinate grasp. Then, towards 2200 hours, Napoleon counter-attacked south of Arcis with a mass of 4,000 cavalry. In the darkness the French threw back some Allied horsemen, veered to the east and charged further units, before being checked by musketry and artillery fire, counter-attacked, and forced to withdraw. *Capitaine* József Grabowski of the headquarters staff described how the clash gradually petered out in disorder:

> It was almost completely dark, and you could no longer make out either the features or the uniforms of the men in front of you. The trumpeters of both sides sounded the retreat. The combatants obeyed these calls, and the officers shouted their orders, which you could hear in French, German and Russian. I found myself in the midst of soldiers of all nationalities, but at this moment, no one thought of cutting or thrusting with his sabre, nor of firing. Keeping his lance, sabre or pistol at ease, each man thought only of trying to find his comrades again. It was a really strange sight, and was illuminated by the flames of Arcis-sur-Aube and of the villages nearby.[12]

Arcis: the second day

Napoleon was reinforced early in the morning of the 21st to a total of 28,500 men, and intended to resume the battle, as he believed that the Allies had fought the previous day merely to cover the *Hauptarmee*'s retreat. In fact, the French position was becoming increasingly dangerous. Whereas Schwarzenberg had so far fought with just a fraction of his army, he could now concentrate the bulk of it on the battlefield, giving him an overwhelming numerical superiority. During the morning his units deployed in a semi-circle before Arcis. He himself was with Alexander and Friedrich Wilhelm III on a height near Mesnil-la-comtesse, 4 miles south-east of Arcis. *Fürst* von Thurn und Taxis noted how:

The point was well chosen for such a conference, as it offered views of the whole area and, in particular, of all the enemy's moves. The enemy stood in concentrated masses close around Arcis. His position seemed in no way advantageous for the defensive, as he had his back so close to the Aube. The heads of our columns crowned all the heights and, I can say, offered an imposing sight. It was, as it were, the first time since the crossing of the Rhine that the army had been concentrated in such a restricted area, and ... [it] was particularly strong in cavalry and artillery. ... Hence, we could hardly doubt that we would be successful.[13]

Napoleon, in contrast, could see little of the *Hauptarmee* from the lower rolling terrain near Arcis. Soon after 1000 hours he pushed *Général de division* Horace, *comte* Sébastiani southwards with 9,000 cavalry, supported by Ney's infantry. The advance finally revealed the gravity of the situation, for as Sébastiani reached the crest of the ridge that had hitherto screened the country further south, he found himself confronted with an entire army.

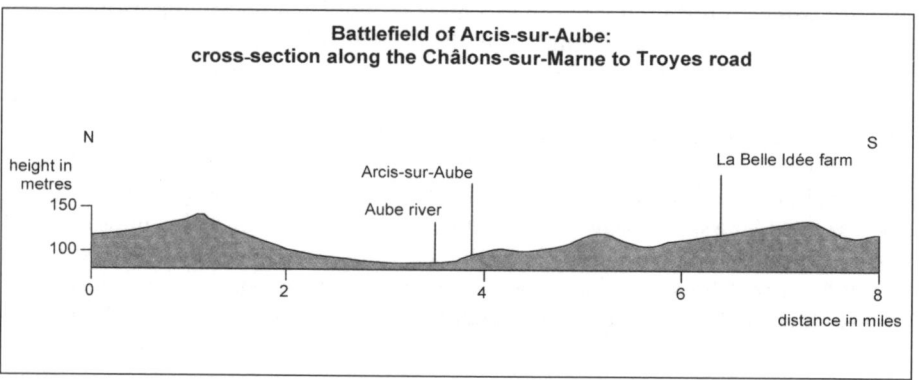

The campaign could have ended that day, with Napoleon trapped and destroyed against the Aube. But Schwarzenberg had reverted to his usual caution and, despite the obvious hesitation in the French lines, had his army rest for two hours instead of ordering an immediate offensive.[14] Napoleon covered his retreat with his cavalry and established a temporary bridge to supplement the permanent wooden one at Arcis.[15] Not until the middle of the afternoon, after seeing French troops withdrawing on the opposite bank of the river, did Schwarzenberg attack. Even then, he was unsure whether Napoleon was retreating north-westwards to cover Paris or heading north-eastwards for Vitry, from where he might threaten the *Hauptarmee*'s supply lines to Basel. At the same time as he attacked Arcis, he therefore covered his communications by detaching the V *Armee-Abtheilung* and the reserves to cross the Aube 14 miles to the south-east.

The town of Arcis was fiercely defended by an infantry division, and at one point *Général de brigade* David, *baron* Chassé famously rallied some men by seizing a drum and beating the charge. By 1900 hours the rearguards had been withdrawn and the bridges destroyed. Napoleon lost 3,400 men in the two-day action, and failed to terrify the *Hauptarmee* into a headlong withdrawal as he had intended. Yet he could still hope to win the campaign, for the battle had been piecemeal and therefore indecisive. Schwarzenberg wrote to his wife on the 22nd that the war could last a long time, that most of the peasants were armed, and that he could not see through the fog of the situation.[16]

Napoleon's gamble

Undeterred by his defeat at Arcis, Napoleon now carried out the bold plan he had long envisaged: a thrust eastwards into the Allied rear. This gamble has been almost universally condemned as an act of desperation, even of madness, the irrational lashing-out of a commander who had exhausted his patience. The theorist *General-Major* Karl von Clausewitz later condemned the move as 'unarguably the worst thing Bonaparte did during the war', while Wellington later claimed that Napoleon's campaign was:

> Excellent – quite excellent. The study of it has given me a greater idea of his genius than any other. Had he continued that system a little while longer, it is my opinion that he would have saved Paris. But he wanted patience – he did not see the necessity of adhering to defensive warfare . . . and he threw himself imprudently on the rear of the Allies.[17]

The remark simply reveals Wellington's superficial understanding of the situation. Napoleon did not make a sudden decision in a fit of impatience, but carried out a long-considered move that he had repeatedly been forced to postpone because of pressures elsewhere. From the very moment he took the field, the campaign had been a subtle interplay of two of his most common campaign strategies: the safer, but less fruitful, use of a central position to attack two enemy armies in turn, and the bolder, and potentially decisive, outflanking bid of the *manoeuvre sur les derrières*.

Napoleon had actually begun his operations at the end of January with a *manoeuvre sur les derrières* when he moved from Vitry against Blücher's rear. A fortnight later, after Vauchamps, he had wanted to complete the overthrow of the *Schlesische Armee* and then sweep southwards against Schwarzenberg's communications, but had been obliged instead to cover Paris more directly. Then, early in March, he had tried to sweep round Blücher's eastern flank and seize the city of Laon in his rear. Even the recent battle at Arcis-sur-Aube followed the failure of another *manoeuvre sur les derrières*, Napoleon's attempt to cut Schwarzenberg's communications by moving south from Reims.

Nor had the strategy been used solely by Napoleon. Blücher had already attempted a *manoeuvre sur les derrières* of his own. Just a month earlier he had marched on Paris, leaving his rear exposed, and had thereby forced Napoleon to abandon the pursuit of Schwarzenberg and move after him. That Napoleon might try a similar manoeuvre deep into their rear had been anticipated by the Allies. At the time of the *Schlesische Armee*'s advance on Paris towards the end of February, Blücher had ordered misinformation to be spread that he had 30,000 men based at Vitry, in order to discourage any attempt by Napoleon to move eastwards against his supply bases.[18]

Napoleon was running out of options, haemorrhaging resources, and leaking his remaining credibility in Paris. In contrast to his stunning succession of six victories the previous month, he had won just two battles thus far in March, at Craonne and Reims, and the former had been a costly and inconclusive clash. Time was not on his side, and using a central position to cover the approaches to Paris would no longer work. The longer the campaign lasted, the more difficult it became for Napoleon to achieve surprise with the same manoeuvres, and his checks at Laon and Arcis-sur-Aube showed that he was now unable to defeat either of the two Allied armies in a frontal battle, even when it was unsupported by the other army. After Arcis-sur-Aube, Napoleon could not continue opposing either Blücher or Schwarzenberg directly by blocking the road to Paris: he would simply have been forced by superior numbers to retreat all the way back to the city. Such was his political insecurity, particularly after the revolt of the southern city of Bordeaux on 12 March and the failure of the Châtillon conference a week later, that it was imperative for him to move the theatre of war away from the capital, instead of bringing the Allies to its very gates.

If Napoleon could induce the Allies to follow him eastwards, he would have more chance of defeating them piecemeal, not least because their lines of communication diverged to the east and south-east. He could establish his army within the belt of frontier fortresses, for instance between Metz and Luxembourg, and use the strongholds to block key roads, protect his flanks, and force the Allies to manoeuvre around them and cross rivers in order to attack him, thus leaving them exposed to a series of counter-strokes against isolated units.[19] He could avoid battle except on favourable terms, and protract the war in the hope that his opponents would become too weary to continue.

By this stage Napoleon could not count on any more reinforcements from the Pyrenees, or large numbers of fresh conscripts from Paris, whereas by moving towards his fortresses he could draw thousands of troops from their garrisons who were now ready to take the field after weeks of training. He could also capture supply magazines, shift the operations away from Paris and the exhausted plains of Champagne, and liberate the frontier regions, thus repairing the disastrous loss of so much territory in the initial stages of the invasion and improving his position in the event of a negotiated peace. Napoleon also knew that he was likely to find more support from the peasantry in eastern France, where the provinces had been under Allied occupation the longest, and where resistance had been sustained by nearby fortresses and favoured by rugged terrain, as in the Vosges and the Ardennes.

A general uprising against the Allies required the supporting presence of a regular army. It would not have been enough for Napoleon to send a mere detachment under a subordinate, while he himself covered Paris, for his *maréchaux* lacked his boldness and the power of his reputation, and splitting the army would have rendered both parts too weak to achieve their objectives. Napoleon had to use his whole army if he was to have the required impact, and to lead it himself, regardless of the consequent risk to the capital.

The manoeuvre that Napoleon now undertook has been misunderstood. He did not simply march headlong on the Allied rear, as is sometimes alleged. Instead, he moved 20 miles eastwards to Saint-Dizier, which he reached on 23 March, and then halted to allow his rearmost units to catch up, and to see how the Allies would react before he took a definitive decision whether to continue. As he awaited reliable intelligence, he pushed light cavalry out to the south, east, and north-east to harass the rear of their armies. He ordered these cavalry units to capture supplies, question messengers and travellers, and rouse entire *départements* by spreading the news of his arrival and having the church bells rung as an alarm signal. They were to open communications with the fortresses and reassert control over previously occupied territory by removing Allied commandants and reorganising the local administration.[20]

Napoleon was torn between either thrusting boldly north-eastwards to his fortresses or moving southwards to intercept the *Hauptarmee*, which seemed (wrongly as it turned out) as if it might be beginning a retreat. He thought that his most judicious option was to head north-eastwards to draw reinforcements from the fortress garrisons, and then give battle using Metz as a base, yet he deferred the decision and spent the 24th waiting for more intelligence.[21] For the moment he compromised by positioning the bulk of his army along a 20-mile stretch of road south of Saint-Dizier, in a central position between the lines of communication of the two Allied commanders. From here he was ready to move in any direction: southwards against Chaumont and the *Hauptarmee*'s magazines; back northwards to Saint-Dizier prior to heading to his fortresses in the north-east; or even, if it became necessary, westwards to Paris along the main road through Troyes.

Thus, far from being a sweeping thrust deep into the eastern provinces, Napoleon's *manoeuvre sur les derrières* turned out to be a shorter, hesitant advance that hovered between progressing to the full, eastward thrust, or returning to the more limited move that he had attempted at the start of his campaign, when he had seized Saint-Dizier with a view to striking against Schwarzenberg's rear at Chaumont. The crux of Napoleon's dilemma was that he was attempting a strategy whose ambition went beyond what he could safely execute with the number of troops at his disposal. This obliged him to check that the Allies were reacting as he wanted before he continued eastwards, even though this robbed his manoeuvre of its full impact by depriving it of the constant motion needed to produce a whole series of psychological shocks to keep the Allies off-balance and incapable of rational decisions.

Napoleon's uncertainty about the Allied moves persisted into the 25th, yet the longer he waited, the more the initiative slipped from him. His confidence also ebbed away, to such an extent that he authorised Caulaincourt to try to re-open the failed peace negotiations at Châtillon.

The Allied response

Whereas Napoleon was beset by doubts, the Allied high command already knew his plan. A letter from him was intercepted by Cossacks on the night of 22/23 March, in which he informed his wife that he was moving on Saint-Dizier in order to draw the Allies away from Paris. This was confirmed in the morning by a captured despatch from *Maréchal* Berthier.

In order to work, the *manoeuvre sur les derrières* depended on Allied sensitivity for their rear. Yet, crucially, it was Napoleon's own communications that were the more vulnerable. The Allies had the whole 200-mile stretch of the Rhine from Huningue to Koblenz as their base of operations, and were able to switch their lines of communication in mid-campaign to the alternative base of the Low Countries. Napoleon, in contrast, was tied to the single point of Paris. He had tactical flexibility, in that he repeatedly transferred his operational base from town to town as he manoeuvred about the campaign area, but strategically he could not afford the loss of Paris because of its political and moral importance.

Despite this fundamental flaw, Napoleon's manoeuvre did, in fact, work, at least initially. In the afternoon of the 23rd a council-of-war met at Pougy, 12 miles south-east of Arcis-sur-Aube, attended by Alexander, Friedrich Wilhelm III, Schwarzenberg, and other senior officers. Some advocated falling back towards Switzerland to cover the *Hauptarmee*'s communications, but a retreat could have demoralised the army and become unstoppable. Instead, the council decided to abandon the existing supply routes, move northwards on Châlons-sur-Marne to join the *Schlesische Armee*, and open a new line of communications through the Low Countries. The two united armies could then follow Napoleon eastwards and defeat him in battle.

More captured despatches reached the *Hauptarmee*'s headquarters during the night of 23/24 March. The authorities in Paris had written to warn Napoleon of the depletion of the city's treasury, arsenals, and magazines, and of growing alarm and discontent. The Allies had already received similar indications of the mood in the

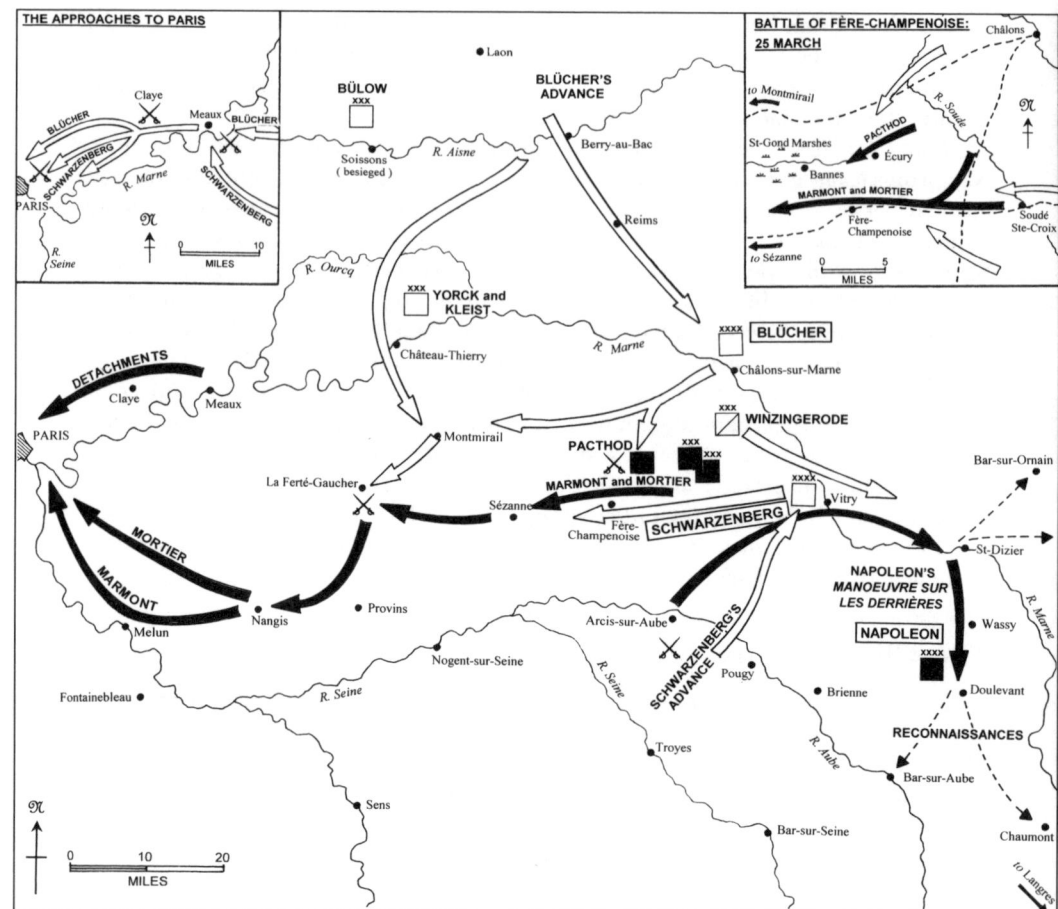

The final Allied advance on Paris: 22–30 March 1814.

capital from a royalist emissary a fortnight earlier, along with a cryptic message. 'You are walking with crutches,' it read, 'make use of your legs, and seek what lies in your power to achieve.'[22]

Such stark warnings actually justified Napoleon's much-criticised decision to strike against the Allied rear in a bid to distract their armies. Even now, Schwarzenberg continued to react as Napoleon hoped: early on the 24th, having linked up with the *Schlesische Armee*, the *Hauptarmee* was ordered to suspend its northward advance and turn eastwards for Vitry.

At this pivotal moment it was Alexander who grasped the full significance of the captured messages, and crushed Napoleon's last chance to avert disaster. The quickest way of deciding the campaign, Alexander realised, lay not in following Napoleon but in occupying Paris. At Sompuis, 10 miles west of Vitry, he consulted four senior Russian officers and received three conflicting recommendations: follow Napoleon; march on Paris; or split the Allied forces and do both. But he himself advocated an advance on the capital, and gradually doubts were surmounted, and agreement secured.

Alexander then joined Schwarzenberg. A further council-of-war at the side of the road overcame Schwarzenberg's caution and opposition from the Austrian staff. Significantly, Metternich and Emperor Franz were unable to influence the debate, since they had been cut off to the rear of the *Hauptarmee* by Napoleon's *manoeuvre sur les derrières*, and forced to withdraw southwards to Dijon.

As a result, the *Hauptarmee* would begin marching westwards on Paris the next day, the 25th. Schwarzenberg wrote and requested Blücher to make a parallel advance, and unite with him at Meaux, 25 miles east of Paris. To cover the move, Winzingerode was detached with 8,000 men, mainly cavalry, and sent eastwards towards Saint-Dizier, where he would shadow Napoleon and try to give the impression that the entire Allied armies were in pursuit.

Battle of Fère-Champenoise

To strengthen his *manoeuvre sur les derrières* Napoleon had even recalled Marmont and Mortier, whom he had previously detached to contain the *Schlesische Armee* on the Aisne. But on 25 March, as the two *maréchaux* moved eastwards to join him, they unexpectedly ran into the Allied advance on Paris in the opposite direction. Some 6 miles further north a French supply convoy also came under attack, and the result was two running engagements, known collectively as the Battle of Fère-Champenoise, as the French beat a fighting retreat that lasted for most of the day.

The *maréchaux*, attacked by the Allied cavalry spearheading the *Hauptarmee*'s advance, withdrew in a series of bounds and rearguard stands that continued for 22 miles. At 1400 hours a storm suddenly unleashed sheets of rain just when they had to cross a deep valley 4 miles east of the town of Fère-Champenoise. The defile was soon jammed with a mass of vehicles and fugitives, and amid the downpour the Allied cavalry managed to break the infantry squares that were covering the retreat, thus capturing 9 guns and most of a brigade.

The two *maréchaux* were fortunate to escape an even worse disaster. At 1500 hours, as the opposing commander, the *Kronprinz* von Württemberg, prepared to attack them again on the hills 7 miles west of Fère-Champenoise, he was diverted by the sound of firing from the north-east, and abandoned the pursuit.

The new threat turned out to be a French supply convoy, which had come under attack that morning from a cavalry corps of the *Schlesische Armee*. The escort, consisting of 4,300 *gardes nationaux* and conscripts under *Général de division* Michel, *comte* Pacthod, retreated south-westwards on Fère-Champenoise, abandoning its cumbersome vehicles on the way. But the action became progressively more serious as Allied units closed in from both sides, forcing Pacthod to veer off and head westwards for the Saint-Gond marshes under a hail of fire. His original six squares were reduced to just three as some broke and others merged. After his line of retreat was blocked, Pacthod was summoned to surrender, but he insisted on the Allied guns ceasing fire before he ordered the capitulation of the square he himself accompanied. Another of his squares laid down its arms after running out of ammunition, the third was finally overwhelmed, and only 500 of his men escaped into the marshes.

The action won the admiration of Alexander, who personally witnessed its closing stages. It has been all the more acclaimed in that such a large proportion of Pacthod's men were *gardes nationaux*, but they actually had more experience than some regular units, given the rawness of many French conscripts.[23]

The numbers of French casualties at Fère-Champenoise are unclear, but the Allies claimed to have taken 6,000 prisoners, several generals, and between 30 and 97 guns.[24] The battle was limited in importance, as it was not a defeat for Napoleon in person, but in terms simply of the losses inflicted, it was as great an Allied success as La Rothière. Even so, it came at a heavy cost for some units: the Württemberg *Jäger*-

Regiment Nr. 4 had gone into battle with 280 horses, and lost 46 of them, along with 31 officers and men.[25]

Throughout the Napoleonic Wars the Allies generally failed to mass their cavalry and use it aggressively as a potentially decisive arm. This is what seems, at first, to make Fère-Champenoise so unusual: they assembled 16,000 horsemen, and won the battle with cavalry and horse artillery alone. Yet they achieved this concentration of cavalry through chance as much as design, and did not use it effectively. Although they gradually brought an overwhelming force to bear against Pacthod, they never had more than 12,000 cavalry deployed in the more important fight further south against Marmont and Mortier's 19,000 troops. The *Kronprinz* von Württemberg repeatedly routed the *maréchaux*'s inferior numbers of horsemen and forced their infantry to retreat through outflanking moves, but rather than hastening their withdrawal in this way, he would have done better to try to pin them down in order to give his own infantry time to arrive. As often happened, the *Hauptarmee*'s corps had received their orders late and so the infantry had been delayed in beginning the advance.[26]

Thus the battle was indecisive: the two *maréchaux* were mauled, but survived to continue their retreat, and this is what enabled the French to fight a final and very bloody battle outside Paris five days later. Despite being celebrated by the Allies as a victory, Fère-Champenoise was actually a missed opportunity that would cost them thousands more casualties.

The Allies advance on Paris

Forced by the battle to abandon their plans of joining Napoleon, Marmont and Mortier withdrew westwards on Meaux, where they hoped to cover Paris by defending the line of the Marne. But on the 26th they found their route blocked at La Ferté-Gaucher by a Prussian division from the *Schlesische Armee*. After several failed attempts to break through, they made a detour to the south through Provins, and reached Paris on the 29th.[27]

Blücher and Schwarzenberg advanced along more northerly routes and converged on Meaux. In the absence of the two *maréchaux*, the only troops available to stop them were a weak force of mainly conscripts and *gardes nationaux*. A brief action on the afternoon of the 27th was enough for the Allies to secure a foothold on the north bank of the Marne and force the French to withdraw.

The Allied armies now descended on Paris in three columns, and, despite a fierce counter-attack at Claye, 9 miles west of Meaux, on the 28th, forced the French to continue a fighting retreat all the way back to the capital. In case Napoleon pursued, the Allies left a rearguard at Meaux: Sacken's corps from the *Schlesische Armee* and Wrede's V *Armee-Abtheilung*. Another corps, under Bülow, was besieging Soissons and Compiègne, 30 miles to the north, while Winzingerode's cavalry had been detached to shadow Napoleon. Even so, the Allies had as many as 107,000 troops when they arrived before Paris on the evening of the 29th.

Chapter 12

Paris

Over half a million people lived in Paris. It had more than twice the population of either Vienna or St Petersburg, and three times that of Berlin. Of all the cities on the continent, only Naples, with 430,000 inhabitants, was anywhere near as populous.[1] For over six years Paris had been the capital of continental Europe, and even now, in the years of defeat, it exerted an unparalleled fascination.

As well as being Napoleon's main arsenal and mobilisation centre, Paris was the heart of his political power. Just 2 per cent of the population of old France lived in the capital, but it had a disproportionate degree of influence because it was more than five times as populous as any other city, and because Napoleon's regime was so centralised. Seizing Paris, as Gneisenau pointed out, would mean more than capturing Vienna or Berlin: 'By occupying the capital, we will paralyse all the nerves of the government and dictate the peace.'[2]

The capital and its defences

Paris was Napoleon's greatest resource but also his most vulnerable point, and it was poorly protected. Since the 1780s it had been surrounded by a stone wall, pierced by over fifty *barrières*, or gates, where duties were paid on incoming goods. But the wall was incomplete, and more useful as a customs barrier than a military fortification, particularly as Paris could be bombarded from the surrounding hills.

Napoleon's immediate reaction to the invasion was to turn his capital into a well-provisioned stronghold, yet he realised that openly erecting fortifications would betray a lack of confidence, take several weeks, and divert funds more urgently needed for the field army. Hence, instead of constructing redoubts and entrenchments on the hills outside the city, he simply secured it against cavalry raids by blocking gaps in the wall and protecting the *barrières* with palisades. Napoleon's victories in February lulled him into believing that Paris was no longer in danger, and so its hills were still unfortified at the end of March. Some batteries were belatedly placed on the heights and trenches dug across roads, but they were not enough.

Only 16,800 troops managed to fall back on Paris in the face of the Allied advance, mainly under Marmont and Mortier from Fère-Champenoise. Another 13,200 were scraped together in the city, including men from the depots, pupils from military schools, and assorted *vétérans*, *invalides*, and volunteers. Even then, the government had to rely on the dubious support of the city's *gardes nationaux*. By the end of March there were still only 12,000 of them, for recruitment had been restricted to respectable men who would be keen to preserve law and order, even if they were unenthusiastic about the Empire or soldiering. Napoleon considered swelling the *Garde nationale* with unemployed workers, but was reluctant to alarm the privileged classes by doing so, and anyway lacked enough firearms. The *gardes nationaux* could not be obliged to fight outside the city, but several thousand volunteered to do so, while the rest occupied the gates, maintained order inside the walls, and freed the regulars to fight.

In all, therefore, the regime had 42,000 men of varying worth to defend the city in either an active or a supporting role.³

Rumours that the Allies were descending on Paris were not immediately believed, since the repeated swings of fortune during the campaign had made people uncertain what information to trust. Yet it was impossible to silence all news of the threat, and inhabitants fleeing the region around Meaux were spreading alarm in the city as early as the 24th, even if the size of the force causing this flight remained unclear.⁴

In Napoleon's absence, the 22-year-old Empress Marie-Louise was the figurehead regent, but his real deputy was his elder brother Joseph. Napoleon was aware of his family's personal defects but trusted his brother more than outsiders, and thought that a prince of his blood could command greater obedience than a lesser dignitary.

By the 26th the authorities knew that Napoleon was not in a position to check the approach of the Allied armies. The regency council initially favoured the Empress and her son remaining in the city to inspire resistance, but was then informed that Napoleon had previously given orders for them and the government to leave for the Loire if the capital was seriously threatened, and this ended the debate. Napoleon feared that their capture would destroy Austria's interest in a negotiated peace, since Marie-Louise was the daughter of Emperor Franz, and hence a hostage and a means of renewing the Franco-Austrian alliance.

The departure of the Empress and her son on the morning of the 29th shook morale. Joseph himself remained behind and issued a proclamation in which he admitted that an Allied column was advancing on the city, but claimed that it was closely followed by Napoleon at the head of a victorious army.

Battle of Paris

The defence of Paris on 30 March has been overshadowed by Napoleon's own actions, and yet it was the largest, bloodiest, and most important battle, and marked the climax of the entire campaign.⁵

Neither side wanted to fight actually within the city. Alexander, playing the role of a magnanimous conqueror, shared the desire of the French authorities to preserve it from destruction; nor were the Allies keen to be drawn into costly street-fighting amidst an enraged populace. Thus, the battle would be fought outside the walls, and decided by control of the hills to the north-east.

Time was not on the Allied side. They needed to capture Paris and its resources quickly, before Napoleon could return from eastern France. A delay of two or three days could leave them exposed outside the city to a counter-attack and beset with logistical problems, since their new supply lines from Belgium had yet to become fully operational to replace the intercepted ones with the Rhine.

Largely because of this need for haste, the Allies suffered heavy losses in a series of disjointed and piecemeal attacks. Commanders struggled to co-ordinate 107,000 men along a semi-circular front of 15 miles, with few reliable maps, and with communications limited to the speed of a horse.⁶ The centre, under the Russian General Mikhail, Count Barclay de Tolly, came into action towards 0600 hours, four or eight hours before the two flanking columns. In the north Blücher did not receive his orders until after 0700 hours, for an advance he was meant to have begun two hours earlier, while the southern column, under the *Kronprinz* von Württemberg, was still more than 12 miles from the battlefield. Not until the afternoon, therefore, did the Allies manage to bring superior numbers to bear all around the northern and eastern sides of Paris and cause the defence to crack.

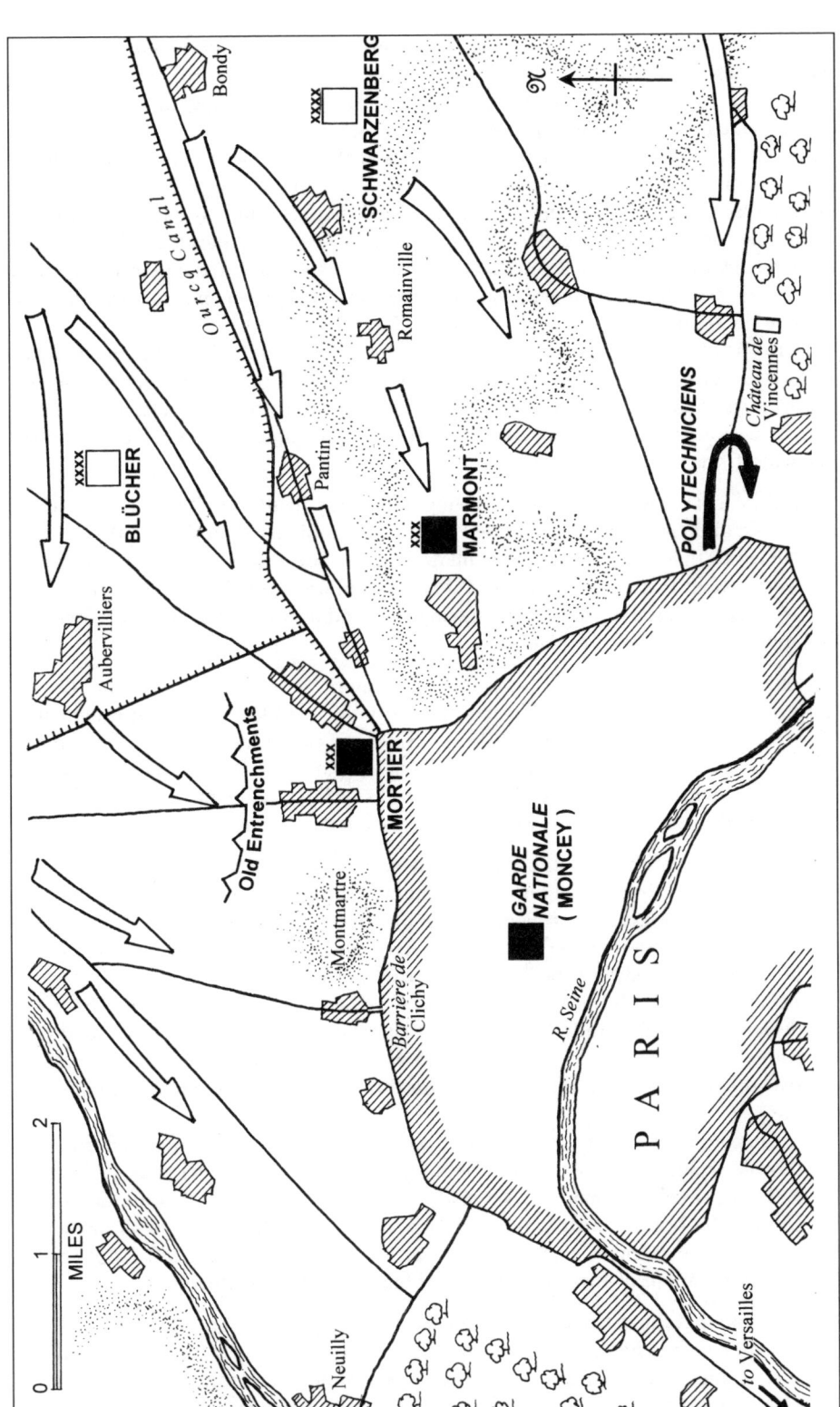

Battle of Paris: 30 March 1814.

Many of the French regular troops had to take up their positions soon after dawn, having reached Paris only the previous day after retreating from the east. Hence, the battle began as an encounter engagement, with both sides struggling to control the Romainville heights 3 miles north-east of the city.

Such was the piecemeal nature of the action that some locations saw little more than skirmishing. Jacques Boucher de Crèvecœur was among the *gardes nationaux* who volunteered to fight outside the city, but admitted that his company had few casualties. 'It is true that we were charged, or rather jostled, by Cossacks,' he added, 'but it would not be strictly accurate to tell you that this jostling was a fight.' At a nearby inn soldiers from both sides were having a drink together and then returning to their units to resume the fight.

Crowds of curious sightseers came from the city to watch. At one point Boucher de Crèvecœur was sheltering behind a wall, when some of them came and perched on top of it to obtain a better view, oblivious to the fact that they were attracting Allied fire. The *gardes nationaux* were about to force them to come down when a cannonball carried off one of the spectators:

> He was cut in two, without even having time to say thank you. Three or four of his neighbours hurriedly jumped down and took to their heels. We told ourselves that the others would follow, and that we would no longer have to worry about them. But not at all! When I poked my head up a moment later, I saw that the existing ones were staying put, and a group of newcomers were arguing over the vacant places.[7]

At other points the fighting was altogether more serious. The Prussian *Garde-Infanterie-Brigade* lost over 1,350 men in two failed attacks after being caught in a vicious crossfire near the village of Pantin. Since the casualties fell unequally, some of its units suffered appallingly, with the *1. Garde-Regiment zu Fuß* losing 67 per cent of its officers and more than half of its other ranks.[8] *Major* Wilhelm von Ditfurth, who commanded its 2nd Battalion, wrote to his wife ten days later:

> Poor thing, you hear of the great battle and read in the newspapers that we were involved, but do not know from them that I am safe and sound and that, luckily, God's grace has again saved me from the dreadful bloodbath of Paris. I have never experienced such hard and fierce fighting. Streams of blood have flowed, but the victory is great and peace certain. Our *Garde* has suffered dreadfully and my heart bleeds when I consider that this final, decisive battle demanded such a great sacrifice. . . . The battalion's losses were very great. Nearly all the officers were killed or wounded, and a good two-thirds of the men put out of action. I myself had two horses shot under me. . . .
>
> I cannot describe to you what our men have achieved once more, after the terrible strains of recent weeks, the privations, cold and hunger that we have endured, the forced marches we made, and finally the result: this murderous battle! The bravery with which my men went into action is above all praise: they are true German heroes! The losses we suffered are great and I still can not get them out of my mind. My heart bleeds to think of them.[9]

It was ironic that the Prussian *Garde* should have taken such losses right outside Paris, for it had been attached to the Russian Guards in the *Hauptarmee*, and hitherto kept in reserve and shielded from action, since Alexander had wanted to preserve his guardsmen for a triumphant entry into the city. In fact, the keenness of the Prussian

Garde to see action for the first time since Leipzig was undoubtedly one reason for the scale of its casualties.

Despite such bloody setbacks, the tide of the battle gradually swung against the French. Shortly after 1000 hours an envoy from the Allies warned Joseph that it would be impossible to prevent their troops from pillaging the city if they had to storm it. At 1215 he sent a note to Marmont, authorising him and Mortier to open negotiations if they could no longer hold their positions, and then, abandoning them, he left Paris to rejoin Marie-Louise.

During the afternoon, as the Allies finally drove the French from the heights, Marmont obtained an armistice to enable the city's capitulation to be negotiated. It proved difficult to implement the ceasefire at the height of the action, and so, like the rest of the battle, it happened haphazardly. The hill of Montmartre, immediately north of the city walls, actually fell to the Russians after the armistice had been arranged, either because the news had not yet arrived, or because it was disregarded. But the fighting finally ended towards 1700 hours, and Marmont concluded the capitulation that night.

The *barrière* de Clichy

Popular accounts of the battle have distorted it by exaggerating trivial incidents into major actions. The most glorious episode was supposedly the defence of the *barrière* de Clichy, on the north-western side of the city, yet it was actually no more than a skirmish that occurred by mistake. The Russian generals on the scene had been instructed to halt their attacks short of the *barrières*, in order to avoid fighting inside the city. As the French defenders outside the walls were driven back, *Maréchal* Bon-Adrien Jeannot de Moncey, the *major-general* of the *Garde nationale de Paris*, prepared to defend the *barrière* de Clichy itself.[10] In the event he did not have to meet a serious attack, for a Russian corps commander, General Langeron, halted his columns short of the city. Firing flared up again temporarily when the defenders mistook a move by Russian skirmishers for a serious assault, but hostilities were soon suspended.[11]

The real reason why this minor incident became so famous was that one of the *gardes nationaux* defending the *barrière* happened to be the artist Horace Vernet. Asked by his commander, *Chef de bataillon* Odiot, to paint the scene, Vernet immortalised it in one of his best-known works.[12] At first glance his painting seems to be a straightforward depiction of a combat, for despite the absence of any corpses, the grim faces and sombre colours hide the artist's underlying message.

It is, in fact, a deeply symbolic image, for the action was supposedly the final episode in the defence of the capital, and the last chance to prevent the entry of the Allies.[13] Vernet's depiction of the *gardes nationaux*, the semi-militarised citizens of Paris, as they heroically protect helpless inhabitants and wounded soldiers makes his painting a celebration of patriotism. Among the men shown are veterans of the great victories of the Revolutionary and Napoleonic Wars. Also present is *Capitaine* Emmanuel Dupaty, who can be seen bringing an abandoned cannon gun back into the city. He had proven his bravery in a naval action against the British in 1794 before becoming a successful playwright, and in 1814 he composed a popular song that urged his fellow *gardes nationaux* to protect Napoleon's son: 'Guard him well, for he's the hope of France.' Nearby is *Colonel* Bon-Marie Jeannot de Moncey, the *Maréchal*'s son and ADC, who is visibly pale because of the pain from a wound he had received at Montmirail: he had to be tied to his saddle to prevent him from falling off. In the background can be seen the *cabaret* of *père* La Thuille, who had encouraged the defenders with the exhortation: 'Drink, my friends, drink for nothing, do not leave a single bottle of my wine to the Cossacks!'[14]

Not surprisingly, the painting was refused entry to the *Salon* of 1822, for under the Restoration scenes of republican and imperial battles had become politically incorrect. Vernet therefore held his own individual *salon*, which naturally acted as a magnet for opponents of the monarchy and contributed to the growing identification of Bonapartism with the liberal and nationalist cause.[15]

Vernet was also fortunate in his timing. A new printing process called lithography had been invented in 1798, and now that its initial technical problems had been overcome it was possible to produce large numbers of inexpensive prints. One of the artists who exploited the new invention was a comrade in the *Garde nationale*, Nicolas Charlet, who can actually be seen in Vernet's painting helping to defend the *barrière* de Clichy. The invention of lithography meant that many of those Frenchmen alienated by the monarchy, even those in the poorer classes, could buy prints of the picture and display them in their homes. Political turmoil and new technology thus combined to give the defence of the *barrière* de Clichy a prominence it did not deserve.[16]

Vernet's patriotic message was reinforced during the Second Empire, when the city of Paris commissioned a monument at the *barrière*. Completed in 1869, it included a bas-relief based on his painting, and three statues depicting Moncey flanked by a personification of the city of Paris and a pupil of the *Ecole polytechnique* collapsing on the limber of a gun.

The *Ecole* provided scientific training for careers in the artillery and in engineering, and the inclusion of the *polytechnicien* was a reminder of another supposedly glorious incident when 28 guns manned by the pupils advanced from the eastern outskirts of the city to take part in the battle, only to be charged by Russian cavalry. The pupils' courage was indisputable: a Russian officer recalled that, although some of them tearfully begged for mercy, others wanted to die rather than abandon their guns. Even so, their short-lived action achieved little. Their battery was left unsupported, and was quickly overrun since the pupils initially mistook the Russians for Frenchmen, had few muskets with which to defend themselves, and had been provided with a motley collection of horses and drivers.[17]

Despite being an élite institution, the *Ecole* had become closely associated with the people of Paris, especially because the pupils joined them on the streets during the 1830 Revolution. Thus, the bravery of the *polytechniciens* in 1814 was incorporated into the myth of an heroic, popular defence of the city by its own citizens.[18] In reality, the brunt of the battle was borne not by the *polytechniciens*, nor by the *gardes nationaux*, but by the regular troops of Marmont and Mortier. Even Vernet's painting, for all its sanitised gloss, includes a hint of the chaos that was as much a part of the battle as courage. The Polish *chevau-léger lancier* in the left foreground, covered in mud and dust, and making his way to the rear, is actually a victim of friendly fire, having been dismounted by a cannonball aimed by some clumsy French gunners.[19]

The outcome

One of the oddities of the battle was the curious reversal of roles between the Allied armies, with the *Hauptarmee* actually doing more of the fighting than the *Schlesische Armee*. The Prussian *Garde-Infanterie-Brigade* suffered three times as many casualties that day as all the Prussian troops in Blücher's army. The *Schlesische Armee* had still not fully recovered from its paralysis following the Battle of Laon three weeks earlier.

Its moves had been slow and disunited, and Blücher had to spend most of the day in his carriage, although he managed to mount a horse in the middle of the afternoon.[20]

The lack of co-ordination was clear from the casualty ratios. The Russians provided half of the Allied troops present at the battle, but suffered 74 per cent of the casualties. The Austrians, in contrast, accounted for 15 per cent of the Allied strength, and yet less than 1 per cent of the losses.[21]

Such problems did not prevent the battle from being claimed as a great victory, or the foremost Russian general, Barclay de Tolly, from being appointed a field marshal the next day. For despite the flawed execution, the battle was the only decisive engagement of the campaign, and its momentous political consequences made it one of the most important actions of the entire Napoleonic era.

During the night that followed the battle, the French army marched out of Paris and headed south-eastwards along the road to Fontainebleau. In the courtyard of the *Hôtel des Invalides*, the Governor, *Maréchal* Jean-Mathieu, *comte* Sérurier, burned 1,417 flags, standards, guidons and kettledrums that the French had captured in various wars. One of the *invalides* recognised a flag that he himself had taken: it had cost him an arm, and he now grasped it with his remaining hand to try to prevent its destruction. 'Weep, my friend,' his *commandant* told him, 'but let us obey'.[22]

For the Allies, in contrast, it was an ecstatic day. 'Hurrah, hurrah. Paris is ours!' wrote *Prinz* Wilhelm, the 17-year-old son of Friedrich Wilhelm III, late that evening. His letter was disjointed with the turmoil of conflicting emotions: grief at the loss of friends among the officers of the Prussian *Garde*; exuberance at the fall of Paris; and the utter numbness of physical exhaustion:

> We now saw the great sink of iniquity [Paris] in its whole length and breadth! For all of us, it seemed like a dream. . . . Now, farewell. I am awfully tired, as for five days we have been on horseback the whole time. Today, we hardly ate, apart from having dined just now at 9.00 pm.[23]

A Russian officer, Staff Captain Eduard von Löwenstern, found himself lost for words as he saw the city for the first time:

> There at our feet Paris lay proudly in a vast amphitheatre. There curved the domes of the numerous churches, the Cathedral of Notre-Dame, the Louvre, the Tuileries, the *Hôtel des Invalides*. How the palaces shimmered in the morning sun, which broke through a heavy mist! I forgot the cannonballs that landed on us and was conscious only of the inestimable Paris that for ten years had laid down the law to Europe. I was proud to be one of the brave men who, with sabre in hand, and covered with blood, dust and powder smoke, had fought their way from the banks of the Volga to Montmartre, and who were now ready to storm the residence of the great [French] military commander. If a mine had exploded beneath me, I would even so have stared in wonder at Paris. Who could really think about death today?[24]

The Allies enter Paris

Not for four centuries had Paris been at the mercy of a foreign ruler, not since the English had lost control of the city in 1436. It was all the more solemn a moment in that less than eight years had passed since Napoleon had marched into Berlin, four since he had last occupied Vienna, and just two since he had entered Moscow.[25]

It was the most visually impressive Allied units, mainly the Russian and Prussian

Guards and reserves, and some Austrian *Grenadiere* and *Kürassiere*, that entered the city with the sovereigns on 31 March. Those that had borne the brunt of the campaign were deemed unfit to appear on parade. In the Württemberg IV *Armee-Abtheilung*, for example, the cavalrymen of the *Jäger-Regiment Nr. 2* had old, patched jackets, and even, in a few cases, trousers made from a green blanket or from the cloth of a billiard table. As a result the Württemberg contingent was represented by the *Infanterie-Regiment Nr. 5*, which had reinforced the *Hauptarmee* on 24 February and, unlike the *Jägers*, had undergone only a month of active campaigning.[26]

Bitter resentment resulted from the *Schlesische Armee* being left outside the city during the parade, but it was a necessary injustice. The Allied leaders had to allay the fears of the Parisians, and convince them that any further support for Napoleon was in vain. They did not want to show them tired and tattered troops, or alienate them by allowing hungry and poorly disciplined men into the city. Napoleon still had an army in being and the Allies could not fight both him and an insurrection within the city at the same time.

Even the Prussian *Garde*, despite all its efforts to smarten itself up, had shabby uniforms and equipment, and ranks depleted by its casualties of the previous day. The companies of the *1. Garde-Regiment zu Fuß* varied between 35 and 67 men, a mere fraction of their full theoretical strength of 200. During the parade the Regiment was followed by the bodies of two slain officers in waggons, for it had not had a chance to bury them and did not want to leave the task to strangers. In contrast, the Russian Guards had a second uniform they were able to put on for this special occasion.[27]

At 1100 hours the parade entered Paris from the north-east and moved through the city to the broad expanse of the *avenue des Champs Elysées* for a final review. As many as 30,000–35,000 troops took part. They were led by Schwarzenberg, Alexander, and Friedrich Wilhelm III, but there were two notable absentees. Blücher remained too ill to take part, and Emperor Franz was still at Dijon, and in any case had no wish to be associated with the humiliation of the French nation.

The onlookers were silent and anxious, for the Allies initially aroused curiosity rather than joy. Earlier that morning some royalist demonstrators had to be rescued by *gardes nationaux* after being attacked by Parisians. It was not until the parade left the working class districts in the east of the city that it was received with vociferous cheers of *Vivent les Bourbons! Vivent les souverains! Vive l'empereur Alexandre!*[28]

Napoleon's propaganda had depicted the Allied troops as brutal barbarians, and the disciplined and impressive parade was therefore reassuring, and produced an outpouring of relief after the tension of the past few days. The cheering was also encouraged by the white armbands worn by the Allied troops. These had actually been adopted in February as a recognition sign to prevent incidents of friendly fire, but were mistaken as an indication of support for the Bourbons and a guarantee that Napoleon would not be left in power to take revenge on those who opposed him.[29]

Paris under occupation

Paris can be occupied, but not conquered. Professor Steffens, who was with Blücher's headquarters, thought that the Allies were overawed by the city, to an extent that reminded him of the barbarian leaders standing before Ancient Rome. Paris certainly had a lasting impact on its occupiers. It was a visit to the city in October 1814 that provided much of the inspiration for the work of the British architect John Nash, who helped transform the appearance of London. He based the design of Marble Arch, for example, partly on that of the *Arc de triomphe du Carrousel*, which Napoleon had erected outside the Tuileries palace.[30]

Seeing Paris, and experiencing the French way of life, are said to have radicalised impressionable young officers from eastern Europe, who subsequently led pressure for political reform after returning home. Stephen Széchenyi, who later became a leading Hungarian patriot, served in Schwarzenberg's headquarters in 1814 as an orderly officer, and complained from Paris that 'we do not have any of this at home and shall never reach this stage; this will always be very sad to me'.[31]

Similarly, Russian officers who took part in the Decembrist revolt of 1825 were often veterans of the 1814 campaign. Kondrati Ryleïev, for example, claimed that it had been during his service in France while fighting Napoleon that he had first been inspired by the cause of liberty. Former Spanish prisoners-of-war are also said to have played a prominent role in the 1820 revolution against the absolutism of Ferdinand VII. Yet these popular assumptions can be misleading, for Allied impressions of France were often negative ones, of harsh treatment or impoverished provincial towns and villages. Not all Russian officers who served in France became Decembrists; many, indeed, saw themselves as the liberators of Europe, and the avengers of the destruction of Moscow, rather than as political and cultural inferiors.[32]

Once the novelty wore off, even Paris could become disagreeable. It was overcrowded with troops and tourists, and seats at theatres or coffee houses were difficult to obtain.[33] Much of it remained a medieval city, with narrow, crooked, and dirty alleyways. The important sights were concentrated in a small area, and Napoleon's attempts to modernise the city by adding fountains and monuments, extending the Louvre, and creating long, straight streets, would have to be completed half a century later by Georges Haussmann.

Paris was also expensive, not just because of the cost of transporting provisions from outside, but because the Parisians exploited their occupiers by inflating the prices. At the end of the occupation, after two months of living like a prince, Lieutenant Boris Uxkull of the Russian *Garde à cheval* was reluctant to leave the city, but knew that he would be bankrupt if he stayed longer, and noted that many of his comrades had caught a venereal disease.[34]

Nor did the initially fulsome welcome from the population last. Within a fortnight the common people were jeering at women who appeared in public with Allied officers. Quarrels with Allied troops became more frequent, and were often sparked by looters bringing plunder back into the city from the surrounding countryside, which they sold at a market in the city centre.[35]

It is sometimes claimed that the occupation left a permanent mark on Paris by inspiring its famous *bistros*. These fast-service *cafés* supposedly took their name from the Russian word for 'quickly', the command that their soldiers were in the habit of shouting when they wanted service. In fact, the story is almost certainly a myth. The real origin of the name *bistro* remains uncertain, but its earliest known record appeared only in 1884, a full seventy years after the campaign.[36] A more reliable sign of Russian influence in Paris was the sudden, temporary passion for *montagnes russes*, steep slopes erected on scaffolding for sledge rides. It was not an entirely new idea in the capital, but caught on after 1814–1815.

Chapter 13

The end of the war

The fall of Paris did not in itself restore the Bourbons, end the war, or ensure a peaceful settlement of Poland and other outstanding issues between the Allied powers. It was not inevitable that all three of these distinct processes should have happened, let alone in that order or at such a pace. A counter-offensive by Napoleon and a further battle for the capital were distinct possibilities, and Schwarzenberg wrote to his wife on 1 April that everything was in a great crisis, that Napoleon had been outlawed and would fight like a desperate man, and that the Allies would have to survive a fierce and decisive battle in the next day or two.[1]

Closing shots

The Allied decision to march on Paris had wrong-footed Napoleon. On 25 March he had still been 120 miles east of the city, hesitant and unsure how the Allies would react to his *manoeuvre sur les derrières*. The next day, at Saint-Dizier, he routed the cavalry force under Winzingerode that had been shadowing him. It was, in fact, his last victory of the campaign, but he failed to establish whether Winzingerode was just an isolated detachment, or the advanced guard of a comprehensive Allied pursuit.

Not until the afternoon of the 27th did Napoleon know for sure that the Allies were advancing on his capital. Next morning he headed back to try to save it, using a route south of the Seine to avoid being delayed by any Allied rearguards, and at the same time he made renewed efforts to obtain peace by sending a captured Austrian diplomat to Emperor Franz. The urgency of the crisis was underlined by a message from the *Directeur général des postes* that Napoleon needed to return immediately to prevent his political opponents from handing the capital over to the Allies.[2]

Travelling ahead of his army, Napoleon reached a posting house at Juvisy, 12 miles south of Paris, during the night of 30/31 March, only to learn that the troops defending the city were already evacuating it. Had he arrived that morning, he could have restored confidence and prolonged the battle, thereby either saving or destroying his capital. But he was half a day too late, and at dawn on the 31st, after learning that the city's capitulation had now been signed, he withdrew to Fontainebleau, 35 miles south-east of Paris, where he reassembled his army over the next four days.

Napoleon still had 70,000 troops, and wanted to fight on.[3] He might have returned eastwards to threaten the Rhine, but that would have exposed the unoccupied rump of the country. Only by remaining near Paris, and immediately trying to retake it, could he intimidate its population into remaining loyal, and retain at least a semblance of authority. Having been hampered throughout the campaign by the need to defend the city, he remained tied to it even after its fall.

The loss of Paris altered the whole balance of the campaign by dislocating Napoleon's government and removing the advantages that had enabled him to defy superior numbers for so long. The obvious alternative as a depot and centre of government was Orléans, but it had a population of just 42,000 and a hinterland to the south that, although protected by the Loire river, was poorly provided with roads and impoverished compared to the north and east of France. It was the Allies who now had the resources of Paris at their backs, and a superior road network on which to manoeuvre and bring up supplies, and this enabled them to keep their two armies united.

Barely three-fifths of old France now remained under Napoleon. Unless he could regain Paris, the shrinkage of his territory would become unstoppable, for with Bordeaux and Lyon in Allied hands, and with the rest of southern France apparently slipping from his control, he could not raise enough resources to continue the war with a reasonable hope of success.[4]

Above all, the fall of Paris was a psychological blow. The question was not simply whether Napoleon had the military means to recapture his capital, or whether its population would rise to support his attack, but whether he could retain the confidence of his key subordinates and convince them that further fighting would not be counter-productive.

Napoleon's downfall

Within a week, therefore, Napoleon was forced to abdicate as the political and military situation unravelled. He grew increasingly sidelined at Fontainebleau, as Paris became the only place that mattered. Its occupation emboldened Napoleon's political opponents, and enabled them to organise themselves and concert their actions with those of the Allies, something that had hitherto been difficult because of police surveillance and the problem of establishing communications across the zone of hostilities.

The two key personalities in Paris were Alexander and one of the most capable French political figures, Charles-Maurice de Talleyrand-Périgord. At this time Metternich, Castlereagh, and Emperor Franz were still absent at Dijon, and yet Alexander was more constrained than he would have been had he occupied Paris six or seven weeks earlier. During the interval the Allies had become more united, and had reached key agreements, including the preservation of France's former frontiers and great power status. Alexander himself had lost many of his illusions.

Talleyrand already knew Alexander well from the Erfurt conference of 1808, and was indispensable because of his experience and pragmatism. He has been seen as a traitor intent on bringing down the Empire, but can be better understood as a corrupt and untrustworthy improviser who kept his options open until the last minute. He would have preferred simply to replace Napoleon with a regency of his son, but had no faith in its viability so long as Napoleon was still alive and able to exert influence. Only reluctantly did he come to accept a restoration as the least worst option.[5]

Talleyrand's actions were guided by self-interest, but also by the interests of France and of Europe as a whole, for unlike Napoleon he pursued realistic and consistent long-term goals. Despite being unscrupulous in his short-term political manoeuvrings, Talleyrand remained faithful to his core political beliefs, including the need for peace, the renunciation of territorial expansion in Europe, and the adoption of political representation of the people on the English model. Unlike most of Napoleon's subordinates, who abandoned him only in 1814, Talleyrand had become disillusioned at least seven years earlier, at the height of the Empire, and in 1808 had openly sought to mobilise opinion in support of a change of policies. It was impossible for him to avoid being accused of treason, since Napoleon had emasculated France's representative institutions and left no legitimate means of expressing dissent.

Talleyrand rightly saw that Napoleon had to be removed before he undermined

France's negotiating position any further by continuing the campaign. His other key objective was to secure the principle of constitutional government, and he had to act quickly. On 31 March, immediately after entering Paris and conferring with Talleyrand, Alexander issued a declaration on behalf of the Allies, ruling out any further negotiations with Napoleon or his family and guaranteeing a constitution that would be chosen by the French nation.[6]

This established the essential framework for the events that followed. Talleyrand intended Alexander's guarantee to safeguard constitutional government even in the event of a restoration, while the refusal to treat with Napoleon gave Frenchmen the confidence to act openly against him without fear of revenge. Thus reassured, the *Sénat* appointed a provisional government under Talleyrand on 1 April, and two days later proclaimed Napoleon's deposition, as did the *Corps législatif*.

Civil war was a real threat, for France now had two governments, and three centres of power: the Provisional Government in Paris, the imperial government at Blois on the Loire under the Empress Marie-Louise, and Napoleon with his army at Fontainebleau, threatening to march on the capital.[7] In addition, there was the Bourbon claimant to the throne, the would-be Louis XVIII, in exile in England, and his representatives in France. So far, the *Sénat* had yet to agree to a restoration, but the position of the Bourbons was strengthened by royalist demonstrations, and by a proclamation in their favour from the *conseil municipal* and the *conseil général* of the *département* of the Seine.[8]

During the course of the campaign the Bourbons gradually emerged as the only acceptable alternative to Napoleon. The other options – either a republic, a regency for his son, or an elected monarch – were too weak or too revolutionary. The Bourbons had legitimacy on their side, had increased their profile, and seemed to have widespread support as a result of the reception given to the Allied troops at Bordeaux and Paris. Yet neither the Bourbon princes nor the secret royalist societies were able to engineer a restoration themselves; they could only influence and constrain Alexander and Talleyrand, who were both wary of them.[9]

Even at this stage, there was an obvious alternative solution: assassinate Napoleon in order to make a regency viable. A potential assassin was identified. Armand de Guerry, known as *Monsieur* de Maubreuil, was a former cavalry officer from a royalist family, who was suitably excitable in character and had fallen into debt. Summoned to meet the Provisional Government's secretary, he was promised money and honours if he assembled 100 men and eliminated Napoleon, but his mission was postponed on the evening of 3 April as it was being overtaken by events.[10]

Abdication

Political developments were now outpacing the military situation, and prevented Napoleon from marching on Paris for a final battle. Opinion in the French army was divided. Some men were exasperated by the welcome the Allies had received in Paris and wanted to take revenge on the city, but others were appalled at the prospect of its destruction.[11] Above all, many of Napoleon's *maréchaux* and generals believed that continuing the campaign would simply weaken France's position. Even a victory would be fruitless, since the Allies had publicly ruled out the possibility of peace with Napoleon. Crucially, the *Sénat* had formally released the French army from its oath of loyalty, and Talleyrand and his associates had been sowing disaffection among Napoleon's subordinates by passing proclamations and newspapers from Paris through the advanced posts.

On 4 April five *maréchaux* balked at the idea of marching on Paris and persuaded Napoleon to abdicate in favour of his son. This step is usually seen as an admission by Napoleon of defeat, but actually makes more sense if regarded as a ploy to divide the Allies and intimidate his political opponents in Paris. If Alexander accepted his conditional abdication, Napoleon could rule by proxy through his son until he was in a position to regain full power. If, on the other hand, Alexander rejected a regency, Napoleon could rally his subordinates by demonstrating the Allied intransigence. This was more astute than demoralising the army by arresting the *maréchaux* and trying to find uncompromised replacements on the eve of a decisive battle.

Hence, Napoleon was far from abandoning the campaign, but his calculations were foiled by a separate development. Another *maréchal*, Marmont, swayed into thinking that he could save France, had already arranged with the Allies to lead his corps through their lines and into Normandy, thus preventing a prolongation of the war by weakening Napoleon and placing an armed force at the disposal of the Provisional Government. Whereas the five *maréchaux* at Fontainebleau wanted to retain the Bonapartist regime, and simply replace Napoleon with his son as a necessary concession for peace, Marmont sought the more sweeping option of a change of dynasty. His actions were not treason, since the *Sénat* had already declared Napoleon's déthronement and a continuation of the campaign was not in France's interests. Yet they did constitute a personal betrayal by a man who had known Napoleon for two decades, had served as his ADC, and owed his advancement to him, and that is what caused such intense bitterness and controversy.[12]

Marmont had planned to defect on the evening of the 4th, but was pre-empted by Napoleon's abdication. With his plans thrown into confusion, Marmont joined Napoleon's emissaries when they passed through on their way to see Alexander in Paris. His subordinates were privy to his scheme, and in his absence they panicked and put it into action by marching his corps out of the French lines. In fact, the defection of Marmont and his generals, if not that of his troops, had become inevitable since he had committed himself in writing, which meant that his undertaking could have been published in the Parisian press to force his hand.

Napoleon's ability to negotiate depended on the existence of a united army capable of taking the offensive, but at a stroke Marmont had revealed the hollowness of his authority and deprived him of one-sixth of his troops. Stiffened by Talleyrand, Alexander now insisted on unconditional abdication.

No longer able to march on Paris, Napoleon decided to withdraw behind the Loire river, convinced that he could still continue a defensive war. But he no longer had the confidence of his corps commanders, and on the night of 5/6 April they resolved to take no further orders from him. It was the end. Next day Napoleon abdicated unconditionally. Many of the French troops reacted with anger and despair, but their commanders were the men who counted, and they left for Paris to rally to the monarchy. Napoleon's entourage, and that of the Empress, shrank as courtiers abandoned the dying government, just as desertion whittled away the army.[13] Marmont's desertion, therefore, was simply one of the first moves in a mass transfer of loyalties from a defeated and discredited regime to one that offered peace and the hope of a more prosperous future.

Under the Treaty of Fontainebleau (dated 11 April, but signed and ratified on the 12th), Napoleon renounced any right of sovereignty. In return, he was given an annual income from the French state and the island of Elba off the coast of Italy, which he would rule as a principality. It is said that Napoleon tried to poison himself in the early hours of the 13th, but such claims are, in fact, dubious. He may simply have fallen ill, or taken opium to calm an attack of nerves. In an atmosphere so tense and full of rumours, it was easy for this to be exaggerated into a suicide attempt.[14] What is certain is that his failure to find death on the battlefield, or end his life rather than survive his fall, caused widespread contempt. 'I confess, Nani, that the man has violently deceived me,' wrote Schwarzenberg to his wife. 'Only a fool could have predicted that Napoleon would creep into a mousehole.'[15] Napoleon was ridiculed by caricaturists, and condemned by *Maréchal* Augereau, who in rallying to the Bourbons stated scathingly that after sacrificing thousands of victims to his ambition, he 'did not know how to die as a soldier'.[16]

Such accusations of cowardice had to be countered, which explains why the story of Napoleon scorning the artillery fire at Montereau became so celebrated, and why accounts later circulated that he had sought death at Arcis-sur-Aube by riding his horse over a shell. Thirteen years after the campaign Louis de Bausset, the *préfet du palais*, claimed in his memoirs that Napoleon had actually told him on 11 April:

> You see what destiny is like! During the fighting at Arcis-sur-Aube, I did all I could to find a glorious death while disputing the soil of the fatherland step by step. I exposed myself carelessly. The musketballs rained around me, my clothes were riddled by them, and none of them could hit me.

Napoleon also rejected the idea that killing himself would have been an honourable end. Whereas death in battle would have been heroic, suicide was shameful, and a failed suicide even more so. 'If I died simply through an act of despair, it would be a cowardly deed,' Bausset recorded him as saying. 'Suicide does not suit either my beliefs, or the position that I have occupied on the world scene. . . . I am a man condemned to live.'[17] Another of Napoleon's close servants, Antoine Chamans, *comte* de Lavallette, asserted that the alleged incident at Fontainebleau, far from being a suicide bid, had been an assassination attempt using poison.[18]

Napoleon had vainly hoped to be reunited with his wife and son, but it became clear that this would not be permitted by his father-in-law, Emperor Franz. On 20 April he finally left Fontainebleau for exile, after bidding an emotional farewell to his Old Guard in a now-famous ceremony that has offset the controversy surrounding his survival.

Peace

On 6 April the *Sénat* had finally decided to summon the Bourbon pretender, Louis, to the throne, but it made his proclamation as king conditional on him accepting the constitution that it now decreed. In fact, Talleyrand would be outmanoeuvred, for rather than have a constitution imposed on him, Louis deftly granted a Charter of his own after returning to Paris on 3 May. The Restoration was still that of a constitutional, rather than absolute, monarchy, but the King ruled by right as Louis XVIII, and not by the choice of the people as Louis-Stanislas-Xavier de France.[19]

The Bourbon Restoration, and Napoleon's removal, eased the process of securing peace between France and the Allies, and a convention formally suspended hostilities on 23 April. The delay that now arose stemmed not from the French, for Louis XVIII had already accepted the principle of the former frontiers, but from disagreements between the Allies themselves. Austria and Prussia wanted issues such as the future of Poland to be settled before peace was signed with France, to ensure that Britain remained involved in, and France excluded from, the shaping of the general European settlement, as this would make it easier to contain Russian ambitions.

But since attempts to craft a comprehensive settlement foundered, a stand-alone peace had to be signed with France on 30 May. It was not punitive, for the Allies wanted a durable settlement, had publicly committed themselves to moderate terms during the campaign, and had no desire to undermine the Bourbons by associating them with national humiliation. France was reduced to her former frontiers, but with the addition of some enclaves and border adjustments, which increased her population by 650,000 inhabitants. She also retained some of her colonies and did not have to pay financial reparations.

Negotiations on the wider, European issues were left to a congress at Vienna, where discussions began in the autumn and continued into 1815. The twin issues of Poland and Saxony were eventually settled, but not before Austria's cautious strategy during the 1814 campaign had been justified by Prussia using the threat of war as a negotiating tactic.

In the spring of 1815 the peacemaking was thrown into chaos when Napoleon boldly escaped from exile and landed in France. He swiftly regained power, for the unrealistic expectations that accompanied the Restoration had given way to widespread disillusionment with the Bourbons as France adjusted to the realities of peace. Once again the European powers mobilised against him, but there was no repeat of the 1814 campaign. Rather than wait on the defensive in a still-devastated region, Napoleon invaded the United Netherlands in June, and was defeated so decisively at Waterloo on 18 June that he abdicated just four days later. The 'Hundred Days', as his brief return became known, were a mere appendix to the Napoleonic Wars and simply reaffirmed the outcome of 1814, except in so far as they increased British prestige and influence, destabilised France and the Bourbons for up to five years, and resulted in harsher peace terms.

Napoleon's final adventure had forced the Allies back together following their dissensions during the Congress of Vienna. In November 1815 Britain, Russia, Prussia, and Austria formally established the Quadruple Alliance, which they had outlined in the Treaty of Chaumont the previous year. It included an additional agreement to hold a regular series of congresses in order to maintain peace in Europe. This system of general security lapsed in the 1820s and was discredited as Alexander's ideal of a 'Holy Alliance' of Christian monarchs became associated with the repression of liberal and nationalist movements. Even so, it was not until 1854 that war once again broke out between the great powers.

The significance of the 1814 campaign lay not just in the downfall of Napoleon, but in the forging of a coalition that, however fractious, encompassed nearly all the important European powers and was ultimately successful. In defeating Napoleon, the Allies established new norms of international co-operation, involving a series of conferences and face-to-face meetings of monarchs and statesmen, and with the four great powers becoming used to thinking and acting on behalf of the whole of Europe. In fact, the campaigns of 1813–1814 were the most intense phase in the emergence since the end of the Seven Years' War in 1763 of a new European order based not on the single-minded pursuit of dynastic self-interest, as exemplified in its most extreme form by Napoleon, but on the quest for international peace and stability. The attitudes and habits forged during the overthrow of Napoleon proved equally effective in securing the peace.[20]

Part Three
Analysis

Chapter 14

Napoleon's finest campaign?

'History will record this campaign around Paris as the most audacious and skilful that has ever been made,' claimed Louis de Bausset, Napoleon's *préfet du palais*.[1] In military terms it was a masterpiece of speed, flexibility, and improvisation, as Napoleon exploited a central position to inflict repeated defeats on two separate armies, and used sweeping, outflanking moves to threaten their lines of communication. Even opponents saw it as his finest campaign.[2]

'He has never shown himself greater'

The struggle has often been compared to that of 1796 in northern Italy, Napoleon's first campaign as an army commander. According to his stepdaughter, he himself made the comparison, soon after the Allied invasion began, by telling his *major-général*: 'Come, Berthier, . . . we must begin the campaign of Italy again'.[3]

On both occasions he commanded a small army, which enabled him to wage a mobile war and exercise a high degree of personal leadership. Yet the comparison with

A captured Allied cuirassier is brought in by peasants for questioning.

1796 actually underrates the more daunting scale and complexity of the situation Napoleon faced in 1814. As well as commanding his army in Champagne, he had to co-ordinate simultaneous operations in multiple secondary theatres, some of which were 500 or 600 miles apart, and mobilise support from a collapsing and near-bankrupt empire. His challenge was never simply a military one, and throughout the campaign he had paperwork brought to him from Paris every week so he could continue to govern his Empire.[4]

It actually makes more sense to see 1814 not as a repeat of 1796, but as a new phase of the struggle to control central Europe in 1813. During that year the Allies had evolved a strategy of avoiding battle with Napoleon in person, thereby forcing him to march backwards and forwards to meet a succession of threats. In doing so they wore down his army and forced him to switch to the defensive behind the Elbe river. This resulted in disaster, for the Allies then seized the initiative, turned his flanks, and closed in on him around Leipzig.

In 1814 Napoleon was more successful at countering the Allied strategy. Lieutenant-General the Hon. Sir Charles Stewart, the British minister to Prussia, emphasised the difference, without grasping the underlying cause, when he wrote on 22 March:

> For myself, I rather like Bonaparte the better for being another Catiline, and the masterly military movements he has of late made, with an inferior army against two armies both superior, must increase his military reputation.
>
> I think he has never shown himself greater, or played a more desperate game more skilfully, than since the battle of Brienne. Before that, I thought he had lost all wits. On the Elbe he was quite insane, and his lengthened stay there was the cause of the battle of Leipsig and all his subsequent misfortunes.[5]

One reason for this change was that the Allies had now become too disunited politically to implement their military strategy effectively: the *Hauptarmee* did not press forward vigorously whenever Napoleon marched against the *Schlesische Armee*. Furthermore, Napoleon had more freedom of manoeuvre in 1814, for he generally had just 30,000 or 50,000 men on a battlefield, barely a third or a quarter the size of his massive forces of the year before. The campaign area itself was at least five times smaller, which made it possible to maintain a high tempo of operations. The distance between the Marne and Seine was only about 40 miles, whereas in the autumn of 1813 Napoleon had to guard the entire length of the Elbe from the North Sea to the Austrian border, a direct distance of 230 miles, and conducted his main operations over a swathe of territory more than 27,000 square miles in extent.[6] In addition, his main base, Dresden, was too near the mountains further south for him to have a real chance of trapping Schwarzenberg's army, whereas in 1814 the configuration of the campaign area enabled him to surprise his opponents piecemeal and threaten their lines of communication.

In short, despite commanding a smaller army in 1814, Napoleon was in a stronger operational situation. He was able to wage a relentlessly active and aggressive defence that boosted the morale of his troops following their dispiriting retreat from the Rhine. He defied the coalition for two months by exploiting both its internal divisions and his three other key advantages: superior mobility, intelligence, and logistics.

Mobility

Significantly, Napoleon fought only one purely defensive battle in 1814, when it was forced on him at La Rothière.[7] Speed, manoeuvre, and unrelenting activity lay at the heart of his campaign. During the sixty-five days between his departure from Paris on 25 January and his arrival at Fontainebleau early on 31 March, Napoleon moved his quarters forty-eight times, or an average of five times a week. He sometimes returned to previous locations but never stayed in the same place for more than four consecutive nights, and his quarters therefore occupied as many as forty-two different places.[8]

Napoleon tended to stay in *châteaux*, in bishop's palaces, with the *maire*, *curé*, or other local notable, in relay houses, or in large residences. He stayed only twice in isolated farms in the countryside, as a default option, and never spent the night in a bivouac, partly because of the cold, although his tent might be erected for temporary halts during the day.[9]

Choosing a *château* or another large building as a residence was sensible, as it offered convenience as well as comfort. Small, isolated peasant huts could not accommodate large personal retinues, whereas large quarters in towns generally offered more than one escape route in an emergency, and enabled Napoleon to receive Allied emissaries or local dignitaries in suitably prestigious surroundings. (The charge of '*château* generalship', which has been flung so wantonly against British commanders in the First World War, ignores the precedent set by great captains like Napoleon, and the practical reasons for choosing such accommodation.)

Some *châteaux* offered a good bed, excellent wine, and beautiful grounds, and made it possible to forget the exhaustion and deprivations of the campaign. It also helped that Napoleon received frequent letters from Marie-Louise, containing not just news of the situation in Paris, but amusing anecdotes about their son, the King of Rome. She described how, in his games, the 2-year-old was always taking flags and prisoners from the Russians, and was particularly hostile to Blücher: 'he does not like him much, for he talks every day of killing him'.[10]

Other of Napoleon's quarters were depressing, uncomfortable, and overcrowded. Corpses had to be removed from the farm of Les Grenaux before he could sleep there after the Battle of Montmirail. *Chef de bataillon* Jean Girod de l'Ain described how:

> The day had been so exhausting that, apart from the sentries who kept watch outside this farm, everyone both indoors and out was fast asleep.... After crossing a large courtyard, which was covered with dung and obstructed by men and horses lying higgledy-piggedly, I entered a small, ground-floor room lit by candles on a small table.
>
> Maps were spread out on the table, and even the floor. Sleeping on the ground, more or less across the doorway, was a man whom I recognised as the Emperor's loyal *mameluck*, while at the end of the room were a small alcove and a bed on which the Emperor himself was lying fully dressed. I remained for a good while, contemplating this fascinating scene, and then withdrew very quietly so as not to wake anyone.[11]

The staircase and the rooms upstairs were crammed with slumbering men, even though the *grand quartier-général*, or army headquarters, as distinct from Napoleon's personal household, occupied a separate farm at La Haute Epine, 2 miles further west.

Security could be a challenge, especially after a battle. At Château-Thierry six Prussian fugitives were found in the relay inn where Napoleon took up his quarters on 13 February, while a seventh remained hidden in the linen attic throughout his stay. Sometimes the more enthusiastic of the local inhabitants could be a nuisance. At Arcis-sur-Aube on 20 March Napoleon established his headquarters at the *Château* de La Briffe. The gardener's young son entered the *château* grounds with two friends and climbed up to the terrace at the rear, where the Old Guard sentries ignored them.

Soon afterwards Napoleon emerged with a group of officers, and the three boys immediately began cheering *Vive l'empereur!* Napoleon looked up from his map, smiled and gave a gesture of acknowledgement. They cheered again, but this time Napoleon did not seem to notice, and the sentries signalled to make them shut up.[12]

During his two months in the field Napoleon covered at least 1,100 miles, or the equivalent of travelling right through the United States from the Canadian border to Mexico.[13] Yet he covered 85 per cent of that distance within the restricted region between the Seine and the Marne, a zone no bigger than Connecticut, the third smallest US state, and a plot of all his movements reveals how intensively he criss-crossed this tiny belt of land.[14]

When he was moving with his army, Napoleon personally covered an average of 17 miles a day, an impressive achievement given the state of the roads and the need to fight actions.[15] Such relentless mobility explains how he repeatedly surprised the Allies and dominated the campaign right into the second fortnight of March. In the same sixty-five day period his two opponents each travelled only half the distance. Blücher moved his headquarters thirty-nine times, nine fewer than Napoleon, between just twenty-seven different places, and remained at Laon for one-and-a-half weeks after collapsing in the middle of March. Schwarzenberg transferred his headquarters a mere twenty-five times, occupied twenty-one different locations, and spent more than half the campaign at just four towns.[16]

Napoleon's sheer activity left the Allies dazed and disorganised, for he moved too fast for them to react. Superior intelligence, the smaller size of his army and logistical tail, the experience and initiative of his subordinates, and the enhanced flexibility of his command and control structure gave him a quicker decision-making loop than those of the Allies. He was able to observe a situation, orient himself, make a decision, and put it into action before his opponents. His dominance was enhanced by the speed with which he moved, which transformed the situation even before his opponents had reacted to his previous punch, and left them bewildered, unable to predict his moves, and overawed by forces less than half the size of their own. One of Blücher's corps commanders, General Langeron, frankly admitted:

> We could not agree anything, for once a plan had been decided or proposed, it was soon foiled by Napoleon. Everyone acted according to circumstances and tried to guess the actions and locations of his ally and enemy. Also, for I have to be honest, the terrible Napoleon had beaten us one after the other in eleven days by the inconceivable boldness and bustle of his moves, just when we had thought that it was all over with him and that he was powerless to offer us the least resistance. He had very disconcerted us, to say the least, and we seemed to see him everywhere.[17]

Napoleon's campaign was an outstanding example of the manoeuvrist approach: the ruthless use of mobility, deception, and the constant searching out of weak points to confuse, intimidate, and paralyse opponents. Momentum, not numbers, was what mattered, for Napoleon was able to magnify his apparent strength through speed, surprise, and sheer moral force. Audacity undermined the nerves of opposing commanders. Determination drove his army forward despite all the difficulties of terrain, weather, and fatigue. Even when he misread a situation, as happened at Arcis-sur-Aube, he was able to escape the consequences because his confidence, reputation, and aggressive attitude kept his opponents disheartened.

But success depended not simply on psychological tricks or brazen propaganda. Napoleon needed a decisive military victory, and it was the quest to fight battles on advantageous terms that shaped his moves. His skill lay in using speed and surprise to negate the Allied advantage of numbers, so that the outcome of an action was decided more by the strategic moves beforehand than by the actual combat. The secret, Napoleon later explained, was to concentrate superior numbers of troops on a battlefield, despite being inferior in the theatre of war as a whole. 'This is what I did in Italy, in my first campaign, and in 1814, in my last.'[18]

At Champaubert, Mormant, and Montereau he enjoyed a crushing numerical superiority, but elsewhere it was enough to achieve a local superiority at the critical point of a battlefield, or in a key arm. At Vauchamps he had only a small, overall advantage of numbers but, crucially, was superior in cavalry and available artillery. At Montmirail he built up his forces more quickly on the battlefield than the Allies and was able to overwhelm Sacken's outnumbered corps with a carefully co-ordinated succession of assaults focused at key points, before it could be properly supported by Yorck.

Even so, hard fighting was required on most battlefields, and even a victory as impressive as Montmirail cost Napoleon 10 per cent of the forces he had present. Outflanking moves on a battlefield were not always possible, and even when they were, Napoleon combined them with frontal assaults and artillery fire to pin down an opponent and obtain a quicker outcome. In any case, the uneven quality of his troops limited his ability to carry out complex deployments on a battlefield. It was easier to manoeuvre spectacularly on the operational level, where the experience and responsiveness of the senior command structure was more significant than the state of training of the troops. On a battlefield Napoleon was particularly reliant on his Old Guardsmen, who had the necessary toughness, reputation, and tactical proficiency to spearhead the crucial, breakthrough attacks.

Some battles fell apart, notably Brienne and Craonne, where the need for haste or the impatience of subordinates caused co-ordination to break down, leading to imprecise, piecemeal assaults, and a bloody and indecisive outcome. But it was not tactical failings on the battlefield that inflicted Napoleon's most serious setbacks. Every one of his defeats – La Rothière, Laon, and Arcis-sur-Aube – was caused by a strategic manoeuvre that miscarried, leaving him outnumbered and confronted by an army that was already united. Only by surprising a scattered enemy could Napoleon hope for victory, and whenever he failed to move fast enough, he found his chances of winning had evaporated even before the start of the battle.

Schwarzenberg's much-criticised hesitations and counter-orders become understandable in this context, as he first extended his army to avoid surprise by guarding against attack from any direction, and then concentrated it again so he could counter Napoleon's thrusts with a defence in depth, and thus prevent a breakthrough that would dislocate his army. He was right to rely on weight of numbers, since his ponderous and loosely assembled coalition army was not suited to manoeuvre or fast-moving battles. Most of its momentum was due to its mass, which meant that it could not react easily to changing circumstances.

With his smaller and more mobile army, Napoleon was able to do the unexpected by using roads that the Allies had assumed were impracticable. In carrying out these manoeuvres he did not even have to move his entire force, since from mid-February, when he adopted a central position between Blücher and Schwarzenberg, he posted covering detachments permanently in the Marne and Seine sectors to cover the main routes to Paris.[19] Thus, Mortier and Marmont remained on the Marne to contain the *Schlesische Armee*, while Oudinot, Macdonald, and the II Corps (initially commanded by Victor) stayed on the Seine to check the *Hauptarmee*. These detached subordinates became familiar with both the geography of their particular sector and the army opposed to them.

Whenever one of these covering forces was threatened by an Allied army, Napoleon was able to march to its aid with a mobile reserve and suddenly gain a local superiority of numbers. Three-quarters of this reserve consisted of Imperial Guard units, and its core was the 1st Old Guard Division, whose 4,000 or 5,000 veterans could quickly cover long distances without shedding large numbers of stragglers.[20] Maréchal Ney, who commanded a Young Guard corps, always formed part of the mobile reserve, for he was a superb combat leader who was better employed under Napoleon's direct supervision than in a detached command where his flaws would be more obvious and where he would see less action. As much as one-third of the mobile reserve consisted of cavalry, and it generally included all three of the Imperial Guard's cavalry divisions.

Napoleon enhanced the mobility of his Old Guard infantry with requisitioned horse-drawn carts. In previous campaigns he had used this so-called *transport en poste* strategically, to whisk units across France for the start of a campaign. In 1814 he exploited it for operational moves actually within the area of hostilities, and even to rush bakers or supplies of shoes to the army from Paris.[21]

Napoleon was unfortunate in his lack of a mobile pontoon train. He also had to compromise between mobility and firepower. When he first took the field he planned to rely heavily on his guns to compensate for the inexperience of his conscripts. 'We will be able to crush the enemy with an immense superiority of artillery,' he wrote on 26 January. 'I am thinking of having 300 pieces in action tomorrow.'[22]

But as the campaign unfolded he did not always have sufficiently good roads available for a mass of heavy guns. His solution was to leave most of his reserve artillery behind whenever he moved north against Blücher along transverse roads, but to collect it again when he returned south for an attack on Schwarzenberg. The reserve artillery would withdraw for safety towards Paris during his absence, but then come forward again in time to join him for his renewed offensive.[23]

Even with this compromise Napoleon managed to deploy a massed battery of 36 guns at Vauchamps, 32 at Mormant, 72 at Craonne.[24] His artillery was particularly effective at Vauchamps, where Blücher could not deploy many guns during his retreat without exposing them to capture, but it never proved decisive. When the Allies managed to field a high proportion of cannon, as at Craonne, Napoleon was unlikely to win more than a bloody and barren victory. Similarly, the terrain at Arcis-sur-Aube worked against him, as it obliged his reserve artillery to fire outwards and upwards at the concave Allied front, rather than inwards for maximum effect.

To enhance his mobility still further Napoleon also left behind in the Seine sector the army's cumbersome main park, the administrative headquarters, and most of his *Maison*, or personal household, under the escort of a Young Guard division. This eased the army's logistics as well as its mobility, since these elements contained a large number of horses. Only a small, tactical headquarters accompanied Napoleon in the field.[25]

Intelligence

The Allies were at a distinct disadvantage in that they lacked Napoleon's detailed knowledge of the theatre of war, and the sources of local intelligence available to him in his own country. During the Battle of Brienne he was guided by *père* Hanriot, who had actually taught him during his schooldays at the town thirty years earlier. At

Craonne it was a local *maire*, David Belly de Bussy, who provided advice: he was a former comrade from Napoleon's time in the *Régiment de La Fère* as a young officer.[26]

Napoleon also had the support of the civilian administrative machine. Both the *Ministre de la police générale* and the *préfets* of unoccupied *départements* sent out agents to the towns held by the Allies to gather intelligence and distribute propaganda.[27] Information could also be obtained by questioning postal couriers and drivers of public transport about what they had seen or heard on the road. Peasants could move about the campaign theatre, and indeed the Allies lacked enough troops to be able to prevent civilian movements altogether. Passports were withheld from vagabonds and disreputable people, but the countryside was crossed by numerous paths that, although unsuitable for an army, were ideal for individual pedlars, smugglers, and agents who wanted to avoid detection.[28]

But the dislocation produced by the invasion hindered attempts to form a clear idea of what was happening. Officials blamed each other, made vague reports, and withdrew too hurriedly in the face of the Allied advance.[29] As the *Ministre de la police générale* complained on 16 February:

> I have much trouble with the *préfets* of the invaded *départements*, who have not preserved a single means of receiving news from their *préfecture*, even though I had previously recommended this to them. They regard it as beneath them.[30]

The value of locally procured information varied. After reaching Arcis-sur-Aube on 20 March Napoleon questioned an *adjoint*, Pierre Finot, and learned that the *Hauptarmee* had between 100,000 and 120,000 men. Finot had noticed a situation report when Schwarzenberg's headquarters had been at the town just two days earlier. Napoleon pretended to dismiss the news – 'you misread' – but was able to gain insights into Schwarzenberg's mindset by asking what he had said about the French army, whether he had believed he had superior numbers, and what the Allies had thought about the Châtillon negotiations.[31]

Yet few civilians had enough training or experience to assess numbers and types of troops, or to give reliable reports. Napoleon's secretary, *baron* Fain, remembered the exuberance at Château-Thierry when the town was freed from occupation in February:

> This general emotion had its effect on the accounts that were given to Napoleon, which were very exaggerated. Ignorance of German, and of the enemy's distinctive insignia of rank, added to the misunderstandings. Everyone, in witnessing the rout on the bridge, also saw the total destruction of the Allies. Everyone, in listing the killed and wounded, innocently made captains into colonels, and colonels into generals, while whoever had housed a wounded general had no hesitation in believing, as his servants confirmed, that it was the commander-in-chief.[32]

It was difficult to sift wild rumours from facts, as *Général de division* Hippolyte, *baron* de Piré found when he reported from Chaumont on 26 March:

> All the inhabitants agree that, forty-eight hours ago, the officers of the Allied troops received important news that threw them into consternation and despair. They all stick to their view that it was the death of the Emperor Alexander. Some think that he has been assassinated, others that he has lost both legs to a cannonball. It is possible that this assumption is inaccurate, but the reports are unanimous about the distress that they witnessed.[33]

To avoid such problems, Napoleon sometimes used *gendarmes* disguised as peasants to act as couriers or spies. He also sought to avoid being reliant on a single source of intelligence by instructing agents to be sent out from both the *Ministère de la guerre* and the *Ministère de la police générale*. He complained that the police were supplying false information because they were too easily alarmed, and were failing to confirm whether the statements obtained during questionings were true. He added that he had given the police a printed interrogation manual designed as a safeguard against such errors, and wanted all their agents to have copies of it.[34]

The Allies faced even more acute frustrations, and often lacked news about their own forces, let alone those of the French. Colonel Hudson Lowe, writing from Blücher's headquarters on 11 March, noted that scarcely any information had been received about the *Hauptarmee*'s movements since the end of February. The intelligence imbalance was particularly obvious in the cautious handling of most of the Allied cavalry, and in the difficulty their armies had in achieving surprise as a result of the inhabitants alerting French troops to their moves.[35]

The Allies drew some benefit from civilian movements, and were able to obtain information from travellers about morale in Paris, Napoleon's defensive preparations, and the locations of his troops. Some local people actively spied for the Allies or guided their columns, and the French government was particularly concerned about immigrants. The *préfet* of the Seine-et-Marne was ordered to have all foreigners in his *département* interrogated, while the authorities at Lyon had German fabric workers placed under surveillance.[36]

In the middle of January the *préfet* of the Aube urged the *maire* of Troyes to redouble precautions against the intrigues of people who might be sent by the Allies to reconnoitre his city. He instructed him to have patrols make frequent visits to all the landlords and innkeepers, but effective surveillance was difficult in such an overcrowded city, especially with the constant turnover of new faces as French troops came and went.[37]

Some Allied spies were ideological opponents of Napoleon's regime, but others were motivated by money rather than idealism. The commander of a Cossack detachment, Major-General Prince Alexander Fedorovich Scherbatov, reported to Schwarzenberg from near Epinal on 10 January: 'I believe I can find as many spies in future as I have found here. However, I must have money, something that I completely lack, and which Your Highness was good enough to promise me.'[38]

Many inhabitants were too afraid of retribution from Napoleon to be swayed by the money on offer. Others would not serve the Allies because of patriotic or Bonapartist loyalties, including the *commandant* of the town of Vaucouleurs, who refused to provide French passes for the *Schlesische Armee*'s spies. He was arrested and threatened with deportation to Russia, but released once Blücher learned of his mistreatment.[39]

In any case, civilians often supplied inaccurate or outdated rumours and reports, perhaps deliberately. 'Since the spies give false news all the time, even when you pay them well, I have to obtain the information we need myself,' grumbled the commander of a flying corps on 10 January.[40] Sometimes the Allies had to resort to using their own soldiers disguised as civilians.[41] Nor did it help that their outposts routinely allowed the French to break contact, or that most of their flying corps failed to act as aggressively as they might have done.

Hence, the Allies were particularly dependent on other sources of intelligence, including interrogations of French prisoners and deserters. Under the Geneva Convention prisoners-of-war are now required to give only their name, rank, service number, and date of birth. Yet in 1814 even officers as senior as colonels sometimes provided useful intelligence under interrogation.[42]

Napoleon often questioned prisoners personally, and did so with skill and persistence. After the Battle of Champaubert he asked Major-General Constantine Markovich Poltoratsky how many Russian troops had been present, the strength of their Guards and their army, and the location of Alexander, but Poltoratsky replied that he did not know.

Napoleon put pressure on him: 'I wanted to speak openly with you, but your replies, "I do not know", prove that you do not want to talk to me.'

When Poltoratsky pointed out that honour would prevent him revealing anything about his army, Napoleon switched to flattery: 'Tell me, please. Why does your Emperor always use his fine troops, and not the German salad dressing that I would have annihilated in half-an-hour, whilst against you I have been obliged to fight for an entire day?'

Alexander, came the reply, used his troops as he saw fit, and would be strictly obeyed.

'So you do not want to talk to me openly?' Napoleon countered in a renewed attempt to break down his resistance. Poltoratsky repeated that honour forbade him to answer, but Napoleon remarked that a brave officer always spoke his mind. He then insulted Blücher by calling him a drunkard, so as to make Poltoratsky feel let down by his own army commander, and closed the interview with a show of confidence by boasting of his strength: 'Fifty thousand men, and myself at their head, that makes 150,000!'[43]

Letters were intercepted throughout the campaign by both sides, and it was captured French despatches that alerted Blücher at the end of January to the fact that Napoleon was descending on him at Brienne. Yet the *Hauptarmee* was generally slow in forwarding intercepted messages to its headquarters. Two letters, captured on 8 January, were sent to Schwarzenberg only on the 12th and 13th.[44] Napoleon repeatedly warned subordinates to encipher key despatches, but it was ironic that the capture on 22 March of his own unciphered letter to Marie-Louise helped reveal his plans and persuade the Allies to march on Paris.

Newspapers made available a surprising amount of information about numbers and locations of troops and the identities of their commanders. On 26 January *Le Moniteur* announced that Napoleon had left Paris the previous morning to take personal command of his army, even though he had written three days earlier to one of his generals at Châlons-sur-Marne: 'Keep the news of my arrival secret. Don't run any risks with your despatches, lest anything is captured and my arrival suspected.'[45] Napoleon was usually careful to avoid releasing valuable information, but occasionally did so inadvertently. In the afternoon of 8 February, he wrote to Joseph:

> I have sent the Empress a notice for *Le Moniteur*. If you receive this letter before 0500, and if the insertion of this article can be delayed, I want you to do so for forty-eight hours, because the enemy would learn of my position and plans too early, and that is always disadvantageous.[46]

Commanders actively sought out information from newspapers, but because of the time delay could make little tactical use of what they learned, however useful it may have been in building up an overall strategic picture.[47] It generally took at least two days for news of a battle to appear in the Parisian newspapers. Nor could all the information be trusted. Napoleon routinely tried to deceive the Allies, particularly about his strength, his personal presence, and the ability of Paris to defend itself.[48] Before leaving Troyes in pursuit of Blücher on 27 February, he gave orders for the troops left behind on the Aube to cheer *Vive l'empereur!* in order to make it seem he was still there.[49]

The Allies' difficulties were compounded by their dearth of good maps, which helps to explain the uninspired handling of their flying corps.[50] At the Battle of Paris Yorck and Kleist had to reconnoitre the ground in person since they lacked any accurate maps, and they saw three members of their staff hit by French fire in the process.[51]

Obtaining maps in French towns was one solution. At Dijon the Austrians requisitioned them from the shops and municipal library. Similarly, within two days of occupying Lyon they published notices requiring the inhabitants to surrender their weapons and maps. Some French commanders sought to deprive the Allies of such sources. When *Maréchal* Macdonald retreated down the Marne valley at the beginning of February, he instructed all the maps in and around Epernay to be burned. Despite this, Yorck's advanced guard managed to obtain an excellent map from an inhabitant of the town.[52]

Some of the most sought-after maps were those of César Cassini de Thury. He was the man responsible for methodically surveying the whole of France to produce the country's first complete detailed map. Drawn on a scale of 1 to 86,400, it showed roads, rivers, woods, and marshes, as well as towns, villages, and even some individual farms. But only a few hundred copies of each sheet had been printed, and so it was expensive and difficult to obtain.[53] At the beginning of February Ney's *chef d'état-major* had to write to the *sous-préfet* at Nogent-sur-Seine:

> The *Maréchal prince de la* Moskowa does not have here, in his collection of Cassini maps, that of Paris. His Excellency directs me to ask if you can give him the one of this *département*: he really needs it, and is unable to obtain it except by applying to you.[54]

A map of Champagne was sent just quarter of an hour after the request was received.[55]

Yet even Cassini's map could be misleading, for the first sheet, showing the region around Paris, was published in 1750, and the rest followed over the course of nearly seventy years. A more recent map, by Louis Capitaine and Pierre de Belleyme, had been produced in 1800, but was less detailed, being on a scale of 1 to 350,000. In any case, many minor roads were mere tracks that defied recording since they were prone to shift or even vanish, while the accuracy of placenames depended on the reliability of local advice. According to Cassini's map, a road ran all the way from Château-Thierry to Montmirail, but in reality the southernmost section became all but impassable during the winter. Moreover, Cassini's sheets gave only a primitive indication of the hills and valleys.[56]

This was why reconnaissances and local guides were so important, and why Napoleon carefully questioned the officers who brought him despatches, and complained when those sent to him from Paris were not educated or intelligent enough to give full and accurate answers.[57]

At Paris a section of a fortifications committee of engineer officers studied the campaign area before the fighting there began, sent out reconnaissances, and advised on the best positions. While operations were in progress, Napoleon's ADCs and *officiers d'ordonnance* who were sent on a mission not only reported on the situation but made recommendations.[58] Napoleon did not, therefore, devise his much-admired operational moves on his own, although he did supply the boldness and resolve needed to carry them out.

Nor did Napoleon make the mistake of relying too heavily on intelligence. An obsession with finding out exact details before making a move would have risked losing the initiative, being misled by counter-intelligence, or over-awed by the actual numerical odds. He was comfortable operating within a degree of uncertainty and exploiting a chaotic situation, instead of seeking to resolve all the contradictions in reports before taking action. In fact he repeatedly misjudged the situation through over-confidence.

Logistics

Logistics have rarely received the high profile they deserve in campaign histories, yet regular supplies were the most effective means of keeping an army together. 'My troops have no bread or rations,' protested the commander of one of Napoleon's cavalry corps at the beginning of February:

> The men are worn down by their duties and complain that they have nothing to eat in France. I request supplies for them as for the infantry. It is the real way to conserve our soldiers' energy and to prevent them from deserting.[59]

It is often alleged that Napoleon neglected logistics and simply made his armies live off the land in the interests of greater mobility. In fact, until the era of mechanised road transport, all armies had to live through a combination of organised supplies and local scavenging or requisitioning. When he invaded Russia, Napoleon actually made painstaking logistical preparations, but knew that there was a physical limit to what his army could take with it.[60]

The challenge in 1814 was not so much finding supplies, since too much food sometimes accumulated at specific locations. The real difficulty lay in transporting stocks over inadequate roads in the middle of winter, using carts pulled by animals that themselves required feeding. When Napoleon joined his field army at Châlons-sur-Marne on 25 January, he had available only 2,500 local vehicles, instead of the 4,000 he needed to supplement the army's transport and distribute its supplies. Even when enough transport was at hand, it increased the congestion and degraded the roads still further. On 4 February, for example, the *intendant général* reported that he was sending as many as 500 sheep, 157 bullocks, and a large convoy of bread, rice, and brandy from Sézanne to Nogent-sur-Seine.[61]

Military *commandants* had to be appointed for towns to supervise the circulation of convoys and avoid delays, but inevitably supplies were lost *en route* through theft, accidents, the difficulty of keeping convoys united, and the negligence of the escorts. Moving supplies by boat eased the pressure on the roads, but the navigable rivers offered access to only some of the towns in the campaign area.[62]

The problem of transport was all the more reason for Napoleon to fight a mobile campaign, in order to avoid burdening a single district for too long. In addition, he ordered military ovens to be built at towns, so that bread could be baked locally for his army instead of being brought from afar. Yet the ovens could take a week to be built and prepared for use, and only if materials and experienced workers were available. In the absence of military ovens, ordinary ones belonging to the inhabitants could be used, but they lacked capacity.[63]

Paris was Napoleon's main supply base, but had only a limited amount of spare transport and required food for its own massive population. When it was decided to requisition the carts in the city's markets in order to send supplies to Meaux, the *préfet de police* described how:

> I had to dash to the *Ministre de l'administration de la guerre*, and tell him that if these carts were not quickly sent back, or if a similar order was issued again, he should expect to see the capital's supplies fail within a week, because the country people would certainly not risk sending their horses or carts there any more.[64]

Similarly, at the beginning of March, when orders were issued for sixty-four bakers to be requisitioned in the capital and sent to Meaux to help feed the army, only forty-eight could be found. They were so discontented that the *préfet de police* feared they would try to escape on the way, for they were escorted by only three *gendarmes*. He added that repeating the step would compromise the baking of bread in Paris, at a time when any failure in the supply could endanger public order.[65]

As it was, shortages in the poorer quarters became pronounced. By 7 February the price of potatoes was causing widespread resentment directed at the wealthier classes.[66] A month later the *préfet de police* reported: 'The destitution in the suburbs, especially in the *faubourg* St Antoine, begins to be felt in the most painful way. The people express themselves very bitterly about it, and ardently long for peace as the only remedy to their misfortunes.'[67]

Gneisenau believed that the Allies could simply starve Paris into surrender by intercepting its supplies. Occupying the strategically sited town of Moret-sur-Loing, 40 miles south-east of the city, would, he thought, block the arrival of food along the Loing canal, and the Seine, Aube, and Yonne rivers.[68]

In fact, Paris drew food along too many routes, and from too extensive a hinterland, to be quickly starved in this way, and the proportion of food brought to the city by river as opposed to road had long been declining. Even so, a partial interdiction could have increased food prices enough to provoke civil disorder, and this was one reason why Napoleon deployed a cordon of troops under *Général de division* Pajol south of the Seine to protect his capital's communications with southern France. During the entire campaign Moret was occupied by the *Hauptarmee* for only four days.[69]

Napoleon's dependence on Paris made him vulnerable. The Allies had a more diffuse base, and three separate lines of communication: that of the *Hauptarmee* running south-eastwards to Basel; that of the *Schlesische Armee* heading eastwards to Nancy and the Rhine; and that of the detached corps from the *Nordarmee* extending northwards to Belgium. When Napoleon manoeuvred in their rear at the end of March, the Allies simply abandoned their communications from the Rhine, and relied on those from Belgium.

Napoleon did have the advantage of shorter supply lines, since his distance from Paris was just two-fifths that of the Allies from the Rhine. Moreover, despite being tied operationally to the capital, he had more flexible communications at the tactical level. By establishing a network of supply dumps, he could repeatedly switch his centre of operations from town to town.[70]

Initially, Napoleon's line of communications ran from Paris along the Marne valley to Châlons, his main supply base, and then followed his advance through Saint-Dizier. But it became too long and exposed after he pursued Blücher to Brienne in the south-west at the end of January. He hence switched to a more direct route, running from the army north-westwards through Sézanne to Epernay on the Marne.[71]

Sézanne was now to be the main supply base, for it was a road hub right at the centre of the campaign area.⁷² Yet it turned out to be unsuitable, for as the *intendant général* pointed out to Napoleon on 3 February:

> Sézanne offers only very feeble resources for the establishments [you] order me to form there. There is just one church, and no magazine. The town, moreover, has no communication, except that with Meaux through Coulommiers. All the others are impracticable when it rains, especially those to Arcis and Brienne.⁷³

Within days Sézanne would also become threatened by Blücher's advance on Paris. Napoleon therefore shifted his supply base to Nogent, 19 miles to the south-west, a safer location linked to Paris by both the Seine and a good road. Thereafter, Napoleon switched his lines of communication to fit his movements, and exploited the magazines he had established in towns dotted around his rear.

The existence of these logistic nodes was essential, particular in barren regions that had already been exhausted. 'If I was obliged to fall back from Troyes on Nogent', wrote Napoleon on 22 February, 'and if these magazines were not formed, the army would die of hunger and all would be lost. . . . We are in danger of not knowing how to survive, for the whole country from [Nogent] to Troyes has been devastated and in any case the soil is not very fertile.'⁷⁴

Yet magazines alone were insufficient to keep the army fed, not least because of the problem of transportation. As a result, units often had to requisition directly from local villages, or simply loot what they needed. *Général de brigade* Ségur explained how:

> While defending the country, our soldiers had no choice but to live off it. They had not been paid for more than a month, and no rations could be distributed during such rapid movements, so they took what they needed where they could, without asking and without any opposition, for necessity took full priority and authorised everything. Our soldiers told themselves, as consolation for contributing to this spoliation, that it was as much a question of taking from the enemy, since he might return.⁷⁵

As in gathering intelligence, Napoleon relied heavily on the local administrative authorities. The *préfet* of the Seine-et-Marne, for instance, was ordered to leave his *chef-lieu*, Melun, and move to Provins, 30 miles nearer the army, so he was in a better position to supply the troops.⁷⁶

Eventually, requisitioning would exhaust a region and drain support for Napoleon. Inhabitants received inadequate indemnities for supplies, which made them even more reluctant to pay their taxes and all the keener to sell their livestock for whatever price they could secure, rather than wait for it to be taken away by the army.

Shoes were a particular problem. The army's demands increased, both because of the arrival of fresh conscripts and because of the ease with which soldiers lost their footwear in the mud.⁷⁷ The *intendant général* informed Napoleon on 30 January that he had been unable to obtain any by making contracts at Reims, Epernay, Châlons, or Troyes. Entrepreneurs were reluctant to risk collecting supplies of raw materials, let alone begin work, because the military situation was so uncertain. Nor could shoes always be requisitioned from inhabitants, since many of the peasants wore clogs, and some troops ended up following their example.⁷⁸

The *intendant général* had no choice but to ask for 40,000 pairs of shoes to be sent from Paris.⁷⁹ Yet by early March even the capital's resources in clothes and equipment were becoming exhausted. Panic caused by the approach of the Allied armies in the middle of February had contributed to the problem, since shops had been closed, goods packed up, and the arrival of fabric from the interior of France interrupted. Suppliers had lost confidence in the government, and would accept only cash payments.[80] 'There was very little urgency among the entrepreneurs,' recalled the *préfet de police*:

> Almost none of them came forward and it was necessary to share the number of shoes and tunics that had to be provided among all the city's cobblers and tailors. This . . . was all the more tiresome since the results were not always satisfactory. When supplies were forthcoming at all, they were too often of wretched quality.[81]

By the end of March, therefore, logistics had become yet another compelling reason for Napoleon to transfer the campaign eastwards and gamble the outcome on a *manoeuvre sur les derrières*. He simply did not have the resources to sustain what was becoming no more than an attritional struggle.

Chapter 15

A protracted, attritional struggle?

Stunning though Napoleon's individual manoeuvres may have been, the campaign as a whole became a bloody, protracted, and indecisive struggle. The scale of his losses has never been fully realised. Nineteen of his *colonels* lost their lives, almost twice as many as had fallen in the 1805 campaign, and at least one-third of those lost in Russia in 1812.[1] Even his victories undermined Napoleon, for they bled and wore down his army at an unsustainable rate, drove the coalition partners together and induced them to agree their war aims.

Coalition warfare

The campaigns of 1813–1814 were an experiment in coalition warfare, and it took time and setbacks for the Allied leaders to understand the evolving situation and formulate a coherent military and diplomatic strategy.[2] Their approach was largely unplanned, and less spectacular than Napoleon's dynamic counter-strokes, and yet it eventually worked. By denying Napoleon the crushing victory he needed, they turned the campaign into a remorseless, attritional conflict. 'What discouraged our soldiers, and even, it must be admitted, the officers,' wrote a French subaltern, *Sous-lieutenant* Lefol, 'was that they saw no end to these marches and counter-marches, nor, it seemed, any result.'[3]

It is true that the political uncertainty of the coalition percolated downwards, and injected disunity, indecisiveness, and a lack of initiative into the military operations of the *Hauptarmee* at every level from the commander-in-chief to the advanced posts. Yet the Allies were not consistently timid. In fact, it was the very inconsistency of their system of command by council-of-war that caused Napoleon to lose the campaign, as it caused him to misjudge how they would react to his manoeuvres. At the same time he himself became more predictable, for only a certain number of times could he achieve surprise with the same methods, and this robbed his final *manoeuvre sur les derrières* of much of the effect it would have had a month or two earlier.

Of Napoleon's immediate opponents the *Schlesische Armee* was the more dangerous, but the defeat of the *Hauptarmee* promised to be more decisive, as it would have made a more immediate impression on the monarchs and diplomats who accompanied it, and put greater pressure on Austria to make a separate peace. Throughout the campaign Napoleon had the general aim of falling on Schwarzenberg's rear, and yet he actually ended up fighting twice as many battles against the *Schlesische Armee* as against the *Hauptarmee*, largely because of Blücher's persistence in seizing the initiative and forcing Napoleon to react to his advance on Paris.

The difference in tempo between the operations of the Allied armies reflected the contrasting political aims of Austria and Prussia as much as disparities in military capability. From the Austrian perspective Blücher was not the dynamic driving force of the campaign, but a maverick who took needless risks and jeopardised the chances of negotiating peace from a position of strength. The *Schlesische Armee* was not even consistently aggressive, for after its headlong advances of January and February it lapsed into the same caution, inactivity, and internal disputes that beset the *Hauptarmee*.

As the campaign progressed, the Allies became more realistic, both politically, as they were forced to moderate their individual ambitions so as to keep the coalition intact, and militarily, as the *Schlesische Armee* matched its operations more sensibly to the resources at its disposal. Napoleon was defeated by both military and diplomatic means, by the pen as well as the sword. The military commander on a battlefield is inevitably a more dynamic and mesmerising figure than a committee of statesmen, but not necessarily a more significant one. Politically the overriding development was the coming together of the Allied leaders and the agreement at Chaumont of their war aims. Thereafter, Napoleon was outgeneralled, outmanoeuvred and outwitted by the Allied commanders and diplomats, and by his enemies in Paris.

For all his flaws Schwarzenberg has been underrated as a commander. Some of his military decisions were fundamental moves that averted disaster and helped swing the campaign in the Allies' favour, such as ordering the *Hauptarmee* to retreat from Troyes on 23 February in order to avoid a battle for which it was not yet fit. A month later his insistence on attacking Napoleon at Arcis-sur-Aube on 20 March inflicted a clear-cut defeat and prepared the way for the resolution of the campaign. Schwarzenberg has been accused of paying too much attention to diplomatic and political considerations. But what leader with any sanity or commonsense would simply seek a quick military decision in blinkered pursuit of regime change, or recklessly invade a country without being ready to restore order and reconstruct the occupied lands? A headlong dash for Paris risked creating a permanent state of regional instability at the very heart of western Europe, and of subordinating Austrian interests to those of a powerful ally without securing any meaningful influence in return.

An immediate invasion of France after Leipzig might have succeeded in reaching Paris and toppling Napoleon, but if it had proved as easy as Blücher and Gneisenau expected, it is unlikely to have produced a stable international order. It may have won the war but is unlikely to have won the peace. Enduring stability can be achieved only by working through international alliances, and Napoleon's most significant, if unintentional, achievement in 1814 was to help forge the Concert of Europe by discrediting the notion that any one power could defeat him on its own.

Napoleon was aware of the fragility of the Allied coalition during the first two months of the invasion, which helps to explain why he hardened his negotiating position following his victories. He actually had a real chance of repelling the invasion by military means, certainly until the end of February, and came nearer to success than is generally realised. Even in March an unexpected event could have intervened, such as the death or capture of Alexander. His confidence has been condemned as arrogance, but was reflected at the time in the bleak outlook of many senior Allied officers. As late as 15 March, *Oberst-Leutnant* Karl von Clausewitz, who was serving in the *Nordarmee*, wrote to his wife from Düsseldorf:

> Only Blücher's bold courage and luck still leave a faint glimmer of hope. Perhaps Blücher will surprise us with a splendid victory, as he has done before. I am now very doubtful about the complete overthrow of Bonaparte. It is most probable that a peace will soon be made with him.[4]

Yet Napoleon never managed to secure a decisive military victory. The successes he did win were ultimately ephemeral, since their impact was mainly psychological, and he proved unable to translate them into a diplomatic settlement before their effect dissipated.

A lasting peace with the entire coalition was, of course, all but impossible, given the incompatibility of the two sides' aims, their mutual distrust, and Napoleon's inability to accept anything less than a position of dominance. Since his system of patronage was so deeply embedded in military glory and conquest, the only peace he could safely accept on a long-term basis was a victorious one. It was obvious to Napoleon that his best chance of securing such a settlement lay in splitting the coalition and detaching Austria, and yet he was too short-sighted to compromise over Austria's key area of interest: he would not give up Italy to save the rest of his Empire. By the time the Allies agreed the Treaty of Chaumont at the beginning of March, the opportunity had passed.

Napoleon's position then progressively worsened during the final month of the campaign. Time was not on his side, for his opponents were steadily reinforced. His February victories were only a momentary swing in the tide after the Allies overstretched themselves. By the middle of March they had recovered and become too strong for him to defeat either of their armies in battle. He had no choice but to take the gamble of marching on their rear, but it was not his abortive thrust towards the eastern frontiers that proved the decisive strategic move of 1814. It was the Allies' own *manoeuvre sur les derrières*, their final, joint descent on Paris, that ended the campaign. Similarly, it was the Allies who won the only decisive battle, when they forced the capital to capitulate, even though the action has often been overlooked by historians because Napoleon was not present.

The Allies had actually stumbled into adopting the manoeuvrist approach. In ignoring Napoleon's field army and occupying his capital, they struck him a devastating psychological blow, displaced his government, and allowed his political opponents in the city to unite and co-ordinate their actions with the coalition.[5]

Paris had been Napoleon's fatal weakness throughout the campaign. It was his indispensable depot and power base, but also a lead weight tied to his ankle. He lacked enough troops to leave behind a sufficient covering force while he attacked one of the Allied armies, and so he repeatedly had to break off a pursuit and return to save the capital. Never, in fact, did he manage to retain the initiative for as long as a fortnight.

Nor did Napoleon feel able to delegate real authority to his government ministers, and allow them to make immediate decisions on their own account. He had too few subordinates who were both loyal and capable, and had become over-dependent on members of his family and on long-serving but mediocre officials. By insisting on blind obedience, he deadened their initiative, while his relentless and unrealistic criticism gradually lost its ability to goad them into action. In theory, Napoleon wielded immense authority, but ultimately his attempt to combine the roles of Emperor and commander-in-chief proved self-defeating, and his over-centralisation of power prevented him from exploiting the manoeuvrist approach to the full limit of its possibilities.

The secondary fronts

However much it has been admired, the campaign that Napoleon ended up fighting was a mere shadow of the larger and more sweeping war of manoeuvre he intended to wage. Only by threatening the Allies' rear and driving them back over the Rhine could he have claimed real victory, or at least rallied France behind him and won time to complete his mobilisation. Despite all his efforts, he never managed to shift the campaign beyond Champagne and thus transform it into this broader, deeper, and more ambitious struggle.

Napoleon's February victories were no more than tactical successes. Even at the time he realised that they were not enough, that they could not be sustained indefinitely, and that only extensive, strategic manoeuvres could tip the balance. His frustration showed in his intemperate, and often unjust, criticism of his generals, and in his changes of mind as he wrestled with the problem of how to increase the tempo and reach of his operations when he was already operating at full pelt.

The widespread condemnation of Napoleon's *manoeuvre sur les derrières* at the end of March overlooks the fact that he originally intended his descent on Schwarzenberg's rear to be just one prong of a giant pincer move. The other prong had to come from his secondary forces outside the main campaign theatre, yet it did not materialise and for this he blamed his subordinate commanders.

Besides his own field army based on Paris, Napoleon had forces defending the Low Countries, south-western France and Catalonia, Lyon and the Rhône valley, and northern Italy. In addition, isolated garrisons still held fortresses on the French frontiers and in central Europe.

Whereas the Allied armies had to operate around the periphery of France, Napoleon had the advantage of holding a central position. French reinforcements from the Pyrenees were able to reach him within a month, whereas it would have taken four times as long for Britain to transfer Wellington's army from the same area by sea and redeploy it in the Low Countries, where her strategic interests were more directly at stake. As Wellington pointed out:

> In a war in which every day offers a crisis, the result of which may affect the world for ages, the change of the scene of the operations of the British army would put that army entirely *hors de combat* for four months at least, even if the new scene were Holland; and they would not then be such a machine as this army is.[6]

Despite being able to draw reinforcements from the secondary theatres, Napoleon could not evacuate them completely without losing territory and resources and weakening his negotiating position. Nor could he supervise his theatre commanders properly from afar, preoccupied as he was by his own operations. He could do little more than bombard them with critical letters or have their relatives write to them from Paris to exert emotional pressure.[7] His exhortations were often out-of-date or inconsistent, not only because it could take a week for them to arrive but also because he continually revised his plans in response to fluctuating fortunes.

His correspondence therefore presents a misleading view, by suggesting that his generals were deadweights fettered to his ankles. In reality, all the French theatre commanders were successful in keeping their armies intact and in tying down superior numbers of Allied troops. *Général de division* Nicolas, *comte* Maison, for example, was unable to prevent the Allied *Nordarmee* from overrunning Belgium, but then waged a skilful defence of the old French frontier with skeleton forces.

The theatre commanders benefited from Allied caution and disunity: Napoleon's stepson, *prince* Eugène, was able to retain most of northern Italy because of the reluctance of the King of Naples (the former *Maréchal* Murat) to co-operate vigorously with the coalition, and the awareness of the local Austrian commander, *Feldmarschall* Heinrich, *Graf* von Bellegarde, that it was not worth incurring heavy casualties in a theatre that was too remote from Paris to decide the outcome of the war.

Some clashes on the secondary fronts were major battles in their own right, notably

Limonest, the culminating action outside Lyon on 20 March, and also Wellington's final battle, Toulouse, on 10 April, where the two sides combined fielded as many as 90,000 troops. They were actually larger than several of Napoleon's own engagements near Paris, and yet none of the secondary theatres had more than an indirect effect on his military fortunes: they simply detained troops who might otherwise have swung the balance in eastern France.

Even Wellington had only a limited impact, despite being the most experienced of the Allied army commanders operating inside France, and having the best-supplied and disciplined forces.[8] A Prussian officer, *Leutnant* von Rahden, noted how little attention was paid in the *Schlesische Armee* to a rumour that the British had crushed the forces opposed to them under *Maréchal* Soult: 'Spain was too far from everyone's outlook at that time, and these victory reports excited little interest, even among the battalion's senior officers.'[9] Nor, for all his advantages, was Wellington any more successful than Napoleon in winning a decisive military victory in his local theatre of operations. He repeatedly failed to cripple Soult's army, and his final attempt to do so resulted in the bloody and mismanaged battle at Toulouse.

In fact, the only events on the secondary fronts with real and immediate significance for Napoleon were the fall of Bordeaux and Lyon, the fourth and second most populous cities of old France, on 12 and 21 March. These were political more than military blows: the apparent enthusiasm of the people of Bordeaux for the royalist cause shook the confidence of Napoleon's regime and established the credibility of the Bourbons. From afar, it seemed that Napoleon had effectively lost the south of France as a base from which to draw resources, and this undoubtedly helped compel him into undertaking his *manoeuvre sur les derrières*.

The thrust from Lyon

Of all Napoleon's secondary front commanders only *Maréchal* Augereau at Lyon could have intervened decisively in the main theatre. Napoleon was bitterly disappointed at his failure to do so, yet had largely himself to blame.

Augereau was unable to launch an offensive until 17 February, partly because he was short of money, transport, horses, weapons, and equipment, and partly because he did not receive until the 10th the experienced reinforcements from *Maréchal* Suchet in Catalonia that were to form the core of his *Armée de Lyon*. Even then, he lacked a clear-cut objective, since his various instructions from Napoleon veered between a thrust north-eastwards against Geneva (which was in Austrian hands), and one northwards up the Saône valley against the *Hauptarmee*'s rear. When Augereau split his forces and pursued both objectives, he attracted further criticism, but in reality he had no choice: he simply could not risk pushing northwards until he had secured his eastern flank by retaking Geneva.

Augereau's advance was therefore too weak, too late, and too dispersed. A concentrated thrust to the north, launched a week earlier, might have posed enough of a threat to make the *Hauptarmee*'s retreat from Napoleon become unstoppable, but the window of opportunity was narrow and fleeting.[10]

Schwarzenberg's response to Augereau's offensive was one of the most effective decisions of the entire campaign. At a stroke his despatch of reinforcements and the creation of the *Südarmee* negated any further threat to his southern flank, for besides the corps that were besieging fortresses such as Besançon, he now had well over 45,000 troops deployed against Augereau's 27,000. Schwarzenberg has been harshly criticised for his concern for his rear, yet he built up his forces in the Lyon theatre more quickly and substantially than Napoleon, and thereby established the essential precondition for a decisive outcome in the war as a whole.¹¹

Consequently, when Napoleon carried out his *manoeuvre sur les derrières* at the end of March, he was deprived of its essential second prong, for by that stage Augereau had evacuated Lyon and was no longer able to mount even a diversion. Instead of being part of a pincer movement, Napoleon's manoeuvre was just an isolated thrust, and hence lacked sufficient tempo. Whereas the Allies should have been swept away by panic and a whole succession of threats, they had time to reconsider their initial decision to follow Napoleon's army, and marched instead on his capital.

The Italian theatre

Augereau, therefore, lacked enough resources for the role assigned to him. What Napoleon had originally envisaged was to collect a powerful army at Lyon, by bringing the whole of *Maréchal* Suchet's troops from Catalonia and if necessary *prince* Eugène's army over the Alps from northern Italy. This would have provided the punch that Augereau was unable to muster on his own.

But in order to release Suchet, Napoleon needed to detach Spain from the coalition with a separate peace. In December 1813 he belatedly tried to end the six-year-old Peninsular War by obliging the detained Spanish King, Ferdinand VII, to sign the Treaty of Valençay, but was unable to compel Spain to ratify it. Hence, only two detachments, each of 10,000 men, could be withdrawn from Suchet. The second of them did not even join Augereau, as it was diverted to Périgueux in south-western France in response to the fall of Bordeaux.

Nor was Napoleon able to withdraw Eugène's army from Italy, for he was foiled by the defection of his brother-in-law, Joachim Murat, the King of Naples. Throughout 1813 Murat had been negotiating with Austria to try to secure his throne, and he continued to do so even as he moved a Neapolitan army up the Italian peninsula, ostensibly to reinforce Eugène.¹² Then, on 11 January he concluded a treaty under which he would field 30,000 troops as part of the Allied coalition in return for Austrian recognition of his right to rule Naples. Yet his position remained insecure, for the treaty had yet to be ratified and he had no agreement with Britain. He did not actually declare war until 15 February and even then did not become seriously engaged.

The uncertainty over Murat's intentions prevented Napoleon from withdrawing Eugène. He had to maintain a presence in northern Italy to impose on Murat, delay his declaration of war, and deny the resources of northern Italy to the Allies for as long as possible. He therefore sent instructions to Eugène on 17 January to cross the Alps, but only after Murat declared war.

A fortnight later Napoleon urgently needed reinforcements following his defeat at La Rothière, and on 8 February he repeated the order for Eugène to evacuate northern Italy.¹³ At the same time he had Eugène's mother and sister write to him from Paris, urging him to comply without delay.¹⁴ Eugène received these letters on 16 and 18 February, and learned of Napoleon's displeasure that he had not already begun his march. He bridled at the criticism and pointed out that his orders to leave had been conditional on Murat declaring war.

Napoleon's idea was for Eugène to leave behind his Italian regiments to hold the key fortresses, so he could quickly recover northern Italy later by pouring troops back into it. Meanwhile, Eugène would march his French units over the Alps, but he would have to do so in the middle of winter, and some of the passes had been blocked by detachments from the *Hauptarmee*.¹⁵ It would, in fact, have taken him three or four weeks to reach the Lyon area, and up to two months to join Napoleon himself in Champagne. He was likely to have arrived with little more than 10,000 men, for even in his French regiments many soldiers had been born in annexed regions of Italy and were likely to desert if he tried to lead them across the Alps.

To have intervened effectively Eugène would have had to join Augereau in time to take part in his offensive in the middle of February, but that would have meant setting out in late January, two or three weeks before Murat declared war. Nor is it certain whether he could have swung the balance if he had arrived in mid-February. Combined with Augereau's army, he would probably have had 35,000 troops, and would still have been outnumbered once Schwarzenberg detached reinforcements from the *Hauptarmee*. Hence, his intervention would have depended mainly on its psychological impact.[16]

Eugène, therefore, was justified in objecting to the idea of leaving northern Italy. Napoleon tacitly admitted as much when, after reversing the situation in Champagne with his February victories, he ordered Eugène to hold Italy for as long as possible, in the hope that a show of boldness might induce Murat to abandon the Allies.

Murat has been condemned for his defection, yet could not realistically be expected to act otherwise. From 1810, after marrying Marie-Louise of Austria and gaining the prospect of a son and heir, Napoleon had begun consolidating his Empire, and imposing more centralised control. In 1810, for example, he annexed the Kingdom of Holland after forcing his brother Louis to abdicate as its ruler, and seemed likely to do the same to other satellite states. Faced with such fundamentally insecure prospects, it was hardly surprising that Murat reacted by identifying more with the Neapolitan people than with France, or that he turned against Napoleon once the balance of power between them altered.[17]

Even so, Murat did not side wholeheartedly against Napoleon. He kept his options open as long as possible, and was reluctant to attack even after declaring war. The reality was that he needed to preserve the balance between Napoleon and the Allies, and exploit both sides in pursuit of his ambitions to become king of a united Italy, or at least to keep the throne of Naples. His political survival rested on his indispensability, and he therefore needed Napoleon to remain in power as a counterbalance to the Allies. Far from being a ruthless and committed traitor, Murat followed a confused and hesitant policy, that of a man out of his depth, driven by an ambitious wife, and worried by an insecure future.[18]

The way that Napoleon effectively goaded Murat into the coalition points to the ultimate causes of his downfall in 1814. Convenient though it was for him to blame the outcome on subordinates such as Marmont and Augereau, they were simply scapegoats for a broader and longer process beyond their control. What really brought Napoleon down was the very nature of his rule, and the political blunders he had made over the course of several years. Rather than suddenly falling, he was steadily undermined by a whole series of military, political, economic, and religious setbacks since 1808. His ill-fated intervention in the Iberian Peninsula, his failure to find a timely political solution to that debilitating war, and his inability to foster genuine loyalty from his satellite rulers all shaped the outcome of the 1814 campaign before it had even begun.

The legacy

All too often the Waterloo campaign has been examined out of context. Far from being an isolated episode, it should be seen as a sequel shaped by the lessons of 1814. The

Langres: the view from the cathedral towers. This walled hilltop town lay on the *Hauptarmee*'s main line of communications from Basel.

Chaumont, 20 miles north-west of Langres, was another fortified town serving as a base for the *Hauptarmee* as it advanced deeper into France.

Metternich.

Tsar Alexander I.

Belfort: the monument commemorating the city's three sieges (1813–1814, 1815, and 1870–1871). Belfort lay on the *Hauptarmee*'s lines of communication, 35 miles west of Basel, and was defended for 113 days by *Commandant* Jean Legrand, whose statue is in the foreground.

The *Château* de Brienne: Blücher's headquarters during the battle of 29 January. The avenue descends to the town, 450 yards behind the camera. French infantry attacked the *château* from the right; others then began advancing up the avenue, forcing Blücher to leave the grounds by an alternative exit more to the south.

La Rothière village: scene of heavy fighting between Russian and French infantry during the battle of 1 February.

La Campagne de France (1814), by Meissonier.

Napoleon's headquarters at Sézanne on the night of 9/10 February, the eve of the Battle of Champaubert.

The battlefield of Champaubert, where Napoleon crushed the Russian 9th Infantry Corps under Lieutenant-General Olsufiev on 10 February.

The crossroads of Champaubert. The monument was erected in 1865–1867 to commemorate Napoleon's victory. The house served as Napoleon's quarters on the night after the battle, but was later enlarged and given an upper floor. The cannonball was apparently added to attract customers when the building became an inn.

The Old Guard at the Battle of Montmirail (11 February). Napoleon relied heavily on the Guard in this campaign.

The battlefield of Château-Thierry (12 February): the scene of Napoleon's opening attack on Yorck's corps, which held the heights on the far side of the Dolloir river. Napoleon drove Yorck back more than 5 miles to the Marne valley.

The escarpment of the *Côte de l'Ile-de-France*, in Blücher's area of operations. The plain below is the western edge of *Champagne pouilleuse*, and the Marne valley lies 11 miles to the north.

The village of Etoges, 7 miles west of Bergères. This was the scene of the final action during the Battle of Vauchamps on 14 February. The *château* in the foreground was the headquarters in turn of Blücher and *Maréchal* Marmont.

The Russian monument in the village of Mormant, scene of Napoleon's victory of 17 February.

The village of Mormant. The surrounding plain enabled Napoleon to deploy overwhelmingly superior numbers of cavalry.

The walls of Provins, 48 miles south-east of Paris. Medieval defences such as these were not proof against artillery, but could protect magazines of food and ammunition from Cossack raids.

Montereau, scene of Napoleon's victory over the *Kronprinz* von Württemberg (18 February). The view is from the heights of Surville on the north bank, which dominate the flat terrain on the far side.

Moret-sur-Loing, 5.5 miles south-east of Fontainebleau. It was occupied by Schwarzenberg's *Hauptarmee* on 15 February, but retaken on the 18th by the French counter-offensive.

A cannonball embedded in a gateway in Moret-sur-Loing.

The battlefield of Craonne: the view from the Russian position, along the *Chemin des Dames*. The French attacked along the top of the ridge, and had to cross this narrow neck of ground at the Hurtebise farm under a hail of artillery fire.

The monument at Hurtebise farm, showing a *Marie-Louise* of 1814 (left) and a soldier of 1914 (right). The *Chemin des Dames* was heavily contested in the First World War.

The view from the hilltop of Laon. Napoleon was checked when he tried to take this strong position from the *Schlesische Armee* (9–10 March).

Napoleon's initial command post during his recapture of Reims (13 March).

Napoleon's headquarters in Troyes. During the campaign he spent eight nights at the city, six of them in this building (3–5 February and 24–26 February).

Ferme du Lumeront: Napoleon's headquarters on the night of 12/13 February. The farm stands on the southern edge of the Marne valley, overlooking the town of Château-Thierry.

The *Château* de La Briffe: Napoleon's quarters during the Battle of Arcis-sur-Aube (20–21 March). Its walls are still scarred from the impact of shots.

The battle-scarred walls of the *Château*.

The battlefield of Fère-Champenoise (25 March). This was the scene of Pacthod's last stand. The Saint-Gond marshes are to the left of the picture.

Maréchal Marmont

Talleyrand

The defence of the *barrière* de Clichy during the Battle of Paris (30 March). This patriotic painting by Horace Vernet was the centre of political controversy under the Bourbon Restoration. Note the wooden fence erected to protect the gate from cavalry raids.

very fact that it was fought at all was the result of Napoleon's determination to strike a pre-emptive blow in Belgium, rather than await the Allied invasion and find himself in the same dilemma as the year before. Similarly, his much-criticised decision not to give a field command to *Maréchal* Davout becomes understandable when it is remembered that he needed a ruthless soldier to govern Paris and prevent it falling as it had done in 1814.

Gneisenau's notorious suspicions of Wellington's reliability in 1815 make sense only when they are seen as a legacy of the year before. He suspected that Wellington deliberately misled the Prussians so that they bore the brunt of the fighting in the opening stages of the Waterloo campaign. This controversial allegation has never been proven, and in fact stemmed largely from Gneisenau's bitter memories of 1814, when the Allies had indisputably deceived each other for political purposes.

Historians have tended to concentrate on Napoleon's manoeuvres and on those battles where he was personally present, in order to gain insights into the art of war. He did not, in fact, invent the basic concepts he used in 1814. Indeed, his defence of France has striking parallels with the 1757 campaign during the Seven Years' War, when Frederick the Great used a central position in Saxony from which to defeat separate enemy armies at Prague, Rossbach and Leuthen. But rarely has a commander managed to apply such methods so intensively as Napoleon in 1814. One of the men most influenced by his defence of France was a 33-year-old *Oberst-Leutnant* in the *Nordarmee*, Karl von Clausewitz. He later emerged as one of the world's greatest military philosophers, and as well as writing a critical analysis of the 1814 campaign, he used examples of Napoleon's manoeuvres to support the arguments in his most famous work, *Vom Kriege* ('On war').

Insights from 1814 may even have guided the Confederate general Thomas J. ('Stonewall') Jackson in his renowned Shenandoah Valley campaign in 1862 during the American Civil War. Jackson had personally studied Napoleon's wars and waged a similar struggle by adopting a central position between several Union forces, dispensing with large supply trains, using local intelligence, and exploiting the stamina of his hard-marching infantrymen to surprise his opponents and defeat their larger forces in detail.

Napoleon's defence of France is still valuable today as a demonstration of just how effective the manoeuvrist approach can be in enabling a small force to impose on larger armies. Yet the lessons of 1814 are about leadership as much as strategy. How did Napoleon keep a largely conscript army motivated in the face of such odds? How did he turn the situation around after his defeat at La Rothière, and galvanise demoralised and disintegrating forces to win six battles and cover over 175 miles in just ten days?[19] How did he overcome the apathy of such a large proportion of the population and contain the hostility of his political opponents for so long? Napoleon's achievement in 1814 was based more on a thorough understanding of human nature than on the more intellectual aspects of generalship. An indomitable character, single-minded determination, and the ability to inspire and lead troops are more important than a knowledge of the art of war.

Part Four
The Civilian Experience

Chapter 16
Occupation

By the end of the campaign the Allies had occupied an area of France the size of the whole of Great Britain.¹ The administration of this vast territory developed out of the arrangements they had made the previous year to govern large areas of Germany as Napoleon's Empire collapsed. Under the Convention of Leipzig of 21 October 1813 they had established a *Zentraldepartment* of provisional administration under Heinrich, *Freiherr* von Stein, a capable administrator who had undertaken a series of reforms in Prussia following her defeat of 1806, and had then entered Russian service.

The administrative structure

The Leipzig Convention applied purely to Germany. It was only on 15 January, three weeks after the *Hauptarmee* had crossed the Rhine, that the Allies agreed a guiding set of principles for France.² The *Zentraldepartment* was given direct responsibility for the occupied regions between the Rhine and Paris. Its remit included Belgium but not Holland, which would be restored to independence, and not the rear area of the *Südarmee*, where separate arrangements were made.

The first regions to be occupied were divided into four general-governments, each containing between two and four *départements*. Austria was entrusted with those general-governments in the south, along the *Hauptarmee*'s line of operations, Russia with those in the *Schlesische Armee*'s rear, and Prussia with the *Nordarmee*'s sector. Stein prepared to establish another eight general-governments, which would have extended the administered area all the way to Paris, but military operations ended so abruptly that only some of them were activated, often in a modified or partial manner.³

The governors-general were hand-picked, experienced, and well-connected administrators. Many were privy or court councillors, or chamberlains, and the Governor-General of Franche-comté, Konrad, *Freiherr* von Andlau-Birseck, was a relative of Metternich. In many cases they had been born in Germany but had taken service with the great powers because they could not find sufficient scope for their talents in their own, small states. They were hostile not so much to France as to the Revolution and Napoleon. One governor-general, *Feldmarschall-Leutnant* Ludwig, *Fürst* zu Hohenlohe-Waldenburg-Bartenstein, actually entered French service after

Gardes nationaux repel a Cossack raid.

Napoleon's fall and became a *maréchal* of France in 1827.

The general-governments were a considerable responsibility. *Niederrhein*, for example, covered an area one-and-a-half times the size of the English counties of Devon and Cornwall combined, and was responsible for 1.25 million inhabitants. (Devon and Cornwall had a total population of 1.6 million in 2006.) The existing French administrative machinery was therefore indispensable because of its wealth of experience, local knowledge, and manpower. In general, it remained in place, but had decapitated itself, since the key officials – the *préfets*, *sous-préfets*, *commissaires extraordinaires*, and the *commandants* of the *divisions militaires* – had either withdrawn as instructed in the face of the invasion or been isolated inside fortresses.[4]

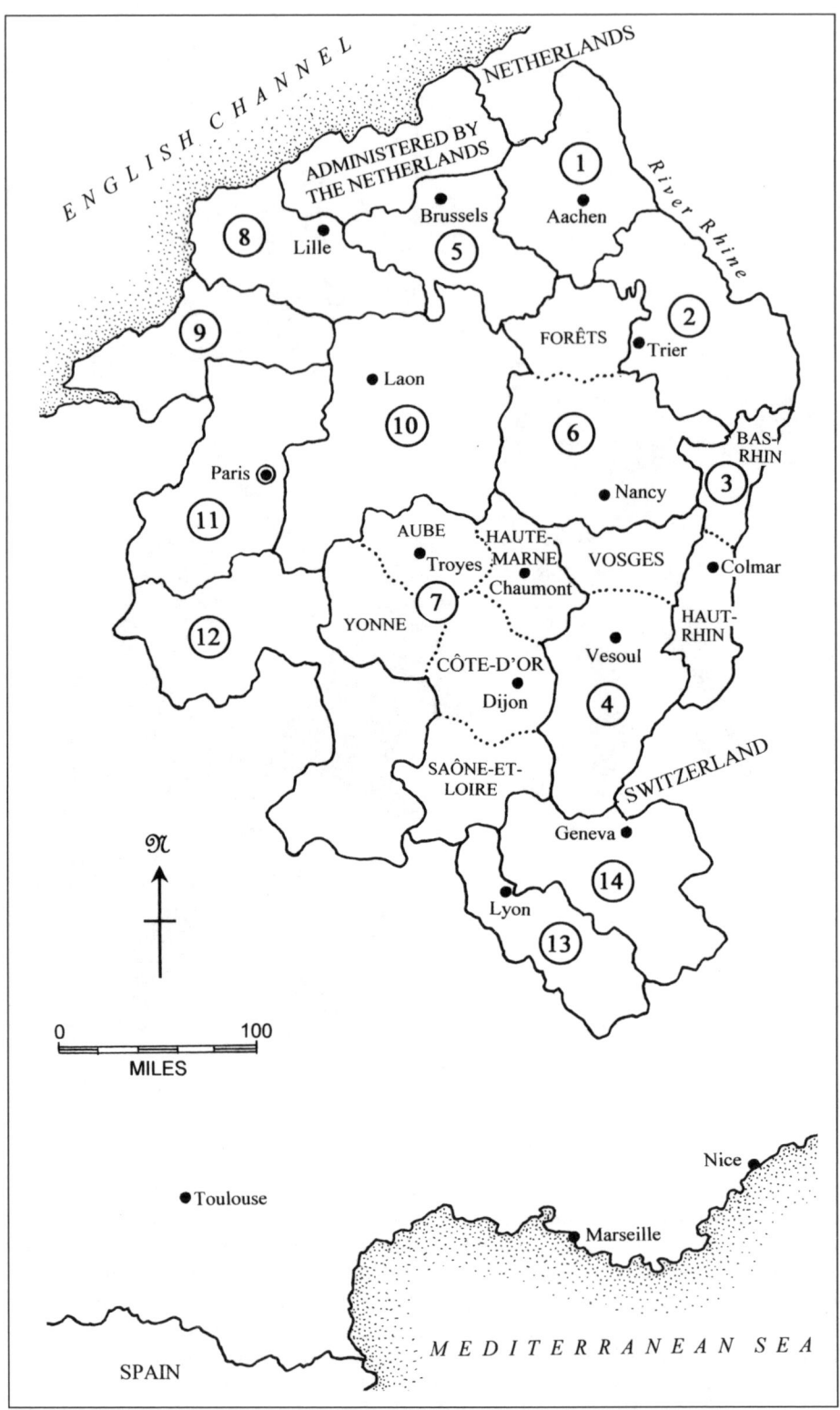

The Allied occupation of France: the general-governments.

Allied General-Governments for the Occupied Regions

Four general-governments were initially established. Each of them can be located on the accompanying map by its identifying number

Identifying no.	General-Government	Governor/Head	Seat of government	Allied power	Notes
1	*Niederrhein* (*départements* of Roer, Ourthe, and Meuse-Inférieure)	von Sack	Aachen	Prussia	Composed wholly of annexed regions of Belgium and the left bank of the Rhine. The government-general was provisionally entrusted to the Governor of Berg (on the eastern side of the Rhine) pending Sack's assumption of his duties in March.
2	*Mittelrhein* (*départements* of Mont-Tonnerre, Sarre, and Rhin-et-Moselle)	Justus Gruner	Trier	Russia	Composed wholly of annexed regions of the left bank of the Rhine. Gruner took up his post early in February. The *département* of Forêts was added to the government-general, as the fortress of Luxembourg made it difficult to be administered by the Governor of Lothringia (Government no.6) to the south.
3	*Oberrhein* (*départements* of Haut-Rhin and Bas-Rhin)	(1) *Feldmarschall-Leutnant* Ludwig, *Fürst zu* Hohenlohe-Waldenburg-Bartenstein (2) Georg, *Freiherr* von Escherich	Colmar	Austria	Hohenlohe-Waldenburg-Bartenstein was the provisional governor pending the arrival of Escherich.
4	Franche-comté and Alsace (*départements* of Jura, Doubs, Haute-Saône, Vosges, and small parts of Swiss territory annexed by Napoleon)	Konrad, *Freiherr* von Andlau-Birseck	Vesoul	Austria	Andlau was appointed on 27/1/1814; and left Vesoul at the end of his tenure on 14/5/1814.

Disputes arose involving Wrede, the commander of the Bavarian V *Armee-Abtheilung*, which had occupied parts of Governments numbers 3 and 4. As a result, changes were made to these two Governments, so that authority was shared between Austria and Bavaria. Government number 3 was divided into two, while one of the *départements* of Government number 4 was detached:

(3)	Lower Alsace (Government) (the *département* of Bas-Rhin)	Hermann, *Freiherr* von Hess	Haguenau	Austria	Resulting from division of Government no.3. Hess took up his office on 10/3/1814.
(3)	Upper Alsace (Commissariat) (the *département* of Haut-Rhin)	Karl, *Freiherr* von Stengel; and von Sonnleithner	Colmar	Bavaria/Austria	Resulting from division of Government no.3. Administered by a joint Austro-Bavarian commission. The former bishopric of Porrentruy was detached from the *département* of Haut-Rhin and had its own administrator.

Identifying no.	General-Government	Governor/Head	Seat of government	Allied power	Notes
(4)	Vosges (Commissariat)	Joseph, *Graf* von Armansperg; and Josef von Polzer	Epinal	Bavaria/ Austria	Vosges was detached from Government no.4. Armansperg had the title of provisional *préfet*. His appointment was officially announced on 16/1/1814. To him was added an Austrian senior commissar, Polzer, whose duties seemed to be minimal. Armansperg and Polzer together formed the *Commission préfectorale*, which ceased its duties on 16/5/1814.

Another three of the planned governments were established later in the campaign, at least in a partial, or modified, form:

5	Belgium (*départements* of Sambre-et-Meuse, Dyle, Jemappes)	*Freiherr* von Horst	Brussels	Prussia	The administration of the Belgian coastal *départements* (Lys, Deux-Nethes and Escaut) was provisionally assigned at British request to the Prince of Orange. In the event, before the Basel arrangements were known, the chiefs-of-staff of Bülow's corps and the 3. Bundes-Corps created a government from the whole of Belgium, under a member of the old, local nobility, the *duc* de Beaufort.
6	Lothringia (*départements* of Meuse, Meurthe, Moselle, Forêts)	David, Count von Alopaeus	Nancy	Russia	Since the French-held fortress of Luxembourg impeded Alopaeus's communications with Forêts, this *département was* added to *Mittelrhein* (Government no.2).
7	Burgundy (*départements* of Haute-Marne, Aube, Yonne, Côte-d'Or)	(1) *Graf* von Auersperg (2) *Feldmarschall-Leutnant* Ludwig, *Fürst* zu Hohenlohe-Waldenburg-Bartenstein	Dijon/Troyes	Austria	Auersperg was the interim governor. Hohenlohe-Bartenstein took up office at the start of February. He was unable to establish permanent, effective control beyond the Côte-d'Or, as the other three *départements* remained contested. On the other hand, he incorporated a neighbouring *département* (Saône-et-Loire), whose inclusion had not been planned at Basel.

Military operations continued in most of Government number 7 until late March. Hence, this government was never fully established. Other arrangements were made for the *départements* concerned:

(7)	Côte-d'Or and Saône-et-Loire *départements*	*Feldmarschall-Leutnant* Ludwig, *Fürst* zu Hohenlohe-Waldenburg-Bartenstein		Austria	

Identifying no.	General-Government	Governor	Seat of government	Allied power	Notes
(7)	Aube and Yonne *départements*	Ferdinand, *Freiherr* von Ulm		Austria	Established after the fall of Paris.
(7)	Haute-Marne *département*	*Generalmajor* Karl, *Graf* von Raigecourt	Chaumont	Austria	Established in January.

In March Stein delegated the overall supervision of the Austrian general-governments in France to Anton, *Freiherr* von Baldacci, the Austrian Army Minister.

The actual extent and degree of control varied between and within the general-governments. Some were established for longer than others; some contained French-held fortresses, and had to contend with widespread armed resistance. Governors sometimes found their radius of effectiveness limited to a small area around their seat of office.

A further five general-governments had been planned, but were not fully established because of the suddenness with which the campaign ended:

Identifying no.	General-Government	Governor	Seat of government	Allied power	Notes
8	Nord, Pas-de-Calais *départements*	*General* von Krusemarck		Prussia	
9	Somme, Seine-Inférieure *départements*	*General* von Kleist		Prussia	
10	Marne, Ardennes, Seine-et-Marne, Aisne *départements*			Russia	
11	Seine-et-Oise, Oise, Eure-et-Loire *départements*			Russia	
12	Loiret, Loir-et-Cher, Nièvre, Allier *départements*	Ferdinand, *Freiherr* von Ulm		Austria	

The Allies agreed at Troyes on 15/2/1814 that if they captured Paris, Russia would appoint a military governor, but actual administrative powers would rest with a commission of Russia, Prussia, and Austria. On 31/3/1814 General Sacken, a Russian corps commander in the *Schlesische Armee*, was appointed military governor of Paris.

Another two governments were established, on the *Südarmee*'s line of operations, but they remained under military control and were not subject to the *Zentraldepartment*:

Identifying no.	General-Government	Governor	Seat of government	Allied power	Notes
13	Rhône and Isère *départements*	*Generalmajor* Kaspar, *Freiherr* von Mylius	Lyon	Austria	
14	Ain, Léman, and Mont-Blanc *départements*	(1) *Feldmarschall-Leutnant* Ferdinand, *Graf* von Bubna und Littitz (2) Alois, *Graf* von Ugarte the younger		Austria	The general-government was abandoned at the end of May.

Notes:
The identifying numbers have been added to clarify this table, and were not used at the time of the campaign.
Sources: Charton, Kielmansegg, Kraehe, Wacker.

The decision to order the *préfets* and *sous-préfets* to withdraw was made at a council of ministers towards the end of December 1813. It was not a unanimous decision, for leaving the officials in place would have mitigated the occupation, discouraged local people from turning away from the imperial regime, and made it easier to organise resistance. It was also recognised that the Allies would be able to find provisional replacements who would be less likely to risk their lives or prospects for Napoleon.[5]

As expected, the Allies simply replaced the absent *préfets* and *sous-préfets*, and supervised the activities of the local administrations with just a few of their own personnel. Before abandoning his *chef-lieu*, the *préfet* of the Aube vainly issued a circular to be displayed in every *commune*, explaining that the *secrétaire-général* and the *conseillers de préfecture* were forbidden to exercise any authority in his absence: 'All the acts they might make are absolutely invalid, and it is forbidden to obey them.'[6] The prohibition was simply ignored, and the *secrétaire-général* was appointed as provisional *préfet*.

Absent officials were replaced from the top down, starting with the appointment of a provisional *préfet* for the *département*, followed by the filling of any vacancies in the *conseil de préfecture* and the election of a *secrétaire-général*. At the next level down *sous-préfets* would be appointed and the *conseils d'arrondissement* completed. The *sous-préfets* would replace any absent *maires*, and complete the *conseils municipaux*. Revenue officials or other public employees could also be appointed. Vacancies would ideally be filled with prominent and respected local citizens who were opposed to Napoleon's regime. Any person who was offered a position had to accept it, unless certified as incapacitated by illness. Inhabitants who disobeyed a summons to serve faced arrest, confiscation of their possessions, or deportation to eastern Europe.[7]

French administrators who worked for the Allies were sometimes made to swear an oath. During the occupation of Dijon a succession of three oaths was imposed, the terms of which became progressively more exacting. At first, on 21 January, the city's officials simply had to swear to help maintain public tranquillity, but on 9 February they were required to submit a written oath. Then, three weeks later, the governor-general wanted them to undertake to obey the Allied powers and place themselves unreservedly under his orders. This final step provoked opposition because of the explicit undertaking to serve Napoleon's enemies, and it had to be replaced with a promise that officials would fulfil their duties in the name of their government and in accordance with French laws.[8] (Compelling inhabitants to swear allegiance to an occupying power is now forbidden under international law.)

In the wake of the total wars of the twentieth century the word collaboration has become confused with treason, and misinterpreted as ideological affinity with an occupier. In fact, it also applied to the more pragmatic maintenance of a working relationship that gave the local authorities considerable negotiating power to mitigate the burden on their communities. The Allies needed to extract resources, lacked enough troops to do so with repression alone, and so had to conciliate the population.

In the Vosges, for example, the head of the Allied *commission préfectorale* in charge of the *département* announced in January that he was reducing the price of salt, and that the inhabitants could expect similar benefits if they continued to deserve them.[9] Since the *commission* wanted the clergy and administrative and judicial officials to help maintain order and tranquillity, it was careful to reassure them that their salaries and pensions would be paid. It also promised to pay the pensions of former soldiers, to ensure that they were not driven by desperation to take up arms.[10]

Collaboration was therefore a two-way process, and a successful, long-term occupation required compromise rather than just brutal oppression. Talleyrand was the supreme example of the usefulness of French officials, and an indication of the influence conferred on them by their indispensability.

By acting as intermediaries the French administrators helped reduce friction between the Allies and the population. Requisitions, for example, tended to be made by the local authorities on the Allies' behalf once a general-government had been established. But, despite the benefits for the population as a whole, the Allied system of indirect government placed a heavy burden on the French officials. They had to reconcile the conflicting interests of the occupiers and occupied, and became an obvious target for violence by Allied soldiers.

When Napoleon appeared before Troyes in the second half of February and the city was at risk of being burned down, it was the *maire* who bravely went through the lines with two colleagues to mediate. As a token of their gratitude, the inhabitants later nominated him and his two *adjoints* for the *Légion d'honneur*, and presented them with gold or silver swords.[11]

Problems

The occupation was not properly prepared. The Allies crossed the Rhine just two months after defeating Napoleon at Leipzig, and during that time the *Zentraldepartment* also had to make arrangements for governing much of Germany. Since the Allies agreed the general principles for the administration of the occupied area only after the start of the invasion, they had to implement them in many areas by correspondence over long distances and insecure roads. Stein accompanied the main Allied headquarters, which limited his control over the more northerly general-governments. Early in March, for example, when he was based at Chaumont, he was over 130 miles from Trier, and 185 from Aachen, the administrative centres of *Mittelrhein* and *Niederrhein*.[12]

Disputes with military commanders forced the *Zentraldepartment*'s plans to be amended. It was a multinational occupation and therefore full of complexities and potential friction. Wrede, the Bavarian commander of the V *Armee-Abtheilung*, asserted his authority over parts of *Oberrhein* and Franche-comté, which his corps had traversed, and defied their Austrian governors-general. Resenting what he viewed as Stein's interference, he sarcastically dubbed him the 'commander-in-chief of the universe' and expressed a wish to 'put him in a cannon and make a present of him to Napoleon'.[13]

When the arrangements were flouted in this way, Stein was dependent on support from a fractious coalition preoccupied with more pressing problems. The *Zentraldepartment* was unable to enforce its authority against Wrede, since Metternich was reluctant to alienate Bavaria. The result was a compromise, with the General-Government of *Oberrhein*, for example, being split into two, and the southern part, Upper Alsace, becoming a joint Austro-Bavarian commissariat.[14]

The *Zentraldepartment*'s core weakness was that it lacked its own military force with which to command obedience from both the civilian population and the various Allied contingents. Thus it faced a spiralling predicament: its inability to prevent troops looting alienated the population, thereby making it more difficult to extract supplies, which in turn increased the likelihood of pillaging. To control their rear effectively, the Allied commanders would have had to deploy an entire reserve army in the occupied regions, yet even if they could have spared the troops, they would have been unable to deploy them because of the problem of finding enough supplies.[15] Instead, security in the rear depended on successive detachments of reinforcements coming forward from the Rhine to join the field armies.

The overriding aim of the occupation authorities was to support the Allied armies by extracting money and supplies. The *Zentraldepartment* did not attempt to implement systematic administrative or legal reforms, as it lacked the time and ability to do anything more than make the existing systems work as effectively as possible for the Allies' benefit.

Yet even in its limited objectives the *Zentraldepartment* was only a partial success. It failed to raise as much money as expected, for France was already exhausted by Napoleon's exactions. The upheaval of the invasion caused many inhabitants to abandon their homes and complicated the collection of taxes. The Allies had abolished the unpopular *droits réunis* as a propaganda gesture, and those revenue officials who remained in post were unlikely to carry out their duties rigorously without close supervision.[16]

Even the four easternmost general-governments, the first to be established, were unable to become fully established. It not until 10 March that the Governor-General of *Niederrhein* took up his duties, just six weeks before the convention of 23 April agreed that the administration of the occupied territory should be returned to French officials.[17]

The *Zentraldepartment* was simply overwhelmed by the scale and complexity of its task. It was difficult to find reliable senior administrators, and Prussia was particularly unhelpful in providing personnel. It was the Austrians who showed most concern for their sector, and the Prussians who were the most neglectful, and this is usually overlooked when Schwarzenberg is criticised for his slower rate of advance.

Local administrations were also swamped by the extra work generated by the occupation. At Bar-sur-Aube the *maire*'s senior secretary spent eleven consecutive nights in his office, while the *maire* of Dijon announced in March that he would receive private individuals only between 1700 and 1900 hours, since he had become overburdened and distracted by mostly pointless requests.[18]

Initial disorder

The experience of occupation consisted of three distinct phases: the initial disorder; the emergence of a more stable and regular administration; and the period after hostilities ended.

The invasion threw a region into confusion by dislocating its administrative structure even before the Allied troops actually arrived. Napoleon's authority, which had already been undermined by unpopular measures such as conscription and taxes, collapsed as the *préfets*, *sous-préfets*, *gendarmes*, tax inspectors, and other functionaries disappeared.[19]

Many inhabitants also fled but others actually wanted the Allies to arrive, as they were tired of the burden of Napoleon's regime and, having been sheltered from the direct effects of war for two decades, had little idea of what occupation would entail.[20] Schwarzenberg encouraged such disaffection by issuing a proclamation at the start of the invasion in December 1813: 'We do not wage war on France; we simply drive far away from us the yoke that your government has sought to impose on our countries, which have the same rights as yours to independence and happiness.'[21]

The Allies, he emphasised, had no desire to avenge the French misdeeds of the previous twenty years; the only conquest they sought was that of genuine peace for the whole of Europe. He urged the inhabitants to remain where they were, and promised that the troops would respect private property and maintain public order.

Some inhabitants were lulled by such assurances. Others made hiding places for valuables in their homes and gardens. At Provins coins were buried by boring deep holes of the same diameter, so that the earth was not visibly disturbed by digging. Entrances to wine cellars were obstructed with large heaps of manure or were walled up, the new mortar disguised by darkening it with dampened soot. Shopkeepers emptied their windows and unhooked their signs, out of fear of being pillaged.[22]

Few inhabitants outside the fortresses thought of resistance. Many open towns capitulated to just a handful of Allied soldiers, for opposition would have won only a temporary delay at the risk of provoking reprisals. Much of the population felt abandoned by the imperial government and was more interested in local everyday concerns.[23] At Tonnerre *gendarmes* barricaded the entrances to the town but 28 January was market day and so the inhabitants unblocked the roads to let traffic circulate. An Austrian cavalry detachment arrived shortly afterwards.[24]

When Allied forces first appeared in a town the mood of its inhabitants varied. 'In the middle of this crisis', wrote a citizen of Tonnerre, 'the inhabitants of every class did not appear terrified. Everyone was curious to see the enemy, and especially the Cossacks; the streets were as full of people as on the day of a fair.'[25] But Allied commanders were nervous about the possibility of resistance. At Dijon the people were forbidden to appear in the streets with sticks or other weapons, and were instructed to stay in their homes until the troops had been billeted.[26]

The sudden passage of an entire invading army was a heavier burden than the subsequent movements of reinforcements and casualties. The initial phase of occupation operated on a day-to-day basis, with the population having to fulfil Allied needs as they arose. An inhabitant might have to feed and lodge as many as twenty or fifty soldiers at a time.[27] Troops forcibly occupied the best lodgings, regardless of which ones had been assigned to them.[28] Different national contingents made overlapping requisitions, and officers often added their own arbitrary demands.

Schwarzenberg genuinely wanted to protect the inhabitants from looting but found it impossible to do so. Inhabitants were informed by official notices of the amount of food they were meant to serve soldiers billeted on them, but in practice were often forced to exceed the legitimate requirements. Some practically became slaves and had to undertake all sorts of menial tasks, such as repairing shoes and fetching water for horses.

Yet it would be misleading to see the entire population as victims, for some people exploited the initial disorder for their own ends. On 11 January the *maire* of Geneva announced an amnesty for the return of items that inhabitants had stolen from the barracks when the Allied troops had entered the city. There were also cases of civilians stealing from Allied officers or beating up soldiers who had been maltreating them.[29]

A more regular occupation

In the easternmost regions the occupation tended to become more regular, even if it was never fully effective. Once the tide of the invasion had swept through a region, the inhabitants were less oppressed. It was in Allied interests to improve discipline so they could mobilise resources more efficiently and avoid anarchy or an uprising.

Early in February Schwarzenberg issued an order of the day informing the *Hauptarmee* of the administrative arrangements made in its rear, and forbidding unit commanders from making requisitions on their own authority where general-governments had been established.³⁰ Requisitions now had to be made, or approved, by the governor and his administration, and requisition slips were often printed rather than handwritten.³¹ Detachments moving between the rear and the army had to remain on prescribed military routes, the *Etappen-Straßen*, where they could be regularly supplied.

Attempts were made to reinforce the authority of the governors-general by providing them with a military force. In February, for example, Blücher appointed a military commandant for the General-Government of Lothringia, *General-Major Fürst* Biron von Kurland, and had him assemble a mobile column of convalescent soldiers, stragglers and detachments with which to restore order.³²

Occasionally the Allies were able to use existing French security forces. Whereas most of the *Gendarmerie* had withdrawn in the face of the invasion, some *gendarmes* returned to the city of Troyes after the Allies' arrival. Along with the local *gardes nationaux*, they were able to protect the city by containing the disorders committed by the Allied garrison.³³

At other towns, such as Nancy, the Allies raised new units of *gendarmes* or *gardes nationaux*.³⁴ In the Vosges the Allied *commission préfectorale* decided to replace the absent *Gendarmerie* with a company of fifty mounted men recruited from among the inhabitants. But this provisional *Gendarmerie* could not be formed, since few suitable men volunteered for a service that would cause the population to see them as Allied spies. Only one or two Bavarian *gendarmes* of French origin were seen in the streets of Epinal, and the *commission préfectorale* relied instead on the *maires*, *gardes champêtres*, and *gardes forestiers* to keep law and order.³⁵

Stein distinguished between the France of the *Ancien Régime* and the more-recently annexed regions of Belgium and the left bank of the Rhine. He believed that reliable collaborators could be found more readily in German-speaking *départements*, and he wanted to detach these areas from France in pursuit of his ambitions for a united German confederation. This was a further incentive for the *Zentraldepartment* to restore order and protect the population from excessive or irregular exactions.

In Germany in 1813 the *Zentraldepartment* had raised not simply supplies and revenue but also troops. This was not possible within occupied France, except for internal security forces created to replace the *Gendarmerie*. Stein did want to raise a *Landwehr* in the German-speaking *départements*, but the initiative had limited success and was dropped following the fall of Paris.³⁶

Paris

Paris was a special case and only ever experienced the regular phase of occupation, with barely any of the initial disorder. Alexander took the city under his protection. Only the most impressive and disciplined Allied units took part in the formal parade into the capital, and the troops bivouacked instead of receiving billets, in order to relieve the inhabitants as much as possible from the burden of occupation. The city simply had to provide provisions and accommodate only officers and staffs. Having the men live in encampments for such long periods was possible because of the milder spring weather, and made it easier for the officers to control their troops than if they had been distributed among numerous houses.

Crucially, the top of the administrative structure in Paris remained in place, in contrast to what happened in the provinces. The city's two *préfets* were left behind and continued their duties, and a provisional government of France was appointed the day after the Allies' entry. The *Gendarmerie* was still present, as was the *Garde nationale*, which jointly patrolled the streets with Allied troops.

A Russian corps commander, General Sacken, was appointed Governor of Paris. Under him was a *commandant*, Colonel Léon, *comte* de Rochechouart, an *émigré* serving as ADC to Alexander. Rochechouart was familiar with Paris and the appointment of a Frenchman was a sign of Alexander's benevolence. Rochechouart began making arrangements for the occupation on 31 March, even before the formal Allied entry. Later that day an additional two *commandants* were appointed, and the city was divided into a Russian, an Austrian, and a Prussian sector.[37]

The campaign zone

Except in Paris, the stability of the Allied occupation progressively lessened to the west. The more forward governments were established later, and since they lay immediately behind the Allied armies, they were heavily burdened by requisitions and exposed to greater risk of a French counter-offensive.

The actual zone of hostilities remained in a permanent state of disorder and oppression. Troyes, for example, changed hands five times during the campaign. This contested area was an administrative void: most of the *maires* were still present, but the *préfets* and *sous-préfets* left before the Allies arrived. Indeed, many imperial officials abandoned their duties too promptly, even before the French army began to retreat, including *commissaires des guerres*, who were supposed to be distributing supplies to the troops; and the *directeurs* and *inspecteurs des postes*, whose departure made it difficult to maintain communications.[38]

The *Zentraldepartment* was unable to establish general-governments in the contested area, or mitigate the excesses suffered by the population. In the absence of a general-government, commissars attached to the Allied armies made provisional administrative arrangements but these lacked the same order and regularity.[39]

The advance and retreat of the opposing armies was followed by rival efforts to insert civil and military authorities, restore order, and extract resources. Napoleon wanted to reimpose his authority on liberated areas as soon as possible. 'It is difficult to be more displeased than I am with your *préfets*', he complained to the *Ministre de l'intérieur* on 21 February: 'They flee when they want, without any need for it. That of the Aube has covered himself in mud. Order him to go immediately to the first village of his *département* that is still in our hands.'[40]

That same day Napoleon gave instructions that all the *préfets* were to remain in the last part of their *département* still held by French forces, and immediately to follow any advance.[41] Five days later the *Ministre de l'intérieur* wrote to the *sous-préfet* of Nogent-sur-Seine to check that he was back in his post:

> I want you, Sir, to give me the assurance, by return of courier, that you have resumed your duties, and that you are in a position to carry out the direct orders you might receive from the *Intendant général* of the *Grande armée*, or from the *prince major général* [Berthier]. You will inform me, at the same time, of the period at which you resumed your duties after the enemy's retreat.[42]

Napoleon was quick to mobilise forces in these liberated regions. On 26 February he signed two decrees for raising new contingents of the *Garde nationale* in all the freed *départements*.[43] The *Ministre de la police générale* pressed the head of the *Gendarmerie* to reorganise his men in these areas, so he could help check desertion from Napoleon's army.[44] Communications had to be restored as well. After the repulse of the *Schlesische Armee* in the middle of February, *Maréchal* Kellermann informed Napoleon that he had sent his *chef d'état-major* to Meaux to re-establish broken bridges and organise the postal relays.[45]

Napoleon had several spare generals attached to his headquarters, so he could immediately replace casualties among his unit commanders. Similarly, he had men available to take up administrative posts. At the beginning of March, for example, he appointed one of his ADCs, *Général de division* Jean-Baptiste, *baron* Corbineau to govern the newly liberated city of Reims. As the *sous-préfet* he inserted Pierre Defleury, who had accompanied his headquarters since the Allied occupation of his previous *arrondissement* in eastern France.[46]

In the middle of March Napoleon wanted several *préfets* who had withdrawn from their invaded *départements* to be sent to him from Paris, clearly in order to have them at hand when he carried out his *manoeuvre sur les derrières* and freed occupied regions in the Allied rear. This was easier said than done. Some of the *préfets* were too old or unfit to ride a horse, while another, Antoine, *baron* Rœderer, left Paris on the night of the 21st/22nd without knowing Napoleon's location, ran into the Battle of Fère-Champenoise, and had to return to the capital.[47]

The Allies found that their attempts to win the co-operation of the population were hampered by the oscillating military fortunes, since those civilians who openly served them were exposed to the threat of reprisals from Napoleon. In ordering *Maréchal* Augereau to recapture Geneva, the *Ministre de la guerre* directed him to take hostage all the men who had formed its provisional government under the Allies. Similarly, the *maire* of Tonnerre was removed for having served the Allied authorities too zealously while under occupation. In trying to protect his town, he had readily complied with their demands, and had even sought contributions from unoccupied *communes* in the area.[48]

The need to intimidate the occupied areas into remaining loyal helps to explain some of Napoleon's most controversial decisions, including his determination to carry out the *manoeuvre sur les derrières* and penetrate deep into the Allied rear. It also sheds light on his much-criticised insistence on the natural frontiers as the basis for peace negotiations, since he thereby prolonged the inhabitants' uncertainty about the fate of Belgium and the left bank of the Rhine.

Battles

Particularly terrifying for civilians was to be caught in the middle of an action. During the Battle of Laon in March the inhabitants of the city were in a state of almost stupefied silence. They could not even hope to be saved by a French victory, as they feared the Allies would sack their homes if forced to retreat. At Arcis-sur-Aube later that month some civilians were so demoralised and weakened by starvation that they seemed oblivious to the shooting, and calmly walked about in the open, as if seeking to be killed. Those inhabitants who remained in their homes often sheltered in their cellars, and might place containers of water by their doors or in their attics in case of fire. Sometimes the inhabitants played a more active role, helping the wounded, or even shooting at the Allies, although this exposed towns, like Nogent-sur-Seine, to being sacked in revenge.[49]

Occasionally a child became lost in the confusion. At Nogent-sur-Seine on 12 February a four- or five-year-old was seen calmly playing in the street and picking up musketballs, which it collected in its pinafore. At Fère-Champenoise a girl was found hiding under a barouche. She explained that, since her mother was dead, she had accompanied her father, a *garde national*, on campaign, but he had been killed in the battle. One of the French prisoners, *Général de division* Pacthod, took charge of her and brought her up.[50]

The Allied withdrawal

The occupation entered its third and final phase after Napoleon's unconditional abdication. A demarcation line was established to separate the occupied regions of the north and east from the rest of France, and the Allied corps were assigned cantonments behind this line.[51]

Hostilities formally ended with the convention of 23 April. The agreement stipulated that the administration of the occupied regions was to be returned immediately to French royal officials, that the Allies would cease their requisitions, and that their troops would be supplied by the royal authorities for the remainder of their presence in France. In practice, the Allied administrators were slow to transfer control and cease their requisitioning. They insisted on the collection of arrears of taxes, on the grounds that they had been decreed before the date of the convention.[52] Yet the French Provisional Government needed to regain control of the occupied territory promptly in order to maintain its credibility and strengthen confidence in the Restoration. It was not in the Allies' interests to undermine the Bourbons' prospects of success, but the convention had indicated that practical arrangements for the transfer of authority could be clarified in a subsequent agreement. Until then, and until they received specific instructions to cede control, Allied governors-general were reluctant to disband their administrations.[53] In fact, it took about three weeks after the convention for the Allied powers to yield to French representations and order the transfer of control.[54]

This final phase of occupation saw a change in the way the Allied troops were supplied. On 30 April, a week after the convention, the Provisional Government instructed the *préfets* of the invaded regions that the Allied forces were now to be fed by contractors, who would be paid by means of a property tax. Requisitions were to be used only to provide transport or to stock magazines if contractors could not be found.[55]

Switching to contractors had the advantage of sharing the burden more widely and bringing supplies from further afield. But in practice it proved impossible to replace requisitioning completely. Few contractors were willing and able to form magazines, especially as the French authorities could not pay them an advance and had difficulty collecting enough revenue to pay for their services. Some entrepreneurs tried to defraud the administration, while speculators manipulated the market price of grain by buying up local supplies.[56]

Extracting the Allied armies from France was a major logistical problem, for tens of thousands of their troops had to pass through an already-exhausted countryside in a limited period. Soldiers looted from magazines or failed to carry out their moves as instructed, with the result that they arrived at villages unexpectedly. But by July the withdrawal was largely complete, except for small detachments and some sick and wounded men, who followed later.[57]

Chapter 17

The struggle to survive

Assumptions about the relationship between the French population and the occupying armies are often misleading, for they underestimate the complexity of the situation. A surprising number of Allied commanders were actually French by birth, and had entered Russian or Austrian service after the outbreak of the Revolution. *Feldmarschall-Leutnant* Ludwig, *Graf* Folliot de Crenneville, an Austrian divisional commander, was born at Metz and served as a French naval officer before emigrating in 1792, while General Langeron, one of Blücher's corps commanders, and Lieutenant-General Karl Osipovih Lambert, leader of a Russian hussar division, were both native Frenchmen who had begun their military careers in Louis XVI's royal guard.[1]

Several other generals had first-hand knowledge of France. Schwarzenberg had served as ambassador to Paris, while the commander of the Russian Imperial Guard cavalry corps, Lieutenant-General Dmitry Vladimirovich, Prince Golitsyn V, had studied at the University of Strasbourg and the *Ecole militaire* in Paris.

'I never saw so filthy a town'

Yet the rank and file did not have this prior acquaintance with France, and few anticipated the deprivations they found. For the past decade France had been the dominant superpower of Europe, and the reality, in many rural regions, of grinding poverty and bad roads came as an unpleasant surprise. 'Our men very much dislike being in France,' noted a Prussian staff officer, *Major* Ludwig von Reiche. 'The local way of life does not appeal to them, and each of them comes to know and appreciate the merit of his German fatherland . . .'[2] He was echoed by a Russian officer, who protested: 'Honestly, these gentlemen we have at home, who admire the French – I do not know why they have so much to say about France. It is a country like any other, and it does not please me in any way.'[3]

Just as dispiriting as the countryside was the destitution in many towns. Troyes used to be a flourishing commercial city, but thousands of its workers were now unemployed. 'It makes one's heart bleed,' wrote Lady Burghersh in February:

> I really do not see how these wretched inhabitants are to escape starvation after we leave them. I never saw so filthy a town as this, and the number of beggars far surpasses that of Dublin: all women and children, for of spare men there are none; but the former follow you about the streets in herds of twenty and thirty together. If you give money to one, the rest all fall on her, and then begins a regular fight.[4]

Many troops despised the inhabitants they met, and described them as a strange and poverty-stricken people, dirty, coarse, lazy, and miserly. Their contempt was often intensified by resentment at the earlier French occupation of their homeland. But miserly often simply meant that the peasants could be obstructive when it came to complying with requisitions, and laziness during the winter was an unavoidable part of their seasonal lifestyle, following a sustained period of activity in the summer.

Besides, the Allies gained a skewed impression of France since they spent so much time in the most impoverished part of Champagne in the winter, which was a stark contrast to the Rhineland in late autumn. A royalist emissary, Jean de Gain de Montaignac, heard a staff officer of the *Schlesische Armee* say that France was a wretched country containing only 'stones, chalk and sand', but it was clear that the man based his assessment simply on the province of Champagne.[5] In reality, there were wide variations between different regions, across the blurred boundaries between town, village, and countryside, and between the great metropolis of Paris and the rest of France.

'Our stay here is dreadful'

The burden of the fighting was borne unevenly by different units, just as the devastation fell heavily on some towns and villages and barely impinged on others. But all the troops, even those generally withheld from combat, had to endure bitter conditions just to survive. The Prussian *1. Garde-Regiment zu Fuß* did not see action for the entire campaign until the final battle outside Paris. Yet by the morning of that day even its strongest company contained only 107 men, little more than half of its full paper strength.[6] One of the regiment's officers, *Major* Wilhelm von Ditfurth, explained on 2 March that the *Hauptarmee* was much reduced:

> This is not from losses in action, since it has still done nothing, but it disintegrates into sick and marauders, who all leave in bands. This is really pitiful. Our stay here is dreadful. All the villages are abandoned and the peasants live in the woods with their livestock. The provisions are buried and, as we do not want to starve to death, we are obliged not only to dig in the ground for treasure troves, but also to break open vaults and newly built walls. . . .
>
> I now have with my battalion a herd of ten cows and oxen, which march with us and are gradually slaughtered. The villages without exception are devastated by the Russians and Austrians, and many are burned down. We wreak no more havoc than the French have done in our country, but the peasants are really infamous rascals, and you can not venture by yourself into a village, still less a wood, for the peasants are hidden there and beat us to death. Often the saddest events occur.
>
> I sent armed detachments into the woods today, and they returned with bread, livestock, and potatoes. Since yesterday, I have had soldiers grind flour in the local mill and bake bread from it. You will see from this that we are badly off in France. Everyone, high and low, longs for peace, and looks forward to it like a child for a doll.[7]

Despite the cold, it was not always possible to house troops indoors by billeting them on the inhabitants. Bivouacking was sometimes the only option, especially in the heart of the campaign theatre during the most active periods of operations. Blücher was obliged in February to rely more heavily on camps, so he could limit disorder, supply his army more regularly, and keep it safer from partisan attacks.[8]

For Allied soldiers the experience of the campaign could veer suddenly between luxury and deprivation. The autumn harvest in 1813 had been abundant, and the French abandoned large magazines as they retreated from the Rhine. Some Allied troops actually over-indulged through looting and extorting supplies. 'The soldiers'

Strength of the Prussian I Corps under *General der Infanterie* Hans, *Graf* von Yorck during the 1814 campaign

Date	Location	Officers	Combatants	Total	Proportion of original strength	Notes
1813, Dec 28	Wiesbaden	635	20,045	20,680	100.0%	
1814, Jan 4	Obermoschel (31 miles SW of Mainz)	597	17,641	18,238	88.2%	I Corps crossed the Rhine on 1 and 2 Jan. A *Streifkorps* of 1,150 men was detached under *Oberst Graf* Henckel against Trier.
1814, Jan 6	Kusel (20 miles SW of Obermoschel)	625	17,568	18,193	88.0%	
1814, Jan 8	Tholey (16 miles N of Saarbrücken)	588	15,976	16,564	80.1%	
1814, Jan 10	Lebach (7 miles SW of Tholey)	594	16,151	16,745	81.0%	
1814, Jan 13	Longeville (21 miles E of Metz)	550	14,986	15,536	75.1%	1,500 men detached under *Major* von Bieberstein to blockade Sarrelibre (Saarlouis).
1814, Jan 18	Boulay (15.5 miles NE of Metz)	655	16,686	17,341	83.9%	The whole I Corps is distributed before the fortresses in the rear of the *Schlesische Armee*. The strengths therefore include Henckel and Bieberstein's detachments.
1814, Jan 25	Pange (8.5 miles SE of Metz)	638	17,488	18,126	87.6%	The I Corps has been strengthened with 1,548 replacements and convalescents, and with the 1,700 men of the 1. *Ostpreußische Infanterie-Regiment*.
1814, Jan 27	St-Mihiel (20 miles SE of Verdun)	640	17,947	18,587	89.9%	
1814, Feb 8	Dormans (11 miles E of Château-Thierry)	613	16,061	16,674	80.6%	
1814, Feb 16	Châlons-sur-Marne	604	13,682	14,286	69.1%	The I Corps has lost 1,432 officers and men at the Battles of Montmirail and Château-Thierry (11 and 12 Feb). The I Corps was re-organised on the 16th, with depleted units being amalgamated.
1814, Feb 18	Châlons-sur-Marne	603	13,715	14,318	69.2%	
1814, Mar 6	Laffaux (7 miles NW of Soissons)	512	13,287	13,799	66.7%	800 replacements and convalescents have arrived under *Oberst* von Lobenthal.
1814, Mar 11	Athies (3 miles E of Laon)	517	13,001	13,518	65.4%	The I Corps has lost only 166 officers and men during its attack on Marmont at the Battle of Laon (night of 9-10 March).
1814, Mar 24	Château-Thierry	487	12,810	13,297	64.3%	
1814, Apr 5	Palaiseau (10.5 miles SW of Paris)	474	11,299	11,773	56.9%	The I Corps has lost 924 officers and men in a series of actions fought between 26 and 30 March, during the march on Paris and the battle outside the city.
1814, Apr 8	Palaiseau	480	11,484	11,964	57.9%	
1814, May 4	Arras (100 miles N of Paris)	588	15,336	15,924	77.0%	The I Corps has been reinforced by the 2. *Ostpreußische Grenadier-Bataillon* and the *Pommersche Grenadier-Bataillon* (total 1,850 men), transferred from the III Corps
1814, July	Arlon (15 miles NW of Luxembourg)	561	20,568	21,129	102.2%	

Sources: adapted from Henckel von Donnersmarck, pp.592-7; Plotho, part 3, appendix XXIII; Weil, *La campagne*, v.3, p.227.

excessive eating and drinking bouts have been so bad that more than 150 men are now in hospital with indigestion,' recorded an inhabitant of Geneva, Jean Janot, on 5 January. 'This has resulted in a decision to place most of them in the barracks, in order to return them to their usual diet.'[9]

A Russian officer, Staff Captain Eduard von Löwenstern, noted how this initial comfortable phase of the invasion came to an end in the last days of January as the rival armies moved closer, putting pressure on a smaller region. He remembered that the day after he had feasted and drunk champagne, he found himself squabbling over half-cooked potatoes. Even so, wine remained plentiful, and the men sometimes cooked everything in it, since it could be easier to find than water. Unexpected delicacies could also turn up: during a lull in the Battle of Paris a group of Russian officers actually dined on roast peacock.[10]

Requisitions

An army could be fed in three ways: by billeting soldiers on the population; by collecting taxes with which to pay contractors for supplies; or by requisitioning. All three methods were used, but only the third way, the authorised requisitioning of supplies to stock magazines, was practicable for lengthy periods. It was difficult to extract taxes from an exhausted region, and contractors rarely had sufficient means to supply all the needs of an army, especially an active or concentrated one. Few inhabitants could afford to feed soldiers billeted on them for long, although they generally had to do so until more regular arrangements could be made.

Requisitioning was therefore the least unsatisfactory option, and besides food and forage it could take the form of clothes, leather, cloth, horses, horseshoes, waggons, lead for musketballs, office stationery, and even services. Men might be required to make equipment, transport supplies, or show a unit the way to its destination. Towns often established a formal service of guides to prevent ordinary inhabitants being suddenly abducted by soldiers for several days without their families knowing what had become of them. At Laon a permanent guides organisation was maintained for two months at the expense of the *mairie*: the men were sometimes mischievous enough to abandon Allied detachments in the middle of the countryside, but the troops simply took out their anger on the local peasants.[11] The Allies also requisitioned labour, for example in repairing bridges. In February they forced three inhabitants of Montereau to help construct fortifications, but let them go after an hour because of their obvious ineptitude.[12]

To requisition supplies, the local authorities would issue *bons*, or slips, stating what was required, and a receipt would be given when the items were provided. If requisitions were not fulfilled, the Allies might resort to demanding money as compensation, threaten simply to let the troops take what they needed, or quarter soldiers on a community at its expense.[13]

Requisitioning was meant to protect inhabitants from the destructiveness and random violence that occurred when troops were simply allowed to pillage, but it was not always done properly. The demands were often distributed unfairly because the authorities were overwhelmed with work, because it was inefficient to transport supplies from a distance, or because inhabitants sought to avoid their share. One *maire* even diverted the Allied troops from his own *commune* by leading them into neighbouring ones and pointing out where they could find supplies.[14] Troops often marauded anyway to supplement their rations, and their officers might make additional unauthorised requisitions by force.

Even if the Allies began with good intentions and made only moderate demands, they were generally forced to become more ruthless and overbearing when people mistook their forbearance for naivety and tried to take advantage of them by being obstructive. A *département* would share requisitions among its *arrondissements*, which in turn cascaded them downwards to the *communes*. But the inhabitants delayed fulfilling the requisitions as long as possible, and then supplied only part of what was demanded, in the hope of evading the rest.[15] Edme-Jacques Gérost, an inhabitant of Villenauxe, explained how:

> Success went to the one who was the best at using trickery, and who acted with the most slyness and subtlety. The regions that had men with talents honed in these sorts of skills were the least exhausted. Not only was all this permissable, it was essential to use these methods, especially in a region like ours, which had neither resources, nor magazines, nor the means of making them.[16]

This obliged authorities to demand more than they needed. As resources became exhausted, and inhabitants hid their remaining livestock in woods, requisitioning became progressively more ineffective. It was quicker and easier for Allied commanders to allow their troops to help themselves, even though this increased the likelihood of violence.[17]

Cultural misunderstandings increased the frustration of the troops. They did not at first realise that the peasants in Champagne rarely drank coffee, tended not to smoke tobacco, and consumed only moderate amounts of brandy. When the soldiers could not find these items, they resorted to violence because they assumed that the peasants were hiding them.[18]

Corruption and wastage increased the burden. Soldiers sold rations, and even equipment, to local people. Supplies were sometimes destroyed deliberately to prevent them falling into enemy hands. In fact, the squandering of resources could be prodigious. When the *Schlesische Armee* rallied around Châlons-sur-Marne on 16 February it found enough forage in the magazines to keep it supplied for ten days, but emptied them in two. Units simply took supplies by force, partly because of language problems since Prussian and Russian contingents received supplies from the same magazines.[19]

Ammunition and equipment accounted for only a small proportion of a unit's logistic requirements, compared to the mechanised and fuel-hungry armies of the twenty-first century. Yet shortages arose because of inefficiency, the difficulty of transport, and the insecurity of the Allied communications from the Rhine. Such problems were eased by captured French supplies and by the capitulation of fortresses such as La Fère at the end of February with its immense stocks of artillery munitions.[20]

Existing hospitals could be supplemented by appropriating large buildings, such as churches, prisons, barracks, former convents, and even theatres. But finding the necessary resources and medical staff for these provisional hospitals proved an insurmountable problem, and transport for the sick and wounded had to compete with an army's logistical needs. Items such as medicines, which could not be requisitioned from the population, had to be bought from suppliers. Since it was difficult and time-consuming to raise the required funds through taxes, a common resort was to extract a contribution from the wealthiest inhabitants using the threat of armed force.[21]

Looting and atrocities

Allied commanders found it difficult to maintain discipline, especially after defeats or when regular distributions of food broke down. Pay was often in arrears, and in the Russian army even officers could rarely afford to buy provisions from their meagre wages.

Lieutenant-General Ivan Fedorovich Paskevich took command of the Russian 2nd Grenadier Division in February, having been appointed to stamp out its notorious indiscipline, which had undermined its combat performance at La Rothière. He found that the heart of the problem was that the men were famished: 'In the morning the soldier leaves even if he has not appeased his hunger the day before. Since no preparations have been made in front, he arrives at the end of the day's march and still finds nothing. So how could he have failed to indulge in pillaging?'[22]

Paskevich began sending detachments ahead of the division to requisition supplies, and insisted that his men should have meat every day instead of just twice a week as was stated in the regulations. He believed that it was his duty to spare his own troops rather than his enemy's country, and that he could not stop his troops pillaging unless they were fed.

Inhabitants suffered at the hands of French as well as Allied soldiers. *Sous-lieutenant* Lefol described how, soon after he left a *château* where he had been generously fed by the occupants, it was thoroughly pillaged by the dregs of Napoleon's army:

> Throughout the campaign, these wretches, who lived by plunder alone and were known at the time as *fricoteurs*, terrorised the places through which they passed. However many were shot, the example simply incited them even more, and they inspired such fear that we often heard the inhabitants wishing for the arrival of the Cossacks in order to be delivered from their odious presence.[23]

Not all Allied troops were disorderly. Charles Charton, a teenager working in the *préfecture* offices at Epinal, recalled that the town's Bavarian garrison was neither brutal nor insolent, and that it sought to avoid provoking clashes.[24] But since the Allies could spare few regular troops for rear-area duties, it was usually their least civilised elements, and units that merely passed through without having time to forge friendships, that had most contact with civilians. Their violence was a sign of insecurity. The soldiers had to struggle to survive the winter conditions, were outnumbered by the population, and risked being killed at any moment either on or off the battlefield. Their fear of partisan attacks and disgust at the poverty of the inhabitants were a potent combination, and encouraged the use of force as a way of asserting authority.

Atrocities occurred on both sides. Cossacks were alleged to have tortured inhabitants by filling their mouths with hay and setting fire to it to make them reveal where they had hidden their valuables. But local peasants finished off wounded Russian soldiers after the Battle of Craonne, having been enraged two days earlier when some of their children suffocated as troops tried to smoke them out of the quarries where they had taken shelter.[25]

Some Allied soldiers did intervene to stop atrocities. A Russian adjutant, Staff Captain Karl von François, rescued a young woman at Troyes who was being chased by two Cossacks, and then evicted a band of their comrades who were looting her house. Fortunately, he noted, 'the word subordination had a very precise and effective meaning in the Russian army'.[26]

But it was difficult to enforce discipline in a multinational force, especially away from the main towns and in remote areas where detachments could not be adequately supervised by senior officers. An Austrian subaltern would have difficulty in making

Cossacks recognise his authority unless he had troops to support him, and even then he might be reluctant actually to fight them. Even the Allied sovereigns were unable to stop the looting and destruction. At Chaumont Emperor Franz personally chased away some hussars who were demolishing a house, but they returned once he had left the scene.[27]

The Allied contingents tended to blame the looting on each other, or claim that they were beyond the authority of another nation's commanders. When the Russian General Sacken issued an order on 4 April to stop troops pillaging the magazines at Versailles, it had only a temporary effect, for the Prussians began again in the evening, claiming that they took orders only from Yorck, their own corps commander.[28]

Some rigorous examples were made. In Franche-comté four Russian soldiers were condemned to death for committing excesses in the *commune* of Vauchoux, and the *maire* and a handful of his inhabitants were invited to the nearby town of Vesoul to witness the execution.[29] Similarly, on 4 March four Bavarian soldiers of the *7. Linien-Infanterie-Regiment* were arrested for pillaging a house in Troyes. On the 10th they were brought before a military commission, and three of them were sentenced to death, the fourth being given a week's imprisonment. The sentence was carried out the same day, widely publicised by both notices and verbal announcements in churches.[30]

But such punishments had little effect given the scale and intricacy of the problem. Since the various Allied contingents had different languages and regulations, it would have been impossible in the middle of the campaign to create a general provostship with the necessary personnel, an agreed penal code, and authority over all the Allied forces.[31] In fact, what proved most effective at countering the disorder was the uprising it helped provoke. One of Blücher's corps commanders, Yorck, was not surprised when he learned that irregulars were threatening the Allied rear, and remarked that it would at least force the troops to remain with their units and stop marauding.[32] At Piney, 12 miles north-east of Troyes, a Russian major actually ordered the inhabitants to take up arms and repel a band of Württemberg looters.[33]

Etappen-Straßen

As part of the process of imposing greater order and stability in the rear areas, Blücher and Schwarzenberg established *Etappen-Straßen*, or military roads. (An *Etappe* was a relay, or a day's march.) The *Hauptarmee* established seven *Etappen-Straßen* as its main lines of communication. Two of the routes connected Basel to Troyes, its most advanced base: one along the *chaussée*, and the other using by-roads.[34] The other five served Dijon (the location of the Austrian reserve) and the detached forces besieging Besançon. The result was an elongated spider's-web of routes. Magazines were established along these roads, with the main logistic base being Langres, and supplies were forwarded to advanced depots and then distributed to the *Hauptarmee*.[35]

To protect the supply magazines and maintain order in the rear areas, four key towns were each provided with a reserve, or *Landwehr*, battalion of an Austrian infantry regiment and a detachment of light cavalry. These towns were Basel, Vesoul, Chaumont, and Dijon, and they each formed the centre of a *Marschbezirk*, or march district.[36] The radius from one of the four key towns to the edge of its *Marschbezirk* could vary between 20 and 55 miles. The director of the *Etappen-Straßen* was the head of the military police, the Russian Lieutenant-General Fedor Fedorovich Ertel, who was based at Basel.

The establishment of the *Etappen-Straßen* was intended to make communications more secure, prevent inhabitants from being unreasonably exploited, and restrict troops to fixed routes, which would also limit the spread of disease. All movements of

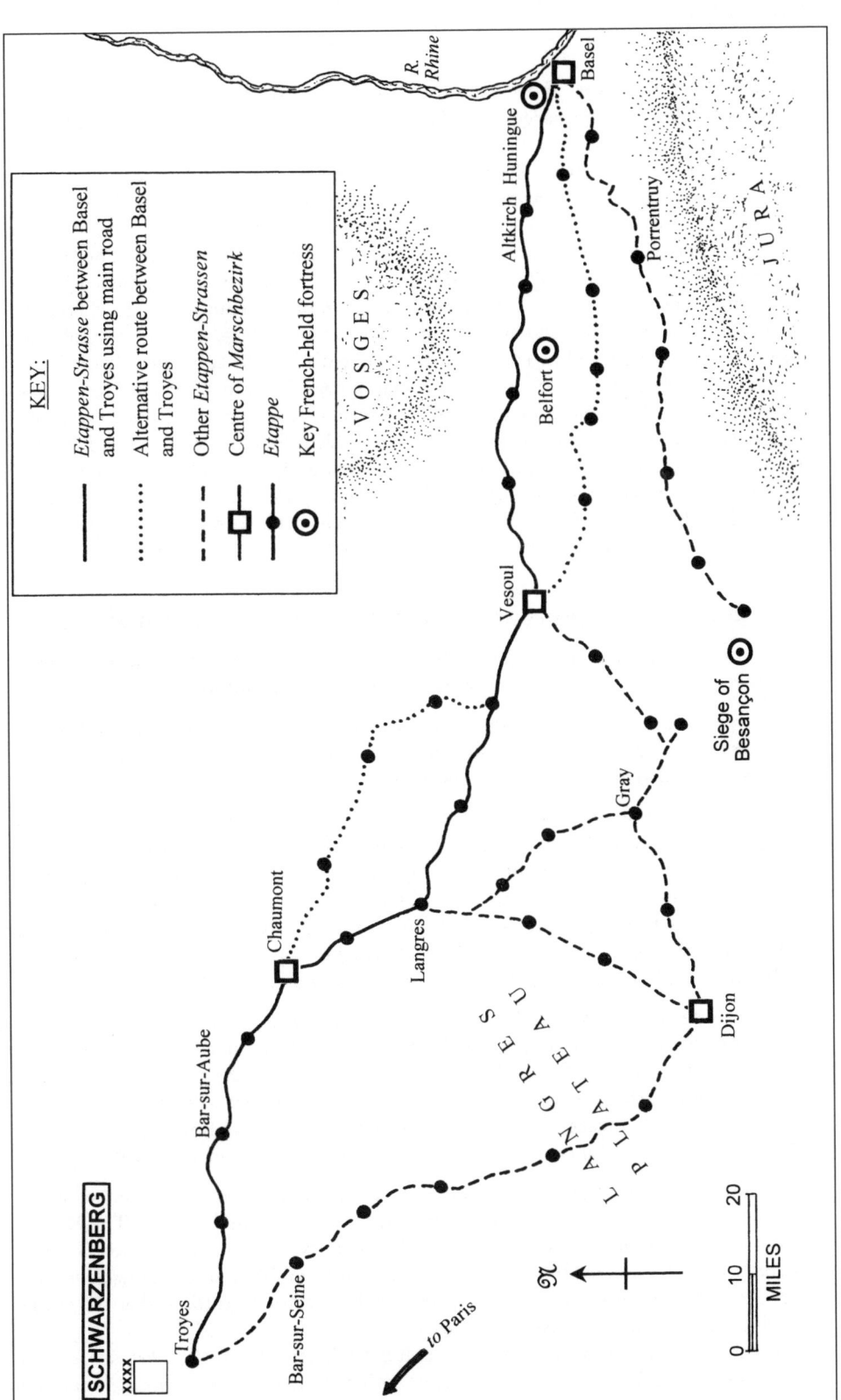

Schwarzenberg's main lines of communication: early February 1814.

supplies, reinforcements, and invalid men would use the *Etappen-Straßen*: civilians could have soldiers who strayed from them arrested by informing the commandant of the nearest military post.

To avoid disputes about the supplies provided by the population, a tariff was posted in every *commune* showing what was due. Each detachment using the *Etappen-Straßen* was provided with two travel warrants. The first was carried by a quartermaster who went on ahead to have rations and billets prepared. The second was with the commanding officer of the detachment, and had to be endorsed by the *maires* of places where it stayed, who could add comments about its conduct. Despite the precautions, pillaging and abuses did occur. At one village a subaltern stole 300 *francs* from the *maire*, and had him beaten so violently that he subsequently died.[37]

Detachments could cover the 195-mile march from Basel to Troyes in fifteen days, with the average day's march being 13 miles. A postal service operated along this route, with inhabitants being forced to serve as *estafettes*. Identified by a sign in their hat, they would take despatches and requisition orders on foot to the *maire* of the next post. The *maires* were responsible for the loyalty of the messengers.[38] Efforts were also made to re-establish the system of relay horses along the main roads by restoring the posts and ensuring that they had enough horses and postillions.[39]

'The contested regions are becoming terribly knocked about'

Volontäroffizier Karl von Raumer, who was serving with Blücher's headquarters, vividly recalled how the cold wind swept across the bare plains of Champagne:

> In the bivouacs on these plains, a soldier could barely find a place at the fire, where the wind did not either blow the flames to scorch him, or deprive him of warmth by driving them to the opposite side.[40]

Firewood became one of the soldiers' foremost priorities, and the search for it left a trail of devastation. Fences were torn up, thatch taken from the roofs of houses, and abandoned Allied bivouacs left littered with beds, mattresses, chairs, doors, wardrobes, and even window frames.[41] Troops often lit fires inside barns or other buildings in order to shelter from the wind and rain, but did not always bother to extinguish the flames when they left, and so many villages burned down. 'France will feel the effects of the war for a long time yet,' wrote *Major* von Reiche to his father:

> The contested regions are becoming terribly knocked about. Since we must obtain what food we need from the land, and since the authorities have usually taken flight, everyone takes what he finds. As a result of the great shortage of wood and fuel that is general here, we remove anything that will burn from the houses to our bivouacs. As a result, you can see whole villages where the roofs have been removed and just the walls are left standing. It's an awful sight.[42]

Men resting indoors had to be careful in case soldiers outside suddenly climbed on to the roof and brought it down, unconcerned if the beams killed anyone. The British liaison officer with the *Schlesische Armee*, Colonel Hudson Lowe, once invited Blücher and his staff to tea and led them to his billet but was bewildered at being unable to find it. He looked as if someone had cast a spell on him, until he realised that the entire building had been demolished during his absence.[43]

French troops played their share in such destruction. An ADC, *Chef de bataillon* Jean Girod de l'Ain, was actually asleep inside a house when *cuirassiers* started demolishing it for firewood. He hurriedly chased them away with blows from the flat of his sword, but had his arm broken when a large stone was thrown at him in return.⁴⁴

Even when trees were nearby, troops preferred to burn dry wood, such as church pews, for damp branches gave off too much smoke and made it necessary to open the windows, which let in the cold. At Laon in March the *Schlesische Armee* fed their bivouac fires in the town with more than fifteen carriages and other vehicles, which they did not bother to dismantle: they simply placed the entire bodywork on the flames.⁴⁵

The forests that did exist were a precious source of wealth because of the widespread demand for timber, not least for shipbuilding, but they suffered serious damage from unauthorised cuttings following the breakdown of law and order.⁴⁶ The Allied authorities issued strict instructions to protect woods in the occupied areas, partly because they wanted to preserve them for future generations and partly because inhabitants who took refuge in them were potential partisans and by their absence reduced the resources that could be extracted from the towns and villages.

'He seems to know only the grossest expressions'

Attempts by the inhabitants and Allied soldiers to communicate produced a confused medley of languages, and sometimes laughable results. Ten-year-old Charles d'Arbois de Jubainville recalled how a group of Russians appeared at his home in Nancy. His father and the Russian sergeant both flattered themselves that they could speak some German. Asked what he wanted, the sergeant replied, *cartoffe*, meaning potato, and ended up with an omelette.⁴⁷

'French is hardly spoken any more in our town, except in private,' explained Pierre Dardenne, a teacher at the secondary school at Chaumont:

> In the squares, in the streets, and on the roads, you hear only the hiss of the Russian language, or the caw of German. The latter language is the most widespread. Those of our fellow citizens who previously knew some words of it strive to remember them, and gabble with the infidels. I, too, try to caw a little, but I make little progress. My throat is not supple enough to lend itself to such a rough pronunciation. However, I can say *Ja, mein Herr* (yes, sir), and *Guten Tag, Gute Nacht* (good day, goodnight). But where I excel is in the words *Fort* (out), *Nicht* (no), and *Nichts* (nothing). For this, I am a real German, and I caw them all the time in the faces of my Cossacks, my Bohemians, my Hungarians, and my Transylvanians. Do they come to take up quarters? *Fort, fort* is my only greeting, but they shut my mouth by showing me a billeting order, or by making a sabre flash in my eyes, and I have to receive these inconvenient guests, these insolent foreigners.⁴⁸

Florentin Fortin, a priest at Auxerre, claimed that the Austrian troops seemed to know only one word of French, which they had learned during Napoleon's occupation of their own lands. It was the word 'immediately', and they added it to each of their demands.⁴⁹ In fact, Allied soldiers also tended to acquire a forceful selection of French oaths. At Geneva a theology student explained that he had an Austrian officer billeted in his house at the end of December 1813: 'I have already tried out my knowledge of German on him, but the outcome has done me no honour. As for him, he seems to know only the grossest expressions in the French language, and is always tossing b__s and f__s out of his mouth.'⁵⁰

In Nancy an *émigré* who had married a Russian woman acted as an interpreter for his fellow citizens, and wrote a useful French, Russian, and German vocabulary of common words and phrases. The *maire* of Epernay maintained official interpreters to support his administration: five for German, one for Russian, and one for Polish.[51]

In fact, the Allied contingents often had as many difficulties communicating among themselves as with the inhabitants, and sometimes had to do so in their enemy's language. When two Cossack regiments were attached to the Austrian I *Armee-Abtheilung* in January, Schwarzenberg instructed that they should include some French-speakers so they could co-operate effectively.[52]

By 1814 French had long been the international language of culture and diplomacy, as a result of the country's enhanced power and influence on the world stage. Almost one-third of Russian officers could speak it, which sometimes amazed the local inhabitants. Ironically, many Frenchmen would not have been able to understand them, for even half a century later a quarter of the population did not know French. Most inhabitants used their local *patois* for everyday speech, with French-speakers being concentrated mainly in the larger towns and cities.[53]

Interestingly, Latin often proved particularly helpful. It had not been officially used by the French government since 1539, but had declined more slowly in eastern Europe. In the sprawling Austrian Empire, for example, it was a neutral language whose use, unlike that of German, did not imply that any of the various subject peoples were inferior.[54]

A Prussian surgeon, Dr Wenzel Krimer, often managed to make himself understood by the inhabitants by picking up a considerable amount of French and mixing it with some broken Latin. If he did have trouble, he would find a priest, talk to him in Latin, and use him as an interpreter. At Chaumont Pierre Dardenne was able, as a schoolmaster, to hold a conversation in Latin with an Austrian doctor from Bohemia. Even Blücher, whose education had been patchy, knew some Latin words, and had actually used them during a private interview with Napoleon in April 1807 after being captured.[55]

It is true that differences in pronouncing Latin could cause difficulties. At Lyon Adèle Audouard de Montviol and her relatives tried talking with the Hungarian officer billeted on them by using a Latin dictionary, but had to switch to a French-German one.[56] Yet on other occasions Latin was startlingly effective. In one incident at Chaumont about fifteen Hungarian hussars entered a house and became frustrated at being unable to communicate with its occupants, two women and a 13-year-old child. They began to smash some of the furniture, so the child fetched his uncle, who worked at the *hôtel-de-ville*. Recognising the soldiers as Hungarians, the uncle shouted at them, 'Quo usque tandem abutemini, o nobilissimi homines?'[57]

It was an adaptation of the first line from Marcus Tullius Cicero's famous denunciation of Lucius Sergius Catilina in the Roman Senate in 63 BC: 'How long, Catilina, will you abuse our patience? How long will your anger continue to mock us? When will your unbridled audacity end?' It had a sudden effect on the hussars, who recognised the allusion. Their anger dissipated, and they protected the house for the rest of their stay.[58]

Champagne

The soldiers' deprivations were offset by the fact that they were fighting in France's champagne-producing region. Napoleon's chief secretary, *baron* Fain, recalled how on 17 March: 'The good inhabitants of Epernay had broken into their hiding places to welcome the army. For some hours, the wine of Champagne made the soldiers forget their exhaustion, and the generals their worries.'[59]

Champagne could even broker local truces. In February a Prussian *uhlan* squadron was surprised to see French sentries sheathing their swords and waving champagne bottles. The *uhlans* joined them for a drink, and afterwards their commander had difficulty persuading them to return.[60]

One of Blücher's most pressing concerns when the *Schlesische Armee* was retreating at the beginning of March was for the safety of his champagne waggon. He did not know where it was, and hoped aloud that it would not fall into French hands. 'I wish they already had it,' retorted Gneisenau. 'Then we would be rid of the troublesome thing once and for all.'[61] A month earlier Alexander had to go and look for Blücher when he failed to appear for a council-of-war at the *Château* de Brienne, and eventually saw him emerge up a spiral staircase, clutching bottles of wine from the cellars.[62]

Champagne encouraged drunkenness to the point where it actually endangered military operations. Part of the problem was that it had to be stored for at least three years before it was ready to drink, which meant that enormous quantities were available for looting, and many Allied troops failed to realise how intoxicating it could be, as they assumed it was just a form of *weiss* beer. Occasionally the consequences were fatal, as Yorck's Prussian corps found when it attacked Châlons-sur-Marne on 4 February. The troops, half-starved and exhausted from several hours of fighting, found champagne and quickly became drunk. Several men were so inebriated that they were shot down after going up to the town wall in a reckless show of bravado, while others went to sleep in dangerously exposed places. Yorck had to relieve the units concerned with a fresh brigade in case the French attempted a sortie, and he later fiercely rebuked the men. In fact the danger was less than it appeared, since at least some of the French soldiers defending the town were also intoxicated.[63]

Looters generally caused less damage in champagne cellars than in wine vaults, for they would find the champagne in bottles stacked along the walls where they could easily help themselves without causing any needless damage. With ordinary wine, in contrast, they would simply stave in the base of the barrels, wasting most of the contents and destroying the whole stock. At one *château* Blücher's staff arrived to find Russian troops wading through a sea of wine, and it was not unusual for soldiers actually to drown in it.[64]

Champagne bottles did become an unexpected obstacle when they were discarded on the march and left the road littered with jagged pieces of glass. 'The quantity of champagne which was consumed that winter was wonderful,' explained Professor Steffens, who was with Blücher's headquarters. 'On the bare and dreary plains round Châlons we found the remains of broken bottles in such thick quantities as to be dangerous to the horses.'[65]

Surprisingly, not all the Allied troops liked the taste. Dr Wenzel Krimer had looked forward to enjoying real champagne at Epernay, but found it a sour and detestable drink.[66] Nor did *Leutnant* Wilhelm von Rahden take to it. He was given champagne when quartered in the home of a wealthy inhabitant of Châlons-sur-Marne: 'But as I have been unable to appreciate it either before or later, I accepted the six bottles intended for me only in the hope that some of my ever-thirsty comrades would visit me and empty them – which, indeed, is what happened.'[67]

When Bar-sur-Aube was ransacked at the end of February individual Allied soldiers were seen taking five or six champagne bottles away with them, which they attached to a string and carried round their shoulders. But they drank so much that they became disgusted with it, and distributed their remaining stocks to other regiments.[68]

Many officers, on the other hand, are said to have acquired a lasting affection for the drink. During the occupation of Epernay the *maire*, Jean-Rémy Moët, who was also a leading champagne merchant, reportedly gave Blücher's army 100,000 bottles, on condition that the rest of his stocks were neither looted nor requisitioned. Soon afterwards, he supposedly added 1 *franc* to the price of a bottle, and quickly recouped his losses as a result of orders from Allied officers who had served in the campaign.[69]

The story does have some basis in fact. Moët was both generous and astute, and he made contacts with officers who passed through Epernay, just as he had previously cultivated the patronage of Napoleon himself. In February, for example, he offered a billet and his best champagne to *Major* Friedrich von Colomb, the commander of a Prussian *Streifkorps*, who had intervened to protect his property from a mob of stragglers. Moët admitted to Colomb that he had already lost more than 40,000 bottles, but thought himself lucky to have escaped so lightly.[70]

Similarly, when Major-General Andrew Thomas, 11th Baron Blayney passed through Epernay in January during the evacuation of the British prisoner-of-war depot from Verdun, Moët gave him a champagne breakfast and insisted on presenting him with a dozen bottles. Blayney's account of his experiences in captivity was published later that year, and did Moët's sales no harm, for, despite mis-spelling his name as 'Mowhil', Blayney praised the excellence of his champagne.[71]

But the fortunes of the great champagne houses were boosted more by the simple fact of peace than by Allied officers' purchases. Champagne was already known in much of Europe before the 1814 campaign: Moët, for example, had established a network of salesmen to collect orders from as far afield as Hamburg and Vienna. His sales did increase immediately after the Napoleonic Wars, but were subsequently dwarfed by the massive expansion of his business in the second half of the nineteenth century.[72]

Chapter 18

Resistance

To offset his disadvantage of numbers, Napoleon had to turn the campaign into an asymmetrical war by outmanoeuvring the Allied forces and wearing them down with the potent combination of irregular forces and a small but highly mobile army. Yet he never managed to complete the transition from an orthodox military campaign to this new and more complex struggle. Resistance to the Allied occupation never became fully effective, partly because hostilities did not last long enough, but also because Napoleon himself was reluctant to instigate a true people's war. He wanted to fan uprisings, but only if they were subordinated to military control and mobilised from the top down, rather than bursting spontaneously into flame.

'What has your war got to do with me?'

The very nature of French society constrained the effectiveness of resistance. France was predominantly a rural country, with less than one-fifth of the population living in a town or city.[1] The isolation of the countryside, combined with low levels of education, inhibited the development of a national consciousness. Few peasants had ever seen a map of France, and in many areas Napoleon had to struggle to impose the notion of national defence on inhabitants whose outlook was altogether more limited.[2] Remote communities tended to be distrustful of the outside world and focused on their local concerns, as a Russian officer, Lieutenant Boris Uxkull, found as he passed through Vesoul. 'The peasants of this part of the country look rather wild and are not very outgoing to strangers,' he noted.[3]

In fact, many inhabitants made little distinction between French and Allied forces, and simply wanted to avoid antagonising whichever troops were in their area. Staff Captain Eduard von Löwenstern wrote that when he was near Provins in February:

> My host, an old farmer, was in the best of moods and little worried by the war around him. He told me: 'What the hell has your war got to do with me? I have no possessions and so nothing to lose. A poor devil like me wins whatever happens, and this war amuses me. One moment I see the French, then Germans and now your funny [Russian] people with your beards and sabres.'[4]

In some secluded areas inhabitants unable to afford light or heating actually went into a form of hibernation during the winter, which hardly favoured Napoleon's attempts to foment an uprising.[5]

France was also a country of strong regional identities, and the attitudes of different areas varied considerably. People in Alsace, Lorraine, Champagne, Dauphiné, the Ile-de-France, and some parts of Gascony tended to be more enthusiastic than those in regions such as the Nord, the Pas-de-Calais, Picardy, Normandy, or some areas in the west and south with a long history of opposition to central authority.

A whole range of local circumstances could determine a region's reaction to the invasion, including the terrain, population density, traditions, levels of education, the influence of the clergy, state of the local economy, and the legacy of the Revolution. Savoy, for example, had been detached from the Kingdom of Sardinia in 1792 and was unenthusiastic about its incorporation into France. 'The fact is that the people at Chambéry have done much more for the enemy than has ever been done for the French,' reported the local *commissaire extraordinaire*. Yet in neighbouring Dauphiné he had nothing but praise for the spirit of the inhabitants, and it is significant that seigneurial dues had been particularly heavy in that province during the *Ancien Régime*, which made a Bourbon restoration an unwelcome prospect.[6]

Interestingly, Napoleon singled out Burgundy as a particularly patriotic province. In May 1815, after regaining power, he awarded the *Légion d'honneur* to three Burgundian towns – Tournus, Chalon-sur-Saône, and St-Jean-de-Losne – for having resisted the Allied invasion. A fourth town, Roanne, 40 miles north-west of Lyon, was granted the same distinction by Napoleon III in 1864. Today the decoration can be seen in the coat of arms of each of these municipalities, and they were the only towns to be awarded the *Légion d'honneur* until after the Franco-Prussian War of 1870–1871. But Napoleon chose them overwhelmingly for political reasons, in order to reward the Burgundians for welcoming his return from exile on Elba and to encourage them to take up arms once again.[7]

Even within a region attitudes varied. The peasantry, for example, were not a uniform bloc and spanned a wide spectrum from labourers, tenants, craftsmen and smallholders to considerable landowners. French society was still deeply divided following the Revolution, and the invasion aggravated these schisms by raising the prospect of a Bourbon restoration. Inhabitants who had benefited from the Revolution feared that the privileges of the *Ancien Régime* would be reinstated, and that confiscated property would be returned to the Church and *émigrés*. When the Allies reoccupied Auxerre in 1815 the common people readily believed a rumour that the local clergy had bribed them to return.[8]

Aristocrats were also vulnerable to wild denunciations. Armand Gayot, *marquis* de Saint-Chamans, lived in a *château* 5 miles from Villenauxe, and used to send his servants to town for provisions. Their questions about the progress of the invasion were enough to cause suspicion that he was helping the Allies, and he was obliged to leave for Paris.[9]

The threat of social disorder undermined the likelihood of communities presenting a united front against the invaders. When Epernay was occupied by the Prussians in February, inmates were released from the town prison and helped to pillage several houses.[10] Inhabitants often exploited the invasion to help themselves to wood from the forests, knowing that the regulations for their preservation could not be enforced. Nor was it just Allied troops who devastated the *Château* de Brienne: it was later noted that wine growers had become the proud possessors of books on advanced science, which they could not even use.[11]

In fact, some people feared bandits almost as much as Cossacks, and the two groups did occasionally merge. The *maire* of Wattwiller, 27 miles north-west of Basel, arrested three young men from neighbouring towns for extortion, along with two Cossacks who had been drinking with them in an inn. But he was forced to release all five, and pay 150 *francs* in damages, when more Cossacks appeared and claimed that the three local men had enlisted in their unit. This was not a unique incident, for other inhabitants disguised themselves as Cossacks in order to extract money from villages by threatening to burn them down.[12]

Yet the invasion could also create a sense of solidarity within a town. At

Fontainebleau inhabitants unable to make secure hiding places in their own homes deposited their valuables with their neighbours. Wealthy inhabitants often made considerable sacrifices to help the less fortunate bear the burden of occupation, and at Troyes some citizens volunteered to replace older men who had been taken hostage by the Allies.[13]

Levée en masse

When the *Hauptarmee* crossed the Rhine Napoleon responded by decreeing a *levée en masse*, a calling to arms of the remaining able-bodied men in the threatened *départements*. Later, as the invasion progressed, the measure was extended to areas nearer Paris.[14]

It was an echo of the famous *levée en masse* of August 1793, when the French Republic had summoned to military service all unattached males between 18 and 25 years of age, with the rest of the population being mobilised in support. But there was an important difference. The main aim of the Revolutionary levy was to increase the strength of the regular army, and it did so by raising men throughout France and amalgamating them with experienced battalions. In contrast, the *levée en masse* of 1814 was designed simply to stoke irregular resistance in specific areas, and it therefore called to arms a wider section of the male population, including married and middle-aged citizens.[15]

During the Revolution Napoleon had seen for himself how the Allied invasion of 1792–1793 had helped tear French society apart by provoking massacres and civil war. This intensified his wariness about devolving any form of power to the people. His attempts to mobilise the population were limited both geographically and in the way in which irregulars were kept firmly subordinated by the appointment in each threatened *département* of a general, a respected local man, to command the insurrection.[16]

Napoleon's attitude was understandable. Even in the Peninsular War, the most famous example in this era of popular resistance, the much-vaunted Spanish guerrillas were often mere bandits, and posed a major threat to the French occupation only when officers were sent to organise and direct them, when regular units were used in close support, and when the guerrilla bands became larger and more militarised as the war progressed. Similarly, when *franc-tireur* companies were raised in France by local initiatives during the German invasion of 1870–1871, they proved so indisciplined that they had to be placed under military commanders.[17]

The *levée en masse* was meant to operate in close conjunction with four regular armies that Napoleon planned to organise in the eastern provinces, and with a corps of *gardes nationaux* attached to each of these armies.[18] Furthermore, the generals commanding the insurrection were given authority over groups of men experienced at handling firearms: the *gendarmes, douaniers, gardes champêtres, gardes forestiers*, and retired or discharged soldiers.[19]

One of the responsibilities of the generals of the *levée en masse* was to authorise the raising of mobile groups of irregulars, to carry out tasks for which regular formations were unsuited. The terms *partisan, corps franc*, and *compagnie franche* tended to be used loosely to describe any such group operating in an irregular role.

A *partisan*, the leader of an irregular detachment, had to be supplied with a letter of marque, a formal licence to carry out attacks, or else he would be regarded as a mere bandit and treated as such if captured. Since Napoleon did not want to create indisciplined groups of brigands or private armies in the wrong hands, he stipulated that a citizen who wanted to form a *partisan* group had to be suitable in background and previous military experience, and undertake to raise at least thirty men.[20]

'These gatherings of men show no backbone'

Yet Napoleon's plans were thrown into disarray by the speed with which the *maréchaux* retreated from the Rhine. As the balanced framework of regular armies and supporting corps collapsed, the *levée en masse* was left paralysed and deprived of a period of undisturbed organisation and training.

Leadership was absent or deficient. The *commissaires extraordinaires* were appointed only after the start of the invasion, and the *préfets* and *sous-préfets* withdrew as instructed in the face of the Allied advance, usually taking their *gendarmes* and *compagnie de réserve* as an escort and thereby removing the men best suited, by training and local knowledge, to act as a nucleus for resistance.[21]

Nobles and clergymen, the natural leaders of a community, were often hostile to Napoleon's government. In Spain the Catholic clergy had inspired, and even led, the guerrilla resistance, but in France religion was a divisive force. Despite the Concordat of 1802, Napoleon had failed to heal the Revolutionary schism between priests who had taken or refused the oath to the Civil Constitution of the Clergy, and in 1809 he had imprisoned Pope Pius VII after being excommunicated. Not until January 1814 did he belatedly try to repair the damage by ordering Pius to be returned to Italy. Many clergymen hoped that a Bourbon restoration would restore the Church to a position of strength, and they often exerted considerable local influence, especially in mountainous areas.

Some regions were too open and sparsely populated to be suitable for irregular warfare, and it was too cold for inhabitants readily to take to the hills unless they had already been driven from their homes by Allied troops. Passive resistance, such as the evasion of requisitioning, was ubiquitous, but sought simply to alleviate the burden on a community. Actively rising in support of Napoleon's regime called for greater motivation, organisation, and resources.

Napoleon lacked enough weapons to arm more than a fraction of the population. In November 1813 he had actually ordered his *préfets* to collect firearms from their *départements* to help equip his regular forces.[22] Much as the weapons were needed by the army, obliging inhabitants to surrender their own muskets, or those that they had collected from the battlefields or taken from deserters, undermined their morale. Even in areas not directly threatened by the Allies, part of the population needed to be armed. When twelve detainees escaped from Orléans prison on the night of 11/12 March, they were all recaptured the next day by peasants who were keeping watch for Cossack raids, fugitives, deserters, and vagabonds. As the *préfet* pointed out, this surveillance could be maintained only if the peasants were allowed to keep their hunting guns.[23]

Merely finding enough fit men for resistance could be problematic in areas already exhausted by levies of conscripts and *gardes nationaux*. Where sufficient manpower was available, implementing the *levée en masse* simply increased the pressure on resources. 'Consider my predicament, Sire,' protested Adrien d'Aucour, *comte* de Plancy, the *préfet* of the Seine-et-Marne, 'if I must feed 6,000 men that I am going to take from working in the countryside, and most of whom are busy at the moment supplying and transporting the food needed by our armies.'[24]

Ordering the *levée en masse* before the Allied armies approached therefore misused manpower required for other, more urgent, tasks; and yet delaying it left insufficient time for organising and training the men. By the time a *général de division* reached the *préfecture* of the Seine-et-Marne on 11 February to organise the levy, three-quarters of the *département* had already been occupied by the Allies. The orders were distributed regardless, but most were intercepted and served only to worry the Allies.

Once Napoleon's victories caused the Allies to retreat, the *levée en masse* became pointless. Plancy believed that the indiscipline of its men would frighten the population and undermine support for Napoleon, and he vainly tried to persuade the government to suspend it. Even the *gardes nationaux* were of dubious value. As Plancy pointed out, their officers were too inexperienced to know how to obtain food, while the generals set too little store on them to bother. As a result, the *gardes* pillaged, consumed twice as much as a similar number of regular troops, and were more fearsome to the inhabitants than the enemy.

Other authorities sent the same message. *Général de brigade* Pierre, *baron* Cassagne, the military commander of the Vosges, complained at the end of 1813: 'These gatherings of men still show no backbone, and can cause disorders because I have no superior officers trained to contain a throng like this, which has no idea of military discipline.'[25]

Similarly, a *commissaire extraordinaire* reported from La Rochelle in March that it was impossible to order a *levée en masse* because of the general discontent, the absence of an immediate threat, and the well-known discipline of Wellington's army:

> I would therefore have preferred to make regular and successive levies, and to have well-organised battalions than disordered and turbulent troops. Besides, the way in which to obtain nobody is to ask for everyone. If we do that, no one remains to force the others to march. In any case, people never take up arms in mass except to defend their own *canton*, and the enemy is still far away.[26]

It was difficult to encourage resistance against the invader, while at the same time enforcing conscription and repressing bands of *réfractaires*. In some *départements* the authorities actually felt obliged to disarm, rather than rouse, the population. The local *commissaire extraordinaire* explained the unwisdom of trying to introduce the *levée en masse* in the area around Luxembourg, which had become part of France only in 1795:

> This measure would not suit the *département* of Forêts. All the inhabitants are very quiet and the least spark could stir them up and then make them turn their weapons against the French. However, the *commandant* of the fortress of Luxembourg intends to have the muskets in their hands taken from them. It will be done gently at first, but force will be used if it proves necessary.[27]

The Allies actually armed the population themselves in some areas, for example on the left bank of the Rhine, where they attempted to raise a *Landwehr*, and in Savoy, where their Governor-General tried to form four regiments in the name of the King of Sardinia, although, significantly, they encountered as much apathy as Napoleon had done. Even in old France, the Allies sometimes kept existing units of *gardes nationaux* to maintain law and order.[28]

'They cost more than they are worth'

The combat value of the irregulars was rarely high. They could harass the Allies by ambushing couriers, capturing baggage, and rounding up defeated troops, but could defend a fixed location only briefly and against a weak force. It was difficult to co-ordinate the actions of different *partisan* bands, and some were little more than a nuisance to both sides.²⁹ In the Lyon theatre of war *Général de division* Jean, *comte* Marchand reported on 2 March that it was time to disband the *compagnies franches*:

> They cost more than they are worth, and I have decided to return them to Grenoble, where you can send each man back to his home. . . . In general, they are bad soldiers, and they are badly commanded, so it is time to get rid of them. If there are any conscripts among them, they could be incorporated into a regiment.³⁰

Such problems were hardly surprising, given the quality of leadership and methods of recruitment. In Paris a *corps franc* was formed by *Monsieur* Simon, but by 4 March it still had little more than half its required strength, and a cavalry element that was yet to be mounted. Recruitment was stymied by the lack of confidence in the government's ability to pay the sums promised to the families of volunteers. Simon drew some of his officers from the gambling and pleasure houses of the *Palais Royal*, and the *quartier-maître* was alleged to have gambled away some of the funds donated for the *corps*. Simon himself had become bankrupt and was reported to be deranged.³¹

The *corps francs* could undermine the field army by attracting deserters and *réfractaires* with the prospect of slacker discipline and personal gain. Some NCOs and men of the *Gardes d'honneur* are known to have left their regiments without authorisation, in order to join the *corps francs*, where they could apparently buy officer commissions.³²

To encourage the formation of *partisan* corps, volunteers were promised that they could keep whatever they took, and this helped to blur the distinction between patriots and mercenaries.³³ A French royalist, Eugène d'Arnauld, *baron* de Vitrolles, was in an Allied convoy attacked by peasants near the Swiss border in March, and later remarked of his captors:

> I would have forgiven them, and even applauded in my heart, if I could have attributed the acts of violence that were going to be inflicted on me to a sense of patriotism or at least to a just resentment of wrongs they had suffered. But it was impossible to have any illusions: they had taken up arms for pillage, not honour. They had risen in order to take loot without danger from defenceless travellers.

When a company of French *chasseurs à cheval* appeared, the peasants became bad-tempered, as they feared that they would have to share their spoils:

> The argument became serious. Suddenly the peasants withdrew to one side of our vehicles, while the *chasseurs* arranged themselves on the other, and they exchanged threats. Some musketshots had been fired behind us, and there was nothing reassuring about our position between two lines of combatants. We had everything to fear, even their clumsiness, but the leaders managed to calm them, and they came to a sort of understanding. It is always easy to agree, when there is a poor third party to plunder.³⁴

The Fismes decrees

Fear of reprisals, and concern about banditry, caused people to have distinctly ambivalent attitudes towards irregulars. When one of Napoleon's chamberlains tried to assemble a *compagnie franche* in a camp in the Morvan region, 40 miles west of Dijon, he had a mixed response. 'Many approve this step', noted a lawyer, 'but others who are no less wise condemn it.' They feared that, by intercepting Austrian communications, the irregulars would provoke an attack, and draw troops into a hitherto unoccupied area without being able to defend it.[35]

Some inhabitants even tried to thwart *partisan* attacks on the Allied forces, but risked being executed if Napoleon returned and liberated the area. The most notorious of his reprisals happened at Troyes, where two local men, the *chevalier* Jacques Gouault and the *marquis* de Widranges, had adopted royalist cockades and medals, trampled on the tricolour, and organised a petition urging the Allies to restore the Bourbons. After reoccupying the city on 24 February, Napoleon had Gouault shot and ordered the compilation of a list of all the Frenchmen who were accompanying, or serving with, the Allied armies. Any Frenchman who wore royalist decorations was to be executed as a traitor, and his property confiscated.[36]

Napoleon already knew that Bourbon princes were entering France behind the Allied armies, and at the same time as he discovered signs of their growing influence, he realised that he himself was not receiving the support he needed.[37] His increased harshness reflected his disappointment that his victories were not in themselves going to end the campaign and that new methods were needed. It was at this time that he began to sack, disgrace, or publicly rebuke a string of subordinates for alleged failings and lost opportunities. They included *Général de division* Claude, *comte* Guyot for causing the loss of some of the Imperial Guard artillery; *Général de brigade* Alexandre, *baron* Montbrun for letting Fontainebleau palace be occupied by the Austrians; *Général de division* Samuel, *baron* L'Héritier for failing to charge as he should have done; *Maréchal* Victor for his lack of drive; *Général de brigade* Armand Digeon for running out of artillery ammunition at Montereau; Charles, *baron* Caffarelli, the *préfet* of the Aube, for failing to return promptly to Troyes once it was liberated; and *Général de brigade* Jean, *baron* Moreau for tamely surrendering Soissons, whom he wanted to have executed in Paris with much publicity.[38]

Not all of these men actually deserved Napoleon's censure. Montbrun, for example, was acquitted by a council of inquiry a month later.[39] But Napoleon was clearly taking a sterner approach, and seeking to escalate the war, and his recent military successes meant he could do so from a position of strength, rather than as an act of desperation.[40] On 5 March he issued two decrees at Fismes, 16 miles west of Reims. The first not merely authorised, but required, all Frenchmen to rush to arms and support his field armies as they approached. The second threatened that any *maire*, public employee, or inhabitant who tried to dampen the spirit of resistance instead of fanning it would be punished as a traitor.

The Fismes decrees were widely publicised. It is difficult to ascertain their effectiveness in actually mobilising resistance, but they certainly alarmed the Allies. What is also clear is that the threats contained in the second decree, about punishing traitors, were not implemented fully. It is true that some men were executed after the decrees were issued, notably Gonzze, *chevalier* de Rougeville, a former *émigré*, who was shot at Reims on 10 March for serving as a guide to the Russians. But the decrees were intended not so much to purge the population as to rouse it against the Allies and intimidate those who might seek to oppose the uprisings. The *département* of the Loire, for example, saw few arrests, even though it contained numerous royalists.[41]

One reason why the Fismes decrees were not implemented in their full rigour was a recognition that the threat to punish traitors was too imprecise and therefore liable to be exploited by people who wanted to settle personal feuds.[42] Besides, treason was not as straightforward as it sounded. Often it was a more complex issue of perceptions, dates, and shifting fortunes. The west bank of the Rhine, for example, had been absorbed into France during the Revolution. But Blücher still regarded it as a German region and threatened that any of its inhabitants who continued to communicate with the French Empire would be executed as traitors. Combined with the Fismes decrees, this put the population in an impossible situation, with both sides demanding their loyalty.

Since the campaign ended with Napoleon's abdication, Frenchmen who had supported the Allied armies could claim that their actions were not treason, but patriotism and fidelity to the legitimate Bourbon monarchy. Acts of resistance, on the other hand, were now seen as crimes and were actually punished by the French royal authorities months after the end of the Allied occupation. In the *département* of the Aube a *garde champêtre*, Jean Jendrié, was executed as late as November for the assassination of an Austrian officer.[43]

Hence, Napoleon could not reasonably expect civilians to risk their lives and property if they saw his defeat as inevitable. The Allied failure to end the campaign quickly was essential in fanning resistance, as it proved that he was still a formidable opponent. It also prolonged the burden on the occupied regions and this was crucial, for Allied pillaging and exactions proved more effective in rousing the population than anything Napoleon did. Etienne Deschamps, a *gendarme* in the blockaded city of Besançon, joined a company of *tirailleurs* out of a desire to avenge his grandfather, a *maire* who had died after being mistreated by Austrian dragoons. 'Wherever the enemy has been, anything can be done,' noted Napoleon on 1 March as he ordered the extension of the *levée en masse* to more *départements*.[44]

It was when they could operate in conjunction with French regular troops that *partisans* were most effective. The resistance in the Ardennes was strong, partly because of the hilly and wooded terrain, but also because it could be sustained by the French-held fortresses in the area. Even small detachments of regulars could provide an experienced and disciplined nucleus around which to mobilise the population.

It was partly because of the need to fan resistance with the close support of the army that Napoleon attempted his *manoeuvre sur les derrières* towards the end of March. It seems strange that he had not already detached a cavalry division to raid behind the Allied armies in a way that would become common in the American Civil War (1861–1865). He did briefly consider sending Ney's corps into Lorraine in the middle of March, but clearly concluded that he had too small an army to afford major detachments.[45]

The Allied response

Since the Allies had only weak forces in their rear, they found it difficult to secure their communications, gather supplies, and stamp out risings. The Governor of Lothringia admitted that he temporarily lost all control over the *département* of the Moselle. But the real impact of the *levée en masse* was psychological. Fear magnified the actual resistance, reinforced the caution of Allied commanders, and added to the discomfort of their troops. Prussian officers later said that when they took up quarters in houses, they had to stay away from the windows in case they came under fire, and that they preferred to bivouac in the fields. Even a courier might have an escort of as many as ten soldiers.[46]

The Allies responded robustly to resistance, both by preventative measures such as placing former French soldiers under surveillance, and by vigorous action against bands that had already formed. One of their first concerns was to disarm the civilian population and *gardes nationaux*, although they had limited success. Many men preferred to hide or bury their weapons, and some actually managed to buy ammunition from Allied soldiers.

Systematic efforts were made to isolate *partisans* from the local communities. Mobile columns swept the countryside, patrols searched forests, and inhabitants who had fled their homes were instructed to return. At Chaumont civilians needed an official pass if they wanted to go to the woods. In the Vosges *communes* that handed over irregular leaders were promised exemption from all requisitions, and *partisans* were offered an amnesty if they abandoned resistance.[47]

Inhabitants caught with unauthorised weapons risked having their houses burned down, and attacks might result in troops being allowed to pillage an entire town. Fines were commonly imposed as a collective punishment, with payment being enforced by the taking of hostages. At Dijon on 21 February, at a time when the *Hauptarmee* was in retreat, the Austrians seized six prominent citizens. One had an attack of gout and was left at home, but the other five were taken away as prisoners-of-war, and freed only on 17 March.[48]

The way the Allies behaved after they reoccupied Troyes on 4 March is a good example of their approach. Since their troops had been attacked while evacuating the city less than a fortnight earlier, the Governor-General ordered searches to be made for the culprits, and threatened to take hostages and impose a collective fine of 1 million *francs*. If the money was not paid, 'the four corners of the city will be set on fire to serve as an example to the whole of France'. At the same time he ordered 6,000 muskets to be surrendered within twenty-four hours, as this was thought to be the number of inhabitants capable of bearing arms, and a sum of 100 *francs* had to be paid for every musket that was not delivered. The Governor-General demanded to be informed of every French soldier who was being hidden by the inhabitants, and threatened to punish any disobedience with death.[49]

A couple of informers did, in fact, claim a reward for the discovery of the culprits, but deliberately misidentified them out of personal hatred, causing two innocent weavers to be shot.[50] This was not an isolated case. A French royalist, Eugène d'Arnauld, *baron* de Vitrolles, had an interview with a senior Austrian commander at Auxerre in March:

> He was particularly struck by the moral depravity he found in France. He gave me, among other examples, the messages from informers that stemmed from local enmities and that were intended to draw the vengeance of the foreigners against hated neighbours.[51]

It was not only in the occupied areas that malicious allegations were made. Towards the end of 1813 a tax inspector at Montargis was said to have criticised Napoleon's government, but the *préfet* believed that the denunciation was unreliable, and pointed out that the employees of the *droits réunis* were unpopular because of the nature of their duties.[52]

Allied attitudes hardened after Napoleon issued the Fismes decrees. Within eight days Schwarzenberg and Blücher had responded with proclamations of their own. First, they rejected Napoleon's claims that they wanted to ravage and dismember France, and repeated their earlier message that they sought only a durable peace, and that he alone was responsible for the continuation of the war. Emphasising the weight of Allied numbers, they claimed that any resistance would be futile, a message that Blücher reinforced with news of his recent victory at Laon. Schwarzenberg tried to contain the risings by threatening to burn *communes* that sounded the tocsin, and to shoot messengers carrying orders for the *levée en masse*. Blücher frankly admitted that his soldiers had committed excesses, but placed the blame on the population for having previously massacred several of their comrades.[53]

In summoning the population to arms, Napoleon had anticipated the obvious Allied reaction by stating that the execution of any French citizen would be immediately avenged by the death of an Allied prisoner. He had also ordered the levies to be dressed in blue peasant smocks, and equipped with shakos and shoes, so they would have a sort of uniform, and some protection from reprisals.[54] His threat was nothing unusual. When King Friedrich Wilhelm III had mobilised the Prussian *Landsturm* in April 1813, he had warned that the severest reprisals would immediately follow if its captured men were treated more harshly than prisoners from the regular army, and he ordered this message to be translated into French and posted up wherever the *Landsturm* was called out.[55]

In response to Napoleon's threat, Schwarzenberg's proclamation stated that French prisoners would answer for any action taken against captured Allied soldiers. But, interestingly, it did distinguish between men caught carrying weapons as part of the *levée en masse*, who would be treated as prisoners-of-war and deported to Siberia or another remote province, and civilians who killed or wounded Allied soldiers, who would be shot within twenty-four hours.[56]

What is particularly striking is how many of the Allied measures were later forbidden under the Hague Conventions (1899 and 1907), or under the fuller provisions of the Fourth Geneva Convention for the protection of civilians in wartime (1949). Reprisals, the confiscation of property, the taking of hostages, and the imposition of fines or other collective penalties all now contravene international law. Yet such rules have often been disregarded, not least during the German occupations of France in both world wars. It should be added that in 1814 the French army itself used many of the same methods on its own people. When the cavalry requisitioned 15,000 *francs* from Nancy in January for shoeing its horses, it took the *maire* and two of his deputies hostage to ensure payment. The Allied authorities intended the more extreme measures, such as the burning of entire villages, as a threat to discourage hostile activity, and rarely carried them out. Nor was it a total war, still less a genocidal one: the Allies did not conscript labour for their home countries, or carry out mass deportations.[57]

Nicolas Wolff

The most famous of the *partisans* was Nicolas Wolff, an Alsatian who became a local folk hero. But his deeds were wildly exaggerated, and deconstructing this legendary figure exposes the real nature and limitations of resistance.

Wolff was one of the emissaries sent by Napoleon at the beginning of March to rouse the occupied *départements* of the Meurthe, Vosges, Bas-Rhin, and Haut-Rhin. He headed for his home village of Rothau, 26 miles south-west of Strasbourg, and on 3 April issued a proclamation in Napoleon's name, calling on the inhabitants to take up arms. He promised the abolition of the *droits réunis*, and a pardon for deserters, but also threatened *gardes forestiers* and members of the *Légion d'honneur* that they would lose their pension if they refused to join him.

Yet the response was poor, for Wolff inspired fear as much as enthusiasm among the population. When the Allies sent out mobile columns, they were able to obtain information from *maires* and spies, even if it was sometimes unhelpful. (Wolff's numbers were variously reported between 300 and 1,500.)

A Bavarian detachment of sixty to seventy men reached Rothau from the south in the night of 6/7 April but withdrew after a clash, as its subaltern commander feared being cut off in unknown country. In the morning another column, this time of Baden troops, attacked Rothau from the east before falling back. These minor temporary successes were later inflated into a major victory over as many as two Bavarian regiments.

Significantly, Wolff's rising was then ended through negotiations initiated by local inhabitants anxious for their homes and livelihoods. The Allies agreed to spare Rothau, provided the population handed over its weapons and remained quiet. Wolff was persuaded to leave, and escaped into the woods with about forty men. The Allies occupied Rothau, ordered the demolition of Wolff's home, and swept the area. Local men volunteered to carry out patrols, and the Allied authorities were confident that the peasants would hand over any remaining resistants. News of the fall of Paris helped complete the pacification.

Even if Wolff had managed to mobilise more men, he would have been too late to affect the outcome of the war, or prevent Napoleon's abdication. Far from being the successful *partisan* leader of popular myth, he in fact epitomised the more general failure of resistance to the invasion.[58]

Chapter 19

The propaganda war

It was not just on the battlefield that Napoleon had to defend France. Inflicting casualties or taking specific locations were less important than establishing his psychological dominance over the opposing forces, and maintaining his credibility with the population. Ultimately, it was moral disintegration, and not military defeat, that cost him the campaign.

All the participants in 1814 employed a combination of hard and soft power, whether it was the Allies seeking to bribe French fortress commanders to capitulate, Napoleon trying to detach the Crown Prince of Sweden and the King of Naples from the coalition, or the Provisional Government attempting to subvert Napoleon's subordinates after the fall of Paris. The way in which commanders consciously strove to undermine their enemy's will is shown by a gleeful note sent in March by the Prussian outpost commander near Courtrai in Belgium to the French opposite him:

> Comrade,
> Not long ago you were good enough to send me some brief accounts of victories that the French army had apparently won. I have the honour to inform you with the greatest pleasure that His Excellency Marshal Blücher has just won a complete victory over the French army commanded by the Emperor of the French, at Laon on the 9th.
> Sir, I have the honour to be . . .[1]

Only by examining these underlying psychological operations can the course of the campaign be understood. Napoleon himself remained acutely conscious of the volatility of morale in Paris, and this influenced his military decisions: one reason why he attacked Reims on 13 March was so he could immediately offset the moral impact of his failure at Laon.

Napoleon's propaganda machine

Whereas the overall quality of Napoleon's army had declined since 1805, his system of controlling information had developed into a formidable machine. He had gradually emasculated the often defamatory press that had sprung into life during the Revolution, and by 1811 had reduced the Parisian political newspapers to just four (the *Journal de l'empire*, the *Gazette de France*, the *Journal de Paris*, and *Le Moniteur*), compared with over seventy-five in 1800.[2] At the same time he ensured that each *département* had a local newssheet or paper of its own, so propaganda could be cascaded from the centre, with *bulletins* printed in *Le Moniteur* automatically being republished throughout the country.

Towards the end of 1813, with invasion imminent, Napoleon tightened his grip even further. The *préfet* of the Seine-et-Marne, for example, was instructed to take personal charge of directing public opinion in his *département*, and to have articles written for the local press to encourage resistance to the invasion. By praising zealous officials, *communes* that readily provided their quota of conscripts, and local men who distinguished themselves in the army, he could encourage a sense of pride in his *département*.³

Emergency controls were also imposed on the national press in Paris.⁴ On 4 February Napoleon decreed the formation of a six-man committee to supervise and edit the newspapers. Prior to publication, it had to approve any article relating to military movements, public morale, or foreign relations.⁵ At the same time Napoleon personally had the papers sent to him so he could monitor them even in the middle of his military operations.⁶ He was often dissatisfied. 'The newspapers are stupidly written,' he berated the *Ministre de la police générale* on 19 February:

> Is it appropriate, at the present moment, to go and say that I had few men, that I won only because I surprised the enemy and that we were outnumbered by three to one? You must really have lost your heads in Paris to say such things, when I say everywhere that I have 300,000 men, when the enemy believes it and when it has to be said until people have had more than enough.
>
> I created an office [committee] to edit the newspapers – so does the office not see these articles? This is how, with strokes of the pen, you destroy all the fruits of victory! You could easily read these things yourself, to know that it is not a question of vainglory and that one of the first principles of war is to exaggerate your strength and not diminish it. But how can you get that across to poets who seek to flatter me and flatter the national pride, instead of trying to do good?
>
> It seems to me that these things are not beneath you, and that, if you paid some attention to them, such articles – which are not simply stupidities, but fatal stupidities – would not be printed. At the very least, if one did not want to say that our strength was immense, nothing should have been said at all.⁷

The *Ministre de la police générale* responded by blaming the committee that Napoleon had appointed to edit the newspapers. He clearly resented the way that it encroached on his functions, and how it sought to obtain his correspondence and interfere in apparently unrelated matters. Its meetings, he claimed, were reduced to fruitless debates by friction between its members and by its president's tendency to regard his task with amused detachment as it interfered with his normal work. 'I have only one view, Sire, on this commission,' the Minister concluded. 'It will not fulfil its purpose, and thus far I see that it has paralysed the already feeble means I had, without substituting anything.'⁸

'The authorities surround you with obscurity'

Bad news was simply suppressed. The fall of Bordeaux on 12 March was not reported in the *Journal de Paris* until 2 April, after the Allied occupation of the capital itself. A leading opposition writer, François-René de Chateaubriand, described how the regime kept the people in ignorance:

> The enemy is at Meaux, but you learn of it only through the flight of the country people. The authorities surround you with obscurity, make light of your worries, laugh at your distress, and scorn what you might feel or think. You want to speak out, but you are denounced by a spy, arrested by a *gendarme*, and judged by a military commission. They do you in, and you are forgotten.⁹

Enforcing silence in this way could actually be more effective than bombarding people with propaganda. Rather than unleashing a torrent of denigration of the Bourbons,

Napoleon followed the precedent set during the Revolution and imposed a blanket of silence. On 27 February, for example, a report in *Le Moniteur* stated that during the Allied occupation of Troyes a former *émigré* and a former *garde du corps* had been condemned to death for declaring themselves 'in favour of the enemy' and for wearing the cross of Saint-Louis. But, significantly, it did not mention either Louis XVIII or the Bourbons by name. This increased the difficulties royalists faced in raising the profile of their claimant to the throne, and establishing him as a viable alternative to Napoleon.

Yet doing no more than suppressing news would have left a vacuum easily filled by damaging rumours. Previously, when the war had been fought beyond France's borders, news had been delayed by distance, but it was no longer so easy to isolate Paris. The authorities did try to control the influx of people, for example by forbidding British prisoners-of-war on parole to enter the capital when their depot was evacuated from Verdun. On 8 March sentries at the city's *barrières* began to check passports, but the sheer number of people entering or leaving made it difficult for this to be done carefully without causing congestion.[10]

The police also intercepted letters coming from the armies, yet Parisians could still learn of events from sick or wounded soldiers, or from the carters who brought supplies to the marketplaces. The *Hôtel des postes* was a hotbed of news about the Allied progress because of the frequent arrival there of couriers and displaced persons. Disaffected political figures, such as the well-connected Talleyrand, could even obtain information and foreign newspapers from officials within the administration.[11]

Thus Napoleon constantly had to spin his own, more optimistic version of events. When Paris was threatened by Blücher's advance at the beginning of February he crushed the idea of the Empress going to pray at the Church of Sainte-Geneviève, the city's patron saint. 'I fear this will do nothing except have a bad effect,' he admonished Joseph, 'so put a stop to these forty-hour prayers and these *Miserere*. If we had to go through so many antics, we would all be afraid of dying. . . . As matters stand, we must show confidence and take bold measures.'[12]

Apart from being his own director of propaganda, Napoleon was even his own war correspondent, for he was a skilled writer and had made a name for himself as early as 1793 with his pamphlet *Le souper de Beaucaire*, with its call for national unity to preserve the Revolution from civil war. He personally dictated *bulletins* of his operations, and reinforced them by ordering abstracts of the same information to be inserted as news items, under the heading of a local town, as if from an independent source. Similarly, when he wrote to his officials at Paris, he had a wider audience in mind. 'Have a summary of this letter inserted as news in *Le Moniteur*,' he instructed Joseph when informing him of the Battle of Craonne.[13]

The influence of Napoleon's propaganda extended beyond France. Translations of his *bulletins*, extracted from *Le Moniteur*, appeared, for example, in the British press, where their significance was intensified by the difficulty in obtaining accurate news. *The Times* complained on 24 February:

> The information which we are enabled to procure of the general positions and movements of the French and Allied Armies is still exceedingly indistinct and obscure. *Moniteurs* of two days later than the last have reached us. We have them now to the 21st instant.[14]

It is too simplistic to regard the reports published in *Le Moniteur* as completely mendacious. Most were partly accurate, difficult to disprove, and reliant on silence and distraction as much as on outright lies. On 22 January an article appeared that did not attempt to conceal the fact that the *Schlesische Armee* had crossed the Rhine, but claimed that it was ravaged by sickness and that all its infantry was blockading fortresses, the implication being that it could advance no further.[15]

The most blatant lies tended to be statistics. Napoleon systematically exaggerated Allied losses and understated his own, claiming, for example, to have taken 10,000 prisoners at Vauchamps, for the loss of just 300 to 400 of his own men. 'Newspapers are not history, any more than the *bulletins* are history,' he explained to Joseph. 'You must always make your enemy believe your forces are immense.'[16]

Napoleon was careful to hover just above the thin line separating the astonishing from the absurd, and realised that some of his figures were difficult to accept. When he reported that he had lost no more than 400 killed or wounded at Nangis and Montereau, he added the assurance 'although this is improbable, it is nonetheless the exact truth'.[17] Previous claims to have destroyed the élite of the Russian army were supported by an announcement that many medals had been taken from the fallen.

Such exaggerations were ridiculed by Napoleon's opponents, as Professor Steffens recorded in the *Schlesische Armee*:

> We learned by degrees how falsely our state after the battles of Brienne and Montmirail had been represented at Napoleon's head-quarters. At first we heard it only by reports, but, when some numbers of the *Journal de l'empire* fell into our hands, the reading of the *bulletins* afforded us immense amusement.[18]

Defeats were misrepresented. Napoleon glossed over the outcome of La Rothière by portraying it as a mere rearguard action, and, at odds of one against five, as 'one of the French army's finest feats of arms'. Despite having lost at least 54 guns, he admitted to the capture of just one Imperial Guard battery, and claimed that it had happened in the darkness, that the gunners had counter-attacked, saving their horses and harnesses, and that they had lost just 15 men killed or captured. He also avoided giving the impression that the battle had ended in a retreat by stating that he had already made up his mind to move towards Troyes so he could operate against Allied columns heading westwards for Sens.[19]

Some setbacks could not be concealed so easily. Napoleon did not try to hide the capitulation of Soissons, but blamed it on 'treason' and a 'cowardice impossible to describe'.[20] By announcing that the *commandant* would be tried before a commission of enquiry, he was able to encourage others to do their duty, and to emphasise that the setback was the result of an individual's failing rather than a symptom of a wider problem. Thus, *Le Moniteur* absolved the people of Soissons from any blame, and stressed the sense of common purpose between them and the garrison: 'There are no praises that they do not give to the *Régiment de la Vistule*, which formed their garrison, and there are no praises that the *Régiment de la Vistule* does not make of the inhabitants.'[21]

Napoleon frequently extolled individual generals or units in this way, knowing that his accounts would be read by his soldiers and their relatives. He specifically mentioned, for example, the *32e Ligne* attacking the village of Mormant on 17 February, and the *7e Chasseurs à cheval* charging across the bridges at Montereau the following day. He sought to create a spirit of emulation not only between regiments but between different towns and regions. He contrasted the example set by the town of Epernay, which had barricaded its streets against an Allied column, to the weakness of Reims in opening its gates to 150 Cossacks.[22]

In describing battles, Napoleon subtly influenced readers by using negatively charged words about the Allies and heroic ones for his own forces. He associated his army with glory, activity, and calmness, and described it vigorously charging and cutting up its opponents without firing a shot. The Allies, in contrast, were disconcerted, unable to gain an inch of ground, driven in, repulsed with great loss, sabred, terrified, completely routed, and entirely destroyed.[23]

In creating a picture of the difficulties experienced by the invaders, Napoleon used covert propaganda by publishing news items that appeared to be from an independent source, but which were either fabricated or carefully selected. Thus, the *Journal de Paris* published extracts from intercepted letters sent to Allied soldiers by their relatives, which expressed a desire for peace and complained about the weight of requisitions in Germany, thus showing the French people that their opponents had to bear similar burdens.[24]

Atrocity stories

Reasoned arguments tend to be less effective in the short term than manipulating emotions, rousing indignation, and playing on fears. Atrocity stories began appearing in the press immediately after Napoleon took the field, with the first communication, published on 29 January, reporting on the joy expressed by the population of Saint-Dizier on being freed after two days of occupation. A further spate of stories followed when Napoleon's victories in the middle of February forced the Allies to retreat. Yet Napoleon believed that opportunities were being missed, and castigated the *Ministre de la guerre*:

> It is impossible for me to be more displeased by the little that is being done for public morale. You can boost it not by verses or odes, but by simple and true facts and details. It's very simple to understand. I do not want articles to be written at Paris. I do not want the public to be deceived, simply the enemy's conduct to be put before everyone's eyes.[25]

Napoleon wanted letters from the occupied regions to be printed in full, including the names, addresses, and any grammatical errors, to show that they were genuine. To reinforce the credibility of the accounts, he ordered *conseillers d'état*, or other prestigious officials, to be sent to the liberated regions to record them.[26]

But as the *Ministre de la police générale* pointed out, few inhabitants would be willing to allow their names to be published, in case it exposed them and their properties to Allied reprisals, and neither would rape victims want to be named.[27] Napoleon was also conscious that the stories would quickly become dated and lose their emotive power, and yet it would take time to produce and disseminate the reports. 'I am no longer obeyed,' he complained: 'You are all more intelligent than me, and I endlessly encounter resistance and objections with buts, ifs, and becauses. The moment has now almost passed: these articles needed to be published immediately.'[28]

In fact, deputations from five liberated towns were received at the *hôtel-de-ville* in Paris that same day, 26 February. The deputies had been chosen from articulate men who could express themselves forcefully in describing their experiences of occupation.[29] Those from Château-Thierry claimed that the Allies had released inmates from jail in order to identify the best places to pillage. One woman, they said, was gang raped and thrown into a lock, while another was violated on the body of her dead husband. Even lunatics and nuns were mistreated, and several children detained by soldiers who wanted to take them back to Russia.[30] A report about the deputies' speeches was printed overnight, posted up in the streets of Paris the next day, and published in the Parisian newspapers on the 28th.[31]

The core message of the atrocity stories was that the capital could expect similar treatment if the Allies arrived, and that no one, of any sex or social rank, would be spared. Napoleon sought to terrify the nobility and bourgeoisie out of any indifference and make them utterly dependent on him, by portraying himself as their only protection. It was a good example of the black-and-white fallacy, when a choice is misleadingly presented of just two alternatives, one of which is too awful to contemplate.

Yet atrocity stories could backfire by cowing people into apathy rather than obedience, or by encouraging them to flee the campaign area, which actually complicated the challenges faced by the authorities in the interior of France, however much it also inconvenienced the Allies.[32] Napoleon was therefore careful to combine reports of atrocities with accounts of ordinary civilians taking revenge, including an incident when they seized some Cossacks who had set a farm alight and threw them into the flames.[33] He thus tried to give the population a sense of empowerment by showing that they could defend themselves.

Napoleon systematically incited hatred in this way. In accusing Lieutenant-General Count Saint-Priest, a French *émigré* in the Russian army, of burning fifty houses, he wrote that 'renegades have always been the cruellest enemies of their country'.[34] According to a subsequent report, the artillery battery that mortally wounded Saint-Priest at Reims was the same one that had felled the exiled *Général de division* Jean Moreau at Dresden in 1813.[35] The claim was dubious, but its implication was clear: any Frenchman who fought against his own country would meet a similar fate.

Napoleon carefully selected the targets at which he directed popular hatred. He tended to blame atrocities on the Cossacks, for their reputation and distinct appearance made them the easiest subgroup to stereotype and dehumanise. Accounts of brutality were more credible if attributed to men already viewed with prejudice, and so the Cossacks became the symbol of all that was negative and fearsome in the Allied armies.

In contrast, Napoleon specifically praised the Austrians in a report published in *Le Moniteur* on 21 February, at a time when he was seeking to detach Austria from the coalition. He stated that an Austrian general had preserved the palace of Fontainebleau during the recent occupation of the town by placing sentries to protect it from the Cossacks, and he added that the inhabitants complained not of the Austrians but of the Tartars, whom he described as 'brigands', 'monsters', and 'true highway thieves'. Thus, Napoleon used his propaganda to support diplomatic efforts to split the Allies, and prepare public opinion for a negotiated peace.

Other propaganda vehicles

It was not just through the press that Napoleon manipulated people's minds, but through posters, proclamations, and public speakers.[36] More subtle than denying rumours in print was to order *préfets* to do so in personal conversation, or to have the police pay literary figures to disseminate a particular version of events in the salons of Paris.[37]

Napoleon personally addressed both soldiers and civilians in countless face-to-face meetings, and tried to gain their loyalty with acts of benevolence. When he passed through the village of Eclaron on 28 January he promised to rebuild the wooden spire of the church, which had been struck by lightning three years earlier, and granted the *Légion d'honneur* to the village surgeon, who had served under him in Egypt.[38]

Oral propaganda had advantages over the press: it could be tailored for a particular audience, produced immediate feedback, and usually made a more forceful impression. But speeches were audible only to a small audience, and could be distorted if repeated second-hand.

Popular prints, in contrast, had a greater reach. When Marie-Louise sent Napoleon a portrait of his son at prayer, he told her to have it engraved with the caption: 'I pray God to save my father and France.' An official proposed changing 'save' to 'watch over'. Napoleon then amended it to the simpler 'I pray God for my father and for France,' and ordered his son to be shown in the uniform of the *Garde nationale*, rather than that of a Polish lancer, so the citizens of Paris saw him as one of their own. As well as having the image sold within France, Napoleon had it sent to the boy's grandfather, Emperor Franz, to remind him of what Austria would lose in a change of regime.[39]

Visual images such as these broadened the propaganda war to embrace non-literate audiences. Similarly, reviews at the Tuileries palace entertained and impressed spectators with a sense of the military power still at the regime's disposal. Salvoes of artillery saluted Napoleon's successes. Ten flags taken in battle were publicly presented to the Empress on 27 February, while the sabres of captured generals were exhibited in the Tuileries. Elsewhere in France the authorities organised demonstrations to increase morale: in the south-west the *préfet* of the Gers distributed funds to his *communes* so they could welcome troops who passed through.[40]

Books were censored. One author, Jacques Quesné, later explained how the censors imposed changes on his novel, the *Mémoires de Céran de Valmeuil*, before it could be published at the start of 1814. In the original version the hero's son died during the retreat from Moscow, but this would have drawn attention to the disastrous outcome of the invasion, so he had to be sent instead to the United States.[41]

Theatres were a particularly powerful medium, since they evoked a mass emotional response. As with the newspapers, Napoleon had reduced the number of theatres in order to improve their quality and make them easier to control. By personally attending shows, as he did at the end of 1813, he could project an air of self-confidence and reassure the social élite, in the same way that he toured the working class districts of Paris before taking command of his army.[42]

Accounts of Napoleon's victories were proclaimed in theatres, just as newsreels would be shown in cinemas during the Second World War. But by assembling large numbers of people in a single place, theatres provided protesters with a degree of anonymity, and could encourage ironic applause. At the town of Blois an actor appeared on the stage and read an official *bulletin*, only to find that some British prisoners-of-war in the audience were mocking the blatant exaggerations with derisive cheers of *Bravo! Vive Napoléon! Encore! encore!*[43]

The plays themselves often evoked the defence of France against earlier invasions, even though this search for historical parallels made it necessary to celebrate royal heroes from the distant past, despite the regime's keenness to avoid mentioning the most recent house, the Bourbons. A common theme was to contrast the paralysing fear of some characters with the heroism of others, and to urge citizens to defend their homes. Ridicule was used in *l'Honnête Cosaque* ('The honest Cossack'), which was subtitled 'Believe that, and drink water'. The moral was that inhabitants who welcomed the Cossacks in the hope of escaping pillage would quickly become disillusioned and be forced to take up arms.

The most notable of the patriotic spectacles was *l'Oriflamme*, which celebrated the success of the Frankish ruler Charles Martel in checking the Saracen invasion of southern France in 732. The opera showed preparations for a wedding suddenly interrupted by the arrival of a terrified crowd of fugitives. They describe atrocities committed by the invaders. Then shouts go up for vengeance and a knight appears, carrying the sacred royal standard or *Oriflamme*. Enthusiasm seizes everyone and redoubles with the announcement that Charles Martel, who had so often led the French to victory, would fight at their head. Swearing to deliver their country from the barbarians, the warriors and inhabitants rush off together to glory.

The key themes of *l'Oriflamme* were that the inhabitants had to defend their country, even at the cost of their lives; that only enthusiasm counted, not the numerical odds; and that Napoleon would arrive as a saviour to lead his people to a final victory that would give peace to the world. The opera therefore responded to the widespread desire for peace and supported the portrayal of Napoleon in the newspapers as the only man able to preserve Paris from the Cossacks.

L'Oriflamme was first staged on 1 February, and the timing of the opening night was fortuitous, for news of Napoleon's victory at Brienne reached Paris that morning. The audience was unusually large, partly because people hoped that details of the battle would be announced in the theatre and that Napoleon's son would appear.[44] But the attendance also reflected the quality of the opera, which had been commissioned by the regime as one of the centrepieces of its propaganda war and was consequently well-funded. It remained popular in the capital, where it was performed right up until 20 March, and was also staged in the main provincial cities.[45]

But the other shows were less successful. Strict state control and pieces hastily composed around the same basic theme were unlikely to produce good theatre. *Les héroines de Belfort* was savaged by reviewers for containing much recycled material. Parisians themselves seem to have wanted to forget the war, as Victor, *duc* de Broglie noted during a performance that showed Cossacks pillaging a village: 'The play was hissed excessively from the start,' he recalled, 'interrupted by protests from the audience, and could not be completed.' In contrast, a comic opera, the *Joconde*, was particularly popular, for audiences simply sought entertainment.[46]

The results

Napoleon's psychological warfare is difficult to assess on its own merits, since it was so closely intertwined with his conventional operations. Even so, some idea of the public mood can be gained from the wild fluctuations in share prices. The stock exchange at Paris hummed with the latest information, and the police were able to take the nation's pulse by monitoring conversations as well as tracking the exchange rates. As in the theatres, Napoleon's *bulletins* were publicly read out to the traders.[47]

Even in London, which was not threatened by hostile armies, the sensitivity of the stock exchange was dramatically demonstrated on 21 February when fraudsters caused a temporary surge in the price of stocks by claiming that an officer had landed in Dover with news of Napoleon's death and imminent peace.

In Paris the swings in public morale are starkly shown by the volatility of 5 per cent consols. Following the Peace of Tilsit they had reached a high point of 93.40 *francs* in August 1807, and had still been over 70 *francs* as late as August 1813.[48] Then they collapsed and by the beginning of 1814 were worth around 50 *francs*.

Public confidence slumped again at the start of February as word spread of the defeat at La Rothière.[49] It did not help that the news of Napoleon's success at Brienne three days earlier had been inflated. Since Brienne and La Rothière were seen as a single battle, hopes were dashed as the victory turned out to be a defeat. That bred

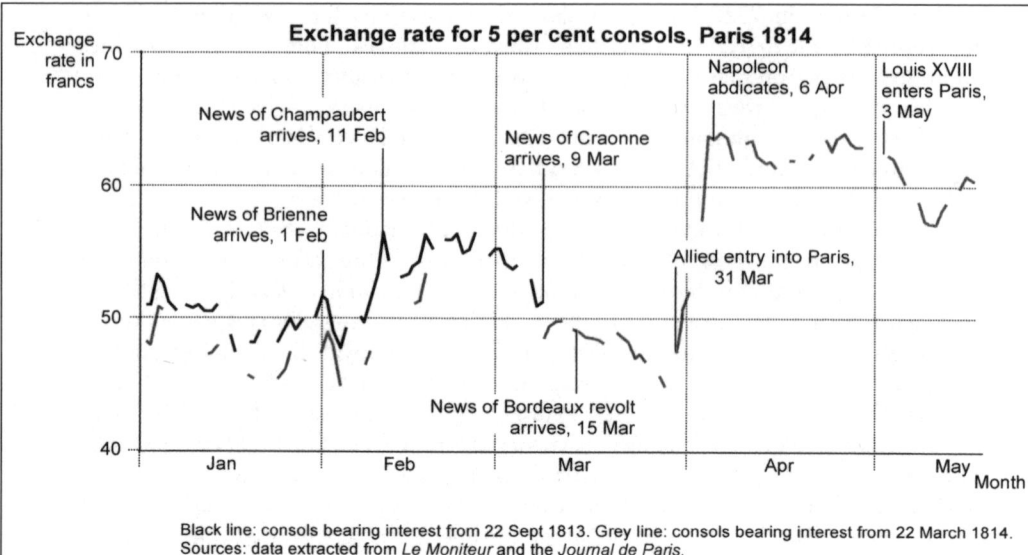

distrust, and caused the setback to be exaggerated into a complete rout. Food was hoarded, craftsmen were kept busy making hiding places for valuables inside homes, and the director of the museum at the Louvre badgered Joseph for permission to prepare the most precious items for evacuation.[50] Napoleon himself gave orders for potential trophies to be quietly removed from his palaces of Compiègne and Fontainebleau, 35–45 miles north-east and south-east of the capital.[51]

Paris remained in a state of panic for over a week, until news came on 11 February that Napoleon had won a victory at Champaubert. Some people were initially sceptical because of their disappointment following Brienne. The architect Pierre Fontaine suspected as late as the 15th that Champaubert and Montmirail were only minor actions that had been exaggerated, and his doubts were reinforced by evidence of the *Hauptarmee*'s advance on Paris along the Seine valley, including the sight of Napoleon's reserve artillery withdrawing to the heights outside the city.[52]

The tighter controls Napoleon had imposed on the press undermined the subtlety of his propaganda, making it too obvious, distracting from the messages he wanted to convey, and encouraging doubt even when the basic facts were true. Once a lie was detected, the official version of events was no longer believed, yet neither could alternative sources of information be trusted, partly as some rumours were invented by speculators.[53] As Wellington explained at the beginning of April:

> You are quite right to put no faith in reports from the coast of France. There are more false reports in France than even in Spain. In fact, between the Government, and those who detest the Government, there is no truth in France. I have been told twenty times that Buonaparte was dead, that he had died of a wound, was poisoned, was dead of the gravel [a disease with small stones being formed in the urine], &c. &c., that the Congress [of Châtillon] was dissolved, that there was an insurrection in La Vendée, in Brittany, &c. &c., the whole being false.[54]

He was echoed by the writer Chateaubriand, who complained of France becoming the 'empire of falsehood', and the widespread scepticism forced Napoleon to provide hard evidence of his claims.⁵⁵ He had prisoners-of-war paraded through Paris, captured guns and caissons parked prominently on the *Champ de Mars*, and abandoned Allied shakos thrown into the Seine after the Battle of Montereau so they would float downriver to the capital.⁵⁶

Yet distrust was too deeply ingrained. Many Parisians dismissed the captured Allied soldiers as police agents in disguise.⁵⁷ Others reacted with pity rather than the exultation on which Napoleon had counted. Seeing that the prisoners were destitute, spectators rushed to give them food, money, and clothing. In trying to convince Parisians of the scale of his victories, Napoleon had ended up undermining his own attempts to dehumanise the Allied troops by portraying them as barbarians. Interestingly, an anonymous letter later appeared in the *Journal de Paris*, purportedly from a subscriber but possibly planted by the government as a damage limitation exercise. It claimed that a group of displaced persons from the countryside had wept on seeing Allied prisoners-of-war being given charity, for they complained that these were the soldiers who had burned their houses and stolen their possessions.⁵⁸

Despite such side-effects and the lingering doubts of individuals, the stock exchange showed that the broad impact of Napoleon's victories in February was one of alarm giving way to relief. It is clear from the price of consols that these battles produced not a bubble of hope that quickly burst but a sustained surge of public confidence that remained high until the 26th and then slowly ebbed away over the following two or three weeks.

Even so, once the subsequent decline set in, it proved inexorable. Parisians refused to believe exaggerated reports of later victories such as Craonne, which barely registered on the exchange rates.⁵⁹ Expectations were too high, for the French people had been spoilt by Napoleon's early years of military glory. Their disillusionment obliged him to produce ever more sensational triumphs, but surpassing his February victories and prolonging their hypnotic spell was physically impossible. By the final week of March morale had returned to the despair of the start of February, and it was this collective nervous breakdown in the capital that drove Napoleon into gambling everything on his *manoeuvre sur les derrières*.⁶⁰

Allied propaganda

Napoleon portrayed his information war simply as the correction of lies spun by the Allies, and yet he was only partly successful at limiting the damage caused by their propaganda. He was adept at the tactical and operational levels, at demoralising Allied units and commanders, and shaping the short-term reactions of the French population, but was outmanoeuvred on the strategic plane.

The very existence and size of the Allied coalition gave it a moral advantage by conferring credibility on its claims about Napoleon's intransigence, the legitimacy of its cause, and the inevitability of the outcome. The inclusion in the Allied ranks of the Crown Prince of Sweden, the former French *Maréchal* Bernadotte, strengthened claims that Napoleon did not represent the interests of his people, and the extent to which the invasion penetrated into France proved his inability to defend them.

At the outset, by publishing the Frankfurt Proposals, Metternich portrayed Napoleon as the only obstacle to peace.⁶¹ Napoleon's attempt to counter that claim by securing an endorsement of his foreign policy from the *Corps législatif* backfired when it used his predicament to demand political concessions. Since he then adjourned it, the *Corps législatif* became a symbol of his isolation, instead of rallying the country around him.

Throughout the campaign Allied proclamations repeated the key message that they were waging war neither to conquer France nor to take revenge, but to secure a just peace. Apart from their obvious propaganda function, such statements publicly committed the coalition to a moderate outcome, by disowning any intention to partition France. They were therefore a means by which Metternich could restrain Alexander's ambitions and shape the post-war settlement while the campaign was still in progress.[62]

The Allies exploited the key reasons for the population's disaffection. Blücher, for example, announced the abolition of the *droits réunis*, the detested indirect taxes, and allowed French deserters to return to their homes.[63] The Allies also sought to reassure the inhabitants that their armies were well-disciplined and would respect private property. Napoleon's response was that these promises were hollow, as was shown by the actual behaviour of the troops, and he used accounts from the occupied areas to try to terrify the French people into seeing him as their only hope of deliverance. The Allies then countered by denying the truth of his atrocity stories, and by claiming that it was Napoleon who was devastating his own country by bringing the war there.[64]

In the end Napoleon over-saturated the French people with atrocity stories and failed adequately to counter the core Allied argument, that they were fighting him and not France, and that, consequently, he alone stood in the way of peace. This was Napoleon's great failure. Scare tactics would have been a useful complement to progress towards a negotiated settlement, but they were an inadequate substitute.

Napoleon did initially encourage belief that peace was imminent. After La Rothière he ordered the insertion of an announcement in *Le Moniteur* that the Châtillon negotiations seemed to be making progress in an atmosphere of goodwill.[65] By insisting on the need to secure an honourable peace, he was even able to demand national support for his military campaign to strengthen his negotiating position. But when peace continued to prove elusive, he had to resort to blaming the Allies and alleging that they were deliberately impeding the talks and making his couriers undertake long detours.[66]

Attempts to short-circuit rational thought became more difficult the longer the campaign lasted. For all Napoleon's efforts to manipulate minds, the stock exchange broadly, if sometimes belatedly, followed the swings in his military fortunes. Psychological operations were force multipliers, able to enhance a victory or mitigate a defeat, but could not turn one into the other. Once the Châtillon conference finally collapsed on 19 March, just a week after the Bordeaux revolt had established the credibility of the Bourbons as an alternative regime, Napoleon's entire position was undermined. It was this realisation that he had lost the propaganda war that impelled him to seek an immediate military solution by marching against the Allied rear. In the end, therefore, he no longer directed public opinion, but became controlled by it, and found his military moves dictated by the meltdown in public trust and the panic in Paris. He even failed to convince key figures within his own government and army. The final tempestuous confrontations at Fontainebleau with his *maréchaux*, the nadir of his relationship with them, revealed how completely he had destroyed his credibility.

Yet although Napoleon's propaganda became counter-productive, it should be remembered that this was largely a consequence of the duration of the military campaign and his failure to win a decisive victory in the field. All he could realistically hope to achieve was to delay the breakdown of public confidence long enough to secure a military solution. Thus, he did not have to persuade the entire population, for simply sowing doubt and confusion was sufficient in the short term. By mounting a sustained programme of propaganda, with its basic themes constantly repeated and reinforced in a variety of media, Napoleon averted a moral meltdown for two crucial months. Without these psychological operations, his much-admired military campaign would been impossible.

The Bourbons

Since they lacked an army of their own, the Bourbons were almost entirely dependent on psychological operations. They had to raise the profile of their pretender to the throne, and convince the Allies, the French population, and key political figures in Paris that the monarchy was a credible alternative to the Empire. This necessitated a degree of deception, first to make the inert mass of the population think that the Allies were committed to a restoration, and then to use the ensuing popular demonstrations of support to convince the Allies that the monarchy was the only viable regime.[67]

The Bourbons had hidden strengths. Republicanism was a spent force following the excesses of the Revolution, and ten years of Napoleon's rule as Emperor had transformed France into an instinctively monarchical country.[68] In the eyes of the French people the only realistic choice was between Napoleon and the Bourbons. Louis increased his acceptability as a ruler by issuing a declaration from his English residence of Hartwell on 1 February 1813. It offered peace, an end to conscription, and reassurances that there would be no purges, no revenge for past actions, and no reversal of the Revolutionary property settlement. Louis thereby allayed concerns that a restoration could endanger the bourgeoisie's social and political gains, and offered the prospect of a monarchy that was more liberal and stable than the Empire.[69]

The Bourbons benefited from the existence of long-established royalist groups within France. The *Chevaliers de la Foi*, for instance, countered Napoleon's propaganda with rumours, placards, anonymous letters, and conversations in *salons*.[70] But royalists found it easier to influence people's attitudes than induce them to take action, and unless they could spark an uprising, they could not persuade the Allies openly to favour regime change.

Hence, the royalists needed figureheads with the prestige to attract popular support and the credibility to command Allied respect. At the end of January Louis sent his brother and two nephews from Britain as his official representatives on French soil. Charles-Philippe, *comte* d'Artois left for the occupied provinces of eastern France; Charles-Ferdinand, *duc* de Berri went to the Channel Islands as a base for rousing Normandy and Brittany; and Louis-Antoine, *duc* d'Angoulême headed for Wellington's army in south-western France.

Yet even royal princes could have little immediate impact. The Allies had yet to agree on their war aims, and kept open the possibility of peace with Napoleon. This prevented them from encouraging revolts, since if Napoleon was left in power, he would be able to take revenge on his own people. The Allies were also concerned that, unless the Bourbons enjoyed widespread popularity, an open declaration of support for a restoration could provoke a rising against the invading armies. Hence, the Austrians tolerated the presence of the *comte* d'Artois in eastern France only if he remained inactive, a restriction that hardly made it easier for him to prove that a restoration was politically viable.[71]

The open demonstrations in favour of the Bourbons that occurred when Bordeaux was occupied by a detachment of Wellington's army on 12 March were therefore crucial, as they followed two months of disappointment elsewhere. Although wary of giving any overt encouragement for an insurrection, Wellington personally favoured a restoration and preserved strict discipline in his army so as not to drive the population into supporting Napoleon's regime, as happened in much of eastern France.

Bordeaux was the tipping point. Coinciding with the collapse of the Châtillon peace talks, it shook the imperial government, encouraged the Allies finally to support the Bourbons, and seemed to signal the imminent loss of the whole of southern France.[72] In fact, far from being spontaneous, the revolt had been carefully orchestrated by royalists, and owed much to specific local circumstances, including strong leadership from the *maire* and the commercial ruin of the port by Napoleon's policies. It did not spark a wider uprising: the inhabitants of Bordeaux soon cooled as they considered the potential consequences of their action, and not until after Napoleon's abdication did mass demonstrations of support for the Bourbons sweep through entire regions. But this did not matter because of the royalists' skill in projecting the Bordeaux revolt as more substantial than it was in reality, and in creating the illusion of unreserved mass support.

Defender of the nation

The propaganda war did not cease as combat operations came to an end. In some ways it actually escalated, as the Provisional Government successfully undermined Napoleon by subverting his senior subordinates and encouraging desertion in his army. The fall of Paris unleashed a torrent of abuse hitherto largely pent-up by Napoleon's grip on the machinery of power. Pamphlets, songs, brochures, and other works insulted him as a cowardly, inept and fraudulent tyrant.

The tightness with which Napoleon had controlled information actually helped his opponents, since it alienated the most talented writers, notably Chateaubriand and Benjamin Constant, both of whom produced scathing indictments of his rule. Other men, who had become accustomed to flattering those in authority, readily switched their loyalties to serve the new regime.

Much of the Bourbon propaganda appeared too late to affect the course of the campaign but did consolidate support for the Restoration. Chateaubriand's *De Buonaparte et des Bourbons* was written during the campaign, but published only in the first week of April.[73] Praising Louis as the legitimate French sovereign, it contrasted him with Napoleon's background as a Corsican outsider. This was a common theme. On 2 April the Provisional Government issued an address to the French armies, reminding them how they had suffered from the tyranny of a man who was not even French.[74] Two days later it issued another proclamation, which claimed that Napoleon was a king of barbarians, a foreigner whose unjust wars had devoured the country's wealth and population. Similarly, Alexander posed as the leader of the civilised world, who had taken Paris under his protection rather than avenge the burning of Moscow. It was a neat reversal of Napoleon's claim that he alone could save the French people from the Cossacks.

Napoleon's very act of abdication was a calculated appeal to public opinion, for he portrayed himself not as a defeated and discredited ruler forced to give up power but as a martyr voluntarily abandoning the throne and being ready to sacrifice even his life in the interests of France.

In fact, Napoleon's defence of his record proved more successful than his propaganda had been during the actual campaign, especially as the unrealistic hopes that accompanied the Restoration gave way to widespread disillusionment with the Bourbons. His defence of France was seen as an heroic failure, more glorious than his loss of central Europe the previous year and less controversial than the Waterloo campaign of 1815. It did much to restore his tattered military reputation, not least because he never suffered a decisive defeat on a battlefield. La Rothière, Laon, and Arcis-sur-Aube could all be portrayed as rearguard actions or reconnaissances in strength, and each was offset within a matter of days by a victory. It was the fall of Paris, not a defeat of the field army, that decided the campaign, and this enabled Napoleon to blame the outcome on treason, just as he had blamed his disaster in Russia on the weather and his defeat at Leipzig in 1813 on the desertion of his foreign troops.

In fact, what Napoleon saw as treason was the consequence, rather than the cause, of his failure to win the campaign, but he needed scapegoats, and in the same way that Grouchy and Ney would be blamed for Waterloo, it was Marmont, Talleyrand, and Augereau who were vilified in 1814. Napoleon thereby diverted anger from his ruinous policies, his failure to protect Paris, and the inadequacies of his brother Joseph.

As a result of the campaign, Napoleon was associated in popular memory not so much with aggressive wars or costly blunders in the Peninsula and Russia as with the defence of the fatherland and the Revolution's achievements in the face of a powerful alliance that subsequently became identified with the repression of liberal and nationalist movements. He became the people's Emperor.[75] Real or imagined incidents of personal bravery and shared danger became enshrined in popular iconography, above all the aiming of the gun at Montereau and the riding of the horse over the live shell at Arcis-sur-Aube, both of which were immortalised in the famous *images d'Epinal*, the popular nostalgic prints produced at a town in the Vosges.

Napoleon's defence of France has been celebrated as his finest military campaign, but was actually more significant in political terms. It was the indispensable element in his transformation from just another ruthless and over-ambitious foreign adventurer and dynastic warlord into the more compelling and tragic figure who has become France's greatest national hero.

Chapter 20

Population displacements and prisoners-of-war

The very fact that the invasion was under way was a psychological shock for France, and the subsequent physical dislocation became far-reaching. As well as displacing part of the population, the Allied advance forced tens of thousands of prisoners-of-war and invalid soldiers to be progressively evacuated into an ever-decreasing rump of the country, putting pressure on its infrastructure and resources, spreading disease, and accelerating the breakdown of the government's authority. Directly or indirectly, the invasion had an impact on the entire country.

Mass displacements

Panic not only caused inhabitants to flee of their own accord, but forced them to leave by paralysing commerce. At Lyon, for example, the big banking houses stopped making payments and entrepreneurs withdrew their investments from business, forcing workshops to close and leaving a mass of workers unemployed. This in turn increased concern among the wealthy that their homes were at risk of attack from hungry mobs. By 4 January the local *commissaire extraordinaire*, *Sénateur* Jean, *comte* Chaptal, was reporting:

> This large and so active and industrious a city no longer seems to have a spark of life. . . . The alarm has reached such a point here that you will find not an *aune* of silk in the shops. Everything has already been removed to the mountains, where large numbers of inhabitants take refuge, and so we will soon be left with only the administration, the *Garde nationale*, and large numbers of unemployed.[1]

In fact, some attempt was made to achieve exactly this sort of void, by removing not just the senior administrative officials but entire populations, and thus make it impossible for the invaders to live off the land. The *Ministre de l'intérieur* instructed the *préfet* of the Aube at the start of January:

> It would be very desirable if we could follow the example of other peoples, and leave the enemy merely an uninhabited land. But in the event of it being impossible to achieve this completely, you will use all your power and influence to try and ensure that every family with sufficient means to live for a while elsewhere should leave its land when it is sullied by the enemy's presence. Loyal subjects would be failing in one of their foremost duties if they lived under his temporary domination.[2]

Yet the authorities gave inconsistent messages. A *commissaire extraordinaire* in Lorraine issued two notices on successive days, the first telling the inhabitants to take up arms and the second urging them to leave so that the Allies would find their towns deserted.[3]

One town where the leading citizens did decide to flee was Villenauxe, 12 miles south-west of Sézanne. But the administrative void created in this way actually worsened the plight of the remaining population, as the Allied troops had to find billets for themselves when they arrived instead of being assigned them in an orderly manner. It took time, and some false starts, to replace absent officials. One inhabitant, Edme-Jacques Gérost, complained that 'scoundrels' sought posts for their own advantage, that they sometimes directed Cossacks to wealthy homes in the hope of obtaining a share of the plunder, and that the post of *maire* was initially filled by a drunkard.[4]

The Allies took steps to check an exodus of the population. At Châlons-sur-Marne, in the wake of the *Schlesische Armee*'s defeats in February, a proclamation forbade the remaining inhabitants to abandon their homes or communicate with the French army. It became rare for people to leave the city because of the insecurity of the countryside and the bureaucracy involved in obtaining a pass. Not until the arrival of French troops on 15 March were the inhabitants again able to emerge from Châlons.[5]

The departure of part of a community increased the burden on those members who remained behind under occupation, and strained the administrative and social fabric of the receiving regions. When peasants flowed into Troyes in the face of the Allied advance, they were ordered to be expelled, as they were seen as contributing nothing to the city while reducing its food supplies. Ironically, it later became the turn of people from Troyes to flee, and as many as 200 of its families withdrew to the forested hills to the south-west, where they survived on roots and a bit of bread from local peasants.[6]

The influx of displaced inhabitants from eastern France did at least enable the imperial authorities to gather intelligence about the progress of the Allied armies and the situation near the frontiers. On 28 December 1813 the *Ministre de la police générale* directed the *préfets* in areas threatened by the invasion to have any new arrivals interrogated. Checkpoints were established at key road hubs, but in the *département* of the Marne they functioned for barely more than a week and did not always provide helpful information. A driver of a *diligence*, on being asked what he had seen, replied: 'I saw a lot of snow.'[7]

It is difficult to ascertain the numbers of displaced persons. Three inhabitants out of every seven were said to have left Châlons-sur-Marne, while in the *commune* of Javernant, 10 miles south of Troyes, more than half the inhabitants had apparently abandoned their homes by 19 February. But both these locations lay in a heavily contested zone, and it seems that only a small minority of *communes* shed a mass of their population.[8]

The main campaign region in Champagne contained at least a million inhabitants. But not all of them fled, possibly because they lacked the necessary money or transport, or because they feared their homes were more likely to be pillaged if abandoned. Those who did flee tended to leave in successive waves rather than all at once: either through fear of the approaching Allied invasion or subsequently as a result of having experienced occupation. Some made considered decisions to leave while others fled in panic.

Much displacement was only local. Rural inhabitants might seek safety in the nearest town, and conversely, the citizens of an oppressed town might leave in order to find refuge with friends or relatives elsewhere, or even to hide in woods and quarries. There were stories of women giving birth in the woods in the bitter cold and with little help. Soissons, which saw heavy fighting, seemed to become deserted as its citizens fled to surrounding towns such as Noyon, Compiègne, and Villers-Cotterêts. Some homeless inhabitants actually followed the French army, in the hope of being protected, but found themselves exposed to both hostile fire and the bitter cold, became too exhausted to continue, and were left behind on the road.[9]

Flight was often temporary, with inhabitants returning even while the campaign was still being fought. They might have fled on the spur of the moment, too terrified to take everything they would need or to know where they were going. Even at Méry-sur-Seine, which was destroyed by fire, inhabitants returned from the woods and took up residence in cellars, in makeshift shelters amidst the ruins, and in nearby villages.[10]

Some inhabitants decided against flight because they lacked a network of personal connections elsewhere. Charles d'Arbois de Jubainville, who was 10 years old at the time, recalled that his father wanted to leave Nancy and withdraw into a fortress such as Metz but was opposed by other members of the family who objected that living in a besieged city would be expensive and disagreeable. Whereas the family lacked connections at Metz, they had family and friends at Nancy, and would be able to help relatives who had decided to remain at the village of Jubainville, 25 miles to the south-west.[11]

At the end of March *Sous-lieutenant* Pierre Auvray of the *23e Dragons* was billeted at Melun on a family that was preparing to leave the town without having a fixed destination. 'We are going where chance takes us,' they explained. Since Auvray's parents happened to live 30 miles to the south, he told the family to go to them, which had the added benefit of ensuring that they received news of him.[12]

Even if inhabitants decided not to flee, they might move their property to safer locations. A family at Brumath deposited its rare wines in the fortress of Strasbourg, 10 miles to the south, for the duration of the campaign. Similarly, some inhabitants from the occupied town of Villenauxe brought their horses to Provins, which was beyond the area held by the Allied forces, for greater security.[13]

It is impossible to assess the degree to which the population displacements spread fear, rumours, and disease. Besides displaced inhabitants, invalid soldiers flooded back from the campaign area, many of whom reached Paris, where they begged in the streets, causing inhabitants to ask why the government did not allocate some public buildings to accommodate them.[14]

Bands of deserters and *réfractaires* stalked the countryside, often surviving as brigands. Desertion remained a critical problem throughout the campaign, for Napoleon's army had been recruited hurriedly, was operating in its home country, and contained numerous provisional units cobbled together from diverse elements. Many stragglers were stopped at the *barrières* of Paris, but others simply flowed around either side of the city in an almost continuous stream. Some men deserted with their horses and sold them to farmers.

The river lines could have been used to stop deserters, or at least to collect their muskets. But in Napoleon's absence from Paris there was much inertia and friction between the various authorities. The *Ministre de la police générale* complained that the head of the *Gendarmerie* was not doing enough, even though the withdrawal of *gendarmes* from the invaded *départements* meant that he had a strong force available. Towards the end of February several hundred deserters were still able to cross the Seine south of Paris every day without being challenged, although steps were then belatedly taken to have the bridges guarded regularly. Napoleon had already ordered deserters to be decimated, and the *Ministre de la police générale* communicated these instructions to Orléans, Chartres, Evreux, and Rouen, which straddled the main roads between 50 and 70 miles south or west of Paris.[15]

A surprising degree of mobility remained possible for civilians while the campaign was in progress. Within the campaign theatre, towns repeatedly changed hands, which provided opportunities for inhabitants to leave the area. The *diligences* were withdrawn to safety in the face of the Allied advance but still operated in unoccupied regions, even if they ran the risk of being stopped by Cossack raids.[16]

Even goods were transported across the war zone. Lyon was known for its silk industry and actually traded with Allied states while it was still in French hands. Exports worth millions of *francs* were sent to Frankfurt-am-Main, using passports issued by *Feldmarschall-Leutnant* Ferdinand, *Graf* von Bubna und Littitz, the local Austrian commander. The trade benefited both sides, as it kept the struggling industry alive in Lyon and provided cheap silks for Germany, where they were in short supply.[17]

Paris

Some civilians fled all the way to Paris. An initial influx came from frontier regions annexed since the start of the Revolutionary Wars, and included administrative officials, French families who had settled in the area, and native inhabitants who feared the consequences of having actively supported French rule. At the same time people who had been exiled from Paris for political reasons took advantage of the disorder to return to the city.[18]

Throughout the campaign it was typical for the approach of Allied forces to be announced at Paris by another wave of displaced persons.[19] According to the *Ministère de la police générale*, they came from a zone extending more than 75 miles around Paris. Another surge in migrants occurred at the end of March as the Allies descended on the capital and those inhabitants who lived closest to it brought even their livestock into the suburbs.

Flight was easier for wealthy and well-connected inhabitants. Charles de Pougens, who had become a distinguished writer despite his blindness, lived at Vauxbuin, 2 miles outside Soissons. Since the countryside was exposed to Cossack raids, in February he and his household took refuge with a friend inside the city. When Soissons itself was stormed by the Russians on the 14th, Pougens returned to Vauxbuin, but his home was pillaged at the beginning of March, leaving his family without food or cooking utensils. They were fortunate to have a friend who sent provisions from his farm, but decided to leave for Paris after a further bout of pillaging. No transport was available from Soissons, but the family friend came to the rescue again and sent vehicles that took them to Nanteuil, 26 miles to the south-west, where they found *diligences* leaving for Paris. They reached the capital on 15 March, three days after leaving their home.[20]

Other displaced persons were less fortunate. Requisitioning left many inhabitants without draught animals or proper transport. One mother and her children were seen in a small cart drawn by a cow and a goat, while another vehicle had an ass and a large dog yoked together.[21] At Paris, the *comtesse* de Boigne described how:

> [The fugitives] walked in the midst of their cows, their sheep and their small, wretched items of baggage. Weeping and wailing, they talked of their losses and fears and, as was only natural, tended to be irritated at those who seemed more fortunate. We could go no faster than a walking pace and our *calèche* was not spared the insults. I had no need of that to begin to realise that the war was very ugly when seen so close.[22]

Despite their wretched state, the displaced persons were regularly exploited. On reaching Paris they were stopped at the *barrières* by the agents of the *droits réunis* and forced to pay duties. Those who could not afford to do so were obliged to sell their possessions for whatever they could obtain.²³

The arrival of these people in the capital caused a shortage of lodgings and apparently also of bread, besides causing concern about potential unrest. 'The *faubourg* St Antoine looked like a bivouac today,' reported the *Ministre de la police générale* on 10 February. When crowds of rural inhabitants gathered in the streets and squares of Paris at the end of March, the *préfet de police* was careful to have them watched and to have patrols undertaken by the *Gendarmerie de Paris*. Napoleon considered keeping the unemployed and the dispersed persons busy by incorporating 30,000 of them into the Parisian *Garde nationale*, but was prevented by the shortage of muskets and doubts about the wisdom of arming dubious elements of society.²⁴

'This withdrawal is a rout'

Paris itself shed part of its population whenever it came under imminent threat. As early as 30 January, even before Napoleon's defeat at La Rothière, many women and children were fleeing the city, partly because of alarm caused by the erection of defences at the *barrières*.²⁵

The departure of the families of ministers and other officials lowered public confidence, and by 8 February so many Parisians were leaving for the regions beyond the Loire that they had trouble obtaining relay horses, causing the authorities to fear that the service might break down altogether. By the 14th the congestion on the roads to the west and south-west had lessened, following Napoleon's victories over the *Schlesische Armee*, but it soon increased again as the *Hauptarmee* neared the city from the south-east.²⁶

The fear penetrated right into the heart of France. Early in February *Capitaine* d'Agout of the *4e Dragons* was moving north with reinforcements detached from Soult's army near the Pyrenees. After passing Guéret and Limoges, a full 200 miles south of Paris, he began to see anxiety spreading:

> The nearer we drew to Paris, the more terrified we saw the inhabitants, and the more serious became the details of the military operations. Soon the number of relay vehicles coming from Paris increased to such an extent that the posts were short of horses. From the direction of Vierzon the movement of travellers looked like a real flight. This gave us reason to reflect.²⁷

By the time d'Agout reached Orléans, 70 miles from Paris, he could see panic on all sides.

Further migrations followed throughout the campaign. On 29 March the Empress herself became a displaced person, along with her son, and she was followed the next day by the imperial government. Her departure was the signal for other individuals to leave, and the towns along the route she had taken, south-westwards to Versailles, Rambouillet and Chartres, became so swamped that some landlords shamelessly overcharged their guests.²⁸ Fugitives also had to put up with insults from malevolent people on the roads. The *diligences* and other means of public transport were inadequate, so people left in boats, waggons, and on foot. 'This withdrawal is a rout,' noted *Colonel-major* Boniface de Castellane of the *1er Gardes d'honneur* on 31 March. 'It is really pitiful to see the unfortunate people who are fleeing, and the congestion of troops and depots is unimaginable. The inns are full of families in flight.'²⁹

The influx of displaced persons into the centre of France did not come solely from the east and north. Despite the discipline of Wellington's army, many inhabitants of south-western France fled from his advance, and committed disorders around Toulouse.[30] Towards the end of March the town of Cahors, 60 miles north of the city, was packed with prisoners-of-war, fleeing civilians, and Spanish refugees who had collaborated with the French occupation of their country during the Peninsular War. Some of the Spaniards were reduced to begging and, to add to the sense of social disintegration, a mass of peasants burned the local government registers at the nearby town of Gourdon out of resentment about the *droits réunis*.

Yet much of the population saw Wellington as a liberator from Napoleonic rule and actually fled towards his forces rather than away from them, in order to escape the indiscipline of their own army. As he himself wrote on 14 January: 'What do you think of the French people running into our posts for protection from the French troops, with their bundles on their heads, and their *beds*, as you recollect to have seen the people of Portugal and Spain?'[31]

Prisoners-of-war

By the end of 1813 there were over 100,000 prisoners-of-war in France, or about one for every 300 inhabitants. In addition to captured soldiers and sailors, Napoleon disarmed and detained those of his army's foreign contingents, such as the Dutch, that he deemed unreliable. By far the largest contingent was Spanish, for by 1814 the Peninsular War had raged for six years and one Spaniard in every 200 had been deported to France.[32]

An estimated 16,000 captives were British. Five times as many French prisoners were in British hands, and Napoleon's untrustworthiness made it impossible to organise large-scale exchanges.[33] Only some individual prisoners were therefore repatriated: even during the 1814 campaign several Britons who were no longer fit to serve their country on active service were sent home, along with a few wives and children of gentlemen prisoners. Morlaix in Brittany was the sole port on the Channel coast designated for such releases, and for the arrival of French prisoners returned by Britain.[34]

To hinder escape attempts British prisoners were held in thirteen fortresses along the eastern and north-eastern frontiers of old France, far from both the coast and Wellington's army in the Iberian Peninsula. (As a result some escapees headed eastwards, through southern Germany and the Austrian Empire to the port of Trieste, and then sailed home through the Mediterranean.)[35] But when the frontiers came under threat after Leipzig, the depots had to be evacuated so the fortresses could be prepared for a siege and the prisoners preserved as bargaining counters in the event of a negotiated peace. Initially, at the end of 1813 the most exposed British depots, such as Briançon, Besançon, and Bitche, were evacuated to more north-westerly ones, but it then became necessary to transfer the prisoners southwards, behind the cover of the Loire.[36] A sailor, John Tregerthen Short, walked more than 970 miles in 108 days, from leaving his depot at Givet in the Ardennes on 7 January until reaching Bordeaux on 27 April. He spent about half of that period on the march, and the rest either in depots or in a hospital after falling ill, apparently with typhus.[37]

Amid the chaos of 1814 the French authorities were overwhelmed by a multitude of problems and were often unable to provide enough food and clothing. Many prisoners died during the transfers or were left permanently crippled by frostbite. One detachment of British captives lost 6 per cent of its strength in being transferred from Givet to Orléans: twenty-one men fell sick and were left behind in hospitals, while another was murdered by a *gendarme*.[38]

The British have often been criticised for the conditions in which they kept prisoners-of-war on board their floating hulks, but they actually held most of them on land and the mortality rate among their captives was only 8 per cent, little more than twice that among British and US prisoners in German camps during the Second World War.[39] In contrast, the sufferings of Napoleon's prisoners have tended to be overlooked. Spaniards suffered particular neglect, and even the British, whose limited numbers made them more valuable than other captives, sometimes endured harsh conditions in the more notorious depots.

Not until the Hague Conventions of 1899 and 1907 would the proper treatment of prisoners-of-war be enshrined in international law. In 1814 conditions of captivity depended on the humanity of the authorities, the availability of resources, the risk of reprisals, and precedents such as the Peace of Westphalia (1648), which had established the principle that prisoners should be freed at the end of hostilities without the payment of a ransom.

Verdun was the depot for socially respectable Britons who had given their parole, a promise not to try to escape in return for a degree of liberty. By the end of 1813 it contained about 950 Britons, who established their own clubs, theatres, and even horse races.[40] They included some *détenus*, or internees, for when the Peace of Amiens collapsed in May 1803 Napoleon had ordered the detention of all male Britons aged between 18 and 60 who were in France. Early in January 1814 the depot was suddenly ordered to leave Verdun in a series of detachments. The population was generally sorry to see the prisoners go, partly because it was thought their presence would prevent the city from being bombarded when the Allied armies arrived, and partly because many of the captives had run up debts. As late as 1839 a deputation from Verdun went to London to try to reclaim the money, but without success. Some Frenchwomen accompanied the depot, as they had fallen in love with British prisoners.[41]

The depot initially moved to Blois. The journey took three weeks, for although Blois lay 215 miles south-west of Verdun in a direct line, the depot had to make a detour around the western side of Paris so as not to pass through the capital or obstruct the passage of troops in Champagne and Burgundy.[42] The evacuation caused much distress, since many families had become incapable of fending for themselves after living in idleness at Verdun for as long as ten years. Children and the older or more infirm captives needed transport but few horses were available and carriages often broke down during the journey. It was money that could most alleviate conditions, yet most captives had few funds. This was particularly true of merchant sailors and civilian *détenus*, who, unlike prisoners-of-war, received no allowance from the French government and had exhausted their resources after years of captivity.[43]

A fortnight after reaching Blois the depot was transferred again when the nearby city of Orléans was briefly threatened by a Cossack raid.[44] This time it moved 120 miles southwards to Guéret in the very heart of France. Prisoners who followed a prescribed route, escorted by *gendarmes*, obtained free lodging while on the march. But many of those on parole made their own way, by easier or less crowded roads, and even disobeyed instructions not to use the main road by Tours (the French authorities were clearly concerned that the prisoners might impede military movements, or cause a shortage of relay horses).[45]

By 11 March Guéret contained 1,064 British prisoners. Yet the town had little more than 3,100 inhabitants, compared to 14,900 for Blois, and this made it even more difficult for the prisoners to obtain suitable lodgings.[46]

Prisoners taken during the course of the campaign were likewise taken into the interior. Lieutenant-General Olsufiev and two other senior Russian officers captured at Champaubert were paraded as trophies through Paris six days later, before being moved southwards. *Prisonniers d'état*, or state prisoners, also had to be evacuated from exposed regions, although their numbers were limited. Some were still held at the *Château* de Vincennes on the outskirts of the capital when the Allied armies arrived, although others had been evacuated into the western provinces.

By moving their captives, the French managed to prevent entire depots from falling into Allied hands, but they did forget some men or perhaps ran out of time. When Blücher occupied Nancy in January he found some Spanish prisoners and formed them into a special battalion for escorting convoys and garrisoning fortresses.[47]

Problems

Such massive evacuations towards the interior of France had a certain propaganda advantage. The sheer number of prisoners could impress the inhabitants, and be taken as an indication of the tide of the war, even though many had been captured before 1814. But the transfers put additional pressure on the roads, which already had to cope with population displacements and the movements of troops and *gardes nationaux*.

Bertrand Barère de Vieuzac, a leading political figure during the Revolution, left the capital on 14 February and found that the traffic on the road to Bordeaux was 'as brisk and heavy as that of the *boulevards* in Paris on holidays'. Similarly, when British prisoners from the depot at Givet were transferred in January around the eastern side of Paris to Orléans, they had to share part of their march with retreating French soldiers, whose guns and vehicles degraded the roads and spattered the captives with mud. One British detachment had to halt in a field near Saint-Dizier for nearly two hours to allow a French formation to pass in the other direction.[48]

Many regions were overwhelmed, for most towns lacked the fortifications and resources to be suitable as depots, and the prisoners were progressively concentrated into an ever-smaller part of France. 'There are too many prisoners-of-war here,' reported *Sénateur* Louis, *comte* de Ségur from Troyes on 2 January:

> There are reckoned to be 1,500 – Spaniards and Austrians. Another 1,600 are expected. Six hundred of them have arrived and are crammed into sheds and stables. The inhabitants are overwhelmed with the sacrifices they make to feed them. They arrive unexpectedly, without the authorities being warned. It is essential to move these men promptly towards the centre of France and far from the threatened points. There are still 950 prisoners in the rest of the *département*, so it is impossible to evacuate those at Troyes to the other towns.[49]

Such large numbers of prisoners became an impossible financial and logistic burden on the state. By 18 February there were 4,492 prisoners-of-war in the *département* of the Eure, or one for every 94 inhabitants. But the despatch of funds by the central government had been interrupted, so the *préfet* was obliged to requisition food from the population instead of paying suppliers. In addition to the prisoners based in his *département*, he had to feed five regimental depots and numerous convoys of prisoners or French troops passing through.[50]

Finding themselves unable to supply, or even guard, the prisoners properly, the authorities shifted the responsibility on to local inhabitants, who had to provide billets.[51] By dispersing prisoners in this way officials could lessen the burden on a single town and provide farmers with a source of labour.

This was not, in fact, a new step. During the Revolutionary Wars the French regarded prisoners as protected by the Rights of Man, and in theory allowed them to work for a living once they had given their word of honour not to escape, although the reality fell short of such ideals. Similarly, during the 1805 campaign Napoleon had planned to put captured Austrian soldiers to work in the countryside to replace absent French conscripts, but it was not until the start of the Peninsular War that the arrival of thousands of Spanish prisoners created a large and permanent labour force. Even then, assigning prisoners to work for private individuals did not operate well in practice, not least because of language difficulties and the security risk in remote rural areas. Hence, Napoleon preferred to use prisoners on large-scale state projects, where they could be supervised more easily. In 1811 he created thirty prisoner-of-war battalions to work on roads, bridges, and fortifications. The work was supposed to subsidise the cost of the prisoners' upkeep, but the viability of the scheme was undermined by their poor physical condition.[52] (The Hague Conventions of 1899 and 1907 ruled that prisoners-of-war could be used for labour, so long as they were not officers, and provided the tasks were not excessive or connected with military operations.)

The reversion in 1814 to private employers was therefore a backward step, and it worked no better than before. The invasion magnified existing fears about prisoners-of-war, who were seen as a threat both to the inhabitants and to establishments such as weapons factories. 'They were an enemy army camped in our midst,' recalled the *préfet* of the Bouches-du-Rhône.[53] Complaints were raised that captives had made veiled threats about the sharpening of daggers, and a plot was discovered at Limoges in March for Spanish prisoners to seize the authorities and make their way southwards to join Wellington's army.

On 10 January the *sous-préfet* at Autun, which was threatened by the Austrian advance, faced a mutiny when he tried to send off 1,400 British prisoners, whose pay was a fortnight in arrears. They refused to leave their barracks and obliged the *sous-préfet* to pay one-third of the arrears before they left. Then 2,000 Spanish prisoners also refused to leave. The inhabitants became alarmed and pressed for the prisoners' demands to be met. The *sous-préfet* knew that the prisoners were likely to desert once they were paid, and he managed to force them to march after summoning *gardes nationaux* from rural *communes* to increase his strength.[54]

On 22 February the *Ministre de la police générale* wrote to inform Napoleon about his concerns for western France:

> I admit that I have some worries about the potential consequences of the accumulation in this part of the country, and in Normandy, of all the English, Spanish, Austrian, and Russian prisoners that we are obliged to send there, without increasing the means of containing them. Not a day goes by without the authorities of these *départements* communicating their fears. The most unfortunate aspect is that it seems the *Administration de la guerre* is not in a position to provide for the feeding of these prisoners, since many of them are entrusted to the inhabitants, who prefer to feed them than risk being maltreated.[55]

The alarm was reinforced by the potential threat of a British or royalist landing on the coast, and by the possibility that prisoners distributed among the *communes* might join bands of deserters and *réfractaires* and contribute to the disorders.[56] Prisoners actively undermined morale by spreading rumours. At Rennes Russian officers loudly stated that the official news was false and that the Allied armies were encountering no opposition. At Périgueux in the south-west Spanish and British prisoners were insinuating early in March that the Allies would soon arrive and that they would be favourable to those inhabitants who welcomed them but merciless to the *gardes nationaux*. Combined with the arrival of displaced persons from Bordeaux, which was threatened by the British forces, such threats had a noticeable effect on the mood in the town.[57]

Napoleon's response to the threat had been to keep prisoners busy and to reinforce security by forming sedentary units of *gardes nationaux*, while withdrawing experienced *gendarmes* from the Peninsular front. His basic principle was that every ten prisoners should always be guarded by one armed man, but in reality many local authorities lacked the necessary manpower.[58]

It was therefore fortunate that most prisoners were too destitute and demoralised to attempt more than survival, and that they tended to be separated from their officers. Although some Spaniards escaped or exulted at French reverses, they rarely tried to take revenge. Despite Napoleon's contempt for the Spaniards, many French people regarded the prisoners with compassion. At Nancy inhabitants invited Spanish officers and priests to dinner as a way of helping them without offering the insult of charity. Similarly, some Frenchmen employed captives on work that did not need doing.[59]

At Richelieu British prisoners became so integrated into the life of the community that they went fishing and shooting with the local people and helped in the fields and vineyards. A band formed from twenty-four of the captives was invited to play in the town's theatre, and regularly practised with a dozen local men in one of their homes.[60] Some captured Allied soldiers actually decided not to return home after the end of the campaign. Ninety-six Spanish and Portuguese prisoners are known to have asked for French nationality in the period up to 1832, and there were undoubtedly others who remained behind without requesting citizenship.[61]

In fact, the prisoners posed more of a threat to health than security. At Sens an *adjoint* at the *hôtel-de-ville* wanted to vomit because of the stench from Russian soldiers held in a garden outside his windows.[62] The Spaniards were particularly vulnerable to disease, as they were usually dirty, destitute, and malnourished, and the massive evacuations of prisoners across France helped spread a deadly typhus epidemic.

Mistreatment

The treatment of prisoners-of-war varied considerably. Much depended on luck, wealth, rank, social status, the availability of resources, and the attitudes of the authorities. French prisoners after the Battle of Leipzig in 1813 even resorted to cannibalism because of the shortage of supplies.[63] During the 1814 campaign prisoners suffered from abuse, neglect, and atrocities, yet mistreatment was not universal. Prussian troops were seen at Châlons-sur-Marne sharing their bread with captured French soldiers. Some of the Württembergers taken prisoner at Montereau had the good fortune to be recognised and protected by Napoleon's *Grand Maréchal du palais*, *Général de division* Henri, *comte* Bertrand, who had been their corps commander the year before when they had still been serving in the *Grande armée*.[64] Similarly, a French actress, *Madame* Louise Fusil, asked to see Lieutenant-General Olsufiev after his capture. She said that she was indebted to the general for having helped her to return to France after she was taken prisoner at Vilnius during the retreat from Moscow.[65]

Allied soldiers captured during the campaign were taken to Versailles, from where they were sent to their respective depots. On their way Napoleon had them paraded through Paris as trophies of his victories, in order to bolster the capital's flagging morale. 'The prisoners are going to be sent to Paris,' he wrote to the *Ministre de la guerre* on 12 February. 'I want you to arrange for them to enter with a bit of pomp and in a way that the public are aware of it.'[66]

Putting prisoners-of-war on display in this manner is now banned under the Third Geneva Convention, which states that they may not be exposed to public curiosity or insults. As it happened, the Parisians who came to watch reacted overwhelmingly with pity.[67] An Allied prisoner described how:

> The Parisians, high and low-born alike, were very curious to see us, but also extremely courteous. No one thought to insult us, not even with words or mockery, as had happened earlier. Instead, they brought our men food and drink, and several women often gave money to soldiers for whom they felt particular sympathy.[68]

Prisoners who had some money could generally obtain better treatment, as could Freemasons. After the Battle of Montereau three captured Allied officers asked to speak to the *préfet* of the Seine-et-Marne. They gave him the Masonic sign, explained that they had lost all their baggage, and asked for a loan of 100 *francs*. The *préfet* was happy to oblige, but was disappointed after the end of the war when they failed to pay him back.[69]

Some prisoners made themselves useful, including a British doctor left on parole at Château-Thierry, who helped care for the wounded during the fighting there on 12 February.[70] Napoleon repeatedly ordered muskets to be collected from the battlefields and greatcoats, shakos, and cartridge pouches taken from the prisoners, in order to equip his own forces. Since he also needed every man he could find, he actually tried to recruit some of the prisoners. He had already had some success in previous years obtaining volunteers from among the Spanish prisoners-of-war, because of the despair to which many of them were reduced by their conditions of captivity. He had also tried to incorporate into a *Légion irlandaise* men of various nationalities who had been captured while serving under the British flag. In March 1814 he ordered Poles to be recruited from the captured Allied soldiers, so as to keep a Polish unit, the *Régiment de la Vistule*, up to full strength. Since Russia, Prussia, and Austria had all absorbed parts of Poland at the end of the eighteenth century, Poles were present in every army in the main campaign theatre.[71]

Escapes

The easiest time for prisoners to escape tended to be immediately after capture, before they reached the rear areas. At the Battle of Laon many of Marmont's men were able to return to their comrades after being captured, because the Allies were keener to pursue than provide escorts for prisoners.[72] Men who escaped did not necessarily rejoin their unit. Nicolas Pénot of the *2e Cuirassiers*, for example, was taken prisoner near Nancy in January, but slipped away and reached Troyes. Since he found himself unable to rejoin his regiment, he instead attached himself to the *Gendarmerie*, and served with it for the rest of the campaign.[73]

Captured French soldiers had the advantage of being in their own country, and were often able to exchange their uniforms for civilian clothes in villages, or were helped to escape by peasants armed with cudgels and pitchforks.[74] In February Cossacks escorted a detachment of French prisoners through the town of Villenauxe. They had originally had as many as 300 or 400 prisoners, but were so negligent in guarding them that no more than 250 were left. At Villenauxe itself a dozen of the prisoners escaped through the crowd, or from garden to garden by jumping over the walls. When the detachment reached a wood 30 miles to the north-east, the Cossacks were ambushed by local peasants. The prisoners joined the attack and afterwards returned to their homes, disguised as civilians.[75]

On 23 February some eighty French prisoners, escorted by Austrians, passed through Brienon-sur-Armançon, 30 miles south-west of Troyes. Some inhabitants noted the weakness of the escort and decided to free the prisoners. They did so and the captives fled. But one of the men, *Lieutenant* Delattre of the *6e Voltigeurs* of the Young Guard, refused to escape, as he wanted to try to shield the town from reprisals. When Russian troops arrived some hours later Delattre asked their commander to spare the town, and was supported by the Austrian escort commander, whose life he had saved. But it was to no avail: Delattre was killed and the town pillaged.[76]

Allied evasion attempts

For captured Allied soldiers escape became a more tempting prospect as they were transferred across France to new depots. Many British prisoners, for example, were moved southwards, closer to Wellington's army, or into Brittany, where they were nearer the coast.[77]

According to regulations issued in October 1806, detachments of prisoners were meant to contain no more than 100 men, and were to be escorted by regular troops and *gendarmes*.[78] Strict security precautions were sometimes taken during the evacuation of the depots in 1814. A British detachment from Givet was initially escorted by troops marching on either side, and it was threatened that any prisoner who left the ranks or strayed from the road without a guard would be shot as a deserter. Repeated musters were held and the detachment spent the nights in prisons, convents, barns, and churches.[79]

Yet detachments were often larger than normal, and might be heavily escorted only during the first phase of a depot's transfer, until at more of a distance from the Allied armies. This was not as risky as it sounded, for even when a convoy was poorly guarded escape could be impracticable. A British sailor, George Casse, described how he was transferred from Saarlouis to Cambrai in the autumn of 1813. After the first two days his convoy was escorted by a single *gendarme*, but he did not try to desert for he was far from the coast, had the French army behind him, and knew that if he strayed from the road he would be heading in the wrong direction and would be deprived of regular distributions of food.[80]

Some escapees were foiled by the bitter cold, such as Richard Langton, a British detainee, who deserted with a naval officer while being transferred from Verdun. They became so badly affected by ague while resting in a wood in the evening that they had to abandon the attempt and report to the nearest authorities, claiming that they had become separated from the rest of their detachment by mistake.[81]

Escaping from a convoy was easier than avoiding recapture and finding a way home. Prisoners who headed for the coast in the hope of embarking for Britain often found it impossible to track down a ship.[82] Others headed back towards the campaign area, including three British prisoners who escaped while being evacuated southwards from Blois to Guéret. They moved north-eastwards to try to join the Allied armies, but were arrested 30 miles south of Montereau on 24 February.[83]

Deserters were often caught again within days, for inhabitants were promised rewards for bringing in fugitives, and *préfets* deployed their local *gendarmes* and *gardes nationaux* to arrest stragglers when detachments were taken through their *départements*.⁸⁴ Yet the vigilance of the civilian population could be lax. The interrogation of a recaptured British prisoner, William Buchell, revealed that he had managed to go from Blois 160 miles down the Loire to Paimbœuf, just 10 miles from the coast, without being asked for his papers. He had left Blois in a boat manned by civilians and had used a fictitious name when registering at an inn. It was clear that *gendarmes*, innkeepers, boatmen, and *maîtres de poste* were neglecting to check travellers' passports.⁸⁵

Gardes nationaux could also be negligent in guarding prisoners, and might even favour their escape in order to reduce the apparent threat to a town's security posed by their presence. As many as 101 British prisoners escaped from Angoulême on the night of 10 March, and 64 from Périgueux.⁸⁶ At Autun some inhabitants helped Spanish prisoners out of friendship rather than fear and even hid them in their homes, for the long presence of the captives had resulted in close ties.⁸⁷

On 8 April the Provisional Government ordered the immediate return of Russian prisoners in France, in response to an order by Alexander for the release of French prisoners. Five days later the Provisional Government widened this to all prisoners-of-war on French territory, and this was confirmed by the convention of 23 April, which ended hostilities.

The problems caused by the population displacements and prisoner-of-war evacuations were not entirely new. During Napoleon's initial victorious campaigns the authorities had been overwhelmed by the number of captured soldiers who suddenly flowed back into France.⁸⁸ Over the years that followed, prisoners were repeatedly transferred around the country and it was common for seasonal workers to migrate temporarily, mainly between different rural regions rather than from the countryside to the cities.⁸⁹ Yet the scale and intensity of the movements that began in the autumn of 1813 were unprecedented, and were compounded by the simultaneous problem of having to evacuate thousands of sick and wounded troops from the campaign area.

Chapter 21

The sick and wounded

Campaigns could be decided by disease and exhaustion as much as by battle casualties. At the end of January one of the Austrian infantry regiments in the IV *Armee-Abtheilung* was reported to have as many men sick as were present in the ranks.[1] The exceptionally cold winter did not help by discouraging bathing and forcing people to huddle indoors in overcrowded and unhygienic conditions.

'I will never forget this horrible sight'

Armies drained by hunger and exhaustion shed thousands of stragglers on the march. An inhabitant was horrified when he saw the road outside Saint-Dizier a day after Napoleon's troops had passed along it:

> You could hardly make it out: the entire road seemed to be just a ploughed field, especially in the places where the batteries had been sited. You could not walk a step without finding horses that had either been killed in the battle or had died from hunger and exhaustion. But what was saddest, what tore your heart, was to see wretched, worn-out soldiers in the abandoned villages, as they looked for bread or a bit of food and fell dead on the main road or in the gardens of the ruined hamlet. I will never forget this horrible sight.[2]

Temporary *ambulances* had to be established to supplement the hospitals in local towns. Inhabitants were asked to supply mattresses, bedsteads, bolsters, sheets, shirts, and nightcaps, and money for more specialised items, such as medicines. It was quicker, and less annoying, to seek donations than to requisition items, but the authorities threatened to billet the sick and wounded on private individuals if voluntary gifts were not forthcoming. Making bandages became a fashionable occupation, and as symbolic an image of the campaign as Cossacks looting or soldiers drinking champagne. The Empress Marie-Louise herself made bandages with her ladies-in-waiting, and donated old linen for the hospitals. Napoleon approved, and ordered any spare beds and other items at his palaces to be given to the army's hospitals.[3]

Mortality rates in the hospitals were high, especially among civilians. Of the 21,373 French and Allied soldiers who entered the *hospices* at Troyes in the first half of 1814, 14 per cent died. Yet the death rate among the 1,191 sick civilians who were admitted was 38 per cent, possibly because the overcrowding left no room for the inhabitants unless they were very ill.[4]

Evacuation

Paris could potentially have absorbed thousands of sick and wounded from the campaign area. In addition to smaller hospices and other establishments, its famous nationalised hospitals were staffed by leading doctors and surgeons, and renowned as centres of research and training, as well as treatment.[5]

Yet the capital's massive and dense population was especially vulnerable to an epidemic. The authorities were reluctant to bring disease into the heart of the capital, and knew that the arrival of large numbers of casualties would have undermined the population's morale and nullified the effect of parading Allied prisoners through the streets. 'The sick must not go by Paris,' Napoleon instructed on 1 February, 'nor the wounded.' Instead, he wanted hospitals organised along a line leading north-westwards from his army at Brienne, through Sézanne and Château-Thierry, bypassing Paris and heading for Picardy in northern France.[6]

But this line of evacuation was exposed within days to the advance of the *Schlesische Armee*. After his defeat at La Rothière, Napoleon instead evacuated his sick and wounded westwards to Troyes. He wanted the walking wounded kept at hospitals there so they could rejoin their units, while the seriously injured were taken in requisitioned carts to Nogent, from where they could be transported down the Seine by boat.[7] Using the river avoided a jolting voyage by road but exposed the wounded to the greed of the bargemen, who stole from the men who died and tipped their bodies overboard. Sometimes, it was alleged, they did not even wait for them to die.[8]

Similarly, carters who were requisitioned to transport the wounded by road might simply dump them in a deserted farm and disappear. They feared that if they reached their destination they would be requisitioned again and perhaps sent even further from their homes. Farmers also hid their horses, making it even more difficult to find enough transport.[9]

Patients were supposed to be evacuated down the Seine only as far as Melun or Choisy, and then sent around the southern side of Paris, either to Versailles or else to Orléans, where they could be embarked again on boats and sent down the Loire.[10] But the reality was that many stricken men were brought right into Paris, or made their own way there, and could be seen begging in the streets.

Napoleon continued to insist on limiting the numbers of patients cared for in the city. When Joseph informed him on 19 February of proposals to establish temporary hospitals in either the *Hôtel des Invalides* or the barracks at Courbevoie, 5 miles north-west of Paris, Napoleon issued instructions not to admit more than 12,000 sick and wounded into the capital.[11]

Instead, two lines of evacuation were established from Paris: one north-westwards down the Seine to Rouen, and the other south-westwards to Orléans and then along the Loire to Tours. He also planned to organise a third line, to Caen in Normandy. Hospitals established along, and near, these three lines would be able to accommodate about 13,500 patients from Paris.[12]

Even though evacuation spread disease more widely, it relieved the overcrowding. Yet the problems in Paris were still acute in mid-March. Patients were transported to the city but then remained several days without food, shelter, or medical attention. François Poumiès de la Siboutie, a hospital intern at the *Hôtel-Dieu*, vividly recalled how:

> We received hundreds of wounded, and were soon overburdened with them. We put them everywhere. The sick people who were in the hospitals were sent back to their families. The poor residents of Bicêtre, of the Salpêtrière, terminally ill people, had to give up their places and cram themselves into tiny dark rooms and attics. We were soon placing two sick men in a bed, and every day we had to find a new way to take in and shelter this ever-increasing flood of sick and wounded men.

These unfortunates dragged themselves along, bolstered by the feverish desire to reach Paris, where they hoped to find help and safety. Several died on the hospital steps, in the halls, or as they got into bed. Many had cuts and wounds that had not been dressed for several days, if at all. Every morning the carts of the *Hôtel-Dieu* took thirty or forty corpses to the cemetery, and it was a similar proportion from the other hospices and hospitals. These men often died without having been able to tell anyone their name, and there was no way of finding it out. In the pervasive confusion it was lucky if they were entered in the hospital registers.[13]

During the battle fought outside Paris at the end of March the French army's surgeons were assisted by civilian colleagues from inside the city. But the battle had been too bloody for all the wounded to receive immediate attention. Many Allied soldiers hid as they did not know the outcome of the action and feared that they would be taken prisoner. Search parties were sent out, but it was days or even weeks before some men received help.[14]

Disease

Disease was the main killer during the campaign. This was hardly surprising, given the insanitary and overcrowded conditions, the intermingling of masses of people from different regions and from both urban and rural environments, the hasty mobilisation of conscripts, the presence of large numbers of dead bodies, the migration of displaced persons and prisoners-of-war, and the continual movements of thousands of troops and animals.

Any sanitary measures were pointless, unless they were enforced throughout the entire region, in the countryside as well as the towns. Effective measures to contain disease depended on the co-operation of poorly educated peasants struggling simply to survive. During the campaign a family at Maizières-la-Grande-Paroisse kept a corpse in a bed for a week to discourage Allied soldiers from staying in their home, and they hid their food inside the straw mattress.[15] Nor did it help when inhabitants looted from slain soldiers on a battlefield. Even while the Battle of Montereau was still being fought, the fallen were robbed of their clothes and several inhabitants died of typhus after buying cheap garments from the thieves.[16]

Warmer weather relieved overcrowding indoors but made it more difficult for troops to keep clean in muddy bivouacs, and increased the rate at which corpses decomposed. Their burial was delayed in many places by apathy or fear of disease and by the reduction in the civilian population through death or flight, and cremation was difficult if firewood was in short supply.[17] At Pontarlier, near the Swiss frontier, the frozen ground made it impossible to dig enough mass graves, and hundred of coffins had to be stored in the stables of the local barracks until a thaw.[18]

Some *maires* were negligent, while others thought that the burials were a task for the military authorities. Efforts to force them to take responsibility were made while the campaign was still under way. On 16 February the provisional *préfet* of the Aube directed the *maires* and *adjoints* to have any dead horses removed from the roads, and renewed orders were given during March for the disposal of bodies.[19] Inhabitants of nearby *communes* could be requisitioned to bury the dead, or workers paid to do the job, which did at least create employment for men deprived of other sources of income.[20]

In April, following the onset of warmer weather, the task became more urgent. On the 14th the *préfets* of *départements* were directed to send commissioners into every contested *commune* to have mass graves dug at least 2 metres deep. The workers were to be kept upwind of the bodies and were to use hooks to avoid direct contact with them. To prevent wild animals digging up the graves, branches of thorns could be planted on top.[21]

Yet the *préfets*' orders were not always carried out. In the Aube putrefying bodies were still lying on the roads on 6 May. When graves were dug, they were often too near the routes and too shallow. Rural inhabitants might simply cover the dead with some earth, which was soon washed away.[22]

The task was complicated as bodies became hidden by growing crops. On 14 July orders were given for all the harvesters around Troyes to be given tools for burying any bodies they found. The harvest was to be done as far as possible in the morning and the harvesters supplied with brandy and vinegar, which were thought to counteract the malignity released by the decomposition.[23]

It was not only dead bodies that posed a health hazard. The armies had left a prodigious amount of manure and excrement, which inhabitants neglected to remove from the vicinity of their homes and stables, partly because of the shortage of horses and carts. The plain around Châlons-sur-Marne was strewn with assorted rubbish, and was described by an eyewitness as being 'no more than a vast dung heap, where you could no longer make out the boundaries between properties'.[24]

The water supply was also contaminated, since items such as cauldrons and cooking utensils had been hidden in wells to save them from being pillaged, and bodies were thrown into rivers as an alternative to burial. Corpses floated downriver to Paris, causing fears of an epidemic there.[25] A letter from experts at the Faculty of Medicine was published in the *Journal de Paris* on 24 March and sought to reassure the inhabitants that it was still safe to drink water from the river. They noted that some citizens were adding vinegar, sulphuric acid, or saline substances. They dismissed the efficacy of these methods and claimed that boiling the water was actually harmful, as it removed the dissolved air:

> In any case, all these methods are totally pointless, since the examination we have made very recently shows that the water of the Seine contains no foreign element and retains its purity and former healthiness. We lack enough space here to report all the researches and experiments that we have carried out in order to be confident of this. But even if we accept that the bodies of some animals may have been thrown into the river, the considerable volume of water that flows past and is constantly replenished, which drags along with it various molecules of earth and sand, and whose surface is ceaselessly agitated and mixed with the air, would have soon dispersed and destroyed these foreign substances, and thus entirely neutralised their effect.[26]

Such reassurances were worthless and many Allied soldiers are known to have suffered from diarrhoea while occupying Paris, as a result of drinking water from the Seine.[27]

Typhus

Unhygienic conditions favoured a mixture of ailments and epidemics rarely involved just one disease. Yet the biggest killer in 1814 was undoubtedly typhus. The cause, an organism similar to a bacterium, was carried by lice, deposited in their faeces, and then rubbed into broken skin when victims scratched their bites. Death could result in a week or two, in between 10 and 60 per cent of those infected.

Typhus was variously known as hospital, prison, or ship fever, as it was common in dirty and overcrowded places. There had already been outbreaks in France during the Revolution and the Empire, especially with the arrival of large numbers of destitute Spanish prisoners from the Peninsular War. But it was Napoleon's invasion of Russia in 1812 that caused the most deadly and widespread epidemic, for typhus was endemic in the east and was brought back into central Europe with the retreat from Moscow.

In 1813 typhus spread rapidly among the thousands of weak and inexperienced young conscripts who filled Napoleon's newly raised army. Not since the Thirty Years' War (1618–1648) had typhus pervaded central Europe to such an extent. It has been estimated than 10 per cent of the German population became infected with the disease in 1813–1814, and that over 1 per cent died from it, including the father of Richard Wagner, the future composer, who was six months old at the time.[28]

After his defeat at Leipzig, Napoleon's army brought the epidemic back into France itself. He wanted hospitals established in the eastern provinces to stop the sick having to be evacuated into the heart of the country, yet the frontier regions lacked the resources to cope and were soon threatened by invasion.[29] At the time it was suspected that typhus was spread by air infected by noxious emanations, for its transmission was known to be possible without people making physical contact, and the role of lice was not realised. Fumigation was therefore a favourite remedy. One method was to push a perforated box of embers around rooms containing any sick people, while casting some pinches of gunpowder on to it. The *Journal de Paris* reported that a mixture of sulphur and powdered saltpetre could be used instead, and claimed that it had some definitive advantages over gunpowder: 'This mixture produces no black smoke to fill the apartments and blacken their contents. It is cheaper than gunpowder, and does not entail the dangers to which carelessness or inexperience expose people using powder.'[30]

Fumigation had some benefit, especially psychologically, but the most effective methods, in the absence of antibiotics or a vaccine, would have been to reduce overcrowding, improve personal hygiene, and kill the rats that helped carry the infected fleas. Steps were, in fact, taken to encourage cleanliness, although apathy and fatalism made it difficult to enforce them. At Metz, for example, notices were posted in the streets at the end of November 1813 informing the inhabitants how to clean houses, clothes, and linen used by patients with dysentery.[31]

In Paris soldiers stricken with typhus were initially isolated inside the *Hôpital Notre-Dame de la Pitié*. Nearly a third of the hospital's patients died, the highest rate in any year between 1809 and 1877 for which data has survived.[32] It became impossible to prevent typhus from appearing elsewhere in Paris, although it was more prevalent within the city's hospitals than outside them. The disease began to abate in May, but at least 7,000 more inhabitants died in the capital in 1814 than in the previous year.[33]

The significance of the epidemic can not be measured solely in terms of mortality rates. Fear inspired by its seemingly unstoppable progress heightened the psychological distress provoked by the invasion. So many people died at Metz that the authorities sought to avert despondency by banning the tolling of church bells and the hanging of black mourning drapes on houses. The *maire* of Chaumont also forbade bells to be tolled, while at Châlons-sur-Marne the dead were buried at night. The authorities at Paris did not inform the public of the presence of typhus but were unable to prevent alarm growing in the city.[34]

Fear was regarded at the time as one of the causes of typhus, and it fed on itself, not least as the possibility of widespread panic raised the spectre of social unrest and added to the unease of the respectable classes. Fear of disease also intensified tensions between soldiers and civilians by making inhabitants more reluctant to lodge troops in their homes.[35]

In previous centuries panic caused by plague and other diseases had contributed to social disintegration, civil war, and even mass conversions to Christianity. It was precisely because fear magnified the actual impact of an epidemic that Napoleon famously visited the plague victims of his army at Jaffa in March 1799, during his invasion of the Holy Land.[36]

No one has fully explored the extent to which pestilences hastened Napoleon's downfall by decimating his armies and paralysing popular support, and yet they were indisputably more deadly enemies than any he met on the battlefield. Even the destruction of the *Grande armée* in Russia was caused not so much by cold, as popular myth would have it, but by disease, fatigue, and demoralisation.

Chapter 22

Reconstruction

The long-term impact of the campaign forms a fascinating study in its own right, and we are fortunate to have a wealth of local histories that trace the repercussions on individual towns, *départements*, or provinces. Yet few, if any, attempts have been made to synthesise these regional accounts and ascertain the effect on the theatre of war as a whole. A wide range of questions demand an answer. For example, how grievous was the devastation, how varied was the impact on different regions, and how long did recovery take?

The devastation

One of the first travellers to pass through the campaign area after the fighting ended was Eugène d'Arnauld, *baron* de Vitrolles. He left Paris on 5 April for Châlons-sur-Marne and found the road cluttered with felled trees, broken waggons, and the bodies of men and horses:

> The places through which I passed were half-deserted: the open houses seemed to be abandoned, and no one was working in either the fields or workshops. The most well-to-do inhabitants wore torn jackets and wretched cloth smocks, and, since they had no hats, they covered their heads with handkerchieves. They wandered around their homes like ghosts.[1]

The invasion was a humanitarian disaster for the communities most directly affected. In the much-contested *département* of the Aube one in eight inhabitants died, and since this was the average rate for the *département* as a whole, some individual towns and villages suffered even worse.[2] In fact, civilian communities such as these lost a higher proportion of dead as a result of the campaign than did many military units.

For Maizières-la-Grande-Paroisse, 20 miles north-west of Troyes, 1814 was the most deadly year of the entire nineteenth century. Out of the *commune*'s 1,000 inhabitants, 117 died. In only two other years did the death-rate rise significantly above the average, and both these spikes were caused by cholera outbreaks, with 46 deaths in 1849 and 61 in 1854.[3]

At Troyes, where more than 3,500 inhabitants died in 1814, the cemeteries were full and many families could not afford a conventional burial, so mass graves had to be dug in a field three-quarters of a mile east of the city. The spot can still be seen at the roadside today, marked by a cross.[4] Similarly, at Saint-Dizier the *conseil municipal* decided in April that it would have to enlarge the existing cemetery and create a new one.[5]

Some towns and villages were all but destroyed during the fighting. Nogent-sur-Seine, for example, was still in ruins in July 1815, by which time an epidemic had killed one in five of the inhabitants. It was rebuilt, but as a British tourist noted in 1841, 'the irregularity of the streets is . . . easily accounted for, and the only surprise is how the fine church escaped at all'.[6]

The destruction had secondary, indirect effects, like the ripples on the surface of a pond disturbed by the dropping of a stone. A 17-year-old medical student in Paris committed suicide on 2 March after learning that his home town, Méry-sur-Seine, had been burned down.[7]

The cultural damage was also grievous. During the fighting at Soissons in March a Roman bas-relief and other relics were lost when the house of a local collector was destroyed by fire.[8] One of the best natural history collections in France was also smashed during the pillaging of the *Château* de Brienne at the end of January. A staff officer, *Capitaine* Józef Grabowski, found that:

> The wooden floor and the tables were strewn with stuffed animals, frogs, snakes, eagles and extraordinary monsters, including a child with two heads. The cabinet of natural history was in a pitiable state. I was surprised by this scene of destruction and at the same time I was struck by an intense smell of alcohol and camphor. The jars were empty or broken and the liquid that had been inside them was spilt on the ground. The books, maps, engravings, globes and various physics instruments – all that had been in this library – lay higgledy-piggledy with the monsters and shards of glass.[9]

Grabowski learned from the *concierge* that the Allied looters had even drunk the alcohol from the specimen jars, not realising that the preservative contained arsenic.

The widespread destruction did at least offer a convenient excuse for clumsy servants. François Fauveau de Frénilly recorded that even ten years after the devastation of his *château* in the Oise valley, whenever anything was lost or broken, his domestics only ever needed the explanation: 'Monsieur, the Cossacks.'[10]

Archives were also lost. Those of the Aube were partly evacuated from Troyes to Nogent-sur-Seine, only to be destroyed there when the *hôtel-de-ville* was burned down during the fighting.[11] The archives were not simply of antiquarian interest, for they were needed by citizens to provide legal proof, for instance that they owned a piece of land. Some records could be replaced. After the *marquis* de Ferreux returned to his *château* in July and resumed his duties as the local *maire*, he found that some of the *commune*'s archives had been stolen or destroyed when his *château* was pillaged. Fortunately, as his *préfet* informed him, the registers of births, marriages, and deaths could be replaced using duplicates kept at the *préfecture*, and the plan showing plots of land with the copy held by the tax director.[12]

It was not always so easy. The archives of Soissons were destroyed during the fighting in March. A commission was established in January 1815 to recreate the births, marriages, and deaths registers using documents such as family papers and parish records, as well as declarations from relatives or older inhabitants, but had only limited success.[13]

In Paris some documents were deliberately destroyed at the end of March on the orders of the Empress Marie-Louise to prevent them from falling into hostile hands. As a result, crucial gaps exist today in the papers of Napoleon's state secretariat at the *Archives nationales*.[14]

The challenge of reconstruction

Even after widespread devastation, the new shoots of life could begin to appear remarkably quickly. The fire at Moscow in September 1812 destroyed 88 per cent of the shops, 70 per cent of the houses, and 43 per cent of the churches. Yet by the end of that year reconstruction was already under way and 70,000 inhabitants, or about a quarter of the former total, had been rehoused in at least temporary accommodation.[15]

In France, too, recovery was soon in progress. Less than two months after the Battle of Paris, the British artist Benjamin Haydon noted that all along the main road immediately north-east of the city 'the houses were ruined; but the workmen were repairing them, singing away, as if everything was a joke'. At Châlons-sur-Marne religious services were suspended during the campaign, partly because the churches were being used as magazines, but at the *maire*'s request the Allied commandant allowed them to reopen in time for Easter Day on 10 April.[16]

When Lieutenant Uxkull of the Russian *Garde à cheval* passed through Meaux at the beginning of June he noted that it had already recovered and bore no visible signs of the war. In fact, many towns had escaped serious physical damage, even when an action raged nearby: Reims changed hands on 13 March with surprisingly little looting or destruction. Yet it was the underlying effects that were most devastating, and they were not always obvious to passing travellers. Apart from at a few specific locations, the actual fighting caused far less harm than the more prolonged burden of requisitioning and the mass culling of people and livestock by disease. It was easier to repair a bridge or restore a damaged *hôtel-de-ville* than to rescue thousands of inhabitants from hunger, destitution, and despair. At Trilport, just 3 miles east of Meaux, nearly forty families were still homeless as a result of the campaign as late as February 1815.[17]

The most obvious physical damage, such as broken roads and devastated forests, were *pertes publiques*: losses borne collectively by the state, *départements*, or *communes*. Yet they were dwarfed by the *pertes particulières*, losses that fell to private individuals. In the *département* of the Aisne, for example, the *pertes particulières* were seventeen times as heavy as the *pertes publiques*.[18]

Some *communes* had lost much of their population through death or flight, which made it difficult to farm fields or rebuild houses. Elsewhere men were left out of work as their employers could no longer afford to pay them. Many vineyards, for example, had been desolated by troops searching for firewood, and simply replacing their stakes was a major expense, for as many as 50,000 might be needed for a single hectare.[19]

In the countryside inhabitants lost not only food and forage but their livestock, tools, and transport, which made it difficult to make a fresh start. Fields usually produced two harvests a year, but the first, immediately after the campaign, yielded little, partly because the armies had trampled the ground. There was still time to sow the land for a second harvest later that year, but in many places the necessary grain, horses, and implements had been requisitioned or destroyed, and the barns had been burned. Even before the campaign many fields in Franche-comté, near the Swiss frontier, had been left fallow because of a lack of manpower.[20]

Reductions in the size of the French army enabled some of its horses to be assigned to landowners. But an epizootic, brought by the oxen accompanying the Allied armies, compounded the losses in livestock. During the campaign animals had often been hidden in woods or quarries, where they were exposed to the bitter winter, and had to be moved repeatedly to avoid detection, which undermined their resistance to disease. It was estimated that in the *département* of the Aisne the Allied armies had taken 6,000 horses, 7,000 bullocks or cows and 40,000 woollen animals, but the epizootic killed another 30,000 horned animals in less than six months.[21]

To combat the epizootic the authorities ordered preventative measures, such as quarantine lines and the slaughter of infected animals, but encountered opposition and negligence. Butchers continued to sell meat from stricken animals. Suspending fairs and markets in an effort to prevent the spread of disease undermined economic recovery. Experts found it difficult to agree on the causes of the epizootic, let alone the remedy. Some thought that the air in specific locations had been contaminated during the campaign, or that cattle were infected after drinking from stagnant water containing corpses. The agricultural society of the *département* of the Marne considered holding a competition to gather ideas, but decided that the results would be too late to help, and instead simply hoped that vets would find a cure after gaining insights from observing the disease.[22]

The depletion of the livestock resulted in difficulties ploughing fields, a lack of manure to fertilise them, and reduced demand for fodder, which depressed the price of hay. At the same time the epizootic aggravated the shortages of food for human consumption and caused prices to rise at a time when inhabitants could least afford them. They found themselves unable to sell possessions, for their neighbours were equally impoverished, or to obtain a loan, for they lacked the necessary credit.[23]

The most pressing problem was having to continue feeding the Allied armies for more than two months after Napoleon's abdication. Taxes were unlikely to be collected, as the threat from looters meant that the inspectors ran the risk of losing large sums.[24] The financial situation was complicated by the existence of more than one currency. In the *département* of the Loire many Austrian and Prussian coins continued to circulate after the Allied armies withdrew, and inhabitants who held foreign money wanted it to be accepted at the artificially high tariff that Schwarzenberg had fixed at the time of the invasion.[25] Many Spanish coins were also in circulation, having been brought by prisoners-of-war or by French soldiers who had served in the Peninsula. One *sous-préfet* proposed having the foreign coins withdrawn, melted down, and made into French pieces.[26]

Communications

Economic recovery required the prompt restoration of links between the main towns and cities. Roads had become degraded by the campaign, compounding the years of neglect that the lesser routes had already suffered since the start of the Revolution.

Communications depended on the staging posts, where travellers could obtain food, accommodation, and fresh horses. Yet the *maîtres de postes* had been an obvious target for requisitioning and looting, since they were situated on the main roads and often needed to maintain a considerable estate to support their posts. A *maître de poste* at Troyes tried to resign on 20 April, explaining that he had lost forty-one horses and all his forage as a result of the war, and that he was unable to re-establish his post without help. He received scant sympathy, being ordered to continue the service for another six months from the date of his resignation, with the threat that otherwise it would be provided for him at his expense.[27]

Towards the end of April the *préfet* of the Seine-et-Marne still found it difficult to correspond with his subordinates because of the irregular nature of the *service de la poste*. At the end of the year he was informed that the *maîtres de postes* had to seek indemnification for their losses by submitting records like any other inhabitants, but that 4,600 *francs* had been allocated to the most severely hit *maîtres de postes* of the *département*, in order to avoid a total interruption in their service.[28]

Broken bridges also had to be repaired. Some were soon back in operation as a result of temporary wooden roadways placed over destroyed arches. Those at Melun and Montereau south-east of Paris were reopened by 10 May. On the Marne, in contrast, only pontoon bridges existed between Paris and Trilport and further east at La Ferté-sous-Jouarre, although engineers were busy identifying the most urgent work.[29]

Reconstruction took even longer elsewhere. As late as November the bridges over the Isère river north of Valence, on the main road between Lyon and Marseille, had not been rebuilt, and travellers instead had to use a ferry. Not until the 1850s were the stone bridges at Vitry-le-François and Moret-sur-Loing properly repaired, a wooden replacement having hitherto sufficed for a broken arch.[30]

Waterways as well as roads were vital to commerce and to the food supply of cities. In addition to repairing a bridge, therefore, the fallen rubble had to be removed from the river so it did not obstruct navigation. As early as 20 April repairs were being made to the three broken locks on the Loing canal, which helped link the Loire and Seine.[31]

Relief

Traditionally help for regions devastated by war came from charities. But in 1792, when northern France was invaded during the Revolutionary Wars, the Republic took responsibility for the losses suffered by its people. In August that year the *Assemblée nationale* gave an undertaking to the inhabitants of the frontier districts:

> Citizens, your location ensures for you the glory of being the first to fight for liberty and equality. The Fatherland relies on your courage; rely on its gratitude. Your children will be its children; it will take care of your wives and, if the tyrants devastate your properties, it will regard it from now on as a sacred debt to indemnify you for the losses you will have suffered.[32]

Initially only partial compensation was considered, but in February 1793 the national *Convention* promised full indemnification for the losses suffered by all its citizens. This pledge was the statement of an ideal, the practical embodiment of the Revolutionary principles of equality and fraternity, and was intended to unite the nation in its moment of peril. But in reality the Republic lacked the financial resources for full compensation and actually paid for barely one-third of the losses, partly as a result of imposing time limits and requiring claims to be verified. Only in the aftermath of the First World War would the French state fully compensate its people.[33]

In 1814 Napoleon tried to relieve the inhabitants even while the campaign was under way. On the day after the Battle of Brienne he sent an ADC to ask the *maire* for details of the inhabitants' losses, but since he soon had to retreat he was unable to provide any immediate relief. Similarly, after the Battles of Montereau and Arcis-sur-Aube he promised to compensate the inhabitants and have their homes rebuilt, but would be unable to do so because of his fall from power.[34]

Any relief, therefore, came initially from local sources. Relatives or neighbours might shelter homeless families, and wealthy Allied officers who were dying in hospital were known to give money to the local *curé* in order to have prayers said for them. When the siege of Huningue ended in April food was sent by the inhabitants of Basel in Switzerland, 3 miles to the south-east. The first battlefield tourists appeared equally quickly, with people flocking to see the damage at another fortress, Belfort, as soon as the fighting stopped, especially from the nearby town of Montbéliard.[35]

Displaced persons who fled the countryside found some charity at Paris. But local authorities were often powerless to help, as their funds for poor relief had been exhausted. Some state intervention was therefore essential, yet it was difficult for Parisians and the central government to comprehend the degree to which the rural population was suffering. The Bourbons faced competing demands, the scale and complexity of which have never been fully appreciated: as well as healing the deeply embedded divisions left by the Revolution, they had to bring France to terms with the loss of her superpower status and adjust her militarised society to peace.[36]

To have any success in meeting these multiple challenges, the government needed money and had to enforce the collection of taxes. It was not in Louis XVIII's interest to see the most badly affected regions permanently crippled, but any tax exemptions in their favour would be at the expense of the financial health of the kingdom as a whole. It was unfortunate that the most devastated regions were also some of the most populous and economically developed, and that the rest of the country had suffered from the indirect effects of the invasion and had only a limited ability to share the burden.

Even so, many inhabitants in the campaign area could pay their taxes only by selling their few remaining animals. Appeals reached the government for tax exemptions or reductions, and the protests made sense, for the local economy could be regenerated more effectively if inhabitants had enough money to rebuild their houses, thus providing employment for workmen. In the *département* of the Aisne the population of La Ville-aux-Bois-lès-Juvincourt threatened simply to abandon their village and migrate to other *communes* if attempts were made to force them to pay their taxes.[37]

Distribution of the *pertes particulières* in the *département* of the Aisne

arrondissement	pertes particulières	proportion of the département's pertes
Laon	22,943,745 francs 91	46.1 %
Soissons	15,985,223 francs 85	32.1 %
Château-Thierry	8,669,182 francs 80	17.4 %
Saint-Quentin	1,186,111 francs 59	2.4 %
Vervins	976,676 francs 68	2.0 %
Total for *département*	49,760,940 francs 83	100.0 %

Source: Fleury, *Histoire de l'invasion*, pp.542-3.

The different degrees of affliction between regions contributed to the complexity of reconstruction.[38] Even within the same *département* the burden varied considerably. Locations near main roads, or near a large, stationary military force, suffered particularly heavily. Of the five *arrondissements* of the Aisne, one, Laon, bore 46 per cent of the *pertes particulières*, partly because it was disproportionately large, but mainly because it hosted two major battles, at Craonne and Laon, and a long occupation by the *Schlesische Armee*. In contrast, two other *arrondissements*, Saint-Quentin and Vervins, had simply seen armies pass through, and they each bore just 2 per cent of the *département*'s total *pertes particulières*.[39]

The inquiry

Simply ascertaining the extent of the losses was difficult, especially in the immediate aftermath of the campaign when *départements* were still occupied by the Allies, and when communications between the *préfet* and his *sous-préfets* and *maires* were still intermittent. In fact, the Bourbons resorted on 22 April to Napoleon's method of sending out *commissaires extraordinaires* to establish their authority and ascertain the reliability of local officials, the state of public opinion, the condition of roads and bridges, and an idea of the losses.[40]

On 18 June the *Ministre de l'intérieur* ordered a more systematic survey. Some *préfets* had anticipated him by making their own arrangements for inquiring into the losses, partly in response to protests about the impossibility of paying taxes. Speed of relief was essential. Problems that could be borne during the summer would become serious with the onset of colder weather from September. Houses without roofs would fall into even greater disrepair the longer they were left. Yet it could take as long as three months for a *département* to submit the results of its inquiry, and the financial problems of the country as a whole made it impossible to do more than alleviate the losses through tax reductions. In short, the state did not send any money to the provinces. Instead, it simply cut the amount that the affected *départements* had to pay in tax, so they could lessen the distress of their own inhabitants. Relief was therefore inadequate and local, and the burden was not shared by France as a whole. Fairness had to be subordinated to the imperative of restoring the nation's finances.

A distinction was drawn between compensation for requisitions and relief for other losses caused by the invasion. Relief for *départements* that had been occupied or contested during the campaign was promised in the finance law of 23 September, and took the form of reductions to the ordinary direct taxes.[41]

On the other hand, compensation for inhabitants who had supplied requisitions was authorised by the *Conseil d'état* in June. It was made by offsetting the amount owed by the state for the requisitions against payments still outstanding from inhabitants for the extraordinary taxes Napoleon had decreed during the winter of 1813–1814. Inhabitants who had supplied requisitions to the French authorities before the invasion were theoretically entitled to full compensation, as were contractors who had supplied the Allied armies during their subsequent evacuation of France. But the state was not legally responsible for requisitions that had been made forcibly by the armies during the campaign, although the *départements* could alleviate those losses by distributing any remaining relief among their worst-hit *communes*.[42]

Within each affected *département* the assistance had to be distributed among the inhabitants, and this was the work of a *commission de liquidation* established to assess and settle claims. The exact way in which the relief was distributed, and the time taken to do so, differed between *départements*, but delays were inevitable because of the scale of the task. Tax inspectors had to visit each *commune* and examine individual claims. In the Aisne it took five months, from 12 September 1814 to 11 January 1815, for the *commission* to complete its work, and appeals continued for another two decades.

The *commissions* were obliged to reduce claims to the lowest possible amount in order to provide even nominal liquidation of all the debts. The *commune* of Festieux in the Aisne lost 330,000 *francs* in requisitions but obtained a reduction of only 1,552 *francs* in the extraordinary taxes. Claims had to be properly certified to prevent fraud, but inhabitants could not always supply acceptable pieces of evidence, perhaps because they had been unable to obtain slips for requisitions carried out by force, or because they had been given forged slips written in Russian or German for unauthorised demands. Indirect losses were unlikely to be granted, such as the claim from a man for loss of earnings while his boats were trapped inside the fortress of Thionville by the invasion.[43]

In the *département* of the Moselle some *communes* had already indemnified their inhabitants with the felling of timber in forests, without having authority to do so. As a result some villages had actually made a profit from the invasion, and the *préfet* insisted that they should not be entitled to tax relief.[44] The authorities were generally reluctant to permit tree felling, as it would undermine prices by putting too much wood on the market and perpetuate a community's problems by ruining its local forests, thus depriving it of future income.

Additional relief

Some efforts were made to provide additional charitable relief, not least because the issue of reconstruction became politicised by the changes of regime in 1814–1815. The *comte* d'Artois and his son Charles-Ferdinand, *duc* de Berri visited the campaign area in the autumn of 1814 and donated money from their private funds. Similarly, Napoleon decreed the establishment of an extraordinary fund in April 1815, a month after he had regained power, half of which would be used to subsidise the rebuilding of homes destroyed by hostilities in the eastern provinces. Napoleon needed to win support, especially in these important frontier districts, and to encourage the payment of taxes.[45]

Later, while in exile on St Helena, Napoleon used his will as a propaganda tool and divided his private estate between soldiers who had fought for France in the recent wars and inhabitants of the provinces that had borne the brunt of the invasions of 1814 and 1815. It was little more than a gesture, however, since his private estate had fallen into the hands of the Bourbon government and been absorbed into the treasury.

Not until 1854, after the establishment of the Second Empire, could Napoleon's legacy be executed, and even then only partially, for the amount set aside, 8 million *francs*, was less than 7 per cent of the value of his private estate. Two million of these *francs* were distributed to the towns and *départements* worst-hit by the Allied invasions. Napoleon's will specifically mentioned both Brienne and Méry-sur-Seine, which had been largely burned down, and at each of them some of the money was used to build a new *hôtel-de-ville*. Elsewhere the funds were used on projects such as hostels for beggars and prizes for inventions. By this stage the money was no longer needed to repair the effects of the wars, and was a thinly disguised means of buying political support for Napoleon III's regime.[46]

Aftershocks

For the inhabitants of the occupied regions the 1814 campaign was neither a short nor an isolated disaster, but part of a prolonged period of troubles that had begun as early as 1810 with an economic crisis and harvest failures.

After 1814 the effects of the invasion ricocheted for years. The impact was aggravated by a second Allied invasion in the summer of 1815 after Napoleon's defeat at Waterloo, which complicated the problems of providing relief. An Allied army of occupation remained in the frontier *départements* until 1818, although its maintenance was more orderly and was borne by the state as a whole. Famine occurred in 1816–1817 when the harvest failed because of unusually cold and rainy weather following the eruption in April 1815 of Mount Tambora in the Dutch East Indies, which dwarfed even that of Krakatoa in 1883. The volcano threw so much dust into the atmosphere that 1816 became known as the 'year without a summer'. It did not help that many peasants lacked food reserves as a result of the Allied invasions.[47]

The experience of 1814 suggests how much greater the suffering must have been in impoverished countries undergoing a longer occupation, notably Spain, Portugal, and Prussia. Even twenty years later inhabitants of Franche-comté still felt the effects of the invasion, and the development of the city of Besançon was delayed by the need to liquidate the debts and repair the damages of war.[48]

Yet the devastation did bring some benefit. The destruction of the village of Torcy-le-Grand during the Battle of Arcis-sur-Aube enabled it to be rebuilt further away from the Aube river, where it was less at risk from flooding. In reconstructing Méry-sur-Seine the *conseil municipal* decided to straighten some streets and ban any thatched roofs because of the fire risk, but other decisions were disregarded, including the creation of a lateral road that would have relieved today's traffic congestion.[49]

Wounds gradually healed with the passage of time and the historian Edouard Fleury noted in 1858:

> All this misfortune has been so forgotten that these details and facts are strange and unknown, as if they were the history of a foreign people. They are totally unknown even at the location where they occurred. People know the broad outline of the invasion and its consequences, but at a time when witnesses of the catastrophe are still alive, the invasion is already almost a myth.[50]

Chapter 23

Bar-sur-Aube: a case study

The full impact of the campaign on the civilian population is easier to grasp by examining a specific community. The town of Bar-sur-Aube makes a particularly interesting case study, since it lay at the heart of the campaign theatre and saw two battles. It was 115 miles east by south-east of Paris, and before the invasion began had a population of between 3,800 and 4,000 people.[1]

'The inhabitants are abandoning their homes'

The first battle was fought outside the town on 24 January as *Maréchal* Mortier's corps fell back on Troyes in the face of the *Hauptarmee*'s advance. He was unable to prevent Bar-sur-Aube from being occupied, and in less than a month the Allies had largely drained the town of supplies. Drawing provisions from the surrounding area was complicated by the shortage of horses and the fact that bands of Cossacks were seizing transport and maltreating farmers. Much of the countryside, far from providing help to the town, actually required assistance, and Bar-sur-Aube was full of displaced families from the surrounding area.[2]

The provisional *sous-préfet* complained bitterly about the Allied pillaging:

> We have a *commandant de place* [town commandant] who does not understand our language, besides being absolutely negligent, [and he] allows the greatest acts of robbery to be committed without standing in their way. All these excesses are reported to him, but he reprimands no one. . . . Most of the inhabitants are abandoning their homes to seek refuge in the woods – they prefer to be exposed to all the horrors of the bad weather and hunger than be left to the brutality of these brigands.[3]

After a month of Allied occupation the tide swung back in Napoleon's favour and French troops retook Bar-sur-Aube on 26 February. Next day the second battle was fought around the town when Schwarzenberg returned to the offensive and defeated *Maréchal* Oudinot's detachment. Bar-sur-Aube was then pillaged by the Bavarians in reprisal for shots that the inhabitants were alleged to have fired earlier at Allied troops.[4]

'What a sight the town offered!' recalled *Rittmeister* Carl von Grüber of the Bavarian *7. Chevaulegers-Regiment*:

> The finest pieces of furniture, pianos, mirrors, and couches lay broken in the streets, while heaps of others had been set on fire and were spreading an acrid smoke. Half-drunk soldiers were pushing wheelbarrows loaded with champagne bottles. After binging on wine, men were sleeping on the road, and against the houses, while others remained dead drunk in the cellars.[5]

Grüber took an officer and six men of his squadron to protect the home of a merchant on whom he had been billeted while staying in the town a month earlier. He saved the house by claiming that it had been reserved as the corps commander's quarters. The friendship he had forged with the merchant transcended the deep divisions that often existed between occupiers and occupied. When he was wounded later in the campaign, he found himself cut off in the Allied rear by local uprisings. He sought sanctuary in Bar-sur-Aube and was hidden by the merchant, who subsequently refused any reward, in case it caused him problems with other inhabitants after the Allies left.[6]

The merchant's wariness was hardly surprising, given the bitterness aroused by the Allies' mistreatment of the town. After Napoleon's forces reoccupied Bar-sur-Aube once more towards the end of March, a Young Guard commander, *Général de brigade* Christophe, *baron* Henrion, reported how:

> The inhabitants of Bar, and those of the surrounding area, could not be better motivated. Immediately after the arrival of the imperial troops, they entreated the commanding officer to seize the weapons that had been confiscated by the enemy and deposited in the community centre. They at once set off in pursuit of various enemy detachments, and in a few hours returned loaded with loot and prisoners. Ten of them particularly distinguished themselves. They fell on a strong detachment of fifty men who were escorting an Austrian 13-pounder gun, took them prisoner, and brought the gun back drawn by four good horses. ... These prisoners were all armed with muskets, which I have left in the hands of the inhabitants. I think that His Majesty could obtain a great advantage if it was possible to arm them.[7]

'I witnessed the most incredible horror'

An eyewitness account suggests that many inhabitants of Bar-sur-Aube were slain during the second battle. A Russian staff officer, Staff Captain Eduard von Löwenstern, claimed to have seen the Bavarians carrying out a massacre on the evening of 26 February:

> In Bar, I saw the terrible action at close quarters and witnessed for myself the most incredible horror. A Bavarian battalion was cut off in Bar and wholly cut down. Their comrades now avenged their deaths. ... Everyone shouted and made a noise, the houses were stormed, women and old men slaughtered, and children thrown out of the upper floor and smashed on the street. The Bavarians took dreadful revenge on the unfortunate town for the deaths of their slain comrades.[8]

Yet the official registers record only five deaths among the inhabitants of Bar-sur-Aube on 27 February and none on the 26th. It is probable that some civilian deaths were not, and indeed could not be, officially recorded. The authorities were overwhelmed with work and some people fled, or were killed, without their fate being known. At Méry-sur-Seine the register was buried for safety during the occupation, and deaths sometimes had to be recorded a year afterwards.[9]

Löwenstern's colourful account was undoubtedly exaggerated, and the destruction caused directly by military action at Bar-sur-Aube was in fact limited. Sixty-five houses in the *commune* were demolished or seriously devastated, causing an estimated loss of 280,000 *francs*, but it could have been far worse, for the town was built largely from wood and was lucky to escape being either burned down or blown up.[10] A fire broke out shortly before the second battle because of the carelessness of some French prisoners-of-war held by the Allies in the former Ursulines convent. Part of the complex burned down, threatening to ignite barrels of powder stored in the cellars.

Fortunately, a civilian managed to flood the cellars with wine and averted a catastrophic explosion.[11]

It was disease, rather than fighting, that proved the real killer for the civilian population. The second battle alone had inflicted over 4,000 military casualties, or more than one for every inhabitant, and left the town overwhelmed with sick and wounded. One of the temporary *ambulances* established to care for them was inside the Church of Saint-Pierre, where wounded French prisoners lit fires to keep warm, leaving cracked and reddened patches on the flagstones still visible today.[12]

Overcrowded and unhygienic *ambulances* established right in the heart of the town favoured the spread of disease. So, too, did Bar-sur-Aube's position on the *Hauptarmee*'s main line of communications, which meant that it was overburdened with requisitions and continuously exposed to diseases such as typhus, which were readily transmitted by reinforcements, prisoners-of-war, and evacuations of the sick and wounded.

Nor was it possible to dispose quickly of the dead, some of whom remained where they had fallen for as long as three months. Claude Girardon, a police commissioner made responsible for ensuring that the dead were buried, visited Bar-sur-Aube on 6 June and told the local *sous-préfet* of the prodigious number of dead men and animals he had seen near the town:

> He had difficulty believing what I reported. He admitted that he had been mistaken and that he had informed the *préfet* that everything had been done in his *arrondissement*. He had no trouble convincing himself of the contrary by going a musketshot outside the town.
>
> I went the same day to the *maire*'s house, as he was detained there by a fairly serious illness. Since he was kept busy with his administrative responsibilities, and could not see to everything himself, he was obliged to entrust the burials to commissioners who lacked the energy and eagerness that should be applied in such circumstances, and who did not consider the unfortunate consequences of their negligence in fulfilling a mission that affected everyone so fundamentally.
>
> The *maire* gave me some workers, but they were too few to accomplish quickly such an important task, which I supervised very closely. I had to turn to the *sous-préfet*, who requisitioned the inhabitants of the neighbouring *communes*, most of whom fled after working an hour or two. I had to bring them round with much care and attention, and I impressed on them how important it was for themselves and everyone else to check the epidemic that was desolating the region.
>
> In truth, it took a great effort of will to remain there. The fact is, on the hill of Ailleville, to the north of the road, the bodies of at least forty men and two *vivandières* had not been buried, besides the carcasses of at least 100 horses. The air was so infected that the wine growers had abandoned the cultivation of their vines.[13]

The epidemic

The devastating course of the epidemic that swept through Bar-sur-Aube can be traced using the *tables décennales*, the ten-year registers of births, marriages, and deaths.[14] The recorded number of deaths among the inhabitants of Bar-sur-Aube in 1814 was more than five times the usual annual total, but it was the four months of March, April, May, and June that accounted for most of this spike.[15] During the first two months of the invasion, January and February, the monthly number of deaths remained below forty. In March it suddenly shot up to over 140. It remained above 100 in April and May, fell to just under 60 in June, and returned to the normal level of below 20 in July, partly because the withdrawal of the Allied troops began to relieve the overcrowding and ease the burden on the population.

Hence, it was the onset of warmer weather in mid-March, following the second battle, that saw the full outbreak of the epidemic. The *maire* was forced to have some of the dead cremated in an effort to combat the problem, but it was too late.[16] The population of Bar-sur-Aube, already weakened by occupation, mistreatment, and bitter cold, was literally decimated. In fact, since not all the deaths were officially recorded, the actual mortality rate would have been even greater, and was reportedly as high as one in six, or even one in four.[17]

Yet the problems connected with the invasion had surprisingly little long-term impact on the death rates, at least in Bar-sur-Aube. During the ten-year period from 1813 to 1822 the monthly number of deaths rose above 20 only between December 1813 and June 1814. Neither the after-effects of the conflict, nor the renewed Allied occupation between July and November 1815, nor the famine of 1816–1817 saw a noticeable rise in mortality. It is true that the *commune*'s population had shrunk, leaving fewer people around to die, especially older and weaker members of the community. This, indeed, helps account for the unusually low number of deaths at another *commune*, Méry-sur-Seine, in 1815 and 1816.[18]

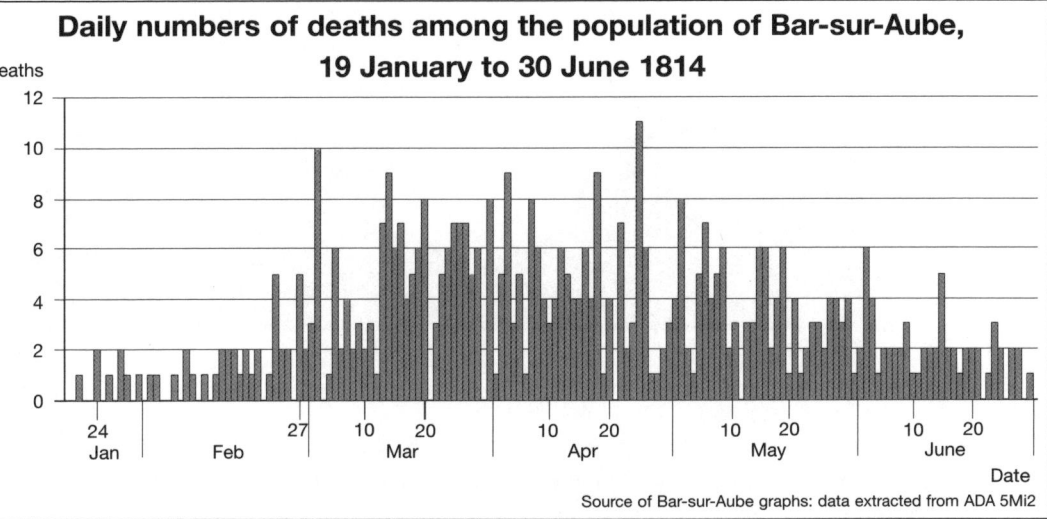

Source of Bar-sur-Aube graphs: data extracted from ADA 5Mi2

Yet neither did Bar-sur-Aube's birth-rate decline in the eight years after 1814, despite the population loss. In fact, there was an average of 116 births a year in 1815–1822, an increase from the average of 103 in 1807–1813. This suggests that the deaths in 1814 carried off mainly older people and the very young. It is known that at Vallentigny, 4 miles north-east of Brienne, twelve of the fourteen inhabitants recorded as having died in 1814 were either children or at least 70 years old.[19]

What is striking about the birth-rate is the temporary dip that occurred in 1814. The number of conceptions steadily declined from October 1813, the month of Napoleon's disastrous defeat at Leipzig, as the inhabitants realised that invasion was imminent.[20] During January and February 1814 there were only two conceptions leading to births registered in the commune. But the conception rate began to pick up

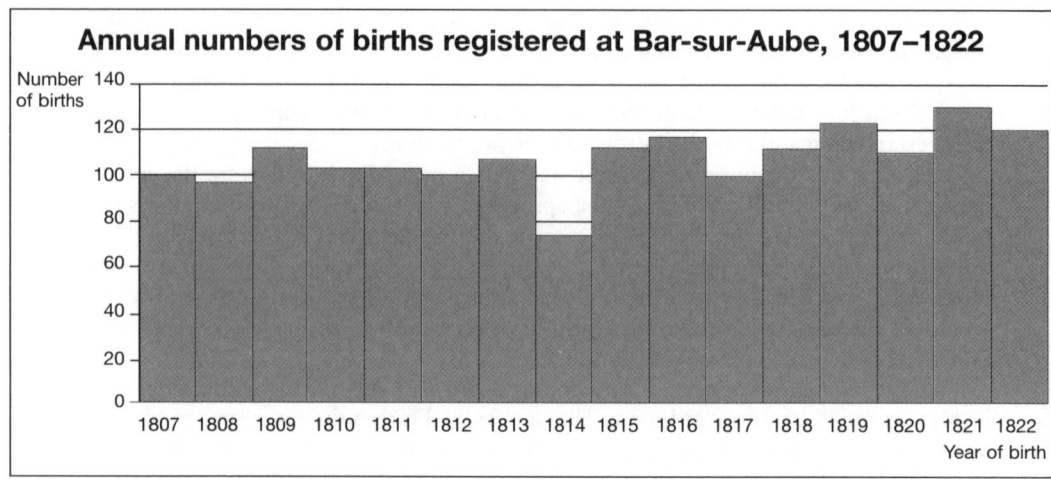

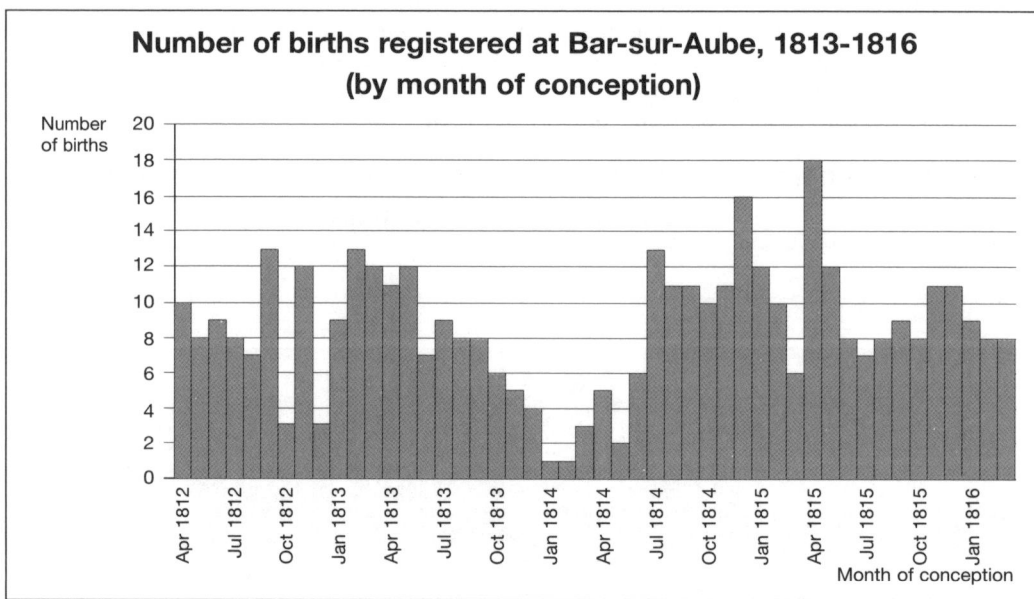

again as early as March, and by July it had already surpassed the October 1813 level.

Similarly, the campaign seems to have had only a limited and temporary effect on the marriage rate. There were no marriages in February to May 1814 inclusive, but this probably contributed to the unusually high number of marriages in 1815–1816. There were fifteen marriages in January 1815, more than in any other month between 1807 and 1822.

The number of marriages might have been expected to increase in the final years of the Empire, as young men sought to avoid conscription. There were 6,585 marriages at Paris in 1813, an increase of 2,024 from 1812, and a level not seen since 1796. In contrast, Bar-sur-Aube did not see a major increase in the number of marriages in 1813, although *Sénateur* Louis, *comte* de Ségur, the local *commissaire extraordinaire*, reported at the start of 1814 that the number of marriages in the *département* of the Aube as a whole was prodigious.[21]

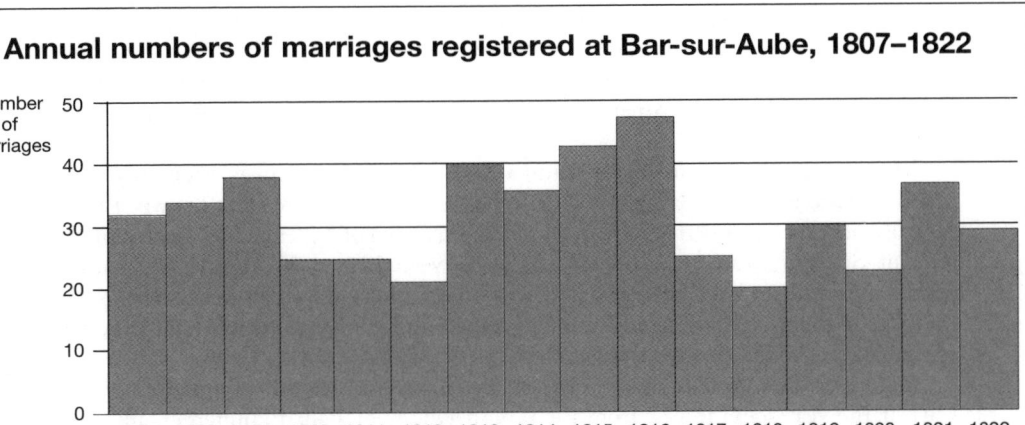

Annual numbers of marriages registered at Bar-sur-Aube, 1807–1822

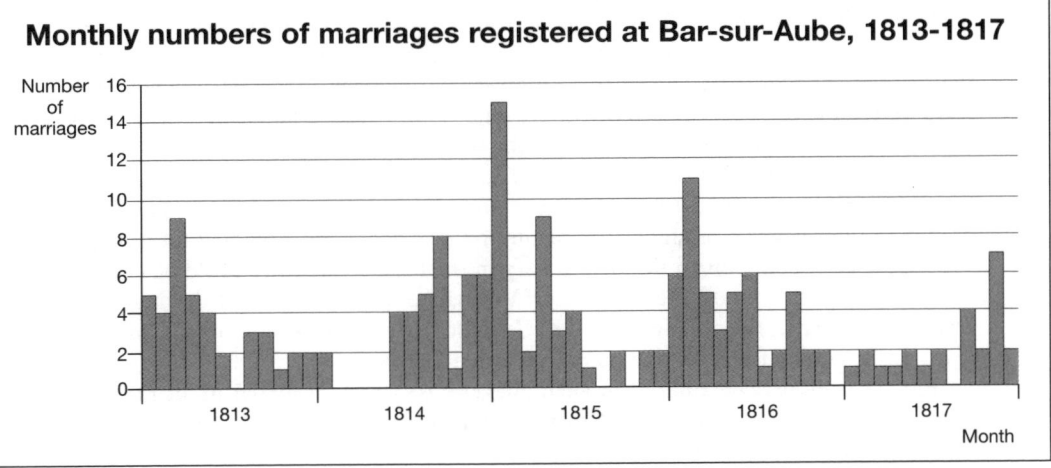

Monthly numbers of marriages registered at Bar-sur-Aube, 1813-1817

Traumas and scapegoats

Other questions remain, and there is scope for further research. For example, how many children were orphaned, and how many babies were fathered by Allied soldiers? What impact did the invasion have on rates of venereal disease? Lieutenant Uxkull of the Russian *Garde à cheval* recorded a succession of flirtations and affairs in his diary, while a Frenchwoman from Saverne is known to have been present at the Battle of Brienne after joining a Russian *jäger* officer who passed through her town during the invasion.[22] The *maire* of Dijon had to issue an official rebuke on 6 March, in which he named and shamed three local women for being too friendly with Allied soldiers:

> Considering that these girls are a source of scandal and that they disturb the peace of their neighbours by the noise they cause, those named below are instructed to behave quietly in future, and no longer to entice foreigners into their home, otherwise they will go to prison.[23]

Prostitutes were convenient scapegoats for the failings of a community as a whole.

After Napoleon retook the city of Reims in March, its earlier capture by the Russians was blamed on treason, and, as *Chef de bataillon* Jean-Marie Girod de l'Ain explained: 'Some whores, who were accused of having betrayed it, were arrested and condemned to be flogged in the public squares, which was carried out. Perhaps they were not the only guilty ones.'[24]

Many women were left deeply traumatised by their experiences, especially those raped by Cossacks or other soldiers, or *femmes cosaquées* as they were known. Edme-Jacques Gérost recorded that several women in his town of Villenauxe, 12 miles southwest of Sézanne, were attacked, especially between 12 and 20 March, when up to eighty were said to have been violated. On one of those days Cossacks went on the rampage through the town, and publicly raped about fifty women whom they had assembled under the covered market.[25]

Rape was often used as a psychological weapon to terrorise the population. At the start of the year some troops from the Grand Duchy of Baden taunted an advanced post of the *3e Gardes d'honneur* on the Rhine and inhabitants from a nearby town. 'Frenchmen', they called, 'it's our turn now to visit you, and to see if your wives and daughters are as good as the German girls.'[26]

At Méry-sur-Seine several young women dressed as men to avoid being attacked, while women elsewhere left their homes and sheltered inside communities of nuns. In the campaign area as a whole many rape victims killed themselves out of a sense of shame, died prematurely, or remained almost continuously ill.[27] The psychological scars were sometimes aggravated by the attitude of husbands, who blamed their wives for causing their own misfortunes. One of the women assaulted at Villenauxe was said to have been verbally abused afterwards by her spouse for not having fled the town with him. She had hoped to earn some money by remaining at home and selling brandy to the Cossacks, as she had done on previous occasions. She died four or five years later, after going into a decline. Gossip in the local community could be equally malicious, and fifteen of the women at Villenauxe were accused of having been attacked only when they really wanted it. 'I particularly heard several people, of both sexes, insist emphatically on this point,' recorded Gérost.[28]

Private enmities contributed to such allegations, which occurred in all ranks of society. Napoleon was informed in February of an attempt to smear the reputations of the daughter-in-law and niece of the *comtesse* de Montesquiou-Fezensac. For safety they had been sent from Paris, properly escorted, to a property near Vendôme, but on the way they met a *sénateur* who falsely told his daughter, Louise de Guéhéneuc, *duchesse* de Montebello, that they had been raped by French soldiers at a relay house. The spiteful gossip soon spread.[29]

The prevalence of such attitudes was not helped by the legal subordination of women to their husbands. The *Code civil des Français*, the unified law code adopted in 1804, reflected Napoleon's own paternalistic views, and curtailed the rights won by women during the Revolution as it sought to safeguard the institution of marriage.

Even so, women were not always passive victims of the invasion. At Avesnes in February a largely female crowd threatened the *commandant* and opened the gates to admit the Allies rather than incur the horrors that usually happened when a town was taken by assault.[30] Similarly, at the beginning of March French troops laughed at the sight of some Allied prisoners being escorted by a body of women armed with scythes and pitchforks. The captives complained of their harshness and asked to be guarded by men.[31]

Apparently none of the women at Villenauxe bore children as a result of the attacks. At Troyes, in contrast, the civil hospice received an average of sixty-eight

A French infantryman.

newborn babies a day towards the end of 1814, and at least two-fifths of them were said to have had foreign fathers, but it is difficult to gain a reliable idea of the numbers of such births in the campaign theatre as a whole.[32]

Nor is it clear how the experience of occupation affected the long-term attitudes of the population of a town like Bar-sur-Aube. *Kaiserlick* was long considered an insult at Dijon, which had been occupied by the Austrians, while in Alsace, where the *8. Bundes-Corps* had helped secure the Allied rear, peasants threatened mischievous children: 'Be quiet, or you will be a Badener.' Yet bitter antagonisms were not inevitable: some Alsatian families formed close ties with the soldiers billeted in their homes, and visited them in Baden, on the other side of the Rhine, after the campaign.[33]

The experience of occupation, in this or any other war, varied by gender, age, class, and location, and defied simple explanations. Yet for all its complexities, and the frequency with which it has been overlooked, it formed an integral part of Napoleon's defence of France.

Appendix I

The weather during the campaign

The following meteorological observations were made at the *Observatoire impérial* in Paris, and have been extracted from the daily reports published at the time in the *Journal de Paris*.

The three readings each day were recorded at dawn, at midday and at 1500 hours, and temperatures would have dipped during the night. It was colder and snowier in many places outside Paris, particularly towards the Langres plateau, and in the heights of the Jura and Vosges. Geneva, for example, saw temperatures as low as –4°C on 23 January; –11°C on the morning of 27 January; and –16°C on 23 February (enough for the Rhône river and Lake Geneva to freeze over).[1]

The *Journal de Paris* did not publish meteorological data for 27 February, for 16, 30 and 31 March, or for 1 April. The last three dates coincide with the Allied occupation of the city. Other sources indicate that there was light mist at Paris on the morning of 30 March, followed by a mild and overcast day, and then a fine evening and superb moonlit night.[2]

Date on which observations were made	Time	Temperature (in °C)	Barometer (millimetres)	Wind direction	State of sky
Fri 31 Dec	0800	–2.8	767.20	NE weak	Some clouds, mist
	1200	1.5	767.04	Same	Fine sky, mist
	1500	3.5	766.64	NNE	Same
Sat 1 Jan	0800	–2.3	764.00	Calm	Fine sky, mist
	1200	0.9	763.50	ENE weak	Same
	1500	2.0	762.40	E	Same
Sun 2 Jan	0800	–4.8	759.04	Calm	Fine sky, mist
	1200	2.0	758.28	SSE	Same
	1500	1.4	757.32	W	Overcast, mist
Mon 3 Jan	0745	1.4	754.24	S	Cloudy, mist
	1200	5.5	753.18	S	Overcast, light mist
	1500	4.0	751.72	S	Same
Tues 4 Jan	0745	3.0	745.02	S	Overcast, mist
	1200	5.3	743.06	S	Cloudy, light mist
	1500	5.0	741.34	S	Overcast, rain at 1300
Wed 5 Jan	0745	1.7	737.96	SE	Cloudy, mist
	1200	6.2	737.34	SE	Same
	1500	7.0	736.52	SE	Overcast, mist
Thurs 6 Jan	0745	4.3	739.30	W strong	Overcast, light mist
	1200	4.5	742.12	Same	Very cloudy
	1500	4.6	743.62	Same	Same
Fri 7 Jan	0745	0.5	747.80	E	Overcast, light mist, ice
	1200	1.5	747.70	E	Overcast, light mist
	1500	1.9	749.90	E	Overcast

The weather during the campaign   239

Date on which observations were made	Time	Temperature (in °C)	Barometer (millimetres)	Wind direction	State of sky
Sat 8 Jan	0745	1.5	746.60	NE	Overcast, mist
	1200	0.2	746.34	NE	Same
	1500	0.6	746.00	NNE	Same
Sun 9 Jan	0745	−2.8	745.40	N strong	Overcast, mist
	1200	1.4	746.40	Same	Same
	1500	2.0	747.50	Same	Same
Mon 10 Jan	0745	−8.3	752.12	NE	Cloudy, mist
	1200	−2.3	753.20	Same	Overcast, gentle snow
	1500	−3.3	754.10	Same	Overcast, mist
Tues 11 Jan	0745	−9.3	756.66	E	Fine sky, mist
	1200	−6.0	757.20	SE	Light clouds, light mist
	1500	−7.0	756.50	Same	Same
Wed 12 Jan	0745	−4.7	745.94	ESE	Snow and hail, mist
	1200	−1.0	744.16	Same	Same
	1500	−0.8	743.94	Same	Drizzle
Thurs 13 Jan	0745	−1.8	753.34	W	Overcast, light mist
	1200	0.4	756.80	NW	Same
	1500	−2.1	759.50	N	Fine sky, light mist
Fri 14 Jan	0745	−10.3	759.60	SE	Cloudy, mist
	1200	−6.3	755.72	Same	Overcast, mist
	1500	−6.5	753.80	ESE	Same
Sat 15 Jan	0730	−3.8	747.80	E weak	Overcast, mist
	1200	1.4	748.12	Same	Same, rain at 1000
	1500	1.2	747.78	Same	Overcast, mist
Sun 16 Jan	0730	1.4	742.00	SSE	Overcast, damp mist
	1200	4.5	738.78	Same	Drizzle
	1500	5.5	737.20	Same	Damp mist
Mon 17 Jan	0730	1.3	749.12	WNW	Overcast, mist
	1200	2.2	751.24	Same	Same
	1500	2.0	751.68	Same	Same, damp mist
Tues 18 Jan	0730	8.8	736.90	S strong	Rain, mist
	1200	11.9	738.36	SW	Some bright spells
	1500	11.3	737.02	Same	Drizzle
Wed 19 Jan	0730	6.0	736.90	SW strong	Agitated and cloudy
	1200	10.5	736.38	Same	Rain
	1500	9.8	736.14	Same	Overcast
Thurs 20 Jan	0730	4.8	738.60	SW	Overcast
	1200	6.3	741.12	SSW	Same
	1500	6.0	742.22	Same	Same, mist
Fri 21 Jan	0730	−1.5	752.78	N	Snow
	1200	−0.4	754.72	Same	Light clouds
	1500	−0.8	755.10	Same	Fine sky
Sat 22 Jan	0730	−4.0	754.16	W	Overcast, mist
	1200	−3.8	753.60	Same	Same
	1500	−5.5	752.75	Same	Same
Sun 23 Jan	0730	−7.8	752.28	N	Cloudy, mist

Date on which observations were made	Time	Temperature (in °C)	Barometer (millimetres)	Wind direction	State of sky
	1200	−4.5	752.00	Same	Same
	1500	−5.2	751.28	Same	Same
Mon 24 Jan	0730	−10.0	752.16	NW	Overcast, mist
	1200	−6.9	751.76	Same	Agitated and light mist
	1500	−4.6	751.32	Same	Snowy spells
Tues 25 Jan	0730	−6.0	754.72	W	Snow, mist
	1200	−2.1	755.44	Same	Same
	1500	−1.2	755.40	Same	Same
Wed 26 Jan	0730	−2.8	753.94	SW	Overcast, mist
	1200	1.4	752.90	S	Very cloudy
	1500	0.4	751.10	Same	Overcast
Thurs 27 Jan	0730	−3.3	743.84	S	Snow, mist
	1200	2.4	742.56	S	Overcast
	1500	2.3	741.70	S	Same
Fri 28 Jan	0730	−0.8	740.34	SE	Overcast, mist
	1200	3.0	741.55	Same	Same, rain at 1000
	1500	2.9	742.40	Same	Overcast, mist
Sat 29 Jan	0715	1.8	735.20	SW strong	Rain, mist
	1200	5.0	728.86	S strong	Overcast, mist
	1500	7.4	726.74	Same	Rainy spells
Sun 30 Jan	0715	2.8	737.62	WSW	Overcast
	1200	5.5	739.44	Same	Cloudy
	1500	5.2	740.00	Same	Same
Mon 31 Jan	0715	−0.4	745.48	W	Cloudy
	1200	2.8	746.72	Same	Snow
	1500	3.2	747.28	Same	Fine sky, cloudy
Tues 1 Feb	0715	0.8	753.00	W	Heavy snow, mist
	1200	3.1	756.60	NW	Cloudy
	1500	2.4	757.88	Same	Same
Wed 2 Feb	0715	−0.5	761.30	WSW	Snow
	1200	3.0	758.48	Same	Overcast
	1500	2.2	757.12	SW	Rain and snow, mist
Thurs 3 Feb	0715	−0.8	759.72	NW	Very cloudy, mist
	1200	2.3	759.90	NNW	Cloudy
	1500	2.6	759.60	NW	Very cloudy
Fri 4 Feb	0715	−1.6	758.24	NE	Overcast, light mist
	1200	−3.1	760.30	Same	Same
	1500	−3.4	760.70	NNE	Some bright spells
Sat 5 Feb	0715	−5.8	764.70	NE	Overcast, light mist
	1200	−2.3	765.84	SE	Cloudy, light mist
	1500	−0.5	764.32	S	Overcast, light mist
Sun 6 Feb	0715	1.5	759.86	SW	Overcast, light mist
	1200	3.5	756.74	Same	Rain
	1500	5.5	753.50	Same	Same
Mon 7 Feb	0715	3.5	753.30	W	Cloudy
	1200	7.0	754.88	Same	Same
	1500	5.0	754.91	NNW	Overcast

The weather during the campaign

Date on which observations were made	Time	Temperature (in °C)	Barometer (millimetres)	Wind direction	State of sky
Tues 8 Feb	0715	4.0	754.40	W	Overcast, mist
	1200	9.1	751.44	Same	Rainy spells
	1500	9.7	750.00	Same	Some bright spells
Wed 9 Feb	0700	5.7	754.80	WNW	Drizzle
	1200	9.5	756.70	Same	Very cloudy
	1500	9.1	757.22	W	Overcast, mist
Thurs 10 Feb	0700	6.4	761.92	NW	Overcast, mist
	1200	11.5	762.90	W	Cloudy
	1500	10.8	763.10	Same	Overcast
Fri 11 Feb	0700	0.7	762.49	SE	Light cloud, hoarfrost
	1200	8.6	762.40	Same	Same
	1500	9.4	761.00	S	Agitated and cloudy
Sat 12 Feb	0700	0.3	760.92	SE	Light clouds, mist
	1200	9.5	760.28	Same	Fine sky, light mist
	1500	10.5	759.90	SW	Slight haze
Sun 13 Feb	0700	1.3	759.00	SW	Haze and light mist
	1200	6.3	759.10	SSW	Same
	1500	5.3	758.74	Same	Cloudy
Mon 14 Feb	0700	−0.5	757.54	SE	Overcast, mist
	1200	2.5	757.88	Same	Same
	1500	3.6	757.72	Same	Some bright spells, mist
Tues 15 Feb	0700	−1.2	759.12	NE	Fine sky, light mist
	1200	3.7	759.44	Same	Same
	1500	6.4	758.70	Same	Same
Wed 16 Feb	0700	−3.3	758.88	NE	Fine sky, light mist
	1200	1.0	760.20	Same	Same
	1500	2.9	760.52	Same	Superb
Thurs 17 Feb	0700	−1.8	765.70	NNE	Overcast
	1200	−0.3	767.20	Same	Very cloudy
	1500	−0.5	767.80	Same	Cloudy
Fri 18 Feb	0700	−6.8	768.92	NE	Superb, light mist
	1200	−2.5	768.72	Same	Same
	1500	−0.7	768.00	Same	Same
Sat 19 Feb	0700	0.0	762.00	NE	Snow, mist
	1200	1.9	762.86	Same	Overcast, mist
	1500	2.3	762.86	Same	Same
Sun 20 Feb	0645	−7.0	766.98	NNE	Superb
	1200	−4.5	768.48	Same	Same, light mist
	1500	−3.3	768.20	Same	Same
Mon 21 Feb	0645	−9.7	767.60	NE	Haze and mist on the horizon
	1200	−4.0	767.40	Same	Same
	1500	−3.7	766.62	Same	Fine sky and mist
Tues 22 Feb	0645	−7.9	765.96	NE	Fine sky, light mist
	1200	−2.2	766.54	Same	Superb, mist

Date on which observations were made	Time	Temperature (in °C)	Barometer (millimetres)	Wind direction	State of sky
	1500	−0.9	765.52	ENE	Cloudy
Wed 23 Feb	0645	−7.7	764.54	NE	Fine sky, light mist
	1200	−4.3	764.46	NNE	Same
	1500	−3.5	763.44	ENE	Same
Thurs 24 Feb	0630	−12.5	763.20	NE	Superb, light mist
	1200	−4.4	763.36	Same	Same
	1500	−3.5	762.96	Same	Same
Fri 25 Feb	0630	−10.5	764.40	N	Fine sky, mist
	1200	−1.5	764.84	Same	Same
	1500	−0.8	763.74	E	Same
Sat 26 Feb	0630	−8.7	759.72	E	Superb, mist
	1200	0.0	758.52	Same	Same
	1500	1.8	757.28	Same	Same
Sun 27 Feb	0630	n/a	n/a	n/a	n/a
	1200	n/a	n/a	n/a	n/a
	1500	n/a	n/a	n/a	n/a
Mon 28 Feb	0630	−6.6	757.84	NE	Slight haze, mist
	1200	3.9	756.68	E	Fine sky, mist
	1500	4.5	755.14	SW	Same
Tues 1 Mar	0630	−2.8	745.56	SW	Overcast, mist
	1200	4.8	737.50	S	Rain, mist
	1500	4.8	753.28	Same	Same
Wed 2 Mar	0630	0.0	737.68	W	Cloudy, mist
	1200	4.2	737.50	SSW strong	Cloudy
	1500	5.0	736.__	SW	Same
Thurs 3 Mar	0630	1.8	727.96	SE	Overcast, snow at 0900
	1200	3.8	726.40	ESE	Overcast
	1500	5.5	726.14	Same	Same
Fri 4 Mar	0630	0.5	735.08	NE	Snow, mist
	1200	2.8	738.04	N	Overcast, mist
	1500	2.9	738.58	Same	Same
Sat 5 Mar	0630	0.0	744.74	NW	Overcast, mist
	1200	1.5	746.60	Same	Same
	1500	1.5	747.30	Same	Same
Sun 6 Mar	0630	−2.0	751.22	NE	Overcast, mist
	1200	−2.5	752.04	Same	Same
	1500	−2.8	751.78	Same	Same
Mon 7 Mar	0630	−6.3	752.06	ENE	Superb, light mist
	1200	−2.0	751.94	Same	Cloudy
	1500	−1.3	751.70	Same	Same
Tues 8 Mar	0615	−5.2	752.40	NE	Overcast, mist
	1200	−2.6	752.16	Same	Snow, mist
	1500	−2.8	751.44	N	Same
Wed 9 Mar	0615	−8.3	750.62	Calm	Fog
	1200	0.1	750.70	SSE	Very cloudy
	1500	−0.3	750.32	Same	Overcast
Thurs 10 Mar	0615	−5.8	746.54	SE	Overcast, light mist
	1200	2.8	746.18	Same	Same
	1500	0.8	745.62	Same	Same
Fri 11 Mar	0615	−2.0	745.96	S	Overcast, mist

The weather during the campaign 243

Date on which observations were made	Time	Temperature (in °C)	Barometer (millimetres)	Wind direction	State of sky
	1200	2.5	746.84	SSW	Same, gentle snow
	1500	2.0	747.20	Same	Continuous snow
Sat 12 Mar	0615	−2.0	750.26	W	Overcast, mist
	1200	7.8	751.92	Same	Same
	1500	2.8	752.52	SSW	Gentle snow
Sun 13 Mar	0615	−0.8	755.60	NE	Overcast, mist
	1200	2.9	757.28	Same	Same
	1500	3.8	757.00	Same	Some bright spells
Mon 14 Mar	0615	−0.5	758.90	N strong	Overcast
	1200	1.0	760.56	Same	Same
	1500	0.5	760.50	Same	Same
Tues 15 Mar	0615	−2.0	762.70	NE	Overcast, mist
	1200	−1.2	763.70	Same, strong	Same
	1500	−0.3	762.90	Same	Same
Wed 16 Mar	0615	n/a	n/a	n/a	n/a
	1200	n/a	n/a	n/a	n/a
	1500	n/a	n/a	n/a	n/a
Thurs 17 Mar	0600	−0.2	764.60	E	Fine sky, mist
	1200	8.2	765.94	Same	Same
	1500	10.5	765.00	ESE	Same
Fri 18 Mar	0600	−0.2	763.70	NE	Fine sky, mist
	1200	6.8	762.88	Same	Same
	1500	7.7	761.70	Same	Same
Sat 19 Mar	0600	−0.8	759.10	NE	Fog
	1200	2.8	758.24	Same	Same
	1500	3.5	756.84	Same	Agitated, mist
Sun 20 Mar	0600	−2.2	755.20	NE	Fog
	1200	11.4	755.90	S	Fine sky
	1500	12.5	754.96	Same	Cloudy
Mon 21 Mar	0600	1.2	753.40	S	Overcast, light mist
	1200	13.8	753.50	SE	Same
	1500	14.5	752.66	Same	Same
Tues 22 Mar	0600	7.5	751.60	SE	Drizzle, light mist
	1200	14.8	752.70	S	Very cloudy
	1500	14.0	752.50	SW	Same
Wed 23 Mar	0600	6.8	754.96	W	Overcast, mist
	1200	11.1	756.50	Same	Very cloudy
	1500	12.0	756.12	Same	Same
Thurs 24 Mar	0545	0.5	757.00	S	Cloudy, mist, hoarfrost
	1200	12.0	755.80	Same	Same
	1500	10.1	755.06	SW	Drizzle
Fri 25 Mar	0545	7.0	753.60	W	Some bright spells
	1200	11.0	753.88	Same	Overcast
	1500	12.0	753.44	Same	Very cloudy
Sat 26 Mar	0545	1.9	752.22	SW	Cloudy, mist
	1200	10.7	752.54	Same	Overcast
	1500	11.7	752.40	S	Cloudy
Sun 27 Mar	0545	5.5	756.82	W	Overcast, mist
	1200	13.7	759.10	Same	Overcast
	1500	13.2	758.80	Same	Same

Date on which observations were made	Time	Temperature (in °C)	Barometer (millimetres)	Wind direction	State of sky
Mon 28 Mar	0545	2.2	758.02	ESE	Fog
	1200	12.0	756.86	SE	Cloudy
	1500	12.1	755.40	Same	Same
Tues 29 Mar	0545	5.5	749.00	ESE	Slightly overcast
	1200	12.8	749.36	S	Overcast, drizzle
	1500	14.2	749.36	Same	Overcast
Wed 30 Mar	0545	n/a	n/a	n/a	n/a
	1200	n/a	n/a	n/a	n/a
	1500	n/a	n/a	n/a	n/a
Thurs 31 Mar	0545	n/a	n/a	n/a	n/a
	1200	n/a	n/a	n/a	n/a
	1500	n/a	n/a	n/a	n/a
Fri 1 Apr	0545	n/a	n/a	n/a	n/a
	1200	n/a	n/a	n/a	n/a
	1500	n/a	n/a	n/a	n/a
Sat 2 Apr	0530	9.7	749.68	SW	Overcast
	1200	11.2	750.68	Same	Same
	1500	13.5	750.00	Same	Very cloudy
Sun 3 Apr	0530	8.2	748.90	S	Rainy spells
	1200	13.9	750.00	Same	Some bright spells
	1500	16.0	748.74	Same	Very cloudy
Mon 4 Apr	0530	10.2	744.90	E	Overcast
	1200	15.8	747.00	Same	Overcast, light mist
	1500	3.5	747.10	SW	Rain
Tues 5 Apr	0530	6.5	752.00	SW	Overcast, light mist
	1200	15.2	753.90	Same	Very cloudy
	1500	14.2	754.08	Same	Same
Wed 6 Apr	0530	8.2	759.00	N	Overcast, light mist
	1200	15.7	760.18	NW	Cloudy
	1500	16.0	760.20	N	Same
Wed 20 Apr	0500	10.5	751.96	E	Rain
	1200	12.5	751.72	Same	Same
	1530	15.5	751.04	Same	Same

Appendix II

Sunrise and sunset at Paris on selected dates

Date	Sunrise	Sunset
Sat 1 Jan	0753	1608
Sun 16 Jan	0741	1620
Tues 25 Jan	0730	1631
Sat 29 Jan	0724	1637
Tues 1 Feb	0719	1641
Thurs 10 Feb	0705	1655
Fri 11 Feb	0704	1657
Mon 14 Feb	0659	1702
Thurs 17 Feb	0654	1707
Tues 22 Feb	0645	1716
Fri 4 Mar	0627	1734
Mon 7 Mar	0622	1739
Wed 9 Mar	0619	1742
Mon 21 Mar	0556	1805
Fri 25 Mar	0549	1812
Wed 30 Mar	0540	1821

Appendix III

Allied order of battle

The following order of battle shows the initial organisation of the main two Allied armies. All strengths are approximate, and fluctuated as a result of losses, sickness, and reinforcements.
Flying corps and other small detached units are not shown.

Hauptarmee

Commander-in-Chief: Schwarzenberg
Chief of the General Staff: Radetzky
Quartermaster-General: Langenau

Austrian *1. leichte Division* (Bubna)
Austrian *2. leichte Division* (Liechtenstein, M.)
I (Austrian) *Armee-Abtheilung* (Colloredo)
II (Austrian) *Armee-Abtheilung* (Liechtenstein, A.)
III (Austrian) *Armee-Abtheilung* (Gyulai)
IV (Württemberg) *Armee-Abtheilung* (*Kronprinz* von Württemberg)
V (Austro-Bavarian) *Armee-Abtheilung* (Wrede)
• Austrian corps (Frimont)
• Bavarian corps
VI (Russian) *Armee-Abtheilung* (Wittgenstein)
• Advanced guard (Pahlen)
• 1st Infantry Corps (Gorchakov)
• 2nd Infantry Corps (Eugen von Württemberg)

Reserves:
Austrian reserves (*Erbprinz* von Hessen-Homburg)
• one division of infantry regiments
• one division of *Grenadier* battalions
• two *Kürassier* divisions
• artillery
Russian troops (Barclay de Tolly):
Russian reserve army (Grand Duke Constantine)
• 3rd (or Grenadier) Infantry Corps (Raievsky)
• 5th (or Imperial Guard) Infantry Corps (Ermolov)
– two Imperial Guard divisions
• Imperial Guard cavalry corps (Golitsyn V)
– three cuirassier divisions
– one light cavalry division
• Prussian *Garde*
– Prussian *Garde-Infanterie-Brigade*
– Prussian *Garde-Kavallerie-Brigade*

- reserve artillery
- Cossack corps (Platov)

Notes:
a. Total strength at the start of the invasion: 200,000 men and 682 guns.[3]
b. This initial order of battle was soon disarranged, as a result of detachments, reinforcements, and reorganisations.
c. Bubna was sent against Lyon. Other units, including the whole of the II *Armee-Abtheilung*, were detached to besiege fortresses and guard communications.
d. Colloredo, the commander of the I *Armee-Abtheilung*, was wounded on 5/2/1814. He was replaced by Bianchi, the commander of an infantry division of the Austrian reserves.
e. Wittgenstein, the commander of the VI *Armee-Abtheilung*, was wounded at Bar-sur-Aube on 27/2/1814. He was replaced by Raievsky. Lambert took Raievsky's place in command of the Russian 3rd (or Grenadier) Infantry Corps.
f. On 21/2/1814 Schwarzenberg decided to create a separate *Südarmee* by detaching Austrian reinforcements from the *Hauptarmee* to join the forces that were already operating against Lyon and besieging the fortresses that lay on his lines of communication.

Schlesische Armee

Commander-in-Chief: Blücher
Chief of the General Staff: Gneisenau
Quartermaster-General: Müffling

Prussian I Corps (Yorck)
four brigades (1st, 2nd, 7th, 8th)
- *Reserve-Kavallerie* (Jürgass)
- *Reserve-Artillerie*

Prussian II Corps (Kleist)
- four brigades (9th, 10th, 11th, 12th)
- *Reserve-Kavallerie* (Röder)
- *Reserve-Artillerie*

Russian corps (Sacken)
- 6th Infantry Corps (Scherbatov)
- 11th Infantry Corps (Lieven)
- cavalry corps (Vasilchikov)
- Cossack corps (Karpov)

Russian corps (Langeron)
- 8th Infantry Corps (Saint-Priest)
- 9th Infantry Corps (Olsufiev)
- 10th Infantry Corps (Kaptsevich)
- cavalry corps (Korf)
- Cossack corps (Grekov)

Another two corps were transferred to the *Schlesische Armee* from the *Nordarmee* during the campaign:

Prussian III Corps (Bülow)
- four brigades (3rd, 4th, 5th, 6th)

- *Reserve-Kavallerie* (Oppen)
- *Reserve-Artillerie*

Russian corps (Winzingerode)
- Infantry corps (Vorontsov)
- Infantry corps (Stroganov)
- cavalry corps (O'Rourke)
- Cossack corps (Chernishev)

Notes:
a. Total strength at the start of the invasion (not including Bülow and Winzingerode): 95,000 men and 448 guns.[4]
b. Of this total, just 50,000 men advanced with Blücher into France in January: Yorck and Sacken's corps, and Olsufiev's 9th Infantry Corps from Langeron.
c. The rest of Langeron's corps was gradually relieved before Mainz by the 5. *Bundes-Corps*, and followed Blücher into France in a succession of detachments. Langeron himself rejoined Blücher's army on the night of 4/3/1814 and resumed command of his corps.
d. The bulk of Kleist's corps joined Blücher by 9/2/1814, along with the main body of Kaptsevich's Russian 10th Infantry Corps (belonging to Langeron's corps).
e. The Russian 8th Infantry Corps under Saint-Priest (part of Langeron's corps) left the area of Mainz on 15/2/1814 and was defeated by Napoleon at Reims on 13/3/1814.
f. Bülow and Winzingerode's corps from the *Nordarmee* began to arrive in northern France in the middle of February. Each had a theoretical total of 30,000 men but each was incomplete. On arrival at Laon on 24/2/1814 Bülow had only 16,000 of his men, as some of his brigades followed him later from Belgium. Winzingerode's corps gradually assembled, with detachments joining it inside France. Stroganov's corps, for example, had been detached from the Russian Army of Poland (Bennigsen).
g. Bülow and Winzingerode united with Blücher's *Schlesische Armee* on the Aisne river only in the first week of March.
h. Olsufiev was captured at Champaubert on 10/2/1814, and replaced in command of the remnants of his corps by Udom.
i. Saint-Priest was mortally wounded at Reims on 13/3/1814, and replaced by Rudzevich.

The German *Bundes-Corps*

The Allies extracted manpower from the German states in order to form eight *Bundes-Corps* to support their three main armies:

1. Bundes-Corps (Wrede)
Units: Bavarian; some Austrian
Destination: Became the V *Armee-Abtheilung* of the *Hauptarmee*.
2. Bundes-Corps (*Herzog* von Braunschweig)
Units: Hanoverian and Brunswick, with smaller contingents from Mecklenburg-Schwerin, the Hanseatic cities, and Oldenburg
Destination: *Nordarmee*. Played no part in the campaign of France.
3. Bundes-Corps (*Herzog* von Sachsen-Weimar)
Units: Saxon, with a small contingent from Thüringia-Anhalt; two Cossack regiments

Destination: *Nordarmee*. Released Bülow and Winzingerode's corps from Belgium to join Blücher; saw action in Belgium against the French *Armée du Nord*.
4. *Bundes-Corps* (*Kurprinz* von Hessen)
Units: Hesse-Cassel
Destination: *Schlesische Armee*. Observed fortresses in Blücher's rear.
5. *Bundes-Corps* (*Herzog* von Sachsen-Coburg)
Units: Berg, with smaller contingents, including from Nassau and Saxe-Coburg.
Destination: *Schlesische Armee*. Relieved Langeron's corps before Mainz.
6. *Bundes-Corps* (Philipp von Hessen-Homburg)
Units: Hesse-Darmstädt, with contingents from Austria, Würzburg, Reuss, Frankfurt, and Isenburg
Destination: *Hauptarmee*. Incorporated into the *Südarmee* operating against Lyon.
7. *Bundes-Corps* (*Kronprinz* von Württemberg)
Units: Württemberg; Austrian units sometimes attached.
Destination: Became the IV *Armee-Abtheilung* of the *Hauptarmee*.
8. *Bundes-Corps* (Hochberg)
Units: Baden, with small contingents from Hohenzollern and Liechtenstein.
Destination: *Hauptarmee*. Besieged fortresses in Alsace, across the Rhine from Baden.

Appendix IV

Napoleon's order of battle

Napoleon did not have a completed army when he took the field, nor did he ever finish its organisation during the campaign. Losses and reinforcements necessitated several reorganisations. To give a detailed snapshot of his order of battle at a specific moment would therefore be misleading. More meaningful is a broad outline of his army's basic organisation and its main changes. The designation of the French formations as corps or divisions was often nominal, reflecting the rank of their commanders rather than their numerical strength. In addition to his field army, Napoleon had second-line formations such as the *Garde nationale*, and the support of irregulars.

The cordon on the Rhine

Towards the end of December 1813 Napoleon had a cordon of troops deployed along the Rhine, but had been obliged to divert part of his reserves to Belgium in response to the Dutch revolt:

Maison
in Belgium:
- I Corps (still being formed; became the *Armée du Nord*)

Maréchal **Macdonald's group**
on the Upper Rhine:
- XI Corps (Macdonald)
- II Cavalry Corps (Exelmans)
- V Corps (Sébastiani)
- III Cavalry Corps (Arrighi de Casanova, duc de Padoue)

Maréchal **Marmont's group**
on the Middle Rhine:
- VI Corps (Marmont)
- I Cavalry Corps (Doumerc)

Morand
at Mainz, where he would become besieged:
- IV Corps

Maréchal **Victor's group**
on the Lower Rhine:
- II Corps (Victor)
- V Cavalry Corps (Milhaud)

Imperial Guard
in reserve:

- Old Guard
  - 1st Old Guard Division (Friant), part of *Maréchal* Mortier's mobile reserve
  - 2nd Old Guard Division (Michel), at Luxembourg
- Young Guard (in process of formation)
  - 1st Young Guard Division (Meunier), at Thionville
  - 2nd Young Guard Division (Decouz), at Paris
  - 3rd Young Guard Division (Boyer de Rebeval), meant to be formed at Lille, but never activated
  - 4th Young Guard Division (Barrois), deployed in Belgium
  - 5th Young Guard Division (Rottembourg), at Paris
  - 6th Young Guard Division (Roguet), deployed in Belgium
- Imperial Guard cavalry
  - Lévesque-Laferrière's division, part of *Maréchal* Mortier's mobile reserve
  - Lefebvre-Desnouëttes's division, at Paris
  - Castex's division, attached to I Corps in Belgium

Notes:
a. *Maréchal* Mortier commanded the mobile reserve, composed of the Old Guard. After reaching Namur in Belgium following the Dutch revolt, it had to return south to Langres, in order to delay the *Hauptarmee*'s advance.
b. The 1st–3rd Young Guard Divisions were sometimes known as the 1st–3rd *Voltigeur* Divisions, and the 4th–6th Young Guard Divisions as the 1st–3rd *Tirailleur* Divisions.

Réserve de Paris

Napoleon formed an *Armée de réserve de Paris* in order to cover the capital and make as much use as possible of the assorted resources in the regimental depots. A succession of its units were pushed forward to reinforce the field army as the campaign progressed.
- Initially, two line infantry divisions were created under the overall command of Gérard. They were sent to the region of Troyes, except for one brigade, which was sent to Châlons-sur-Marne.
- Two line cavalry divisions were also formed:
  - a heavy division (Bordesoulle) was sent forward to Arcis-sur-Aube, in order to cover Mortier's northern flank.
  - a division of *dragons* and light cavalry (Pajol) was organised south of the Seine, to cover the southern approaches to Paris.

More line formations were created later.

The *Réserve de Paris* also contained provisional Imperial Guard formations, and units of the *Garde nationale*.

Napoleon takes command

Napoleon took personal command of his army when he reached Vitry-le-François on 26/1/1814.

Major-général: *Maréchal* Berthier
Commander of the reserve cavalry: Grouchy

Artillery commander: Ruty
Engineer commander: Rogniat

The formations immediately available to Napoleon were:
Maréchal Victor's group:
- II Corps
- V Cavalry Corps (Milhaud)

Maréchal Marmont's group:
- VI Corps (less Ricard's detached division)
- I Cavalry Corps (Doumerc)

Maréchal Ney's Young Guard corps:
- two infantry divisions (Meunier, Decouz)

Maréchal Oudinot's Imperial Guard corps:
- 5th Young Guard Division (Rottembourg)
- an Imperial Guard cavalry division (Lefebvre-Desnouëttes)
- Imperial Guard artillery (part)

Napoleon's most important detached forces were:
Général de division Gérard:
A provisional corps, in the Aube valley. It joined Napoleon in time for the Battle of La Rothière.
- 1st Division of the *Réserve de Paris* (Dufour)
- Ricard's infantry division, detached from Marmont's VI Corps
- a cavalry brigade (Piquet), from the I Cavalry Corps

Maréchal Mortier:
A reserve corps, based on Troyes.
- 1st Old Guard Division (Friant)
- 2nd Old Guard Division (Michel)
- an Imperial Guard cavalry division (Lévesque-Laferrière)
- Imperial Guard artillery (part)
- *113e Régiment de ligne*
- the 2nd Division of the *Réserve de Paris* (Jan de la Hamelinaye), garrisoning Troyes
- a provisional cavalry division (Bordesoulle), in the Aube valley
- a provisional Imperial Guard cavalry division (Colbert), in the Aube valley

Maréchal Macdonald:
The northernmost section of the cordon along the Rhine, still retreating southwards from the Belgian *départements*.
- V Corps (Sébastiani)
- XI Corps (Macdonald)
- II Cavalry Corps (Exelmans)
- III Cavalry Corps (Arrighi)

A cordon covered the south bank of the Seine:
- the troops of the *18e division militaire* (Allix), based on the Yonne river
- a corps of observation, in process of being formed (Pajol)

- a provisional cavalry division (Pajol)
- a division of *gardes nationaux* (Pacthod)
- *gendarmes*
- irregulars

Note:
a. On 14/2/1814 Jan de la Hamelinaye left the army because of illness and was replaced by one of his brigade commanders (Jarry).

Reorganisation after La Rothière

By retreating after his defeat at La Rothière (1/2/1814), Napoleon was able to collect reinforcements, including *Maréchal* Mortier's group at Troyes. He then reorganised his army. The key changes included:

1. The establishment of a new VII Corps. This was created on 8/2/1814 from two Peninsular infantry divisions which were arriving from Soult's army in south-western France:
VII Corps (*Maréchal* Oudinot):
- 7th Division (Leval)
- 9th Division (Pierre Boyer)

2. A new organisation for the line cavalry under *Général de division* de Grouchy. It would now have four cavalry corps, each of which combined a light division with one or two heavy divisions:
- I Cavalry Corps (Doumerc)
- II Cavalry Corps (St-Germain)
- V Cavalry Corps (Milhaud)
- VI Cavalry Corps (Kellermann)

The reorganisation was ordered on 9/2/1814 but took a couple of weeks to implement. On 19/2/1814 Napoleon issued a further order as part of this process. The old III Cavalry Corps and the provisional cavalry divisions of the *Réserve de Paris* were disbanded and incorporated into the four corps.

3. Cavalry reinforcements from the Peninsula. A division of Peninsular *dragons* from Soult's army arrived under Trelliard in time for the Battle of Mormant (17/2/1814) and was added to the VI Cavalry Corps. Another brigade of Peninsular *dragons* (Sparre) would arrive towards the end of February. This would help form a second *dragon* division (Roussel d'Hurbal) in the VI Cavalry Corps. Roussel's division would be immediately detached to the Marne sector.

4. Imperial Guard: the Imperial Guard cavalry was commanded by Nansouty and its three divisions in the main campaign theatre were grouped together. Attached to them was the division of *Gardes d'honneur* (Defrance). This was created by uniting Piquet's brigade (which had been on the Rhine with the I Cavalry Corps) and Ségur's brigade (which had been part of the V Cavalry Corps).

The commander of the 2nd Young Guard Division (Decouz) had been mortally wounded at Brienne and was replaced by Curial.

Napoleon defeats the *Schlesische Armee*

Napoleon now inflicted four defeats on the *Schlesische Armee* (10–14/2/1814). He left Victor and Oudinot behind in the Seine valley to contain the *Hauptarmee*, but did not appoint an overall sector commander to co-ordinate their actions.

Maréchal Victor's group:
- II Corps
- two line infantry divisions of the *Réserve de Paris* (Gérard)
- V Cavalry Corps

Maréchal Oudinot's group:
- VII Corps
- 5th Young Guard Division (Rottembourg)
- the cordon south of the Seine (Pajol)

The 5th Young Guard Division was used to escort the army's cumbersome elements, including the parks and reserve artillery. These withdrew from Provins on Paris for safety.

On 11/2/1814 Oudinot detached Leval's division of experienced Peninsular infantry from VII Corps, and sent it northwards to help Napoleon defeat the *Schlesische Armee*. At this time Macdonald's group was withdrawing down the Marne valley in the face of the *Schlesische Armee*'s advance. To attack the *Schlesische Armee*, Napoleon moved northwards from the Seine valley with a mobile reserve under his direct command:

- 1st Old Guard Division (Friant)
- 2nd Old Guard Division (Michel)
- *Maréchal* Ney's Young Guard corps
- Nansouty's three divisions of Imperial Guard cavalry (Colbert, Lévesque-Laferrière, Guyot)
- *Gardes d'honneur* cavalry division (Defrance)
- Imperial Guard artillery (part)
- *Maréchal* Marmont's group
  – VI Corps
  – I Cavalry Corps
  – a temporarily attached force of 400 cavalrymen (Maurin)

The corps that *Maréchal* Mortier had hitherto commanded was effectively dissolved when Napoleon formed this mobile reserve. Mortier himself accompanied the 2nd Old Guard Division.

Napoleon returns to repel the *Hauptarmee*

After defeating the *Schlesische Armee*, Napoleon returned to the Seine sector with his mobile reserve (arrived 16/2/1814). He left *Maréchaux* Marmont and Mortier behind in the north to contain the *Schlesische Armee*. (Mortier now received a new command composed of Imperial Guard elements.) The two *maréchaux* remained in this sector until late March, when they were summoned eastwards to join Napoleon's *manoeuvre sur les derrières*:

Maréchal Marmont's group:
- VI Corps
- I Cavalry Corps

Maréchal Mortier's Imperial Guard corps:
- 2nd Old Guard Division (Christiani, replacing Michel, who had been wounded at Montmirail)
- an Imperial Guard cavalry division (Colbert)
- the division of *Gardes d'honneur* (Defrance)

Napoleon also left Grouchy in the Marne valley with the II Cavalry Corps (St-Germain), and Leval's division from the VII Corps, but this was a temporary detachment.

Maréchal Macdonald, who had initially operated in the Marne valley, had already been sent on 13/2/1814 to reinforce Victor and Oudinot against the *Hauptarmee*. He joined them at Guignes on the evening of 14/2/1814, and would remain in the Seine sector for the rest of the campaign. Following the losses he had suffered in retreating from the Rhine, Macdonald amalgamated the remains of his V Corps into his XI Corps.

Reorganisation after Montereau

Line cavalry
The reorganisation of the line cavalry, ordered on 9/2/1814, continued. As part of this process, Pajol's corps of observation was disbanded. The regiments of his provisional cavalry division were now more organised and ready to join the permanent corps; he himself had been wounded at Montereau and could no longer continue in active service.

Pacthod's division of *gardes nationaux*, which had also belonged to Pajol's corps, became part of VII Corps. Allix continued to maintain a cordon along the Yonne river south of the Seine.

II Corps
Maréchal Victor was removed from command of II Corps on 18/2/1814 and replaced by Gérard. The two infantry divisions of the *Réserve de Paris* (Gérard) were now incorporated into II Corps.

Réserve de Paris
A third line infantry division of the *Réserve de Paris* was activated. It was known as the 1st Division, since the original two divisions had become part of II Corps. It was commanded by Arrighi de Casanova, *duc* de Padoue, and would join *Maréchal* Marmont's group in the first days of March.

The *Réserve de Paris* also provided three new infantry divisions of the Young Guard. Two of them had been pushed forward from Paris to help block the *Hauptarmee*'s advance along the Seine in the middle of February:
- 1st Provisional Young Guard Division (Charpentier)
- 2nd Provisional Young Guard Division (Boyer de Rebeval)

These two Young Guard divisions were now organised into a corps commanded by

Maréchal Victor. Napoleon would be able to supervise Victor more closely than before, since the corps formed part of the mobile reserve under his direct command.

Another newly formed division reinforced Mortier's Imperial Guard corps in the Marne valley on 1/3/1814:
- 3rd Provisional Young Guard Division (Poret de Morvan)

Two days later Joseph informed Napoleon that it would be difficult to form a 4th Provisional Young Guard Division, or a fourth line division of the *Réserve de Paris*, because of the shortage of conscripts, weapons, and funds.[5]

Nonetheless, a fourth line division (Souham) was, in fact, formed in the middle of March and became known as the 2nd Division of the *Réserve de Paris*. It was left behind to cover the bridges of the Seine valley when Napoleon launched his *manoeuvre sur les derrières*.

A fifth line division (Ledru des Essarts) was activated on 22/3/1814 and fought in the Battle of Paris on 30/3/1814. This was known as the 3rd Division of the *Réserve de Paris*.

A weak Young Guard division (Henrion) left Paris and joined Napoleon's army at the time of the Battle of Arcis-sur-Aube (20–21/3/1814).

Note:
a. Once activated, the provisional Young Guard divisions were sometimes known by their numerical order after the original six divisions. For example, the 1st Provisional Young Guard Division was also known as the 7th Young Guard Division.

Napoleon's second pursuit of the *Schlesische Armee*

At the end of February Napoleon left the Seine sector with his mobile reserve in pursuit of the *Schlesische Armee*, which was again advancing on Paris. He left covering forces, under *Maréchal* Macdonald's overall command, to contain the *Hauptarmee*:

Maréchal Macdonald's group:
- XI Corps
- V Cavalry Corps

Maréchal Oudinot's group:
- II Corps (Gérard)
- VII Corps (less a brigade of Pierre Boyer's division)
- II Cavalry Corps
- VI Cavalry Corps
- 5th Young Guard Division (Rottembourg)

Of these forces, the VII Corps and VI Cavalry Corps were composed largely of Peninsular troops.

Napoleon's mobile reserve consisted of:
- 1st Old Guard Division (Friant)
- two divisions of Imperial Guard cavalry (Exelmans and Lévesque-Laferrière)[6]
- Imperial Guard artillery (part)
- *Maréchal* Victor's Young Guard corps
  - 1st Provisional Young Guard Division (Charpentier)
  - 2nd Provisional Young Guard Division (Boyer de Rebeval)
- *Maréchal* Ney's Young Guard corps:

- 1st Young Guard Division (Meunier)
- 2nd Young Guard Division (Curial)

Provisionally attached to *Maréchal* Ney's corps for the pursuit were:
- Arrighi's infantry division of the *Réserve de Paris*
- Bordesoulle's cavalry (about 800 men, belonging to I and II Cavalry Corps)
- a division of Peninsular *dragons*, detached from VI Cavalry Corps (Roussel d'Hurbal)
- one brigade of Pierre Boyer's infantry division, detached from VII Corps

Of these units attached to *Maréchal* Ney:
- the brigade under Pierre Boyer would become part of *Maréchal* Ney's corps
- Arrighi and Bordesoulle would join *Maréchal* Marmont
- Roussel d'Hurbal would join *Maréchal* Mortier

Napoleon collected *Maréchaux* Marmont and Mortier in the Marne valley and pursued the *Schlesische Armee* northwards to Laon.

Maréchal Marmont's group contained:
- VI Corps
- I Cavalry Corps (now commanded by Bordesoulle, replacing Doumerc)
- 1,100 cavalry reinforcements from Paris (Boulnois)

Maréchal Mortier's group contained:
- 2nd Old Guard Division (Christiani)
- 3rd Provisional Young Guard Division, newly arrived from Paris (Poret de Morvan)
- one Imperial Guard cavalry division (Colbert)

Reorganisations after the Battle of Laon

As a result of his losses, Napoleon had to reorganise his army in the middle of March:
Young Guard:
The Young Guard had suffered particularly heavily, in both men and commanders. Its five infantry divisions that had been serving under Mortier, Ney, and Victor were therefore amalgamated into just two (Curial, Charpentier).[7] The 5th Young Guard Division (Rottembourg) was still with Oudinot in the southern sector.

As a result, *Maréchal* Ney's Young Guard corps no longer existed and he had to be given a weak corps cobbled together from assorted line units.

Maréchal Victor, who had also held a Young Guard corps command, could no longer serve, having been seriously wounded at Craonne.

Maréchal Mortier's Imperial Guard corps now included:
- 2nd Old Guard Division (Christiani)
- two Young Guard divisions (Curial, Charpentier)
- Roussel d'Hurbal's division of *dragons*

Line cavalry:
Grouchy, the overall commander of Napoleon's line cavalry, had been wounded at Craonne, and was replaced by Belliard, formerly the *aide-major-général* of the cavalry.

Mobile reserve:
Napoleon's mobile reserve, with which he moved southwards from Reims against the

Hauptarmee, contained:
- 1st Old Guard Division (Friant)
- three Imperial Guard cavalry divisions (Sébastiani)
  – 1st Division (Colbert), including 600 Poles under Pac
  – 2nd Division (Exelmans)
  – 3rd Division (Letort)
- Imperial Guard artillery (part)
- a provisional cavalry division of *escadrons réunis* (amalgamated squadrons) newly arrived from Paris (Berckheim)
  – 1st (heavy) brigade (Mourier)
  – 2nd (light) brigade (Curély)
- *Maréchal* Ney's corps
  – an infantry division composed of reinforcements that had broken out of the frontier fortresses and joined the field army (Janssens)
  – an infantry brigade detached from VII Corps (Rousseau)
  – *Régiment de la Vistule* (a Polish regiment, formerly garrisoning Soissons)
  – *122e Régiment de Ligne* (from Paris)
- Defrance's division of *Gardes d'honneur*

Lefebvre-Desnouëttes joined Napoleon at Arcis-sur-Aube with reinforcements from Paris:
- 1,500 Imperial Guard cavalrymen
- a provisional Young Guard infantry division containing 3,000 men from the depots (Henrion)

Maréchal Macdonald's group moved eastwards, up the Aube, to rejoin Napoleon.

Notes:
a. Sébastiani had replaced the original commander of the Imperial Guard cavalry, Nansouty, who had become unfit for further active service after Craonne.
b. Letort had replaced Lévesque-Laferrière, who had been wounded at Craonne.
c. Janssens was wounded at Arcis-sur-Aube and replaced by Lefol, who had hitherto been attached to Napoleon's headquarters as a spare general.
d. Rousseau had replaced Pierre Boyer.
e. Lefebvre-Desnouëttes had been wounded at Brienne while commanding an Imperial Guard cavalry division, but had now recovered and returned from Paris.

Battle of Paris

After Arcis-sur-Aube (20–21/3/1814) Napoleon carried out his *manoeuvre sur les derrières*. He summoned *Maréchaux* Marmont and Mortier to join him with their detached forces that had been covering the *Schlesische Armee* on the Aisne. They encountered the Allied advance at Fère-Champenoise (25/3/1814) and retreated on Paris. Various other detachments fell back on Paris in the face of the Allied advance:
- On 22/3/1814 Ledru des Essarts had been appointed the commandant at Meaux, 25 miles east of Paris, and commander of the 3rd Division of the *Réserve de Paris*.
- On 25/3/1814 Compans reached Sézanne and collected various isolated detachments that had been on their way to join Napoleon's army. He fell back on Meaux and then Paris.

- Vincent commanded a detachment of Young Guardsmen and *Gardes d'honneur*, and rallied 1,000 fugitives from the Battle of Fère-Champenoise.

At Paris two more provisional divisions of the Imperial Guard were scraped together and entrusted to generals who had been wounded earlier in the campaign (Michel, Boyer de Rebeval).

French forces available to defend Paris:
Commander-in-chief: Joseph Bonaparte
Total strength: 42,000 men, including second-line units.

Right wing (*Maréchal* Marmont):
- Provisional corps (Compans)
  – three infantry divisions (Compans, Ledru des Essarts, Boyer de Rebeval)
  – one cavalry division (Chastel)
- VI Corps
  – three infantry divisions (Ricard, Lagrange, Arrighi)
- I Cavalry Corps
  – two divisions (Merlin, Bordesoulle)

Left wing (*Maréchal* Mortier):
- Imperial Guard corps
  – 2nd Old Guard Division (Christiani)
  – two Young Guard divisions (Curial, Charpentier)
  – a division newly formed from the Imperial Guard depots (Michel)
- Cavalry corps (Belliard)
  – one cavalry division (Roussel d'Hurbal)
- A detachment of 320 men formed from the Imperial Guard depots (Ornano)

Reserve (*Maréchal* Moncey):
- *Garde nationale de Paris*

Garrisons of outlying villages or forts: St-Maur, Charenton, Vincennes, St-Denis, Neuilly.

Glossary

French words are indicated by (F), and German by (G).

adjoint (F)	deputy (mayor).
adjudant (F)	warrant officer.
adjudant-major (F)	staff officer with equivalent rank to *major*.
l'administration de la guerre, Ministère (directeur du département) de (F)	Minister (directing the department) of war administration (responsible for food, forage, remounts, hospitals, clothing, transport, etc.).
ambulance (F)	(1) casualty post/field hospital; or (2) vehicle(s) for evacuating wounded.
Ancien Régime (F)	'Former Regime', the monarchy before the Revolution.
armée (F)	army.
Armee (G)	army.
Armee-Abtheilung (G)	corps.
arrondissement (F)	administrative subdivision of a *département*, headed by a *sous-préfet*. *Arrondissements* were divided into *cantons*, which in turn were divided into *communes*.
Ataman	Cossack leader.
auditeur (F)	professional administrator attached to the *Conseil d'état*.
aune (F)	a unit of measurement, equivalent to 1.20 metres.
bataillon (F)	battalion.
biens nationaux (F)	lands confiscated by the state during the Revolution, for example from the Crown or the Church, and often sold in due course to private acquirers.
bulletin (F)	Napoleon's official communiqué of news from his army. In 1813 and 1814 these accounts were no longer formally called *bulletins*, as they took the form of official letters to the Empress Marie-Louise.
Bundes-Corps (G)	Federal Corps. Contingents supplied by German states were used to form eight of these corps in support of the Allied invasion of France.
butte-témoin (F)	isolated hill, like Montmartre, that had resisted the erosion of its surroundings.
cadre	nucleus of officers, NCOs and men around which a unit can be formed and trained.
capitaine (F)	captain.
capitaine de vaisseau (F)	naval captain.
centime (F)	coin. One hundred *centimes* equalled one *franc*.
Champagne humide (F)	damp Champagne, a zone covered with ponds and lakes.
Champagne pouilleuse (F)	barren Champagne, a zone of infertile ground sweeping past Châlons-sur-Marne.
chasseur à cheval (F)	light cavalryman (a *chasseur* literally means a hunter).
chasseur à pied (F)	light infantryman.

chaussée (F)	main road.
chef de bataillon (F)	battalion commander (the holder of this rank did not always lead a battalion).
chef d'escadron (F)	squadron commander (the holder of this rank did not always lead a squadron).
Chef des Generalstabes (G)	Chief of the General Staff.
chef d'état-major (F)	chief of staff of a division or corps (the chief of staff of Napoleon's army was known as the *major-général*).
chef-lieu (F)	administrative centre (chief town of a *département*).
chevau-léger lancier (F)	light horse lancer.
colonel (F)	Colonel, the commander of a regiment.
commandant (F)	commander.
commandant de place (F)	town commandant.
commissaire extraordinaire (F)	extraordinary commissioner, sent by Napoleon at the end of December 1813, after the start of the Allied invasion, into the provinces in an attempt to overcome the inertia of the local administration. A *commissaire extraordinaire* was appointed to a *division militaire*.
commission préfectorale (F)	prefectoral commission, as set up by the Allies in, for instance, the *département* of the Vosges.
commune (F)	the lowest administrative subdivision in the French Empire, headed by a mayor.
compagnie de réserve (of a *département*) (F)	created in 1805 so the *préfet* of each *département* had a company of reservists as a local military force.
compagnie franche (F)	an independent company, commonly formed in order to undertake reconnaissance or irregular missions. This was necessary in the eighteenth century because an army generally lacked its own, permanent units of light troops.
comte (F)	count.
conseil d'arrondissement (F)	advisory council for the *sous-préfet* of an *arrondissement*.
conseil de préfecture (F)	prefectory council, to settle a *département*'s litigious matters, for example those relating to the *biens nationaux*.
conseil d'état (F)	Council of State.
conseil général (F)	general council of a *département*.
conseil municipal (F)	town council.
conseiller d'état (F)	councillor of state.
corps (F)	(1) army corps, or *corps d'armée*, the largest component part of an army, containing infantry and cavalry divisions, artillery and supporting services; or (2) more generally, a distinct administrative or tactical unit, large or small.
corps franc (F)	free corps, so-named because it was free from normal military discipline, and permitted to live off the country without paying for supplies. It might be composed of either regulars or irregulars, but was used for irregular missions.
Corps législatif (F)	Legislative Body, existed from 1795. Under Napoleon the *Corps législatif* enacted laws

	proposed by the Council of State but did not debate them.
Cortes	Spanish parliament.
côte (F)	escarpment or hill.
coucou (F)	small slow coach.
cuirassier (F)	heavy, armoured cavalryman, considered as an élite within the line.
département (F)	the key administrative division of the French Empire, including its *pays réunis*. The central government's representative in each *département* was the *préfet*.
diligence (F)	public conveyance for long-distance travel.
Directeur général des postes (F)	Postmaster-General.
division (F)	(1) tactical formation formed from one or two *pelotons*; or (2) a higher formation between brigade and corps level.
division militaire (F)	mobilisation district, usually containing between two and six *départements*.
douanier (F)	customs officer.
dragon (F)	dragoon, originally intended as a mounted infantryman who would fight on foot but use his horse for mobility. In practice, *dragons* became ordinary cavalry, a medium form between the heavy and light.
droits réunis (F)	indirect taxes, one of the main reasons for popular discontent in Napoleon's Empire in 1814.
Ecole militaire (F)	Military School in Paris.
émigré (F)	French exile, not necessarily noble, who had emigrated during the Revolution.
Erbprinz (G)	hereditary prince.
escadron (F)	squadron. A cavalry regiment contained two or more squadrons.
escadron de service (F)	duty squadron, for escorting Napoleon.
estafette (F)	messenger.
étape (F)	relay, or a day's march.
Etappe (G)	relay, or a day's march.
Etappen-Straße (G)	military road, officially designated for the movements of troops, supplies, and casualties to and from the army.
état-major (F)	staff.
Feldmarschall (G)	Field Marshal.
Feldmarschall-Leutnant (G)	general, usually a divisional commander.
Feldwebel (G)	sergeant.
Feldzeugmeister (G)	general, usually a corps commander.
fermier (F)	tenant farmer.
forestier (F)	forester.
franc (F)	introduced as the French national currency in 1795.
franc-tireur (F)	irregular (literally, free-shooter).
Freiherr (G)	baron.
fricoteur (F)	pillager.
Fürst (G)	Prince. In German a distinction was drawn between royal and other princes, a royal prince having the title of *Prinz*.
garde (F/G)	Guard.

Glossary 263

garde champêtre	rural guard.
garde d'honneur (F)	guard of honour. Four regiments of *Gardes d'honneur* were raised by Napoleon in 1813 to provide more cavalry and a source of officers, and to tie the nobility and upper bourgeoisie more closely to his regime. They were not formally part of the Imperial Guard but were attached to it.
garde forestier	forestry warden.
Garde impériale (F)	Imperial Guard (1804–1814 and 1815).
Garde nationale (F)	National Guard, initially a citizen's militia organised during the Revolution. Napoleon neutralised it as a political force and converted it into a territorial reserve that could be selectively mobilised when necessary for home defence. Part of it was used to help rebuild the *Grande armée* after the Russian campaign; other units saw action in 1814.
Gendarmerie (F)	militarised police force.
général de brigade (F)	general of brigade (the holder of this rank did not always lead a brigade); known as *maréchal de camp* under the Bourbon Restoration.
général de division (F)	general of division (the holder of this rank did not always lead a division).
General der Infanterie (G)	General of Infantry, usually a corps commander.
General der Kavallerie (G)	General of Cavalry, usually a corps commander.
General-Major (G)	Major-General, usually a brigade commander.
Generalstab (G)	General Staff.
General-Quartiermeister (G)	Quartermaster-General.
génie (F)	engineers.
Graf (G)	count.
Grande armée (F)	Grand Army, Napoleon's main field force.
Grand Maréchal du palais (F)	Grand Marshal of the Palace, responsible for Napoleon's personal security and for the efficient running of the imperial household.
grand prévôt (F)	Chief Provost.
grand quartier-général (F)	army headquarters.
Grenadier (G)	grenadier.
grenadier à cheval (F)	mounted grenadier.
grenadier à pied (F)	foot grenadier.
guerre, Ministre (du département) de la (F)	Minister (of the department) of War (responsible for levies, organisation, discipline, army movements, fortifications, pay, retirements, prisoners-of-war, etc.)
Hauptarmee (G)	Grand Army (or Main Army), commanded by Schwarzenberg. Known in 1813 as the Army of Bohemia.
Herzog (G)	duke.
Hôtel des postes (F)	Post Office.
hôtel-de-ville (F)	town hall.
hussard (F)	hussar (light cavalryman, considered in the French army as an élite).
Infanterie (G)	infantry.
intendant général (F)	quartermaster-general.
l'intérieur, Ministre de (F)	Minister of the Interior.

Invalides, Hôtel des (F)	home for invalid soldiers, founded by Louis XIV in 1674. Besides the main *hôtel* in Paris, there were secondary establishments, for example in Louvain and Avignon.
Jäger (G)	light infantryman.
Jäger zu Pferde (G)	light cavalryman.
Kavallerie (G)	cavalry.
Korporal (G)	corporal.
Kronprinz (G)	Crown Prince.
Kürassier (G)	cuirassier.
lancier (F)	lancer.
Landsturm (G)	home defence force.
Landwehr (G)	militia.
légère (F)	light: infantry/cavalry/artillery units that had an emphasis on mobility or were specially trained to scout, skirmish or reconnoitre. Abbreviated titles have been used for regiments, eg *37e Légère*, rather than the full *37e Régiment d'infanterie légère*.
Légion d'honneur (F)	Legion of Honour, a prestigious order instituted by Napoleon in 1802 to reward soldiers and civilians.
leichte Division (G)	light division.
Leutnant (G)	*lieutenant*.
levée en masse (F)	mass levy. In theory, the mobilisation of much, or all, of the civilian population in response to an invasion. In practice, was more limited in scope, and was used during the Revolution as a method for increasing the regular army's manpower.
lieutenant (F)	*lieutenant*.
ligne (F)	line. Abbreviated titles have been used for regiments, eg *59e Ligne*, rather than the full *59e Régiment d'infanterie de ligne*.
Line	ordinary troops of the army (the word comes from 'the line of battle'). In other words, those men not part of either crack corps, reserve formations, or irregulars.
maire (F)	mayor.
mairie (F)	town hall.
Maison (F)	Household.
maison de poste (F)	posting house or relay inn.
maître des postes (F)	postmaster.
major (F)	usually the second-in-command of a regiment, entrusted with the administrative duties carried out during the *Ancien Régime* by a *lieutenant-colonel*.
major-général (F)	chief of staff of Napoleon's army.
maréchal (F) (plural *maréchaux*)	marshal (a dignity, not a rank).
maréchal des logis (F)	cavalry sergeant.
maréchal des logis chef (F)	cavalry sergeant-major/first sergeant.
marin (F)	seaman.
Marschbezirk (G)	march district.
métayer (F)	sharecropper.
militia	non-regular, second-line troops raised for home defence.
ministère (F)	(government) ministry.

Glossary 265

ministre (F)	(government) minister. (See also under names of government departments.)
Nordarmee (G)	Army of the North, commanded by the Crown Prince of Sweden.
Oberst (G)	colonel.
Oberst-Leutnant (G)	lieutenant-colonel.
Observatoire impérial (F)	Imperial Observatory.
officier d'ordonnance (F)	orderly officer or despatch rider.
opolchenie	Russian militia.
palanque (F)	see *tambour*.
palisade (F)	see *tambour*.
partisan (F)	leader (or sometimes just a member) of a war party, licensed to carry out attacks in an enemy's rear.
pays réuni (F)	foreign region annexed ('re-united') by France.
police générale de l'empire, Ministre (du département) de la (F)	Minister (of the department) of the general police of the Empire.
préfet (F)	prefect, the administrative head of a *département*, and representative of the central government.
Préfet de police (F)	Prefect of Police, responsible for security and law enforcement. Paris had two *préfets* because of its size and importance: the *préfet de la Seine* and the *préfet de police*.
Préfet du palais (F)	Prefect of the Palace, assistant to the *Grand Maréchal du palais*.
prévôt (F)	provost.
Prinz (G)	(royal) prince.
réfractaire (F)	man evading summons for conscription (as opposed to a deserter, who had already joined a depot or unit).
représentant-en-mission (F)	representative on mission, or political commissar. The direct agent of the central government, sent into the provinces or to French armies during the Revolutionary Wars.
Réserve de Paris (Armée de) (F)	Reserve army of Paris, created to cover the capital and mobilise the resources of its depots.
Rheinbund (G)	Confederation of the Rhine: Napoleon's collection of German satellite states in central Europe, established in 1806.
route départementale (F)	local road, maintained at the expense of the *département*.
route d'étape (F)	military road, officially designated for the movements of troops, supplies, and casualties to and from the army.
route impériale (F)	main road, maintained wholly or partly at the expense of the imperial government. There were three classes of *routes impériales*, the first two being the Empire's great strategic or commercial arteries.
Schlesische Armee (G)	Army of Silesia, commanded by *Feldmarschall* Blücher.
secrétaire général (F)	secretary general.
Sénat (F)	Senate, successor to the *Conseil des Anciens* (the upper house of the *Corps législatif* before Napoleon's coup of 1799). By 1814 the *Sénat*

	contained 180 senators, who were aged at least 40. It was replaced in 1814 by the *Chambre des pairs*.
soldat (F)	soldier (private).
sous-lieutenant (F)	second lieutenant.
sous-préfet (F)	sub-prefect. The administrative head of an *arrondissement*.
Streifkorps (G)	flying corps.
Südarmee (G)	Army of the South, commanded by the *Erbprinz* von Hessen-Homburg.
tambour of *palanques* (F)	a stockade of tree trunks, planted in two rows and with the defenders able to fire over the top.
tambour of *palisades* (F)	a fence made from planks of wood planted in the ground, with narrow gaps through which the defenders could fire.
tirailleur (F)	literally, shooter. Applied broadly to designate a skirmisher or light infantryman, or an ordinary soldier used in such a role. Sometimes refers to an irregular.
transport en poste (F)	relays of requisitioned vehicles used to transport infantry quickly.
Uhlan (G)	lancer.
Vice grand électeur (F)	Vice-Grand Elector, one of the ten grand dignitaries of the Empire. The office was held by Talleyrand in 1814. The *Grand électeur* was Napoleon's brother Joseph.
voiturier (F)	carriage-hirer.
Volontäroffizier (G)	volunteer officer.
weissbier (G)	light, effervescent beer made from barley and wheat.

References

Archive sources:
ADA: *Archives départementales de l'Aube*, at Troyes.
AN: *Archives nationales*, at Paris.

Introduction
(pages x–xii)
1. Hungerford, p. 128; Gréard, pp. 222, 240–1. Other senior officers shown riding behind Napoleon include *Maréchal* Berthier (the *major-général*), and two of Napoleon's ADCs: *Général de division* Auguste, *comte* de Flahaut de la Billarderie, and *Général de division* Antoine, *comte* Drouot.
2. Gréard, pp. 226–7, 241, 366. Meissonier wrote that he thought of Napoleon 'returning from Soissons' after Laon, but probably meant to Soissons.
3. The battle casualties of the corps during the 1814 campaign as a whole were just 15 per cent of those it had suffered in central Europe the previous autumn. Calculated from Plotho, part 3, appendix XXIII.
4. Estimate based on the area of operations of the *Hauptarmee* and *Schlesische Armee*. Many more civilians, in more distant regions, would have been affected indirectly. It should be noted that the distinction between French civilians, soldiers, and irregulars was sometimes blurred.

Chapter 1: 'No language can describe the horrible devastation'
(pages 1–8)
1. Smith, *1813 Leipzig*, p. 298.
2. Bockenheimer, p. 43.
3. Fane, *The letters*, pp. 66–7.
4. Sherwig, pp. 353–4.
5. Nesselrode, v. 5, p. 152.
6. Castlereagh, v. 9, pp. 212–13.
7. Schwarzenberg, *Briefe*, p. 360.
8. Reinhard, pp. 383–4.
9. Müffling, p. 396; Metternich, v. 1, p. 178.
10. Kraehe, p. 255.

Chapter 2: France in 1814
(pages 9–17)
1. The Nord, for example, for all its aversion to conscription, showed little opposition to taxes or requisitions. Bruchet, pp. 23–4.
2. Benaerts, pp. xiii, xxii.
3. Underwood, p. 2.
4. Chamans de Lavallette, pp. 84–5.
5. Savary, v. 6, pp. 320–1.
6. Houssaye, p. 2; Belhomme, v. 4, p. 643.
7. In mid-February the *Ministre de l'intérieur* sent several *auditeurs* with funds to visit the battlefields, in order to collect and buy abandoned Allied muskets from the peasants. This step was intended to provide firearms for the *Garde nationale de Paris*, but had still produced no result by the 24th. AN AF/IV/1669B (2), doc 309, Mortemart to Napoleon, 24/2/1814.
8. Houssaye, p. 13; Marmont, v. 6, p. 320; AN AF/IV/1669B (2), doc 279, Victor to Berthier 23/2/1814.

9. These eleven *maréchaux* do not include Massena, who commanded the *Armée d'Italie* south of the Alps.
10. Of the four honorary *maréchaux*, Kellermann in January was entrusted with the defence of the Marne valley. Moncey was appointed *major-général* of the *Garde nationale de Paris* on 8/1/1814. Sérurier had been Governor of the *Invalides* since 1804. Pérignon had not been employed since March 1813.
11. Fabvier, p. 63.
12. Analysis of the careers of forty-six divisional commanders who served under Napoleon in the main campaign theatre in 1814, using the data in Six. Similarly, two out of the seven *maréchaux* serving directly under Napoleon (not including Berthier) were wounded in the 1814 campaign: Victor at Craonne and Oudinot at both Brienne and Arcis-sur-Aube. Martinien, p. 11.
13. Lefebvre de Béhaine, v. 3, p. 412.
14. The calculation of the proportion of Napoleon's field army provided by the Imperial Guard was based on the situation on 17/3/1814. It is for the field army under Napoleon's direct command in eastern France. Janson, v. 2, appendix XXXII.
15. Weil, *La campagne*, v. 2, p. 169.
16. Fabvier, p. 6.
17. Fabvier, pp. 32–3; Marmont, v. 6, pp. 51–2.
18. Napoleon ordered daily target practice for the *Garde nationale* at the camp of Meaux. Du Casse, *Mémoires*, v. 10, p. 71.
19. Napoleon, v. 26, no. 20835.
20. Houssaye, pp. 8–9.
21. Their indiscipline was caused partly by their arrears of pay. AN F/7/3782, *bulletin* of the *police générale*, 30 and 31/1/1814; AN F/7/6603, dossier 4295; AN AF/IV/1534, *bulletin* of the *préfecture de police*, 10/2/1814.
22. Bertrand, v. 3, p. 44.
23. Some batteries were even drawn by unbroken horses. Fabvier, p. 61.
24. AN F/7/6603, dossier 4292. Caupeil's invention was not entirely unprecedented. For example, Leonardo da Vinci (1452–1519) had drawn a design for a tank.
25. Fiévet, *Histoire*, v. 2, p. 200.
26. Napoleon, v. 27, no. 21057.
27. Du Casse, *Mémoires*, v. 10, pp. 51, 52, 78.
28. Levavasseur, pp. 205–6. Napoleon tried to limit the upheaval caused by changes. In replacing Victor at the head of II Corps on 18/2/1814, he directed the new commander, Gérard, to keep all the *état-major* of the corps, all the relevant paperwork, and a record of the orders that Victor had received. Weil, *La campagne*, v. 2, p. 303.
29. Marmont, v. 6, p. 273; Du Casse, *Mémoires*, v. 10, pp. 52, 98.
30. AN AF/IV/1667 (2), docs 295 and 329, Berthier to Napoleon, 21 and 27/2/1814; AN AF/IV/1669 (2), doc 260, Friant to Berthier, 21/2/1814.
31. Grivel, p. 298.
32. Napoleon, v. 27, no. 21185.
33. Napoleon, v. 27, no. 21403.
34. Descaves, pp. 198, 206.
35. Lefol, pp. 15–16.

Chapter 3: The Allied armies
(pages 18–24)
1. Leggiere, p. 132.
2. The total includes Bülow and Winzingerode's corps, detached from the *Nordarmee*, but not the supporting *Bundes-Corps*, except for the two that were formally incorporated into the *Hauptarmee*'s order of battle.
3. Schwarzenberg, *Briefe*, pp. 332–3.
4. Reiche, part 2, pp. 42–3.

5. During the spring 1813 campaign Blücher led a formation of corps strength (about 25,000 men) that operated as part of the Russo-Prussian army. Only in August did his command become a large independent army of more than 100,000 men. Unger, v. 2, pp. 10, 37, 54, 56.
6. The analysis includes Winzingerode and Bülow, whose corps were transferred to the *Schlesische Armee* from the *Nordarmee*.
7. Before August 1813 Blücher's command had been of corps strength and had operated as an integral part of a coalition army. Unger, v. 2, p. 54.
8. Similarly, Napoleon had used contingents from his German allies to help protect his lines of communication during the 1805 campaign. From 1809, faced with greater demands on his manpower, he incorporated large numbers of his German contingents into his field army, rather than using them merely as rear-area auxiliaries. In 1814 the Allies used the *Bundes-Corps* in both active and support roles, with two of them forming an integral part of the *Hauptarmee*.
9. Rothenberg, *Napoleon's great adversary*, p. 233.
10. Keep, pp. 153–4.
11. Württemberg, *Journal des campagnes*, p. 184.
12. Rahden, part 1, pp. 238–9.
13. Mikhailovsky-Danilevsky, p. 356; Müffling, pp. 34–5.
14. Prussian infantry brigades tended to have a balanced mix of regular, reserve, and *Landwehr* regiments, and by 1814 the differences in combat capabilities had narrowed.
15. Mikaberidze, pp. xxix, xxxiii; Zhmodikov, p. 25.
16. The corresponding figures for the Russian divisional commanders who took part in the invasion of France were 55 per cent and an average of five years. Analysis of a sample of fifty-two Russian generals serving in 1814 in the *Hauptarmee* or *Schlesische Armee* (including units transferred from the *Nordarmee*), using the information in Mikaberidze. The sample does not include the Cossack commanders. The figure for the corps commanders includes Barclay de Tolly, who commanded the Russian army as a whole and was in overall charge of the Russian and Prussian reserves within the *Hauptarmee*.
17. Kleist's corps was transferred from the *Hauptarmee* to the *Schlesische Armee*, while Bülow's corps was detached from the *Nordarmee*. Only the Prussian *Garde* remained in the *Hauptarmee*.
18. Müffling, pp. 34–5, 44, 296.
19. Starklof, *Geschichte . . . Zweiten Reiter-Regiments*, p. 536.
20. Pertz and Delbrück, v. 4, p. 218, Gneisenau to Boyen, 20/3/1814. Lieutenant-General Illarion Vasilievich Vasilchikov I commanded the cavalry in Sacken's corps and Lieutenant-General Feodor Karlovich, Baron Korf that of Langeron's corps. General Ferdinand Fedorovich, Baron Winzingerode commanded a corps detached from the *Nordarmee* and joined the *Schlesische Armee* at the beginning of March.
21. Underwood, p. 44; Gain de Montaignac, p. 7.
22. Weil, *La campagne*, v. 2, p. 100.
23. Weil, *La campagne*, v. 3, pp. 295–300, 538; v. 4, p. 262.

Chapter 4: Invasion!
(pages 25–31)
1. Schroeder, pp. 492–5; Oechsli, p. 55.
2. Some divisions of the Austrian reserves also remained in the main theatre, but not the reserves as a whole.
3. Another 21 per cent of the garrison deserted, while hundreds more troops were sick or wounded. Chuquet, pp. 219, 255–6, 449. The Austrians used Swiss artillery against Besançon in particular, because of the difficulty and expense that would have been involved in bringing their own heavy guns from central Europe. The Bavarian siege artillery was used against Huningue. Oechsli, pp. 99–100.
4. Schwartzkoppen, pp. 242–3.
5. The original Austrian reserves ceased to exist as a formation, having been completely divided between the I *Armee-Abtheilung* and the new central reserve. (This new reserve was formed

largely from elements of the I and II *Armee-Abtheilungen*, and two divisions of the Austrian reserves. As a result, the I *Armee-Abtheilung* was left with just two of its three divisions, so it had to be reinforced by the 2. *leichte Division* and the remainder of the original Austrian reserves.)
6. Leggiere, p. 267.
7. Weil, *La campagne*, v. 1, pp. 10, 178.
8. Gneisenau, *Briefe*, no. 109, p. 140.
9. Schwarzenberg, *Briefe*, p. 370.
10. Weil, *La campagne*, v. 1, pp. 254–5. The proportion does not include officers.
11. Roloff, p. 41.
12. Leggiere, pp. 91–2, 177, 179, 364. Mortier showed with his fighting retreat before the *Hauptarmee* what could have been achieved, but it would have been more difficult to replicate his success against the more determined advance of the *Schlesische Armee*, and with troops who lacked the Old Guard's experience and cohesion.

Chapter 5: The campaign theatre
(pages 32–41)
1. Nesselrode, v. 5, p. 151.
2. The study compared standardised temperatures for Kew Observatory. The coldest month of the period 1783–1942 was January 1795, when the monthly mean temperature was –2.6°C. But it was 1814 that had the lowest mean temperature for the winter as a whole (1.1°C). The temperatures fluctuated, but overall the winter of 1814 constituted an unusually prolonged period of cold conditions. Drummond, pp. 24–5.
3. The location of the eruption is still unknown, but the evidence for its occurrence comes from ice-core samples and tree-rings. Briffa, Jones, et al., p. 452.
4. Couper-Johnston, p. 102; Diaz and Markgraf, pp. 123, 126, 152; Grove, pp. 318–19.
5. Jordan, p. 221; Steffens, p. 148; Raumer, pp. 224–5; Bourqueney, p. 235; Pétiet, pp. 18–19. French units often lacked not only the funds to shoe their horses for ice, but also sufficient numbers of blacksmiths. Weil, *La campagne*, v. 1, p. 120; Grüber, p. 209; Levavasseur, p. 223.
6. Faré, p. 321; Grivel, p. 297.
7. Alberti, pp. 93–4.
8. Sometimes the travellers would find some *buttes-témoins*, or isolated hills that had resisted erosion, like Montmartre immediately north of Paris.
9. Costello, v. 1, pp. 195–6.
10. Most of the settlements that do exist are strung along the river valleys.
11. Thurn und Taxis, pp. 235–6.
12. There were three classes of *routes impériales*. The first two classes, which were maintained wholly at the expense of the central government, totalled twenty-seven in 1811. Over 200 third-class roads linked the cities and large towns, and were maintained at the expense of both the central government and the *départements* through which they passed. The local roads, entrusted to the care of the *départements*, were known as *routes départementales*.
13. France, *Almanach*, p. 949. The distance between Paris and Strasbourg in a direct line is 250 miles.
14. Robb, pp. 143–4; Litre, p. 382; Rembowski, p. 464; Mathieu, *Dernières*, p. 59.
15. Planat de la Faye, p. 180.
16. The Austrian III *Armee-Abtheilung* reported from Bar-sur-Aube on 28/1/1814 that the road between Châtillon and Troyes was broken up and barricaded. Weil, *La campagne*, v. 1, pp. 393–4; v. 2, p. 29. At the end of January Napoleon wanted a usable road established from Arcis-sur-Aube, leading north-westwards through Sézanne to La Ferté-sous-Jouarre in the Marne valley. He also wanted a road to link Arcis-sur-Aube and Paris without crossing the Aube river. Napoleon, v. 27, no. 21162.
17. The Marne valley was flooded at Château-Thierry during the campaign, whereas the rivers were often reduced to a derisory stream in summer. A traveller noted in 1818 that the Seine at Paris was 'so diminutive, that one fancies it would have been cheaper to have filled it up

than bridged it over'. To prevent such problems, reservoirs were created between 1949 and 1990 to regulate the flow of the Marne, Seine, Aube and Yonne rivers. Hall, p. 63; Mathieu, *Dernières*, p. 22.
18. The ferry was brought from Ramerupt. ADA 14R69, Guillaumot to provisional *préfet* of the Aube, 18/2/1814.
19. ADA 14R3, *arrêté* of provisional *préfet* of the Aube, 15/2/1814; ADA 14R69, Guillaumot to provisional *préfet* of the Aube, 18/2/1814; Beuve, p. 5; Oisy, p. 18.
20. Auvray, p. 550.
21. The reserve cavalry of Kleist's Prussian corps was delayed by four days by ice in the Rhine, and crossed the river only on 13/1/1814. Meier, p. 136; Weil, *La campagne*, v. 1, p. 213; Müffling, pp. 406, 456; Schubert, pp. 336–7.
22. AN AF/IV/1669B (2), doc 259, report of 21/2/1814; AN AF/IV/1534, *bulletin* of the *préfecture de police*, 23/2/1814.
23. Napoleon, v. 27, no. 21379.
24. Napoleon, v. 27, nos 21420 and 21481; AN AF/IV/1667 (2), docs 342 and 349, Berthier to Napoleon, 6 and 9/3/1814. The bridging train reached Meaux from Paris on 4/3/1814; La Ferté-sous-Jouarre on the 5th; and was due to reach Château-Thierry on the 6th. It reached Fismes on the morning of 9/3/1814, from where it was to join Napoleon at Soissons.
25. The *Hauptarmee* found itself checked when the French burned the permanent wooden bridge at Lesmont after the Battle of La Rothière, for the Austrian bridging train was at Chaumont, 40 miles to the south-east. Weil, *La campagne*, v. 2, pp. 7–8.
26. Gneisenau, *Briefe*, pp. 154, 156.
27. Gourgaud wrote to Napoleon from Paris on 15/2/1814 that Joseph Bonaparte had ordered two pontoon bridges to be established on the Seine at Villeneuve and at the junction of the Marne, so as not to be reduced to just the bridge at Choisy should the one at Corbeil be lost to the Allied advance. Napoleon wrote to Joseph that same day that it was pointless to establish new bridges immediately outside Paris. AN AF/IV/1669B (1), doc 224, Gourgaud to Napoleon, 15/2/1814; Du Casse, *Mémoires*, v. 10, p. 121; Godard d'Aucour, pp. 173–4, 184.
28. France: Ministère de la guerre, *Instructions . . . bridges*.
29. At Melun the French took the precaution of cutting one of the arches of the stone bridge, and replacing it with a wooden roadway that could be destroyed more quickly in the event of an attack. Godard d'Aucour, p. 126; Humbert, pp. 28–9.
30. Müffling, p. 451.
31. Bertrand, v. 2, p. 394.
32. A *tambour* of *palisades* was a fence made from planks of wood planted in the ground, with narrow gaps through which the defenders could fire. The *tambour* of *palanques* was a stockade of tree trunks, planted in two rows and with the defenders able to fire over the top.
33. ADA 14R3, second-in-command of the engineers to the *sous-préfet* of Nogent-sur-Seine, 7/2/1814; ADA 14R4, order from the *sous-préfet* of Nogent-sur-Seine, 5/3/1814.
34. Versailles had originally been a mere village, but grew into a city once Louis XIV relocated the court there from Paris. Its population was about 60,000 inhabitants by 1789, but then shrank by almost two-thirds as a result of the Revolution.
35. Blayney, v. 2, p. 307; Alison, Alison et al., v. 2, p. 15.
36. Gain de Montaignac, p. 34.
37. Dry, p. 70.
38. France: Ministère de la guerre, *Instructions . . . towns and villages*.
39. Pougiat, p. 70; Faucheur, pp. 281–2; Macdonald, p. 244.
40. Las Cases, *Suite*, v. 2, p. 82.
41. The southern flank of the line of the Yonne rested on Auxerre and the hills of the Nivernais.
42. Humbert, pp. 24, 27–8. Kellermann withdrew from Châlons-sur-Marne to Meaux as the Allies advanced. Meaux served as an intelligence-gathering post, from where Kellermann was ordered to keep Napoleon informed of developments to the east. After Macdonald reached Meaux, Kellermann wrote to Napoleon on 10/2/1814 that he regarded his own mission as finished and was returning to Paris. His arrival at Paris was reported in the

general police *bulletin* of 6 and 7/2/1814. It was claimed that his departure from Meaux disorganised all the services, as everyone followed him. He wrote to Napoleon on 14/2/1814 to counter this claim, and stated that he had left his *chef d'état-major* at Claye to organise the *forestiers* of Louvre, Versailles, and Boulogne to halt fugitives and escort prisoners. AN AF/IV/1669B (1), docs 169 and 219, Kellermann to Napoleon, 10 and 14/2/1814; AN F/7/3782, *bulletin of the police générale*, 6 and 7/2/1814.
43. Godard d'Aucour, pp. 117, 131; Napoleon, v. 26, no. 21052.
44. The main two camps had been Châlons and Soissons, which covered the north-eastern approaches against the Allied invasion, which moved through the area of the Argonne. Las Cases, *Suite*, v. 2, p. 68.
45. Lefebvre de Béhaine, v. 4, p. 311.

Chapter 6: Napoleon takes command

(pages 42–9)

1. The bulk of the Allied forces was dispersed between Luxembourg and the Langres plateau, a distance of more than 150 miles, with detached corps even further afield.
2. Lefebvre de Béhaine, v. 4, p. 251; Weil, *La campagne*, v. 1, p. 356.
3. Napoleon, v. 27, no. 21135.
4. Weil, *La campagne*, v. 1, pp. 357, 359.
5. Napoleon, v. 27, no. 21135.
6. Fain, p. 76.
7. Levavasseur, pp. 194–5.
8. Pahlen commanded the advanced guard of the Russian VI *Armee-Abtheilung*, part of the *Hauptarmee*, but had temporarily joined Blücher that morning.
9. Löwenstern, *Mit Graf Pahlens Reiterei*, pp. 201–3.
10. Nostitz, part 5, p. 76. Nostitz wrongly claimed that this was the first time Blücher had seen Napoleon so closely. In fact, Blücher had personally had an interview with Napoleon in 1807.
11. Levavasseur, pp. 195–6.
12. The famous story of how Nostitz rescued Blücher at Ligny on 16/6/1815 ignores the role of a cavalry officer, *Major Freiherr* von dem Bussche of the *Elb-Landwehr-Kavallerie-Regiment*, who ensured that Blücher and Nostitz then headed off in the right direction to avoid falling into French hands. In 1819 Napoleon claimed that he recalled, from his schooldays, a track that led behind the *château*, and that he sent an acquaintance from that time to lead a French column along it. As with many of Napoleon's claims, it can not be accepted without reservations. The man supposedly guided the French troops into the basement of the *château* from the north, but Prussian eyewitnesses agree that the alert was caused by French troops firing from outside the *château*. A news item in *Le Moniteur* of 3/2/1814 shows that the French were aware of Blücher's escape from capture as he descended from the *château*. But Napoleon's official report, published in *Le Moniteur* on 6/2/1814, made no mention of Napoleon personally sending one of his fellow pupils from Brienne as a guide for the French troops. It simply stated that *Général de brigade* Louis Huguet-Châtaux led two battalions round to the right and entered the *château* through the park. Bernard, 'Du nouveau', pp. 10–11; Raumer, pp. 209–10; Pougiat, pp. 69–70; Nostitz, part 6, pp. 96–7.
13. Löwenstern, *Mit Graf Pahlens Reiterei*, pp. 201–3.
14. Lefol, p. 18; Du Casse, *Mémoires*, v. 10, pp. 39–40.
15. Napoleon, v. 27, no. 21150.
16. Napoleon himself said in March 1817 that he could not remember Gourgaud saving his life. Gourgaud, v. 1, p. 531; Marnat, 'Gourgaud'; Las Cases, *Mémorial*, v. 2, p. 118.
17. Weil, *La campagne*, v. 1, p. 426.
18. Levavasseur, pp. 201–2.
19. Bernhardi, v. 4, p. 282.
20. Wellington was similarly reluctant to allow his army to be used as a reserve to Blücher at

Ligny on 16/6/1815. Blücher and his command team pressed their troops too hard and were not good at controlling a battle coolly and rationally.
21. Weil, *La campagne*, v. 1, p. 459. The Allies had 200 guns available but could put only 150 into the line because of the state of the ground.
22. The driving snow also muffled the sound of the guns, which could be heard only faintly even a short distance from the battlefield. Raumer, p. 211.
23. Starklof, *Geschichte . . . Zweiten Reiter-Regiments*, pp. 464–5.
24. Müffling, pp. 109–10.
25. Thurn und Taxis, p. 202; Müffling, pp. 111–12.
26. Weil, *La campagne*, v. 1, p. 493. The uncertainty about the number of captured guns stemmed from conflicting claims by units and the fact that some guns were probably counted more than once.
27. Marmont, v. 6, pp. 36–7.
28. The figure is for the generals in Napoleon's army in eastern France, not including the forces in the secondary theatres. Bertin, p. 1.

Chapter 7: 'Where will we stop?'
(pages 50–5)
1. Blücher, p. 226.
2. Plotho, part 3, v. 1, p. 194.
3. It was on the Voire that the French *132e Ligne* earned the motto 'one against eight'. More research is needed on this action. Marmont held the Voire at the village of Rosnay but was outflanked when Allied detachments crossed another, unguarded, bridge to the west. According to the regimental history, the *132e* was ordered by Marmont to counter-attack, and threw back the Allies. (Another regimental source states that a *sous-lieutenant* of a different regiment joined the *132e*, had the charge beaten, and cut up the Allies.) In his memoirs Marmont attributed this counter-attack to the *131e* rather than the *132e*. Today plaques at the bridge at Rosnay pay tribute to both regiments, but the counter-attack described by Marmont actually occurred towards the other bridge to the west. In any case the odds have been exaggerated, for only limited numbers of Allied troops managed to cross the river. Interestingly, Marmont did not mention either the *131e* or the *132e* when he described the action in a letter written that evening to Berthier. He did mention the *1er* and *3e Régiments de marine*, which he used to repel the Allied forces that crossed the abandoned bridge to the west. He also mentioned the *121e* and *70e Ligne* for defending the bridge at Rosnay. AN AF/IV/1669 B (1), doc 15, Marmont to Berthier, 2/2/1814; Fabvier, pp. 27–8; Maindreville, *Historique du 132e régiment*, pp. 46–7; Mir, *Mémento*, p. 59; Marmont, v. 6, p. 42; Weil, *La campagne*, v. 1, p. 516; Hennequin, pp. 80, 86; Crossard, v. 6, p. 194.
4. Granier, p. 202.
5. Fabvier, p. 29; Weil, *La campagne*, v. 2, p. 8.
6. Fabvier, p. 29.
7. AN AF/IV/1668 (1), doc 98, printed order, 7/2/1814.
8. Fabvier, p. 29.
9. Houssaye, p. 94.
10. Hennequin, p. 196.
11. Fain, p. 91.
12. At the same time Napoleon expected to be able to draw considerable reserve forces from Paris in the middle of February. Weil, *La campagne*, v. 2, p. 43.
13. Fain, pp. 93–7, 111.
14. The calculation includes the division of *Gardes d'honneur* with the Imperial Guard. The *Gardes d'honneur* did not formally belong to the Guard, but were attached to it.
15. Ségur, v. 6, p. 314.
16. Napoleon, v. 27, no. 21227.
17. Kaptsevich commanded the Russian 10th Infantry Corps, which formed part of Langeron's corps.
18. Müffling, p. 119. The bulk of Winzingerode's corps reached Laon, 30 miles north of the

Marne, on 13/2/1814, but was still incomplete, as other elements joined it later in February.
19. Müffling, p. 435.
20. Janson, v. 2, p. 257; Weil, *La campagne*, v. 2, pp. 183–5; Müffling, pp. 124, 126, 437–8.

Chapter 8: A salvo of victories

(pages 56–68)

1. Müffling, p. 438; Weil, *La campagne*, v. 2, p. 180; Langeron, pp. 392–3.
2. Fabvier, pp. 32–3. About 7,000 or 8,000 of Napoleon's troops actually took part in the battle, about double Olsufiev's total strength. Mathieu, *Dernières*, p. 106.
3. Langeron, p. 394.
4. Weil, *La campagne*, v. 2, pp. 194–5; Müffling, p. 127.
5. Napoleon could still surprise his opponents on a tactical level, by doing the unexpected on a battlefield. He regained operational surprise three days later when Blücher mistakenly concluded that the French army had begun withdrawing on Paris. This enabled Napoleon to fall on Blücher at Vauchamps on 14/2/1814.
6. Napoleon inflicted larger numbers of casualties at Vauchamps, Montereau, and Craonne. But he defeated fewer troops at each of these battles, and suffered heavily himself at Craonne. He was able to exploit his victory at Montmirail by pursuing Yorck and Sacken over the Marne the next day. In contrast, he had to break off the pursuit of Blücher on the evening of Vauchamps in order to counter Schwarzenberg. It is true that Blücher had about 30,000 to 35,000 troops at Brienne, but that battle was only a marginal victory for Napoleon and soon negated by La Rothière.
7. Napoleon's plan to crush Sacken from several directions did not work. Berthier wrote to Oudinot at 2000 on 10/2/1814. Oudinot received this letter at 1130 on 11/2/1814, at Provins, and accordingly ordered Leval to leave with his division and reach La Ferté-Gaucher that evening. (Oudinot did not know the location of Boyer's division. Rottembourg's Young Guard division was allocated to guarding the *Grand quartier-général* and the parks of the army.) In the event Leval's division was able to leave Provins only at 1800 on 11/2/1814, and was further delayed by the state of the roads. Leval wrote at 2200 that he counted on being at La Ferté-Gaucher at dawn on 12/2/1814, from where he would march on Viels-Maisons. Nor was Macdonald able to advance against Sacken's rear from the west, since he had previously destroyed the bridge at Trilport. AN AF/IV/1669B (1), doc 183, Oudinot to Berthier, 11/2/1814; and doc 193, letter from Leval, 11/2/1814; Weil, *La campagne*, v. 2, pp. 183–4.
8. Henckel von Donnersmarck, p. 279.
9. The *8. Brigade* was left at Château-Thierry with the heavy artillery. Only the *1. Brigade* was seriously engaged, and it bore almost all of Yorck's losses. Janson, v. 1, p. 271.
10. Napoleon, v. 27, no. 21231.
11. The pursuit force did include Defrance's division of *Gardes d'honneur*, who were informally attached to the Guard rather than formally part of it. Defrance's division included a line regiment, the *10e Hussards*. Not all the Guard was used in the pursuit: part of the 1st Old Guard Division and some Young Guard infantry were left behind to rest near Montmirail.
12. Griois, v. 2, pp. 286–7.
13. Mathieu, *Dernières*, p. 172.
14. *Capitaine* Levavasseur, ADC to *Maréchal* Ney, thought that Napoleon's arrival paralysed Ney and thus lost the opportunity to crush the Allies against the Marne. But it was actually the terrain that checked the French. Levavasseur, pp. 207–8; Koch, v. 1, pp. 251–2.
15. A previously broken arch of the stone bridge had been repaired with wood. The Allies now set fire to this repaired arch and used artillery fire to prevent the French from extinguishing the flames.
16. Napoleon blamed Macdonald for not cutting the Allied escape route at Château-Thierry by thrusting north-westwards up the north bank of the Marne. On the evening of 12/2/1814 he wrote to the *Ministre de la guerre*: 'If [Macdonald] had gone from La Ferté-sous-Jouarre on the right bank of the Marne, as he should have done, not a man would have escaped.' As usual, Napoleon was simply venting his frustration about the outcome of an action at one of

his subordinates, regardless of the fairness of the criticism. Macdonald was actually too weak to have cut Yorck and Sacken's escape route, partly because he had received orders on 11/2/1814 to join Napoleon, who at the time was fighting at Montmirail, and had consequently pushed Saint-Germain's cavalry across the Marne to the south bank. Napoleon, v. 27, no. 21235; Weil, *La campagne*, v. 2, p. 195; Mathieu, *Dernières*, pp. 177–9.
17. Marmont, v. 6, pp. 188–9; Napoleon, v. 27, no. 21232.
18. Colomb, pp. 247–8.
19. Blücher, pp. 228–9. On 13/2/1814 a Frenchman, the *comte* de Ferrières-Saurebœuf, informed Blücher's staff that Napoleon had marched westwards for La Ferté-sous-Jouarre. The *comte* later disappeared, which caused suspicion that he had deliberately spread misinformation to lure Blücher into a trap. In fact, the reason why he disappeared was that he had been murdered. His information was accurate in the sense that Napoleon had moved westwards after the Battle of Champaubert, and it seems simply to have been misinterpreted by Blücher's staff. Mathieu, *Dernières*, p. 210; Pertz and Delbrück, v. 4, p. 241; Lawford, p. 83.
20. At this stage Napoleon did not realise that the corps at Etoges was the tail of the *Schlesische Armee*, and actually thought it could be the Russian VI *Armee-Abtheilung*, detached from the northern flank of the *Hauptarmee*. He did think that Blücher personally might be with Wittgenstein's corps. Napoleon, v. 27, nos 21253, 21254; Weil, *La campagne*, v. 2, p. 209.
21. Zelle, pp. 138–9, 144.
22. Levavasseur, p. 210.
23. Nostitz, part 5, p. 96.
24. Nostitz claimed that, after breaking through the French cavalry on the main road, Blücher rode back westwards, as he did not want to survive such a defeat. Nostitz claimed to have saved Blücher's life yet again by persuading him to move to the rear. But Nostitz tended to exaggerate his own role in such incidents, and so it remains unclear whether Blücher really tried to get himself killed. Raumer, who was with Blücher's headquarters, also stated that Blücher tried to get himself killed, but may simply have been told this by Nostitz. Nostitz, part 5, pp. 97–8; Raumer, p. 212.
25. Rahden, part 1, pp. 244–7.
26. Müffling, pp. 135, 444; Zelle, p. 142; Raumer, p. 213.
27. Rahden, part 1, pp. 250–1.
28. Secondary sources vary considerably regarding the Allied losses at Vauchamps, from 3,200 to over 6,000. The proportion of a quarter of the total strength was given in a letter from Gneisenau of 28/4/1814, and falls in the middle of the more extreme figures given by historians. Pertz and Delbrück, v. 4, p. 242.
29. The figure of 55 miles is the direct distance from the Marne at La Ferté-sous-Jouarre, which was reached by the head of Sacken's advance, to Châlons-sur-Marne, where Blücher rallied his army. It is unclear how many guns the *Schlesische Armee* lost between 10 and 14/2/1814. According to a letter from Gneisenau on 28/4/1814, the total was only twenty-seven. The higher figures usually quoted include three French guns previously taken from Macdonald that were then lost to Napoleon. Some captured guns were probably double-counted: for example, those lost during Sacken's retreat on the night of 11–12/2/1814 could have been included in the total for either Montmirail or Château-Thierry. Pertz and Delbrück, v. 4, p. 242; Müffling, p. 446; Unger, v. 2, p. 187.
30. Napoleon, v. 27, no. 21255. Napoleon's massed battery had in fact contained just 36 guns, but it helped him to dominate the battlefield.
31. *The Times* (London), 28/2/1814.
32. Unger, v. 2, p. 189; August von Preußen, p. 61. The other brigade, the 9th, reinforced the corps from the Rhine on 24/2/1814.
33. Blücher, pp. 229–30.

Chapter 9: 'They were swept away in the whirlpool'

(pages 69–81)

1. Thurn und Taxis, p. 213.

2. Kraehe, pp. 297–8.
3. The figure of 50,000 includes Oudinot, Victor, and Macdonald, and Napoleon's mobile reserve. It does not include Pajol, Pacthod, Allix, and two newly formed provisional Young Guard divisions, which were covering the country south of Guignes and guarding the Seine bridges near Paris.
4. Weil, *La campagne*, v. 2, pp. 134–5, 278; Janson, v. 1, p. 279. The forces opposed to the *Hauptarmee* did not include Marmont and Mortier's corps in the Marne sector, as they were containing the *Schlesische Armee*. Some of Napoleon's 50,000 troops did not reach Guignes in time for the Battle of Mormant, hence his local superiority over Pahlen was ten to one.
5. Fain, p. 109; Paulin, p. 279.
6. Griois, v. 2, pp. 296–8.
7. Lemaitre, p. 261.
8. Lemaitre, pp. 264–5.
9. Löwenstern, *Mit Graf Pahlens Reiterei*, pp. 210–12.
10. Weil, *La campagne*, v. 2, p. 278.
11. Castéras-Villemartin, p. 157.
12. Victor's new corps was composed of Charpentier and Boyer de Rebeval's Young Guard divisions. Napoleon had initially intended to give Victor a command outside the army. But Victor wrote on 21/2/1814 requesting to serve with him as he regarded it as every Frenchman's duty to make a supreme effort to expel the Allied invaders. AN AF/IV/1669B (2), doc 262, Victor to Napoleon, 21/2/1814.
13. Bertin, p. 134. Villaron is now Les Ormeaux, a tower-block estate.
14. Biot, pp. 181–2.
15. Biot, pp. 186–7.
16. AN AF/IV/1667 (2), doc 297, Berthier to Napoleon, 21/2/1814; Braive, p. 499.
17. The Yonne bridge had been blown up by the French before they abandoned Montereau on the night of 13–14/2/1814, and the Allies had temporarily repaired the destroyed arch with a wooden span. Some accounts suggest a series of cavalry charges, including units other than Pajol's men. Subervie's light cavalry brigade from the V Cavalry Corps may have charged into the suburb, with a handful of men of the *3e Chasseurs à cheval* penetrating up to the bridges before being forced to withdraw. Napoleon committed most of his escort squadrons to exploit Pajol's success. Anon, *De la campagne de Saxe*, p. 124; Rembowski, p. 456.
18. Fain, pp. 113–14.
19. Beauchamp, v. 2, pp. 233–4; Pougiat, p. 403; Anon, *De la campagne de Saxe*, pp. 127–8.
20. When the gun began to fire, he was actually at some distance from it and observing the Allies through a telescope. Anon, *De la campagne de Saxe*, pp. 127–8. However, Boulart of the Guard artillery claimed that Napoleon personally aimed the guns of one of his batteries that he, Boulart, had established on a terrace beside the *Château* de Surville. Boulart did not mention Napoleon's supposed remark about the cannonball that was to kill him. Boulart, p.315.
21. Pillersdorff, pp. 433, 436.
22. Pillersdorff, pp. 438–9.
23. Napoleon, v. 27, no. 21327.
24. Du Casse, *Mémoires*, v. 10, p. 139; Anon, *De la campagne de Saxe*, pp. 133–4.
25. Weil, *La campagne*, v. 2, p. 326.
26. Schwarzenberg, *Briefe*, pp. 376–7.
27. Rahden, part 1, pp. 255–6.
28. Thielen, pp. 221–2.
29. Ditfurth, p. 155.
30. By setting fire to the city Wrede would have deprived Napoleon of its resources and made it dangerous to bring ammunition through the streets for a close pursuit.
31. The treaty was dated 1/3/1814. Some sources give 9/3/1814 as the date on which it was signed. But rather than signing a single document, the plenipotentiaries of the four powers signed separate documents, each between two powers, so that the treaty could be ratified by the respective monarchs. Therefore, the treaty may have been signed during the course of several days. Lamarre, pp. 70, 78, 86, 136–9.

Chapter 10: Stalemate

(pages 82–99)

1. The *Schlesische Armee* was about 56,000 men strong immediately before its defeats by Napoleon on 10–14/2/1814. It lost about 13,000 men in those defeats but was restored within days to about 53,000 men as reinforcements arrived from the Rhine. Then, at the end of February and beginning of March, Blücher not only united with the 44,000 men under Winzingerode and Bülow, but was joined by another part of Langeron's corps from the Rhine. (Langeron's final element, the Russian 8th Infantry Corps under Saint-Priest, had to halt at Vitry and served to connect Blücher and Schwarzenberg's armies.)
2. Henckel von Donnersmarck, p. 291. *Aböllino der grosse Bandit* was a famous romantic novel written by Heinrich Zschokke and published in the 1790s. The hero of the story, a Neapolitan count, had two guises, one of which was Aböllino, a big outlaw.
3. Napoleon, v. 27, no. 21439. Moreau was brought before a council of war, but survived because Paris fell before he could be shot.
4. Petre, *Napoleon at bay*, pp. 113–16.
5. Varnhagen von Ense, *Leben des Generals Grafen Bülow*, pp. 361–2.
6. Henckel von Donnersmarck, pp. 591–7; Varnhagen von Ense, *Leben des Generals Grafen Bülow*, pp. 362–3; Müffling, pp. 149, 151–2; Nostitz, part 5, pp. 121–2.
7. Napoleon, v. 27, nos 21416, 21449.
8. Napoleon, v. 27, no. 21453.
9. Mikhailovsky-Danilevsky, pp. 221–2.
10. Mikhailovsky-Danilevsky, pp. 223–4; Löwenstern, *Mémoires*, v. 2, p. 337.
11. Mir, *La Garde impériale*, p. 24.
12. Litre, p. 355.
13. Mikhailovsky-Danilevsky, p. 225.
14. Mikhailovsky-Danilevsky, p. 229.
15. Henckel von Donnersmarck, p. 296.
16. The Ailette was a minor stream but was hemmed in by hills, so the ravine as a whole was difficult to cross. Winzingerode would have done better simply to order his cavalry to cross wherever it could and reunite at a fixed location by a certain time. Müffling, p. 480; Langeron, p. 419.
17. Löwenstern, *Mémoires*, v. 2, p. 338.
18. Napoleon, v. 27, no. 21454; Houssaye, p. 192. Napoleon had another 8,000 men (Christiani and Poret de Morvan's divisions) in reserve. The Russian total of 22,500 comprised Vorontsov's units and Sacken's cavalry under Vasilchikov, but not Sacken's infantry in reserve.
19. Rembowski, p. 471.
20. At Vauchamps the Allies had lost a quarter of their men, but French losses had been far lighter.
21. Martinien, pp. 16, 26.
22. Weil, *La campagne*, v. 3, pp. 182–3.
23. Some Prussians even suspected that Winzingerode's mistakes had been deliberate. Müffling, pp. 474, 483–4; Rahden, part 1, p. 282.
24. Petre, *Napoleon at bay*, p. 199. In order to concentrate as many troops as possible, the *Schlesische Armee* had abandoned the fortress of Soissons.
25. Petre, *Napoleon at bay*, pp. 116, 138.
26. Alberti, p. 88. Alberti was in Kleist's corps.
27. Reiche, part 2, p. 75; Müffling, p. 484; Unger, v. 2, p. 211.
28. Fabvier, p. 50.
29. Henckel von Donnersmarck, pp. 300–1.
30. Müffling, pp. 157–8; Schwarzenberg, *Briefe*, pp. 383–5; Marie-Louise, p. 154.
31. Steffens, p. 152.
32. From 27/2/1814 to 9/3/1814 inclusive.
33. Napoleon, v. 27, no. 21461.
34. The debris of one of the five divisions, Meunier's, was used to help garrison Soissons and

Compiègne. The other four divisions (from Ney and Victor's corps, and Poret de Morvan's division from Mortier's corps) formed two divisions under Curial and Charpentier. Weil, *La campagne*, v. 3, p. 262.
35. Müffling, p. 173.
36. Pertz and Delbrück, v. 4, p. 211.
37. *The Times* (London), 18/3/1814.
38. Nostitz, part 5, p. 136; Müffling, pp. 173, 516.
39. Langeron, p. 482.
40. Reiche, part 2, p. 82.
41. Schwarzenberg, *Briefe*, pp. 382–3. Unofficial reports of Blücher's victory at Laon reached Troyes that day, 12/3/1814. Thurn und Taxis, pp. 267–8.
42. Granier, pp. 219–20.
43. Golitsyn, pp. 101–2.
44. Zhmodikov, v. 2, p. 23; Lomier, *Histoire*, p. 410; Ségur, v. 7, pp. 17–18.
45. *Le Moniteur*, 5/11/1813 and 27/2/1814; Lomier, *Histoire*, p. 411.
46. Pelleport, v. 2, p. 109. Ségur claimed that he was not properly supported, but his memoirs are not always reliable and in the thick of the fight he could not be expected to take a balanced overview of the situation.
47. Napoleon did push some cavalry across a repaired bridge to the north bank of the Vesle, to encourage the Russians to evacuate Reims by threatening their line of retreat. But it would have taken too long for his entire army to cross. Weil, *La campagne*, v. 3, p. 269.
48. Weil, *La campagne*, v. 3, p. 269.
49. The victory at Reims had no impact on the Paris stock market, where share prices had been falling since the beginning of March and would continue to do so for the rest of the month.
50. Faré, p. 321.

Chapter 11: 'We are afraid of fighting'
(pages 100–12)
1. Castlereagh, v. 9, pp. 336–7, letter of 12/3/1814.
2. Napoleon, v. 27, no. 21506.
3. Houssaye, pp. 284–5.
4. At La Rothière Schwarzenberg had delegated control of the battle to Blücher.
5. The *Kronprinz* would run into a separate fight that afternoon, 6 miles west of Arcis, when his leading units repelled a cavalry division that was marching to join Napoleon.
6. Ségur, v. 7, pp. 49–50.
7. Thurn und Taxis, p. 276.
8. Ségur stated that the explosion merely wounded the horse. Ségur, v. 7, pp. 49–50.
9. Fain, p. 191. Ségur, not always a reliable witness, claimed that Exelmans was going to shout a warning but Sébastiani supposedly told him not to do so, as Napoleon clearly wanted to get himself killed.
10. Schwarzenberg, *Briefe*, p. 387.
11. Griois, v. 2, pp. 317–18; Thurn und Taxis, pp. 278, 282.
12. Grabowski, pp. 225–6.
13. Thurn und Taxis, p. 284.
14. Schwarzenberg, *Briefe*, p. 386.
15. According to Pierre Finot, an *adjoint* at the *mairie*, the French crossed the Aube at three points: the main bridge in the town; a pontoon bridge near Villette; and the bridge of the *moulin* de Cherlieu above Arcis. Beuve, p. 25.
16. Schwarzenberg, *Briefe*, p. 387.
17. Stanhope, pp. 7–8; Clausewitz, *La campagne*, p. 148.
18. Müffling, pp. 457–8.
19. Müffling, pp. 402–3.
20. Napoleon, v. 27, nos 21535 and 21536; Fain, pp. 195–6; Pétiet, p. 72.
21. Napoleon, v. 27, nos 21536 and 21538.

22. Houssaye, p. 444.
23. Pacthod's division, and the smaller one under Amey which came under his overall command at Fère-Champenoise, had existed for less than two months. But they had already seen action in minor combats, and at Montereau and Bar-sur-Aube in February.
24. Weil, *La campagne*, v. 4, pp. 30–1.
25. The regiment mitigated its losses in horses by capturing twenty from the French. Starklof, *Geschichte . . . vierten Reiterregiments*, pp. 211–12.
26. Weil, *La campagne*, v. 4, p. 2; Janson, v. 2, p. 357.
27. Houssaye and Weil criticised Marmont for not retreating directly on Sézanne on the evening of 25/3/1814, but his troops had already covered over 22 miles and therefore halted on the high ground at Allemant. Houssaye is more reasonable when he criticises Mortier for attacking La Ferté-Gaucher frontally and then deciding to retreat on Provins. Houssaye, p. 385; Weil, *La campagne*, v. 4, p. 16.

Chapter 12: Paris

(pages 113–21)
1. Bairoch, Batou, and Chèvre, *passim*.
2. Klein, p. 355.
3. Houssaye, p. 489.
4. Marie-Louise, p. 170; Marigny, p. 49.
5. Laon was almost as large a battle in terms of the total numbers of troops on both sides, but was fought on a much narrower front and directly affected far fewer civilians. Craonne was a more intense battle in that a higher proportion of those engaged became casualties. But Paris was bloodier in terms of the total numbers of casualties.
6. Wellington would encounter similar problems when attacking the city of Toulouse from three sides on 10/4/1814, along a semi-circular front nearly 10 miles long. Major-General Ange, *baron* de Damas led a Russian grenadier regiment into action at the Battle of Paris and later recalled how he was not entirely sure where he was, for 'I had no map, the region was unknown to me, and Paskevitch [my divisional commander] knew no more than me'. Damas, v. 1, p. 169.
7. Boucher de Perthes, v. 3, pp. 50–3, 67–71.
8. Reinhard, pp. 391, 414–15.
9. Ditfurth, pp. 159–63.
10. Napoleon himself was the commander-in-chief of the *Garde nationale de Paris*, but had entrusted its command to Joseph on leaving the capital. Moncey was the second-in-command but the effective commander.
11. Houssaye, p. 518; Langeron, pp. 469–70; Löwenstern, *Mémoires*, v. 2, pp. 380–1.
12. Odiot was the acting commander of the *2e légion* of the *Garde nationale de Paris*.
13. In reality, resistance continued elsewhere even after the incident at the *barrière* de Clichy. For instance, the garrison of the town of Saint-Denis, 5.5 miles north of Paris, capitulated only on 31/3/1814.
14. Blanc, p. 124. La Thuille's establishment is said to have had increased numbers of customers after 1814, as they were drawn by popular interest in its role during the battle. Its site, at no. 7, *avenue* de Clichy, is now occupied by a cinema.
15. Blanc, pp. 110, 115–16.
16. La Combe, p. 9; Blanc, pp. 124–5; Beulé, pp. 8–9.
17. A statue of a *polytechnicien* was erected in the courtyard of the *Ecole* in 1914 to commemorate the 100th anniversary of the defence of Paris. Five years later a replica was presented to the US Military Academy at West Point. Callot and Journau, p. 158; Löwenstern, *Mit Graf Pahlens Reiterei*, pp. 230–1; Löwenstern, *Mémoires*, v. 2, pp. 374–5; Sautai, pp. 17, 22–5, 75.
18. Duchesne de Gillevoisin, pp. 454–6.
19. Etienne de Jouy, p. 37. The *chevau-léger lancier* is from a Polish regiment of the line and not the famous regiment of the Imperial Guard.
20. Reinhard, pp. 391, 414–15; Nostitz, part 5, p. 136.

21. Calculated from statistics in Janson, v. 2, p. 439, and Pfister, p. 429. The losses given by Janson include those suffered in the actions on 29/3/1814.
22. Bégis, pp. 14–20.
23. Granier, pp. 228–9.
24. Löwenstern, *Mit Graf Pahlens Reiterei*, p. 230.
25. Moscow was Russia's religious capital, St Petersburg being the political capital. Some of the Allies' more experienced German soldiers would have been the only troops in history to have marched triumphantly into both Moscow and Paris, having entered the former in 1812 as part of Napoleon's *Grande armée*.
26. Girod de l'Ain, p. 350; Starklof, *Geschichte . . . Zweiten Reiter-Regiments*, pp. 552–3.
27. Reinhard, pp. 415–16, 418.
28. Pasquier, v. 2, pp. 254–5; Le Borgne, v. 1, p. 331.
29. Löwenstern, *Mémoires*, v. 2, p. 372, 388; Chuquet, pp. 88–9; Houssaye, p. 560; Rochechouart, p. 365; Pétiet, p. 37.
30. Steffens, p. 162. Marble Arch was originally an entrance gateway for Buckingham Palace, but was moved to the north-eastern corner of Hyde Park in 1851. Nash built a house for himself on Regent Street in 1818–23, which had shops on the ground floor, as he had seen in Paris. Morley, p. 273.
31. Barany, p. 55.
32. Montclos, p. 15; Aymes, p. 31; Keep, pp. 254–7.
33. Blayney, v. 2, p. 428; Reinhard, p. 423.
34. Rodriguez, pp. 81–2; Uxkull, pp. 184, 186, 192.
35. Rodriguez, p. 92; Poumiès de la Siboutie, pp. 138–9; Pasquier, v. 2, p. 274.
36. Gold, pp. 425–8.

Chapter 13: The end of the war
(pages 122–7)
1. Schwarzenberg, *Briefe*, p. 388; Quesné, v. 2, p. 277.
2. Houssaye, p. 413.
3. Weil, *La campagne*, v. 4, p. 250.
4. According to *Maréchal* Macdonald, a shortage of ammunition (and the difficulties of replenishing it in the event of a major battle) cast doubt on the feasibility of an advance by Napoleon on Paris. Arms manufactories had been lost as a result of the invasion. The *préfet* of the Loire had tried to evacuate the manufactory from St-Etienne after the Austrians occupied the nearby city of Lyon. He promised the workers the same pay at the new seat of his *préfecture*, but found it impossible to evacuate all the wood and tools, which were dispersed since many of the employees worked from home. Gras, *L'invasion . . . 1814*, pp. 38, 44. Macdonald, p. 265.
5. The significance of the cryptic message sent to the Allies from an associate of Talleyrand, urging them to stride boldly forward, has been exaggerated. The Allies did not advance on Paris until a fortnight later, after intercepting despatches from the capital's authorities that informed Napoleon of the unstable situation there.
6. Webster, *The foreign policy of Castlereagh, 1812–1815*, p. 248.
7. The Empress stopped at Rambouillet palace on 29/3/1814; Chartres on the 30th; Châteaudun on the 31st; Vendôme on 1/4/1814; and reached Blois on the 2nd. Tours had originally been selected as the Empress's new residence, but was crammed with sick and wounded, and stricken with an epidemic. Blois was therefore chosen instead, and Corvisart, Napoleon's *premier médecin* who was attending the Empress, asked for the hospitals and prisoner-of-war depots there to be transferred before her arrival. Ganière, p. 235; Bausset, v. 2, pp. 251, 254.
8. Fleury and Gille, p. 14.
9. Bertier de Sauvigny, p. 96.
10. After the Treaty of Fontainebleau Maubreuil was apparently sent to assassinate Napoleon on his way through France into exile, as his presence on Elba would be too close to France

for the Bourbons to be secure. Maubreuil was also authorised to recover state property in the hands of the Bonapartes, and this was intended to serve as a cover for his real mission. Maubreuil later claimed that he was reluctant to carry out the assassination. On 21/4/1814 he intercepted and robbed Catherine, the wife of Napoleon's brother Jérôme, of her diamonds. He probably took this action as a way of extracting himself from the undertaking he had given to assassinate Napoleon. Vizetelly, p. 179; Houssaye, p. 595.
11. Levavasseur, pp. 238–9.
12. Vanity, the major flaw in Marmont's character, helps explain his actions. But it should also be noted that he was the only one of the *maréchaux* in a position to defect with his corps, since he was deployed at the head of the army, nearest Paris.
13. Bausset, v. 2, p. 299.
14. Hillemand, pp. 71–8.
15. Schwarzenberg, *Briefe*, p. 393; Semmel, p. 152.
16. Zins, p. 103.
17. Bausset, v. 2, pp. 286–7.
18. Chamans de Lavallette, v. 2, p. 102.
19. Thus established by the Restoration, parliamentary government would survive in France until 1848. Mansel, *Louis XVIII*, p. vii.
20. Webster, *The foreign policy of Castlereagh, 1812–1815*, p. 229; Schroeder, *passim*.

Chapter 14: Napoleon's finest campaign?

(pages 128–41)
1. Bausset, v. 2, p. 242.
2. Langeron, pp. 399–400; Stanhope, pp. 7–8.
3. Hortense, v. 2, pp. 174–5. Napoleon again compared the two campaigns while on St Helena: Bertrand, v. 1, p. 219.
4. Fain, p. 177.
5. Castlereagh, v. 9, p. 373. Catiline (Lucius Sergius Catilina) was an Ancient Roman politician. He had won a reputation as a soldier but is best remembered for conspiring against the aristocratic Senate.
6. The main campaign theatre of 1814 covered some 4,800 square miles.
7. Arcis-sur-Aube began with both sides on the offensive, and it was only part of the way through the second day that Napoleon finally abandoned the idea of attacking and sought simply to cover his retreat.
8. Napoleon returned (sometimes more than once) to four locations he had previously occupied: Troyes, Nogent-sur-Seine, Doulevant and Saint-Dizier. He spent four nights at Troyes, on 23–26 February, and four nights at Reims, on 13–16/3/1814. (On 23/2/1814 he stayed at the *Château* de Pouilly on the outskirts of Troyes before moving to the town centre for the next three nights, but I have counted these four nights as being at the single location of Troyes.) Even on days when Napoleon did not transfer his quarters, he sometimes made excursions. While based at Chavignon on 8–10/3/1814, he moved forward on both the 9th and 10th to direct the Battle of Laon before returning to his quarters in the evening.
9. Napoleon spent the night in isolated farms on 11 and 12/2/1814, after the Battles of Montmirail and Château-Thierry.
10. Marie-Louise, pp. 103, 157; Girod de l'Ain, p. 348.
11. Girod de l'Ain, pp. 346–7.
12. Bertin, p. 221; Fain, p. 103.
13. The total distance of 1,100 miles refers to the displacement of Napoleon's quarters from one location to the next, following the route on the ground, not as the bird flies. It includes the main excursions that Napoleon made, for example to the Battlefield of Laon during his stay at Chavignon on 8–10/3/1814, but does not include his minor movements, for example rides around a battlefield. The overall distance he travelled would, therefore, have been even higher.
14. The land area of Connecticut. Equivalents in the United Kingdom would be three times the

distance between London and Edinburgh, largely contained within an area little more than half of Wales.

15. Napoleon travelled an average of 17 miles a day between the morning of 25/1/1814 and the morning of 31/3/1814. But this included days when he moved particularly fast to join his army on 25/1/1814, and to precede it back towards Paris on 30 and 31/3/1814. During the time he was actually with his army, he covered an average of 14 miles a day, but this included twelve days when his headquarters were stationary. On the days that he was in movement with his army, he covered an average of 17 miles a day.
16. Schwarzenberg transferred his headquarters an average of 2.7 times a week. The four towns were Troyes, Chaumont, Colombey-les-deux-Eglises, and Bar-sur-Aube. Blücher transferred his headquarters an average of 4.2 times a week.
17. Langeron, p. 425.
18. Bertrand, v. 1, p. 219.
19. Napoleon had begun the campaign with a *manoeuvre sur les derrières* but its failure resulted in his defeat at La Rothière and subsequent adoption of the central position.
20. The proportion of Imperial Guard units in the mobile reserve remained consistent at between 70 and 75 per cent throughout the campaign. Not all the Imperial Guard was used in the mobile reserve, partly because it had grown so large compared to the line and partly because the detached covering corps needed to be stiffened with some Imperial Guard units. The 2nd Old Guard Division (which contained more junior regiments than the 1st Division) formed the core of Mortier's detached group in the Marne sector. In fact, Mortier's group was composed almost wholly of Imperial Guard formations, although only the 2nd Old Guard Division remained under him throughout the campaign. The 5th Young Guard Division remained in the Seine sector as it had been assigned to Oudinot's group when Napoleon first took the field. The experienced Peninsular troops of the VII Corps and the VI Cavalry Corps also remained under Oudinot in the Seine sector, except for Leval's division (detached briefly in February), Roussel's *dragon* division (detached to the Marne at the end of February), and a brigade of Pierre Boyer's division (attached to Ney's corps in March).
21. AN AF/IV/1668 (2), doc 17, Marchand to Napoleon, 3/2/1814; AN F/7/3835, report of 3/3/1814. It was not just the Old Guard infantry that benefited from *transport en poste*. For example, Napoleon informed Joseph on 7/2/1814 that he was going to have some *Garde nationale* battalions transferred from Soissons to Meaux by *transport en poste*. Requisitioned carts were also used to move infantry reinforcements from Soult's army, but rain, bad roads, and inadequate numbers of horses caused delay. Du Casse, *Mémoires*, v. 10, p. 55; Lefebvre de Béhaine, v. 4, p. 314.
22. Napoleon, v. 27, no. 21138.
23. Litre, pp. 346, 366, 370–1, 373; Boulart, pp. 317–18.
24. Litre, pp. 326, 356.
25. AN AF/IV/1669B (1), doc 172, Oudinot from Provins, 10/2/1814; Du Casse, *Mémoires*, v. 10, p. 74.
26. Fain, p. 78; Pougiat, p. 72; Martin, p. 236.
27. AN AF/IV/1043, *Ministre de la police générale* to Napoleon, 23/2/1814; Godard d'Aucour, p. 197.
28. Robb, p. 146; Charton, pp. 258–9.
29. AN F/7/3782, *bulletin* of the *police générale*, 6 and 7/3/1814.
30. AN AF/IV/1043, *Ministre de la police générale* to Napoleon, 16/2/1814.
31. Beuve, pp. 20–2.
32. Fain, pp. 103–4.
33. Steenackers, pp. 106–7.
34. Napoleon, v. 27, no. 21531; Du Casse, *Mémoires*, v. 10, pp. 55, 73, 113. Savary wrote to reassure Napoleon on 8/2/1814 that he was better served than he thought. Savary explained that he had agents east of Paris, for example at Meaux and between Lagny and Coulommiers. Savary also had information from travellers on the road from Châlons to Paris. AN AF/IV/1043, *Ministre de la police générale* to Napoleon, 8/2/1814.

35. ADA 14R69, Jan de la Hamelinaye to *préfet* of the Aube, 24/1/1814; *The Times*, London, 18/3/1814.
36. Godard d'Aucour, p. 117; Benaerts, p. 166; Weil, *La campagne*, v. 1, p. 237.
37. Foncin, pp. 65, 70.
38. Weil, *La campagne*, v. 1, p. 95.
39. Nostitz, part 5, p. 75; Müffling, p. 439.
40. Weil, *La campagne*, v. 1, p. 95.
41. Janot, p. 103.
42. A Russian colonel captured at Etoges during the Battle of Vauchamps on 14/2/1814 provided intelligence to his captors. AN AF/IV/1669B (1), doc 215, Marmont to Napoleon, 14/2/1814. Late in March groups of prisoners were brought in at all hours of the day to the *Schlesische Armee* and were sent to an officer with the task of interrogating them. Müffling, p. 500.
43. Poltoratzky, pp. 2–5.
44. Weil, *La campagne*, v. 1, p. 71.
45. Napoleon presumably calculated that by the time the Allies secured a copy of *Le Moniteur* of 26/1/1814, he would already be attacking them. Napoleon, v. 27, no. 21131. It was rumoured in the Bourse on 24/1/1814 that Napoleon would leave Paris that night. AN F/7/3835, report of 24/1/1814.
46. Du Casse, *Mémoires*, v. 10, p. 64.
47. When the commander of the III *Armee-Abtheilung* sent a report to Schwarzenberg from Bar-sur-Aube on 28 January, he attached the latest issues of the *Journal de l'Empire*. Weil, *La campagne*, v. 1, pp. 393–4.
48. Du Casse, *Mémoires*, v. 10, pp. 39–40.
49. Napoleon also instructed Caulaincourt, who was at the Châtillon congress, to say that the Emperor was at Bar-sur-Aube, and to send the couriers to him there. Napoleon, v. 27, nos 21393 and 21397.
50. Even on 8/1/1814, a week after the *Schlesische Armee* crossed the Rhine, Yorck was asking his advanced guard and flying corps to send him maps, since he had no knowledge of the land on the far side of the Saar river. The *Schlesische Armee* did have some plans of fortresses by the middle of January, including those of Thionville and Saarlouis. Janson, v. 1, pp. 322–3.
51. Henckel von Donnersmarck, p. 312.
52. Gaffarel, p. 30; Anon, *1814: résistance et occupation*, p. 167; Fiévet, *Histoire*, v. 2, p. 168.
53. Robb, p. 207.
54. ADA 14R3, Ney's *chef d'état-major* to *sous-préfet* of Nogent-sur-Seine, 7/2/1814.
55. The *Ministère de la guerre* had provided Ney on 5/1/1814 with some Cassini maps before his departure from Paris for Nancy. Leggiere, p. 342.
56. Robb, pp. 196–7; Müffling, p. 436.
57. Du Casse, *Mémoires*, v. 10, pp. 101–2.
58. AN AF/IV/1669 B (1), doc 224, Gourgaud to Napoleon, 15/2/1814.
59. Weil, *La campagne*, v. 1, p. 522.
60. Creveld, p. 59.
61. AN AF/IV/1668 (2), doc 18, *intendant général* to Berthier, 4/2/1814; Godard d'Aucour, p. 184; Napoleon, v. 27, no. 21164; Lefebvre de Béhaine, v. 4, p. 249.
62. Napoleon, v. 27, no. 21347. The *intendant général* reported on 27/2/1814 that supplies would be moved from Nogent-sur-Seine to Troyes mainly by river. AN AF/IV/1668 (2), doc 51, Marchand to Napoleon, 27/2/1814.
63. The ovens could not have been established earlier, for it had not been known that the campaign would be waged so close to Paris. Fiévet, *Histoire*, v. 2, p. 166. Lefebvre de Béhaine, v. 4, pp. 223–4; AN AF/IV/1669B (1), doc 92, Léry to Berthier, 7/2/1814; AN AF/IV/1669B (1), doc 97, report of an *officier d'ordonnance* to Napoleon from Nogent, 7/2/1814; AN AF/IV/1668 (2), doc 2, report on the services at Châlons, 24/1/1814 (stating that the twelve ovens being built at the town would probably not be ready for use until 30/1/1814).
64. Pasquier, v. 2, p. 201.
65. AN F/7/3835, report of the *préfet de police*, 3/3/1814.

66. AN AF/IV/1534, *bulletin* of the *préfecture de police*, 7/2/1814.
67. AN F/7/3835, report of the *préfet de police*, 3/3/1814.
68. Gneisenau, *Briefe*, no. 108, pp. 138.
69. Kaplan, pp. 88, 90–1, 103–5; Lioret, p. 40.
70. But it was difficult to evacuate large depots quickly and valuable supplies could be lost if positioned too far forward.
71. On 4/2/1814 the *comité de défense* heard several orders from Napoleon dated 1/2/1814. Sézanne was the *grand quartier-général*. All evacuations were to go to Epernay, Château-Thierry, La Ferté-sous-Jouarre, and then to the depots of Aisne and Seine-et-Oise. From Sézanne to the field army at Brienne the *ligne d'étapes* was to go through Plancy, Luistre, Dampierre. Las Cases, *Suite*, v. 2, p. 100.
72. Napoleon, v. 27, no. 21164.
73. AN AF/IV/1668 (2), doc 17, *intendant général* to Napoleon, 3/2/1814.
74. Napoleon, v. 27, no. 21352.
75. Ségur, v. 6, p. 341.
76. Napoleon, v. 27, no. 21347; Godard d'Aucour, pp. 130–1.
77. The Allies also needed large numbers of shoes. Every cobbler in the *département* of the Haute-Marne was ordered on 18/2/1814 to make two pairs of shoes for the Allied forces. Steenackers, p. 253.
78. AN AF/IV/1668 (2), doc 24, *intendant général* to Napoleon, 30/1/1814; Uxkull, p. 171; Weil, *La campagne*, v. 4, p. 222; Pfister, p. 415.
79. AN AF/IV/1668 (2), doc 17, *intendant général* to Napoleon, 3/2/1814. On 9/2/1814 the *intendant général* explained to Berthier that he was writing again to the *Ministre directeur* about this request. AN AF/IV/1668 (2), doc 45, *intendant général* to Berthier, 9/2/1814.
80. AN AF/IV/1670 (1), doc 111, Mortemart to Napoleon, 8/3/1814.
81. Pasquier, v. 2, pp. 149–50.

Chapter 15: A protracted, attritional struggle?
(pages 142–9)
1. Quintin, p. 25. The figure of nineteen *colonel*s for 1814 is for the *Grande armée* under Napoleon's command. The figures are those of *colonel*s who were killed or mortally wounded, or who went missing or died on campaign from disease, exhaustion, or accidents.
2. Kissinger, p. 127.
3. Lefol, p. 33.
4. Schwartz, v. 2, p. 109. As late as 17/3/1814 the Russian diplomat Karl, Count von Nesselrode thought that it would take some more months of war to finish Napoleon. Nesselrode, v. 5, pp. 179–80.
5. Napoleon has been criticised for occupying enemy capitals rather than concentrating on destroying the field army, but occupying a capital is often justifiable for its psychological effect, its control of the central road hub (as with Madrid in 1808), and its attack on the enemy's cohesion.
6. Wellington, *The dispatches*, v. 11, pp. 384–7, Wellington to Bathurst, 21/12/1813.
7. In February, for example, Napoleon instructed Marie-Louise to tell Augereau's wife to write and spur him into action. He also ordered Joseph to talk to Augereau's wife, and to have the *dames du palais* talk to her. Zins, p. 131; Napoleon, v. 27, no. 21356.
8. Blücher had longer experience of military service than Wellington, but not of army command: he had actively commanded an army for just half a year.
9. The rumour spread on 9/3/1814, the first day of the Battle of Laon. Rahden, part 1, p. 284.
10. Zins, p. 153.
11. On 27/2/1814 Napoleon instructed the *Ministre de la guerre* to have Suchet send a second division of 10,000 men to Lyon. It would, in fact, be diverted on the way to help counter the fall of Bordeaux on 12/3/1814. A division sent from the French Empire's *départements* in north-western Italy reached Chambéry only after 19/3/1814, followed by another at the start of April. Zins, p. 153.

12. Connelly, *Napoleon's satellite kingdoms*, p. 301.
13. Weil, *Le prince Eugène*, v. 4, p. 105.
14. Weil, *Le prince Eugène*, v. 4, pp. 105–6.
15. Weil, *Le prince Eugène*, v. 4, pp. 213–14.
16. Lefebvre de Béhaine, v. 4, pp. 317–29; Weil, *Le prince Eugène*, v. 4, p. 105.
17. Connelly, *Napoleon's satellite kingdoms*, p. 122.
18. Connelly, *Napoleon's satellite kingdoms*, pp. 307, 310.
19. The period of ten days from 9 to 18/2/1814 inclusive.

Chapter 16: Occupation

(pages 150–63)
1. Calculation based on the occupied areas of old France, and the Swiss, Rhenish, and most of the Belgian *départements*. The area occupied by the *Südarmee* is included, but not the Dutch and north German *départements*, nor the area occupied by Wellington.
2. These *Principes généraux sur l'organisation des autorités administratives des provinces françaises occupées par les troupes alliées* were amplified in a detailed instruction for the governors-general issued at Basel on 17/1/1814. Kielmansegg, p. 98.
3. Kielmansegg, p. 101.
4. Similarly, in the occupied areas of France in the First World War the Germans installed regional governors, with subordinate local commandants. Only one French *préfet* remained, and the burden of the occupation fell heavily on the local *maires*. McPhail, p. 32. In 1814 even some *maires* were ordered to leave: the *maire* of Tonnerre was instructed to withdraw to Auxerre when the *Hauptarmee* approached. Rouyer, pp. 6–7, 10.
5. Savary, v. 6, pp. 247–50, 343–4. Similarly, in Prussia in 1813 senior officials were ordered to leave when the French armies approached, but to delay their departure until the last possible moment. The local police, justice officials, and municipal officials (except for the provincial councillors) were to remain behind under occupation. Edict of 17/7/1813, quoted in Blumenthal, pp. 178–83.
6. ADA 14R1, circular of Caffarelli, 5/2/1814.
7. Steenackers, pp. 240–1; AN AF/IV/1667 (1), doc 181, copy of the *Journal de la Meurthe*, 30/1/1814.
8. Gaffarel, pp. 36–7.
9. Charton, p. 223.
10. Charton, p. 225.
11. Anon, *Relation de la cérémonie*, pp. 10, 34.
12. Kielmansegg, p. 121.
13. Weil, *La campagne*, v. 1, pp. 112–13.
14. Kielmansegg, pp. 110, 128.
15. Klein, pp. 377–8; Schwarzenberg, *Briefe*, pp. 378–9.
16. Kielmansegg, p. 113.
17. Kielmansegg, p. 139.
18. Pougiat, p. 52; Gaffarel, p. 49.
19. ADA 14R1, *préfet* of the Aube to the *maires*, 23/1/1814; ADA 14R2, *Ministre de l'intérieur* to the *préfet* of the Aube, 27/1/1814.
20. Benaerts, pp. 148, 150.
21. Pougiat, p. 468.
22. Anon, *1814: résistance et occupation*, p. 184; Descaves, p. 213; Richard, p. 362; ADA 2J502, pp. 13–14.
23. Oyon, p. 217.
24. Rouyer, p. 3.
25. Rouyer, pp. 3–4.
26. Gaffarel, p. 20.
27. ADA 14R5, undated report from *maire* of Arcis-sur-Aube to *préfet* of the Aube.
28. Noailly, p. 61.
29. Janot, pp. 32–3; Latouche, p. 583.

30. Kielmansegg, p. 109.
31. In the Aube some requisition slips were still handwritten, even in April. ADA 14R10.
32. Kielmansegg, pp. 132–3; Weil, *La campagne*, v. 2, p. 221.
33. Anon, *Relation de la cérémonie*, p. 30.
34. Arbois de Jubainville (1925), p. 20; Arnaud, v. 1, p. 180.
35. Charton, pp. 248–50.
36. Kielmansegg, pp. 119–20.
37. Rochechouart, pp. 360–2, 365–6.
38. Godard d'Aucour, pp. 189–91.
39. Kielmansegg, p. 99.
40. Napoleon, v. 27, no. 21340. Napoleon sacked Caffarelli, the *préfet* of the Aube, three days later, on 24/2/1814. Napoleon appointed Rœderer as his replacement, with Haw, an *auditeur* in the *conseil d'état*, acting as provisional *préfet* in the meantime. As early as 13/1/1814 the *Ministre de l'intérieur* had asked Napoleon to transfer Caffarelli for being unequal to the critical situation. The police *bulletin* of 10/2/1814 reported that Caffarelli had not only reached Paris, but left it for Orléans. AN F/7/3782, *bulletin* of the *police générale*, 10/2/1814.
41. Napoleon, v. 27, no. 21341.
42. ADA 14R3, *Ministre de l'intérieur* to the *sous-préfet* of Nogent-sur-Seine, 26/2/1814.
43. Carrot, p. 133.
44. AN AF/IV/1043, *Ministre de la police générale* to Napoleon, 19/2/1814.
45. AN AF/IV/1669B (1), doc 219, Kellermann to Napoleon, 14/2/1814.
46. Lefol, p. 15; Dry, p. 135. Defleury is better known as Fleury de Chaboulon.
47. Anon, *1814: résistance et occupation*, pp. 217–19.
48. Zins, p. 27; Rouyer, pp. 6–7, 10.
49. Oyon, pp. 229–30; Fiévet, *Histoire*, v. 2, p. 202; Pougiat, p. 374; Beuve, p. 26, 62; Bertin, pp. 98–9; Boulart, p. 299.
50. Schwartzkoppen, pp. 247–8; Rochechouart, p. 353.
51. Wacker, pp. 73–4.
52. Contamine, p. 23; Chuquet, p. 361.
53. Wacker, p. 77.
54. Wacker, p. 76.
55. Steenackers, pp. 295–6.
56. Bruchet, pp. 58–9.
57. Borrey, *La Franche-comté*, p. 246.

Chapter 17: The struggle to survive

(pages 164–76)

1. In contrast, *Général de division* Nicolas, *baron* Roussel d'Hurbal had been born in 1763 at Neufchâteau (now in the *département* of the Vosges but at the time in the Duchy of Lorraine, which became part of France only in 1766). Roussel entered Austrian service in 1782 and fought against France during the Revolutionary and Napoleonic Wars until the end of the 1809 campaign. After Napoleon made an alliance with Austria, Roussel entered French service in 1811 and fought for him in 1814.
2. Reiche, part 2, pp. 87–8.
3. Mansuy, p. 293.
4. Fane, *The letters*, p. 167. Beggars were also common at Nancy. Mansuy, p. 296.
5. Gain de Montaignac, pp. 38–9.
6. Reinhard, p. 391.
7. Ditfurth, pp. 156–7.
8. Müffling, pp. 118, 434.
9. Janot, p. 30.
10. Löwenstern, *Mit Graf Pahlens Reiterei*, p. 200; Jordan, p. 226; Löwenstern, *Mémoires*, v. 2, pp. 375–6.

11. Beuve, p. 77; Fleury, *Histoire*, p. 551.
12. Anon, *De la campagne de Saxe*, p. 103.
13. Borrey, *La Franche-comté*, pp. 76–7; Contamine, p. 14.
14. Fleury, *Histoire*, p. 551.
15. Guyot, pp. 13–14.
16. ADA 2J502, pp. 5–6.
17. Guyot, pp. 17–18; Reiche, part 2, pp. 48–9.
18. Raumer, p. 227; Gain de Montaignac, pp. 39–40.
19. Charton, pp. 242–3; Fiévet, *Histoire*, v. 2, p. 206; Borrey, *La Franche-comté*, p. 286; Müffling, pp. 138, 470–1.
20. Mikhailovsky-Danilevsky, pp. 9–10, 13; Müffling, pp. 116–17; Weil, *La campagne*, v. 3, p. 9.
21. Steenackers, pp. 253–5; Borrey, *La Franche-comté*, p. 169.
22. Shcherbatov, v. 1, p. 170.
23. Lefol, p. 32.
24. Charton, p. 214.
25. Houssaye, p. 58.
26. Schwartzkoppen, pp. 248–50.
27. Steenackers, p. 219.
28. Anon, *1814: résistance et occupation*, p. 260.
29. Apparently only one was shot, the other three being reprieved on the request of the *maire*. Borrey, *La Franche-comté*, p. 197.
30. Charton, pp. 257–8.
31. Arnaud, v. 1, p. 112.
32. Reiche, part 2, p. 48.
33. Pougiat, pp. 138–9; Anon, 'Les misères de l'invasion de 1814 dans l'Aube', in *La Vie en Champagne* (Dec. 1991), 39th year, no. 426, p. 7.
34. The *chaussée* was obstructed between Basel and Vesoul by the fortress of Belfort, which had to be bypassed since it refused to capitulate until after Napoleon's abdication.
35. Borrey, *La Franche-comté*, p. 168. Besides these main lines of communication, secondary routes existed, for instance through the Vosges on the line of advance of the Bavarian V *Armee-Abtheilung*. Charton, pp. 219, 239, 245–6.
36. Plotho, part 3, appendix XIV.
37. Borrey, *La Franche-comté*, pp. 167, 171.
38. Hennequin, pp. 214–15; Pétiet, pp. 68–9.
39. ADA 14R4, order of the provisional *préfet* of the Aube, 16/3/1814.
40. Raumer, p. 224.
41. Rembowski, pp. 458–9.
42. Reiche, part 2, p. 87.
43. Raumer, pp. 224–5.
44. Girod de l'Ain, pp. 353–4.
45. Steenackers, pp. 199–202; Dry, pp. 91–2; Gain de Montaignac, p. 29; Oyon, p. 230.
46. ADA 14R3, letter from Troyes to the *sous-inspecteurs forestiers*, 18/2/1814.
47. Arbois de Jubainville (1925), p. 18.
48. Steenackers, pp. 224–5.
49. Fortin, p. 180.
50. Bertin, pp. 22–3.
51. Arbois de Jubainville (1925), pp. 18–19; Fiévet, *Histoire*, v. 2, pp. 169–71.
52. Weil, *La campagne*, v. 1, p. 161.
53. Planhol and Claval, p. 280; Bertin, p. 340; Mikaberidze, p. xxvii.
54. Ostler, p. 294.
55. Krimer, v. 2, p. 100; Steenackers, p. 211; Janot, p. 37; Unger, v. 1, p. 322.
56. Anon, *1814: résistance et occupation*, p. 169; Wolfe, p. 47.
57. 'How long, most noble men, will you abuse [us]?'
58. Steenackers, p. 211.
59. Fain, p. 185.

60. Weil, *La campagne*, v. 2, p. 166.
61. Unger, v. 2, p. 202.
62. Schubert, p. 343.
63. Beuve, p. 60; Rahden, part 1, p. 272; Klein, p. 365; Steffens, p. 143; Weil, *La campagne*, v. 2, pp. 154–5.
64. Schubert, p. 166; Steffens, p. 147.
65. Steffens, p. 143; Weil, *La campagne*, v. 2, pp. 154–5.
66. Krimer, v. 2, p. 100.
67. Rahden, part 1, p. 241.
68. Grüber, p. 221.
69. Grabowski, pp. 222–3.
70. Colomb, pp. 245–6.
71. Blayney, v. 2, pp. 302, 305.
72. Desbois-Thibault, pp. 32–3, 36–7, 333; Fiévet, *Madame Veuve Clicquot*, p. 59–61; Grabowski, p. 223.

Chapter 18: Resistance

(pages 177–87)
1. The ratio is for old France. 'Town' is defined as a settlement of over 2,000 inhabitants, concentrated in one place rather than scattered throughout a commune. Lepetit, p. 399.
2. Robb, p. 53.
3. Uxkull, p. 171.
4. Löwenstern, *Mit Graf Pahlens Reiterei*, p. 209.
5. Robb, pp. 75–6.
6. Benaerts, pp. xvi, xxii, 22, 32.
7. Napoleon passed through two of the three towns on his way from Elba to Paris. Burgundy was likely to bear the brunt of the Allied invasion in 1815, since Napoleon intended to take the offensive on the other major front, in the north. Gras, *L'invasion . . . 1814*, p. 56.
8. Houssaye, p. 35; Fortin, p. 208.
9. ADA 2J502, pp. 30–3; Godard d'Aucour, pp. 193–4.
10. Fiévet, *Histoire*, v. 2, pp. 168–9.
11. Pougiat, p. 88.
12. Latouche, pp. 347–50.
13. Lioret, p. 19; Anon, *Relation de la cérémonie*, p. 17; Pougiat, pp. 58–60.
14. Napoleon, v. 27, nos 21061, 21403. On 14/1/1814 Napoleon ordered the *levée en masse* to be authorised in the Ardennes and the Marne. Leggiere, p. 365.
15. The Revolutionary *levée en masse* fell short of its rhetoric about mobilising the entire population. Griffith, pp. 80–1. There were even earlier instances of the *levée en masse*, during the *Ancien Régime*. King Philippe IV, for example, called to arms all Frenchmen aged between 18 and 60 after a disastrous battlefield defeat at Courtrai in 1302.
16. Napoleon, v. 27, no. 21061.
17. Howard, *The Franco-Prussian war*, p. 252.
18. Napoleon, v. 27, no. 21055.
19. Napoleon, v. 27, no. 21070.
20. In the twentieth century *partisans* have become seen as ideologically motivated guerrilla fighters. But previously, they could be either regular troops or volunteers used in an irregular role.
21. Leggiere, p. 298; Benoit, pp. 236–7.
22. Leggiere, p. 73.
23. AN AF1667 (2), doc 372, letter from La Ferté-sous-Jouarre, 13/3/1814; AN F/7/3782, *bulletin* of the *police générale*, 14/3/1814.
24. Godard d'Aucour, pp. 149, 161–4; Benaerts, p. 6.
25. Benoit, p. 263.
26. Benaerts, pp. 80–1.

27. Benaerts, p. 10.
28. Roux, v. 2, pp. 224, 238, 241–2; Weil, *La campagne*, v. 1, p. 328; Beauchamp, v. 1, pp. 404–5; Lefebvre de Béhaine, v. 4, pp. 353–4; Gras, *L'invasion . . . 1814*, p. 43.
29. Chuquet, pp. 79, 345. Wolff and Brice tried to concert their operations and passed information to each other, but were too distant to be able to do so effectively.
30. Roux, v. 2, pp. 210–11.
31. AN F/7/3835, report of 18/1/1814; AN AF/IV/1534, *bulletin* of the *préfecture de police*, 4/3/1814.
32. Lomier, *Histoire*, p. 429.
33. Foncin, pp. 59–60.
34. Arnaud, v. 1, pp. 259, 263–4.
35. Montenay, no. 163, pp. 180–1.
36. Beauchamp, v. 1, pp. 487–8. Widranges had fled to Chaumont. For the debate on whether Napoleon decided too late to spare Gouault's life, see Lenotre, pp. 214–20; and Marnat, 'Napoléon a-t-il voulu la mort de Jacques Gouault?'.
37. AN AF/IV/1043, *Ministre de la police générale* to Napoleon, 27/1/1814.
38. Du Casse, *Mémoires*, v. 10, p. 183; Beauchamp, v. 1, p. 327.
39. Montbrun had fallen back from Moret-sur-Loing only when forced to do so, and after both his flanks were threatened. He had received no orders to defend the forest of Fontainebleau tenaciously, and would have been unable to do so because of the quality of his troops and *gardes nationaux*. He believed that he had to establish communication with Napoleon's army as soon as the *Hauptarmee* forced the passage of the Loing, and he could do so only by falling back to Essonnes, since the Melun bridge was cut. Similarly, Sorbier, the *premier inspecteur général de l'artillerie*, pointed out to Napoleon on 19/2/1814 that the artillery ammunition of II Corps had not, in fact, failed at Montereau. The artillery reserves of the corps had simply withdrawn temporarily from the line of batteries when the French infantry fell back in the face of a counter-attack. Lioret, p. 75; AN AF/IV/1669B (2), doc 249, Sorbier to Napoleon, 19/2/1814.
40. Another reason for Napoleon to foment risings at this time was to make it easier for troops from his fortresses to come and reinforce his field army by breaking through the Allied units left to observe them.
41. Fain, pp. 161–2; Dry, pp. 166–7; Gras, *L'invasion . . . 1814*, p. 32.
42. AN F/7/3835, report of 8/3/1814.
43. Beauchamp, v. 1, pp. 99–100; Hennequin, p. 264.
44. Napoleon, v. 27, no. 21403; Deschamps, pp. 112–13. Deschamps won promotion to *sous-lieutenant*, and, interestingly, was transferred later in the campaign to a regular regiment, the *2e Ligne*.
45. At the end of March Napoleon was sent a proposal for using Piré's light cavalry division to foment a general insurrection, but he was preoccupied by the need to return to his threatened capital. Borrey, *La Franche-comté*, p. 183; Fain, p. 182. Pétiet, p. 73.
46. Kielmansegg, p. 137; Grabowski, p. 211; Chuquet, p. 330.
47. Steenackers, pp. 142–3; Charton, pp. 253, 255–6.
48. Chuquet, pp. 328–30; Gaffarel, pp. 38–9.
49. Pougiat, pp. 271–2; ADA 14R10, Hohenlohe-Bartenstein to the *préfecture* of the Aube, 6/3/1814; and order of provisional *préfet* of the Aube, 6/3/1814.
50. Foncin, pp. 50–1.
51. Arnaud, v. 1, p. 74.
52. AN F/7/6600, dossier 4099.
53. Gaffarel, p. 42; Steenackers, pp. 143–4; Beauchamp, v. 1, pp. 540–4.
54. Mir, *La bataille de Paris*, p. 25.
55. Article nine of the Edit about the *Landsturm*, 24/3/1813, quoted in Blumenthal, pp. 163–78.
56. Gaffarel, p. 42.
57. Leggiere, pp. 369–70; Steenackers, p. 257.
58. Chuquet, pp. 326–30, 338–40, 342, 344.

Chapter 19: The propaganda war

(pages 188–201)

1. Weil, *La campagne*, v. 4, p. 308.
2. Cabanis, p. 41.
3. Godard d'Aucour, pp. 515–16.
4. The emergency controls were apparently due in part to Napoleon's dissatisfaction with blunders. AN AF/IV/1043, *Ministre de la police générale* to Napoleon, 2/2/1814 and 4/2/1814.
5. AN AF/IV/852, file 6846, docs 41 and 42. This decree, dated 4/2/1814, was sent the same day from Napoleon's headquarters at Troyes to Paris. On 7/2/1814 it was transmitted to the *Ministre de la police générale*, who was entrusted with its execution. The committee was composed of the chief editors of three newspapers, a censor, a councillor of the *Université*, and a president, Antoine, *comte* Boulay de la Meurthe, a *conseiller d'état*. The decree specified that the controls were to be applied only during the existing circumstances and were not to be publicised.
6. Napoleon complained in a letter to Joseph at 2000 on 1/3/1814 that 'the *estafette* who should have left Paris yesterday morning with my newspapers has still not reached me'. Napoleon, v. 27, no. 21404.
7. Napoleon, v. 27, no. 21316.
8. AN AF/IV/1043, *Ministre de la police générale* to Napoleon, 20/2/1814.
9. Chateaubriand, *De Buonaparte*, pp. 11–12.
10. Blayney, v. 2, p. 308; AN F/7/3782, *bulletin* of the *police générale*, 9/3/1814.
11. Vidal de la Blache, v. 2, p. 279; Rodriguez, pp. 10–11; Méneval, v. 3, p. 366; Houssaye, pp. 441, 445, 448; Dufour de Pradt, pp. 44–5; AN F/7/3835, report of 18/1/1814.
12. Napoleon, v. 27, no. 21205, Napoleon to Joseph, 7/2/1814. The *Ministre de la police générale* had written to Napoleon on 6/2/1814 to inform him that a mass that day had been followed by forty-hour prayers and a *miserere*, which had disheartened people. AN AF/IV/1043, *Ministre de la police générale* to Napoleon, 6/2/1814.
13. Du Casse, *Mémoires*, v. 10, pp. 140, 188; Napoleon, v. 27, no. 21454. Napoleon's official accounts had been called *bulletins* before 1813, and continued to be known as such informally. But in 1813 and 1814 they took the form of reports to the Empress, since he had appointed her as Regent in his absence from Paris, following an attempted *coup d'état* in October 1812.
14. *The Times* (London), 24/2/1814.
15. *Le Moniteur*, 22/1/1814.
16. Napoleon, v. 27, no. 21360, Napoleon to Joseph, 24/2/1814.
17. *Le Moniteur*, 21/2/1814.
18. Steffens, p. 144.
19. *Le Moniteur*, 6/2/1814.
20. *Le Moniteur*, 7 and 12/3/1814.
21. *Le Moniteur*, 14/3/1814.
22. *Le Moniteur*, 21/2/1814.
23. Official accounts of Leipzig and Hanau, in *Journal de Paris*, 31/10/1813 and 6/11/1813.
24. *Journal de Paris*, 25/3/1814.
25. Napoleon, v. 27, no. 21375.
26. Du Casse, *Mémoires*, v. 10, p. 108. Reports from the *auditeurs en mission* to the liberated towns were supported by systematic written evidence of the losses, signed by inhabitants and witnesses, although the versions of the reports that appeared in the newspapers were edited. AN F/7/7031, dossier of work of Adrien Cochelet, *auditeur*, on mission to Nogent-sur-Seine.
27. AN AF/IV/1043, *Ministre de la police générale* to Napoleon, 27/2/1814.
28. Napoleon had instructed Joseph on 23/2/1814 that the deputies from the liberated towns were to be heard in Paris, and their addresses displayed publicly. Napoleon, v. 27, nos 21356 and 21375.

29. AN AF/IV/1669B (2), doc 295, letter from *Général de division* Allix.
30. *Le Moniteur*, 28/2/1814.
31. AN F/7/7031, *Ministre de l'intérieur* to the *préfet* of the Seine, 27/2/1814. The report covered four sheets, so it took the whole of the 27th to post up all the copies in the streets.
32. Las Cases, *Suite*, v. 2, pp. 284–5.
33. *Le Moniteur*, 24/2/1814.
34. *Le Moniteur*, 14/3/1814.
35. *Le Moniteur*, 16/3/1814. Napoleon had claimed in a letter to Joseph of 14/3/1814 that Saint-Priest was mortally wounded by the very same gunner who had felled Moreau. This appeared in *Le Moniteur* as the same battery, apparently so as not to overstretch readers' credibility. Houssaye, p. 269.
36. Du Casse, *Mémoires*, v. 10, p. 155.
37. Beauchamp, v. 1, pp. 173–4.
38. Napoleon, v. 27, no. 21145; AN AF/IV/852, file 6846, docs 53 and 54. Napoleon instructed the *Ministre des cultes* on 30/1/1814 to prepare a draft decree for the rebuilding of the steeple. He signed a decree on 4/2/1814 for funds to be allocated for the repairs, but Eclaron remained under Allied occupation for nearly the whole of the remainder of the campaign. Napoleon III had the spire rebuilt in 1856–7.
39. Proofs of the engraving reached Napoleon on 3/3/1814. Marie-Louise, pp. 83, 96, 99, 101, 102, 103, 117, 125; Du Casse, *Mémoires*, v. 10, pp. 163–4; *Journal de Paris*, 21/3/1814.
40. Houssaye, p. 41; Méneval, v. 2, pp. 35–6; Vidal de la Blache, v. 2, pp. 279–80.
41. Quesné, v. 2, pp. 270–1.
42. Lecomte, p. 265.
43. Blayney, v. 2, pp. 343–5; Du Casse, *Mémoires*, v. 10, p. 93; Marie-Louise, p. 70.
44. AN F/7/3835, report of 2/2/1814; AN AF/IV/1534, extract of reports of 2/2/1814.
45. Bartlet, p. 336. Boucher de Perthes, v. 3, p. 6 (the letter as published is incorrectly dated 26/2/1813, instead of 1814). The *Ministre de la police générale* wrote to Napoleon on 1/2/1814 that within two days the music for *l'Oriflamme* would be engraved and the work sent to be played in the theatres of all the large towns in France. AN AF/IV/1043, *Ministre de la police générale* to Napoleon, 1/2/1814.
46. Broglie, v. 1, pp. 251–2; Welschinger, pp. 258–9; *La Gazette de France*, 17/2/1814, review of *Les héroines de Béfort*.
47. Houssaye, pp. 36–7; AF/IV/1534, *bulletin* of the *préfecture de police*, 9/3/1814. It is true that the fluctuations in share prices were sometimes based on just a few transactions, that they could be distorted by transfer and payment dates, and that they did not necessarily reflect opinion outside Paris or across the entire social spectrum. Nonetheless, the traders were from the politically important classes.
48. Marion, v. 4, pp. 345–6, 366–7, 371.
49. The news of La Rothière circulated at the Stock Exchange on 4/2/1814. Fontaine, v. 1, p. 385; AN AF/IV/1043, *Ministre de la police générale* to Napoleon, 3/2/1814; AN AF/IV/1534, *bulletin* of the *préfecture de police*, 4/2/1814.
50. Some statues and paintings were already being removed from display when Napoleon instructed the precautions to be suspended. Fontaine noted on 10/2/1814 that exhibits were replaced. Fontaine, v. 1, p. 385; Rodriguez, pp. 14–15; Du Casse, *Mémoires*, v. 10, pp. 68, 80.
51. Du Casse, *Mémoires*, v. 10, p. 73. Napoleon's fears had some justification. His mother's *château* at Pont-sur-Seine was burned down in March, and according to reports had been deliberately set on fire as an act of revenge against the imperial family. On 15/11/1813 Napoleon instructed the *Château* de Marrac near Bayonne to be burned if Wellington's army approached it, to prevent the British from sleeping in his bed. Bernard, 'Le *Château* de Pont-sur-Seine', pp. 9, 11; Napoleon, v. 26, no. 20895.
52. Fontaine, v. 1, pp. 385–6. The fact that the courier bringing the news of Champaubert arrived in the middle of a review at the Tuileries aroused suspicion that it had been staged for maximum impact. Yet the timing actually seems to have been fortuitous, since the *Ministre de la police générale* wrote to inform Napoleon of it. AN AF/IV/1043, *Ministre de*

la police générale to Napoleon, 11/2/1814; AN AF/IV/1534, extract of reports of 11/2/1814; Le Borgne, v. 1, pp. 319–20.
53. Fontaine, v. 1, p. 385.
54. Wellington, *The dispatches*, v. 11, pp. 617–18, Wellington to Bunbury, 1/4/1814.
55. Chateaubriand, *Of Buonaparte*, p. 13.
56. Cabanis, pp. 315–16; Bertin, p. 135; Underwood, pp. 37–8; AN AF/IV/1669B (2), doc 309, Mortemart to Napoleon, 24/2/1814. Bodies, either from the Battle of Montereau or from hospitals on the Seine, are known to have reached Paris by floating down the river.
57. Boucher de Perthes, v. 3, p. 7 (the letter as published is incorrectly dated 26/2/1813, instead of 1814).
58. *Journal de Paris*, 13/3/1814.
59. The effect of Craonne was lessened by rumours that Schwarzenberg's army was advancing along the Seine. AN F/7/3782, *bulletin* of the *police générale*, 8/3/1814.
60. News of the end of the Châtillon conference reached Paris on 22 or 23/3/1814, according to the *Ministre de la police générale*, but it was not announced in the newspapers. Houssaye, pp. 449, 455; Savary, v. 6, p. 349.
61. Allied propaganda was able to penetrate into the heart of France. A former French soldier was arrested in Alsace with Schwarzenberg's proclamation of 21/12/1813. He admitted that he had been sent by the Allies and was going through *communes* telling the inhabitants to welcome the Allies. Copies of the proclamation soon reached Paris. Allied proclamations were also distributed in France by smugglers, and even through the French postal system. Leggiere, p. 113; Benoit, pp. 265–6; Houssaye, p. 16; Müffling, p. 99.
62. In their efforts to win over the population the Allies used the existing local newspapers and also established their own. From 20/3/1814 the *Journal de la Meurthe* became the *Journal de la Lorraine et du Barrois*, and published articles critical of the Revolution and Empire. At the same time they sought to monopolise the means of communication. At Troyes, for example, the provisional *préfet* forbade all the printers in the city to print anything without the governor-general's permission. ADA 14R3, instruction from provisional *préfet* of the Aube, 12/2/1814; Perrin, p. 29; Cabanis, p. 308; Borrey, *La Franche-comté*, p. 186.
63. Müffling, pp. 98–9, 408–9.
64. Fiévet, *Histoire*, v. 2, pp. 183–94.
65. Du Casse, *Mémoires*, v. 10, pp. 56, 63.
66. *Le Moniteur*, 24/2/1814.
67. Although much of the population did not know the identity of the Bourbon pretender, the politically significant classes would have been aware that an exiled brother of the guillotined Louis XVI claimed the throne. Mansel, *Louis XVIII*, pp. 157–8; Bertier de Sauvigny, p. 114.
68. Mansel, *Louis XVIII*, p. 171.
69. Mansel, *Louis XVIII*, p. 162.
70. Bertier de Sauvigny, p. 74.
71. Bertier de Sauvigny, pp. 83–4.
72. Bertier de Sauvigny, p. 95; Boudon, p. 407.
73. Vimont, p. 154.
74. AN AF/IV/1670 (2), doc 11, provisional government address to the French armies, 2/4/1814.
75. During the Hundred Days in 1815 Napoleon reinforced this image by experimenting with a more liberal empire and identifying himself more with the common people. This reinterpretation of the campaign as a national war was strengthened by the invasions of 1870 and 1914. Monuments at La Rothière, Craonne, and Chalon-sur-Saône all link the fallen of 1814 with those of subsequent invasions.

Chapter 20: Population displacements and prisoners-of-war

(pages 202–14)
1. Benaerts, p. 156.
2. Foncin, p. 60.

3. Richard, p. 355.
4. ADA 2J502, pp. 7–9.
5. Beuve, pp. 83–4, 95–7.
6. Beuve, p. 51; Foncin, p. 16; Arpin, p. 22.
7. Richard, p. 362.
8. Beuve, p. 83; ADA 14R57, Javernant to provisional *préfet* of the Aube, 19/2/1814; Hantraye, *Les Cosaques*, p. 101.
9. Steenackers, p. 278; Martin and Jacob, Appendix, p. 61; Lefol, p. 29.
10. Beuve, pp. 63–4; Maindreville, 'Incendie de Méry-sur-Seine', pp. 308–9.
11. Arbois de Jubainville (1925), p. 17.
12. Auvray, pp. 557–8.
13. Coulmann, v. 1, p. 60; Descaves, p. 208.
14. AN AF/IV/1534, *bulletin* of the *préfecture de police*, 9/2/1814.
15. Godard d'Aucour, pp. 167–8; AN AF/IV/1043, *Ministre de la police générale* to Napoléon, 8, 19, and 20/2/1814.
16. On 12/3/1814, for example, Cossacks stopped the *diligence* from Compiègne to Noyon. The last *diligence* left Metz for Paris at dawn on 13/1/1814, as Marmont's rearguard left the city. Richard, p. 359; Montenay, no. 163, pp. 172, 178; Anon, *1814–1815: souvenirs des régions envahies*, p. 66.
17. Benaerts, pp. 166–7, 170–1, 174.
18. Savary, v. 6, p. 314.
19. For example, a wave began reaching Paris on 27/2/1814 as a result of Blücher's second advance on the city. AN AF/IV/1534, *bulletin* of the *préfecture de police*, 28/2/1814.
20. Pougens, pp. 260–72.
21. Blayney, v. 2, p. 282.
22. Le Borgne, v. 1, p. 320.
23. Rodriguez, p. 40.
24. Savary, v. 6, p. 320; Rodriguez, p. 39; Godard d'Aucour, p. 169; Houssaye, pp. 426–7; Du Casse, *Mémoires*, v. 10, pp. 192, 199; AN AF/IV/1043, *Ministre de la police générale* to Napoléon, 10/2/1814; AN F/7/3835, report of 28/3/1814.
25. Marie-Louise, p. 48.
26. AN AF/IV/1043, *Ministre de la police générale* to Napoléon, 8/2/1814; Castellane, v. 1, p. 248; Du Casse, *Mémoires*, v. 10, pp. 80, 90; Barère de Vieuzac, v. 3, pp. 182–3; Beauchamp, v. 1, p. 318.
27. Lemaitre, pp. 261–2.
28. Savary, v. 7, pp. 5, 58; Oudinot, pp. 307, 312–13; Hortense, v. 2, p. 192. The road to Etampes and Orléans was less congested.
29. Castellane, v. 1, p. 253; Du Casse, *Le général Arrighi*, p. 442; Las Cases, *Suite*, v. 2, pp. 284–5.
30. AN F/7/3782, *bulletin* of the *police générale*, 16/3/1814.
31. Wellington, *Supplementary despatches*, v. 8, p. 510.
32. The often-quoted figure of 100,000 Spanish prisoners in fact included other nationalities. By November 1813 there would have been about 60,000 Spanish detainees, but also about another 35,000 prisoners-of-war from other countries. Aymes, pp. 170–2, 258; Lefebvre de Béhaine, v. 3, pp. 396–7; Napoléon, v. 26, no. 20893.
33. Lewis, pp. 48, 264–6.
34. AN F/7/3311, dossier 2, docs 318, 319, 340; AN F/7/3782, *bulletin* of the *police générale*, 30 and 31/1/1814.
35. Short, p. 15; Langton, v. 1, pp. 81–2. The thirteen British depots were: Arras, Bitche, Cambrai, Givet, Longwy, Sarrelibre (now known as Saarlouis), Sedan, Valenciennes, and Verdun along the north-eastern frontier; Auxonne and Besançon near the Swiss border; and Briançon and Mont-Dauphin further south, near the Alps. Bitche, Sarrelibre, and Sedan were punishment depots, for men who had previously tried to escape or were difficult to control. Verdun was the most comfortable depot and held the socially respectable captives. Briançon was the main depot for Britons captured in the Mediterranean, so they did not have to be marched all the way to north-eastern France.

36. AN F/7/3309, dossier 2, docs 58 and 60, *Ministre de la guerre* to *Ministre de la police générale*, 11 and 18/11/1813.
37. Short gave the total number of days inaccurately as 110. Short, p. 69.
38. Wetherell, p. 329.
39. Lewis, p. 172. The figure of 8 per cent is for captives of all nationalities held during the war of 1803–14.
40. There were 958 British prisoners at Verdun on 30/11/1813 and 957 on 20/12/1813. AN F/7/3312, docs 847 and 851.
41. Langton, v. 1, p. 268; Elton, p. 257; Boys, p. 255; Blayney, v. 2, pp. 284–5.
42. The depot was ordered through Château-Thierry, Senlis, Mantes, Chartres, and Chateaudun. AN F/7/3309, dossier 4, docs 246 and 248, note of 13/1/1814, and *Ministre de la guerre* to *Ministre de la police générale*, 7/1/1814.
43. Blayney, v. 2, pp. 283–7, 301; Boys, p. 255. Some money, raised by subscription in Britain, was forwarded to a committee of responsible prisoners at Verdun, which distributed it to the needy and the other depots. Until the French Revolution it had been customary in Europe to repatriate non-combatants, such as surgeons, captains of merchantmen, and other civilians. Wolfe, pp. 2–3, 66.
44. Seslavin summoned Orléans to surrender on 18/2/1814 but immediately had to leave before he could force it to comply. The *Hauptarmee*'s defeats at Napoleon's hands had resulted in his recall.
45. Blayney, v. 2, p. 347.
46. Blayney, v. 2, p. 379; France, *Almanach*, p. 909; AN F/7/3782, *bulletin* of the *police générale*, 17/3/1814. In addition to the Verdun depot, seventeen British prisoners from various depots had reached Guéret, making a total of 1,064.
47. Weil, *La campagne*, v. 1, pp. 157, 237. According to a local account, the Spaniards had hidden until the *Schlesische Armee* arrived, and their knowledge of the French language made them useful in gathering intelligence against partisans. Arbois de Jubainville (1924), p. 584.
48. Barère de Vieuzac, v. 3, pp. 182–3; Wetherell, pp. 192, 200, 207.
49. Benaerts, pp. 134–5.
50. AN F/7/3312, doc 441, *préfet* of the Eure to *conseiller d'état*, 18/2/1814. By 20/3/1814 there were over 3,800 prisoners-of-war, mostly British, in the western *département* of the Maine-et-Loire, or one for every 106 inhabitants. The nearby *département* of Ille-et-Vilaine likewise had one prisoner for every 106 inhabitants by 20/3/1814. AN F/7/3309, docs 65 and 240.
51. Blayney, v. 2, p. 409; Short, pp. 53–4, 62.
52. Porée, pp. 21–2, 32, 34, 45, 47, 54–5, 62, 64; Gras, *L'invasion . . . 1814*, p. 33; Short, p. 21. British prisoners sometimes made French uniforms and equipment, but were rarely allowed to work outside their fortresses, partly because they might try to escape.
53. Thibaudeau, pp. 379–80; Vidal de la Blache, v. 2, pp. 368–9.
54. AN F/7/6603, dossier 4298, *sous-préfet* of Autun to *Ministre de la police générale*, 16/1/1814.
55. AN AF/IV/1043, *Ministre de la police générale* to Napoleon, 22/2/1814.
56. AN F/7/3782, *bulletin* of the *police générale*, 8/2/1814.
57. AN F/7/3782, *bulletin* of the *police générale*, 16/3/1814; AN F/7/3309, doc 66.
58. Napoleon, v. 26, nos 20893, 20920; Benaerts, p. 111.
59. Aymes, pp. 238, 461; Arbois de Jubainville (1924), p. 582.
60. Wetherell, pp. 240–1.
61. A foreigner had to have resided in France for ten consecutive years to become a French citizen. Caucanas, Cazal, and Payen, eds, pp. 245, 255.
62. Porée, pp. 65–6; Vidal de la Blache, v. 2, pp. 368–9; Barère de Vieuzac, v. 3, pp. 192–3.
63. Brett-James, p. 241.
64. Löwenstern, *Mit Graf Pahlens Reiterei*, p. 218; Beuve, p. 110; Paulin, p. 280; Pfister, *Denkwürdigkeiten*, p. 432.
65. AN F/7/6603, dossier 4328.
66. Napoleon, v. 27, no. 21235. Napoleon had wanted the *Garde nationale de Paris* to go to

Meaux, 25 miles east of Paris, to receive the prisoners and then escort them to the capital. But Moncey knew that the *gardes nationaux* would fear they were being lured out of the city so they could be incorporated into the field army. Hence, the *Garde nationale de Paris* instead received the prisoners at the *barrières* of Paris and escorted them to Versailles. Duchesne de Gillevoisin, p. 451.
67. Underwood, pp. 28–30.
68. Pfister, *Denkwürdigkeiten*, pp. 432–3.
69. Godard d'Aucour, p. 215. In Napoleon's France Freemasons were found predominantly in the bourgeoisie and administration.
70. Bertin, p. 107.
71. Napoleon, v. 27, nos 21296 and 21482; Marmont, v. 6, p. 320; Blayney, v. 2, pp. 225–6.
72. Müffling, p. 487.
73. ADA 14R5, certificate dated 2/5/1814. Pénot joined the company of *Gendarmerie* of the *département* of the Aube on 24/1/1814 and transferred to the company of the Haute-Marne on 28/2/1814.
74. Steenackers, p. 164; Godard d'Aucour, pp. 215–16.
75. ADA 2J502, pp. 45–7.
76. Delattre was ceremoniously reburied in the town cemetery in 1865, when his original burial place was about to be built on. Guimard, pp. 1–4.
77. AN F/7/3309, dossier 4, doc 240, situation of prisoners-of-war in the Ille-et-Vilaine, 20/3/1814.
78. If the detachments were no more than ten men strong they would be escorted by *gendarmes* alone. Prisoners on parole could leave for their destination on their own, after signing an obligation not to stray from the route, but might be escorted for part or all of the way if the military commander thought it necessary. Porée, p. 54, 83–90.
79. Wetherell, pp. 192–3, 195. The escort apparently left on 23/1/1814 to concentrate with other troops at Troyes. The British detachment was then guided by an invalid officer.
80. Casse, p. 103.
81. Langton, v. 2, p. 15.
82. AN F/7/3782, *bulletins* of the *police générale*, 28/1/1814 and 4/2/1814.
83. AN F/7/3782, *bulletin* of the *police générale*, 3/3/1814.
84. AN F/7/3312, docs 467 and 468, *préfet* of the Eure-et-Loire to *conseiller d'état*, 24/2/1814 and 8/3/1814.
85. AN F/7/3309, dossier 4, doc 293, letter from *auditeur* at Nantes, 1/3/1814.
86. AN F/7/3782, *bulletins* of the *police générale*, 3/3/1814, 16/3/1814, and of 20 and 21/3/1814.
87. AN F/7/6603, dossier 4298, *sous-préfet* of Autun to *Ministre de la police générale*, 16/1/1814; Arbois de Jubainville (1924), p. 584.
88. Aymes, p. 181; Porée, p. 50.
89. Chatelain, v. 2, pp. 581–2.

Chapter 21: The sick and wounded
(pages 215–20)
1. Weil, *La campagne*, v. 1, p. 434.
2. Steenackers, p. 276.
3. The *intendant de la Couronne* subsequently reported that none of the items could be spared. Marie-Louise, pp. 112, 114, 122, 125; Godard d'Aucour, p. 117; Campan, p. 130; *Journal de Paris*, 11/2/1814.
4. Anon, *Relation de la cérémonie*, p. 16.
5. Ackerknecht, p. 18.
6. Napoleon, v. 27, no. 21164. These instructions were put into effect, at least in part. The *intendant général* wrote to Napoleon from Sézanne on 3/2/1814 confirming that he had given the orders for the lines of evacuation, forbidding any sick to be taken to Paris. AN AF/IV/1668 (2), doc 17. Within days the towns of Meaux and La Ferté-sous-Jouarre in the

Marne valley were designated to receive 1,700 sick and wounded. Godard d'Aucour, pp. 139–40.
7. Dubois, pp. 33–5.
8. Godard d'Aucour, pp. 168–9.
9. Hapdé, pp. 23–4.
10. The only exceptions were to be patients whose corps were stationed in the *1re division militaire* (the regions around Paris). Dubois, pp. 36–7.
11. Napoleon, v. 27, no. 21319; Du Casse, *Mémoires*, v. 10, pp. 142–4.
12. Dubois, pp. 38–40; Du Casse, *Mémoires*, v. 10, p. 157; Pasquier, v. 2, pp. 201–2; Anon, *1814: résistance et occupation*, p. 246.
13. Poumiès de la Siboutie, pp. 133–4.
14. Lagneau, pp. 284–5; Reinhard, pp. 416–17.
15. Jamerey, p. 179; Arpin, pp. 37–9.
16. Anon, *De la campagne de Saxe*, pp. 129–30; Prinzing, p. 135.
17. The *préfet de police* preserved Paris from an epidemic after the battle of 30/3/1814 by having more than 4,000 corpses burned in a fortnight at ten furnaces. Tulard, *Nouvelle histoire*, p. 375.
18. Borrey, *La Franche-comté*, pp. 254–5.
19. ADA 14R3, order issued at Troyes for burial of dead horses, 16/2/1814; ADA 14R67, *Colonel* Aunervadel to provisional *préfet*, 16/2/1814.
20. ADA 14R10, order of Hohenlohe-Bartenstein, Troyes, 8/3/1814; ADA 14R67, order of provisional *préfet* of the Aube, 17/3/1814; ADA 14R54, extract from deliberations of the *Conseil municipal* of Bar-sur-Aube, 10/8/1816.
21. ADA 14R1, Beugnot to *préfets* of *départements*, 14/4/1814.
22. ADA 14R67, Koenigsbrunn to provisional *préfet* of the Aube, 6/5/1814.
23. ADA 14R67, letter signed by Gayot, *secrétaire-général* of the *préfecture* of the Aube, 14/7/1814.
24. Beuve, pp. 95–7.
25. Underwood, pp. 37–8.
26. *Journal de Paris*, 24/3/1814.
27. Meier, p. 136.
28. Prinzing, pp. 163–4. There is some doubt whether Richard Wagner's natural father was an actor called Ludwig Geyer.
29. Napoleon, v. 26, no. 20986.
30. *Journal de Paris*, 26/3/1814.
31. Anon, *1814: résistance et occupation*, p. 144.
32. Guillier, fold-out table entitled *Population de l'Hôpital de la Pitié: relevé des comptes moraux depuis 1803 (an XI) jusqu'en 1877*. The exact mortality rate in 1814 was 1 in 3.28.
33. Pasquier, v. 2, pp. 201–2; Prinzing, p. 157. It is unclear how much of this increased death rate was due to typhus.
34. Anon, *1814: résistance et occupation*, p. 148; Lamarre, pp. 26–7.
35. Beuve, p. 39.
36. Prinzing, p. 120; Zinsser, pp. 129, 139; Schur, p. 69.

Chapter 22: Reconstruction
(pages 221–9)
1. Arnaud, v. 1, pp. 352–4.
2. Noailly, p. 67.
3. Jamerey, p. 92.
4. Pougiat, pp. 363–5; Groley, p. 50. The current cross, a metal one with a stone base, was erected in 1897 to replace a wooden one. It can be found on the southern side of the *avenue lieutenant* Michel Taittinger (the D619), and to the east of the *rue* Jules Pochinot.
5. Steenackers, p. 272.
6. Costello, v. 1, p. 197; Aufauvre, p. 301.
7. AN F/7/3835, report of 3/3/1814.

8. Martin and Jacob, Appendix, p. 63.
9. Grabowksi, pp. 195–6; Pougiat, pp. 87–8.
10. Frénilly, p. 279.
11. Bernard, *Guide des archives*, p. 7; ADA 14R8, *préfet* of the Aube to *Ministre de la guerre*, 2/9/1820.
12. ADA 14R6, *marquis* de Ferreux to *préfet* of the Aube, 15/7/1814; and reply, 21/7/1814.
13. Martin and Jacob, Appendix, pp. 60, 65–6.
14. Boulay de la Meurthe, p. 6.
15. Nazarevski, p. 236; Olivier, p. 185. As in France, devastated regions in Russia were given tax relief. The needs of the rural populations were subsidised, and livestock, wheat, and wood distributed in the form of loans, repayable in a period of seven years. Shcherbatov, pp. 194–5.
16. Haydon, v. 1, pp. 267–9; Beuve, p. 111.
17. Uxkull, p. 193; Fain, p. 175; Fleury, *Histoire*, p. 546; Humbert, pp. 212–13.
18. Fleury, *Histoire*, pp. 542–3.
19. Noailly, p. 66; Humbert, pp. 214–15; Fleury, *Histoire*, p. 556.
20. Borrey, *La Franche-comté*, p. 260; Noailly, pp. 65–6.
21. Gras, *L'invasion . . . 1814*, p. 109; Pietresson de Saint-Aubin, p. 28; Fleury, *Histoire*, pp. 551–2; Borrey, *La Franche-comté*, pp. 298–9.
22. Arpin, pp. 37–9; Gras, *L'invasion . . . 1814*, pp. 130–1; Alison, Alison et al., v. 2, p. 25; Mathieu, *Comte sommaire*, pp. 9–10.
23. Pietresson de Saint-Aubin, p. 24; Janot, p. 116; Alison, Alison et al., v. 2, p. 25; Noailly, p. 65.
24. Godard d'Aucour, p. 256.
25. The exchange rate of Austrian and Prussian coins with French ones was fixed in a tariff issued by Schwarzenberg on 27/12/1813. A tariff was also issued in May 1814, with updated rates.
26. Gras, *L'invasion . . . 1814*, p. 92.
27. ADA 14R5, letter to Bourlier La Prairie, 6/5/1814; letter to *maire* of Troyes, 9/5/1814; undated note.
28. Godard d'Aucour, p. 270; Humbert, pp. 205–6.
29. *Le Moniteur*, 20/4/1814; *Journal de Paris*, 20/4/1814; Godard d'Aucour, pp. 548–9.
30. Alison, Alison, et al., v. 2, p. 39; Oisy, pp. 11–12, 19–20; Lioret, p. 46.
31. *Le Moniteur*, 20/4/1814. The French had breached the dykes of the ponds of the canal in order to try to submerge the fords of the Loing river from Nemours. Humbert, p. 33.
32. Berland, *Les dommages de guerre*, p. vii.
33. Berland, *Les dommages de guerre*, pp. 111, 260.
34. Pougiat, pp. 77–8; Beuve, p. 25; Anon, *De la campagne de Saxe*, pp. 133–4.
35. Pougiat, p. 91; Chuquet, pp. 255–6; Anon, *1814: résistance et occupation*, pp. 50–1.
36. Godard d'Aucour, pp. 244–6; Gabiou, pp. xii–xiii.
37. Fleury, *Histoire*, p. 568.
38. Arnaud, v. 2, p. 59.
39. Fleury, *Histoire*, p. 553.
40. Godard d'Aucour, p. 542.
41. France, *Collection*, v. 19, p. 191.
42. Fleury, *Histoire*, p. 573.
43. Fleury, *Histoire*, p. 571; Contamine, pp. 30–1.
44. Contamine, p. 29.
45. Steenackers, pp. 314–15, 317; France, *Collection*, v. 19, p. 388; ADA 14R1, decree of 6/4/1815.
46. Gras, *L'invasion . . . 1814*, pp. 87–8.
47. Stommel, p. 49; Chevalier, p. 273; Briffa, Jones, et al., p. 452.
48. Fohlen, p. 294; Deschamps, p. 127.
49. Groley, p. 47; Porcheret, p. 37.
50. Fleury, *Histoire*, p. 575.

Chapter 23: Bar-sur-Aube: a case study
(pages 230–7)
1. Pougiat, p. 53.
2. ADA 14R18, provisional *sous-préfet* of Bar-sur-Aube to provisional *préfet* of the Aube, 18/2/1814.
3. ADA 14R3, provisional *sous-préfet* to provisional *préfet* of the Aube, 18/2/1814.
4. Anon, *1814: résistance et occupation*, pp. 194–5.
5. Grüber, p. 219. Grüber was confused as to the sequence of events during the campaign. He stated he was wounded in the Battle of Paris but was in fact describing Arcis-sur-Aube.
6. Grüber, pp. 240–1.
7. AN AF/IV/1670 (1), doc 224, report of 26/3/1814.
8. Löwenstern, *Mit Graf Pahlens Reiterei*, pp. 215–16.
9. Pougiat, p. 53; Beuve, p. 38; Porcheret, p. 42.
10. ADA 14R41, record of houses and buildings burned or demolished by the events of war, May 1815; Chevalier, p. 263. In contrast, the cost of the destruction to properties in the *commune* of Brienne-le-Château was valued at 632,849 *francs*, for the town had been largely destroyed by fire in the battle of 29/1/1814. Another *commune* in the same *département*, Bar-sur-Seine, had a loss estimated at just 6,484 *francs*.
11. Chevalier, p. 265; Anon, *1814: résistance et occupation*, p. 192. Part of the convent had already been demolished during the Revolution. The surviving buildings today form the *hôtel-de-ville*.
12. Attempts were later made to repair the damage, by replacing the most damaged flagstones in the centre of the marked patches. It has been suggested that the heat alone was unlikely to have caused the cracks, and that powder from cartridges may have been used to start the fires. In fact, the combination of the cold winter temperatures, the hot fires, and possibly cold water to quench the flames could have been sufficient.
13. Arpin, pp. 41–2.
14. ADA 5Mi2. The *tables décennales* were lists of births, marriages, and deaths kept by the municipalities. The deaths of a few French or Allied soldiers were included, presumably as they had been left behind sick or wounded by their units. The real number of deaths among the inhabitants would have been even higher than that recorded in the registers. For instance, deaths among those inhabitants who fled the town, or those that occurred during the fighting, might not have been recorded officially.
15. Analysis of the number of deaths in 1814 compared to the annual totals between 1813 and 1822.
16. Pougiat, pp. 52–3.
17. Chevalier, p. 266; Arpin, pp. 41–2; ADA 14R54, extract from deliberations of the *Conseil municipal* of Bar-sur-Aube, 10/8/1816.
18. Porcheret, p. 43.
19. Cartault, p. 16. At Méry-sur-Seine at least 67 per cent of the recorded civilian deaths in 1814 were of inhabitants aged under 11 or over 50. Porcheret, p. 42.
20. At least, there was a decline in the number of conceptions that led to births registered at Bar-sur-Aube.
21. Tulard, *Nouvelle histoire*, p. 20; Benaerts, p. 134.
22. Löwenstern, *Mit Graf Pahlens Reiterei*, p. 202.
23. Gaffarel, p. 48.
24. Girod de l'Ain, p. 355.
25. ADA 2J502, pp. 90–4.
26. Mauduit, p. 451.
27. Maindreville, 'Incendie de Méry-sur-Seine', p. 308; Rouyer, p. 4; Arpin, p. 24.
28. ADA 2J502, pp. 92, 95.
29. AN AF/IV/1043, *Ministre de la police générale* to Napoleon, 27/2/1814; Mathieu, *Dernières*, pp. 323–5. The *comtesse* de Montesquiou was the governess of the King of Rome. The *duchesse* de Montebello was the widow of *Maréchal* Lannes, and a *dame d'honneur* of the Empress Marie-Louise.

30. AN F/7/3782, *bulletin* of the *police générale*, 3/3/1814.
31. Rembowski, p. 464.
32. Pougiat, p. 207. It is unclear whether the proportion of foreign fathers was taken from reliable data, or was the result of assumptions based on the babies' physique.
33. Gaffarel, pp. 23–4; Chuquet, pp. 374–5.

Appendices

(pages 238–59)
1. Janot, pp. 41, 47, 69.
2. Rembowski, p. 488; Le Borgne, v. 1, p. 323; Löwenstern, *Mit Graf Pahlens Reiterei*, p. 231; Houssaye, p. 519; Rémusart, p. 60.
3. Weil, *La campagne*, v. 1, p. 9.
4. Weil, *La campagne*, v. 1, p. 10. Including Yorck, Sacken, Kleist, and Langeron, but not the *4.* or *5. Bundes-Corps*.
5. Du Casse, *Mémoires*, v. 10, p. 175.
6. Exelmans initially commanded a provisional division with Macdonald, into February. He replaced Guyot, who was blamed by Napoleon for the capture of some Imperial Guard guns at the time of the Battle of Montereau.
7. The five divisions were the 1st and 2nd Young Guard Divisions, and the 1st, 2nd, and 3rd Provisional Young Guard Divisions.

Bibliography

Newspapers
Gazette de France. Paris.
Journal de Paris. Paris.
Journal des débats politiques et littéraires. Paris.
Le Moniteur universel. Paris.
The Times. London.

Books
Ackerknecht, Erwin Heinz. *Medicine at the Paris hospital, 1794–1848.* Baltimore, 1967.
Alberti, Heinrich Wilhelm. *Kriegsbriefe des Leutnants Wilhelm Alberti aus den Befreiungskriegen.* Ed. Rudolf Brieger. Breslau, 1913.
Alison, Sir Archibald, William P. Alison, John Hope and Alexander Fraser Tytler. *Travels in France, during the years 1814–15: comprising a residence at Paris during the stay of the Allied armies, and at Aix, at the period of the landing of Bonaparte,* 2 vols. Edinburgh, 1815.
Alison, Sir Archibald. *Lives of Lord Castlereagh and Sir Charles Stewart, the second and third Marquesses of Londonderry,* 3 vols. London, 1861.
Andolenko, Serge. *Histoire de l'armée russe.* Paris, 1967.
André, Roger. *L'occupation de la France par les Alliés en 1815, juillet–novembre.* Paris, 1924.
Anon. *Relation de la cérémonie qui a eu lieu le dimanche 13 novembre 1814, pour la distribution des épées d'honneur offertes à MM. les maire et adjoints de la ville de Troyes, par les habitans de cette ville, en reconnaissance des services qu'ils ont rendus pendant la dernière guerre.* Troyes, 1814.
Anon. *J.R. Moët et ses successeurs.* Paris, 1864.
Anon. 'Les misères de l'invasion de 1814 dans l'Aube', in *La vie en Champagne* (Dec. 1991), 39th year, no. 426, pp. 6–9.
Anon. *1814–1815: souvenirs des régions envahies, extraits du Carnet de la Sabretache.* Paris, 1999.
Anon. *De la campagne de Saxe à la campagne de France: lettres et souvenirs, 1813–1814.* Paris, 2000.
Anon. *1814: résistance et occupation des villes françaises.* Paris, 2001.
Antoine, Alfred. *La sous-préfecture d'Auxerre, 1811–1816.* Auxerre, 1908.
d'Arbois de Jubainville, Charles-Joseph. 'Souvenirs d'un avocat de Nancy (de la Révolution au Second Empire)', in *Le pays lorrain* (1924), 16th year, pp. 513–25, 578–85; and (1925), 17th year, pp. 17–25.
d'Arnaud, Eugène-François-Auguste, baron de Vitrolles, *Mémoires et relations politiques du baron de Vitrolles,* 3 vols. Pub. Eugène Forgues. Paris, 1883–4.
Arpin, Charles. *Les horreurs de la campagne de 1814 dans le département de l'Aube.* Troyes, 1910.
Aufauvre, Amédée. *Histoire de Nogent-sur-Seine.* 1859. Reissued Paris, 1989.
August von Preußen, Prinz. 'Aus dem kriegsgeschichtlichen Nachlasse Seiner Königlichen Hoheit des Prinzen August von Preußen', in *Kriegsgeschichtliche Einzelschriften* (1883), no. 2.
Auguste Caroline Sophie, Herzogin von Sachsen-Coburg-Saalfeld. *Auszüge aus dem Tagebuch der Herzogin Auguste von Sachsen-Coburg-Saalfeld, geb. Prinzessin Reuß-Ebersdorf, aus den Jahren 1805–1821.* Darmstadt, 1893.
Austria (Army, Kriegsarchiv). *Befreiungskrieg 1813 und 1814: einzeldarstellungen der entschiedenden Kriegsereignisse,* 5 vols. Vienna, 1913. Part of *Geschichte der Kämpfe Österreichs,* 20 vols. Vienna, 1896–1914.
Auvray, Pierre. 'Souvenirs militaires de Pierre Auvray, Sous-lieutenant au 23e régiment de dragons (1807–1815)', in *Carnet de la Sabretache* (1914–19), pp. 533–83.
Aymard, Paul. *Souvenirs d'un gamin de Lyon de 1814.* Lyon, 1878.
Aymes, Jean-René. *La déportation sous le premier empire: les Espagnols en France, 1808–1814.* Paris, 1983.
Bairoch, Paul, Jean Batou and Pierre Chèvre. *La population des villes européennes: banque de données et analyse sommaire des résultats, 800–1850.* Geneva, 1988.

Barany, George. *Stephen Széchenyi and the awakening of Hungarian nationalism, 1791–1841*. Princeton, NJ, 1968.
Bardin, Etienne-Alexandre, baron. *Dictionnaire de l'armée de terre, ou recherches historiques sur l'art et les usages militaires des anciens et des modernes*, 16 parts. Ed. Pierre Jean Alexandre Mollière. Paris, 1841–51.
Barère de Vieuzac, Bertrand. *Mémoires de B. Barère, membre de la Constituante, de la Convention, du Comité de salut publique, et de la Chambre des représentants*, 4 vols. Paris, 1842–4.
Bartlet, Elizabeth C. 'Opera as patriotic ceremony: the case of *L'Oriflamme*', in Marc Honegger, Christian Meyer and Paul Prévost, ed. *La musique et le rite sacré et profane: actes du 13e congrès de la Société Internationale de Musicologie, Strasbourg, 29 août–3 septembre 1982* (1986), vol 1, pp. 327–38.
Barton, Sir Dunbar Plunket, *Bernadotte: prince and king, 1810–1844*. London, 1925.
de Bausset, Louis-François-Joseph. *Mémoires anecdotiques sur l'intérieur du palais*, 2 vols. Brussels, 1827.
de Beauchamp, Alphonse. *Histoire de la campagne de 1814, et de la restauration de la monarchie française*, 2 vols. Paris, 1815.
Bégis, Alfred. *Curiosités historiques: invasion de 1814, destruction des drapeaux étrangers et de l'épée de Frédéric de Prusse à l'hôtel des Invalides d'après des documents inédits*. Paris, 1897.
Belhomme, Victor-Louis-Jean-François. *Histoire de l'infanterie en France*, 5 vols. Paris, 1892–1902.
Belliard, Augustin-Daniel, comte. *Mémoires du comte Belliard, lieutenant-général, pair de France, écrits par lui-même*, 3 vols. Ed. J. Vinet. Paris, 1842.
Bellot de Kergorre, Alexandre. *Un commissaire des guerres pendant le premier empire: journal de Bellot de Kergorre*. Paris, 1899.
Benaerts, Louis. *Les commissaires extraordinaires de Napoléon Ier en 1814, d'après leur correspondance inédite*. Paris, 1915.
von Bennigsen, Levin August Gottlieb, Count. *Mémoires du général Bennigsen*, 3 vols. Ed. E. Cazalas. Paris, 1907–8.
Benoit, A. 'Invasion de 1814 dans le département des Vosges: correspondance inédite du général Cassagne', in *Annales de la Société d'émulation du département des Vosges* (1877), pp. 233–326.
de Béranger, Pierre-Jean. *Ma biographie*. Paris, 1858.
Berland, Just. *Histoire d'un monument: la colonne commémorative de Champaubert, 1839–1895*. Reims, 1912.
Berland, Just. *Histoire d'un monument: la colonne commémorative de Montmirail, 1864–1867*. Reims, 1914.
Berland, Just. *Les dommages de guerre après Valmy*. Châlons-sur-Marne, 1931.
Bernard, Gildas. 'Evocation historique du Château de Brienne', in *La vie en Champagne* (June 1959), 7th year, no. 69, pp. 2–6.
Bernard, Gildas. 'Du nouveau sur Napoléon à Brienne et sur la retraite de Lesmont', in *La vie en Champagne* (May 1961), 9th year, no. 90, pp. 10–11.
Bernard, Gildas. 'Le Château de Pont-sur-Seine', in *La vie en Champagne* (May 1963), 11th year, no. [112], pp. 4–11.
Bernard, Gildas. 'Une évasion de prisonniers français au temps des Cosaques', in *Almanach de l'Est-Eclair: le grand quotidien de l'Aube* (1966), pp. 99–100.
Bernard, Gildas. *Guides des archives départementales de l'Aube*. Troyes, 1967.
Bernard, Gildas. '1814: la campagne de France', in *Napoléon et la Champagne*, special issue of *La vie en Champagne* (June 1999).
Bernard, Gildas. 'L'enjeu de la campagne de France: la frontière du Rhin', in *Napoléon et la Champagne*, special issue of *La vie en Champagne* (June 1999).
von Bernhardi, Felix Theodor. *Denkwürdigkeiten aus dem Leben des Kaiserl. russ. Generals von der Infanterie Carl Friedrich Grafen von Toll*, 4 vols. Leipzig, 1856–8.
Berthelot, Claude-Philibert, comte de Rambuteau. *Mémoires du comte de Rambuteau*. Ed. Georges Lequin. Paris, 1905.
Bertier de Sauvigny, Guillaume. *Le comte Ferdinand de Bertier, 1782–1864, et l'énigme de la congrégation*. Paris, 1948.

Bertin, Georges. *La campagne de 1814 d'après des témoins oculaires*. Paris, 1897.
Bertrand, Henri-Gratien, comte. *Cahiers de Sainte-Hélène*, 3 vols. Ed. Paul Fleuriot de Langle. Paris, 1949–59.
Best, Geoffrey. *War and society in revolutionary Europe, 1770–1870*. 1982. Reissued Stroud, 1998.
Beugnot, Jacques-Claude, comte. *Chambre des députés: opinion de M. le comte Beugnot, ministre d'état, député du département de la Haute-Marne, sur l'exécution de la loi du 23 septembre 1814*. Paris, undated.
Beulé, Charles-Ernest. *Eloge de M. Horace Vernet*. Paris, 1863.
ed. Beuve, Octave. *L'invasion de 1814–1815 en Champagne: souvenirs inédits* (Paris, 1914)
Bianchi, Serge, and Roger Dupuy. *La Garde nationale entre nation et peuple en armes: mythes et réalités, 1789–1871*. Rennes, 2006.
Bibolet, Françoise, Chantal Rouquet, André Boisseau and Emmanuel Saint-Mars. *Histoire de Troyes*. Troyes, 1999.
Bienvenu, Jacques. *La campagne de France: la bataille de Montereau, 18 février 1814*. Montereau, 1964.
Biot, Hubert-François. *Campagnes et garnisons: souvenirs anecdotiques et militaires du Colonel Biot*. Ed. comte Fleury. Paris, 1901.
Blanc, Alexandre-Auguste-Philippe-Charles. *Une famille d'artistes: les trois Vernet, Joseph, Carle, Horace*. Paris, 1898.
Blayney, Andrew Thomas, Baron. *Narrative of a forced journey through Spain and France, as a prisoner of war, in the years 1810 to 1814*, 2 vols. London, 1814.
Blücher von Wahlstadt, Gebhard Leberecht, Prinz. *Blüchers Briefe*. Ed. W. von Unger. Berlin, 1913.
Blumenthal, Maximilian. *Der Preußische Landsturm von 1813*. Berlin, 1900.
Bockenheimer, Carl Georg. *Erinnerungen an die Geschichte der Stadt Mainz in den Jahren 1813 und 1814*. Mainz, 1863.
Bodart, Gaston. *Militär-historisches Kriegs-Lexikon, 1618–1905*. Vienna, 1908.
Borrey, Francis. *La Franche-comté en 1814*. Paris, 1912.
Borrey, Francis. *L'esprit public chez les prêtres francs-comtois pendant la crise de 1813 à 1815*. Paris, 1912.
Boucher de Perthes, Jacques. *Sous dix rois: souvenirs de 1791 à 1860*, 8 vols.
Boudon, Jacques-Olivier. *Histoire du consulat et de l'empire, 1799–1815*. Paris, 2000.
Boulart, Jean-François, baron. *Mémoires militaires du général baron Boulart sur les guerres de la République et de l'empire*. Paris, 1892.
Boulay de la Meurthe, Alfred. *Société de l'histoire de Paris: séance annuelle du 14 mai 1889, discours du président*. Nogent-le-Rotrou, 1889.
de Bourgoing, Paul-Charles-Amable, baron. *Souvenirs militaires du baron de Bourgoing*. Paris, 1897.
de Bourqueney, Marie-Victor-Clément. *Historique du 25e régiment de dragons, 1665–1890*. Tours, 1890.
Boutiot, Théophile. *Histoire de la ville de Troyes et de la Champagne méridionale*, 5 vols. Troyes, 1870–80.
Bouvier, Félix. *Les premiers combats de 1814: prologue de la campagne de France dans les Vosges*. Paris, 1895.
Boys, Edward. *Narrative of a captivity and adventures in France and Flanders: between the years MDCCCIII and MDCCCIX*, 2nd ed. London, 1831.
Braive, Gaston. *Duhesme, 1799–1815: né à Mercurey, blessé à mort à Waterloo, décédé à Genappe, enterré à Ways*. Baisy-Thy, 2001.
Brett-James, Antony. *Europe against Napoleon*. London, 1970.
Briffa, K.R., P.D. Jones, F.H. Schweingruber and T.J. Osborn. 'Influence of volcanic eruptions on Northern Hemisphere summer temperature over the past 600 years', in *Nature: international weekly journal of science* (4 June 1998), vol. 393, pp. 450–4.
de Broglie, Achille-Léonce-Victor-Charles, duc. *Souvenirs, 1785–1870*, 4 vols. Paris, 1885–6.
Bruchet, Max. *L'invasion et l'occupation du département du Nord par les Alliés, 1814–1818: extrait de la Revue du Nord*. Lille, 1920.
Buxbaum, Emil. *Das Königlich Bayerische 3. Chevaulegers-Regiment 'Herzog Maximilian', 1724 bis 1884*, 2 parts. Munich, 1884.
Cabanis, André. *La presse sous le Consulat et l'Empire, 1799–1814*. Paris, 1975.
Callot, Jean-Pierre and Philippe Journau. *Histoire de l'Ecole polytechnique*. Paris, 1982.

Campan, Jeanne-Louise-Henriette. *Correspondance inédite de Mme Campan avec la reine Hortense*, 2 vols. Ed. Jean-Alexandre C. Buchon. Paris, 1835.
Campbell, Sir Neil. *Napoleon at Fontainebleau and Elba, being a journal of occurrences in 1814–1815 with notes of conversations*. London, 1869.
Carrot, Georges. *La Garde nationale, 1789–1871*. Nice, 1979.
Cartault, Jean. 'Vallentigny et ses environs: en marge de la grande histoire', in *La vie en Champagne* (Feb. 1964), 12th year, no. 120, pp. 10–16.
Casse, George Richard. *Authentic narrative of the sufferings of George Richard Casse, as a prisoner of France, during the late war; and of his escape to the Allied army near Clermont: with some particulars of his apprenticeship at sea*. London, 1828.
de Castellane-Novejan, Esprit-Victor-Elisabeth-Boniface, comte de Castellane. *Journal du Maréchal de Castellane*, 5 vols. Paris, 1895–7.
de Castéras-Villemartin, Jacques, vicomte. *Historique du 16e régiment de dragons*. Paris, 1892.
Castlereagh, Robert Stewart, Viscount. *Correspondence, despatches, and other papers, of Viscount Castlereagh, Second Marquess of Londonderry*, 12 vols. London, 1853.
ed. Caucanas, Sylvie, Rémy Cazal and Pascal Payen. *Contacts entre peuples et cultures: les prisonniers de guerre dans l'histoire*. Toulouse, 2003.
de Caulaincourt, Armand-Augustin-Louis. *Mémoires du général de Caulaincourt, duc de Vicence, grand écuyer de l'empereur*, 3 vols. Ed. Jean Hanoteau. Paris, 1933.
Cavaillès, Henri. *La route française: son histoire et sa fonction*. Paris, 1946.
Chalmin, P. 'Les luttes psychologiques à l'occasion de la campagne de 1814', in *Revue historique de l'armée* (August 1959), 15th year, no. 3.
Chamans de Lavallette, Antoine-Marie, comte. *Mémoires et souvenirs du comte Lavallette, aide-de-camp du général Bonaparte, conseiller-d'état et directeur-général des postes de l'empire*, 2 vols. Paris, 1831.
Chandler, David. *The campaigns of Napoleon*. London, 1966.
ed. Chandler, David. *Napoleon's marshals*. London, 1987.
Chappey, Jean-Luc and Bernard Gainot. *Atlas de l'empire napoléonienne, 1799–1815*. Paris, 2008.
Chaptal, Jean-Antoine, comte de Chanteloup. *Mes souvenirs sur Napoléon*. Paris, 1893.
Charton, Charles. 'L'administration bavaroise dans les Vosges en 1814', in *Annales de la Société d'émulation du département des Vosges* (1864), v. 12, 1st journal, pp. 213–67.
de Chateaubriand, François-Réne, vicomte. *De Buonaparte, des Bourbons, et de la nécessité de se rallier à nos princes légitimes, pour le bonheur de la France et celui de l'Europe*. Auxerre, 1814.
de Chateaubriand, François-Réne, vicomte. *Of Buonaparte, and the Bourbons, and of the necessity of rallying round our legitimate princes for the happiness of France and that of Europe*, 2nd ed. London, 1814.
Chatelain, Abel. *Les migrants temporaires en France de 1800 à 1914*, 2 vols. Villeneuve-d'Ascq, 1976.
Chevalier, L. *Histoire de Bar-sur-Aube*. Bar-sur-Aube, 1851.
Chuquet, Arthur. *Alsace en 1814*. Paris, 1900.
Church, Ronald James Harrison, et al. *An advanced geography of northern and western Europe*, 3rd ed. Amersham, 1980.
Clark, Peter, and Bernard Lepetit. *Capital cities and their hinterlands in early modern Europe*. Aldershot, 1996.
von Clausewitz, Karl. *La campagne de 1813 et la campagne de 1814*. Trans. Commandant Thomann. Paris, 1900.
von Clausewitz, Karl. *On war*. Ed. and trans. Sir Michael Howard and Peter Paret. Princeton, NJ, 1976.
Clement, Félix and Pierre Larousse. *Dictionnaire des opéras (dictionnaire lyrique)*. Paris, 1905.
Cohen, Bernard. *Compendium of finance: containing an account of the origin, progress, and present state of the public debts, revenue, expenditure, national banks and currencies . . . .* London, 1822.
de Coigny, Aimée de Franquetot, duchesse de Fleury. *Mémoires de Aimée de Coigny*. Ed. Etienne Lamy. Paris, 1906.
von Colomb, Friedrich. *La guerre de partisans contre Napoléon: carnet de campagne d'un officier prussien, 1813–1814*. Trans. Edouard Minart. Paris, 1914.

Combe, Julien. *Mémoires du Colonel Combe sur les campagnes de Russie 1812, de Saxe 1813, de France 1814 et 1815*. Paris, 1853.
Connelly, Owen. *Napoleon's satellite kingdoms*. London, 1965.
Connelly, Owen. *Blundering to glory: Napoleon's military campaigns*. Wilmington, 1987.
Constant de Rebecque, Henri-Benjamin. *Journaux intimes: édition intégrale des manuscrits autographes publiée pour la première fois*. Ed. Alfred Roulin and Charles Roth. Paris, 1952.
Contamine, Henry. 'Les conséquences financières des invasions de 1814 et de 1815 dans les départements de la Moselle et de la Meurthe', in *Annuaire de la Société d'histoire et d'archéologie de la Lorraine* (1933), 46th year, vol. 42, pp. 1–103.
Cooper, Duff. *Talleyrand*. 1932. Reissued London, 1964.
Costello, Louisa Stuart. *A pilgrimage to Auvergne, from Picardy to Le Velay*, 2 vols. London, 1842.
Coulmann, Jean-Jacques. *Réminiscences*, 3 vols. Paris, 1862–9.
Couper-Johnston, Ross. *El Niño: the weather phenomenon that changed the world*. London, 2000.
Cox, Gary P. *The halt in the mud: French strategic planning from Waterloo to Sedan*. Boulder, 1994.
Craig, Gordon A. 'Problems of coalition warfare: the military alliance against Napoleon, 1813–14', in *War and diplomacy: selected essays*. London, 1966.
Crepon, Tom. *Leberecht von Blücher: Leben und Kämpfe*. Berlin, 1988.
van Creveld, Martin. *Supplying war: logistics from Wallenstein to Patton*, 2nd ed. 1977. Reissued Cambridge, 2004.
Cronin, Vincent. *Napoleon*. 1971. Reissued Glasgow, 1990.
de Crossard, Jean-Baptiste, baron. *Mémoires militaires et historiques pour servir à l'histoire de la guerre depuis 1792 jusqu'en 1815 inclusivement*, 6 vols. Paris, 1829.
Curély, Jean-Nicolas. *Le général Curély: itinéraire d'un cavalier léger de la Grande armée, 1793–1815*. Paris, 1887.
de Dainville, François, and Jean Tulard. *Atlas administratif de l'empire français, d'après l'atlas rédigé par ordre du duc de Feltre en 1812*. Paris, 1973.
de Damas, Ange-Hyacinthe-Maxence, baron. *Mémoires du baron de Damas, 1785–1862*, 2 vols. Paris, 1922.
Dändliker, Karl. *A short history of Switzerland*. London, 1899.
Dayot, Armand. *Les Vernet: Joseph, Carle, Horace*. Paris, 1898.
Dechamps, Jules. *Sur la légende de Napoléon*. Paris, 1931.
de Dedem de Gelder, Antoine-Baudouin-Gisbert. *Un général hollandais sous le premier empire: mémoires du général baron de Dedem de Gelder, 1774–1825*. Paris, 1900.
Delorme, J.S. *Rambouillet devenu chef-lieu d'arrondissement: document historique et d'administration locale*. Paris, 1839.
Desbois-Thibault, Claire. *L'extraordinaire aventure du Champagne: Moët & Chandon, une affaire de famille, 1792–1914*. Paris, 2003.
Descaves, Lieutenant-Colonel. 'Journal de Provins (janvier–avril 1814 – juillet–octobre 1815), extrait du manuscrit de l'abbé Pasques', in *Carnet de la Sabretache* (April 1929), 4th series, pp. 195–234.
Deschamps, Etienne-Maurice. *Souvenirs militaires, persécutions sous la restauration, songe, etc.* Pontarlier, 1835.
Desmarest, Pierre-Marie. *Témoignages historiques, ou quinze ans de haute police sous Napoléon*. Paris, 1833.
ed. Diaz, Henry F., and Vera Markgraf. *El Niño: historical and paleoclimatic aspects of the Southern Oscillation*. Cambridge, 1992.
von Ditfurth, Wilhelm Arthur. *Aus sturmbewegter Zeit: Briefe aus dem Nachlasse des Generals der Infanterie von Ditfurth 1808–1815*. Berlin, 1912.
Druhen, Ignaceraîné. *Etude sur la mortalité de la population civile en Franche-comté pendant la dernière invasion allemande: deux époques médicales à Besançon, 1814–1815 et 1870–1871*. Besançon, 1881.
Drummond, A.J. 'Cold winters at Kew Observatory, 1783–1942', in *Quarterly Journal of the Royal Meteorological Society* (1983), vol. 69, pp. 17–32.
Dry, A. *Reims en 1814, pendant l'invasion*. Paris, 1902.

ed. Du Casse, Pierre-Emmanuel-Albert, baron. *Mémoires et correspondance politique et militaire du roi Joseph*, 10 vols. Paris, 1854.
Du Casse, Pierre-Emmanuel-Albert, baron. *Le général Arrighi de Casanova, duc de Padoue*, 2 vols. Paris, 1866.
Dubois, A. 'Les ambulances versaillaises de 1814', in *Revue de l'histoire de Versailles et de Seine-et-Oise* (Feb. 1914), 16th year, I, pp. 32–55.
Duchesne de Gillevoisin, Claude, duc de Conegliano, *Le Maréchal Moncey, duc de Conegliano, 1754–1842*. Paris, 1902.
Duffy, Christopher. *Russia's military way to the west: origins and nature of Russian military power, 1700–1800*. London, 1981.
Dufour de Pradt, Dominique. *Récit historique sur la restauration de la royauté en France le 31 mars 1814*. Paris, 1816.
Ellis, Geoffrey. *The Napoleonic empire*. Basingstoke, 2003.
Elting, John. *Swords around a throne: Napoleon's Grande armée*. London, 1988.
Elton, Letitia. *Locks, bolts and bars: stories of prisoners in the French wars, 1759–1814*. London, 1945.
England. *A complete collection of the treaties and conventions at present subsisting between Great Britain and foreign powers . . .* 2 vols. Ed. Lewis Hertslet. London, 1820.
Englund, Steven. *Napoleon: a political life*. Cambridge, Massachusetts, 2004.
Esdaile, Charles J. *The Spanish army in the Peninsular war*. Manchester, 1988.
Esdaile, Charles J. *The wars of Napoleon*. London, 1995.
Esdaile, Charles J. *Napoleon's wars: an international history, 1803–1815*. London, 2007.
Esposito, Vincent and John Elting. *A military history and atlas of the Napoleonic wars*. 1965. Reissued London, 1999.
d'Estre, Henry. *Bourmont: la Chouannerie, les Cent Jours, la conquête d'Alger, 1773–1846*. Paris, 1934.
Etienne, Charles-Guillaume, and Baour-Lormian. *L'Oriflamme: opéra en un acte, représenté pour la première fois, sur le théâtre de l'académie impériale de musique, le 1er février 1814*. Paris, 1814.
Etienne de Jouy, Victor-Joseph and Antoine Jay. *Salon d'Horace Vernet: analyse historique et pittoresque des quarante-cinq tableaux exposés chez lui en 1822*. Paris, 1822.
Eustace, John Chetwode. *A letter from Paris, to George Petre, Esq.*, 3rd ed. London, 1814.
Eve, Antoine-François. *Tableau historique des prisons d'état en France sous le règne de Buonaparte; par M. Eve, dit Démaillot, vieillard infirme, et prisonnier d'état pendant dix ans*. Paris, 1814.
Ewald, Johann. *Treatise on partisan warfare*. Trans. Robert A. Selig and David Curtis Skaggs. New York, 1991.
Fabvier, Charles-Nicolas, baron. *Journal des opérations du sixième corps pendant la campagne de France, en 1814*. Paris, 1819.
Fain, Agathon-Jean-François, baron. *Manuscrit de mil huit cent quatorze*. London, 1823.
Fane, John, Earl of Westmorland. *Memoir of the operations of the Allied armies, under Prince Schwarzenberg, and Marshal Blücher, during the latter end of 1813, and the year 1814*. London, 1822.
Fane, Priscilla Ann Wellesley, Countess of Westmorland. *The letters of Lady Burghersh, afterwards Countess of Westmorland, from Germany and France during the campaign of 1813–14*. Ed. Lady Rosé Weigall. London, 1893.
Faré, Charles. *Lettres d'un jeune officier à sa mère 1803–1814*. Paris, 1889.
Faucheur, Narcisse. *Souvenirs de campagnes du sergent Faucheur*. Ed. Jacques Jourquin. Paris, 2004.
Fauvelet de Bourrienne, Louis-Antoine, *Memoirs of Napoleon Bonaparte*, 4 vols. London, 1836.
Fave, Ernest-Honoré. *Campagne de 1814, II: les premières opérations militaires dans la vallée de l'Aube, du 27 janvier au 6 février 1814*. Paris, undated.
Fiévet, Victor. *Madame Veuve Clicquot, née Ponsardin: son histoire et celle de sa famille*. Paris, 1865.
Fiévet, Victor. *Histoire de la ville d'Epernay depuis sa fondation jusqu'à nos jours*, 3 vols. Epernay, 1868.
Fleury, Edouard. *Histoire de l'invasion de 1814 dans les départements du nord-est de la France*. Paris, 1858.
ed. Fleury, Michel, and Bertrand Gille. *Dictionnaire biographique du conseil municipal de Paris et du conseil général de la Seine*. Paris, 1972.

Fohlen, Claude. *Histoire de Besançon de la conquête française à nos jours*. Paris, 1965.
Foncin, Pierre. *L'invasion de 1814: Napoléon et les alliés à Troyes et dans le département de l'Aube, conférence faite au Cirque, à Troyes, le 20 juin 1866*. Troyes, 1866.
Fontaine, Pierre-François-Leonard. *Journal, 1799–1853*, 2 vols. Paris, 1987.
Fortin, Florentin-Jean-François. *Souvenirs*. Paris, 1865–7.
Fournier, Edouard. *L'esprit dans l'histoire: recherches et curiosités sur les mots historiques*. Paris, 1857.
France: Administration des postes. *Etat général des postes du royaume de France, avec les routes qui conduisent aux principaux villes de l'Europe, dressé par ordre du conseil d'administration, pour l'an 1814*. Paris, 1814.
France. *Almanach impérial pour l'année M.DCCC.XIII*. Paris, 1813.
France. *Collection complète des lois, décrets, ordonnances, réglemens, avis du Conseil-d'état*, 2nd ed. Ed. Jean-Baptiste Duvergier et al. Paris, 1834 onwards.
France: Corps royal des ponts et chaussées. *Annuaire du corps royal des ponts et chaussées, pour les années 1814 et 1815*. Paris.
France: Ministère de la guerre. *Instructions issued by the French imperial Minister at War for the defence and destruction of bridges, in 1814*. Trans. Brevet Major William Reid. Chatham, 1823.
France: Ministère de la guerre. *Instructions issued by the French imperial Minister at War for the defence of open towns and villages, in 1814*. Trans. Brevet Major William Reid. Chatham, 1823.
de Frénilly, François-Auguste Fauveau. *Mémoires, 1768–1828: souvenirs d'un ultraroyaliste*. Ed. Frédéric d'Agay. Reissued Paris, 1987.
von Freytag-Loringhoven, Hugo, Freiherr. *Kriegslehren nach Clausewitz aus den Feldzügen 1813 und 1814*. Berlin, 1908.
Frye, William Edward. *After Waterloo: reminiscences of European travel, 1815–1819*. London, 1908.
Fusil, Louise. *Souvenirs d'une actrice*, 2 vols. Brussels, 1841.
Fustier, Pierre. *La route: voies antiques, chemins anciens, chaussées modernes*. Paris, 1968.
Gabiou, Jean-Frédéric. *Nouveau système de finance et projet de liquidation générale fondés sur la Charte*. Paris, 1816.
Gaffarel, Paul. *Dijon en 1814 et en 1815*. Dijon, 1897.
de Gain de Montaignac, Jean-Romain. *Journal d'un Français, depuis le 9 mars jusqu'au 13 avril 1814*. Paris, 1817.
Gallery, Roger. *1814: l'Aube se lève*. Paris, 2002.
Ganière, Paul. *Corvisart: médecine de Napoléon*. Paris, 1951.
Gates, David. *The Spanish ulcer: a history of the Peninsular war*. London, 2002.
de Gerbaix de Sonnaz, Hector. *Une panique militaire à Piney, 2 février 1814*. Troyes, 1914.
Gerrare, Wirt. *The story of Moscow*. London, 1900.
Geyl, Pieter. *Napoleon: for and against*. 1949. Reissued Harmondsworth, 1986.
Gildea, Robert. *Marianne in chains: in search of the German occupation 1940–45*. London, 2002.
Giraud, Pierre-François-Félix-Joseph. *Histoire générale des prisons sous le règne de Buonaparte, avec des anecdotes curieuses et intéressantes sur la Conciergerie, Vincennes, Bicêtre, Sainte-Pélagie, La Force, le Château de Joux, etc., etc., et les personnages marquans qui y ont été détenus*. Paris, 1814.
Girod de l'Ain, Jean-Marie. *Dix ans de mes souvenirs militaires de 1805 à 1815*. Paris, 1873.
von Gneisenau, August Wilhelm Anton, Graf Neidhardt. *Briefe Generals Neidhardt von Gneisenau 1809–1815*. Ed. Julius von Pflugk-Harttung. Gotha, 1913.
von Gneisenau, August Wilhelm Anton, Graf Neidhardt. *The life and campaigns of Field-Marshal Prince Blücher of Wahlstadt*. Trans. and revised James Edward Marston. 1815. Reissued London, 1996.
Godard d'Aucour, Adrien, comte de Plancy. *Souvenirs du comte de Plancy, 1798–1816*, 2nd ed. Paris, 1904.
Gold, David L. 'More on the alleged Russian origin of French *bistro/bistrot*', in *Romance philology* (May 1991), vol. 44, no. 4, pp. 425–8.
Golitsyn, Prince N.B. *Souvenirs et impressions d'un officier russe pendant les campagnes de 1812, 1813 et 1814 avec la relation de la bataille de Borodino*. St Petersburg, 1849.

Görlitz, Walter. *The German General Staff: its history and structure*. Trans. Brian Battershaw. London, 1953.
Gourgaud, Gaspard, baron. *Sainte-Hélène: journal inédit de 1815 à 1818*, 2 vols. Ed. Emmanuel de Grouchy and Antoine Guillois. Paris, undated.
Grabowski, Jozef Ignacy Tadeuz, Count. *Mémoires militaires de Joseph Grabowski*. Trans. Jan V. Chelminski and Alphonse Malibran. Paris, 1907.
Granier, Herman. *Hohenzollernbriefe aus den Freiheitskriegen 1813–1815*. Leipzig, 1913.
Gras, Louis-Joseph. *L'invasion du Forez en 1814*. Saint-Etienne, 1922.
Gras, Louis-Joseph. *L'invasion du Forez en 1815*. Saint-Etienne, 1923.
Gréard, Octave. *Jean-Louis-Ernest Meissonier: ses souvenirs, ses entretiens, précédés d'une étude sur sa vie et son oeuvre*. Paris, 1897.
Griffith, Paddy. *The art of war of Revolutionary France, 1789–1802*. London, 1998.
Griois, Charles-Pierre-Lubin. *Mémoires du général Griois, 1792–1822*, 2 vols. Ed. Arthur Chuquet. Paris, 1909.
Grivel, Jean, baron. *Mémoires du vice-amiral baron Grivel*. Paris, 1914.
Groley, Gabriel. *La campagne de France dans l'Aube*. Troyes, 1972.
Groupe d'histoire des forêts françaises. *Histoire des forêts françaises: guide de recherche*. Paris, 1982.
Grove, Richard H. 'Global impact of the 1789–93 El Niño', in *Nature: international weekly journal of science* (28 May 1998), vol. 393, pp. 318–19.
von Grüber, Carl Johann, Ritter. *Sous les aigles autrichiennes: souvenirs du chevalier de Grueber, officier de cavalerie autrichien, 1800–1820*. Trans. Charles Tardieu de Maleissye-Melun. Paris, 1909.
Guidon, Jean-François. *Notes et souvenirs, 1794–1848*. Coutances, 1894.
Guilbert, Aristide. *Histoire des villes de France, avec une introduction générale pour chaque province*, 6 vols. Paris, 1844–8.
Guillier, Octave. *Histoire de l'hôpital Notre-Dame de Pitié, 1612–1882*. Paris, 1882.
Guimard, M.V. *Episode de l'invasion de 1814 à Brienon-sur-Armançon, d'après Pierre-Jacques Bridier*. Auxerre, 1916.
Guizot, François-Pierre-Guillaume. *Mémoires pour servir à l'histoire de mon temps*, 8 vols. Paris, 1858–67.
Guyot, Charles. *Souvenirs de la première invasion, d'après le journal de Charles d'Espinchal, maire de Fouchécourt, 15 décembre 1813–1er mai 1814*. Nancy, 1913.
Halevy, Elie. *England in 1815*. Trans. E.I. Watkin and D.A. Barker. Reissued New York, 1968.
Hall, Francis. *Travels in France, in 1818*. London, 1819.
Hantraye, Jacques. *Les Cosaques aux Champs-Elysées: l'occupation de la France après la chute de Napoléon*. Paris, 2005.
Hantraye, Jacques. 'Les morts des champs de bataille champenois de 1814', in *La vie en Champagne* (Oct.–Dec. 2006), new series, no. 48, pp. 9–12.
Hapdé, Jean-Baptiste-Augustin. *Les sépulcres de la Grande armée, ou tableau des hôpitaux pendant la dernière campagne de Buonaparte*. Paris, 1814.
Haydon, Benjamin Robert. *Life of Benjamin Robert Haydon, historical painter, from his autobiography and journals*, 2nd ed. 3 vols. Ed. Tom Taylor. London, 1853.
Haythornthwaite, Philip. *Napoleon's military machine*. Reissued London, 1988.
Haythornthwaite, Philip. *The Napoleonic source book*. London, 1990.
Haythornthwaite, Philip. *Who was who in the Napoleonic wars*. London, 1998.
Henckel von Donnersmarck, Wilhelm Ludwig Victor, Graf. *Erinnerungen aus meinem Leben*. Zerbst, 1846.
Henckens, J.L. *Mémoires se rapportant à son service militaire au 6ème régiment de chasseurs à cheval français de février 1803 à août 1816*. The Hague, 1910.
Hennequin, Emile. *Les opérations de 1814 dans l'Aube*. Troyes, 1921.
Hillemand, P. 'Napoléon a-t-il tenté de se suicider à Fontainebleau', in *Revue de l'Institut Napoléon* (April 1971), no. 119, pp. 71–8.
von Hoen, Maximilien. *Die Hauptarmee 1814*. Vienne, 1912. Vol. 5 of Alois Veltzé. *1813–1815: Österreich in den Befreiungskriegen*.
Horne, Alastair. *The fall of Paris: the siege and the Commune 1870–71*. 1965. Reissued London, 1967.

Horricks, Raymond. *Marshal Ney: the romance and the real.* Tunbridge Wells, 1982.
Hortense, Queen of Holland. *Mémoires de la reine Hortense*, 3 vols. Ed. Jean Hanoteau. Paris, 1927.
Hosking, Geoffrey. *Russia: people and empire, 1552–1917.* London, 1997.
Hourtoulle, François-Guy. *1814: la campagne de France.* Paris, 2005.
Houssaye, Henry. *1814.* Reissued, Paris, 1947.
Howard, Martin. *Napoleon's doctors: the medical services of the Grande armée.* Stroud, 2006.
Howard, Sir Michael. *The Franco-Prussian war.* 1961. Reissued, London, 2001.
Huard, Pierre. *Sciences, médecine, pharmacie de la Révolution à l'empire, 1789–1815.* Paris, 1970.
Hüffer, Alfred. *Kriegsfahrten einer Preußischen Marketenderin während der Feldzüge von 1806 bis 1815.* Münster, 1863.
Humbert, Frédéric. *L'invasion de 1814 en Seine-et-Marne.* Melun, 1885.
Hungerford, Constance Cain. *Ernest Meissonier: master in his genre.* Cambridge, 1991.
Jamerey, Emilien. *Histoire de Maizières-la-Grande-Paroisse, arrondissement de Nogent-sur-Seine, Aube.* Romilly-sur-Seine, 1918.
Janot, Jean. *En 1814: journal d'un citoyen genevois.* Geneva, 1912.
von Janson, R. August. *Geschichte des Feldzuges 1814 in Frankreich*, 2 vols. Berlin, 1903. In *Geschichte der Befreiungskriege 1813–1815.*
Johnson, Ray. *Napoleonic armies: a wargamer's campaign directory, 1805–1815.* 1978. Reissued London, 1984.
von Jordan, Heinrich. *Erinnerungsblätter und Briefe eines jungen Freiheitskämpfers aus den Jahren 1813 und 1814.* Berlin, 1914.
Josselson, Michael and Diana. *The commander: a life of Barclay de Tolly.* Oxford, 1980.
Kaplan, Steven Laurence. *Provisioning Paris: merchants and millers in the grain and flour trade during the eighteenth century.* London, 1984.
Keep, John Leslie Howard. *Soldiers of the Tsar: army and society in Russia, 1462–1874.* Oxford, 1985.
von Keyserling, Archibald, Graf. *Aus der Kriegszeit: Erinnerungen von Archibald Grafen von Keyserling.* Berlin, 1847.
von Kielmansegg, Peter. *Stein und die Zentralverwaltung 1813/14.* Stuttgart, 1964.
Kissinger, Henry. *A world restored: Metternich, Castlereagh and the problems of peace 1812–22.* 1957. Reissued London, 1999.
Klein, Tim. *Die Befreiung 1813, 1814, 1815.* Munich, 1913.
von Knobelsdorff-Brenkenhoff, Benno. *Briefe aus den Befreiungskriegen: ein Beitrag zur Situation von Truppe und Heimat in den Jahren 1813/14.* Bonn, 1981.
Koch, François. *Mémoires pour servir à l'histoire de la campagne de 1814*, 3 vols. Paris, 1819.
Kraehe, Enno Edward. *Metternich's German policy, volume I: the contest with Napoleon, 1799–1814.* Princeton, NJ, 1963.
Krimer, Wenzel. *Erinnerungen eines alten Lützower Jägers 1795–1819*, 2nd ed. 2 vols. Ed. Adolf Saager. Stuttgart, undated.
Krones von Marchland, Franz Xaver. *Zur Geschichte Österreichs im Zeitalter der französischen Kriege und der Restauration, 1792–1816.* Gotha, 1886.
de La Barre de Nanteuil, Hugues. *Le comte Daru, ou l'administration militaire sous le Révolution et l'Empire.* Paris, 1966.
de La Combe, Joseph-Félix le Blanc. *Charlet: sa vie, ses lettres.* Paris, 1856.
Lachouque, Henry. *The anatomy of glory: Napoleon and his Guard, a study in leadership.* Trans. Anne S.K. Brown. London, 1961.
de Ladoucette, Jean-Charles-Francois, baron. *Voyage fait en 1813 et 1814 dans le pays entre Meuse et Rhin.* Paris, 1818.
Lagneau, Louis-Vivant. *Journal d'un chirurgien de la Grande armée.* Ed. Eugène Tattet. Paris, 1913.
Lamarre, Leo. *La diplomatie et la guerre: 1814, le traité de Chaumont en Bassigny.* Colombey-les-deux-Eglises, 1988.
Lambart, Christian. 'Troyes en 1814, une ville au coeur d'une campagne d'hiver', in *Napoléon et la Champagne*, special issue of *La vie en Champagne* (June 1999).
Lamon, Siméon. 'Souvenirs d'un chasseur de la vieille Garde', in *Soldats suisses au service étranger*, vol. 7. Geneva, 1916.

Langeron, Louis-Alexandre-Andrault, Count. *Mémoires de Langeron, général d'infanterie dans l'armée russe: campagnes de 1812, 1813, 1814*. Paris, 1902.
Langton, Richard. *Narrative of a captivity in France, from 1809 to 1814*, 2 vols. London 1836.
de Lanzac de Laborie, Léon. *Paris sous Napoléon*, 8 vols. Paris, 1911.
Larreguy de Civrieux, Silvain. *Souvenirs d'un cadet, 1812–1823*. Paris, 1912.
Larrey, Dominique-Jean, baron. *Mémoires de chirurgie militaire et campagnes du baron D.J. Larrey*, 4 vols. Paris, 1817.
de Las Cases, Emmanuel-Auguste-Dieudonné, comte. *Mémorial de Sainte-Hélène, ou journal où se trouve consigné, jour par jour, ce qu'a dit et fait Napoléon durant dix-huit mois*, 8 vols. Paris, 1823–4.
de Las Cases, Emmanuel-Auguste-Dieudonné, comte. *Suite au mémorial de Sainte-Hélène, ou observations critiques, anecdotes inédites pour servir de supplément et de correctif à cet ouvrage*, 2 vols. Paris, 1824.
de Latouche, Henri-Louis-Joseph-Xavier. 'Souvenirs de 1813 et 1814: journal d'un habitant de Cernay', in *Revue d'Alsace* (1903), 4th series, 4th year, pp. 337–56 and 576–98.
Laurillard-Fallot, Louis. *Les frères Laurillard-Fallot: souvenirs de deux officiers du temps de l'empire*. Brussels, 1904.
Lawford, James. *Napoleon: the last campaigns, 1813–15*. Maidenhead, 1977.
Le Barbier, Louis. *Petites pages d'histoire: une commune de l'Oise pendant l'invasion de 1814–1815*. Paris, 1909.
Le Borgne, Charlotte-Louise-Eléonore-Adélaïde, comtesse de Boigne. *Récits d'une tante: mémoires de la comtesse de Boigne, née d'Osmond*, 4 parts. Paris, 1907.
Lecomte, Louis-Henry. *Napoléon et le monde dramatique*. Paris, 1912.
Lefebvre, Charles-Stanislas. *Campagnes et missions, 1793–1821*. Paris, 2001.
Lefebvre de Béhaine, Edouard Alphonse, comte. *La campagne de France*, 4 vols. Paris, 1913–35.
Lefol, Monsieur. *Souvenirs sur le prytanée de Saint-Cyr, sur la campagne de 1814, le retour de l'empereur Napoléon de l'île d'Elbe, et la campagne de 1815, pendant les Cent-Jours*. Versailles, 1854.
Leggiere, Michael V. *The fall of Napoleon, volume 1: the Allied invasion of France, 1813–1814*. Cambridge, 2007.
Lemaitre, L. *Historique du 4e régiment de dragons, 1672–1894*. Paris, 1894.
Lenotre, Georges. *En suivant l'empereur: croquis de l'épopée*. Paris, 1947.
Lepetit, Bernard. *Les villes dans la France moderne, 1740–1840*. Paris, 1988.
Levavasseur, Octave-René-Louis. *Souvenirs militaires d'Octave Levavasseur*. Paris, 1914.
Lewis, Michael. *Napoleon and his British captives*. London, 1962.
de Lignières, Marie-Henry, comte. *Souvenirs de la Grande armée et de la Vieille Garde impériale*. Paris, 1933.
Lioret, Georges. *1814–1815 à Moret-sur-Loing et dans les environs*. Moret-sur-Loing, 1904.
Litre, Emile-François. *Les régiments d'artillerie à pied de la Garde, le régiment monté de la Garde et le 23e régiment d'artillerie*. Paris, 1895.
Lomier, Eugène. *Le bataillon des Marins de la Garde, 1803–1815*. Saint-Valery-sur-Somme, 1905.
Lomier, Eugène. *Histoire des régiments de Gardes d'honneur, 1813–1814*. Paris, 1924.
Longford, Elizabeth. *Wellington: the years of the sword*. London, 1969. Reissued with its sequel, *Wellington: pillar of state*, as an abridged one-volume edition in 1992.
Lot, Henri. *Les deux généraux Ordener*. Paris, 1910.
von Löwenstern, Eduard. *Mit Graf Pahlens Reiterei gegen Napoleon: Denkwürdigkeiten des russischen Generals Eduard von Löwenstern, 1790–1837*. Berlin, 1910.
von Löwenstern, Woldemar, baron. *Mémoires du général-major russe baron de Löwenstern, 1776–1858*, 2 vols. Ed. Maurice H. Weil. Paris, 1903.
Macdonald, Etienne-Jacques, duc de Tarente. *Souvenirs du Maréchal Macdonald, duc de Tarente*, 6th ed. Paris, 1892.
McPhail, Helen. *The long silence: civilian life under the German occupation of northern France, 1914–1918*. 1999. Reissued London, 2001.
Madelin, Louis. *Histoire du consulat et de l'empire*, 4 vols. Paris, 2003.
Magraw, Roger. *France, 1800–1914: a social history*. Harlow, 2002.

de Maindreville, Charles-Maurice Doë, *Historique du 132e régiment d'infanterie rédigé d'après les documents officiels*. Reims, 1890.
de Maindreville, Général, 'Incendie de Méry-sur-Seine (22 février 1814)', in *Carnet de la Sabretache* (1914–19), 3rd series, pp. 305–11.
Malte-Brun, Victor-Adolphe. *Géographie complète de la France et de ses colonies*. Paris, 1857.
Mändler, Friedrich. *Erinnerungen aus meinen Feldzügen in den Jahren 1809 bis 1815*. Nuremberg, 1854.
Mansel, Philip. *Paris between empires, 1814–1852*. London, 2001.
Mansel, Philip. *Louis XVIII*. 1981. Reissued London, 2005.
Mansuy, Abel, 'Les Russes en Lorraine en 1814: mémoires du général Kahovsky sur la campagne de 1814', in *Le pays lorrain* (1914–19), vol. 11, pp. 292–8.
Marie-Louise, Empress of the French. *Marie-Louise et Napoléon, 1813–1814: lettres inédites*. Ed. Carl Fredrik Palmstierna. Paris, 1955.
de Marigny, Marie-Anne-Françoise. *Paris en 1814: journal intime de Madame de Marigny*. Paris, 1907.
Marion, Marcel. *Histoire financière de la France depuis 1715*, 6 vols. Paris, 1925.
Markham, J. David. *Imperial glory: the bulletins of Napoleon's Grande armée, 1805–1814*. London, 2003.
de Marmont, Auguste-Frédéric-Louis Viesse, duc de Raguse. *Mémoires du Maréchal Marmont, duc de Raguse de 1792 à 1841*, 9 vols. Paris, 1857.
Marnat, Jacques. 'Gourgaud a-t-il vraiment sauvé Napoléon à Brienne?', in *La vie en Champagne* (Sep. 1990), 38th year, no. 412, pp. 316–21.
Marnat, Jacques. 'L'invasion de 1814 dans l'Aube: III. La bataille d'Arcis-sur-Aube', in *La vie en Champagne* (Dec. 1992), 40th year, no. 437, pp. 5–10.
Marnat, Jacques. 'Une anecdote de la campagne de France: Napoléon à Herbisse', in *La vie en Champagne* (May 1993), 41st year, no. 442, pp. 15–18.
Marnat, Jacques. 'Napoléon a-t-il voulu la mort de Jacques Gouault?', in *La vie en Champagne* (Jul.–Aug. 1994), 42nd year, no. 455, pp. 3–6.
Marnat, Jacques. 'Campagne de France: Napoléon à Piney', in *La vie en Champagne* (Apr.–June 1995), new series, no. 2, pp. 18–21.
Marquis, César-Henry. *Considérations sur le typhus observé dans l'arrondissement de Tonnerre* . . . . Paris, 1816.
Marshall-Cornwall, Sir James. *Napoleon as military commander*. London, 1967.
Martin, Commandant Emmanuel. 'Le Colonel d'artillerie Belly de Bussy (David-Victor), aide-de-camp de Napoléon 1er (1768–1848)', in *Carnet de la Sabretache* (1914–19), pp. 232–9.
Martin, Henry and Paul L. Jacob. *Histoire de Soissons, depuis les temps les plus reculés jusqu'à nos jours*. Soissons, 1837.
Martinien, Aristide. *Tableaux par corps et par batailles des officiers tués et blessés pendant les guerres de l'empire, 1805–1815*. Paris, 1899.
Masson, Frédéric, *L'affaire Maubreuil*, 4th ed. Paris, 1907.
Mathieu, Marguerite Robert. *Dernières victoires 1814: la campagne de France aux alentours de Montmirail*. Paris, 1964.
Mathieu, Monsieur. *Compte sommaire des travaux de la Société d'agriculture, commerce, sciences et arts du département de la Marne, depuis le 2 novembre 1813, jusqu'au 25 août 1814*. Châlons, 1814.
de Mauduit, Hippolyte. 'Cent jours d'arrière-garde et d'avant-garde: récit dramatique de l'invasion de 1814', in *Carnet de la Sabretache* (Nov.–Dec. 1921), vol. 24, vol. 4 of 3rd series, p. 445.
Maurice, Barthélemy. *Histoire politique et anecdotique des prisons de la Seine*. Paris, 1840.
Maycock, Frederick William Orby. *The invasion of France, 1814*. London, 1914.
Maze-Sencier, Alphonse. *Les fournisseurs de Napoléon 1er et des deux impératrices*. Paris, 1893.
Mazeret, Constantin and C.V. Monin. *Panorama descriptif, historique, anecdotique des rives de la Seine de Paris à Montereau*. Corbeil, 1836.
Meier, Wilhelm. *Erinnerungen aus den Feldzügen 1806 bis 1815 aus den hinterlassenen Papieren eines Militärarztes*. Karlesruhe, 1854.

de Méneval, Claude-François, baron. *Napoléon et Marie-Louise: souvenirs historiques*, 3 vols. Paris, 1843–5.
Menuau, Charles-Maurice. *Historique du 14e régiment de dragons*. Paris, 1889.
Mercier, Jean. *Les dalles tumulaires de l'église Saint-Pierre de Bar-sur-Aube en Champagne*. Bar-sur-Aube, 1989.
von Metternich-Winneburg zu Beilstein, Klemens Wenzel Nepomuk Lothar, Fürst. *Mémoires, documents et écrits divers laissés par le prince de Metternich*, 8 vols. Paris, 1880.
Meynert, Hermann. *Kaiser Franz I: zur Geschichte seine Regierung und seiner Zeit*. Vienna, 1872.
Michalski, Serguisz. *Public monuments: art in political bondage, 1870–1997*. London, 1998.
Mikaberidze, Alexander. *The Russian officer corps in the Revolutionary and Napoleonic wars, 1792–1815*. Staplehurst, 2005.
Mikhailovsky-Danilevsky, Alexander Ivanovich. *History of the campaign in France in the year 1814*. London, 1839.
Miquel, Pierre. *Napoléon: la campagne de France*. Paris, 2003.
Mir, Jean-Pierre. *La Garde impériale et la campagne de 1814: dictionnaire des morts et blessés au combat*. Paris, 2001.
Mir, Jean-Pierre. *Mémento sur la campagne de France de 1814: la Grande armée du 1er janvier au 6 avril 1814, suivi du dictionnaire des officiers tués ou blessés au cours des combats*. Paris, 2002.
Mir, Jean-Pierre. *La bataille de Paris, 30 mars 1814: ouvrage suivi du dictionnaire biographique des pertes pour l'infanterie et la cavalerie des troupes de ligne au cours de la campagne de 1814*. Paris, 2004.
Mistler, Jean, François Blaudez and André Jacquemin. *Epinal et l'imagerie populaire*. Paris, 1961.
ed. Mollat, Michel. *Histoire de l'Ile-de-France et de Paris*. Toulouse, 1971.
de Montclos, Brigitte. *Les Russes à Paris au XIXe siècle*. Paris, 1996.
de Montenay, Solange. 'Les deux invasions de 1814 à 1815 et les Cent Jours en Bourgogne d'après les archives Bureau', in *Annales de Bourgogne* (July–Sept. 1969), vol. 41, no. 163, instalment 3, pp. 169–97; and (Oct.–Dec. 1969), vol. 41, no. 164, instalment 4, pp. 1–246.
Morin, Louis. *Souvenirs de 1814: Charles-Antoine de Widranges*. Troyes, 1914.
Morley, John. *Regency design, 1790–1840*. London, 1993.
von Müffling, Carl, baron. *The memoirs of Baron von Müffling: a Prussian officer in the Napoleonic wars*. 1853. Reissued London, 1997.
Muir, Rory. *Britain and the defeat of Napoleon, 1807–1815*. London, 1996.
Muller, Paul. *L'espionnage militaire sous Napoléon 1er*. Paris, 1896.
Murray, John (Firm). *A handbook for travellers in France: being a guide to Normandy, Brittany; the Rivers Seine, Loire, Rhône, and Garonne; the French Alps, Dauphiné, Provence, and the Pyrenees; their railways and roads*, 6th ed. London, 1856.
Nafziger, George F. *The Wurttemburg army, 1793–1815*. Leeds, 1987.
Nafziger, George F. and Marco Gioannini. *The defense of the Napoleonic kingdom of northern Italy, 1813–1814*. London, 2002.
Napoleon I, Emperor of the French. *Correspondance de Napoléon 1er publiée par ordre de l'empereur Napoléon III*, 32 vols. Paris, 1858–70.
Nazarevski, V.V. *Histoire de Moscou depuis les origines jusqu'à nos jours*. Paris, 1932.
Nerlinger, Charles. *Nicolas Wolff et la défense des Vosges, 1814–1815*. Strasbourg, 1897.
von Nesselrode, Carl Robert, Count. *Lettres et papiers du chancelier comte de Nesselrode, 1760–1850*, 11 vols. Paris, 1904–11.
Newcourt-Nowodworski, Stanley, *Black propaganda in the Second World War*. Stroud, 2005.
Nicolson, Harold. *The Congress of Vienna: a study in Allied unity: 1812–1822*. 1946. Reissued London, 1948.
Nicolson, Harold. *Benjamin Constant*. London, 1949.
Noailly, Adeline. 'Les relations entre les armées alliées et les populations envahies en 1814', in *Napoléon et la Champagne*, special issue of *La vie en Champagne* (June 1999).
von Nostitz, August Graf, 'Das Tagebuch des Generals der Kavallerie Grafen v. Nostitz', in *Kriegsgeschichtliche Einzelnschriften* (1885), vol. 1, part 5, pp. 30–138; and part 6, pp. 1–97.
Oechsli, Wilhelm. *Le passage des Alliés en Suisse, 1813–1814*. Trans. Francis Borrey. Paris, 1912.
d'Oisy, Husson. *Souvenirs de 1814*. Vitry-le-François, 1862.

Oliver, Michael and Richard Partridge. *Napoleonic army handbook: the British army and her allies*. London, 1999.
Olivier, Daria. *The burning of Moscow, 1812*. London, 1964.
Oman, Carola. *Napoleon's viceroy: Eugène de Beauharnais*. London, 1966.
Oman, Sir Charles. *Wellington's army, 1809–1814*. 1913. Reissued London, 1993.
Oman, Sir Charles. *A history of the Peninsular war*, 7 vols. 1902–30. Reissued with two additional volumes London, 1995–9.
Opoix, Christophe. *Histoire et description de Provins*. Paris, 1823.
Ostler, Nicholas. *Ad infinitum: a biography of Latin*. London, 2007.
Otto, Hans. *Gneisenau: Preußens unbequemer Patriot*. Bonn, 1979.
Oudinot, Marie-Charlotte-Julienne-Eugénie, duchesse de Reggio. *Récits de guerre et de foyer: le Maréchal Oudinot, duc de Reggio, d'après les souvenirs inédits de la Maréchale par Gaston Stiegler*. Paris, 1894.
Oyon, Jean-Auguste. *Campagnes et souvenirs militaires, 1805–1814*. Paris, 1997.
Ozanam, Jean-Antoine-Frédéric. *Histoire médicale, générale et particulière des maladies épidémiques, contagieuses et épizootiques, qui ont régné en Europe depuis les temps les plus reculés jusqu'à nos jours*, 2nd ed. 4 vols. Paris, 1835.
Paimblant de Rouil, Adrien. *Le 131e d'infanterie: historique du régiment*. Paris, 1891.
Pajol, Charles-Pierre-Victor, comte. *Pajol: général en chef*, 3 vols. Paris, 1874.
Paris (France). *Paris and its environs*, in Bogue's Guides for travellers. London, 1855.
Parkinson, Roger. *Hussar general: the life of Blücher, man of Waterloo*. London, 1975.
Pasquier, Etienne-Denis. *Mémoires du chancelier Pasquier*, 6 vols. Paris, 1893–5.
Paulin, Jules-Antoine, comte. *Les souvenirs du général baron Paulin, 1782–1876*. Paris, 1895.
Peiffert-Henriot, Irene, *Histoire des Champenois*. Paris, 1980.
de Pelleport, Pierre, vicomte. *Souvenirs militaires et intimes du général vicomte de Pelleport de 1793 à 1853*, 2 vols. Paris, 1857.
Périvier, A. *Napoléon journaliste*. Paris, 1918.
Perrin, René. 'L'esprit public dans le département de la Meurthe de 1814 à 1816', in *Annales de l'Est* (1913), 27th year, instalment 1.
Pertz, Georg Heinrich and Hans Delbrück. *Das Leben des Feldmarschalls Grafen Neithardt von Gneisenau*, 5 vols. Berlin, 1864–80.
Pétel, Auguste. *Essoyes pendant la Révolution et pendant les invasions de 1814 et de 1815*. Troyes, 1895.
Pétiet, Auguste. *Journal historique de la division de cavalerie légère du 5e corps de cavalerie, pendant la campagne de France en 1814*. Paris, 1821.
Petit, L.-M. *Histoire d'Epernay et de l'invasion 1870–1871 dans l'arrondissement*, 2 vols. Epernay, 1898.
Petot, Jean. *Histoire de l'administration des ponts et chaussées, 1599–1815*. Paris, 1958.
Petre, Francis Loraine. *Napoleon's last campaign in Germany, 1813*. 1912. Reissued London, 1974.
Petre, Francis Loraine. *Napoleon at bay, 1814*. 1914. Reissued London, 1994.
Peyrusse, Guillaume-Joseph Roux, baron. *1809–1815: mémorial et archives de M. le baron Peyrusse, trésorier-général de la couronne pendant les Cent-Jours*. Carcassonne, 1869.
von Pfister, Albert. *Denkwürdigkeiten aus der württembergischen Kreigsgeschichte des 18. und 19. Jahrhunderts im Anschluß an die Geschichte des 8. Infanterieregiments*. Stuttgart, 1868.
Philip, Raymond-Marie-Alphonse de. *Etude sur le service d'état-major pendant les guerres du premier empire*. Paris, 1900.
Pietresson de Saint-Aubin, P. *Le voyage du comte d'Artois dans l'Aube en 1814*. 1926.
Pillersdorff, Albert, Freiherr. *Das 57. Infanterie-Regiment Fürst Jablonowski und die Kriege seiner Zeit*. Vienna, 1857.
Planat de la Faye, Nicolas-Louis. *Vie de Planat de la Faye . . . souvenirs, lettres et dictées, recueillis et annotés par sa veuve*. Paris, 1895.
Planhol, Xavier de and Paul Claval. *An historical geography of France*. Trans. Janet Lloyd. Cambridge, 1994.
von Plotho, Carl. *Der Krieg in Deutschland und Frankreich in den Jahren 1813 und 1814*, 3 parts. Berlin, 1817.

Poltoratzky, Serge Dmitrievitch. *Conversation de l'empereur Napoléon avec le général russe Constantin Poltoratzky, en 1814, après la bataille de Champaubert, extrait de la 'Revue d'Alsace'*. Colmar, 1855.
Porcheret, Pierre. *Il était une fois . . . l'époque napoléonienne à Méry-sur-Seine et aux environs*. Méry-sur-Seine, 1990.
Porée, Charles. *Les prisonniers de guerre dans l'Yonne, de Louis XIV à Napoléon, 1643–1814*. Auxerre, 1916.
de Pougens, Marie-Charles-Joseph. *Mémoires et souvenirs*. Paris, 1834.
Pougiat, F.-E. *1814–1815: invasion des armées étrangères dans le département de l'Aube*. Troyes, 1833.
Poumiès de la Siboutie, François-Louis. *Souvenirs d'un médecin de Paris*. Paris, 1910.
Prinzing, Friedrich. *Epidemics resulting from wars*. Ed. Harald Westergaard. Oxford, 1916.
Prod'homme, J.R. 'L'administration préfectorale de l'Aube et les préfets impériaux', in *La vie en Champagne* (Dec. 1957), 5th year, no. 52, pp. 11–18.
Quantin, Raoul, 'Napoléon à Troyes en 1814', in *La vie en Champagne* (Mar. 1954), 2nd year, no. 11.
Quesné, Jacques Salbigoton, *Confessions de J.S. Quesné, depuis 1778 jusqu'à 1826*, 2 vols. Paris, 1828.
Quintin, Danielle and Bernard. *Dictionnaire des colonels de Napoléon*. Paris, 1996.
Raffles, Thomas. *Letters during a tour through some parts of France, Savoy, Switzerland, Germany, and The Netherlands, in the summer of 1817*. Liverpool, 1818.
von Rahden, Wilhelm, Baron. *Wanderungen eines alten Soldaten*, 3 parts. Berlin, 1846–51.
Raikes, Thomas. *A portion of the journal kept by Thomas Raikes, Esq. from 1831 to 1847: comprising reminiscences of social and political life in London and Paris during that period*, 4 vols. London, 1856–7.
von Raumer, Karl. *Karl von Raumer's Leben von ihm selbst erzählt*. Stuttgart, 1866.
ed. Rehtwisch, Theodor. *Aus dem Tagebuch eines Freiwilligen: Bilder aus den Jahren 1813 und 1814*. Leipzig, undated.
von Reiche, Ludwig. *Memoiren des königlich preußischen Generals der Infanterie Ludwig von Reiche*, 2 parts. Ed. Louis von Weltzien. Leipzig, 1857.
von Reinhard, Carl. *Geschichte des Königlich Preußischen Ersten Garde-Regiments zu Fuß*. Potsdam, 1858.
Rellstab, Heinrich Friedrich Ludwig. *Aus meinem Leben*, 2 vols. Berlin, 1861.
Rembowski, Aleksandre. *Sources documentaires concernant l'histoire du régiment des Chevau-légers de la Garde de Napoléon I*. Warsaw, 1899.
de Rémusart, Charles. 'L'invasion vue par un lycéen (1814): souvenirs inédits de Charles de Rémusart', in *La revue de Paris* (April 1958), 65th year, pp. 52–63.
Richard, Gabriel. 'L'exode sur les routes de Lorraine lors de l'invasion de 1814', in *Annales de l'Est* (1954), 5th series, 5th year, no. 4, pp. 355–64.
Riley, Jonathon P. *Napoleon and the world war of 1813: lessons in coalition warfighting*. London, 2000.
Riley, Jonathon P. *Napoleon as a general*. London, 2007.
de Rivaz, Charles-Emmanuel. *Mes souvenirs de Paris, 1810–1814*. Ed. Michel Salamin. Martigny, 1967.
Robb, Graham. *The discovery of France: a historical geography from the Revolution to the First World War*. London, 2007.
Roberts, Andrew. *Napoleon and Wellington*. London, 2001.
Robertson, Ian C. *Wellington invades France: the final phase of the Peninsular war, 1813–1814*. London, 2003.
ed. Robin, Pierre. *1814: la guerre racontée par des témoins*. Paris, 2004.
Robinaux, Pierre. *Journal de route du Capitaine Robinaux 1803–1832*. Paris, 1908.
de Rochechouart, Louis-Victor-Léon, comte. *Souvenirs sur la Révolution, l'empire et la restauration*. Paris, 1933.
Rodriguez, Julien-Antoine. *Relation historique de ce qui s'est passé à Paris*. Paris, 1814.
Rogers, Hugh Cuthbert Basset. *Napoleon's army*. London, 1974.
Rogue, Nicolas-Pierre-Christophe. *Souvenirs et journal d'un bourgeois d'Evreux, 1740–1830*. Evreux, 1850.

Roloff, Gustav. *Politik und Kriegführung während des Feldzuges von 1814*. Berlin, 1891.
Rothenberg, Gunther E. *The art of warfare in the age of Napoleon*. 1978. Reissued Staplehurst, 1997.
Rothenberg, Gunther E. *Napoleon's great adversary: Archduke Charles and the Austrian army, 1792–1814*. 1982. Reissued Staplehurst, 1995.
Rothwiller, Antoine-Ernest, baron. *Histoire du deuxième régiment de cuirassiers, ancien Royal de Cavalerie, 1635–1876*. Paris, 1877.
Rougier de la Bergerie, Jean-Baptiste, baron. *Les forêts de la France*. Paris, 1817.
Roux, Xavier. *L'invasion de la Savoie et du Dauphiné par les Autrichiens, en 1813 et 1814*, 2 vols. Grenoble, 1892.
Rouyer, Camille. *L'invasion de 1814 à Tonnerre*. Auxerre, 1915.
Sagnac, Philippe. *Le Rhin français pendant la Révolution et l'empire*. Paris, 1917.
de Saint-Just, Victor-Ernest-Marie. *Historique du 5e Régiment de dragons*. Paris, 1891.
Sautai, Maurice. *L'école polytechnique pendant la campagne de France, 1814*. Paris, 1910.
Savary, Anne-Jean-Marie-René, duc de Rovigo. *Mémoires du duc de Rovigo, pour servir à l'histoire de l'empereur Napoléon*, 8 vols. Paris, 1828.
Schama, Simon. *Patriots and liberators: revolution in the Netherlands, 1780–1813*. London, 1977.
Schneider, Louis. *Aus dem Leben Kaiser Wilhelms, 1849–1873*, 3 vols. Berlin, 1888.
Schoeps, Hans Joachim. *Aus den Jahren Preussischer Not und Erneuerung*. Berlin, 1963.
Schroeder, Paul W. *The transformation of European politics, 1763–1848*. 1994. Reissued Oxford, 1996.
von Schubert, Friedrich. *Unter dem Doppeladler: Erinnerungen eines Deutschen in russischem Offizierdienst 1789–1814*. Ed. Erik Amburger. Stuttgart, 1962.
Schur, Nathan. *Napoleon in the Holy Land*. London, 1999.
Schwartz, Karl. *Leben des Generals Carl von Clausewitz und der Frau Marie von Clausewitz*, 2 vols. Berlin, 1878.
von Schwartzkoppen, Clotilde. *Karl von François: ein deutsches Soldatenleben*. Schwerin, 1873.
zu Schwarzenberg, Carl Philipp, Fürst. *Briefe des Feldmarschalls Fürsten Schwarzenberg an seine Frau, 1799–1816*. Ed. Johann Friedrich Novak. Vienna, 1913.
Schwarzenberg, Charles. 'Considérations sur la campagne de France', in *La vie en Champagne* (Dec. 1964), 12th year, no. 129, pp. 12–14.
Scott, John. *Paris revisited in 1815, by way of Brussels: including a walk over the field of battle at Waterloo*, 3rd ed. London, 1816.
Seaton, Albert. *The Cossacks*. Reading, 1972.
Seeley, Sir John Robert. *Life and times of Stein, or Germany and Prussia in the Napoleonic age*, 3 vols. Cambridge, 1878.
de Ségur, Philippe-Paul. *Histoire et mémoires*, 7 vols. Paris, 1873.
Semmel, Stuart. *Napoleon and the British*. London, 2004.
Shcherbatov, Prince Aleksandr Grigorevich. *Le Feld-Maréchal Prince Paskévitsch: sa vie politique et militaire d'après des documents inédits*, 6 vols. St Petersburg, 1888–93.
Sherwig, John M. *Guineas and gunpowder: British foreign aid in the wars with France, 1793–1815*. Cambridge, Massachusetts, 1969.
Short, John Tregerthen. *Prisoners of war in France from 1804 to 1814, being the adventures of John Tregerthen Short and Thomas Williams of St Ives, Cornwall*. London, 1914.
Simpkin, Richard E. *Race to the swift: thoughts on twenty-first century warfare*. London, 1985.
Six, Georges, *Dictionnaire biographique des généraux et amiraux français de la Révolution et de l'empire, 1792–1814*, 2 vols. Paris, 1934.
Smallman-Raynor, Matthew and Andrew David Cliff. *War epidemics: an historical geography of infectious diseases in military conflict and civil strife, 1850–2000*. Oxford, 2004.
Smith, Digby. *The Greenhill Napoleonic wars data book*. London, 1998.
Smith, Digby. *1813 Leipzig: Napoleon and the Battle of the Nations*. London, 2001.
von Stadlinger, Leo Ignaz. *Geschichte des Württembergischen Kriegswesens von der frühesten bis zur neuesten Zeit*. Stuttgart, 1856.
Stanhope, Philip Henry, 5th Earl Stanhope. *Notes of conversations with the Duke of Wellington 1831–1851*. 1888. Reissued London, 1938.

Starklof, R. *Geschichte des Königlich Württembergischen Zweiten Reiter-Regiments, ehemaligen Jäger-Regiments zu Pferde Herzog Louis.* Darmstadt, 1862.
Starklof, R., *Geschichte des Königlich Württembergischen vierten Reiterregiments Königin Olga, 1805–1866.* Stuttgart, 1867.
Steenackers, François-Frédéric. *L'invasion de 1814 dans la Haute-Marne.* Paris, 1868.
Steffens, Henry. *Adventures on the road to Paris, during the campaigns of 1813–14.* London, 1848.
Stein, F. von. *Geschichte des Russischen Heeres vom Ursprunge desselben bis zur Thronbesteigung des Kaisers Nikolai I Pawlowitsch.* Hanover, 1885.
Stewart, afterwards Vane, Charles William, 3rd marquis of Londonderry. *Narrative of the war in Germany and France in 1813 and 1814*, 2nd ed. London, 1830.
Steyert, André. *Nouvelle histoire de Lyon*, 4 vols. Lyon, 1899.
Stommel, Henry and Elizabeth. *Volcano weather: the story of 1816, the year without a summer.* Newport, Rhode Island, 1983.
Strack von Weißenbach. *Geschichte der Königlich Württembergischen Artillerie.* Stuttgart, 1882.
Suchet, Louis-Gabriel, duc d'Albuféra. *Memoirs of the war in Spain, from 1808 to 1814*, 2 vols. London, 1829.
Susane, Louis-Auguste-Victor-Vincent. *La Champagne pouilleuse.* Metz, 1857.
Tanski, Joseph. *L'entrée des russes à Paris et l'armée russe.* Paris, 1864.
Taylor, Alan John Percivale. *The Habsburg monarchy, 1809–1918: a history of the Austrian Empire and Austria-Hungary.* 1948. Reissued London, 1990.
Thévenot, Arsène. *Histoire de la ville et de la chatellenie de Pont-sur-Seine.* Nogent-sur-Seine, 1873.
Thibaudeau, Antoine-Claire, comte. *Mémoires de A.-C. Thibaudeau, 1799–1815.* Paris, 1913.
von Thielen, Maximilien Friedrich. *Erinnerungen aus dem Kriegerleben eines 82jährigen Veteranen der österreichischen Armee.* Vienna, 1863.
Thiers, Louis-Adolphe. *Histoire du consulat et de l'empire*, 20 vols. Paris, 1845–62.
Thomas, Donald. *Cochrane: Britannia's sea wolf.* 1978. Reissued London, 2002.
Thompson, James Matthew. *The French Revolution.* 1943. Reissued Stroud, 2001.
Thompson, James Matthew. *Napoleon Bonaparte.* 1952. Reissued Oxford, 1990.
Thouvenel, Pierre-Sébastien. *Traité analytique des fièvres contagieuses et sporadiques, simples et compliquées, qui ont régné dans le département de la Meurthe, vers la fin de 1813, et au commencement de 1814.* Pont-à-Mousson, 1814.
von Thurn und Taxis, Fürst August. *Aus drei Feldzügen 1812 bei 1815.* Leipzig, 1912.
Tiersot, Edmond-Pierre-Lazare. *La Restauration dans le département de l'Ain: l'invasion – les cour prévôtales, 1814–1815–1816.* Paris, 1884.
de Tournon, Philippe-Antoine, comte. *Notes sur l'invasion du Lyonnais en 1814.* Lyon, 1887.
Tulard, Jean. *Nouvelle histoire de Paris: le consulat et l'empire, 1800–1815.* Paris, 1970.
Tulard, Jean. *La vie quotidienne des Français sous Napoléon.* 1978.
Tulard, Jean and Louis Garros. *Itinéraire de Napoléon au jour le jour 1769–1821.* Paris, 1992.
Uffindell, Andrew. *The eagle's last triumph: Napoleon's victory at Ligny, June 1815.* 1994. Reissued London, 2006.
Uffindell, Andrew. *On the fields of glory: the battlefields of the 1815 campaign.* 1996. Reissued London, 2002.
Uffindell, Andrew. *The National Army Museum book of Wellington's armies.* London, 2003.
Uffindell, Andrew. *Great generals of the Napoleonic wars and their battles, 1805–1815.* Staplehurst, 2003.
Uffindell, Andrew. *Waterloo commanders: Napoleon, Wellington and Blücher.* Barnsley, 2007.
Uffindell, Andrew. *Napoleon's immortals: the Imperial Guard and its battles, 1804–1815.* Stroud, 2007.
Underwood, Thomas Richard. *A narrative of memorable events in Paris . . . in the year 1814; being extracts from the journal of a détenu, who continued a prisoner, on parole, in the French capital, from the year 1803 to 1814.* London, 1828.
von Unger, Wolfgang. *Blücher*, 2 vols. Berlin, 1907–8.
Uxkull, Boris. *Arms and the woman: the diaries of Baron Boris Uxkull, 1812–1819.* London, 1966.
Varnhagen von Ense, Karl August. *Geschichte der Kriegszüge des Generals Tettenborn während der Jahre 1813 und 1814.* Stuttgart, 1814.

Varnhagen von Ense, Karl August. *Leben des Generals Grafen Bülow von Dennewitz.* Berlin, 1853.
Véron, Louis-Désiré. *Mémoires d'un bourgeois de Paris*, 6 vols. Paris, 1853.
Vichier-Guerre, Jean-Louis-Victor. *1814: opérations en Savoie et en Dauphiné.* Paris, 1910.
Vidal de la Blache, Henri-Joseph-Marie-Casimir. *L'évacuation de l'Espagne et l'invasion dans le Midi, juin 1813–avril 1814*, 2 vols. Paris, 1914.
de Villefosse, Louis and Janine Bouissounouse. *The scourge of the eagle: Napoleon and the liberal opposition.* Trans. and ed. Michael Ross. London, 1972.
Vimont, Jean-Claude. *La prison politique en France: genèse d'un mode d'incarcération spécifique XVIIIe – XXe siècles.* Paris, 1993.
Vizetelly, Ernest A. *The wild marquis: the life and adventures of Armand Guerry de Maubreuil, marquis d'Orvault.* London, 1905.
Wacker, Volker. *Die alliierte Besetzung Frankreichs in den Jahren 1814 bis 1818.* Hamburg, 2001.
von Waldersee, Alfred Heinrich Carl Ludwig, Graf. *Denkwürdigkeiten des General-Feldmarschalls Alfred Graf von Waldersee*, 3 vols. Ed. Heinrich Otto Meisner. Berlin, 1925.
Weber, Eugen. *Peasants into Frenchmen: the modernization of rural France, 1870–1914.* London, 1977.
Webster, Charles Kingsley. *The foreign policy of Castlereagh, 1812–1815: Britain and the reconstruction of Europe.* 1931. Reissued London, 1950.
Webster, Charles Kingsley. *The foreign policy of Castlereagh, 1815–1822: Britain and the European alliance.* London, 1934.
Weil, Maurice H. *La campagne de 1814 d'après les documents des archives impériales et royales de la guerre à Vienne: la cavalerie des armées alliées pendant la campagne de 1814*, 4 vols. Paris, 1891–6.
Weil, Maurice H. *Le prince Eugène et Murat, 1813–1814: opérations militaires, négotiations diplomatiques*, 5 vols. Paris, 1902.
Weller, Jac. *Wellington in the Peninsula.* 1962. Reissued London, 1992.
Weller, Jac. *On Wellington: the Duke and his art of war.* Ed. Andrew Uffindell. London, 1998.
Wellington, 1st Duke of. *The dispatches of Field Marshal the Duke of Wellington during his various campaigns in India, Denmark, Portugal, Spain, the Low Countries, and France, from 1799 to 1818*, 13 vols. Ed. John Gurwood. London, 1837–9.
Wellington, 1st Duke of. *Supplementary despatches, correspondence, and memoranda of Field Marshal Arthur Duke of Wellington, KG*, 15 vols. Ed. 2nd Duke of Wellington. London, 1858–72.
Welschinger, Henri. *La censure sous le premier empire.* Paris, 1882.
Wetherell, John Porritt. *The adventures of John Wetherell.* Ed. Cecil Scott Forester. London, 1954.
Wilson, Sir Robert Thomas. *Private diary of travels, personal services, and public events, during mission and employment with the European armies in the campaigns of 1812, 1813, 1814: from the invasion of Russia to the capture of Paris*, 2 vols. London, 1861.
Winters, Harold A. et al. *Battling the elements: weather and terrain in the conduct of war.* London, 1998.
Wolfe, R.B. *English prisoners in France, containing observations on their manners and habits, principally with reference to their religious state.* London, 1830.
Württemberg: Army. *Das Commando des Kronprinzen von Württemberg in den Feldzügen von 1814 und 1815 gegen Frankreich.* Stuttgart, 1841.
von Württemberg, Prince Eugen. *Journal des campagnes du prince de Wurtemberg, 1812–1814.* Ed. Georges Fabry. Paris, 1907.
Zaluski, Jozef. *Les Chevau-légers polonais de la Garde, 1812–1814: souvenirs.* Paris, 1997.
Zelle, W. *1814: Der Zusammenbruch des I Kaiserreichs.* Leipzig, 1906.
Zhmodikov, Alexander and Yurii. *Tactics of the Russian army in the Napoleonic wars*, 2 vols. West Chester, Ohio, 2003.
Zins, Ronald. *1814: l'Armée de Lyon, ultime espoir de Napoléon.* Massieux, 1998.
Zinsser, Hans. *Rats, lice, and history: being a study in biography, which, after twelve preliminary chapters indispensable for the preparation of the lay reader, deals with the life history of typhus fever.* London, 1937.

Index

Agout, Capt d' (Fr 4e Dragons), 73, 206
Alberti, Lt Wilhelm (Pr 6. Res-Inf-Regt), 33–4, 93
Alexander I, Tsar of Russia, 136; war aims, 4, 6, 8, 50 (becomes more realistic, 123, 143, 198); role in Allied decision-making, 19, 82, 123 (desires to be commander-in-chief, 18; decision to march on Paris, 109, 110); disputes with Metternich, 25, 28, 30–1, 69–70; delays and shields Russ Guards and reserves, 28, 116; reaches Langres, 29; at La Rothière, 48, 49; searches for Blücher at Château de Brienne (2/2), 175; attitude to Châtillon peace conference, 31, 69, 80–1; receives news of Laon, 97; at Arcis-sur-Aube, 105; at Fère-Champenoise, 111; false rumour of death, 134; enters Paris, 120; poses as leader of civilised world, 200; protects Paris, 114, 160, 161; wary of Bourbons, 124; influenced by Talleyrand, 123, 124, 125; orders release of Fr POWs, 214
Allix de Vaux, GdeB Jacques, 40, 252, 255
Andlau-Birseck, Konrad, Freiherr von (Gov-Gen of Franche-comté), 150, *153*
Arbois de Jubainville, Charles d' (civilian), 173, 204
Arcis-sur-Aube (Aube), 40, 101, 105, 134, 140, 225; Nap's headquarters, 130-1
Arcis-sur-Aube, Battle of (20–21/3), 76, 101–3, *104*, 105–6, 107, 131, 132, 143, 229, 281; effect of terrain on artillery fire, 105, 133; Nap rides horse over shell, 103, 105, 126, 201, 278; Nap downplays defeat, 201; civilians traumatised, 162
armoured personnel carrier invented for Nap, 14–15
Arnauld, Eugène, baron de Vitrolles (royalist), 182, 185, 221
Artois, Charles-Philippe, comte d' (later King Charles X), 199, 228
Audouard de Montviol, Adèle (civilian), 174
Augereau, Maréchal Pierre, 12, 79, 80, 126, 162, 284; fails to intervene decisively, 146, 147, 148; vilified for outcome, 148, 201
Austrian army, 23; quality, 21, 22; conduct at Montereau, 77; behaviour praised by Nap, 193; reinforcements detached from HA to help form Südarmee, 80; contribution to Battle of Paris, 119; shielded from heavy losses, 4, 19, 28, 80, 145; Fr-born generals, 164; Landwehr, 22, 170, 264def
- *units*: 1. leichte Div, 246; 2. leichte Div, 246, 270; Inf-Regt Josef Colloredo, 77; Ferdinand-Husaren, 23; *see also under Hauptarmee for corps and reserves*
Autun (Saône-et-Loire), 210, 214
Auvray, Sous-lt Pierre (Fr 23e Dragons), 37, 204
Auxerre (Yonne), 40, 173, 178, 185, 271
Avesnes (Nord), 236

Balisson de Rougemont, Michel (journalist), 76
Bar-sur-Aube (Aube), 102, 158, 230–7, 282; sacked by Bavarians, 175, 230, 231; birth, marriage, and death rates, 231, 232–4, *235*; long-term impact of campaign, 233, 234, 237
Bar-sur-Aube, Battles of (24/1 and 27/2), 29, 100, 230, 231, 232, 247
Barclay de Tolly, FM Mikhail, Count, 114, 119, 246
Barère de Vieuzac, Bertrand (politician), 209
Bausset, Louis de (Préfet du palais), 126, 128
Bavarian army, 20, 28; attack on Rothau, 186–7; occupation areas, *153*, *154*, 157; pillaging, 170, 230, 231; moderation at Epinal, 169; siege artillery, 269
- *units*: 7. Linien-Inf-Regt, 170; 7. Chevaulegers-Regt, 230; *see also* V Armee-Abtheilung, *under* Hauptarmee; *and* Wrede
Belfort (territoire de Belfort), 29, 225, 287
Berry-au-Bac (Aisne), 86, 91, 96
Berthier, Maréchal Louis, 74, 76, 109, 128, 251, 267, 274
Bertrand, GdeD Henri, comte, 211
Besançon (Doubs), 29, 146, 170, 184, 207, 225, 269, 293
Biot, Capt Hubert (ADC to Pajol), 76
Biron von Kurland, GM Fürst, 160
bistros (aka bistrots), origin, 121
Blayney, Maj-Gen Andrew Thomas, eleventh Baron, 176
Blois (Loir-et-Cher), 124, 194, 208, 213, 214, 280
Blücher, FM Gebhard Leberecht von, 19–20, 64, 68, 130, 135, 185–6; interview with Nap (1807), 174, 272; limitations as commander, 20, 30, 84, 96, 142–3, 269, 273; aims, 6–7, 143; alcohol, 175, 176; headquarters, 131; mobility in 1814, 41, 131, 282; at Brienne, 44–6, 175, 272; at La Rothière, 47, 48, 49, 50; allegedly seeks death at Vauchamps, 275; injured at Méry-sur-Seine, 79; collapses at Laon, 93, 94, 96, 131; at Battle of Paris, 114, 119; misses entry into Paris, 120; rescued at Ligny (1815), 272
Bonaparte, Joseph (elder brother of Nap), 114, 117, 196, 201, 216, 256, 259, 271, 279, 284
Bordeaux (Gironde), 207, 209, 211; impact of revolt, 108, 123, 124, 146, 147, 189, 198, 199–200, 284
Boucher de Crèvecœur, Jacques, 116
Bourbons (Fr royal family): royalists in France, 110, 199; wariness of population, 178, 199; information suppressed by Nap, 189–90, 194; Allied attitude, 120, 124, 163, 199–200; credible alternative to Nap, 70, 124, 146, 180, 183, 198; problems after restoration, 127, 200, 225–6; *see also under* psychological operations
Boyen, GM Hermann von, 85
Boyer, baron de Rebeval, GdeD Joseph, 88, 251, 255, 256, 259
Brienne (Aube), 139, 140, 216; burned (29/1), 40, 45, 298; Nap compensates inhabitants for losses, 225, 228
Brienne, Battle of (29/1), 44–6, 52, 129, 132, 133, 136, *235*; army strengths, 274; losses, 46, 49, 191, 253; impact in Paris, 195, 196
Brienne, Château de, 44, 50, 175, 178, 222; Blücher flees (29/1), 45, 272
Brienon-sur-Armançon (Yonne), 213
Broglie, Victor, duc de (civilian), 195
Brumath (Bas-Rhin), 204
Bubna und Littitz, FML Ferdinand, Graf von, *155*, 205, 246, 247
Buchell, William (British POW), 214
Bülow, GenLt Friedrich Wilhelm von, 112, *154*, 247, 248; independent outlook, 20, 84, 85; at Laon, 91, 94, 96
Burghersh, Col John Fane, Lord, 100
Burghersh, Priscilla Fane, Lady, 3, 164
Burgundy, Nap awards Légion d'honneur to three towns (1815), 178, 288

Caffarelli, Charles, baron (préfet of Aube), 183, 286
Cambronne, GdeB Pierre, baron, 76
Cassagne, GdeB Pierre, baron, 181
Casse, George (British POW), 213
Castellane-Novejan, Col-maj Boniface, comte de (Fr 1er Gardes d'honneur), 206
Castlereagh, Robert Stewart, Viscount (British Foreign Secretary), 6, 8, 30, 70, 123
Caulaincourt, GdeD Armand, marquis de, 52, 109
Caupeil, Jean (inventor of an

armoured personnel carrier), 14–15, 268
Chalon-sur-Saône (Saône-et-Loire), 178, 292
Châlons-sur-Marne (aka Châlons-en-Champagne, Marne), 36, 64, 70, 100, 109, 175, 211, 218, 219, 223; population size and displacements, 39, 203; supply base, 68, 139, 140, 168; Fr camp, 41, 272; concentration point of Nap's army (late Jan), 30, 136, 138; Allies threaten to burn down (Feb), 40
Chambéry (Savoie), 178, 284
Champaubert (Marne), 53, 55
Champaubert, Battle of (10/2), 13, 56, 57, 58, 132, 136; scale and significance, 56, 58, 84, 196, 274, 291
Chaptal, Sénateur Jean, comte (commissaire extraordinaire), 202
Charlet, Nicolas (artist), 118
Charton, Charles (civilian), 169
Chassé, GdeB David, baron, 106
Château-Thierry (Aisne), 58, 59, 64, 137, 216, 270; population size, 39; Nap's quarters, 130; inhabitants' reaction to liberation, 134; deputation in Paris describes Allied atrocities, 192; losses of arrondissement, 226
Château-Thierry, Battle of (12/2), 13, 61, 62, 63, 98, 212, 274
Chateaubriand, François-René (writer), 189, 196, 200
Châtillon-sur-Seine (Côte-d'Or): peace conference, 31, 52, 53, 69, 74, 80–1, 134, 196, 198 (collapses, 98, 108, 109, 198, 200, 292)
Chaumont (Haute-Marne), 42, 95, 97, 109, 155, 157, 170, 173, 174, 185, 282; moral impact of epidemic, 219
Chaumont, Treaty of (1/3), 81, 127, 143, 144, 276
Chemin des Dames, 86, 89, 90, 91
Chevaliers de la Foi (royalist society), 199
civilians: experiences in 1814, 150–237; caught up in battle, 69, 116, 162–3, 217; loyalty demanded by both Nap and Allies, 156, 183–4; mixed reliability as source of military intelligence, 134, 135, 137; solidarity in face of invasion, 179; social tensions, 139, 178, 182; clergy, 156–7, 174, 178, 180, 225; nobility (attitude to Empire, 180, 193; vulnerable to denunciations, 178); informers and malicious allegations, 183, 185, 236; attitudes towards irregulars, 182–3, 187; mortality rates (at Bar-sur-Aube, 232–3; at Huningue, 29; at Troyes, compared with military, 215); disposal of dead bodies, 217–18, 221, 232, 233, 296; poverty and begging, 34, 139, 164–5, 172, 177, 206, 207, 221, 223, 286; compensation for losses, 225–8; not always passive victims of campaign, 159, 170, 178, 182, 216, 236

- *Allied occupation arrangements*: 150–63; Fr administrators as intermediaries, 151, 156, 157, 162, 202–3; size of occupied area, 150; initial disorder, 158–9, 178, 203; emergence of more regularity, 159–60, 170, 172; occupation following end of hostilities, 163, 224
- *relations with Allied forces*: diverse reactions to Allied arrival, 29, 51, 158–9 (hide valuables, 159, 196; at Paris, 120–1); friendships with Allied soldiers and POWs, 176, 208, 211, 230–1, 237
- *relations with Fr forces*: local guides for Nap, 133–4; reaction to liberation, 98, 134; reception of Nap, 51, 98, 130-1; hide Fr soldiers at Troyes, 185; help Fr POWs escape, 212–13; abandon Fr wounded, 216; pillaging by Fr soldiers, 169, 172, 207; relations strained by risk of disease, 220
- *see also*: irregular forces; Paris; population displacements; préfets; psychological operations; reprisals; requisitioning; resistance; sick and wounded; *and* women

Clausewitz, GM Karl von, 107, 143, 149
Clichy, barrière de (at Paris), 117–18
Colomb, Maj Friedrich von (Pr Streifkorps), 64, 176
Compiègne (Oise), 112, 196, 204, 278
Constant, Benjamin (writer), 200
Corbineau, GdeD Jean-Baptiste, baron, 162
Craonne (Aisne), Battle of (7/3), 34, 86, 87, 88–91, 107, 132, 133, 292; strengths and losses of armies, 88, 90, 169, 277; reported in Parisian press, 190, 197; monument, 292
Curély, Col Jean (Fr 10e Hussards), 63, 258

Dardenne, Pierre (schoolteacher), 173, 174
Davout, Maréchal Louis, 11, 12, 149
Defleury, Pierre (sous-préfet, aka Fleury de Chaboulon), 162
Delattre, Lt (Fr 6e Voltigeurs), 213, 295
Delort, GdeB Jacques, baron, 75–6
Deschamps, Etienne (gendarme), 184, 289
Digeon, GeB Armand, 183
Dijon (Côte-d'Or), 29, 79, 111, 120, 123, 154, 170, 237; Allies extract hostages and oaths of obedience, 156, 185; inhabitants forbidden to appear with weapons, 159; maire's workload, 158; women consort with Allied soldiers, 235
Ditfurth, Maj Wilhelm von (Pr 1. Garde-Regt zu Fuß), 79–80, 116, 165
Doulevant (Haute-Marne), 41, 281
Duhesme, GdeD Philibert, 76
Dupaty, Capt Emmanuel (Garde nationale), 117

Eclaron (Haute-Marne), 193, 291

Ecole polytechnique, 118, 279
El Niño Southern Oscillation (ENSO), linked to harshness of winter, 32
Emmanuel, Maj-Gen George Arsenyevich, 97
Epernay (Marne), 34, 137, 139, 140, 178, 191; official interpreters, 173–4; champagne industry, 174, 175, 176
Epinal (Vosges), 29, 135, 154, 160, 169; images d'Epinal, 201
Ertel, Lt-Gen Fedor Fedorovich, 170
Etoges (Marne), 40, 64, 67, 72
Eugen von Württemberg, Lt-Gen Prince, 21–2, 246
Eugène, prince (Viceroy, Kingdom of Italy), 145, 147–8

Fabvier, Col Charles, baron (Fr VI Corps), 13, 51–2, 94
Fain, Agathon, baron, 52, 76–7, 103, 134, 174
Faré, Capt adj-maj Charles (Fr 2e Gren à pied), 99
Ferdinand VII, King of Spain, 11, 121, 147
Fère-Champenoise (Marne), Battle of (25/3), 111–12, 113, 162–3, 259
Festieux (Aisne), 94, 227
Finot, Pierre (adjoint), 134
Fismes decrees (5/3), 183–4, 185–6
Flahaut de la Billarderie, GdeD Auguste, comte de, 267
Folliot de Crenneville, FML Ludwig, Graf, 164
Fontainebleau (Seine-et-Marne), 69, 119, 122, 123, 124–5, 126, 179, 198; palace, 183, 193, 196
Fontainebleau, Treaty of (11/4), 125
Fortin, Florentin (priest), 173
François, Staff Capt Karl von (Russ VI Armee-Abtheilung), 29, 169
Frankfurt-am-Main (Germany): imports silk from Lyon, 205; Allied conference (1813), 3, 6–8
Frankfurt Proposals (1813), 8, 31, 52, 197
Franz I, Emperor of Austria, 4, 18, 25, 80, 97, 114, 122; unable to prevent disorders, 170; Nap sends picture of King of Rome, 194; forced to withdraw on Dijon by Nap's m/derrières, 110–11, 123; absent from Allied entry into Paris, 120; prevents reunion of Marie-Louise with Nap, 126
French army, 11–17; conscription, 9, 10, 12, 158, 181 ('Maries-Louises', 13; age of conscripts, 14); clothing inadequate, 11, 17, 73, 99, 212; foreign elements, 16, 148, 212; deserters, 31, 51, 95, 135, 182, 186, 198 (attempts to check, 51–2, 180, 204); réfractaires, 181, 182, 204, 265def; morale, 16, 51–2, 124, 125, 142, 220; quality, 11, 12–14, 15, 17, 44–5, 46, 52 (in defending a town, 69; limited tactical manoeuvrability, 13, 88); re-organised frequently, 15, 95, 250, 268; mobility, 37, 72, 95, 97, 128, 129–33, 149, 282; mobile

reserve's composition, 53, 74, 133, 254, 256–7, 258, 282; pontoon train, 38, 84, 101, 133, 271
– *strength*, 11, 14, 15, 42, 128, 129, 146; at La Rothière, 47; at Champaubert, 274; at Montmirail, 59; at Mormant, 71; at Montereau, 75; in front of Troyes (late Feb), 79; at Laon, 93; at Arcis-sur-Aube, 101, 105; at Battle of Paris, 113–14; after fall of Paris, 122, 125; units smaller than usual, 15, 250; reinforcements, 15, 52, 72, 82, 108, 145
– *commanders*: quality, 12, 15, 145; attitudes after fall of Paris, 124–5; losses of maréchaux and generals, 12, 49, 90, 162, 268; losses of colonels, 142, 284; *see also names of individual commanders*
– *cavalry*: quantity and quality, 12, 14, 67, 73, 75; skill of commanders, 12–13, 96; dragons from Peninsula, 73
– *artillery*: quantity and quality, 14, 47, 52, 133, 268; effect of fire at Arcis-sur-Aube, 133; massed batteries, 48, 66, 73, 89, 133, 275; reserve artillery, 72, 89, 133, 196, 254
UNITS: *see also* Garde nationale; *and* Imperial Guard
– *infantry regts*: 1er and 3e Régts de marine, 273; 32e Ligne, 191; 37e Légère, 51; 70e Ligne, 273; 113e Ligne, 252; 121e Ligne, 273; 122e Ligne, 258; 131e Ligne, 273; 132e Ligne, 273; Régt de la Vistule, 191, 212, 258
– *cavalry regts*: 2e Cuirassiers, 212; 3e Chasseurs à cheval, 276; 4e Dragons, 73, 206; 7e Chasseurs à cheval, 191; 10e Hussards, 63, 274; 16e Dragons, 74; 23e Dragons, 37, 204
Frénilly, François Fauveau de (civilian), 222
Friant, GdeD Louis, comte, 72, 251, 252, 254, 256, 258
Friedrich Wilhelm III, King of Prussia, 4, 49, 70, 97, 105, 109; mobilises Landsturm (1813), 186; enters Paris, 120
Fusil, Louise (actress), 211

Gain de Montaignac, Jean de (royalist), 39, 165
Garde nationale, 10, 38, 40, 41, 93, 112, *151*, 209, 263def; selective mobilisation, 16, 17, 161; varied quality, 17; target practice, 268; at Lyon, 202; at Fère-Champenoise, 111, 163; sedentary cohortes urbaines, 17, 211; as support for levée en masse, 64, 179, 180, 181; guards Allied POWs, 210, 211, 213–14; uses transport en poste, 282; uniform worn by King of Rome, 194; in occupied areas, 160, 181, 184
Garde nationale de Paris, 113, 116, 206, 259, 267, 268, 279; escorts POWs, 294–5; at barrière de Clichy (30/3), 117, 118; after fall of Paris, 120, 160–1
Gayot, Armand, marquis de Saint-Chamans (civilian), 178
Geismar, Col Fedor Klementievich, Baron von (flying corps), 24
Gendarmerie, 14, 16, 139, 160, 161–2, 189, 206, 212, 263def; counters desertion, 51, 204; guards POWs, 17, 207, 208, 211, 213, 214, 295; gathers intelligence, 135; meant to support levée en masse, 159, 179, 180; in occupied areas, 160, 161
Geneva (Switzerland), 79, 146, 159, 167, 173, 238; Augereau ordered to take hostages, 162
Gérard, GdeD Etienne, baron, 74, 76, 251, 252, 254, 255, 256, 268
Gérost, Edme-Jacques (civilian), 168, 203, 236
Girardon, Claude (police commissioner), 232
Girod de l'Ain, Chef de bataillon Jean (ADC), 130, 172–3, 236
Givet (Ardennes), 207, 209, 213, 293
Gneisenau, GenLt August Neidhardt von, 20, 38, 68, 113, 175, 247; believes Paris can be starved into surrender, 139; becomes cautious (Mar), 85, 94–5, 96; views on coalition strategy, 30, 143; low opinion of HA, 96; concerns about Crown Prince of Sweden, 96; suspicions of Wellington (1815), 149; friction with SA's corps commanders, 20, 85, 96; poor opinion of SA's cavalry commanders, 23–4; respect for Fr cavalry commanders, 96
Golitsyn, Prince (Russ officer), 98
Golitsyn V, Lt-Gen Dmitry Vladimirovich, Prince, 164, 246
Gonzze, chevalier de Rougeville (royalist), 183
Gouault, chevalier Jacques (royalist), 183
Gourgaud, Col Gaspard, baron (officier d'ordonnance), 46, 272
Grabowski, Capt Józef (Fr staff officer), 105, 222
Griois, Col Charles, baron (Fr IG artillery), 61, 63, 72, 105
Grivel, Capt de vaisseau Jean (Fr IG Marins), 16
Grouchy, GdeD Emmanuel, comte de, 66, 201, 251, 253, 255, 257
Grüber, Rittmeister Carl von (Bav 7. Chevaulegers-Regt), 230–1, 298
Guéret (Creuse), 206, 208, 213, 294
Guerry, Armand de (hired assassin, aka Monsieur de Maubreuil), 124, 280–1
Guignes (Seine-et-Marne), 71, 72
Guyot, GdeD Claude, comte, 183, 254, 299
Gyulai, FZM Ignaz, Graf, 19, 246

Hardenberg, Karl August von (Pr Chancellor), 4, 70
Hauptarmee, 38, 132, 139; composition, 18–19, 246–7; strength, 134, 165 (at Mormant, 71; at Montereau, 75; at Troyes in late Feb, 79, 80; problems caused by size, 100, 102); indiscipline, 24, 159–60, 168, 169, 170, 172, 230; role in invasion, 7; Nap's main target, 142; fails to support SA adequately, 69, 85, 96, 100, 129; slow communications, 112, 136; age of corps commanders, 20; inter-operability of contingents, 23; cavalry (poorly led, 23, 135; massed, 48–9, 111, 112); main lines of communication, 139, 170, *171*, 172, 287
– *operations*: crosses Rhine, 25, 26–7, 28, 179; advance from Rhine, 28, 29, 36; central reserve created at Dijon, 29; during Brienne and La Rothière, 46, 47; separates from SA in early Feb, 50, 52, 53, 55; advances on Paris, 69, 196, 206 (becomes over-extended, 70); retreats, 74, 146, 185 (helped by freeze to escape, 33, 77); resumes offensive at end Feb, 82, 100, 230; visual impact at Arcis-sur-Aube, 106; bears brunt of Battle of Paris, 118
UNITS: *see also individual units under national armies; and names of unit commanders*
– *Austrian corps*: I Armee-Abtheilung, 18, 174, 246, 247, 269, 270 (detached to Südarmee, 80); II Armee-Abtheilung, 18, 246, 270 (besieges fortresses, 29, 247); III Armee-Abtheilung, 18, 28, 29, 47, 80, 246
– *IV (Württemberg) Armee-Abtheilung*: 18, 21, 23, 29, 47, 120, 246, 249; bears brunt of fighting, 28
– *V (Bavarian) Armee-Abtheilung*: 18, 19, 21, *153*, 157, 248, 287; bears brunt of fighting, 28, 70; composition, 23, 246; sickness rates, 215; at La Rothière, 47; action on the Voire, 51, 273; at Nogent-sur-Seine, 69; at Nangis and Villeneuve, 74; covers HA's retreat from Troyes, 80; at Arcis-sur-Aube, 103, 106; left as rearguard at Meaux (end Mar), 112
– *VI (Russian) Armee-Abtheilung*: 18, 29, 70, 71, 246, 247, 275; as link with SA, 28; advanced guard bears brunt of fighting, 28; at Nogent-sur-Seine, 69
– *Reserves*: Austrian reserves, 18, 80, 170, 246, 269, 270; Russ Guards and reserves, 18, 19, 31, 246–7 (belatedly cross Rhine, 28; at La Rothière, 47, 48; at Arcis-sur-Aube, 105; at Paris, 116, 119–20)
Henckel von Donnersmarck, Oberst Wilhelm, Graf (Pr I Corps), 58–9, 90, 94, *166*
Henrion, GdeB Christophe, baron, 231, 256, 258
Hessen-Homburg, Gen der Kav Friedrich, Erbprinz von, 80, 246
Hohenlohe-Waldenburg-Bartenstein,

FML Ludwig, Fürst zu (Gov-Gen of Burgundy), 150, *153*, *154*
Huguet-Châtaux, GdeB Louis, 272
Huningue (Haut-Rhin), 29, 225, 269

Imperial Guard (of Nap), 67, 75, 250–1, 253; proportion of Nap's army, 13, 61; proportion of mobile reserve, 53, 133, 282; losses, 68; looting, 51
– *Old Guard*, 95; importance, 52, 132; delays HA at Langres, 29; absence from Nap's first battles, 42, 46, 49; at Montmirail, 61; at Arcis-sur-Aube, 103, 130; Nap's farewell at Fontainebleau, 126; Grenadiers à pied, 61; transport en poste, 72, 133, 266def, 282
– *Young Guard*, 72, 74, 231, 252, 254, 256, 258, 259; at Brienne, 44; at La Rothière, 48; at Craonne, 88; quality, 13; 'melts away like snow', 95; divs amalgamated after Laon, 95, 257
– *cavalry*, 12, 95, 253; awards, 16; in mobile reserve, 72, 101, 133, 254, 258; at Montmirail, 59, 61; at Château-Thierry, 61; at Vauchamps, 66; at Craonne, 88; at Arcis-sur-Aube, 103
– *Gardes d'honneur*, 53, 236, 253, 254, 255, 258, 259, 263def, 274; at recapture of Reims, 97–8; men join corps francs, 182
– *artillery*, 76, 89, 183, 191
– *divisions*: 1st OG Div, 251, 252, 254, 256, 258, 274 (as core of mobile reserve, 72, 97, 101, 133; awards, 16); 2nd OG Div, 59, 64, 251, 252, 254, 255, 257, 259, 282; 1st YG Div, 251, 257; 2nd YG Div, 251, 253, 257; 3rd YG Div, 251; 4th YG Div, 251; 5th YG Div, 251, 252, 254, 256, 257, 263def; 6th YG Div, 251; 7th YG Div, 256; 1st Prov YG Div, 255–6; 2nd Prov YG Div, 255–6; 3rd Prov YG Div, 256, 257
– *regts*: 2e Gren à pied, 99; 2e Chass à pied, 59; 6e Voltigeurs, 213; 14e Voltigeurs, 88; Dragons, 59, 61, 63; Gren à cheval, 61; 1er Gardes d'honneur, 98, 206; 3e Gardes d'honneur, 98, 236
– *other IG units*: Marins, 16
irregular forces: compagnies franches, 179, 182, 261def; corps francs, 179, 182, 261def; partisans, 179–80, 181–2, 183, 184, 185, 288; raised, 179–80, 182, 184; disadvantages, 181–2; allowed to keep loot, 182; popular attitudes to, 182–3; Allied responses, 165, 169, 173, 184–6, 187; *see also* levée en masse; *and* Wolff

Janot, Jean (civilian), 167
Jendrié, Jean (garde champêtre), 184
Joachim Napoleon, King of the Two Sicilies (King of Naples, formerly Maréchal Murat), 145, 188; joins Allied coalition, 12, 147, 148

Jordan, Lt Heinrich von (Pr 1. Garde-Regt zu Fuß), 32

Kaisarov, Maj-Gen Paisii Sergeyevich, 24
Kaptsevich, Lt-Gen Peter Mikhailovich, 55, 64, 66, 67, 68, 247; joins Blücher, 53, 248
Kellermann, Maréchal François, 12; entrusted with defence of Marne valley, 40, 268; returns from Meaux to Paris, 271–2; helps re-establish communications in liberated areas, 161–2
Kellermann, GdeD François, comte de Valmy (son of maréchal), 73, 253
Kleist, GenLt Friedrich von, 22, 85, 247, 271; joins Blücher, 53, 248; detached to reinforce HA, 55; at Vauchamps, 64, 66, 67, 68; at Battle on the Ourcq, 82; at Laon, 91; at Battle of Paris, 137
Korf, Lt-Gen Feodor Karlovich, Baron, 23, 247
Krimer, Dr Wenzel (Pr infantry surgeon), 174, 175

La Ferté-Gaucher (Seine-et-Marne), 112, 279
La Ferté-sous-Jouarre (Seine-et-Marne), 84, 224, 295–6
La Rothière (Aube), Battle of (1/2), 28, 46–9, 52, 91, 132, 169, 273; Nap's only purely defensive battle in 1814, 129; effect of outcome, 50, 51–2, 69, 147, 149, 195–6; defeat downplayed by Nap, 201; losses, 49, 95, 191; evacuation of Fr sick and wounded, 216; monument, 292
Lambert, Lt-Gen Karl Osipovih, 164
Langeron, Gen Louis Alexander, Count, 68, 91, 96, 117, 164, 247, 248; describes Nap's manoeuvrist approach, 131
Langres (Haute-Marne), 8, 29, 42, 80, 95, 170, 238
Langres Protocols (end Jan), 30–1, 69
Langton, Richard (British detainee), 213
Laon (Aisne), 85, 86, 90, 91, 107, 248; appearance during campaign, 39; carriages burned by SA, 173; guides for Allied forces, 167; losses of arrondissement, 226; population size, 39
Laon, Battle of (9–10/3), 34, 91, *92*, 93–5, 107, 131, 132, 185, 188; losses, 94, 95, *166*, 212; civilian experience, 162; defeat downplayed by Nap, 201; worsens friction between Russ and Pr contingents of SA, 96; reinvigorates Allies, 97, 278
Lavallette, Antoine Chamans, comte de (directeur-général des postes), 122, 126
Lefol, Sous-lt (nephew and ADC of general), 17, 46, 142, 169
Lesmont (Aube), 37, 44, 46, 51
Letort, GdeB Louis, baron, 63, 258
Levavasseur, Lt Octave (ADC to

Ney), 42, 44–5, 46, 274
levée en masse, 179–81, 184, 264def; Revolutionary (1793), 179; ordered by Nap (1814), 17, 184, 288; problems, 180–1; clothing, 186; reprisals threatened, 185–6
L'Héritier, GdeD Samuel, baron, 183
Limonest (Rhône), Battle of (20/3), 146
logistics, 133, 138–41; importance, 138; pillaging and wastage, 168, 170, 181; problem of transport, 138, 230 (use of transport en poste, 133); Fr camps 40–1; resources of towns, 39, 41, 138–9, 140–1; *see also* requisitioning
– *Nap*: cause losses after La Rothière, 51; limit pursuit after Montereau, 77, 79; as reason for m/derrières, 108, 141; centre of operations repeatedly switched, 139–40, 284
– *Allies*: restrict options after La Rothière, 41, 50; contribute to Schw's caution, 51, 79–80, 100; restrict SA after Laon, 96; new supply lines opened from Belgium, 84, 109, 114, 139; some troops eat too much, 165, 167
London Stock Exchange fraud (21/2), 195
Louis XVIII, King of France, 124, 126, 190, 199, 200, 226, 292
Lowe, Col Hudson (British observer with SA), 68, 96, 135, 172
Löwenstern, Staff Capt Eduard von, 44, 45, 73–4, 119, 167, 177, 231
Löwenstern, Lt-Col Vladimir Ivanovich, Baron von (brother of Eduard), 90
Lusigny (Aube), ceasefire talks (late Feb), 80–1
Luxembourg (Grandy Duchy of Luxembourg), 30, *153*, *154*, 181, 251
Lyon (Rhône), 12, 16, 79, 145, 146, 147, 148, *155*, 174, 182; silk trade with Allied states, 205; German fabric workers, 135; inhabitants flee, 202; falls to Südarmee, 137; impact of fall, 123, 146

Macdonald, Maréchal Etienne, 13, 42, 250, 252, 255, 258; at Châlons-sur-Marne, 40; withdraws down Marne before SA, 53, 55, 137, 254; during Montmirail and Château-Thierry, 58, 274–5; at Guignes, 71, 72; assigned to Seine sector, 132; left to contain HA (end Feb), 82, 256; driven back from Seine, 100, 101; falls ill, 12
Maison, GdeD Nicolas, comte, 145, 250
Maizières (Aube), 46
Maizières-la-Grande-Paroisse (Aube), 217, 221
manoeuvre sur les derrières, 50, 70, 101, 107–11 122, 142, 282; Nap justified in attempting, 107–9, 110, 141, 144, 146, 162, 184, 197, 198;

Index 321

intended as part of pincer move, 145, 147
manoeuvrist approach, 131, 144, 149
Marchand, GdeD Jean, comte, 182
Marie-Louise, Fr Empress, 148, 190, 284; decrees levies of troops (1813), 13; correspondence with Nap, 109, 130, 136, 290; sends Nap portrait of son, 194; makes bandages, 215; destruction of government papers, 222; leaves Paris (29/3), 114, 117, 206, 280; after fall of Paris, 124, 125, 126
Marmont, Maréchal Auguste, 15, 46, 47, 98, 250, 252, 254, 255, 257; headquarters, action on the Voire, 51, 273; at Champaubert, 56, 58; at Vauchamps, 64, 66, 67; assigned to Marne sector, 72, 132; at Battle on the Ourcq, 82, 84; at Laon, 91, 93–4, 212 (criticised by Nap, 95); left to contain SA on Aisne, 101; recalled to join Nap's m/derrières, 258; at Fère-Champenoise, 111, 112, 279; retreats on Paris, 113; at Battle of Paris, 117, 118, 259; defection, 125, 281; vilified for outcome, 148, 201; erratic performance, 12
Maubreuil, Monsieur de (hired assassin), 124, 280–1
Meaux (Seine-et-Marne), 72, 82, 101, 112, 114, 139, 162, 189, 258; military significance, 39; Fr camp, 40–1, 268; casualty evacuation centre, 295–6; intelligence-gathering post, 271–2; recovery from campaign, 223
Melun (Seine-et-Marne), 140, 204, 216; Fr camp, 40–1; bridge over Seine, 224, 271
Méry-sur-Seine (Aube), 38, 79, 101; largely burned down, 40, 222, 229; Nap's legacy, 228; civilian registers buried, 231; mortality, 233, 298; women dress as men to avoid attacks, 236; population displacements, 204
Metternich, Klemens, Fürst von (Austrian Foreign Minister), 6, 8, 19, 29, 150, 197; war aims, 4, 8, 198; understanding with Castlereagh, 30; disputes with Alex, 25, 28, 30–1, 69–70; reluctant to alienate Bavaria, 157; forced to withdraw on Dijon by Nap's m/derrières, 110–11, 123
Metz (Moselle), 30, 108, 164, 204, 219
Milhaud, GdeD Edouard, comte, 73, 250, 252, 253
Moët, Jean-Rémy (maire of Epernay), 173–4, 176
Moncey, Maréchal Bon-Adrien Jeannot de, 12, 117, 259, 268, 279; statue at the barrière de Clichy, 118
Moncey, Col Bon-Marie Jeannot de (son and ADC of maréchal), 117
Montbrun, GdeB Alexandre, baron, 183, 289
Montereau (Seine-et-Marne), 39, 40; inhabitants forced to construct fortifications, 167; Nap undertakes to indemnify inhabitants, 225; repair of bridges, 224
Montereau, Battle of (18/2), 74–7, 79, 132; alleged shortage of Fr artillery ammunition, 183, 289; losses, 77, 191; Nap's alleged remark ('cannonball that is to kill me'), 76–7, 126, 201, 276; Nap orders shakos thrown into Seine, 197; Pajol seizes bridges, 75–6, 77, 191, 276; infected clothes taken from dead, 217; treatment of Allied POWs, 211, 212
Montier-en-Der (Haute-Marne), 42, 44
Montmirail (Marne), 53, 67, 72, 137
Montmirail, Battle of (11/2), 58–9, *60*, 61, 64, 117, 130, 132; scale and significance, 58, 59, 61, 196, 274; losses, 59, 61, 132, 191
Moreau, GdeD Jean (killed at Dresden), 193, 291
Moreau, GdeB Jean, baron (surrenders Soissons), 84–5, 183, 277
Moret-sur-Loing (Seine-et-Marne), 289; ability to interdict food supplies to Paris, 139; bridge repaired, 225
Mormant (Seine-et-Marne), Battle of (17/2), 72–4, 191; losses, 74; Nap's massed battery, 73, 133; odds, 71, 132
Mortier, Maréchal Edouard, 251, 252, 253, 254, 255, 256, 257, 282; delays HA at Langres, 29, 270; fights battle at Bar-sur-Aube, 29, 230; based at Troyes, 42, 51, 52; at Château-Thierry, 61; pursues after Château-Thierry, 64; assigned to Marne sector, 72, 132; at Battle on the Ourcq, 82, 84; left to contain SA on the Aisne, 101; recalled to join Nap's m/derrières, 258; at Fère-Champenoise, 111, 112; retreats on Paris, 113, 279; at Battle of Paris, 117, 118, 259; assessment, 12
Müffling, GM Karl von, 20, 85, 94, 247
Murat, Joachim, *see* Joachim Napoleon

Nancy (Meurthe-et-Moselle), 39, 186, 204, 286; Spanish POWs, 209, 211; under occupation, *154*, 160, 173; as base for SA, 30, 139
Nangis (Seine-et-Marne), 74, 191
Nansouty, GdeD Etienne Champion, comte de, 12, 253, 254, 258
Napoleon I, Emperor of the French: Corsican origins, 9; health, 94; fails to explain counter-invasion plan to maréchaux, 42; takes command of field army, 42; escapes capture at Brienne, 46; decides to strike against SA (early Feb), 52–3; supposedly aims gun at Montereau, 76–7, 276; considers options against HA (mid Mar), 101, *102*; rides horse over shell at Arcis-sur-Aube 103, 105, 278; prime reasons for downfall, 148; over-centralises power, 9, 10, 113, 144; abdicates, 125; alleged suicide attempt, 125–6; assassination plots, 124, 280–1; scorned for surviving his downfall, 126; farewell to OG at Fontainebleau, 126
– *assessment as commander*, 128–49; comparison with 1796 and 1813, 128–9, 281; chances of repelling invasion, 143; never fights a campaign in smaller zone, 34; knowledge of campaign theatre, 133–4; does not devise operational moves on own, 137–8; headquarters, 36, 130–1, 133, 281; personally interrogates POWs, 136; distance covered during campaign, 131, 281, 282; concentrates superior numbers on battlefield, 68, 71, 132–3; fights most battles against SA, 142; over-confidence, 81, 93, 94, 105–6, 138; fails to detach Austria from coalition, 142, 144, 193; successes drive Allies together, 142; increasingly difficult to achieve surprise, 107, 142; harshness in seeking to increase tempo (Feb), 183; fails to turn campaign into sweeping war of manoeuvre, 144–5, 146, 147–8
– *leadership*: determination, xiv; rewards promptly and generously, 16, 76, 98; criticises subordinates unjustly, 145, 183, 274–5, 289; under fire at Château-Thierry, 61; command and control at Mormant, 73; example of bravery at Arcis-sur-Aube, 103, 126
– *popular support*: extent of support, 9–11, 123–6; tours working-class districts of Paris, 194; evokes Revolutionary precedents, 10; prorogues Corps législatif, 10, 197; military decisions influenced by state of public morale, 108, 146, 188, 197, 198; seeks to reimpose authority on liberated areas, 161–2; reasons for insisting on natural frontiers, 8, 80–1, 143, 162; indemnifies inhabitants for losses, 225, 228; wary of encouraging a people's war, 16, 177, 179
Napoleon II, *see* Rome, King of
Nash, John (architect), 120-1
Nesselrode, Karl, Count von (Russ diplomat), 4, 32, 284
Ney, Maréchal Michel, 44, 72, 252, 256, 257, 258, 274; assigned to mobile reserve, 133, 254; requires maps, 137; at Montmirail, 59; at Craonne, 86, 88; at Arcis-sur-Aube, 103, 105; possibility of being detached into Lorraine (mid Mar), 184; impatience, 12, 88; blamed for outcome of Waterloo (1815), 201
Nogent-sur-Seine (Aube), 36, 74, 138, 140, 216; population figure, 39; Nap at, 52, 281; fighting at, 69, 162; burned, 40, 162, 222; rebuilt,

221; difficult access to temporary bridge, 38; sous-préfet supplies Ney with a map, 137; sous-préfet returns after liberation of town, 161

Nordarmee, 19, 24, 25, 55, 84, 96, 139, 145, 247; role in invasion, 7, 18; rear areas, 150; *see also* Bülow; *and* Winzingerode

Nostitz, Maj August, Graf von (Blücher's adjutant), 66, 272; exaggerates role in saving Blücher, 45, 272, 275

Odiot, Chef de bataillon (Garde nationale), 117, 279

Olsufiev I, Lt-Gen Zakhar Dmitrevich, 209, 211, 247, 248; at Champaubert, 56, 58, 64

'Oriflamme' (opera), 194–5, 291

Orléans (Loiret), 39, 180, 204, 206, 207, 209, 216; threatened by Cossacks (18/2), 208, 294; inadequate as an alternative centre of government, 122–3

Oudinot, Maréchal Nicolas: assigned to Seine sector, 53, 69, 132; detaches a division for Montmirail, 58, 274; on the Yerres river, 71, 72; defeated at Bar-sur-Aube, 100, 230; unfit for independent command, 12; wounded, 268

Ourcq, Battle on the (28/2 and 1/3), 82, 84, 96

Pacthod, GdeD Michel, comte, 111, 112, 163, 253, 255, 279

Pahlen III, Lt-Gen Peter Petrovich, Count, 44, 71, 73, 74, 246, 272

Pajol, GdeD Claude, comte, 40, 72, 139, 251, 252, 254, 255; seizes bridges at Montereau, 75–6, 77, 276

Panchulidzev I, Lt-Gen Ivan Davydovich, 97

Paris: appearance, 119, 121; corps franc formed, 182; defences, 113, 206; marriage rate high (1813), 234; population size, 36, 39, 113; weather data, 238–44; benefits for Nap (road hub, 36, 41; logistical base, 36, 41, 139, 140–1; reinforcements from depots, 72); drawbacks for Nap (heart of centralised regime, 113; food supply for population, 138–9; restricts freedom of manoeuvre, 109, 122, 139, 144; vulnerable to epidemics, 216, 218, 219; difficult to insulate from bad news, 190)
– *morale*: volatile, 38, 70, 109–10, 114, 188, 197, 198, 206, 216, 218, 219, 290; Nap seeks to terrify out of indifference, 192–3, 195; sympathy for POWs, 197, 212; affected by Fr wounded begging in streets, 204, 216
– *under Allied occupation*: final Allied descent (end Mar), 113–14, 144, 205, 222; Allied entry, 119–20; occupation arrangements, 155, 160–1; relations with Allied troops,

120–1, 160; effect of fall, 122, 123, 124, 201
– *see also*: bistros; population displacements; *and* sick and wounded

Paris, Battle of (30/3), 28, 112, 114, 115, 116–19, 137, 144, 167, 279, 296; repair of houses, 223; wounded, 217; *see also* Clichy

Paskevich, Lt-Gen Ivan Fedorovich, 169, 279

Pelleport, GdeB Pierre, baron, 98

Peninsular war (1807–1814), 11, 73, 147, 148, 207, 210, 211, 224; spreads typhus, 219; popular resistance, 179; indiciplinе of Fr troops, 14, 268

Pénot, Nicolas (Fr 2e Cuirassiers), 212, 295

Périgueux (Dordogne), 147, 210–11, 214

Piney (Aube), 170

Piré, GdeD Hippolyte, baron de, 134, 289

Planat de la Faye, Capt Nicolas (ADC to Drouot), 36–7

Plancy, Adrien d'Aucour, comte de (préfet de Seine-et-Marne), 140, 180, 181, 224; lends money to Freemason POWs, 212; directs public opinion in Seine-et-Marne, 188–9

Plancy (Aube), 101, 102

Platov, Gen Matvei Ivanovich, Count, 24, 247

police générale, Ministre de la, 10, 161, 192, 204, 205, 206, 290; fears about number of POWs in western France, 210; role in intelligence gathering, 134, 135, 203, 282; resents committee editing Parisian newspapers, 189

Poltoratsky, Maj-Gen Constantine Markovich, 56, 58, 136

Poncet, Maj-Gen Mikhail Ivanovich, 89

population displacements, 158, 193, 202–7, 214, 217; in dépt of Aube, 202; stemmed by Allies, 203; as source of military intelligence, 203; homeless civilians follow Fr army, 204; local, 203–4, 230; temporary, 204; threaten disorder, 206, 207; impede recovery, 223; to Paris, 114, 205–6, 225, 293; from Paris, 114, 206

Pougens, Charles de (writer), 205

Poumiès de la Siboutie, François (hospital intern), 216–17

préfets of dépts, 180, 193, 213, 265def; support Nap with intelligence and logistics, 134, 140, 203; ordered to withdraw in face of invasion, 151, 156, 158, 180; flee too soon, 134, 161; replaced by Allies, 156; sent to Nap from Paris (late Mar), 162; organise relief for population, 227

prisoners-of-war (and civilian detainees), 207–14, 295; threatened with execution, 186; interrogated, 135–6, 283; escape, 212–14
– *Allied*, 17, *128*, 293; paraded

through Paris, 197, 209, 211–12; escorted by women, 236; responsibility shifted from Fr authorities to population, 209–10; seen as threat to Fr population, 210–11, 214; health risk, 11, 211; recruited into Fr army, 212; some later settle in France, 211
– *British*, 207, 208, 209, 210, 212, 213, 214, 293, 294; repatriations, 207, 294; losses during transfer of depots, 207; mock Nap's bulletins, 194; on parole, 176, 190, 208, 295; relations with Fr population, 208, 210–11
– *French*: conditions of captivity in British hands, 208; cannibalism after Leipzig, 211; at Bar-sur-Aube, 231, 232
– *Spanish*, 207, 208, 209, 210, 211, 219, 293; relations with Fr population, 210–11, 214; formed by Blücher at Nancy into a battalion, 209, 294; role in 1820 revolution, 121

Provins (Seine-et-Marne), 101, 112, 140, 159, 177, 204; appearance, 39; walls, Garde nationale, 17

Provisional Government of France, 163; appointed (1/4), 124; undermines Nap, 124, 125, 188; orders release of Allied POWs, 214

Prussian army: attitude of generals alarms FWIII, 4; corps concentrated in SA, 23; limited impact of reforms, 21; quality, 22, 269; General Staff, 20; Landwehr, 22, 264def; in 1815, 38, 149; *see also* Schlesische armee
– *corps*: I Corps, *166*, 247, 267; II Corps, 247; III Corps, 247; *see also names of corps commanders*
– *brigades*: Garde-Inf-Brigade, 116–17, 118, 119–20; 1. Brigade, 274; 8. Brigade, 274; 9. Brigade, 275
– *regts*: 1. Garde-Regt zu Fuß, 7, 32, 116, 120, 165; 1. Schlesische Inf-Regt, 66; 2. Schlesische Inf-Regt, 22, 67; 6. Res-Inf-Regt, 33, 93; 7. Res-Inf-Regt, 66

psychological operations, 188–201; Allied, 158–9, 185–6, 188, 236, 292; Bourbon, 199–200, 292; Nap, 95, 120, 188–97, 198–9, 200–1, 228, 292 (false statistics, 46, 58, 61, 64, 90, 136–7, 189, 191); Fr Provisional Government, 200

Radetzky, FML Josef, Graf zu Radetz, 246

Rahden, Lt Wilhelm von (Pr 2. Schlesische Inf-Regt), 22, 67, 79, 146, 175

Raumer, Volontärofficier Karl von (HQ, SA), 172, 275

Reiche, Maj Ludwig von (Ober-Quartiermeister, Pr III Corps), 164, 172

Reichenbach, Maj Graf (Pr 2. Schlesische Inf-Regt), 67

Reims (Marne), 15, 40, 101, 140,

162, 183, 281; size and significance, 39, 41, 97; opens gates to Cossacks, 191; prostitutes flogged, 236; recaptured by Nap (13/3), 22, 34, 97–9, 107, 188, 223, 278
reprisals: by Nap, 162 (at Troyes, 183, 190); by Allies (at Bar-sur-Aube, 230, 231; at Brienon, 213; at Troyes, 185); threatened in response to Fismes decrees, 185–6; during Bourbon Restoration for resistance to Allied occupation, 184
requisitioning, 9, 140, 157, 161, 167–8, 169, 205, 224; attempts to evade, 164–5, 168, 180, 216; becomes more regular, 159–60, 172, 286; partly replaced by contractors after end of hostilities, 163; civilian labour, 39, 167; compensation, 227
resistance from population to Allied invasion, 6, 106, 165, 177–87, 289; in Ardennes, 108, 184; in Marne valley, 64; requires support of Nap's army, 108; limited by local concerns, 159, 177–8; open towns readily capitulate, 159; Allied reactions, 159, 170, 184–6, 187; *see also* irregular forces; *and* reprisals
Roanne (Loire), 178
Rochechouart, Col Léon, comte de (ADC to Alex), 161
Rœderer, Antoine, baron (préfet), 162, 286
Rome, King of (Nap's son), 4, 117; awareness of campaign, 130; popular print, 194; leaves Paris (29/3), 114, 206; possibility of regency, 123, 124, 125
Rosnay (Aube), action at (2/2), 273
Rothau (Bas-Rhin), 186-7
Rouen (Seine Maritime), 204, 216
Russian army: present at nearly all battles, 23; bears brunt of Battle of Paris, 119; quality, 21, 22, 191; drunkenness, 175; long-term impact of serving in France, 121; officers and commanders, 22, 23, 90, 169, 269 (Fr-born, 164; Fr-speaking, 174); infantry, 22, 88; cavalry, 97–8, 118; artillery, 22–3 (massed at Craonne, 88, 89, 90); pontoons, 37–8; opolchenie (militia), 22; Bashkirs, 24
– *Cossacks*, 1, 24, 45, 151, 174, 205, 247, 248; occupy Hamburg (1813), 6; occupy Reims, 191; threaten Orléans, 180, 208, 294; endanger Nap (29/1), 46; intercept despatches, 109; escort POWs, 212–13; excite curiosity of Fr civilians, 159; dehumanised by Nap, 193, 197, 200; portrayal in Fr theatres, 194, 195; accused of looting and atrocities, 24, 118, 169, 230, 236; loot in conjunction with Fr civilians, 178, 203; blamed for items broken by clumsy servants, 222
– *corps*: 2nd Inf Corps, 21–2; 8th Inf Corps, 97, 248, 277; 9th Inf Corps, 56, 248; 10th Inf Corps, 248
– *other units*: Army of Poland, 248; 2nd Grenadier Div, 169; Ryazanskii Inf Regt, 98; Tchougouiev Uhlans, 44; *see also* VI Armee-Abtheilung *and* Russ Guards and reserves, *under* Hauptarmee; Schlesische armee; *and names of corps commanders*
Ryleïev, Kondrati (Decembrist plotter), 121

Sacken, Gen Fabian, Baron von der Osten-, 30, 53, 64, 247; at Brienne and La Rothière, 44, 47; at Montmirail, 58, 59, 61, 132; at Craonne, 88, 89, 90; at Laon, 91; left as rearguard at Meaux, 112; Governor of Paris, 155, 161, 170; friction with Yorck, 58
Saint-Dizier (Haute-Marne), 17, 34, 42, 108, 109, 111, 139, 192, 209, 215, 281; cemetery full, 221
Saint-Dizier, Battle of (26/3), 122
Saint-Jean-de-Losne (Côte-d'Or), 178
Saint-Priest, Lt-Gen Emanuel, Count, 193, 247, 248, 277; mortally wounded at Reims, 22, 97, 98, 193, 291
Saverne (Bas-Rhin), 235
Savoy (Fr province), 178, 181
Scherbatov I, Lt-Gen Prince Aleksey Grigorievich, 247
Scherbatov, Maj-Gen Prince Alexander Fedorovich (Platov's Cossack Corps), 135
Schlesische Armee, 19–20, 132, 146; role in invasion, 7, 29, 143; greater threat than HA, 19, 61, 85, 129, 142 (not consistently aggressive, 143); order of battle, 247–8; corps commanders, 20 (*see also individual names*); addition of Pr corps, 23; pontoon train, 37–8, 82; rear areas, 150, 170 (lines of communication, 84, 107, 139)
– *strength*, 19, 30, 53, 248; at Brienne, 274; at La Rothière, 47; at Champaubert, 56; at Montmirail, 59; at Vauchamps, 64; at Craonne, 86, 88; at Laon, 91, 93, 95, 96; reduced by mid Feb defeats, 68, 275, 277; almost doubles at start of Mar, 84, 91, 277; misinformation about detachment at Vitry, 107
– *cohesion*: friction in high command, 20, 85, 143; friction between Russ and Pr contingents, 20, 23, 85, 90–1, 96, 168, 170; limited inter-operability of contingents, 23; challenge of integrating fresh corps, 85
– *cavalry*: initial shortage, 23, 53, 64, 68, 95; poor handling, 23–4, 89–90, 91, 135; massed (at La Rothière, 48–9; at Craonne, 86, 89–90; shadows Nap's m/derrières, 111; at Fère-Champenoise, 111, 112)
– *operations*: crosses Rhine, 26–7, 29, 191; advance from Rhine, 30; advance to Brienne, 42; separates from HA (early Feb), 50; bivouacs more often (Feb), 165; first advance on Paris causes overextension (early Feb), 53, 55, 56; command and control dislocated by Champaubert, 58; defeats influenced by weather (Feb), 33; rallies at Châlons-sur-Marne, 64, 68, 168; second advance on Paris (end Feb), 82, 107; retreats north of Marne (early Mar), 82, 84–5; state of troops at Soissons (early Mar), 85; plan for Craonne, 86; at Laon, 91, 93–7; paralysed after Laon, 90, 95–6, 98, 118; at Battle of Paris, 118; not included in entry to Paris, 120
– *see also*: Prussian army; Russian army; *and names of battles*
Schwarzenberg, FM Karl Philipp, Fürst zu, 4, 6–7, 18–19; diplomatic experience, 18, 164; limited experience of army command, 18; limited authority, 18–19; frustrations, 6, 19; views on Blücher and Gneisenau, 30, 97; proclamations to Fr people, 158–9, 185, 292; tries to prevent looting, 159–60; fights only one battle with Nap, 101; less mobile than Nap, 131, 282; reasons for slowness and caution, 18–19, 28–9, 37, 51, 69, 70, 100, 106, 127, 132, 142–3, 158; underrated, 143, 146–7; opinion of Nap's survival, 126
– *operations*: at La Rothière, 46–7; pursues Nap, 51, 53; outflanks Troyes, 52, 55; instructed not to cross Seine (13/2), 70; requests armistice (17/2), 74, 80; abandons plan to fight at Troyes (23/2), 79, 143; creates Südarmee, 80, 146, 148, 247; defeats Oudinot at Bar-sur-Aube, 100; ill (mid Mar), 94; at Arcis-sur-Aube, 101, 105, 106, 143; role in final advance on Paris, 109, 110, 111; enters Paris, 120; expects battle after fall of Paris, 122
Sébastiani, GdeD Horace, comte, 106, 250, 252, 258, 278
Ségur, Sénateur Louis, comte de, 209, 234
Ségur, GdeB Philippe, comte de, 53, 140, 253, 278; charge at Reims (13/3), 97–8, 278
Sens (Yonne), 40, 69, 211
Sérurier, Maréchal Jean-Mathieu, comte, 12, 119, 268
Sézanne (Marne), 34, 36, 40, 101, 138, 216, 258; unsuitability as supply base, 139–40; Nap at, 55
Short, John Tregerthen (British POW), 207
sick and wounded, 167, 215–20; evacuation, 168, 215–17, 295–6; reach Paris, 190, 204, 215–17; murdered, 169; *see also* typhus
Simon, Monsieur (raises a corps franc), 182
Soissons (Aisne), 36, 86, 95, 97, 112, 258, 277; size and significance, 39; Fr camp, 41, 272; stormed by

Russians (14/2), 205; capitulates to Allies (3/3), 84–5, 183, 191; damaged, 222; losses of arrondissement, 226; population displacements, 203–4, 205
Soult, Maréchal Jean-de-Dieu, 11, 12, 72, 146, 206, 253, 282
Steffens, Professor Henrik (HQ, SA), 95, 120, 175, 191
Stein, Heinrich, Freiherr von, 150, *155*, 157, 160, 181
Stewart, Lt-Gen the Hon Sir Charles, 129
Strasbourg (Bas-Rhin), 36, 164, 204
Suchet, Maréchal Louis, 11, 12, 146, 147, 284
Südarmee, 80, 146, 150, *155*, 247
Sweden, Crown Prince of (formerly Maréchal Bernadotte), 12, 18, 25, 84, 96, 188, 197
Switzerland, 9, 25, 28, *153*; artillery used against Besançon, 269; Swiss in Fr army, 15
Széchenyi, Stephen (Hungarian patriot), 121

Talleyrand-Périgord, Charles-Maurice de (Vice grand électeur), 10, 280; well-informed, 190; wary of Bourbons, 123, 124; actions after fall of Paris, 123–4, 125, 157; psychological operations to undermine Nap, 124; vilified for outcome, 123, 201
Thionville (Moselle), 227, 251, 283
Thurn und Taxis, August, Fürst von, 34, 69, 103, 105–6
Toll, Lt-Gen Karl Fedorovich (Alex's Adj-Gen), 48
Tonnerre (Yonne), 159, 162, 285
Torcy-le-Grand (Aube), 103, 105, 229
Toulouse (Haute-Garonne), Battle of (10/4), 146, 279
Tournus (Saône-et-Loire), 178
Tours (Indre-et-Loire), 208, 216, 280
Trelliard, GdeD François, baron, 72, 253
Trilport (Seine-et-Marne), 223, 224, 274
Troyes (Aube), 100, 101, *154*, *155*, 183, 282; size and military usefulness, 36, 39, 52; Fr camp, 41; Mortier at, 42, 52; Fr counter-intelligence measures, 135; Allied POWs at, 209; changes hands five times, 161; Nap at, 36, 52, 137, 281 (unenthusiastic welcome, 51; reprisals against royalists, 183, 190); HA's advanced base, 79, 102, 170, 172; Allied political crisis at (Feb), 69, 70; unfought battle (Feb), 79, 143; Wrede threatens to burn, 40, 80, 157, 276; Allied pillaging and reprisals, 160, 169, 170, 185; restrictions on printers, 292; volunteers replace hostages, 179; maire nominated for Légion d'honneur, 157; population displacements, 203; destitution, 164; evacuation centre for Fr sick and wounded, 216; mortality rates, 215, 221; burial of dead, 218, 221; babies fathered by Allied soldiers, 236–7; maître de poste tries to resign, 224
typhus epidemic, 218–20; in Germany (1813), 3, 219; in France (1813–1814), 207, 211, 217, 232–3; infection and mortality rates, 218, 219; moral impact, 219–20; popular remedies, 219

Urusov, Maj-Gen Alexander Petrovich, Prince, 67
Uxkull, Lt Boris (Russ Garde à cheval), 121, 177, 223, 235

Valençay (Indre), Treaty of (1813), 11, 147
Vasilchikov I, Lt-Gen Illarion Vasilievich, 23, 247
Vauchamps, Battle of (14/2), 64, *65*, 66–8, 70, 107; losses, 67–8, 275; Blücher allegedly seeks death, 275; Nap's advantages, 68, 91, 132, 133; Nap exaggerates results, 191
Vauxbuin (Aisne), 205
Verdun (Meuse), 176, 190, 208, 213, 293, 294
Vernet, Horace: paints defence of barrière de Clichy, 117-18
Versailles (Yverlines), 39, 170, 206, 211, 216, 271, 272
Vesoul (Haute-Saône), *153*, 170, 177
Victor, Maréchal Claude, 29, 44, 250, 252, 254, 257; abandons Saint-Dizier, 42; left to contain HA (mid Feb), 53, 69, 132; on the Yerres river, 71, 72; at Mormant, 73–4; sacked, 12, 74, 183, 255, 268; appointed to a YG command, 74, 256, 276; at Craonne, 88, 90, 268
Villenauxe (Aube), 168, 178, 204; administrative void, 203; Fr POWs escape Allied escort, 212–13; rapes, 236
Villeneuve (Seine-et-Marne), action at (17/2), 74
Villers-Cotterêts (Aisne), 72, 204
Vitry-le-François (Marne), 17, 42, 51, 70, 106, 107, 110, 225
Voire river, action on the (2/2), 51, 273
Vorontsov, Lt-Gen Mikhail Semenovich, Count, 88, 89, 90, 248
Vuich, Maj-Gen Nikolay Vasilievich, 89

Wattwiller (Haut-Rhin), 178
Wellington, Arthur Wellesley, 1st Duke of, 6, 12, 18, 145, 210, 279; limited impact of operations in France, 146; distrusts reports from France, 196; attitude to Bourbons, 199–200; discipline and cohesion of army, 20, 181, 200, 207; advance causes population displacements, 207; rope bridges, 38; opinion about Nap in 1814, 107; relations with Blücher and Gneisenau (1815), 149, 272–3
Widranges, marquis de (royalist), 183, 289
Wilhelm, Kronprinz von Württemberg (IV Armee-Abtheilung; later King Wilhelm I), 48, 246, 249; at Montereau, 74, 75, 76, 77; at Arcis-sur-Aube, 103, 278; at Fère-Champenoise, 111, 112; at Battle of Paris, 114
Wilhelm, Prinz (son of FWIII; later Emp Wilhelm I of Germany), 51, 97, 119
Winzingerode, Gen Ferdinand Fedorovich, Baron, 23, 85, 248; detached from Nordarmee, 55, 84; captures Soissons with Bülow, 84; entrusted with massed cavalry force (6–7/3), 86, 89–90, 91, 277; at Laon, 91, 94, 96; detached to shadow Nap, 111; routed at Saint-Dizier (26/3), 122
Wolff, Nicolas (partisan), 186–7, 289
women in 1814 campaign, 169; accompany Allied soldiers or POWs, 121, 208, 235; rebuked at Dijon for behaviour with Allied soldiers, 235; traumatised, 236; rapes, 192, 236; give birth in woods, 203; not always passive victims, 236; sutlers and vivandières, 84, 232; prostitutes as scapegoats, 235–6
Wrede, Gen der Kav Karl, Graf von, 74, 246, 248; at La Rothière, 47, 48; threatens to burn Troyes, 80, 276; at Arcis-sur-Aube, 103, 105; left as rearguard at Meaux (end Mar), 112; abrasive, 19; opinion of Stein, 157; asserts authority over some occupied areas, *153*, 157
Württemberg, Kronprinz Wilhelm von, *see* Wilhelm, Kronprinz von
Württemberg (Kingdom) army, 20; bears brunt of HA's campaign, 28; pillages, 170; light cavalry at La Rothière, 49; POWs at Montereau protected by Bertrand, 211
– *units*: Inf-Regt Nr. 5, 120; Jäger-Regt Nr. 2, 23, 120; Jäger-Regt Nr. 4, 111–12; *see also* IV Armee-Abtheilung, *under* Hauptarmee

Yorck, Gen der Inf Hans, Graf von, 53, 137, 170, 247, 283; detached to observe fortresses in SA's rear, 30, 50; attacks Châlons-sur-Marne, 175; at Montmirail, 58, 59, 132; at Château-Thierry, 61, 63, 64; at Laon, 91, 94; at Battle of Paris, 137; strength of corps, 30, *166*; enforces discipline, 84, 170; friction with Sacken, 58; friction with Blücher and Gneisenau, 20, 85, 96

Zentraldepartment of provisional administration, 150, *155*, 157–8, 160, 161
Zieten, GenLt Hans von, 66, 68